BUYING & RENEWING CANADIAN GROUP INSURANCE PLANS: A PRACTICAL GUIDE

Richard Ackroyd

CCH CANADIAN LIMITED
6 Garamond Court, North York, Ontario M3C 1Z5
Telephone: (416) 441-0086 Toll Free: 1-800-268-4522
Fax: (416) 444-9011 Toll Free: 1-800-461-4131
Internet: http://www.ca.cch.com

Now You Know™
"Now You Know" is a trademark owned by CCH Canadian Limited

B154

Published by CCH Canadian Limited

USA	CCH Incorporated, Riverwoods, Illinois.
UK and EUROPE	CCH Editions Limited, Bicester, Oxfordshire.
AUSTRALIA	CCH Australia Limited, North Ryde, NSW.
NEW ZEALAND	CCH New Zealand Limited, Auckland.
SINGAPORE, MALAYSIA and BRUNEI	CCH Asia Limited, Singapore.
JAPAN	CCH Japan Limited, Tokyo.

Canadian Cataloguing in Publication Data

Ackroyd, Richard, 1951–
Buying & renewing Canadian group insurance plans

Includes index.
ISBN 1-55141-767-7

1. Insurance, Group — Canada. I. Title. II. Title: Buying and renewing Canadian group insurance plans.

HG8058.A35 1995 368.3'00971 C95-932168-3

ISBN: 1-55141-767-7

Typeset and printed in Canada.

EXPLANATION

Information in this book is subject to change without notice. Underwriting information, renewal formulas, policy wording, policy terms, policy conditions, tax and legislation information are constantly changing. Users of information provided in this book are encouraged to check with insurers and to review legislation prior to making any changes to their own employee benefit policies and programs. The sections on taxation and legal implications are not intended to be used as interpretations of the law. These chapters are intended as introductions only to very complex areas. Specific interpretations should be referred to experts in those areas. Ideas expressed in this book are solely those of the author. The author and the publisher assume no liability whatsoever for the accuracy of any of the information contained in this book, or for the reliance by any person on the information. Reproduction of any part of the book, with the exception of the sample form letters, requires the express written permission of the author and the publisher.

DEDICATION

This book is dedicated to all of the people who have the courage and faith to reach their goals. Many thanks are extended to Debbie Carroll, Mike Lewington, and Jett Britnell for their encouragement in writing this book. Special thanks to Dr. Colin Soskolne, Ivan Docker, Mike Naugler, Charmaine Johnson, and Tom Certain for their friendship over the years.

A special note of thanks is extended to Charmaine Johnson, who provided content editorial assistance. The editor of this book, David Iggulden of CCH Canadian Limited, is also thanked for seeing it through to its completion.

WHO CAN MAKE USE OF THIS BOOK

Every person who owns, controls, does accounting, manages human resources, keeps books, or assists with any of these areas for a company or an organization can make use of this book. Any organization that wants to market a group insurance plan, with or without the assistance or the cost of an agent, broker or consultant, can use this book.

This book will also be useful to the insurance community at large. For the independent agent, broker, or consultant, this book will serve to level the playing field between those few people who know how to properly provide group insurance marketing services and those who would like to provide a better and more competitive service for their clients. For insurance company human resources and training departments, this book will add some valuable basic information about these products and how they are marketed.

The book will be particularly useful to agents, brokers and consultants who wish to update their skills and knowledge. Since all agents, brokers and consultants are at different skill levels, no matter what they tell their clients, this book will assist them to do a more complete and better job. If your organization chooses to hire an agent, broker or consultant, I hope this book will assist you in understanding the products and the processes involved, so that you can better assess the qualifications of the agents, brokers and consultants.

TABLE OF CONTENTS

Paragraph

THE PURPOSE OF THE BOOK

Nearly every Canadian corporation employing five or more people has a group insurance program in place for its employees. Unions, major associations, all levels of government and professional sports teams use some form of group insurance program to provide benefits to employees, members and their families. These "group benefits" are offered through life insurance companies, and other benefit suppliers who are not insurance companies, but who provide similar benefits. (In this book, the use of the word "insurer" will also mean benefit supplier.) The purpose of this book is to provide the professional and the layman with a basic understanding of what is covered under Canadian group insurance and benefit plans, how they work, how they are funded, and how to shop the market for the best products and services available. The main focus of the book will be on group life, health and disability benefits.

Traditionally, group insurance plans have been purchased with the help of life insurance agents, insurance brokers, or specialist group insurance consultants. This book will examine their roles, how they operate, how they get paid, when to use their services, and when to do the work yourself. If you own or operate a company, or have the authority to act on behalf of your company in the purchase or administration of these plans, you will find enough information inside to shop the market for the best plan, with or without using the services of an agent, broker or consultant. You will also find a checklist of questions which will help your organization find the agent, broker or consultant that best suits your needs.

Readers of this book will have different levels of experience and knowledge about the insurance industry. Those with little experience in the area of group insurance would be advised to start at the beginning of the book. People who know the basics can proceed directly to the section on marketing a plan, renewing a plan, or choosing the best available agent, broker of consultant.

THE SET-UP OF THE BOOK

This book is set up to enable the reader to:

1. Obtain an insight into the politics, underwriting and administration of a group insurance policy.

2. Hire the best available agent, broker or consultant to assist with a marketing or a renewal.

3. Assist an agent, broker or consultant to market or renew a group insurance policy for a client.

4. Take the steps necessary for the successful marketing or renewal of a group insurance policy with or without using an agent, broker or consultant.

Each chapter is self-contained. For example, if an organization wishes to review their renewal, simply turn to the chapter on renewals. Renewal formulas can be compared with those provided by your present insurance company. Note that the formulas included in this book are representations, and not necessarily the exact formulas of a particular insurer.

The beginning of the book contains several checklists. The checklists provide suggested steps for taking action.

It will be helpful to review the commentary on specific topics. Commentaries are designed to give a more complete explanation of the rationale behind the scenes. Although there are programs (such as automobile and home owner) available in Canada which are referred to as a "group insurance" or "group plans", these terms refer only to group life, health, and disability in this book. Also, the term "employer" is occasionally used to denote a "group insurance policyholder", when, in fact, a group policyholder may also be a union or an association.

CHAPTER 1

¶1000 INTRODUCTION TO GROUP INSURANCE

¶1005 WHAT IS INSURANCE?

In Canada, people have come to expect that "insurance" is one of those facts of daily life that takes your money and rarely gives anything back in return. Rates for all types of insurance keep rising and they appear to be beyond our control. We pay and complain about the cost to whoever is prepared to listen. But when was the last time you sat back and reflected about what you were paying for, and how insurance actually works?

Insurance, similar to investment in the stock market, can be considered a form of gambling. The insurance company bets that you will not claim, at least in the short term, and you, by paying premiums, bet that you, or other members of your group, will claim. Like a gambling casino, the insurance company knows that it will have to pay out a certain percentage of its income on claims. And like a casino, insurance companies are not in business to lose money.

Basically, insurance works like this: people put their money into a pot, thinking that a major or minor catastrophe will, or will not happen. The insurance company pays claims from the pot. Anything left over is kept as profit, or redistributed as dividends to the shareholders. However, the situation is slightly more complicated. The money in the pot is invested by the insurance company. The investment income is also put into the pot.

From the pot, all claims, operating expenses, overhead, commissions, taxes, profits, dividends paid to shareholders, investment losses and contingency monies are taken out. The insurance companies, as big as they are and as old as some of them are, have little control over certain things that affect their bottom line. Increases in corporate or premium taxes, increases in operating expenses, or having to pay out a series of large, unexpected claims over a short time frame cannot always be foreseen by insurance companies. Increases are passed on to you, the buyer, after the fact. In other words, the insurance company looks at past events and its past experiences, ties in its other costs, and determines what rates it will charge in the year to come. It uses a "best guess" approach to funding the policies for the following year. It is only at the end of the year, and maybe after many years, that it will know if a profit has been made.

Insurance comes in all sorts of guises and for all sorts of purposes. There are insurance "pools" for automobiles, for buildings, for liability, for boats and planes, to cover the loss of one's life, the loss of one's ability to work, or the loss of one's fingers and toes. In fact, if you can think of something or some action that you would like insured, you can probably find someone somewhere willing to take a chance and "insure" that probability. Of course, you may not want to pay the premiums that are quoted!

¶1010 WHAT IS GROUP INSURANCE?

Group insurance is, quite simply, a method of insuring a group of individuals, almost always a group of employees, association members, or union members, for certain benefits, under one master contract, or policy.

Group insurance started as a method of insuring a group of employees, for the loss of their lives, under one contract or policy. This was considered an innovation at the time. Setting up one policy to cover a group of employees saved the additional task of setting up individual policies for each individual in the group. Theoretically, this should reduce the insurer's expenses, and hence the rates offered. The appeal of this approach soon spread and other companies started to set up group life insurance contracts for employee groups.

Not content to rest on their laurels, life insurance companies started to get requests for, and to look for ways to insure other risks, such as disabilities. Some of the first disability type policies were actually additions, called "riders" by the insurance community for some long forgotten reason, to life insurance policies. The "rider" would read something like this: If an insured person becomes totally and permanently disabled prior to age 60, the face amount of the policy will be divided and paid out to the certificate holder in 60 equal monthly instalments.

Today, group insurance contracts (still called policies) comprise a whole range of services from the traditional benefits like life insurance and disability insurance, to dental plans, plans to supplement Medicare, accident plans, travel plans, short-term disability plans, dependant life insurance plans, plans to assist groups of people through personal counselling, legal plans, and group automobile plans. Want a group health plan to cover veterinarian's bills for your pets? You can probably arrange such a plan!

¶1015 WHAT IS SELF-INSURANCE?

What if we want to cover our group of employees or members but we do not want to use an insurance company? If you decide that you can afford, as an organization, to cover certain types of losses yourself, instead of paying an insurance company to cover the risk, you can set up your own policy to do so. This is called "Self-Insurance". The policy that you set up can be formal or informal. However, there are consequences for you and your employees to consider, from liability and taxation points of view. (See Chapter 14, Legal Responsibilities, and Chapter 15, Taxation.)

Can an organization take on any of the risks? The premiums that one pays to insurance companies, for certain benefits, can be expensive. If the insurance company is taking a large percentage of the premium dollar to administer and pay the claims (the insurance industry calls this figure the "retention"percentage), then this will be reflected in the rates. For certain benefit items, it can pay to self-insure. Let us examine a benefit which pays for the replacement of eye glasses every two years. If the benefit paid to the employee (or dependant) is (a maximum) $100 every two years, then the insurance company will take the actual claim amount multiplied times the retention percentage to pay that claim. If your organization is being charged a high retention rate (say 25 per cent of the claims), then it could cost your organization $25 for the insurance company to write that one cheque, once every two years; an expensive cheque indeed. Extended health care (sometimes called supplementary health care) plans, dental plans and short-term disability plans are pay-for-service type plans. The more you use, the more you pay.

There are certain risks such as life insurance, accidental death, and long-term disability which are not recommended for self-insurance unless: (a) your organization is large; (b) the premium that you are paying for the benefit is in excess of $500,000 per year; and (c) your organization has the financial resources to pay in the case of a high claims year. Even in these situations, it is possible to use insurance companies to insure risks over large amounts, while self-insuring smaller claims amounts. Self-insured plans, like those offered by insurance companies and other benefit providers, require a description of the benefits, as well as a description of the terms and the conditions under which those benefits will be paid. Extended health care and dental benefits can be received by employees as non-taxable benefits, according to Revenue Canada Interpretation Bulletin IT 339R2 (see Appendices at ¶17,095), if the employer is required to provide these benefits as part of an employment contract, or a union contract.

¶1020 HOW DO INSURERS DIFFERENTIATE THEIR PRODUCTS AND SERVICES?

One of the most difficult things to do in a mature and overcrowded market, such as that of the present group insurance providers, is to assess which of the insurers is better than the others and why. The policies look and sound the same. There are seemingly imperceptible differences in the levels of service offered by the competitors. All of the insurers will tell you that they are the "best". How do they see themselves?

Life insurance companies are mostly old, large, staid and bureaucratic organizations run mainly by actuaries. These companies are heavily regulated by bureaucratic government rules and regulations and old legislation that basically inhibits the way they operate and invest their (read your) money. The legislation exists, at least partially, to help ensure that the insurers' policyholders are protected from any potential insolvency of the insurers.

Marketing is a relatively new idea to many insurers. It is not a main emphasis in actuarial studies. Product and service differentiation is difficult for most insurers. Given the combination of bureaucracy and restricting legislation, life insurance companies are forced to keep "reinventing the wheel" in order to continue "progressing". For these reasons, it is difficult for the buying public to tell the insurers apart.

In fact, insurers can only tell themselves apart by pointing to how long they have been in business, how the rating agencies have placed their claims-paying abilities, how many countries they operate in, how large their accumulated surplus is, and how many people they employ. They may also point to the fact that they are the "largest group health insurer in Canada" or the "largest annuity underwriter in Canada". But talk about products or services? It is a tough call to tell them apart. For the insurers themselves, there is always controversy internally over whether or not they should advertise (their differences) at all. It is little wonder that the buying public has a difficult time choosing between them. It should be no surprise to the insurance companies that, time and time again, purchasers buy policies almost solely based on price.

The life insurance business, including the field of group insurance, is one of the most complex financial services industries in business today. To be a life insurance professional in today's market means that one has to know not only life insurance products, but also such an incredible range of products and services that most agents, brokers and consultants (the ABCs) choose to specialize in four or five product lines. One of Canada's major life insurance companies touted, in 1988, that it offered 65 different products for sale, but that its agents could usually only keep up on five or six of them! How's that for efficient use of resources!

¶1025 WHY MARKET A GROUP INSURANCE PLAN?

Group insurance, like other products and services, is purchased. At present, there is a lot of competition for your business among the insurers. Products and services offered by the various insurers look very similar to the layman. But there can be substantial differences between the plans themselves, their particular wording, their intent, the way they are funded, the rates, and above all, the attitudes of the various insurers competing in the marketplace.

There is a constant turnover, within the insurance industry, of financial circumstances inside each insurer, of insurer attitudes toward acquiring and maintaining books of business, of budget and profit forecasts, of staff and of systems. Each insurer reviews and predicts where it wants to be over the next year, the next few years. Depending on the prevalent views of the members of the boards of directors, the senior executives, senior and middle management, your organization can be either the "belle of the ball" or yesterday's dinner in terms of how the insurer values your business. At the local level, insurer group sales offices and their representatives can turnover, move, become content with their level of service, and some have the ability to change, within limits, a policyholder's rates. Shopping the market every three to five years will help to keep your costs in line and will serve to keep your insurers and their representatives more conscious of the rates that are being charged, and of the levels of service that are being provided.

¶1030 WHO OR WHAT IS AN AGENT?

An "agent" is paid, generally on a commission basis, by a specific insurance company to place business with that company. Commissions are a portion of the selling price(s) paid to the salesperson(s) for their work in selling the policies. Agents can work for many companies if they have permission to do so from their primary sponsoring company. Agents are sometimes referred to as being "captive" agents when their primary responsibilities and the majority, if not all of their business, goes to their primary sponsoring insurance company. In some jurisdictions, life insurance agents who are relatively new to the business, will be restricted by conditions of their provincial licensing, and by their sponsoring companies, from doing business with other insurers for a set time period (i.e., two years from initial licensing date).

The concept of "agency" is well set out in legal circles. An agent can fill out applications for insurance and can accept money on behalf of an insurance company. It is always best to make sure that group insurance premiums are paid, in cheque form, and made payable directly to the insurance company and not to the agent, unless there is a "third-party administration" agreement in place between the agent (broker or consultant) and the insurance company.

Agents work on behalf of the client and are supposed to hold the clients' best interests foremost. In the past, this situation has caused some conflicts between agents and insurers. Some agents believe that a client "belongs" to them; some insurers believe that the client belongs to the insurer. Both the agent and the insurer may have different beliefs as to what is "best" for the client. When these conflicts occur, the clients can be drawn into the fray, but these situations rarely result in group insurance coverage being put into jeopardy.

¶1035 WHO OR WHAT IS A BROKER?

An insurance broker is an insurance agent. The difference between a broker and an agent, in practical terms, is becoming lost, though the brokers will tell you differently. A broker is an agent who will place contracts for several insurance companies. Brokers, like agents, generally get paid commissions by the insurers for placing policies with them. Commissions and other remuneration will be discussed in a later chapter.

¶1040 WHO OR WHAT IS A CONSULTANT?

This question has been treated as a bit of a joke over the last few years as many white-collar professionals, recently laid off, have gone out on their own and called themselves "consultants" in whatever business they happened to be in. A consultant, for group insurance purposes, is someone usually with an insurance background, who will provide insurance advice and/or services for your organization on a "fee-for-service" basis. Some consultants will work for commissions and fees or any combination that is agreeable to both parties.

Consultants, especially those who work for what are termed the "alphabet houses" — the major firms — usually have a background specialty in a certain product line such as group insurance, pension plans, or human resources. Some may have specialty degrees in other areas such as actuarial sciences, mathematics, law, or have practical experience with an insurance company.

¶1045 INSURANCE: WHY THE BAD IMPRESSION?

What is one of the first questions asked when a worker dies? "Oh, I'm sorry to hear that. Did that person have any life insurance?" Or when someone gets disabled, "Does that person have a disability 'pension' at work?" Why, then, do some employees consider the prescription drug and dental benefits as more important than life and disability benefits? The answer is in the perception of the benefits and how they have historically been sold. We are not talking just about group insurance here. Life insurance agents and their personal insurance policies occasionally fell into disrepute through incomplete explanations of what was being sold and how the plans worked. They were often sold as "savings plans". And, of course, they were, if you considered a bank savings account rate of return as "savings". Enter the days of inflation. Old style life insurance policies, designed in the days of little to no inflation, were still being sold even when inflation was hitting 10 plus per cent. Rates of return were very poor in comparison to other types of savings accounts available on the market at that time. Even when the insurers increased their dividend scales to account for their increased profits, they acted too slowly to overcome the negative impression that had been created of them offering poor rates of return. More recently, life insurers have decreased their dividend scales on personal life insurance policies because of lower overall rates of return on their investments. This has resulted in policyholders receiving lower rates of return than were originally shown (although not guaranteed), in the illustrations used to sell the policies initially.

Sales approaches designed by the insurance companies in the 1950s were still being taught in the late 1970s and early 1980s to new agents. Agents were forced to continue to sell these older design products either because it was all that they were provided to sell, or because these products offered the highest commission rates. An agent trying to exist solely by selling the least expensive term policies would rarely be in the business two years down the road. Insurance companies continued to expand and sell variations on these "savings" type products, while the public began to tire of the sales pitch. This attitude continues to this day on both sides of the fence. In group insurance plans, some employees care more for benefits, such as prescription drug or dental coverage, in which they see an immediate return. There is little thought given to dying or disability. For people trying to "just make ends meet", the consequences of dying or becoming disabled are too far into the theoretical, and perhaps the metaphysical, realm to be of much use, as they see it. Who can take time to care about a possible death tomorrow if one is having trouble feeding the family today?

The trouble with this approach to viewing benefits is that employees tend to lose the perspective of what is really important. The immediate returns of dental and prescription drug plans are very small for the average employee, especially in comparison to the benefits of a properly designed disability plan or life insurance plan. There is very little, if any, insurance element in extended health care and dental plans. In fact, if employees share premiums with the employer, some employees may put more into these health and dental plans than they take out! Their "overpayments" go to pay the insurers' overhead, taxes, the ABC's commissions, and to offset the high claims of other employees within their group.

Up until very recently, the Canadian perspective was to put as many benefits as possible into the benefits program, without really looking at the reasons or the costs. Employers, who recently had to downsize because of economic conditions, still viewed certain benefits as a "right" of the employees. They complained about the rising cost of group insurance programs, yet were unwilling to consider dropping a dental benefit, the last benefit added to the program in many cases. And dental benefits alone can cost up to 40 per cent of a complete benefits package. Most employers and many employees forgot the basic rule of the insurance purchaser: *Buy to cover the catastrophe.*

Why emphasize coverage for the catastrophe? First of all, we should ask the question "What would be the worst thing that could happen to an employee or his or her family while they are working for our organization?" Is the answer "dental work"? Or is it a "prescription drug" claim? Perhaps it is a "chiropractor's bill"? Or an "ambulance charge"? Yes, these things can be expensive. And yes, these things can be very costly to the person who has a severe ongoing medical problem. But for the average employee, a couple of hundred dollars here or there will only mean some short-term suffering. An unexpected death or disability, by comparison, can mean severe hardship on the family of the affected employee. Where does a family turn when the breadwinner dies? If there is no life insurance, there is often no alternative (i.e., enough family savings to carry the family through the crisis and beyond). If there is no disability insurance, the chances are that there will be no continuing source of income, other than Canada Pension Plan's (CPP) disability benefit, or welfare. The chances of collecting welfare if your spouse is working are negligible. And if you have not contributed to CPP for a significant number of years, your disability benefit can be very low. Most employees do not purchase personal disability policies due to the cost. Most employees consider their group life insurance plans as an integral part of their families' financial planning. To die or to become disabled is a significant catastrophe! Maximum available coverage for these two benefits should be considered paramount when designing a group insurance plan. The other benefits should be considered as icing on the proverbial cake.

¶1050 CHECKLIST: WHAT DO YOU WANT TO DO? STEPS TO TAKE

¶1055 HIRE OR CHANGE AN AGENT, BROKER OR CONSULTANT

1. Review need for an ABC. ☐
2. Decision to hire an ABC. ☐
3. Confirmation of decision by management. ☐
4. List of candidates compiled. ☐
5. Basic information requested from candidates. ☐
6. Short list of candidates chosen. ☐
7. Short list candidates interviewed. ☐
8. Winner selected. ☐
9. ABC remuneration and services confirmed. ☐
10. Write new Agent of Record letter; confirm commissions, if applicable, to new insurer. ☐

¶1060 REMOVE AND NOT REPLACE AN AGENT, BROKER OR CONSULTANT

1. Review need for an ABC. ☐
2. Decide to remove ABC. ☐
3. Write letter to insurance company, advising them of the decision. Include request to put policy on a "net commission basis". ☐
4. Advise ABC by telephone. ☐

¶1065 MARKET A GROUP INSURANCE POLICY BY USING AN AGENT, BROKER OR CONSULTANT

1. Decision to market policy. ☐
2. Decision to do work yourself, or hire an ABC. ☐
3. Choose present ABC, or hire new ABC. ☐
4. Write new Agent of Record Letter, if a new ABC is chosen (see Sample Agent of Record Letter at ¶3095). ☐
5. Confirm commissions or fees in writing to ABC. ☐
6. Confirm all services to be provided with ABC. ☐
7. Compile and confirm employee data list with ABC. ☐
8. Provide ABC with copies of all policies, amendments, and employee booklets. ☐
9. Meet with ABC to discuss alternative benefits. ☐
10. ABC writes to present insurer to obtain up-to-date experience and rates. ☐
11. ABC prepares specifications; possible review by employer. ☐
12. ABC mails, or couriers specifications to insurers (addresses in the Appendices at ¶17,055). ☐
13. ABC receives responses. ☐
14. ABC analyzes responses, obtains clarification. ☐
15. ABC prepares spreadsheets. ☐
16. ABC prepares report. ☐
17. ABC sets up meeting and reviews report with employer. ☐
18. Employer and ABC agree on shortlist. ☐
19. ABC sets up meetings with shortlisted insurer group offices. ☐
20. ABC and employer interview shortlist insurers. ☐
21. Employer chooses winner. ☐
22. Winner advised; unsuccessful insurers advised and thanked by letter. ☐

¶1070 MARKET A GROUP INSURANCE POLICY WITHOUT USING AN AGENT, BROKER OR CONSULTANT

1. Decision to market policy. ☐
2. Decision to do work without the services of an agent broker, or consultant. ☐
3. Compile an Employee Data List (see example at ¶8155). ☐
4. Review list of possible insurers (see ¶17,035 in Appendices). ☐
5. Obtain up-to-date experience and rate information from present insurers. ☐
6. Make copies of Master Policies, all amendments and employee booklets to send to insurers. ☐
7. Write brief "introduction to specifications" letter (see example at ¶8135). ☐
8. Write alternative quote requests; include blank spreadsheets, questionnaire in proposal. ☐
9. Mail or courier specifications to insurer group offices (see addresses at ¶17,055 in Appendices). ☐
10. Receive responses. ☐
11. Analyze responses, obtain clarifications. ☐
12. Compile spreadsheets; spreadsheets will be the "report". ☐
13. Choose and contact group offices of shortlist candidates (suggest a maximum of three). ☐
14. Interview shortlist candidates. ☐
15. Choose winner. ☐
16. Advise winning group office; send thank you letter to unsuccessful insurers. ☐

¶1075 REVIEW A RENEWAL

1. Insurer requests up-to-date employee data list. ☐
2. Provide insurer with up-to-date data list. ☐
3. Insurer prepares renewal. ☐
4. Insurer sends renewal to policyholder or ABC. ☐
5. Review renewal. ☐
6. Compare renewal to last year's renewal and the examples in this book. ☐
7. Question group representative about renewal, if not satisfied. ☐
8. Group representative provides answers. ☐
9. Renewal renegotiated, or benefits amended to meet requirements and budget. ☐
10. Renewal accepted or decision made to market policy. ☐

CHAPTER 2

¶2000 THE POLITICS OF GROUP INSURANCE

¶2005 INTRODUCTION

Politics play a large role with group insurance programs. There are many levels of politicking that go on within the group insurance industry. One major Canadian life insurance company lost up to one-third of its Quebec business when its head office moved out of Quebec in the late 1970s. In addition, the same company was replaced by a Quebec-based life insurance company as underwriter of the federal government's group life insurance policy. Politics can run deep when dealing with multi-millions of dollars at stake on the large policies. On the local level also, politics can play just as important a role. Historically, life insurance companies obtained new group insurance clients through the contacts made by their own life insurance agents. The agent made the contact, brought in the (salaried) group representative, who explained the policy, and the administration procedures, presented the proposal, and signed up the account. The agent was reimbursed for his or her efforts by means of a commission. Today, the business still operates in much the same way. Agents, brokers or consultants (ABCs) ask the various insurers for quotes on a client's behalf, gather and analyze the quotes, and then show their choices to the client. The client then makes the decision as to which insurer to use.

The agents, brokers and consultants are all competing against each other for your group's business. They guard their contacts, their clients and their knowledge with tenacity. One of the main concerns they have is "control" over their clients. This control is most often exercised by the amount of knowledge they provide to their clients, and even to their own colleagues! After all, people always ask successful people about the secrets of their success. One of the main secrets to success is in keeping information to oneself. This is a main ingredient in becoming successful in knowledge-based industries. How, then, has this affected the group insurance purchaser?

All ABCs have two things that they guard: their knowledge and how much time it really takes to provide their services. The reasons are simple. If someone else knows how to do their job, or to provide their service, that someone will find ways to improve or better the job. With the dollars up for grabs, in terms of commissions or fees, for each client, it is also an advantage to the ABC to keep information, and how much time it takes to do each project close to the chest. Consumers may become quite upset if they realize that they have given thousands of dollars to an ABC for projects that required very little effort on the part of the ABC. On the other hand, some consumers are more than willing to pay for the level of expertise that they are receiving.

Within a group insurance purchaser's organization, the control over an employee benefits program is sometimes used as protection for one's position within the company. A review of the group insurance program is also used by people new to the controlling position to prove their worth within the organization. A marketing and change of insurers can result in a savings, at least in the short term, in many situations. The result can be a feather in the cap of the person in the new position. For the group insurance purchaser, these factors affecting the purchase decision are referred to as "internal politics". Factors outside of the purchasing organization, which influence the purchasing decision, including those within the insurance companies and benefit providers, are referred to as "external politics".

In the United States, where group insurance premiums are very high in comparison to Canada (because there is no universal Medicare), a much larger percentage of the group insurance business is conducted directly (without the use of an agent, broker or consultant) between the insurance companies and their clients. Almost every group policy in Canada, on the other hand, uses some form of intermediary employed to act on the "insured's" behalf. Canadian group insurance policyholders pay out millions to agents, brokers and consultants annually, to perform this intermediary function. These millions are paid out in the form of commissions built directly into the rates, or in the form of consulting fees, which are billed separately. In odd situations, some unethical ABCs have billed fees at the same time as they have collected commissions! In effect, their clients have paid twice for the same services.

This control, by the agents, brokers and consultants, has hidden the fact that many organizations can choose to deal directly with insurance companies, and benefit provider group offices, without using the services of the ABCs. Insurance companies may have a minimum size limit, in terms of the number of employees that a group must have before it will offer this service, but that minimum is low. It is usually in the range of ten to 20 employees. Anything over that number, depending on the insurer, will allow the insurer to offer group insurance rates directly to your organization on a "net commission" basis. By asking an insurer's group office to cut out the commission payments from the rates, an organization can save up to 10 per cent or more, depending on the benefit, of the group insurance costs! This will mean though that the group will lose whatever services the agent, broker or consultant offers, particularly if they are paid strictly on a commission basis. If a group wants to keep these services, it is often possible to offer the ABC an hourly rate on a retainer basis for his or her services.

Why do the insurance companies and their group insurance offices, not offer these "net commission" rates to the consumer more often? The answer is simple. First of all, many agents, brokers and consultants are seen to provide a valuable intermediary service between the policyholders and the insurance companies. Second, some policyholders do not have the time or do not make the time to set up group plans this way, preferring the status quo to the "fear" of doing something they perceive as different. Third, the majority of an insurer's business comes through the ABCs. The insurers fear that if they start to offer and to advertise net commission rates, the ABCs will stop putting business through them. Most group insurers as well, are not set up to deal directly with prospects and clients in terms of marketing. But if the client tells the insurer that they no longer require the services of their ABC and requests in writing a change to net commission rates, many insurers will comply.

Agents, brokers and consultants also play "politics" in whom they recommend to their clients in terms of insurers. One insurer's representative may have a better working relationship with a particular ABC than another. This insurer is more likely to show up favourably on a spread sheet than someone else, even if the services and rates are comparable. Some insurers offer sales bonuses to ABCs as incentives to place business with that insurer. These bonuses are rarely billed back through, in the rates, to the policyholder. But the offer of a bonus can cause an ABC to call up a particular insurer, advise the insurer's representative of its place on the spreadsheet, and negotiate a better rate or two. Both ABCs and insurers can have preferences with whom they like to negotiate business.

Insurer group insurance representatives also are forced to play the political game within their own offices, and between themselves and their underwriters. A group representative that has placed business, for his insurance company, that has lost money or caused administrative grief, is less likely to get a break from the underwriters on the next piece of business. An underwriter in the head office may not trust the information that has been provided by the group representative on the next case and could therefore offer a very conservative (i.e., high rates) quote. This can be detrimental to any purchasing organization that is trying to procure the best combination of rates benefits, and service available.

Group insurance underwriters, especially the junior ones, may not understand particular industries. A junior underwriter, straight out of school and who has lived in Toronto for his or her lifetime, is less likely to understand regional differences and attitudes than a senior person in the same position. The junior underwriter, with little experience, is also less likely to know anything about a particular industry and may well charge higher than necessary rates to compensate for this lack of knowledge. Remember that one of the main functions of a group insurance underwriter is to look for reasons *not* to underwrite a piece of business! They will tell you that they just want to underwrite the policy at the correct rates. But the reality is that they are in the last position of protecting the insurer's underwriting profit. Getting an inexperienced underwriter can cause incorrect rates to be charged to your policy.

Inside an insurance company, there can be a division between the "group insurance" side of the business, and the "agency", or "individual" side of the business, concerning offering group insurance packages for smaller organizations. This is the result of concern for the bottom line in each of these divisions. Group insurance policies, for smaller groups, are more expensive to set up on a "per employee" basis. For example, the cost to print a policy, to compile the administration data, and to send an administration kit, is virtually the same for a group containing ten employees, as for a group containing one hundred. The total premium differs substantially, however. The "Group Division" of an insurance company, may want to withdraw from offering group packages to smaller organizations because the profits are too small, or because there are underwriting losses with their smaller group clients. The "Agency Division" will oppose any withdrawal, citing that loss of the ability to offer group insurance to small businesses will jeopardize its ability to underwrite and sell other types of insurance, such as life/disability insurance, funding for buy/sell agreements to these same business owners. The compromise, reached within the insurance company, may be that the Agency Division agrees to assume any loss or profit on the small group insurance product line. Unless watched carefully, this type of arrangement can cause rifts within the insurer, inflexible products, uncompetitive rates (either too high or too low), poor policyholder service, and underwriting losses. Insurers sometimes attempt to overcome this by transferring a "group" person, to the Agency Division, to oversee the product line. This person can be viewed as an outsider by the Agency Division and also by the Group Division, and runs the risk of running up against walls with any attempt to change things for the better. These internal rifts, can, and do, affect everyone concerned, including the policyholders.

¶2010 EXTERNAL POLITICS

¶2015 THE SET-UP OF INSURANCE COMPANIES

Life insurance companies are organized internally into different divisions. Each division is normally responsible for its own growth and profitability. The divisions are: (1) individual life insurance; (2) group insurance; (3) pensions; (4) investments; and (5) property management. Some insurance companies specialize in one or two areas only. Others, such as the larger companies, try to offer all products. Although these divisions may be part of the same company, it is not necessarily true that each division knows what the other divisions are doing. Therefore, an insurer may refuse to acknowledge that providing the investment management for your pension plan should affect the rates that it is offering on the group insurance policy.

Within the group division of an insurance company, there are several sections: underwriting, claims, administration, sales and marketing. Almost all of the positions within this division are salaried. There may be incentive bonuses for the field positions, such as group representatives, to put new policies on the books. There may also be incentive bonuses to the field representatives, the senior underwriters and senior management based on growth and profitability. ABCs are not considered, by most insurance companies, to be part of the group insurance division of the company.

¶2020 THE WAYS THAT INSURERS MARKET GROUP INSURANCE PLANS

Most insurance companies market the majority of their group products to corporations and organizations through agents, brokers and consultants. They are also able to market their products and services directly to the customer, although some may choose to market only through the ABCs for political reasons. At present, there is little effort by insurance companies to market directly to organizations requiring group insurance programs. This is basically because of a fear factor. The fear is that should an insurer start to actively solicit business directly, without going through the very well-established ABC network, then there is a chance that it will lose more than it gains. A direct marketer of products is not as likely to retain present business gained through the ABC network, and it is just as unlikely to "be recommended" by the ABCs for a new account, especially if there would be no commissions payable! Organizations, which have gone directly to the insurance companies to underwrite their group insurance plans, in the past, can still employ the services of agents, brokers, or consultants at a later date, if required, for a fee or commissions.

It should be noted that direct sales in the United States have been around for years, and where commissions are paid, the scale is generally much lower, while medical premiums are higher.

¶2025 INTERNAL POLITICS: INSIDE THE POLICYHOLDER'S ORGANIZATION

The control of the employee benefits program within the group policyholder organization is seen, on the one hand, as an extremely important task, and on the other hand, as just another task and bill to pay. How the benefits are viewed depends on the size of the organization, its sophistication, whether or not there is a union or employee association involved, and the attitudes of the owners and senior managers. A new company, rapidly growing with a strong focus on obtaining new business may not spend as much time on the benefits programs, as an older company, with an older workforce. Nor does it have to spend as much time! A program that is properly set up for a new, smaller company, should only need a review once or twice per year for an hour or so. A program for a larger, older organization may require more review, because of its corporate culture, the needs of its employees, and the tendency of "older" organizations towards bureaucracy and formality.

¶2030 CORPORATE GOALS

There has been much written about the importance of corporate goal planning within a successful organization. The corporate mission statement should state how the organization deals with its own employees. A mission statement that states this up front sets the tone for how it intends to treat its employees. A mission statement can also be used as a reference source for management when it is asked to review future situations and opportunities. The bottom line is "write it down". It will assist those who tend to politic at length to keep the corporate goals in focus.

¶2035 WHO IN THE ORGANIZATION IS RESPONSIBLE AND WHY?

In an organization of five to ten employees, the question of responsibility is generally a moot point. It will fall to the person doing the books or perhaps the person running the paperwork end of things. In a larger organization, the senior manager of human resources, the controller, director of administration, the accountant, or the bookkeeper is usually assigned or takes up the duties.

For an organization that looks at a group insurance program as just another expense, it is extremely important to ensure that this "expense" item is handled in an appropriate manner. This means that time must be spent in the beginning, and on a continuous basis, to make sure that the company puts the most appropriate benefits in place and administers them correctly. A program that omits important benefits, or that fails to have the eligible employees enrolled may place the organization in potential legal hot water, in a liable situation, or may adversely affect corporate morale. It is important, therefore, that enough attention be paid to the program to keep these potentialities at bay.

The larger organization also must place these reasons high on the priority list. Attention should be paid to which department and to which position the responsibility is to be placed. It is generally advisable to keep all employee benefit responsibilities together under one department, i.e., keep the pensions area with the group insurance benefits area. Employee communications are less complicated when only one department is involved. It is also advisable to have someone who is interested and in favour of employee benefits to be in charge of the plan. Being in favour of benefits should also mean being in favour of cost-effective benefits. Be wary of appointing an individual who wants to add more benefits than may be necessary or cost effective.

¶2040 MORE POLITICS

The tendency over the last 25 years or so has been to increase benefit plans and to expand the range of services that they cover. Examples of the types of services commonly covered in plans now that were not commonly covered years ago, range from things such as coverage for "masseurs", to other paramedical practitioner services, to dental plans. Companies, generally, need to take a harsh look at the types of benefits that they are offering, the internal clauses within the policies, whether or not each benefit item is required and how much each of these benefits costs. There has been little suggestion by the insurance companies to reduce benefits because their income and profit figures rely on total premium dollars; the more premium, the more they show growth, and, theoretically at least, the more profit they could show.

Similarly, the ABC's commission income increases if the premiums increase. On top of all of this, in every province there is a "hidden" premium tax amounting to a minimum 2 per cent of the premium dollar. Governments are gaining income by means of this tax. Recently, in Quebec, the provincial government declared that premiums paid by an employer on behalf of an employee are to be considered as a taxable benefit for provincial tax purposes! The higher the premiums are, the more tax is paid to the various provincial governments. So one can see that there has been little incentive in the insurance industry or in government circles to reduce the cost of these plans.

The end result has been a huge increase in the number of plans and of their "complexity", especially in terms of including rarely used benefit clauses. The insurance industry has not encouraged its clients to look into the concept of "self-insurance" because this concept does not put any income into the insurers' pockets. Self-insurance, in a nutshell, is "insuring" a risk on one's own. But why do this if the insurance is available from the insurance marketplace? The answer is simple. Because it can save money!

Much of the so-called insurance in today's group insurance programs is more of an administration function than real "insurance" per se. For example, in the typical extended health care plan or dental plan, the insurer takes a policyholder's total claims for each benefit, at the end of the policy year, multiplies the total by their "retention" percentage and determines what the rates for the next year will be. "Retention" is the insurance industry word for "what percentage of the premium dollar the insurer takes" to pay the claims, administer the policy, pay the commissions, pay the taxes and make a profit. This percentage can range as high as 35 per cent to as low as 8 per cent, and is generally dependent on the size of the policyholder's annual premium. The more premium paid the lower the percentage charged. It works like a form of volume discount purchasing. The more one purchases, the lower the cost of the servicing element of the policy. The insurance premium is comprised of amounts to pay the actual claims, plus amounts to pay for the administration of paying the claims. If you know that you are going to have to pay a claim anyway, why pay someone else the administration expense to pay that claim?

For certain benefits, especially those of low frequency and of low dollar value, such as "vision care", it may be less expensive to self-insure. On the other hand, you may consider the services of the insurer to be well worth the administration cost.

CHAPTER 3

¶3000 THE ABCs: AGENTS, BROKERS AND CONSULTANTS

¶3005 ABCs: HOW THEY OPERATE AND GET PAID

Agents and brokers are best termed as "individual entrepreneurs". Most are "sponsored" by an insurer, but in effect, they work for themselves. Agents and brokers are responsible for their own production, their own income, and their own expenses. Consultants may be reimbursed for expenses if they are paid on a salary plus bonus basis. Every province in which ABCs operate, licensed ABCs sell life or accident insurance on a commission basis. In order to be licensed, one must pass a general knowledge test about the life insurance industry and its products. The licensing is not specific to group insurance. In fact, the licensing is aimed at individual life and disability insurance sales agents; one would be hard pressed to find much in the licensing study material, or on the licensing examinations, which pertains to employee benefit plans.

An agent, broker or consultant, by law, must be sponsored by a life insurance company in order to obtain life and accident insurance licences. Agents, brokers and consultants who are licensed, must be bonded. Once the licences are obtained, an ABC can sell and consult on any individual or group life and health insurance product. When a group plan is sold to an organization, then commissions can be paid to the ABC. Anyone can consult on group insurance plans without a licence and without formal accreditation. However, without the licences, they cannot accept commissions from insurers. There may be rules within the provincial insurance licensing bodies' regulations that restrict "new-to-the-business" agents from selling any other products than their own licensing insurer's products, for a period of up to two years after date of hire. These restrictions can be circumvented by the new agent, with the approval of the sponsoring company, or by the agent funnelling the commissions through an agent who has been around longer than two years.

Consultants operate in a way similar to agents and brokers. They will assist an organization in designing and implementing a group insurance program, and when this project is completed, they receive any commissions payable. A big difference is that consultants will give the purchasing organization another payment option besides commissions. Consultants generally offer either a fee-for-service billing arrangement, a commission-only arrangement, or a combination of the two. Agents and brokers rarely offer to work on a fee-for-service arrangement; most prefer to work for commissions.

Whether an organization decides to use an agent, a broker, or a consultant, it will find that none of them operates for free. Insurance companies have standard commission scales. These commissions are included in the rates unless a written request is made to take them out, or to change them. Insurance companies' scales are not all the same. Depending on the benefit, there may be up to a five or more per cent difference between the scales. A knowledgeable and reputable ABC will include in any program marketing specifications, the specific commission scale, if any, to use when requesting group insurance quotes from the various insurers. Asking all quoting insurance companies to use a standard commission scale will enable a more fair comparison of rates and retention percentages between the insurers.

Consulting firms which have negotiated not to receive commissions operate on an hourly rate, a daily rate, a weekly rate or a project rate, in much the same manner as law and accounting firms. The key term for consultants is "billable hours". All employees of consulting firms are evaluated on how many hours they can "bill" to clients. One of the ways for clients to control consulting fees is to establish and confirm the rates for completed projects in advance. Most of the front-end work — that of meeting clients and procuring new business — is done by the senior partners or consultants in the firm. The actual group insurance marketing is normally carried out by the assistants. This can serve to reduce project costs to the consultant, but not necessarily reduce billed costs to the client. Consumers must be aware of being billed at the senior partner rate, while having the work done by the more junior staff.

Consultants who are not partners generally receive one-third of the new income that they bring into the consulting firm. The remaining two-thirds are split equally, with one-third going for expenses and the other third going for profit. Consultants who are new to the game should be aware of two things. The first is to confirm what constitutes "new business" and, secondly what defines a "new" client. If a consulting firm takes the attitude that any income derived from a "client" in the last five years, even if it was only a one-time $500 project, means that that organization is still considered a "client", it will be extremely difficult for you as the new consultant to bring in any new clients. One should also be aware of what constitutes a sales territory and who gets to keep what prospect on their exclusive list, and for how long. New consultants can get quickly frustrated by the established status quo unless they are careful. A regular turnover of consultants is required by some senior consultants and partners in order to keep up their own income levels, as the senior people get to pick over the best accounts when a consultant leaves.

There are several ways in which ABCs can tilt the scales to increase their income. One of these is to request a commission scale which pays more than the insurers' standard scales, when asking for quotes. Another is to charge clients on a fee-for-service basis, ask for net-commission rates in the specifications, and then change the rates to include commissions without the client's knowledge. A method that has been widely used was to ask the insurers to quote benefits separately so that the commission scales start at the highest level for each benefit. An alternative to this method is to place benefits with different insurers, i.e., place the group life insurance with one insurance company, the long-term disability with another, and the health benefits with another. Each way increases the commission income to the ABC. This extra cost is ultimately borne by the consumer.

Insurers allow this situation to exist. In their attempts to obtain business, insurers will offer incentives to an ABC in order to place the business. These incentives can include the addition of extra benefits at "no cost" to their standard wording. No cost, that is, until there are claims. Extra claims at renewal, mean extra premium next year; extra premium means more commissions. Or it can mean extra fees charged to the client to analyze why the rates have increased so dramatically.

The size of the commissions directly affects the rates. Some insurance companies also offer bonus incentives to place business their way. These bonuses are generally paid in the form of increased commissions. An example might be that if an ABC placed three group insurance policies with a particular insurer, and a minimum of, say, $100,000 of premium, then the ABC would be eligible to receive an extra 2 per cent of the commissions paid as a bonus. (These bonuses may not be directly charged to the policyholder through the rates, but they are part of the overall expenses of the insurer. As such, they ultimately affect the amounts charged to each policy.) This type of incentive scheme is geared by the insurance company to increase its sales. It is not geared to the consumer. ABCs who are offered this type of bonus may be tempted to bend their interpretations of the spreadsheet data, or their presentations, to lend a bias towards the insurer offering the bonus. This can have the negative repercussion of the purchaser not being made aware of all of the facts. It should be mentioned that not all insurers offer these bonuses. Neither do all ABCs manipulate rates and commissions. But it is best to be aware that these things can, and do, happen.

¶3010 COMMISSIONS

Group insurance commissions are normally paid annually, in advance, to the agent, broker or consultant. A portion of the commission scale is allocated for the "sale" of the policy. Another portion is allocated for "servicing" the policy. Servicing should include assisting the policyholder's administrator in understanding policy administration procedures, holding employee meetings, clarifying policy terms with the underwriter and acting as an intermediary between the insurer and the policyholder. First-year commissions for the policy sale, and for first-year policy service, are paid after the underwriters have accepted the risk, the first month's premium cheque has been received, and the policy is well on its way to being finalized. It is not usually required that the final policy wording be approved and the policy issued prior to paying the commissions.

Renewal commissions are normally paid the month after the policy has entered into the next policy year. Most of today's commission scales are called "level" scales. This means that the same commission percentages are paid year after year, regardless of the amount of work put in by the ABC. In the past, commission scales were set up on a "high/low" basis; higher in the first year than in subsequent years. This took into account that most of the work done by an ABC was done in the first year. Commissions paid on a high/low basis were higher in the first year and significantly lower in succeeding years. The unfortunate thing about these latter scales was that some ABCs advised their clients to change insurers, even if a change was not warranted. Changing insurers meant that the ABC would continue to be paid at "top of scale", and could, thereby, obtain more commissions on the plan.

The life insurance industry generally allows the more successful agents, brokers and consultants to request that insurers include higher, non-standard commission scales in their group insurance quotes. The insurers oblige by increasing the scales and pay for this by increasing the rates charged to the purchasers. Even if the policyholder is made aware of the scale being implemented, the significance of the larger scale can be glossed over by the ABC. Commission scales paid to ABCs are still considered to be a subject that is rarely discussed outside of the life insurance industry itself. The ability to implement larger commission scales for group insurance is unlike virtually every other line of insurance or investments offered to the public. It is also possible for ABCs to request lower than standard commission scales, either when doing a marketing or at policy renewal.

Group insurance policyholders should be aware that they, ultimately, have control over whether or not commissions are paid, and what scale is to be paid. Only the smallest groups — those with below 15 to 20 employees — are normally protected by the insurance companies' insistence that only their standard scales be used. Policyholders, especially those with over 20 employees, have the right to choose their ABC, and to negotiate the fees and the commission scale to be used. ABCs and some policyholder employees, who ignore the scales as "insignificant" so that they can keep their income levels up, or, in the case of the employees, keep their work levels low, are downplaying a very important fact. If the commission was coming out of your own personal pocket and you had a choice, would you pay it? The argument put up by some ABCs is that "their" services are worth it, and then they will show you in detail how many "billable" hours were put into your account. Group policyholders can save ABC costs, on a marketing, by doing some, or all of the work themselves, or with the help of the insurance companies group representatives. Not only can group representatives help, but they can assist with much of the comparison work at no charge. However, the majority of groups in Canada today believe in, trust, and use an ABC to assist them with the purchase and service of their group insurance policies.

A comparison of the two commission scales below shows the costs, in premium, that can be built into group insurance policies by ABCs.

¶3015 SAMPLE COMMISSION SCALES FOR GROUP INSURANCE PLANS

The following are two commission scales. The second is a standard scale used by an insurance company. The first is an example of another scale that an ABC could request. Rates shown to a client might include a scale such as one of these, or another. Scales are not consistent between insurers, providers, or even ABCs. Notice that the differences in the examples appear small, but when worked out based on an annual premium over a number of years, can be quite significant.

Example #1: ABC Special Commission Scale

1. Group Life, Weekly Indemnity, Health and Dental insurance, paid *per benefit*

Annual Premium Total	*Commission Scale*
First $ 20,000	10%
Next $ 15,000	7.5%
Next $ 25,000	5%
Next $ 50,000	3%
Next $150,000	2%
Next $250,000	1%

2. Group Long-Term Disability

Annual Premium Total	*Commission Scale*
All premium	15%

Example #2: Insurance Company Commission Scale

Group Life, AD&D, Weekly Indemnity, Health and Dental insurance paid on *combined premium*

Annual Premium Total	*Commission Scale*
First $ 10,000	10%
Next $ 15,000	7.5%
Next $ 25,000	5%
Next $ 50,000	3%
Next $150,000	2%
Next $250,000	1%

Group Long-Term Disability

Annual Premium Total	*Commission Scale*
First $50,000	10%
Over $50,000	0%

¶3020 COMMISSION SCALE COMPARISON: THE EFFECT ON WHAT YOU PAY

Let us compare the two scales over the course of a year. The difference is the extra premium paid by the employer and the employees, (if the premiums are shared) over the course of that year.

ABC Special Commission Scale		*Example Scale #1*	
Benefit	*Annual Premium*	*Commission Produced* Combined Benefits and Premium Basis	Per Benefit Basis
Group Life	$ 5,000		$ 500
AD&D	500		50
Dependant Life	500		50
Health	20,000		2,000
Dental	25,000		2,375
Subtotal	$51,000	$3,925	$4,975
LTD	8,000	1,200	1,200
		TOTAL: $5,125	$6,175

Insurer Standard Commission Scale		*Example Scale #2* Combined Benefits and Premium Basis
All Benefits except LTD combined	$51,000	$3,405
LTD	$ 8,000	800
		TOTAL: $4,205

¶3025 CONSULTANT CHARGES

Independent consultants, and often senior consultants within major consulting firms, are free to charge as high or as low as they want. *A high chargeable rate is not a guarantee that the person charging it knows what he or she is doing.* Many consultants specialize in pension plans and issues. Consultants may or may not know anything at all about the particulars of designing, funding and marketing a group insurance plan, although they may well be experts in another benefits area. A later chapter will examine how to choose the best available ABC.

The following chargeable rates are representative for a major employee benefits consulting firm.

Sample Fee-For-Service Rates

Actuarial Services	$250 per hour
Actuarial Assistant	$165 per hour
Group Insurance Consultant	$165 per hour
Consulting Assistant	$140 per hour
Support Staff/Secretarial	$ 60 per hour

¶3030 ABC GAMES AND MARKETING STRATEGIES

Agents, brokers and consultants who are successful are so because of three things. First, they have a consistent prospecting system, including follow-up. Second, they have a reputation. Third, they have information and know-how to market it. The majority of life insurance agents and brokers sell group insurance as one of many products in their portfolio. Unless they make a particular effort to learn about, prospect for, and market group insurance plans, an agent or broker may only sell those plans that he or she happens to come across. Since agents and brokers in these situations may not be completely up to date in terms of group insurance knowledge, they tend to rely on insurer group representatives. Newer agents historically have brought in group representatives whenever there was a technical question or problem.

Specialist agents and brokers, on the other hand, may be of more assistance, but only if they have the experience. Some agents and brokers either do not have, or have only a limited, marketing program and follow-up for group insurance unless they specialize in this area. Employee benefits consultants tend to have a greater focus on group insurance. Here again, individual consultants may specialize in one area, such as pensions, and have only general knowledge of another area of benefits, such as group insurance. In terms of marketing, some consulting firms have very little knowledge, surprisingly enough, of who, what and where their prospective clients are. The essence of marketing is knowing one's clients and prospects. That includes, knowing about their organizations, their personnel, their competition, and their corporate goals. The reason why ABCs may not have this basic type of information is because it takes time to put the information together, and there is no immediate payback, nor billable hours to be charged.

ABCs use membership in professional organizations to further their marketing efforts. These organizations are good sources of information. From a marketing perspective, many of these organizations are composed mostly of their peers and competitors. It is very difficult to market one's services to the competition! On the purchasing end of things, it is surprising the number of organizations that require group insurance plan assistance, who will just call up who they know and ask them who they consult. This can be an expensive crap shoot; acceptable, perhaps, in an expanding economy where the emphasis is on growth, but definitely not the most recommended way of controlling expenses, or hiring the best available.

¶3035 HIRING AN ABC

¶3040 INTRODUCTION

One of the quickest ways to find out who is available locally is to consult the *Yellow Pages* of your local telephone directory. Should you live in a smaller centre, your local public library will have telephone books for the larger centres nearest your location. Look under the titles of "Employee Benefits Consultants", or, under "Life Insurance (Agencies)" and pick a company. Try also to locate a copy of a magazine specializing in Canadian employee benefits. In addition to advertisements, every year these magazines publish lists which contain the names and addresses of the majority of the largest consulting firms in Canada. Another alternative is to join the local chapter of the Canadian Benefits and Pensions Conference (the C.B.P.C.). Any local actuarial and benefits consulting firms will be able to give the names and numbers of the C.B.P.C. people to contact.

Hiring an ABC to shop the market for your group insurance program is as easy as writing a letter. An ABC will require what is called an "Agent of Record" letter. This letter is written on your organization's letterhead, and is signed by an executive. It specifies that the ABC is appointed and that the ABC is allowed access to all pertinent information on file with the present insurers, including premium and claims information. A sample Agent of Record letter is included at ¶3095 in this chapter. Note in the sample that there is a portion to be signed by the appointee, guaranteeing that the appointee will keep all information strictly private and confidential. A copy of the letter should be kept on file by the appointing organization.

The hardest part of hiring an ABC is in picking the best. The next section will discuss what to look for when hiring an ABC.

¶3045 HOW TO CHOOSE AN AGENT, BROKER OR CONSULTANT

¶3050 Where to Find Out Who Is Available

1. Yellow Pages.
2. Libraries.
3. Board of Trade or Chamber of Commerce directories.
4. Associations, i.e., local human resources association.
5. Professional associations.
6. Business associates.

7. Business competitors.
8. Referrals.
9. Tender advertisements in the newspaper.
10. Want ads.

¶3055 How Can You Tell Which ABC Is Best for Your Organization?

Once you have compiled your list of potential ABCs, ask for their brochures and annual reports of their organizations, either by letter or by telephone. These may tell you something about the head offices of the ABCs' organizations, but generally have little to do with the people that you will eventually deal with on a day-to-day basis.

Telephone and ask for a partial list of their clients and for three client references. Be aware that they will give you references of organizations with which they have good relationships. See if you can find out which clients they have lost lately and ask these people their opinion about the ABC's service.

Now you can call up three to five ABCs and get to know them. Set appointments to see all of them on one day, or at least on two consecutive days. It is generally accepted that being either the first or the last to be interviewed is the best position. Be aware that the ABCs may try to adjust your schedule to fit them into one of these two positions.

Choose your ABC based on what services are offered, how well they know your business, your industry, and your business environment. You will have an idea of how well they know their own business through the references and through your discussions.

Some organizations use ABCs as consultants, for reasons that may be unnecessary. For example, "consultants" can be used to postpone, delay, or avoid major human resources decisions concerning the organization. Decisions such as whether or not to drop an expensive benefit, i.e., a dental plan, can be placed on the shoulders of a consultant. The consultant's recommendations and report can take months to prepare, if need be. After the report, the decision can be delayed longer by marketing the benefits program.

ABCs can also be used if the organization needs a scapegoat. This can serve as protection for a middle manager who does not want to, is not confident to, does not have the time to, or is not competent to learn the specifics involved in benefits programs.

ABCs are used to provide the person doing the hiring of the ABC with an outside source of agreement with his or her views. If required, ABCs can provide answers to specifics in a format which reflects the views of the person doing the hiring.

ABCs should be hired to educate, to provide an independent set of ideas, to act in place of having to hire a full-time person, and to provide facts and opinions in order that management be able to make informed management decisions.

All potential ABCs wishing to act for your organization should be interviewed. To assure a form of consistency in your interview process, use the questionnaire provided in this book (see ¶3065 below).

¶3060 CHOOSING AN ABC: QUESTIONNAIRE

The following questionnaire is designed to assist an organization in choosing the best agent, broker or consultant to handle the marketing and servicing of a group insurance policy.

¶3065 How to Use the Questionnaire

Every organization purchasing a group insurance plan will have different priorities. Therefore, each question in the questionnaire will have a different level of importance to each organization. For this reason, the first step is to rank the importance of each question. To do this, place a "10" beside each question that is very important to your organization, a "5" beside each question that is somewhat important, and a "3" beside each question that your organization considers to be least important. Do this prior to the interviews. The questionnaire is designed to be used during a face-to-face interview. It can be adapted to receive written answers.

The questionnaire is now ready to be used. Ask each ABC to answer the questions one at a time. Rank each answer by putting a number beside the question. For example, if the question, in terms of importance, has been given a maximum score of 10, and your organization liked the ABC's answer, you might assign a 10 as a score for that question. If the answer was not totally to your liking, then the score might be a 5, or a 3, or perhaps a 2. After the interview has been completed, total the score. Use the same questions on each of the ABCs being interviewed. A simple comparison of the scores will assist in the decision process.

It is possible to forgo the interview process, and assign an ABC based on gut instinct. Should circumstances change, thereby causing you to revise your decision, remember that an ABC, hired on a commission-only basis, can be replaced at any time, unless there is also a signed contract in place that stipulates a notice period be given.

The Agent, Broker, Consultant Questionnaire

	Maximum Score Allowed	*#1*	*#2*	*#3*
1. From where do you provide your services?	______	____	____	____
2. What are your professional qualifications?	______	____	____	____
3. What is your group insurance experience?	______	____	____	____
4. Who are your clients?	______	____	____	____
5. How much experience do you have with our type of business?	______	____	____	____
6. What are your technical resources?	______	____	____	____
7. Do you (operate by) have a professional code of ethics? Whose?	______	____	____	____
8. How do you market your services?	______	____	____	____
9. How do you differentiate your services from your competitors?	______	____	____	____
10. How many clients do you service, in total, in your local office?	______	____	____	____
11. How many group insurance plans do you personally service?	______	____	____	____
12. What type of back-up technical support, i.e., computers do you use?	______	____	____	____
13. What back-up personnel are available?	______	____	____	____

	Maximum Score Allowed	*#1*	*#2*	*#3*
14. Do you offer toll-free numbers?	______	____	____	____
15. How do you assure consistency?	______	____	____	____
16. What type of reports will you provide? When do you present the reports?	______	____	____	____
17. What type of training of our staff do you provide? At what cost?	______	____	____	____
18. What do you do internally to ensure education and improvement of your staff?	______	____	____	____
19. Describe your quality control system.	______	____	____	____
20. What "added value" (i.e., free) services do you offer?	______	____	____	____
21. How do you want to be paid?	______	____	____	____
22. Are your remuneration requirements flexible?	______	____	____	____
23. Describe how you will provide your services. Describe how you will handle this project.	______	____	____	____
24. Will you do our project for the fee we want to pay you?	______	____	____	____
25. What follow-up services do you provide?	______	____	____	____
26. Describe any staff turnover that you have had during the last three years.	______	____	____	____

	Maximum Score Allowed	*#1*	*#2*	*#3*
27. Describe the steps that you and your organization take to ensure the privacy and confidentiality of client information.	______	____	____	____
28. Do you provide insurer rating agencies figures in your reports?	______	____	____	____

¶3070 ABC Questionnaire Answer Guide

The following are suggested aids to the analysis of responses received from the ABCs during the interview process.

1. Location is important in terms of ability to analyze local needs. Someone living in another province is less likely to understand local language, customs and lifestyle. Costs may be increased if one has to deal at long distance. The ability to deal with emergencies is more difficult from a distance. Dealing locally helps the local economy. Dealing locally, on the other hand, may increase slightly the chances of release of confidential information.

2. Professional qualifications are an indicator of commitment to the insurance business. Letters after one's name do not automatically mean knowledge in a subject. Actuaries and ABCs may not work on group insurance programs during their entire career. It is possible to obtain other types of professional designations, such as F.L.M.I. or C.L.U. without obtaining any practical experience in this area. Accountants and lawyers are generally not specifically educated in the area of group insurance, although some may have obtained practical experience.

3. Practical experience is often more useful, in group insurance marketing, than professional qualifications. But experience, like professional qualifications, may not guarantee quality or technical competence. This question should be scored out of 10.

4. This question may trigger a defensive response. The question could be rephrased as "Who can you give as references?" Answers that include organizations within your industry are important. Answers may be given that are strictly the names of organizations that you have never heard of, or that are located out of your province. Answers may include pension clients, and exclude group insurance as an attempt to hide the lack of clients in that area. The response can be analyzed as a means of determining

whether or not the ABC will be able to keep your corporate information confidential.

5. Experience with your type of business will be important, especially in the ability to assist with claim problems. A knowledge of your type of business will also assist in the negotiation of renewals.

6. Access to technical resources in this case, means access to people who have the knowledge, experience and power to resolve potential problems quickly and without fuss. These resources may be internal to the ABC's firm, or external, such as having the names and numbers of the people with these qualities. It is not vital to know everything; it is vital to know where to get the answers.

7. This question should be easily answered. The Life Underwriters Association has a code of conduct, as does the Society of Actuaries. In addition, major ABC firms may have developed their own. All insurance companies have, at least, a rudimentary code of ethics to which their employees and agents should abide. It is surprising how many ABCs have never read their companies' codes. You may be interested in the responses to this question.

8. This question is geared to get a reaction and to generate conversation. Conversation can lead to a better idea of the type of organization, or individual, with whom you will be dealing.

9. This question is also geared to starting a conversation. Many ABCs have little idea of how their competitors operate, and hence, they have difficulty in differentiating their services.

10. This question will give you an idea of how much time is spent specifically in group insurance, and in other areas. A successful life insurance agent will have 500 or more personal life insurance clients, but may have only one or two group insurance clients. On the other hand, the agent may specialize in group insurance, service 25 groups, and have few individual insurance clients. Consulting firms may have 85 per cent of their business in the pensions area, and very little in the group insurance area. Or they may specialize in group insurance. In general, the more group insurance clients, the better. Look for a minimum of ten group insurance clients.

11. The number of group plans personally serviced is an indicator of work load. Some senior consultants may spend the majority of their time looking after three or four clients. They may employ junior consultants or consulting assistants to look after the smaller cases. If this is the case, your interview should include the person who will be looking after your account, not just the senior person. It is extremely difficult for one full-time person

to personally service by him or herself more than 50 small- to medium-size groups.

12. Nearly every ABC has a computer on his or her desk, and probably one at home as well. What you need to know is whether or not there is a back-up system available should their main system fail. A failure of a computer system at renewal can cause delays in receipt of new rates, or cause a crisis within the ABC's firm, which could affect the amount of time that your staff have to spend rebuilding files and data. Also important is the ability of the ABC to access a fax machine and a telephone. Nothing is more frustrating than needing an answer immediately and being unable to reach the ABC or the appointed support person, to get that answer. Generally, more and better technology indicates that the ABC wants to be competitive in the business.

13. Back-up personnel are important when there is a crisis. Not having back-up slows down the process. Generally, many agents, brokers and consultants do most of the work on their clients' cases themselves. A back-up person may not have to know the details of your account, but must at least know how to get hold of the ABC. Most emergencies will be handled by your organization directly with the insurance company's group or claim's representative.

14. Toll-free numbers are more convenient and quicker to use than calling collect. Dialling long distance direct to the ABC costs your organization money. Look for toll-free telephone and fax numbers, or e-mail addresses.

15. This is another question designed to provide a forum for discussion. Look for mention of a quality control system, a minimum standards manual, training programs for staff and a contingency program (for such things as staff resigning in the middle of a project).

16. Some ABCs provide huge reports, containing filler, used to impress the readers. Your organization needs readable marketing and renewal reports that give the facts, the reasons for the decisions and alternative approaches to review. A comparison format for rates, benefits, claims and employee statistics works best. Look for a willingness to provide quarterly, or semiannual, premium/claim reports. Look for a question or mention of your organization's year-end. The last thing that your organization needs is to look at a group insurance renewal during the middle of a fiscal year-end. Many ABCs are not aware enough of the operations of group insurance plans to realize that the best time to have a renewal is when your organization does its budget for the next year. Knowing about rate changes at budget time will enable expense projections to be more accurate. Getting a rate change, especially to higher rates, in the middle of

your fiscal year, when it has not been budgeted, could otherwise cause headaches for your organization.

Renewal reports need to be presented as far in advance as possible so that your management team can review the changes and their causes, changes to payroll can be made, and employees can be advised. The life insurance industry, including the ABCs, is famous for waiting until the last minute to review changes and to do reports. Look for a written commitment, or a guarantee that renewal reports will be in your organization's hands with a minimum of 45 days prior to the rate change date, whether you need them at that time or not.

17. Any training that an ABC is willing to extend to your firm without extra charge is a bonus. In reality, the insurance company's salaried representatives will provide most of the technical training for free. Their costs are included in the rates charged by the insurer. The question is to see how much and how willing the ABC is to spend time with you, teaching you what he or she knows.

18. A commitment to ongoing training for all ABC staff and consultants shows that an ABC considers education to be important. Ask what courses have been offered or encouraged within the firm during the last two years. Answers such as "we leave the staff to educate themselves" show a disrespect for those employees and may be an indicator of internal problems within the ABC's firm.

19. Few ABCs have quality management systems in place. Award extra points if the ABC's organization has a program in place. Look for mention of systems such as ISO 9004-2, which is an internationally recognized standard of quality management for service firms.

20. Look for "free" employee meetings, regular benefits newsletters, the promotion of your organization by the ABC in their business rounds, support for your local charity, support for your annual company golf day, or even positive mention of your organization in any relevant articles written by the ABC.

21. If the organization needs a lot of assistance, it is better to have the work done using a standard level commission scale basis, for the first year. If the organization only requires a one shot marketing of the group insurance plan, or perhaps only requires assistance at renewal, it may be better off paying on a project basis, assuming that the ABC's cost is less than that paid using (the) insurer standard annual commission scales. Some consultants do not work on a commission basis because they feel that there is too much room for abuse in that system; others work on a non-commission basis because they are not licensed to collect commissions in the province. Working on a fee-for-service basis can become expensive, especially if the whole scope of the project has not been covered in the fee agreement. An

example of this is contracting for the marketing of a group insurance program and failing to include installation costs, employee booklet costs, travel costs, or the costs charged by the consultant to conduct employee meetings. An ABC may keep the selected insurer's representatives away from your organization if he or she has the possibility of providing extra billable services. The ABC may not tell you that some of the services offered for an extra fee are included for free by the insurance company. You may, in effect, pay double for these services.

22. Look for flexibility here. You should be willing to pay for good service, including an ABC's intermediary services, but if ABC service is only required once or twice a year, there is little use in paying for a full-service package every year through commission rates.

23. This question will provide the ABCs with the opportunity to explain not only what they will do with the project, but may include how they operate in terms of your project versus others. The question should provide you with an idea of the steps that will be taken and the timeframe. The question may need to be clarified to the ABC who may interpret the question to be one about ethics.

24. This is designed to provoke a response to see how the ABC will respond. Give extra marks for humour. Take marks away if the ABC is shocked into silence, or tries too hard to convince you that their fees are warranted.

25. Look for regular telephone calls and follow-up for your plan's administrator. Also look for a willingness to advise you in advance of any changes or new situations which have come up in legislation, are being discussed by regulators, or are being reviewed in the courts.

26. Staff turnover is an indicator, especially in the larger brokerage and consulting firms, of the potential of something being wrong in the organization. Ask about the turnover of senior consultants and partners in particular. Agents and brokers, however, generally work independently. Therefore, the turnover of other agents, within a branch for example, will have little consequence to the group insurance purchaser.

27. Changes in the financial services industry are happening constantly. ABCs and employees, within financial institutions, have access to an incredible amount of information about people and their organizations. Although the Canadian Life and Health Association has developed and amended a privacy code (see Appendices, at ¶17,050) for use by all of its members (and member employees), little attention is paid to this issue by management, or by industry training programs. Why is privacy important? Can you imagine the consequences of your organization attempting to close a big deal, and personal claims information, such as the pending disability claim of one of the key members of your team, being leaked out,

perhaps jeopardizing the entire deal? The potential is there, unless closely watched by the insurance industry. It pays to be aware and to choose an ABC carefully.

28. After the recent collapse of Confederation Life, it is very important to have information as to the claims-paying ability and the financial background of the insurers and the benefit providers, especially with regards to life insurance and long-term disability benefits. You need to know that all benefit amounts will continue to be paid if the insurer/provider collapses. This is extremely important to all employees who are covered for over $2,000/month of benefit under long-term disability benefit, or over $200,000 under a life insurance benefit. (These are the maximum amounts for benefits guaranteed by Comcorp — the life insurance industry's version of the Canada Deposit Insurance Corporation.)

¶3075 USING MORE THAN ONE ABC

Using more than one ABC to review different group insurance benefits is of little practical use, with the possible exception of the largest size groups. Most ABCs who know the ins and outs of one group insurance benefit will be able to advise your organization on the other group benefits.

Some ABCs specialize in group insurance; some specialize in other benefits or other types of insurance. An ABC who handles the organization's group insurance may not be the best person to handle the pension benefits or the individual insurance required to fund a buy/sell agreement, and vice versa.

¶3080 CHANGING AN ABC

An organization can normally change agents, brokers or consultants at any time, with a simple letter called an "Agent of Record" letter. If the ABC is being paid on a commission basis, a signed and dated letter appointing another Agent of Record should be drawn up, signed and sent to the present insurers. The new Agent of Record letter can include a different commission scale. There will be pressure from the new Agent of Record to do a marketing of the group insurance plan as soon as is possible. The new ABC may suggest changing insurers. This change may be suggested as much for the new ABC to gain control, and to cut all ties with the last ABC, as it is to see if there is a better package available. A change of insurers may not be in the best interest of your group and should not be undertaken just to allow the new ABC to gain more control.

If you are using an ABC on a fee-for-service basis, unless there is a penalty clause in the consulting agreement, you should be free to terminate the agreement at any time, for whatever reason you choose. Before terminating an ABC's services, have the ABC provide you with all of the personal and confidential data, such as claim reports, as well as copies of the master policies, plus amendments, and the last three years' renewal reports for your group plan. Some ABCs keep all of their client's records and policies instead of passing these on to the client. Keeping written documentation is occasionally used by ABCs as a method of keeping control over their clients. Should the fired or replaced ABC be unable, or refuse, to provide this information, it can usually be obtained with a telephone call to the insurer's group office. The object of obtaining this information is to have it on hand in case the plan is to be marketed in the future, and to assist in the understanding of policy issues.

¶3085 THE AGENT OF RECORD LETTER

The Agent of Record letter is an important document. It is far more important to the ABC than to the appointing organization, because this is the document that is used to allow payment of commissions by the insurance company to the ABC. The Agent of Record letter, in effect, is the document that tells the insurance company to pay commissions.

The Agent of Record letter is often used to serve other purposes. Besides commissions, the letter is used by the ABC as written confirmation and permission from the client to obtain copies of the master policies, employee booklets, renewal information, employee data lists (sometimes called "nominal lists" in the insurance industry), and general claims information.

Today's Agent of Record letter, in reality, is worth little more than the paper it is written on. An organization can replace an Agent of Record at any time by writing and signing a more currently dated Agent of Record letter appointing someone else, or no one else, as the need may be.

In the sample Agent of Record letter supplied in this book, there is a section for the ABC to sign. This is an agreement by the ABC to keep all information concerning the policy strictly private and confidential. This information includes the claims, the claimants, information on all employees and dependants, financial information and other data. This signed section of the agreement is new to the insurance industry. The purpose of this section is to have the ABC acknowledge and agree to keep all information gathered, as a result of being the Agent of Record, strictly private and confidential. ABCs often discover confidential information about the organizations when they are appointed as Agent of Record. This information can be detrimental to the organization if it were leaked, even inadvertently, to the public, to other employees, or to the competition. Having the ABC sign this section will bring the subject of privacy and confidentiality into the open.

It is possible to appoint more than one Agent of Record. For example, it is possible to have one ABC handle the group life and long-term disability benefits, while another ABC is appointed to look after the health and dental benefits. This serves the political purpose, especially for those organizations located in a smaller centre, of appeasing more than one local ABC. Simply draw up two Agent of Record letters, covering different benefits, and appointing the two different ABCs. It is also possible to appoint an insurance brokerage firm, a consulting firm, or more than one agent, as Agent of Record on the group insurance policy.

An Agent of Record letter may not be necessary in all circumstances. For example, if an agent of XYZ Insurance Company sells an XYZ Insurance Company group insurance policy to an organization, the insurance company may not require the letter.

Some insurance companies require you to use their own agents to obtain a quote. This is particularly true if your organization has below 15 to 20 employees. One major insurance company will not offer quotes through anyone except their own agents, if your organization has under 100 employees. This is done, they say, to protect their own agency force. It has been the experience of the insurance industry in the past, that group insurance business stays on their books longer if it has been placed there by the insurer's own agents. Benefit providers, who are not insurers, may quote quite readily to most organizations either directly or through an ABC, and with or without commissions.

Finally, it is to your organization's advantage not to issue an Agent of Record letter to every ABC that walks through the door, especially if you are in the midst of a search for a new insurer. Each ABC to whom you give a letter, will try to submit the specifications to the same insurers for a quote. Insurers, who see this happening, will think that your organization does not know what it is doing and may decline to quote. Or at best, if a quote is offered, it may not include the best rates possible, because the representatives are wary. If you do not understand how to market a group insurance plan, you may make other mistakes, such as in the administration of the policy, which might be very costly to the insurer. Besides the lack of trust that may be established, you will create a lot of duplicated work for the ABCs, the insurance companies, and more importantly, for your own organization. The time that you take to appoint more than one ABC, the duplication of material and records to be provided, the number of interviews, and the number of reports to be analyzed will increase. The worst part about this is that, in the end, it will be more difficult to ensure that you are comparing "apples to apples" quotes.

The only situation in which you may have to accept more than one quote from more than one ABC, is if your organization is small, i.e., under 15 to 20 employees, or if it has under 100 employees and you wanted to obtain a quote from one of the insurers that only deals through its own agents. Be extra careful in this situation, to ensure that "every apple is compared to every apple" before making a decision. Be sure not to be bowled over by slick sales presentations without checking all of the facts. Be sure to confirm every statement and obtain written confirmation on every question that you ask, prior to making a decision. Some insurers' proposals are so devoid of information as to make a comparison, solely based on the explanations in the proposal, impossible.

¶3090 HOW TO REPLACE YOUR ABC

Occasionally, an organization may want to replace an ABC. The reason for replacement is strictly a decision of the policyholder. A common reason to replace an ABC is the perception that the organization will receive more value or expertise from someone else. Or, an organization may find, after comparing the latest renewal presented by the ABC, to the formulas presented in this book, that the ABC could have negotiated better rates on the organization's behalf, but did not. Or, the organization may want to release the ABC in order to save the commissions or fees. These are all reasonable grounds for replacement.

In most group insurance situations, the most formal piece of documentation, between the purchaser and the ABC, is the Agent of Record letter. This letter can be rescinded at any time. The replaced Agent of Record, generally, has no comeback on the organization. It is common courtesy to advise the Agent of Record that he or she is being replaced or let go, and why, but the organization is under no obligation to do so.

To replace one ABC with another, if they are being paid on the same commission basis, the only thing necessary is to write a new Agent of Record letter, naming the new ABC. Be sure to date and sign the letter. It is more professional to type the letter on your organization's letterhead, although this is not a specific requirement. This letter is then presented to the new ABC who will promptly forward it to the current insurers. If you want to remove an ABC, without replacing him or her, write a letter on your organization's letterhead, dated and signed, asking the insurance company to put the policy onto a "net-commission" basis, and to place the policy onto a "direct" (without an agent) basis. This will remove the Agent of Record as such, and will stop commissions being paid out. At the same time, you may ask to have your rates reviewed and adjusted to reflect the fact that commissions will no longer be paid. (Your current rates will be reduced, unless the policy is close to the renewal date, in which case the renewal rates should be reduced). Most group insurance commissions are paid up front, in advance, for the year. If a policy cancels, for any reason, or if the agent gets replaced, the agent will normally have to pay back the portion of the commissions which was paid, but not earned, for the year. If you wish to keep the ABC (i.e., on a fee-for-service basis) as Agent of Record, write the same letter asking that the policy be put on a "net-commission" basis, and stating that the Agent of Record is to remain as such, but on a fee-for-service basis. Note that on those policies which cover under 15 employees (in insurance industry terminology, those that are in the "small group", or "group package" market), it may not be possible to replace the Agent of Record with an ABC who works for a different company. The rules and regulations for the small group market, on this issue, are much more restricting than on the larger group market. The insurance company, also, may not allow a "small group" to be placed on a net-commission basis. Some insurance companies, or their local representatives, may consider that it is politically better for them, internally, to refuse a request to put a group insurance policy on a net-commission basis. In these situations, they will take a chance that the group policy will stay on the books, and not be marketed, rather than make waves with the status quo. Any life insurance company, or benefit provider, has the ability to offer policies direct to the consumer. Some choose not to do this. A letter to an insurance company's vice-president of group insurance may help to clarify specific situations and requests. In these cases, it may also pay to shop around.

¶3095 SAMPLE AGENT OF RECORD LETTER

Corporate Letterhead

To: Mr./Ms. (*ABC Insurance Representative*)
123 Anystreet
Bestville, Province
Postal Code

Re: Group Insurance Plan(s) #__________(s)

Dear Sirs,

This letter will serve to appoint Mr./Ms. (*ABC Insurance Representative*) as our Agent of Record on our group insurance plan(s). The appointment is to be effective immediately (or target date).

This letter will also serve as authorization to our present or future insurers to release all information required by the Agent of Record to perform its duties on our behalf. By requesting any information, the Agent of Record agrees to abide by all relevant legislation on rights to privacy and confidentiality issues in respect to individual employee and dependent claims. Any commissions included in the rating structure of the group insurance benefits are to be paid to the Agent of Record (as per the attached scale. Benefits not included in the attached scale are to be implemented using a "net commission" rate basis).

We reserve the right to rescind this appointment at any time without advance notice to the Agent of Record.

Yours truly,

Name, Title

CHAPTER 4

¶4000 TYPES OF GROUP INSURANCE PLANS

¶4005 INTRODUCTION

There are three main types of group insurance plans available in today's marketplace: those sold to corporations (including those sold to government organizations), those sold to unions, and those sold to associations. The next section looks at the similarities and differences between the plans.

¶4010 CORPORATE GROUP PLANS

The most common types of group insurance plans are those sold to corporations. By corporation, I mean an incorporated or limited company which employs people in an employer/employee relationship. Many life insurance companies and benefit providers prefer to deal with this type of group over any other. In fact, many life insurance companies underwrite only a few, if any, union-only or association-type group plans. Government organizations, especially municipalities and government-sponsored social agencies, can also be viewed by the underwriters as "less than desirable" risks. Some insurers have an inherent fear that if they underwrite union business, for example, then corporations will refuse to put business their way. Governments and their sponsored agencies are renowned in the insurance industry for a high overall level of claims, especially long-term disability claims. Government organizations include school boards and social work agencies. A high level of overall claims in any type of industry will limit the number of underwriters who are willing to look at the risk.

Corporations, in comparison to other types of groups, are run as businesses. They understand finance and tend to be concerned over the state of health of the employees that they hire. They understand, but will not generally admit (because of fear that they will be reported to a human rights agency) that hiring unfit people will drive up their group insurance costs. Insurers believe that it is easier to sell policy renewals to corporations, as they tend not to have as many chiefs in the decision-making process. The chiefs may be too busy trying to make more money for the corporation to overly concern themselves with expense items such as group insurance renewals. Organizations other than corporations, such as governments, unions or associations, are thought by some insurers to have less judicious hiring practices, which in turn lead to higher group insurance claims, especially for life insurance and long-term disability.

Corporations are named as the “policyholder”. This means that the corporation and its signing officers can ask the insurance companies to put the policy into force and to amend the policy at any time, without the employees’ prior knowledge or agreement. Employees will have to sign an enrolment card or a beneficiary card when the plan is first put into effect (this is called the “inception date” of the policy). After this, unless an employee wishes to change a beneficiary, employee responsibility is only to sign the occasional claim form.

Employees of a corporation rarely have anything to do with the design, funding or renewal of a group insurance plan. This is almost always done by management. Employees are left at the mercy of the employer in terms of plan design and funding. The employee hopes that the employer is honest, acts in the best interests of the employees, and continues to deduct any employee premium share based on the correct rates.

¶4015 UNION GROUP PLANS

The benefits for union group insurance plans are much the same as they are in corporate group programs. Union plans differ, if at all, in the levels of benefits that are negotiated. They also can differ in the way that they are administered. In a union plan, the union, or union local, as the case may be, is named as the policyholder on the actual policy.

Union group insurance plans operate, in many cases, on an “hour-bank” system. This means that the number of hours worked by a union member are accumulated (banked as it were) in his or her account. The method of banking was designed to ensure that a union member would be able to accumulate enough hours to keep group insurance benefits in force during times of seasonal layoffs, or temporary layoffs between jobs. Employers contribute so much money per hour worked for each employee. During periods of high activity (i.e., with lots of overtime), the employer, in effect, over-contributes to the group insurance plan on behalf of the employee. This over-contribution is banked to provide and to help pay for benefits in times of layoff.

A new union member is first eligible to join the benefits plan when he or she has accumulated or worked a set number of hours. The minimum number of hours is set as a "waiting period" by the insurance company, in the group insurance policy, after consultation with the union executive. This minimum can vary by contract or by policy. The minimum number of hours set in the policy's waiting period before benefits coverage begins is similar to the minimum time set in corporate group insurance policies. The difference is that corporate group insurance policies generally set the waiting period in terms of months (instead of hours) before new employees will be eligible. And unions negotiate this waiting period for their members, whereas with a corporate plan, the employer normally picks the term of the waiting period for the employees.

Benefits may differ under union-type plans. They can differ between unions, between locals of the same union, between provinces, and certainly between policies. Sometimes these differences are small, such as the amount that is reimbursed for something like orthopaedic shoes. Other times, the differences have more important implications, such as the amount to be received for long-term disability claims. In almost all situations, it is a combination of the importance put on benefits by the union's negotiators and the cost of each benefit that determines the level of benefits. If union negotiators think that money is more important than a long-term disability plan (LTD), then they might place more emphasis on getting a higher hourly rate of pay, than implementing a higher maximum in the disability benefit. Hence, even today you can find LTD plans which pay low levels of benefits on disability, because negotiators gave priority to wages or to other benefits.

There is no doubt that people's attitudes towards benefits heavily influence the makeup of a group insurance plan. Someone who dislikes insurance companies, for whatever reason, is less likely to work with an insurer or benefit provider to install a properly designed program, than someone who is more tolerant concerning the issues. This is true for all types of benefits programming.

¶4020 ASSOCIATION GROUP PLANS

There are two main types of "association" group insurance plans. The first is an association of employers, such as the Canadian Manufacturers' Association, where each member of the association is a corporation that employs groups of people. The second type of association is an association of individuals, such as the Canadian Bar Association, whose members can be individuals rather than groups of people. Both of these types of associations, the association of employers and the association of individuals, can set up group benefit programs for their members. The benefits of association purchase, to the associations themselves, are principally twofold: to add an incentive to membership to join the association, and to receive "volume discounts" on the purchase of group insurance programs. Let us examine both types of association plans.

¶4025 ASSOCIATIONS OF EMPLOYERS: GROUP PLANS

The idea behind every association of employers, in terms of group insurance, is to produce volume discounts and better benefits for member companies. Certain ABC firms in Canada have been very successful in marketing this type of group insurance plan over the last ten to 15 years. The concept can work, especially in the short term. In the long term, however, there can be serious problems for the insurers, unless the plans are monitored closely.

The first problem is that most association member companies have their own group insurance schedules that they do not really want to change, unless they can get "more for less". ABCs, in charge of marketing these plans, have to first convince the member companies that the association group insurance policy is a good one. The member companies can be skeptical about the promises, about the ABCs, about the possible ramifications of a change, about the amount of extra work involved, about the possibilities of something, or someone falling through the cracks, about having to gather and provide confidential employee information to unknown people, about the loss of control over their own program, and about the long-term success of the program. The association members are usually committed to their current ABCs, who could be friends, relatives or golf buddies. It is quite a job for the association executive to get and keep the interest of the member companies.

The ABCs gather up what information they can for each of the groups in the initial survey, including the paid premiums and paid claims experience per employer group. A set of specifications is designed, which includes the insurance schedule for each group in the survey, along with the employee data per group. The specifications are, then, sent to every life insurance company that they are in contact with, including the ones with whom they have little other business. Not many life insurance companies actively pursue association business.

Some insurers look at association group plans with a suspicious eye. The main problem with association-type groups is that there is nothing, generally, in the association's bylaws, that forces a member company to use the group insurance program, or to stay with the program. Employer members will stay with the program as long as they can get a break on the rates, via the volume discounts, or in the case of the smallest of employers, as long as they can get better benefits than they can on their own. ABCs, who are typically paid on a commission basis for association plans, are constantly trying to add new members to the program, as old ones drop out. They are also constantly trying to encourage the larger association members to join the plan, because without these larger members, there is less profit to be made by the consultants and by the insurers.

By joining the program, larger members can help the smaller members of the association to procure better rates and benefits. Unless there are many large member groups participating, there is not necessarily much to be gained by the larger employer members in terms of benefits or rates by being a member of a particular association group insurance plan. (See the comments on Size of the Group at ¶5070, in Chapter 5.)

The major problem with association (of groups) plans is that the plans tend to lose the members that have good experience because these members can obtain, from time to time, better rates outside of the association plan, despite the volume discounts applied to that plan. This is because any bad apples in the association's group insurance barrel (i.e., those groups with high claims experience) may require higher premiums from the other groups in the plan in order to offset the losses. Companies with good experience may find that they can get better rates elsewhere, on their own.

A way to get around this, is to underwrite each company belonging to the association as a separate group, with separate rates based on each group's experience alone, but with the total premium for all groups being used to determine the volume discounts and policy maximum benefits. The association's master policy can be set up as one policy, with standard policy wording for all groups. The master policy can have a separate policy subdivision with a separate (and individually designed) schedule for each member company. This method can appease a potential underwriter, but will not necessarily be incentive enough to get association member groups to join the plan. Individual members, especially the large ones, have their own agendas and political games to play. There is nothing to "force" an association member to join an association group insurance plan. That is the major failing of these types of plans.

¶4030 ASSOCIATIONS OF INDIVIDUALS: GROUP PLANS

Group insurance for associations of individuals are considered by insurers more as sales to "individuals" than to groups. The products which are more often offered are policies, such as long-term disability, life insurance, and registered retirement savings plans, rather than the extended health care and dental benefits. These latter benefits can also be structured and financed into association group plans.

The "savings", over the purchase of personal policies, can be found, depending on the plan itself, in the association member not having to pay high commissions and other high set-up charges that are part and parcel of personal policies. On the negative side, group policy set-up is usually compromised to provide better average benefits to the group as a whole. Personal policies, especially for disability, can be more closely tailored to suit the needs of the individual, but they are expensive!

¶4035 GROUP INSURANCE: NON-MEDICAL LIMITS

Personal policies are only issued to you if you can pass a medical examination. The same can be said for many associations of individual's plans. An individual belonging to an association of individuals group plans may only be issued a policy if the individual can pass a medical examination. Group insurance plans issued to corporations on the other hand, except for the smallest of groups, are issued without the employees having to pass a medical. There can be situations in all group plans, where the highest wage earners request additional life insurance and disability benefits which are over and above the standard benefits issued for that size of group. For these additional benefits, the insurer can request the employee to pass a medical examination. If an employee cannot pass the medical examination, and knows in advance that he or she cannot, then the employee should not try to apply for the extra. Sometimes, insurers have been known to decline any future across-the-board (i.e., for all employees) increases in benefits to any individual who has previously been declined for benefits, unless the individual can prove thoroughly to the insurer that the condition that originally caused the declination no longer exists. This is usually a big hassle to say the least, and when it happens to top executives, it can be more so.

If a top executive is stuck in the trap of being unable to increase benefits because of an inability to pass a medical examination, and he or she is at the maximum allowed without a medical examination, then this excuse is sometimes enough for the employer or group to have the group insurance plan marketed. Of course, the insurance companies are aware that certain groups' top wage earners who cannot pass medical examinations want more coverage. They can and will decline to issue the coverage if they know that someone is dying, for example. It may be essential for the group policyholder then, to keep this fact confidential. The objective, for the underwriters, is to find out what they can do to limit the risk, all without annoying any group which wants larger benefits, and where everyone is healthy.

Some ABCs in the past have been particularly adept at providing insurers with the minimum required information. Since most ABCs do not share directly in underwriting profits (unless they have shares in the insurer or a "participating life insurance policy"), they may not request from their clients, or provide to insurers any information which may jeopardize the chances of obtaining a competitive quote or higher benefits for their client. Hence, underwriters must fulfil their jobs by sorting out which are the best risks and which are not. ABCs can and do lose their credibility with the underwriters if the underwriter suspects that the ABC cannot be trusted. A group trying to procure the best rates and policies for a client through using this type of ABC may not be able to get quotes from certain of the insurance companies. And all that will show on the ABC's spreadsheets will be a note that the insurer has declined to quote (due to the "nature of the group", or due to the "experience"). Not all declines to quote are based on a lack of trust, however.

CHAPTER 5

¶5000 POLICY REVIEW AND DEVELOPMENT

¶5005 INTRODUCTION

The following section details how to develop a group insurance policy. Whether there is a plan in place or not, it is in an organization's best interests to look at why a program is needed, and then to prioritize those needs. The first step in the review and development process is for management and the employees or members to ask themselves the following questions:

¶5010 PLAN DEVELOPMENT QUESTIONS

A: If Your Organization Has a Present Policy

1. Why did our organization implement this benefit?
2. Who does this actually benefit?
3. Does this benefit still fulfil its purpose in the most efficient and cost-effective way?
4. Is this benefit funded properly? Can we improve the funding?
5. Is this benefit worth retaining?

B. If Your Organization Does Not Have a Policy

1. Why do we need this benefit?
2. Who will this actually benefit?

3. Will this benefit fulfil its purpose in the most efficient and cost-effective way?

4. Will this benefit be funded correctly? How do we stand to win or lose?

Ask the above questions for each benefit: life insurance; accidental death and dismemberment; dependant life insurance; voluntary employee life insurance; voluntary employee accidental death and dismemberment; voluntary dependant life insurance; voluntary dependant accidental death and dismemberment; short-term disability; long-term disability (LTD); extended health care; travel emergency medical; vision care; and dental.

Employers will find that group insurance plans work best if they keep the needs of employees, as well as their own, in mind. Employee surveys are one of the best, and easiest, ways for an employer to gain an understanding of these needs. Employee surveys should be performed every five years or so, or more regularly, if there is a high turnover of staff. After a merger, or after downsizing, it is also recommended that a survey be completed.

Surveys can be quite simple in nature. A one- or two-page letter can be sent to each employee household asking for comments on what the employee and the dependants like, do not like, how the plans fit into their personal financial plans and goals, and what changes they would like to see. An employer can distribute the survey forms to the employees at the workplace. But it is better to involve the dependants as well, for they are also recipients of the benefits. Sample or example survey forms are available in many compensation and employee benefits textbooks. Your public library would be one source for these books.

What are the most important benefits? Ask 100 different employees or 100 different employers, and you can expect to receive as many different answers. Basically, if an employee is paying a portion of the premiums, and this employee has dependants, then the extended medical benefit, especially the prescription drug benefit, and the dental benefits will generally be the ones most utilized and "appreciated" by that employee. If, on the other hand, the employee is the owner of the organization, and he or she has health problems, or has had a family history of health problems, then perhaps high, non-medical maximums on the group life and LTD benefits will be the most appreciated. Or perhaps, young, single employees, participating in sports, may think that a good disability plan is the most important benefit.

¶5015 IF YOU DO NOT HAVE A PRESENT PLAN

Starting a new organization and hiring employees will eventually bring employers to the problem of designing and implementing a group insurance program. Most employers in this position have historically relied on the services of an agent, broker or consultant (ABC) to procure a quote or two, explain how the benefits work, what someone can expect to receive, and how much the plan will cost. Entrepreneurs and new business owners are busy and often do not take the time to review which are the best benefits to have and why. Also ignored by many employers are the questions of how the benefits are funded, and what will be the effects of high claims experience over the years that the policy is in effect. If the ABC is doing a proper job, the purchaser will be advised in advance how the renewals will be calculated in the future, and what the purchaser can do to affect those renewals right now. In insurance language, this is called "selling the renewal at inception". In other words, advise the policyholder of how the benefits are underwritten and funded when the plan is originally put into effect. Then, by keeping the policyholder informed of his or her claims experience at regular intervals during the year, the ABC can generally gain the trust of the client and can suggest adjustments to control costs at renewal. At worst, the ABC can prepare the client in advance for the rate changes.

As an employer, you can do many of the things that an ABC does for you if you have the time. Before you advance any further down this road, note two things. If your group of employees is under 15 to 20 or so people, your ability to obtain quotes may be limited, especially if you would like to obtain a net-commission quote. Many insurers only issue quotes for smaller size groups through ABCs, and these insurers may not be willing to quote without commissions. Also, if your new organization is in this size category, it may be worthwhile to let an ABC assist you with putting the first policy into place. However, you will save money and future aggravation by understanding how to set up the plan, and why to do it that way.

¶5020 ESTABLISHING A GROUP INSURANCE POLICY

A benefits plan stipulates what benefits are to be covered. It must also stipulate who is to be covered. Insurance, benefit provider and self-insured policies state who is to be covered, when their coverage is to begin and end, what occupations are covered, what the minimum number of hours worked per week will be, and what employee locations are covered. These factors are termed the "eligibility" provisions of the policies.

¶5025 STEP 1: WHOM DO YOU WANT COVERED?

Employees covered under a group insurance plan are called "eligible employees". Eligibility is very important because it defines who is to be covered and, hence, who is not. An organization can "discriminate" by occupation, in a group insurance contract. It is possible to cover only certain positions within the organization (i.e., cover only the office staff and management). It is also possible to cover some employee positions (called "classifications" in insurance language) for greater amounts than others (i.e., cover management for twice as much life insurance as for other occupations). It is possible to cover certain classifications, such as management, for 100 per cent of all dental work, including orthodontic, while covering other classifications for lesser amounts, or even while not covering other employees at all. Coverage of employees, in certain locations only, is also possible, depending on the location and circumstances. Before determining a group's eligibility, check provincial regulations with respect to coverage for certain employee classifications, such as "part-time" employees.

¶5030 ELIGIBILITY CHART

Who Is to Be Covered?

All employees or

1. Executives ______
2. Management ______
3. Office staff ______
4. Union ______
5. Staff association members ______
6. Certain occupations (list them in the next question) ______

What Occupations Are to Be Covered?

All Employees or

1. Executives ______
2. Management ______
3. Office staff ______
4. Union members ______
5. Other . . . . ______
6. Other . . . . ______
7. Other . . . . ______
8. . . . . ______
9. . . . . ______

What Locations Are to Be Covered?

1. Provinces ______
2. United States ______
3. Expatriates ______
4. Other countries ______
5. Other . . . . ______

¶5035 MINIMUM (AVERAGE) WORK WEEK

It is possible to stipulate, in a group insurance policy, the minimum number of hours that have to be worked, on average, for someone to be eligible. Typically, group insurance policies state the minimum (i.e., an employee must work a minimum of 24, 27.5 or 30 hours per week in order to qualify). An employer can control eligibility and costs by asking the insurance company to set a minimum number of hours for eligibility. Insurance companies, on smaller policies, normally require a standard minimum of not less than 20 hours per week. Check provincial regulations with respect to part-time and other classifications of employees.

¶5040 EMPLOYMENT CLASSIFICATIONS

Historically, group insurance policies have been set up for "permanent, full-time employees, working a minimum of (20, 24, 27.5 or 30) hours per week". Part-time employees have been included on the larger policies. Seasonal employees are rarely, if ever, covered. Temporary employees are almost never covered. Temporary employees working through a temporary agency are rarely covered, except perhaps through the temporary agency itself.

Contract employees can be covered as long as the insurance company agrees to do so. Obtain this agreement in writing from the insurer. An example of a contract employee would be an engineer hired to work on a specific project. Note that employees on short-term contract (i.e., a contract of under six months' duration) may not be accepted for coverage by the insurer. The insurer's reason is that it will receive only six months in premium, but may get up to two years' worth of claims, especially for dental, within those six months. This will affect an organization's renewal rates. Coverage of short-term contract employees under the contractor's group insurance plan is, therefore, not financially advisable in most situations. Contract employees can be paid extra to cover the purchase of benefits on their own. However, coverage may be compromised by this method, if the contracted employee cannot purchase benefits because of a medical condition.

It is often less expensive from a contract employee's viewpoint to purchase benefits through the contractor's group insurance plan, especially if coverage is not available from the contractee's association group plan. Group insurance policies can stipulate, however, that an employer must contribute to the premiums for the group insurance policy. The intention of this clause is to make sure that the employer takes an interest in the policy. It is rarely stated what amount the employer must contribute, or to which employees, so there is some room for interpretation here.

Probationary employees are not normally covered. It should be clear in the administrative rules, discussed and confirmed in writing with the insurer, whether or not there will be a policy *waiting period* at the end of the probation period. Does the waiting period occur during the probation period, or does it start on the day that the probation period ends?

Subcontract employees are rarely covered, as they do not, in reality, work for the organization. They usually work for themselves or another company.

Directors of the organization may be covered if they are full-time employees and on the regular payroll. If a director is not a full-time employee and coverage is still required, check with the underwriter prior to making a commitment or change to a policy that would affect that director.

¶5045 CHECKLIST: EMPLOYMENT CLASSIFICATIONS

Type of Employees to be Covered

Full-time Employees . . . . ☐
Part-time Employees . . . . ☐
Seasonal Employees . . . . ☐
Temporary Employees . . . . ☐
Contract Employees . . . . ☐
Probationary Employees . . . . ☐
Subcontract Employees . . . . ☐
Company Directors . . . . ☐
Minimum number of hours worked per week to be eligible . . . . . ___

¶5050 CLASSIFICATIONS: SEPARATING THE EXECUTIVES, AND OTHER OCCUPATIONS

Executives and working owners of corporations may have needs that differ from those of other employees within the organization. It is possible to separate the executives, and any other discernible group within the company, from the other people covered, and to offer this separate group a different level of benefits. In this manner, the working owners and the senior management can be provided with higher, or lower, levels of benefits, yet remain under the same master policy. Administratively, this is done by establishing a separate "classification" for these employees. The following is an example of a group life insurance benefit schedule that contains two classifications.

Class A: President, Vice-presidents and Controller:	Two times annual earnings adjusted to the next highest $1,000, if not an even number, maximum $150,000
Class B: All other employees:	One times annual earnings adjusted to the next highest $1,000, if not an even number, maximum $150,000

Insurers sometimes stipulate that a minimum number of employees be in a classification before they will agree to separating classifications. This number may be as high as five, but may be as low as one, depending on the insurer.

Insurers will allow up to a two times annual earnings differential between the classifications for group life insurance, but usually not any higher. In other words, in the above example, Class A would be allowed to have a schedule of three times annual earnings, but not four times, assuming Class B stays at one times annual earnings.

A group insurance policy cannot be set up where the majority of the benefits are provided for one or two individuals.

¶5055 PROS AND CONS OF SEPARATING CLASSIFICATIONS

Other employees, especially those who share premiums with their employers, sometimes end up subsidizing the older, senior people in the organization. Group life insurance and long-term disability rates are based on the average age and level of benefits for the employee group. An older executive, with a high benefit, can drastically affect the average rate charged to a group. The effect is greatest in small groups. Setting up separate schedules for higher paid senior employees can increase the effect on the rates.

Separate classifications can be drawn up for each benefit within a group insurance policy. For example, different deductibles can be set up in the dental or extended health care benefits for each classification.

Insurance companies can provide separate rates for each classification. The insurers can often keep experience separate for each classification. Request this when a policy is initially set up. Separate rates by classification can be requested after the inception date of the plan, but the insurers may only be willing to separate the rates and the experience starting in the month after your request or at the next renewal date.

Advise the insurance company if any employees covered under a plan (i.e., the executives) are not covered by Workers' Compensation, as this can affect the risk and the rates for certain benefits, especially short- and long-term disability.

Insurers can produce separate employee booklets and separate billings for each classification, if requested. There may be a small extra cost, in the neighbourhood of $5 to $10 per month, for each separate billing required, although this extra is sometimes "hidden" by the insurer. It is hidden by being averaged into one of the rates. The advantage of separate billings is that confidential information, such as amounts of life and disability insurance on the executives, can be kept private. There is normally no extra charge to have separate employee booklets for each classification, especially if the booklets are requested at the policy's effective date, unless the policy covers a small group under 15 to 20 employees.

Occasionally, executives and business owners elect not to be covered under group insurance plans for short- and long-term disability benefits because they have purchased personal disability policies which offer more extensive benefits. These disability policies are specifically designed for business owners and contain more bells and whistles than a typical group insurance policy's disability benefits. But they can be expensive depending on age, occupation, type of business, and medical condition of the applicant.

If you are covered under a group insurance policy's long-term disability (LTD) benefit, a personal disability insurance (called DI in the insurance industry) policy's underwriter will limit the amount that you can purchase under a personal policy. The total benefit allowed by the personal DI underwriter, between the group and the personal policies combined, is usually limited to 66.67 or 70 per cent of predisability income. If executives decide that the benefits of the personal DI policy are worth the cost, they can ask the group insurance company to exclude them from the classification for the LTD benefit (or LTD plus short-term disability) only. The exclusion should only be requested after the executives have been approved in writing, for the entire amounts applied for under the personal DI policy. Also make sure that you request a quote for the DI based on your dropping out of the group plan.

It is not necessary to advise a group insurer that you have a personal DI policy, as this will have no effect on the group rates, unless you drop out of the group plan's disability benefits. Group insurance LTD policies include what are called "all-source maximum" benefit limits. These, in effect, limit the amount of total money that can be received by a claimant to a percentage somewhere between 75 per cent of predisability net (after-tax) earnings and 85 per cent of predisability gross earnings, depending on the policy. This clause in a group policy, unless clarified in advance, could be used to reduce the amount paid under the group LTD policy by the amount paid under a personal DI policy (although I have not heard of this happening).

All-source maximum benefits, and their interpretations, are one of the most confusing areas in Canadian group insurance plans. Each insurer has a different definition of "all-source maximum", and there is no common industry consensus of these limits. Personal DI policies, and group insurance policies, should both be reviewed for their treatment of possible offsetting benefits. The definition of all-source maximum benefit can be clarified by asking the DI insurer and the group insurer for their interpretations.

Pros and Cons of Separating Classifications

Pros

1. Allows individual employer and employee benefit needs to be met.
2. Reduces group insurer risk for certain classifications if (older) higher paid employees opt to purchase individual DI coverage.
3. Allows classifications of employees to have different benefits schedules (within the same policy), thereby decreasing administration costs.
4. Allows more privacy for senior executives.

Cons

1. Possible antagonism from employees with fewer, or smaller, benefits.
2. More administrative complexity.
3. More complex employee communications.
4. Increased possibility of administrative errors.

¶5060 THE BENEFITS: WHAT SHOULD BE IN THE PLAN?

Someone could spend a lifetime studying the ins and outs of what to put into group insurance plans, and determining what benefits are more important. It is theoretically possible to put any type of medical or dental coverage into a plan, as long as one can afford the premiums, or can otherwise finance the benefits. An insurer's basic rule of thumb is that the size of the overall premium determines the options available for benefits and the options that are available for benefit financing.

Today's tough economic climate has forced many organizations to take a second look at their benefit plans. However, there are "core" benefits which appear in the majority of employer-sponsored group benefit plans and which can have a big effect on employees if decreased or dropped. These benefits are: 1. life insurance; 2. long-term disability; and 3. extended health care. Dental and short-term disability also appear in many plans, but not as often as the first three benefits.

Other benefits available are: 1. basic employee accidental death and dismemberment (AD&D); 2. dependant group life insurance; 3. employee and dependant optional (voluntary) group life insurance; and 4. employee and dependant voluntary AD&D.

If benefit dollars are in short supply, the best advice is to cover the employees for catastrophic losses first. This means coverage should be primarily aimed at protecting the employees and their dependants from financial ruin because of death or disability. Group life insurance and long-term disability should be considered as the primary building blocks because they cover catastrophic situations for both the employee and for the employer, and they are inexpensive, in comparison to health and dental benefits. The last thing that an employer wants to tell a grieving spouse is that there is no life insurance. Similarly, the last thing that an employer wants to tell a disabled employee is that there is no disability coverage. In situations where benefit dollars are tight, a dental plan is not as important. What is a dental claim for a couple of hundred dollars maximum when compared to a claim which could amount to hundreds of thousands of dollars in the case of a long-term disability claim for a young employee?

Benefits to be installed in order of importance are: 1. long-term disability; 2. group life insurance; 3. extended health care; 4. short-term disability; 5. dependant group life insurance; 6. basic employee AD&D; and 7. dental.

The Canada Employment and Immigration Commission (CEIC) has an accident and sickness plan which will pay a percentage of weekly earnings (55 per cent after the February 22, 1994 Federal Budget) to an ill or disabled employee for up to 15 weeks. This can be used to substitute for an insurance company or self-insured short-term disability policy. The pros and cons are discussed in Chapter 6, Benefits.

Dependant group life and AD&D are inexpensive benefits which can be added to a group life insurance policy. The cost makes them very attractive additions, and it is rare to see policies without, at least, the AD&D benefit. Implementing these two benefits is not required by insurers unless your organization has fewer than 15 to 20 employees, and the insurer requires their implementation as part of the package.

Dental policies were the newest additions to group insurance plans, when they became more generally available 25 years ago. They have since become a fixture of group insurance plans, especially in Western Canada. Yet in the Maritime provinces, dental policies took longer to catch on. Maritimers seemed to prefer installing a good pension plan, adequate life insurance and a good LTD plan before considering a dental plan. Corporations in Alberta, in contrast, preferred to implement a dental plan, including orthodontics, before considering a pension plan. Dental plans are expensive. They can cost up to 40 per cent of an organization's total group insurance premium. If benefits money is tight, the dental plan is the place to start looking at cuts. If things are really tight and you do not want to drop the dental plan completely, consider heavily revising it, or adding high deductibles. The same can be said of the extended health care benefit.

Benefits, which can be installed at no cost to the employer, are LTD, short-term disability, optional employee and dependant life insurance, and optional employee and dependant AD&D insurance. All of these benefits can be structured to have the employees pay 100 per cent of the premium. The advantage to the employees of these group benefits, is that all are much less expensive to purchase than similar personal policies.

Except for small groups — those under 15 to 20 employees — it is possible to underwrite just the benefits that your organization requires. Small groups may have to purchase group life, AD&D, and dependant group life benefits in order to purchase any of the other benefits. Insurers differ on which benefits are required in order to implement a particular policy. Some insurers may not offer an LTD benefit without a group life benefit. Selling more than one benefit to a group has advantages to the insurer of being able to bring in more premium, and of increasing the chances of keeping the policy on the books. To the policyholder, it is sometimes an advantage to place certain benefits with the same insurer. For example, a claim for long-term disability benefits usually means a claim for the waiver of premium under the group life insurance benefit. Also, short-term disability claims sometimes become LTD claims. The claims process can be easier and result in fewer delays or errors if the life and LTD benefits are with the same insurer. With the latter benefits, a short-term disability claim can be passed on to the LTD claims area within the same insurance company much more easily than having to set up the claims process with two different insurers. Claims for accidental dental, covered under an extended health care benefit, will be delayed less often if the same insurer covers the (standard) dental benefit.

¶5065 UNDERWRITING CONSIDERATIONS

The choice of what benefits an organization can choose and what insurers are available to provide the benefits may be limited. Insurers are not required to underwrite any group that they feel uncomfortable in underwriting. There are many reasons that the insurance companies use to decline certain types of organizations for group insurance. For example, some (not all) organizations have not been very careful when hiring people (at least in the past) and have suffered a high incidence of disability claims. This has resulted in the insurers refusing to offer quotes to other groups in the same industries. There are many factors, other than indiscriminate hiring practices, that also affect organizations' claims. These include high stress jobs, poor safety practices, exposure to environmental risks, and poor management practices. Whatever the cause, higher claims mean higher future rates. Certain groups have the habit of changing insurers and leaving insurance companies with losses if the insurers asked for rate increases to cover underwriting losses. No insurer will tolerate many losses without re-evaluating its underwriting of that type of business. Hence, many insurers decline to underwrite areas in which they suffer too many losses.

Not all corporations make good risks in the eyes of the insurers, especially for group life and long-term disability benefits. Small corporations, governments, groups employing under 15 to 20 employees, higher risk organizations such as social work agencies, the arts community, retail stores, underground mines, automobile dealerships, and trucking firms, especially those that use contract drivers, are types of organizations that draw limited enthusiasm in terms of insurer interest. Types of occupations can also cause insurers to decline to underwrite business. Underground miners, 100 per cent commissioned salespeople, a high percentage of low-paid workers (i.e., such as in a retail store), or any organization with a high turnover of employees, can cause an insurance company to decline to offer a quote.

The size of the organization may cause an insurer to decline an invitation to underwrite a group. Some insurers only underwrite larger groups. The smallest group underwritten is typically three employees. The smallest group underwritten without the insurer asking for medical examinations from the employees is normally around ten employees. Insurance companies' policies for groups of under 100 employees, for most industry groups, are often underwritten in the local group offices. It is important, if your organization has under 100 employees, to use experienced group insurance representatives. They are able to use their expertise to your best advantage, as they know their systems and how to work these systems to get the better rates. The difference in obtaining better rates may well be in how the duties of the various employees within your organization are coded into the computer in terms of occupations. For example, if your organization is a machine shop, and the employee data sheet states that everyone is a "blue-collar" worker, rates will be generated on that basis. By changing the owner's title to President and the partner's title to Controller (assuming that is what they spend the majority of their time doing), instead of calling them blue-collar workers, the rates can be adjusted to reflect the employees' true duties. An experienced underwriter or group insurance representative will know to do this in advance of calculating the rates. The result is a more accurate set of rates for your firm, leading to more predictable renewals, lessening the chance of huge rate increases in later years and increasing the immediate chance of lower rates.

¶5070 SIZE OF THE GROUP CAN DETERMINE THE BENEFITS

The larger the group, the more options the insurer will provide in terms of benefits and financing options. What constitutes a "large" employer depends on the insurance company. Insurers tend to group group insurance risks by number of employees within a group, and by the total premium dollars per group and per benefit type. The breaks tend to be along the lines of

a. Number of Employees:
   1. 3 to 9 employees;
   2. 10 to 19 employees;
   3. 20 to 49 employees;
   4. 50 to 99 employees;
   5. 100 to 249 employees;
   6. 250 to 499 employees;
   7. 500 to 999 employees;
   8. 1,000 plus employees;

   or

b. Annual Premium per Benefit ($):
   1. less than 500;
   2. 500 to 999;
   3. 1,000 to 2,499;
   4. 2,500 to 5,000;
   5. 5,001 to 7,500;
   6. 7,501 to 10,000;
   7. 10,001 to 20,000;
   8. 20,001 to 50,000;
   9. 50,001 to 100,000;
   10. 100,001 to 250,000;
   11. 250,001 to 500,000;
   12. 500,001 and up.

The above are examples of where insurers arbitrarily set their break points when determining whether to underwrite a business. A group that has nine employees may not be allowed to buy the same LTD benefit that a group of ten employees in the same industry and the same location could buy. Similarly, a group wishing to purchase a specific benefit may have better luck if their total annual premiums add up to $20,001, as the insurer may have a minimum premium limit set before the sale of a particular benefit will be allowed. If minimum premium is a problem, a group representative may boost the rate, or perhaps a rate on one of the other benefits, to ensure that the minimum premium is met.

Size of the group has a lot to do with the type of benefits and the benefit clauses underwritten. For example, a group with 19 employees may be allowed a maximum benefit of $150,000 per employee for group life insurance. If the group had 20 employees, a maximum of $250,000 might be allowed. Other areas of group insurance plans that are affected by the size of the group are: maximum amounts available without having to pass a medical examination (especially for group life insurance and LTD), the availability of certain benefits such as dental crowns, bridges, dentures, or orthodontics, and coverage for glasses and contact lenses. Not only can the benefits be affected by the size of the group, but as importantly, the way in which they are financed. Finally, some agents, brokers and consultants may not be willing to assist your organization unless there is a certain minimum amount of premium involved, unless they are working on a fee-for-service basis.

¶5075 INTERNAL COMMUNICATIONS

In order to be effective, a benefits program should contain regular employee communications. Employees who understand what benefits are available and how they are funded will appreciate more what they have. Employees, who understand that abuse of their sick-leave program by one of their members, will have a direct effect on all of their pocketbooks, will want to have a more active role in the group insurance plan's claim control process. Employee peer pressure can have a significant effect on plan abusers who tend to take more time off on sick-leave than other employees. Peer pressure can also take the form of employees advising their peers to get professional counselling, or advising the management team of a potential safety problem that could result from employees drinking on the job, for example. Peer pressure can reduce claims and expenses.

It is important to communicate with employees through meetings. These are best conducted over the lunch hour, before or after work, or during regular association or union meetings, in order to reduce the down-time costs. Insurance company group representatives will make presentations to the employees for free (the cost is actually built into the rates whether you use their services or not). It may be possible as well to have the group representative make a presentation on other benefit-related subjects, such as pension planning, again for free. Alternatively, insurance company group offices may be able to provide you with enough information to do your own presentations. The "Agent of Record", or other local insurance agents, brokers and consultants may also be willing to make a presentation to your employees for free, if they think that they have a chance to get some business out of it in the future. A word of caution here. Make sure that meetings have a set time limit. This will allow the employees time to prioritize their work so as to have the least disruption to their day. It will also enable them to be attentive and comfortable during the presentation itself. Any complex questions can be addressed by the presenter at a later time. Another reason to keep the meetings short: the presenters are generally technicians — they know the material well, but are not trained as entertainers!

Employee letters are a useful and inexpensive method of communicating. They can be designed to let employees know of any changes that are taking place, or as a format to ask for opinions and suggestions for improvements in the plan. The letter format is an excellent method of advising employees on how to save money, both for themselves, and for the plan. The use of generic drugs, as opposed to name brands, is one way to assist in reducing expenses. Employees may wish to know the pros and cons of this cost-saving measure, and the employee letter is a good format for this type of information. Sample employee letters can sometimes be obtained from the insurer group insurance offices, for free. Ask for them first before spending the time to develop your own. Another source of this type of letter, or at least of information to put into the letters, is from large corporations that already produce their own. These companies may be willing to share their literature for free if your organization is willing to acknowledge the source. Written permission should be obtained prior to reproducing any information.

Also look to the large employee benefit consulting firms for free information. These firms generally produce information in the form of newsletters for their clients and their prospective clients. Phone and ask to be put on their client newsletter mailing list. If you are a competitor of one of these large consulting firms and cannot get on the mailing list, check your local library or a friendly insurance company's group representative for a copy to read.

¶5080 MOST COMMON POLICYHOLDER ERRORS: GROUP INSURANCE DESIGN

Organizations can make errors in the design of group insurance plans. The following errors are common.

1. Failure to design eligibility to meet the organization's needs.

2. Failure to ask for written insurer consent prior to agreeing to individual employee, union or association demands for changes in the group insurance plans.

3. Failure to review the potential future financial ramifications of policy additions or amendments.

4. Failure to provide up-to-date experience and rate information to an ABC, for group insurance plan marketing purposes.

5. Failure to advise the insurer of group life insurance waiver of premium claims for employees on Workers' Compensation, or on long-term disability.

6. Failure to check the references, credentials and experience of new potential ABCs.

7. Failure to review the organization's needs for, or use of, the current ABC.

8. Failure to treat employee benefits as a financial requirement, not solely as an expense.

9. Failure to review the benefits schedule annually, with advice from the covered employees.

10. Failure to keep cost control features, such as deductibles, on pace with inflation.

CHAPTER 6

¶6000 THE BENEFITS

¶6005 THE BASIC BENEFITS

¶6010 GROUP LIFE

Group life insurance is one-year renewable term insurance. It pays the benefit amount (called the "face amount of the policy"), stated in the insurance schedule, to a named beneficiary. The group life benefit is paid out upon death from any cause, including, unless specified, suicide. The rate is determined on the average age, sex, and insurance amounts for the group as a whole. The average rate can be adjusted by insurers to compensate for industrial risks, occupational risks, location, and claims experience of the group. Rates can also be adjusted by the insurers to compensate for changes in the rate basis (the rate charged per $1,000 for each age), and for overall insurer group life insurance experience. The rate for this benefit is expressed as a rate per $1,000 of coverage per month.

Most group life insurance policies in Canada, with the exception of policies bought in Quebec, allow the employee to change beneficiaries (the person(s) who will get the money when the employee or member dies), at any time, to anyone. For policies bought in Quebec, and for employees who are considered Quebec residents, an employee must have the written consent of the named beneficiary before a change can be put through. Beneficiaries that can be changed at any time are called "revocable" beneficiaries. If one needs the beneficiary's consent first, before changing to a new beneficiary, then the beneficiary designation is called "irrevocable". Irrevocable beneficiaries might still be found in very old policies in other provinces, but this would be a very rare situation today, as these old policies have almost all been changed to new wording. Charities and schools can be named as beneficiaries, but naming the "estate" as beneficiary should be avoided, unless absolutely necessary (as in the case where there are no close relatives). In Quebec, the class of "protected" beneficiaries is extended to included any ascendants or descendants. Life insurance left to an estate cannot be released by the insurer until the will has been probated. In addition, life insurance in an estate can be seized by creditors. Creditors can also seize life insurance proceeds left to anyone other than a spouse, child (natural or adopted), grandchild or parent.

Naming children under the age of 18 as beneficiaries can also cause claim problems. Correct wording of the beneficiary nomination is important to avoid these problems. Life insurance companies will provide the proper wording to nominate "minors" as beneficiaries. Examples may be given in the group insurance administration manuals provided by the insurers. It is judicious, and recommended, that a trustee be nominated for the children, either directly on the beneficiary card, or in a will.

Group life insurance is usually set up in the policy on a "times annual earnings" basis, or on a "level" basis. A sample "times annual earnings basis" is shown on page 59 (see ¶5050, "Separating the Executives" in Chapter 5, Policy Review and Development). An example of a level benefit is "Each employee is covered for $25,000". A benefits schedule on a "times annual earnings basis" is considered a more "fair" schedule because it provides more benefits to the higher wage earners and it can automatically keep up with wage increases. (It could be argued though, that the lowest wage earners require the largest amounts of insurance. This is an argument for economists and political philosophers and as such, will not be discussed here.)

Group life and disability benefits are usually stated as having two "maximum" benefits: an overall maximum benefit, and a non-medical maximum benefit. The overall maximum will match or be greater than the non-medical maximum. The overall maximum is the greatest amount of insurance coverage allowed under the policy. The non-medical maximum is the maximum allowed without having to pass a medical examination. A "medical" may be just a questionnaire related solely to health matters, or a full-blown medical examination by an insurer-approved doctor, an insurer-approved medical specialist, or the employee's family physician. These medicals can include blood and urine tests and may request the release of medical information from doctors to the underwriter. A "medical" may also include a "lifestyle" test which could contain questions on participation in adventure sports, such as scuba diving, parachuting and automobile racing.

Coverage can be declined based on these medicals or on these lifestyle answers. The non-medical benefit can be quite crucial, especially for smaller companies, and more so if those companies employ people with health problems. If the non-medical maximum is not high enough in the policy, an employee can be eligible for more coverage than the insurer is willing to allow, based on the examination of the employee's medical information. This situation can lead to inequity of coverage between employees in the same classification. The non-medical maximum usually affects the higher wage earners, and executives of an organization. This situation can become quite a problem for an insurer, who wishes to keep a policy on the books, but who does not want to take a larger risk because of the poor health of one of the employees. *The non-medical and overall maximums are critical areas to examine within group life, short-term disability, and long-term disability benefits.*

Group life contains a waiver of premium clause. An employee who is permanently and (considered by the insurer to be) "totally disabled" can apply to have the group life insurance amount, as per the schedule, continued, but with the premiums waived. This means that if an employee was covered for $50,000 prior to the date of disability, the $50,000 coverage amount, once approved by the insurer, would be continued, as if the employee was still actively at work full-time, without the disabled employee or the group policyholder having to pay premiums. The coverage amount is frozen at the amount insured as of the date of disability. The disability must normally take place prior to age 65. Premiums may only be waived until age 65 (age 60 under some very old group life contracts), even if coverage for actively-at-work employees is continued past age 65.

Insurers differ on the definition of what constitutes "total disability". Two interpretations are the most common. The first says that premiums will be waived if the employee is disabled and unable to perform "any occupation" for wage or profit. The second interpretation is that the employee must be unable to do his or her "own occupation" for a certain length of time (usually for the first two years), and thereafter must be unable to perform any occupation. The better interpretation is the second. Except for smaller groups, the second definition mimics the time periods in the definition of disability under many long-term disability (LTD) plans. It is easier for everyone to understand when someone claims LTD benefits, that both the premiums for the LTD benefit and group life benefit will be waived. Ask the insurer to have the "group life waiver of premium definition match the (two-year own occupation) definition of disability under the LTD benefit".

If an employee is permanently disabled, not at work and not likely to return to work, and is drawing Workers' Compensation benefits, the employee can still apply for the waiver of premium benefit. All waiver of premium claimants are generally requested by the insurer to provide doctors' statements once a year, verifying that the claimants are still disabled.

The insurance company(ies) contracted to provide the group life and the LTD benefit(s) should be advised of all employees who are off work with any disability that has the potential of becoming a long-term claim, even if the claim is an obvious Workers' Compensation claim. Advising the insurer will result in fewer payment delays should a claim become long term, and will assist in the claims process should the Workers' Compensation Board deny the claim, thereby forcing the employee to claim under the LTD benefit.

There is an extra added to the group life rate to include waiver of premium. All waiver of premium claims are considered as a claim against the life insurance policy by insurers. For all but the very largest of policies, having either one group life claim, or one waiver of premium claim, will not, typically, affect the rate at renewal. The rate is more likely to be affected by an increase in the overall rate basis of the insurer, by underwriting losses in the insurer's overall "pool", or by poor returns in the insurer's investments. Insurers regularly re-evaluate the number of claims that they receive for each age and sex category. Regularly means every five to ten years. When the review indicates that a certain age and sex has had fewer claims, or more claims as the case may be, then the insurer may adjust that specific rate to compensate for the experience. Changes of this nature are called changes to the "rate basis".

For all but the largest organizations, the standard method of funding group life insurance is to have the insurer deposit a group's premium in a "pool" with all other groups' premiums. The money in the pool is invested by the insurer and investment income may be credited to the pool. Claims, taxes, administration expenses and commissions come out of the pool. Insurance companies institute across-the-board rate increases if more comes out of the pool than goes in. These increases are kept tightly under wraps as long as possible. Any outside knowledge of "pooled" increases usually send ABCs scurrying to put their clients' plans out to market to see how the new rates stand up. An increase in the rate basis, or an across-the-board increase in the pooled rates, is a major reason to market a group insurance plan. Even if the increases are under 10 per cent and appear insignificant, the effect of the increase over a number of years can be costly to an organization. Increases in the rate basis, and in the pooled rates, also call into question the overall underwriting practices of the insurance company. Are they underwriting poorer risks at standard rates? If they are, your rates could go up.

Group life also contains "reduction clauses". These clauses specify what happens to employee coverage at "normal retirement age", at early and postponed retirement ages. Usually, the life amount reduces to one-half at age 65 for active employees and coverage cancels at age 70, regardless of whether or not the employee is still working. Larger group employers can opt to continue coverage for retired employees. Some employers do continue coverage, but the effect of older individuals on the average group rate can be drastic. Because of this, coverage of retired employees in the same group contract with active employees is not recommended. As premiums paid by an employer to an employees' group life insurance plan are a taxable benefit to the employee, the higher the group life rate, the more tax employees must pay. It is therefore important to keep group life rates as low as possible. Retired employees can be covered under special paid-up policies for life insurance.

Paid-up life insurance policies for retirees are set up through an insurance company. Organizations having retired employees covered under the same policy as active employees, can ask insurers to provide quotes for a "group paid-up life policy" for the retirees. Rates can be requested on a "no commission" basis directly from the insurers' group offices, thereby reducing the costs to your organization. Paid-up life insurance policies are also available for other classifications, or groups. Because the premiums are generally fully paid in advance, the cost of these policies can make them too expensive for many organizations.

All group life insurance policies must contain, by law, a conversion privilege. This is a benefit that allows an employee, who has stopped working for any reason whatsoever, to purchase a personal life insurance policy from the underwriter of the group life benefit, without having to pass a medical. In years gone by, when employers used to receive what amounted to refunds of premiums for having good claims experience, unscrupulous employers might fire an employee who was about to die or become disabled. By firing the employee prior to the death or disability, the employer would be able to collect the "favourable" experience refund. (Some employers collected and kept these refunds for themselves, even if the employees had contributed towards the premiums.) Thus, a disabled employee would be out of work and would lose the life insurance benefit as well. The law allowing the employee 31 days to convert to a personal policy came about as a result of this type of situation.

The waiver of premium benefit is only useful to an employee who cannot pass a medical when he or she terminates service. Although conversion allows the terminated employee to purchase an individual policy without a medical, the policies available are limited to the more expensive "whole life" types, unless the policy has the option which enables the employee to purchase a one-year, non-renewable convertible term policy (meaning that a purchaser can turn the policy into a whole life policy). The problem with having to convert, is that insurers restrict the types of policies that you can convert to, and they only allow you to purchase a policy at standard rates. Standard rates, in insurance language, means smoker rates, regardless of whether or not you smoke. Someone who converts the group life insurance coverage to a personal policy, purchases the individual policy at high rates, in comparison to typical group insurance rates, and typically, must pay "standard" rates. An employee who can pass a medical, and whose lifestyle is considered "standard risk" by the insurer (meaning someone not participating in any hazardous activities, or sports, and who is planning on staying in Canada), can usually purchase any number of policy types at various rates, including non-smoker rates, if applicable. There is no reason for this employee to convert, unless the medical for the new policy turns up a previously unknown problem. All conversions must be insured through the same insurance company that underwrites the group insurance policy and must be applied for within the 31 days after leaving the employer. If the terminated employee wants to use a different insurance company for the personal insurance policy, as a safety precaution in case that policy is turned down, an application can also be submitted to the group policy insurer. Mark at the bottom of the latter application that the policy is a "group conversion from group policy number____".

The life insurance (conversion) application must be written up by a licensed life insurance agent. Most insurance companies do not pay commissions to agents for writing these policies on a conversion, unless the applicant can pass a medical. This situation is sometimes resented by ABCs who must take the time to fill in the forms and meet with the applicant, but for no pay.

From the financial perspective of the group insurance policy, any conversion is considered a claim against the group policy. The amount charged to the policy is generally minor, except for the largest policies, where the financial agreement between the insurer and the policyholder may stipulate the terms of the claim allocation.

¶6015 ACCIDENTAL DEATH AND DISMEMBERMENT

Group accidental death and dismemberment (AD&D) pays an amount (called the "face amount of the policy") to the beneficiary named in the group life insurance benefit, if the employee dies accidentally. There are also specific amounts paid to the employee if the employee loses an eye or a limb in an accident. The amounts, like life insurance, are stated in the schedule. The benefit is sometimes called "basic" AD&D. There are also other types of group AD&D, such as "voluntary".

The most common way of setting the schedule for basic AD&D is to have the face amount, on an accidental death, match the amount paid under the group life benefit. In other words, if the group life schedule states that the coverage is "two times annual earnings", and the employee dies accidentally, then the beneficiary will receive two times annual earnings under the group life benefit, and an additional two times annual earnings under the AD&D benefit. It is not necessary to have the schedule match the group life schedule. Occasionally, the AD&D benefit schedule may be greater than the life schedule; occasionally it pays a smaller amount.

AD&D benefits are sold through most life insurance companies as a "rider", or an addition to the group life benefit. Many insurers will limit the maximum accidental death benefit to the same maximum as is payable under the group life benefit. However, there are specialty insurers who may often offer more in terms of "side" benefits and who may offer better rates. The market has been very competitive for this benefit over the last few years. The reason for this is that the AD&D benefit is one of the most profitable for the insurers. The chance of dying sometime is 100 per cent. The chances of dying in an accident can be 5 per cent or less.

Specialty insurers are worth looking at from a benefit point of view because they often offer more "bells and whistles" on their policies and can also be less expensive. These insurers generally require a minimum premium per month. Because of this, smaller organizations will find that the "extras" offered by the specialty insurers may not be worth the cost to fund the minimum required premium. These organizations will find that the AD&D benefit offered by the group life insurer is a better option. Implementing an AD&D benefit through a specialty insurer will also require slightly more administration. An additional premium cheque will have to be prepared and sent each month.

Policyholder administration for the specialty insurer AD&D coverage is as easy as multiplying the total insurance volume times the rate and sending a cheque to the insurer for the balance, once a month. There will be slightly more administration in the case of a claim, than if this benefit is insured by the same insurance company as the group life benefit, because a proof of claim must be sent to two different insurers.

The benefit's rate is expressed as a rate per $1,000 of coverage per month. The rate is affected by the occupations of the employees covered. The insurers, when rating the benefit, consider that the people employed in certain occupations lead more "adventurous" lives. The insurers load the rates accordingly.

Over the last 15 plus years, certain ABCs have used the AD&D benefit to add bulk to their marketing reports when attempting to gain new clients. Because of the large number of minor riders that can be added by the specialty insurers, an ABC can write several pages comparing the specialty insurer products to those of other insurers. This has contributed to the success of these ABCs, usually to the detriment of other ABCs who did not know about the specialty products.

Most AD&D benefits include a waiver of premium if the employee becomes totally and permanently disabled. The AD&D definition of disability should match the definition under the group life benefit, even if two separate insurers are used.

AD&D usually covers employees 24 hours per day, both on and off work. In older AD&D policies, in order for a dismemberment claim (i.e., the loss of a limb) to be paid, the limb would have to be completely severed in an accident. Most modern policies will also pay if there is a permanent "loss of use" of a limb (or an eye), instead of the complete and irreparable severance due to an accidental cause. Insurers differ as to the time limit set in the policy in which the loss must occur after an accident. The loss must generally occur between six months and one year after the accident, depending on the policy, in order for a claim to be paid.

Exclusions differ between insurers. Insurers do not normally consider death or dismemberment to be accidental if the employee is committing a crime. Some policies consider that having a blood alcohol count over 0.08 per cent to be a crime. Others do not specifically state this. AD&D benefits are not paid due to acts of war, participating in a riot, or in the case of suicide, unless these restrictions have been waived.

¶6020 DEPENDANT GROUP LIFE

The purpose of this benefit is to assist the employee with the last expenses, in the case of the death of a dependent spouse or a dependent child. Amounts of coverage for the spouse range from $1,000 to $20,000. Coverage for dependent children is normally one-half of the spousal amount. Claims are paid to the employee. There is no beneficiary nomination.

The spouse must be by marriage, or by common-law arrangement, and must currently be of the opposite sex. (Human rights advocates have yet to challenge and win the same-sex spouse issue in all areas of the country.) Insurance companies have allowed coverage to be extended to spouses in the case of separation. Coverage is not normally allowed for "ex" spouses, or those who are no longer considered to be a "husband" or "wife", such as in the case of divorce. Older policies state that a common-law relationship must have existed for a minimum time period, usually for at least one year. Newer policies do not generally have this stipulation.

The employee can only have coverage for one spouse. It is important to point this out to a separated, but not yet divorced employee who has entered into a common-law relationship. The employee can cover any number of dependent children with no affect on the rate. The basic rule of thumb to use when determining if there is coverage for a dependent child, is to ask if the employee can obtain a "child" income tax deduction. If the answer is yes, then in most circumstances, the child will be considered eligible. Check with the insurance company for its ruling. Natural and legally adopted children are eligible. There may be restrictions on whether coverage is extended to other children.

Coverage is normally cancelled at age 65 for spouses. Coverage for dependent children is normally to age 19. Today, child coverage is usually extended to age 21, or age 25 if a full-time student is dependent on the parent for support. There is a small extra charge applied to the rate for this extension. The minimum age for coverage of dependent children is either "birth", age 24 hours, or age 15 days. (Stillborn children are not usually covered.) The younger the age that coverage starts, the higher the extra applied to the rate. The cost of the extras is minimal. Organizations, whose employees are young, may want the coverage to start at birth. The death of a child at any age is too traumatic to have to tell an employee that there is no coverage.

Coverage for children, under some policies, is extended past the age of 19 or 21 if the "child" is mentally or physically disabled, and still dependent on the parent for support. The insurance company should be advised in writing immediately of any children in this situation, when the child reaches age 19 (or 21 depending on the policy). This extension to the definition of dependent child can be agreed to, normally, at no charge to the dependant life rate. The extension can also be applied to medical and dental benefit definitions, but in these cases, future claims by these "dependent children" will continue to affect renewal rates.

Older policies' dependant life benefits had limited coverage for dependent children under one year of age. An example of one of these older schedules would see the spouse covered for $2,000 and dependent children over one year of age covered for $1,000. Coverage for children aged 15 days to one year might be $500. These older schedules are becoming rare.

Under some insurer wording for this benefit, if the employee is totally disabled and premiums have been waived for the group life benefit, the dependant life benefit will continue as if the employee was still actively at work, and the dependant life premiums will be waived. Each insurance company differs on this point. Some require dependant life premiums to be paid even if the employee group life premiums have been waived.

There is a "conversion privilege", similar to one under group life, in this benefit. The spouse of a terminated employee has 31 days (one month) to apply for a personal policy. This policy will be issued at standard rates regardless of whether or not the spouse can pass the medical, or participates in activities that are perceived by the insurers as hazardous. Because the amounts which are issued are so low (maximum coverage on any conversion is limited to the benefit maximum), and generally below most insurers' current, minimum policy amounts, there is normally no option as to the type of policy issued. It will be a "whole life" type. If the spouse can pass a "medical", there is little reason to convert the group policy amount. Simply apply for another type of personal policy.

From the insurer's financial perspective, conversions are set up as "claims" against the group life insurance policy. However, unless there has been a rash of dependant conversions or deaths, a conversion will, usually have little or no effect on the group rate.

There are two ways in which insurance companies rate a dependant life benefit. The first is by what is called a "flat" rate, or a "book" rate. Insurers, who rate in this manner, do not individually rate the benefit for each group. A rate is simply set and then applied to all groups. The other way to underwrite the benefit, is tie the basic rate charged to the group life rate. A higher group life rate will result in a higher dependant life rate. A lower group life rate will result in a lower dependant life rate. The reasoning behind tying the two rates together is that a higher group life rate generally means a higher overall average age of the group. Theoretically, an older group of employees should have older spouses. Insurers may increase the dependant life rates across the board if the dependant life pool loses money. If the dependent life rate is tied to the group life rate, an increase to the group life benefit rate may increase the dependant life rate.

Insurance companies do not normally ask for information on the age of the spouse in order to underwrite this benefit.

Dependant life is not considered as important a benefit if the employees have optional employee and optional dependant group life insurance at their disposal. Optional life for dependants can include coverage for dependent children. The main advantages of optional life insurance for dependants are that it is inexpensive in comparison to personal policies, easy to buy (typically only a one-page form to be completed) and maximum amounts available for purchase are much higher than a standard group dependant life benefit. On the downside, the optional coverage may be subject to obtaining underwriting approval, which may not come if the dependant cannot pass a medical examination. Dependant life, except for the smallest of group policies, on the other hand, is underwritten without medicals. Optional dependant life is usually paid for 100 per cent by the employee, while employers pay at least a portion of the premium for other (non-optional) benefits.

¶6025 LONG-TERM DISABILITY

Long-term disability (LTD) pays a monthly benefit to an employee who is disabled. The benefit is usually paid as a percentage of monthly earnings. It is occasionally paid as a "level", or flat, benefit, i.e., the level benefit might be $500 per month, regardless of earnings. The percentage of monthly earnings paid varies, but is usually set at between 50 per cent and 75 per cent of monthly earnings. The benefit percentages seen most often are 66.67 per cent and 70 per cent. Earnings used for calculation of employee benefits do not include overtime pay or bonuses, unless negotiated and agreed to by the insurance company.

The benefit begins to be paid after the "elimination" period has been satisfied. The elimination period states the time after the date of disability that benefits begin to be paid. The elimination period should fit with what ever short-term disability program is in place. An elimination period of 17 weeks, for example, means that benefits will begin after 17 weeks of being off work because of a disability. The elimination period is sometimes confused with the benefit's "waiting period". The waiting period is the time that a new employee must wait before becoming eligible to be enrolled in the plan.

Insurers generally offer a choice of elimination periods when underwriting a policy. The most common are 15, 17, 26, and 52 weeks. Insurers may allow different elimination periods for each classification of employee, within the same policy. This allows an employer to set up separate short-term disability programs for the various classifications of employees. For example, an employer may have a self-insured, paid sick-leave program for its management staff, with a six-month maximum accumulation. This same employer may have an insured short-term disability program for the field employees with a maximum paid period of 17 weeks. Both elimination periods can be accommodated within the same LTD policy, set up under the separate classifications.

One relatively common problem for employers is trying to set an elimination period to co-ordinate with a self-insured accumulative sick-leave program. For employees who have built up to their maximum accumulation (i.e., six months), there will not be a problem with the (six-month) elimination period. For a new employee who has not built up his or her time, there is a chance that a disability will go into long-term, and the employee will run out of accumulated sick-leave credits and have to wait, without income, for the LTD benefit payments to begin. The longer the period of accumulation allowed under the sick-leave program, the more chance there is for this situation to become a problem. For employers in this situation, there are three possible courses of action. The first is to continue paying sick leave as if the employee had the credits. This is the most paternalistic of the approaches. The second is to say "tough luck" and have no payment (although Unemployment Insurance sick leave may be an option) during this period. The third option, and certainly the most complicated, is to try and handle the difference within the wording, or administration of the LTD benefit. It can be done by providing the insurer with a list of all employees and the number of accumulated sick leave days, once per year, and having the insurer adjust the elimination period, and the rate, to accommodate. This is messy to administer and difficult for the insurer to rate. An alternative to the mess would be to shorten the accumulation period to 17 weeks, and set the elimination period at 17 weeks.

There has been much contention over the years, as to what is the best percentage of monthly earnings to be reimbursed. Should it be 55, 60, or 70 per cent? The situation has been made more complicated by Revenue Canada. They say that if employees pay 100 per cent of the premium for a short- or a long-term disability plan (the employer cannot even put one cent into the benefit in this case), then benefits, when received, will be tax free. This tax rule is used by employers who wish to share premiums for the whole benefits package with their employees. These employers use the non-taxable point to help sell the premium-sharing arrangement to employees. The merits of the taxable versus the non-taxable have been debated amongst actuaries for years. There are proponents for both approaches.

In a premium-sharing arrangement with an employer, employees pay for their share of the premiums with after-tax dollars. An employee, in a 40 per cent income tax classification, enrolled in an LTD plan which has a rate of $0.50/100, could end up having to earn ($0.50 × 1.4 =) $0.70 to pay for that $100 of benefit, depending on other allowable deductions. The employer can deduct any premiums paid into a group insurance program. If the employer pays for 100 per cent of the premium, the employer can deduct the whole amount. It can be argued that it is better, from an employee's perspective, to have a group insurance program that is 100 per cent paid for by the employer, because the cost is less expensive to the employee.

To confuse the matter even more, many insurers think that employees who receive money on a non-taxable basis, are less likely to return to work. Insurers, therefore, load the rate to take care of this possibility. In addition, insurers also use a little-understood catch-all clause to limit the amount that disabled employees can receive. It is called the "all source maximum benefit" clause, sometimes referred to as the back-end cap. This cap, in effect, limits the total amount of income that can be received from all sources, to a maximum of 85 per cent of an employee's predisability earnings. The percentage can be lower, depending on the policy.

An 85 per cent of gross earnings cap is usually set by insurers on taxable plans. Taxable LTD plans are those in which the employer contributes to the premium. Non-taxable plans — those where employees pay 100 per cent of the premiums — are limited to 75, 80 or 85 per cent of predisability "net" (after tax deductions) earnings. In the past, some insurers only allowed a 75 per cent of net cap on non-taxable plans. Today, some insurers may increase the cap from 75 to 85 per cent for a 10 to 15 per cent load on the rates. Other insurers do not offer any choice. Their policy wording simply states that taxable plans have an 85 per cent of gross cap, while non-taxable plans have an 85 per cent of net earnings cap. The cap really comes into effect if the disabled employee is drawing income from other sources. An insurer usually defines "income" as per the definition of income in the *Income Tax Act*. An employee who is drawing a pension from the Armed Forces (for example) may stand a risk, if disabled, of having the LTD benefit reduced by the pension amount. This issue is further confused by each insurer having a different definition of what constitutes "net income". The definition of net income should be standardized in the industry to ease comparisons. In the meantime, any prudent marketing of the group insurance policy must include a careful review of this clause.

From an overall employee tax perspective, it has been argued that the best plan to have is a 75 per cent benefit, plus 5 per cent payable to a registered retirement savings plan (RRSP) or pension plan, employer pay-all benefit with an 85 per cent of gross predisability earnings all-source maximum.

The definition of disability is extremely important in any disability policy. Groups with below 15 to 20 employees will generally have to settle for a more limited definition. This definition pays an employee if the employee is disabled and unable to perform "any occupation". The word "occupation" means occupation that one can perform through "education, training or experience".

The more standard definition of disability, available to most other groups, is that a disabled employee will be paid for up to two years if unable to perform one's "own occupation". At the end of the two-year period and a re-evaluation of the claim (if the employee is still disabled), he or she will continue to receive benefits if unable to perform "any occupation". More than one major insurance company has tried to differentiate its LTD product from others, by changing the definition slightly, from "own occupation", to the substantial duties of one's "own job". Although this sounds like it may be a more accurate way of treating the definition of disability, this definition really serves to define disability the way that the insurance company treats disabilities from a claims administration point of view. Insurance companies, which originally changed their definitions from an "own occupation" to an "own job" definition, were quite successful for a while with the change, in terms of new policy sales. This success had as much to do with ABCs having something different to talk about than the product being that much different.

LTD benefits are usually paid to age 65. This is termed the "maximum age". The maximum age can be age 60 or any other age. It is possible to purchase a benefit that has a maximum payout of only five years. The higher the maximum age, or the longer the benefit payment period, the higher the rate. The maximum age for LTD plans in the United States typically extends beyond age 65 if people are actively at work. In Canada, there has not yet been much call for benefits to extend past age 65.

LTD is rated in much the same manner as a group life benefit. For every age and sex there is a rate. The calculations are done by multiplying the rate times the volume for each employee, adding up the results and taking the average. This result is then loaded for type of industry, occupation and location. The rate will be increased or decreased, at renewal, depending on the average age, sex, and occupational make-up of the group. Like the group life benefit, LTD premiums are generally "pooled", for small- to medium-sized organizations. The pool is then invested and investment earnings may be added to the pool. Administration expenses, commissions, profit, taxes and claims come out of the pool. When more comes out than goes in, the insurer usually has a pooled rate increase. Every group in the pool will get an increase. A rate increase can be given to a particular group within a pool if that group has had exceptionally poor experience, without giving the same increase to every other group in the pool. Pooled rate increases are a good reason to market the benefit (to test the new rate's competitiveness). When there is a claim, the underwriters calculate from tables, called "reserve tables", what amount the insurer will have to put aside to pay the benefit if it were to go for the maximum length of time. This reserve amount is treated by the insurer as a claim against the policy. An employee who returns to work, or gets another job and goes off claim causes a "release of the reserve". This release is then credited to the policy. Most insurance companies use some form of reserve formula based on "Commissioners' Reserve" (actuarial) tables which are adjusted to the insurer's own overall experience.

The LTD rate is expressed as a rate per hundred dollars of benefit. To obtain an employee's benefit amount, multiply the benefit percentage times the employee's regular monthly earnings. An employee who earns $2,000 per month and has a benefit percentage of 66.67 per cent would receive a benefit of ($2,000 × 66.67% =) $1,333.40 (less any amount paid by CPP or WCB). If the LTD rate was $0.50/$100 of benefit, then the monthly premium would be ($1,333.40 × .50/100 =) $6.67.

Occasionally, LTD plans are set up with cost-of-living adjustments (COLAs) built into the benefit formulas. For example, a benefit might be set up as 66.67 per cent of predisability gross monthly earnings plus a 3 per cent COLA. The COLA is intended to increase the benefit amount paid to a claimant to help the claimant keep up with inflation. The COLA clause can be set up to pay the stated amount (i.e., 3 per cent), or to pay the lesser of the stated percentage and the annual inflation rate as stated by Statistics Canada. COLA increases are typically determined once per year, normally at January 1. The advantage of one of these clauses to a claimant is obvious. It helps a claimant's income keep up with inflation. The disadvantage is the cost. Insurers increase the LTD rate by approximately 5 per cent for every one per cent of COLA protection. A 3 per cent COLA clause can therefore add 15 per cent to the rate charged.

Poor hiring practices can lead to high LTD claims. If an employer is lax in this area, or if the employer has poor safety practices, claims will cause the rates to go up. It is important, therefore, for both the employer and the employees to understand how these benefits are rated, and what high claims can do to the rates. Employees should become more careful and more vigilant, and should let employers know if they are unhappy with the quality of people being hired. This is especially important where the employees are paying for the benefit. (Hiring practices should be based on ability to do a job. Employers have to pay attention to the possibility of increased benefit costs when hiring people with medical problems.) With the exception of the smallest groups, policies do not discriminate as to the health condition of an employee. Therefore, hiring employees who are not healthy increases the chances of increased claims, and increased future rates.

Exclusions are another area where policies differ. It is important to review all exclusions when comparing policies. Acts of war, participation in a riot, self-inflicted injuries, and disabilities caused as a result of performing a criminal act are common exclusions. Some policies exclude disabilities caused as a result of having a blood alcohol content of over 0.08 per cent. Certain disabilities, such as those caused by mental illness, drug or alcohol abuse were at one time treated differently in LTD policies. Today, as a result of human rights legislation, these disabilities should be treated as any other illness. The insurance company, understandably, does not want to pay people to stay home and drink or take drugs. They, therefore, will require people in these situations, to be involved in insurer-approved rehabilitation programs.

The larger insurance companies are proud to point out their "rehabilitation" programs. A good rehabilitation program can have positive results for everyone concerned. People on disability can easily be left to themselves, which may not be the best for them, will not get them back to work and will not get them off claim. People staying on claim hurt employers in three ways. The employer loses a valuable employee. The more ongoing or open claims that an organization has, the greater the effect on the LTD rates. Also, too many open claims will scare away many insurers when a program is marketed. A proper rehabilitation program is an integral part of any LTD benefit.

Some insurers employ their own rehabilitation counsellors. Others employ independent counsellors. The success of either approach depends on the experience and workload of the people involved.

¶6030 Canada/Quebec Pension Plan Disability Benefit Integration

The long-term disability amount is reduced by amounts received from the disability benefit of the Canada/Quebec Pension Plan (CPP/QPP). CPP/QPP pays an amount to a permanently disabled employee that is dependent on how much and how long an employee has contributed over his or her lifetime. There is also a separate amount paid for every dependent child. With the exception of the occasional level benefit schedule (e.g., all members are covered for $750/month), usually underwritten for a union, almost all group long-term disability plans contain a CPP/QPP offset. What this means in a nutshell, is that all accepted claimants will receive their LTD benefit percentages, less what CPP/QPP pays.

The CPP/QPP offset is called a "primary" offset if only the portion paid by CPP/QPP on behalf of the disabled employee is subtracted from the benefit paid by the insurer. It is called a "full" offset if the insurer subtracts all monies, including those paid on behalf of the dependent children, from the benefit it pays. An LTD benefit which uses full offsets is less expensive than one using primary offsets. The difference in rates between the two is between 5 and 10 per cent. A plan with full offsets can be seen to discriminate against employees with dependent children. The rate is the same for single employees and for employees with dependent children, yet an employee with dependants, insured under a full offset plan, will potentially receive less than from the LTD benefit than a single employee.

Groups contemplating the installation of a long-term disability plan should review the benefits paid by CPP/QPP for disability. To qualify for a disability pension, the applicant must be suffering from a mental or a physical disability that is both *severe* and *prolonged*. A disability is *severe* if it renders the individual regularly incapable of pursuing any substantial gainful occupation, and *prolonged* if it is expected to be of infinite duration, or is likely to result in death.

CPP/QPP disability maximum age: disability must occur prior to age 65. Disability payments are only made until age 65, at which time they then become a CPP/QPP retirement pension.

CPP/QPP disability applicants must have valid contributions in five of the last ten years, or in two of the last three years in order to be considered. Contributors must have contributed to CPP/QPP for the Minimum Qualifying Period, be disabled as defined in the CPP/QPP legislation, and be under age 65.

CPP/QPP disability benefits, when approved, will begin four months following the month in which disability is considered to have commenced. Benefits will end when the individual is no longer considered to be disabled as defined by the plan, or age 65, whichever is earliest. The CPP/QPP disability benefit is calculated according to the individual's own earnings and CPP/QPP contributions. There is also a benefit payable if the claimant has qualifying dependent children under the age of 18. The maximum benefit as of January 1995 is $854.74 per month. The maximum dependent child benefit is an additional $161.27 per child per month. Benefits are paid for qualifying dependent children, up to age 25, attending full-time education courses (i.e., university, or community colleges) and who are living at home. CPP/QPP disability benefits are taxable, but the child benefit is non-taxable up until the dependent child reaches age 18.

¶6035 Workers' Compensation Offset

Workers' Compensation benefits are another offset from the amount paid by the insurer. The Workers' Compensation Board (WCB) pays for on-the-job disabilities only. It may not pay if someone is disabled on the way home or on the way to the job site. Workers' Compensation pays the majority of claims on the job. There are, however, situations where WCB will cut someone off claim for a variety of reasons. The claim may then turn into an LTD claim, especially for the duration of the two-year, own occupation period. LTD coverage is for 24 hours per day under most policies. Employees who are disabled while working for wage or profit for another employer may not be covered under their primary employers' LTD plans.

¶6040 Working for Two Employers

Claim payments from another group insurance plan are normally used as an offset to the employer's group disability plan. This is an important point to note if an employee is moonlighting and covered under another group insurance plan.

¶6045 Personal Disability Plan Integration

Group LTD claimants who have a personal disability policy, should not have their group insurance claim amount affected or reduced by any claim on their personal policy. A claim on the personal policy may be affected by the group claim amount. Individual policies should be reviewed to determine whether or not a group claim will act as an offset to the personal disability policy.

Any employee who has both personal and group disability coverage, should obtain written confirmation (if it is not already clear in the master policy or employee booklet), from the group insurer, that any benefits paid under the personal disability insurance (DI) policy will have no affect on the benefits paid under the group disability policy, particularly with respect to the "all-source maximum" benefit restriction in the group policy.

¶6050 Association Disability Plan Integration

An employee who has a disability policy through a professional association group plan should check the association policy wording to see whether or not other LTD group claims payments will affect payments under the association policy. Unlike life insurance policies, both group and individual, which will pay the total face amount of all life insurance policies issued, disability policies may offset each other. Because of this, it is important to ensure that employees and employers do not pay for coverage that cannot be collected.

¶6055 Pre-Existing Conditions

There is a clause added to many LTD benefits that can restrict payment in the event of certain types of disability. This clause is called a pre-existing (pre-x) conditions clause. It normally works like this. If a new employee has sought advice for a medical problem prior to being hired, and the employee becomes disabled because of that problem after being hired, then he or she will not receive any benefits if a disability results from that specific medical condition. It is critical for new employees to realize that there can be a "pre-x" clause in group insurance contracts. It may make the difference as to whether or not they leave their old employer. An employee who has had a "minor" heart problem, may find, upon taking another job, that there is no coverage for this pre-existing condition under the new group insurance contract. Luckily, the majority of these clauses contain time limits. If a new employee has not sought medical advice and has not been on medication for the last three months prior to being hired, for example, then, depending on the policy, the clause will have no effect on that employee. Also, if the employee has sought advice or has been on medication and becomes disabled as a result of this condition one year or more after the date of hire, depending on the policy, benefits will be paid. The policy, and the proposals should be reviewed to see whether there is a clause included and to see what time restrictions are given. Pre-existing conditions clauses usually only turn up, in Canadian group insurance policies, in the LTD benefit, but may be contained in other benefits as well. They are common in other types of policies, besides group, such as travel policies.

Pre-existing conditions clauses are written into most group insurance policies automatically, unless the purchasing organization requests that they be removed. Removal may cost anywhere from an extra 5 per cent load on the rates, to no load. The size of the group will dictate whether or not removal is an option. Insurance companies will not normally remove these clauses if a group has 20 or less employees. The purpose of the clause is to protect the insurance company from having employees hired, going through the waiting period, getting onto the group insurance plan, and then going off on claim immediately. This clause also helps to protect the rates of the group policyholder and its employees: those who pay the premiums. If an employer is not being careful in its hiring practices, and hires people who become claimants, especially right after joining the plan, the rates will go up. Whoever pays the premiums will end up with rate increases.

Insurers may think that smaller companies tend to hire relatives and friends more often than larger companies. Some insurers believe that the possibility of a small company hiring a very ill relative, just to get the relative onto the group insurance plan, is greater than with a larger company. That is one of the reasons insurers can give for not removing the clause on smaller policies. If an organization wishes to remove the clause, contact the insurer's group representative.

(See also: Non-medical Maximum Benefits at ¶6065 below.)

¶6060 SHORT-TERM DISABILITY (WEEKLY INDEMNITY)

Short-term disability insurance, often referred to as weekly indemnity (WI), is a group insurance benefit that offers coverage for short-term disabilities or sickness. Coverage is usually expressed as a percentage of employee weekly earnings. The percentages, offered by insurers, range from 50 to 75 per cent. The most common are 60, 66.67 and 70 per cent. Occasionally, short-term disability plans are set up to pay "level" amounts, i.e., all employees will receive $450/week, but outside of plans underwritten for unions, these are rare. The coverage is put into place for injuries and sickness that occur anytime but on the job. Workers' Compensation is used to cover on-the-job injuries and sickness.

Short-term disability insurance can be set up to pay disabled employees for periods of up to 104 weeks. Most policies are set up to pay for periods of 15, 17, 26 or 52 weeks. The 15 and 17-week maximum benefit periods are used to coincide with the maximum sick leave period payable under unemployment insurance (UI). This is called UI integration.

When do benefits start being paid? You can set the starting day of benefit payments to begin whenever you wish, as long as the insurance company approves. Most benefits begin paying on the first, the eighth, or the fifteenth day of disability. The earlier the benefits begin to be paid, the more expensive the premiums. Benefits can start being paid on different dates, depending on the cause of the disability. A typical plan design might have benefits beginning on the first day of an accident, and the fourth or eighth day from the onset of sickness. As an option, benefits can begin on the first day of hospitalization, for extra premium of course.

A short-term disability benefit is described in terms of numbers. For example, a 1-8-17 week plan, means that the plan's benefits begin on the first day of an accident, the eighth day of sickness, and continue for 17 weeks. A 1-1-8-17 plan is the same but includes first-day hospitalization. A 8-8-26 plan pays benefits beginning on the eighth day after an accident, after the eighth day of a continuing sickness, and benefits continue for up to 26 weeks.

The maximum benefit stated in the policy is important. A low maximum benefit typically cuts off the highest wage earners in terms of percentages that can be received. For example, if a plan was set up to pay 66.67 per cent of weekly earnings, with a maximum benefit of $450, then anyone earning over $675 per week will be cut off. The president of the company may earn $1,000 per week. If the president went off ill, the maximum benefit that he or she would receive would be $450 per week, which means that the reimbursement level will only be 45 per cent! The maximum is a very critical component of the benefit.

¶6065 Non-Medical Maximum Benefits

An important point in the design of a benefit is the "non-medical" maximum benefit. This is the maximum benefit allowed by the underwriters, without employees having to pass a medical before approval. In the above example, if the non-medical maximum weekly indemnity benefit was set at $450, and the maximum benefit was set at $600, there is the problem of the higher wage earners (i.e., the president) not being covered for the full 66.67 per cent. There is the additional problem of having to have the president take a medical (a hassle at the best of times, let alone at a busy period) in order to qualify for the benefit amount between the $450 and the $600. If the president, for some reason, cannot pass the medical, then there can be real problems. Compounding the problem is the clause, written into most group short-term disability (and LTD) benefits, that any amount paid by the employer to the disabled or ill employee will be deducted from the amount paid in benefit by the insurer. So topping-up a benefit plan is technically not allowed. Policyholders have been known to ignore this clause by not telling the insurance company that any top-up is being paid, but this is technically not allowed. Insurance companies can stipulate in their policies that they retain the right to audit policyholder records. Although audits are rarely performed, an audit of payroll records could turn up discrepancies. Insurers can demand repayment of overpayments.

¶6070 Using UI for Short-Term Disability

The Canada Employment and Immigration Commission underwrites a sick-leave benefit, which employees and employers pay for as part of their unemployment insurance (UI) premiums. It pays (January 1995) a maximum of 55 per cent of weekly earnings, to a maximum benefit of $448/week, for a maximum period of 15 weeks. A claimant on this program must wait two weeks from the onset of an illness, or disability, before benefits begin. There are no benefits paid by UI for these first two weeks. Short-term disability benefits on group insurance policies are designed to replace the UI benefits for those 15 or 17 (15 plus the two-week wait) weeks.

Why use a group insurance policy when we have UI? The answer is that group insurance policies are more flexible. Short-term disability policies can:

1. start paying benefits earlier;
2. pay a higher benefit percentage;
3. pay for a longer time period;
4. pay quicker;
5. pay a higher maximum benefit (important for higher wage earners);
6. can be more easily integrated with a long-term disability benefit; and
7. the employer can receive a UI rate reduction on the employer portion if there is a short-term disability plan in place that at least matches the UI sick-leave benefit.

For an employer, there can be a reduction in the employer premium rate percentage to implement a short-term disability policy (STD) that at least matches the sickness benefit offered by UI. A portion (5/12's) of the savings obtained by the employer through this rate reduction is supposed to be returned to the employees, at least "in kind", according to UI rules and regulations. The employer rate reduction can mean a savings of up to approximately $140 per year for each employee who is contributing the maximum to UI. Not having a short-term disability plan, and opting to use UI sick benefits instead, will mean the loss of this employer rate reduction.

Occasionally, short-term disability plans are set up to "wrap around" the UI sick-leave benefit. This allows an employer to set up a disability program which covers the first two weeks of disability or sickness. At the end of those two weeks, UI then pays for 15 weeks, after which the insurer continues payments. This effectively reduces STD premiums, but it is a complicated, hard to explain, and hard to administer method of setting up benefits. Some insurers refuse to underwrite a "wraparound", or "UI carve-out" STD plan because of these reasons.

What are the disadvantages of installing a short-term disability program instead of using the UI sick leave? First, it can cost more. Also, if a short-term disability plan is used and the claims are greater than the premium plus the insurer retention, then short-term disability rates will increase.

What are the advantages of installing a short-term disability program besides the UI rebate? Installing an insured short-term disability benefit can replace a self-insured, sick-leave program, and in certain situations, be less expensive. Why less expensive? Many self-insured plans pay 100 per cent of an employee's earnings during the time off. Insured policies pay a maximum of 75 per cent of pre-disability earnings. Insured plans also give the employer the advantage of having a third-party adjudicate a claim. This can bring to light more information about a specific employee's condition, as claims are usually submitted through the employer. To claim on an insured plan, the employee and the employee's doctor must complete claims reports, which are much more detailed than the typical doctor's "note".

There may be initial employee dissatisfaction if an organization tries to replace a self-insured, accumulative sick-leave program with an insured program that pays less.

¶6075 Definition of Disability

The normal definition of disability for a short-term disability benefit is "disabled and unable to perform one's own occupation". The coverage is termed "non-occupational", meaning that benefits are not paid for on-the-job injuries or illness (unless agreed to by the insurer in advance). Smaller organizations, which are only able to purchase an "any occupation" definition of disability under an LTD benefit because of their size, can get around the LTD limitation by installing a short-term disability program that covers employees for 52 or 104 weeks, before the LTD benefits begin. Under a 26-week, short-term disability program, you receive up to 26 weeks of claim payments if you are disabled and unable to perform your own occupation. Or, extend the STD coverage to 52 or 104 weeks and you have a way of, at least partially, getting around the LTD definition limitation.

¶6080 Personal Disability Policy Integration

Income from a personal disability policy generally does not affect the benefit payments under the group plan unless specified otherwise. Personal disability plan benefits may, however, be affected by group disability claim payments. Personal disability plans should be integrated with the group coverage to ensure that you are not overinsuring yourself, or having to pay for benefits that you may be unable to collect.

¶6085 EXTENDED HEALTH CARE

Extended health care (EHC) plans, also called Medicare supplement plans, are best described as plans which cover medical services not typically covered by Medicare. EHC plans are comprised of five main benefit types: hospital coverage; prescription drug coverage; other services; travel benefits; and vision care.

EHC plans can include a large number of benefits, which are not paid for within provincial Medicare programs. Hospital coverage for semiprivate or private rooms, prescription drugs, ambulance charges, artificial limbs and eyes, paramedical practitioners (i.e., chiropractors, naturopaths, podiatrists, masseurs, etc.), out-of-country emergency treatment, coverage for eye glasses and contact lenses. The list is virtually endless. You can generally add on as many items as you are willing to pay for, as long as the underwriter agrees. The key words here are "as you are willing to pay for".

Benefits such as EHC and dental are "dollar-in, dollar-out benefits". You pay your dollar in premium, and you take out a dollar in claims. Except it does not work quite that way. The insurer has its cost of providing the benefit — the retention — taken directly off of the premium dollar before, or as you claim. You can claim what is left without your rates going up. Remember that retention can be as low as 8 per cent on the largest of policies, and as high as 35 per cent on the smaller policies. This means that your organization actually loses, or has to pay, if you like, up to 35 cents on the dollar, for the insurer services, the ABC services, and the taxes.

Because of the cost of the retention, and because of the rapidly rising price of medical services, the emphasis on these benefits over the last few years has been to control costs. Control of costs has traditionally been by three main methods: the use of deductibles; limiting the percentages reimbursed (called co-insurance factors); and reducing the number of benefits included, or at the very least, reducing their internal maximums. Virtually no one in Canada has sought to cancel these benefits altogether, yet.

Deductibles have always been a popular method of controlling costs. These are typically written as follows: nil, \$10/\$20, \$25/\$50, \$50/\$100. The first number is the annual deductible that a single employee must pay. The second number is what an employee with dependants must pay. In a $10/$20 deductible policy, the single employee has to pay for the first $10 of his or her total each year; an employee with dependants is responsible to pay the first $20. Occasionally, the second deductible figure refers to the amount that each family member must pay before receiving benefits (i.e., the claims for the parent must add up to $20 before the balance is reimbursed, and the claims for each child must be $20 before the balance of that individual's claims will be paid). This latter interpretation is rare in today's marketplace.

The higher the deductible, the lower the premium rates. Deductibles still abound that were designed 25 years ago. A $10/$20, or a $25/$50 deductible meant that the employees shared a much larger portion of the cost years ago, when prescription costs were a lot lower. Today, a $10/$20, or even a $25/$50 deductible is almost useless if an organization wants to control costs. Yet the deductibles have not been changed in many plans to keep up with inflationary trends. Deductibles, to be more effective at controlling costs, should start at $50/$100, and go up from there. There is a problem with the concept of deductibles, however. With this type of benefit, if employees all contribute to the premium, not all employees will claim enough to be reimbursed. Employees may all pay the same premiums, yet those who claim little or nothing are, in fact, penalized because they receive less back in return for those premiums. An organization can reduce this problem, and reduce costs, by changing the percentage reimbursed to the employee, instead of using a deductible to reduce costs.

Although the percentage reimbursed, or the co-insurance, can be set at any percentage that the underwriters agree to, the three most common are 80, 90, and 100 per cent. The latter means that 100 per cent of the claims, up to the policy maximum benefit, will be reimbursed. Reduce the co-insurance from 100 to 80, or 90 per cent and there will be a drop in the rates. There is however, a catch in doing this. EHC plans cover a wide variety of claims, some of which can be very expensive. If one wants to continue coverage for the catastrophic scenario, the percentage reimbursed for the high dollar value claims, as compared to ones with high usage and lower per claim values, should be kept at 100 per cent. Not many employees can afford an out-of-country hospital bill, or an air ambulance bill. Claims of this sort can run from thousands to hundreds of thousands of dollars. Who on your payroll can afford to pay 10 or 20 per cent of a claim which is that large? How do you set your plan to reduce costs, by lowering the amount reimbursed, yet still be able to cover the catastrophic scenario?

The answer is to look at the structure of most EHC benefits. There are five main components, as mentioned earlier. The first component is hospital room coverage; the second is prescription drugs; the third is other; the fourth is travel; and the last is vision care. Where would the majority of high expense claims fall under? Yes, a semiprivate or private room can be expensive over a long time period. And so can prescriptions if someone is trying to control a serious medical condition. But the catastrophic claims that we are referring to are out-of-country medical, air ambulance, private duty nursing, dental work required as the result of an accident, and artificial limbs and their replacements. These benefits are usually placed under the "other" section of an EHC plan. The trick then, to reduce overall costs yet cover the employees for a catastrophe, is to reduce the percentage reimbursed for hospital room coverage and prescription drugs only. In other words, set up the policy to reimburse 80 or 90 per cent on semiprivate or private hospital and prescription drugs, all the while leaving the co-insurance at 100 per cent on the "other" benefits. Alternatively, because prescription drugs can be expensive for employees needing long-term drug therapy, co-insurance can be set at 70, 80 or 90 per cent for the first $2,000 or $3,000 of annual drug bills, then be reimbursed at 100 per cent after those amounts. Except for the smallest groups, most insurance companies should be able to set up plans this way.

The number of benefits and the scope of the coverage can be viewed by looking at the sample spreadsheets enclosed in the Appendices of this book. We will examine these benefits by category, starting with hospital room coverage.

Under large benefit plans, in-Canada hospital room coverage is generally set up as semiprivate or as private. Private room coverage is more expensive than semiprivate. It is often very difficult to get a private room in a hospital unless it is requested by a doctor. Requests by doctors should be because the room is required for medical reasons, and if this is the case, provincial Medicare may pick up the cost. In addition, private rooms are not often available anyway. Paying for private room coverage can be, therefore, a waste of money.

The drug portion of an EHC benefit can be set up to include coverage for just those drugs legally requiring a prescription, or for all drugs that a doctor has "prescribed", i.e., written down the name of the drug on his or her prescription pad and handed to the employee, including those drugs that an employee can get without a prescription. It is not in the best interests of claims control to set up a plan to cover anything more than the former definition. There is too much room for abuse using the latter definition, and premiums for the latter definition can be up to 30 per cent higher. A middle way of setting up the prescription drug benefit is to cover all drugs legally requiring a prescription and include all non-prescription drugs which are required because of life-threatening illnesses. Because this wording helps those who really need it, and also gets rid of the smaller "nuisance" claims from the experience, it is a way of setting up a benefit to help solve both the problem of controlling claims and the problem of providing a "real" benefit to the employees.

Another way of paying for prescription drugs within an EHC benefit is by use of a prescription drug card. Control of costs with these cards can be a problem, especially without proper claims adjudication and control systems in place. The problem with them, historically, was that the majority of the claims control was left to the people working at the dispensing pharmacies. The insurance companies had less control over what was paid for at the time of the sale of the prescription. With a reimbursement system, the insurance company makes the decision as to whether or not the claim is in fact reimbursable. With a card, the insurance company may not make the decision. One method of trying to control costs while using a drug card is to include a co-pay amount such as $1.00, $2.00, $3.00 or $5.00 per prescription. In other words, the employee has to pay whatever the co-pay amount is for every prescription. There is no denying the popularity of the card system, at least in some areas of the country. Yet, many major insurance companies have done studies that show there is anywhere from a 5 to 15 per cent increase in claims by using cards! Insurance companies, which use a third party to administer a drug claims system, have to pay that company for every claim processed, and those costs are passed on to their policyholders. Benefit providers, who prefer a card system, do not seem as bothered by these increases. Of course, these providers may be "non-profits" who do not pay provincial premium tax, so they may get a partially offsetting break, immediately, which can be passed on to their clients.

Prescription drug coverage generally excludes anything available "over the counter", unless the policy is specifically set up to cover "prescribed" drugs — an expensive inclusion which is avoided by most cost-conscious groups. Examples of typical exclusions are patent and proprietary drugs, baby food and formulas, cough medicine, minerals, proteins and vitamins, collagen treatments, anti-obesity treatments, and fertility treatments. They can also be set up to exclude "contraceptives" such as "the pill" and IUDs, although this is rarely requested, except by some religious organizations. Diabetic and colostomy supplies are covered under some policies and not under others. Some insurers state that they have this coverage, while others may cover them, but do not state it directly. If in doubt, obtain clarification in writing.

The area in most EHC policies which contains the benefits most likely to cover catastrophic claims, is the section called "other", or "extended health". Here we find three benefits which cover catastrophic type situations: air ambulance, private duty nurses, and artificial limbs. The odds of needing one of these services are very small, but if you do, the costs will be very high. Let's examine each one.

Ambulance services are covered under the majority of policies. Coverage for air ambulance services may not be as common. Air ambulance services can be very expensive, ranging into the thousands of dollars. Sometimes it is covered by provincial Medicare, but Medicare may only cover the first leg of the journey, i.e., to the first hospital. The first hospital may not be able to offer the proper care, however, and another flight may be necessary to a larger centre. Costs for these services vary, as they are usually dependent on distance. Coverage for air ambulance services is important. What is covered under some policies, but not others, is the charge for some method of public transportation, such as a taxi, if an ambulance is not available. Many insurers do not cover this because the insurer has no way of determining whether or not the services are actually required. They do with an ambulance, however. Another problem for insurers is that they do not want to have to pay claims for every taxi trip to a doctor's office. However, the cost of a ground ambulance trip anywhere in Canada will be at least a couple of hundred dollars. And a taxi may be less expensive! Of course, a taxi will not be able to offer the emergency equipment that is carried by some ambulances, and hence travel by public conveyance may endanger the life of the patient.

Private duty nurse charges are expensive. An employee or dependant requiring these services can run up a substantial bill, because people who need private duty nurses are usually very ill. If a private duty nurse has to come to someone's home twice a day for half-an-hour each day, the cost over one year can be $25,000, which is a large claim to put into any group insurance policy! Many insurers have now put dollar limits on the amount they will reimburse each year, both to save themselves losing money on these claims, but also to save the policyholders from the large rate increases which would be required at renewal. This limit varies between insurers. It can be as low as $5,000 per year, or as high as an unlimited maximum. If you were the person requiring the services, what would you want? What would you be able to afford? Would you prefer to stay at home, with your family and the help of a private duty nurse, or, because there is no option (who would take care of you otherwise?) be put into an institution? Tough choice. I would take the home stay if I could afford it, or if there was insurance coverage to help out. Putting limits on this benefit limits your choices.

Artificial limbs are also expensive, with the cost of an artificial leg easily running over $12,000. But here is where insurance companies differ. Some cover the "initial" artificial limb only. Others cover the initial limbs "plus replacements"; others specifically include adjustments and repairs as well. Artificial limbs may need to be replaced quite often at the beginning, because the area that they are attached to changes, or, later, because they wear out due to usage. Therefore, it is important to cover the replacements. Insurers have been slow to embrace coverage for "myoelectric" limbs — those which work via small servo motors and electric impulses generated from wires attached to other parts of the body. You may find that these benefits may specifically be excluded.

There are other benefits, within extended care, that differ between insurers. They are services such as accidental dental, which covers dental treatment required as a result of an accident. Look for two things here. First, insurers have a time limit in which the services must be performed, usually one year, but sometimes six months. Pick the one year limit if possible. Psychologists' charges are sometimes covered under extended health, as are physiotherapists, up to certain annual limits. Physiotherapist coverage is sometimes covered under provincial health care, so may not be much of a benefit. Similarly, psychologist coverage is not something that is often claimed, because there is no privacy and confidentiality in having to submit a claim form through an employer for this type of claim. If there is a claim, however, it can be large. Psychologist rates are in the $85 per hour range. The maximum benefit paid under EHC policies is typically $300 to $500 currently. Because of the confidentiality issue, it is preferable to investigate an Employee/Family Assistance Program (EFAP), instead of using the EHC benefit for this sort of claim.

Paramedical practitioners coverage is also included in most extended health care benefits. Many services provided by "parameds", as they are called, are not generally paid for by provincial Medicare plans, although this differs by province. Examples are naturopaths (treating via herbs, etc.), chiropractors, chiropodists, masseurs, acupuncturists, Christian Science practitioners, speech therapists, and osteopaths. Insurance companies differ in which services they cover. They also differ in the maximum coverage that they offer. Insurers express these coverages as either a maximum per employee for all parameds combined, or as a maximum per practitioner per employee (or dependant). The latter generally offers more coverage, and is better from a benefit perspective. The former is better wording from the cost reduction point of view. The claims can be expensive if there is no internal maximum set up in a policy. Another area of difference between insurers is whether or not they cover "paramedical X-rays", and to what maximum. Some insurers do cover these, or put in internal limits, such as $15 per X-ray, maximum one per year per practitioner.

The following are items sometimes covered under EHC policies.

1. Convalescent hospital is occasionally covered under the hospital benefit along with semiprivate room, etc. Other times it is offered as an option for extra premium. Compare the maximum paid per day, the max-

imum number of days paid, and the overall maximum. Convalescent care may not include "nursing home" costs.

2. Radiotherapy, coagulotherapy, blood, plasma, oxygen, tests done in doctors' offices, laboratory tests are generally covered by provincial Medicare. Although they may be used as "filler" in the benefit wording, they are obviously of little use, unless one requires the services while outside of Canada.

3. Some services are offered as optional coverage. These are coverage for such things as hearing aids, orthopaedic shoes, wigs after chemotherapy, surgical stockings. A comparison between insurers will turn up differences generally in the maximum benefit paid per year, or the number of claims allowed per year. If your organization requires the coverage, then ask for the insurers to write the ones needed into the policy. If not required, it is not necessary to put them in, which will reduce the initial premiums.

4. Travel insurance is something that can be purchased on its own, as either a separate rider on a group insurance policy, or it is sometimes included in standard EHC benefit wording. It covers doctor and hospitalization costs if one is injured, or falls ill, out of the country. The biggest problem location is the United States, because the expenses there are considerably higher than they are presently in Canada. If you are injured or fall ill anywhere else but the U.S.A. or Europe, you may want to return home as quickly as possible. Many places in the world are not up to our standards of treatment, but they also do not have our associated costs either. Setting a broken leg in Russia, for example, may only cost $100 (today at least), so cost reimbursement may not be a big issue. The trouble is that you generally do not know before you travel what these costs could be. The major difference between the benefits included in most group insurance plans, and the benefits offered through policies bought in your local travel agency, is this: "pre-existing conditions". Group insurance coverage is most often bought without a medical, and an employee will not be turned down for the EHC benefit (unless the group is under five or ten employees, depending on the insurer). Even if an employee is suffering from a heart condition and suffers a heart attack in the U.S.A., most group policies will cover the costs up to their policy limits. Other travel insurance plans generally have an exclusion for illnesses of any kind that one has before leaving on the trip. This is the single most important item to review in a travel policy. Little items, such as "return of luggage", are minor in comparison. If a travel policy has a pre-existing conditions clause, it can cause severe problems down the road, especially if the insured person has a "pre-x" condition and needs medical help while out of Canada.

Travel policies within group insurance contracts differ in the following ways: some cover only up to the ward rate; others to the semiprivate or private room rate. Some limit the number of days covered outside of the country; others do not. Some cover medical evacuation to Canada, something that provincial Medicare may help arrange, anyway, to reduce its own costs. Coverage for group travel policies only pays the difference between what is paid by provincial Medicare and the actual costs, up to the policy maximums. The out-of-country maximum should be adequate to cover a long hospital stay in the U.S.A., at least $500,000, with $1 million a better alternative for the difference in premium. The balance of the "benefits", such as return of the vehicle, loss of luggage, hospital visits and flight for a relative, return home of dependants, and repatriation of the body, vary quite extensively by insurer, and should be viewed as to their usefulness to you. Return of the vehicle coverage is not important if you are flying and renting a car, instead driving your own.

Travel claims can be reimbursed in Canadian dollars calculated with the exchange rate in effect on the date of the actual claim, not as of one or two months later, when the claim is submitted. When exchange rates are fluctuating, any delay in submission of the claim forms, bills, receipts, etc., may result in less than the actual cost to the claimant being reimbursed. People who travel should be prepared to pay travel medical expenses when they occur and at the location that they occur. Travel medical expenses are reimbursed by provincial Medicare first, then the travel insurer second, upon submission of the claim forms and receipts. Where there is coverage under a group insurance plan's travel policy, and duplicate coverage under a separately purchased travel accident or medical policy, any claims should be submitted to both insurers with the explanation that there is double coverage. The insurers can then sort out who pays what between themselves, without jeopardizing claim payments, should one of the insurers refuse to pay. Common reasons for refusal to pay are pre-existing conditions, time limits on the coverage, time limits for the submission of claims, and claims for non-insured services.

Insurance companies now often include a "travel assistance" program, which offers help to people who are injured or who fall ill while out of the country. This assistance takes the form of toll-free or collect numbers to call to ask for help. A travel assistance provider will act as a co-ordinator to see that you are taken care of, and will arrange, if necessary, to evacuate you to the closest hospital that can give you the required services. The bills for the evacuation may be paid for by the assistance provider, or will be billed to you later. You can then submit these to your provincial Medicare and to your insurance company for reimbursement. Travel assistance can help if you or other members of your organization do a lot of travelling, especially overseas.

"Political evacuation" programs are not part of a standard group insurance policy. They can be purchased from organizations such as S.O.S. International Assistance®, normally on an annual premium basis. A political evacuation program will help to evacuate employees who find themselves in situations where a foreign country's political stability creates a potentially dangerous situation.

¶6090 Coverage While on Disability

The question of what happens to EHC and dental benefits when employees go on to long-term disability claim is one that is often overlooked during the benefits review process. Many insurers leave the decisions of whether or not coverage is allowed to continue for the disabled employee and his or her dependants, and who is responsible for paying the premiums — employee or the employer — to the policyholder. If LTD claimants are allowed to continue to be covered under one or both of these benefits, the insurer will sometimes establish a separate administration classification for the claimants, because disabled employees, technically, no longer qualify for coverage under the "actively-at-work" eligibility clause in the policies. If group policyholders allow benefits to continue for one disabled employee, then they should allow benefits to continue for all disabled employees who were on the plan prior to the date of disability. EHC and dental claims submitted by the disabled employees will be calculated as claims against the policy in the same manner as claims by actively-at-work employees. Claims made by disabled employees can be high if there are private duty nurse charges, artificial limb charges, or heavy prescription drug charges.

¶6095 VISION CARE

Vision care is a benefit that reimburses a set amount for the purchase of eye glasses and contact lenses. The benefit is normally sold by the insurers as a rider on the EHC benefit. The maximum reimbursed is generally in the range of $60 to $250. Occasionally, this benefit can be set up to include the cost of eye examinations, where not covered by provincial Medicare, and where reimbursement is allowed under legislation.

The benefit is usually paid once every two years for adults and once per year for dependent children. There is typically a maximum age of 18 or 19 for children. In order to be paid, the policy may require that a change in the prescriptive strength of the lenses is necessary. This clause helps to reduce the number of claims for employees who just want to change their "looks" by purchasing new lenses and frames.

Of all of the benefits, vision care is the one that can be most easily self-insured. This is because of two factors. First of all, not all employees and their dependants need glasses, so the number of claims is limited. In addition, benefit terms usually state that an employee or dependant can only claim once a year, or every two years, at the maximum. The number of reimbursement cheques needed, therefore, can be small. Second, the insurance companies charge the same retention percentage for vision care as for the other, more labour intensive, parts of the EHC benefit. This limit to the number of claims paid results in higher profits for the insurer. The lack of complexity makes vision care an easy benefit to administer, to adjudicate and to pay.

¶6100 DENTAL CARE

Dental programs became a common benefit in Canadian group insurance policies in the 1970s. Dental plans have remained basically the same since that time. They cover employees and their dependants for the costs of dental services. Dental plans contain three sections: basic services, including diagnostic, preventative and minor restorative work; major services which include work on crowns, bridges and dentures; and orthodontic services which cover braces for teeth. Today, dentists' charges are suggested by provincial dental associations, and most dental plans only reimburse up to that limit. A dentist is free to charge more than the dental association's fee guide, but the insurance company will not generally reimburse for the "overcharge". (My suggestion is that if you are being overcharged, ask your dentist's office to check to see if there was a mistake on the service number of the work performed that was put down on the claim form. If there was, resubmit the details to the insurance company if the insurer owes you money, or get the dentist to reimburse you for the overcharge. If the dentist refuses and you have an alternative, consider changing dentists. But before you change, ask the former dentist for your X-rays, and take them to the new dentist. This will save you and the insurance company additional costs.) Dentists have been reported to be a little more flexible on price and payment schedules if you do not have a dental plan. Dentists like dental plans because they know that they can bring patients in on a more regular basis, and can perform expensive procedures without the patient hesitating due to the cost.

A group dental policy can be purchased to cover just basic services. The first dental plans split basic services into two parts: diagnostic and minor restorative. Diagnostic services include such services as checkups, and X-rays. Minor restorative services include teeth cleaning, extractions, and fillings. Most basic plans cover root-canal work and treatment of gum disease under the minor restorative section. Rebasing, relining and repairs to dentures are also often covered under a minor restorative plan, particularly if the plan only covers basic services. Treatment of gum disease (periodontics), treatment of root canals (endodontics), and rebasing, relining and repairs to dentures can often be moved to the major dental benefits section of the plan to reduce premium rates. Premiums are reduced because the percentage of the claim amount reimbursed under a major dental section is usually lower than the percentage reimbursed under the basic portion.

Coverage for major work — crowns, bridges and dentures — is an option which can be added to a plan. If a plan has basic and major coverage, it may be possible to opt to include orthodontics. (Specialty benefit providers, in comparison to many insurers, may allow more flexibility in plan design, such as the implementation of orthodontics without the implementation of major dental.) Obviously, the more benefits that are covered, the higher the rates. If an organization is considered by insurers to be "too small" to implement a major or an orthodontic benefit, it can sometimes purchase a plan that includes these benefits through one of the cost-plus benefit providers. The advantage of using a cost-plus provider is that a smaller employer is allowed to deduct these cost-plus payments as "premiums" for corporate tax purposes. In the case of an employee of one of these firms, it is advantageous to have the employer pay the cost-plus fees, rather than the employee have to pay the dental expenses with after-tax dollars. The same situation can apply to larger organizations. Groups can opt to have coverage for dental programs provided by a separate benefit provider, without jeopardizing other coverage under their other group benefits. Opting to take the dental benefit out of an existing policy and place it with another provider, may cause the EHC and short-term disability rates to rise in the existing policy, but the increase is rarely more than 3 to 5 per cent. The increases to other "health" rates are due to the lower volume discounts which result from decreased insurer premium totals.

Dental rates can be partially controlled in three ways, in much the same way as control of EHC costs. Including deductibles, reducing the percentages reimbursed, imposing lower maximum benefits, and limiting benefits covered are the traditional ways of controlling costs. Lately, insurance companies have been offering an alternative method of controlling costs, that of limiting, not the services, but the number of times in a year that you can be reimbursed for the services. Some organizations have also been experimenting with maximum overall benefit dollar amounts which are allocated to each employee to spend as the employee wants. For example, if an organization sets up an account of $2,500 per year per employee, the employee and the employee's dependants can be reimbursed for up to that amount for all EHC, dental, and perhaps even short-term disability expenses. This type of flexible benefits system is far from being the norm at this time, but it does have its share of proponents, especially among organizations that self-insure.

Typical annual deductibles are nil, $25/$50, and $50/$100, The first figure (i.e., the $25) is the single person's annual deductible; the second figure is the deductible for the dependants. The dependant deductible can be a "combined" deductible for all dependants, or under some policy wordings it can be applied to each dependant separately. The latter is the better way to control costs of the plan, but it is rarely seen. Most deductibles are of the former nature. Lately, deductibles of $100/$200 are being seen, but they are still not common. Level, or flat, deductibles, such as $25 or $50 per year for both single and for employees with dependants, are available for dental and EHC benefits, but they are rarely implemented. Level deductibles discriminate against the single employee. Regardless of the type of deductible used, the higher the deductible, the lower the rates.

Co-insurance, or reimbursable percentages, are another way to control costs. Basic services are typically reimbursed at 80, 90, or 100 per cent. The higher the reimbursement, the higher the rates. Some insurers split the basic services into two parts: diagnostic and preventative, and minor restorative. These insurers can set up the basic benefit to pay 100 per cent reimbursement on the diagnostic and preventative, and 80 per cent on the minor restorative, which will reduce rates. Unfortunately, this can be confusing to employees, and thereby cause dissatisfaction with the plan. Minor restorative covers fillings and extractions. It also, typically, covers root canals (endodontics) and treatment of gum disease (periodontics), both well-known services to the baby boomer generation. These two services are expensive. It is not uncommon to see repairs and relines to bridges and dentures covered under the basic section of a plan. These were originally added to the basic portions of dental plans to entice employees, who had few if any teeth, to join the plans, especially if the policy only included basic benefit coverage.

Major services are usually reimbursed at 50 per cent, but there are some plans that cover 60 per cent. The latter are rare due to the additional cost. Orthodontic services are also generally reimbursed at 50 per cent. Again, the higher the reimbursement, the higher the rates. Orthodontic benefits were originally set up to cover dependent children. Some plans have been extended to cover adults as well. Extending the coverage to adults can drive up renewal costs.

Another way of controlling costs is to implement a maximum annual benefit. Insurers will set up maximums for each of the benefit areas within a dental plan. In other words, you can set up a maximum for the basic benefits, a separate maximum for the major benefits, or a combined maximum for the basic and major benefits. A combined maximum is more common. Typical maximums for the combined plan are $1,000, $1,500, and $3,000. Occasionally, it is possible to see limits for the first year of coverage which are prorated based on the amount of time left in a "benefit", or "policy", year. In this situation, an employee who joins a plan, whose policy year-end is December 31, on September 1, might only be able to claim 25 per cent (three months' worth) of the maximum.

Although employee claims are controlled by these annual maximums, an employee who has a claim which will go over the maximum, can have the services performed over two "benefit" years, and hence get around the maximum. For example, if the benefit maximum is $1,000 per year, and the policy year ends on December 31, the employee could arrange to have half of the work completed and billed prior to December 31, and the other half completed and billed after that date. In this way, the purpose of implementing these maximums does not work, but the claim is spread over two policy years, which may help the rate renewals. Some insurers used to sell an "unlimited maximum" as being a "real" benefit to purchasing their policies. In times of fiscal restraint, this is not a recommended way to set up a dental policy.

Orthodontics have lifetime maximum benefits. The typical maximums found for these benefits are $1,000, $1,500, or $2,000. The higher the maximum, the higher the rates.

Yet another way to reduce premium costs, is to reduce the frequency that employees will be reimbursed for dental services. "Recall" oral examinations and routine X-rays are normally covered once every five or six months through dental plans. Some insurers are now offering dental plans which limit services to once every nine months or to once every year. These plans are less expensive than the ones which allow five or six months between recall visits. Other plans can be set up which do not cover certain services, such as oral hygiene instruction (how to brush your teeth, etc.), pit and fissure sealants, and topical fluoride applications. Some plans also do not cover dental "specialist" services. Dental specialists can have a separate fee guide. Some dental plans only cover up to the regular provincial dental fee guide, not up to the specialists' fee guide.

Claims under the major dental benefit can be controlled in one of two ways. First, limit the claims for major benefits by putting in a waiting period of at least one year before a new employee can claim these benefits. Second, a "missing tooth exclusion" can be written into the plan. This latter exclusion means that the policy will not pay to replace a tooth which was missing prior to the employee coming to work for your organization.

Overall dental plan costs can also be reduced by the following:

1. move the coverage for rebasing and relining of dentures, and repairs to bridges and dentures from the basic section of the plan to the major section, which is reimbursed at a lower percentage;

2. move coverage for root canals and treatment of gum disease from basic to major;

3. reduce the maximum coverage for basic benefits (i.e., to $1,000 or $750 per year if currently higher); alternatively, reduce the plan's overall maximum;

4. change the frequency allowed for reimbursement between recall exams from once per five or six months, to once per nine or 12 months;

5. drop coverage for oral hygiene instruction, topical fluoride applications and pit and fissure sealants;

6. consider self-insuring all dental benefits, or those benefits which have less frequent claims, such as major and orthodontic procedures;

7. consider removing the orthodontics and the major dental coverage; or

8. consider dropping the dental plan.

There are some benefit providers that operate on a fee-for-service basis. These providers will set up a dental plan to cover any dental benefits that you want at whatever co-insurance factors, with whatever maximums. These plans operate like bank accounts. You tell them what you want covered; they write up the benefits as if it was an insurance company arrangement, and they draw up an "underwriting" agreement. The agreement works like this. When claims are submitted, the provider adjudicates, compiles and bills your organization for the claim cost plus an administration fee. The administration fee is approximately 8 per cent of the total bill, plus up to 7 per cent to pay commissions, if an ABC has assisted you by setting up the plan. In many cases, setting up this type of arrangement may reduce retention costs, unless you cover a large group of employees. Another advantage of this type of arrangement is that it is possible to cover the owner and senior executives, or any other occupational class, for 100 per cent of all dental work, all the while still covering the "other" employees with a standard contract. Owners and executives, thereby, can get the organization to pay the claims, instead of them having to pay for their portion of the expenses for things like major dental, with after-tax dollars. Of course, arrangements of this type can be made for all employees, if an employer can afford it.

The major disadvantage of this type of arrangement is that at the end of the policy year, if there is a deficit, the organization will have to pay it to the benefit provider immediately. The benefits providers say, in response to criticism of this method, that you would have to pay any deficits eventually, even if you use an insurance company; insurers would just increase rates the next year. What the insurance companies cannot argue is that unless you have a fully experience-rated policy, you are not credited with any surplus, except perhaps in the lowering of next year's rates. Another disadvantage of replacing an "insured" dental policy with a fee-for-service arrangement is that by dropping an insurance company's dental plan, the total premium for the overall policy drops, and this may cause the overall retention on the EHC and short-term disability benefit to increase or the volume discounts applied to decrease. Any comparison of the benefits of a fee-for-service, or "cost-plus" arrangement and an insured dental policy should take into consideration the effects on the other benefits' rates.

Comparisons between dental plans should include looking at all exclusions, including the standard exclusions of dental work for cosmetic purposes, temporal mandibular joint (TMJ) dysfunction services, and lost or stolen prosthodontics.

For Coverage While on Disability see ¶6090.

¶6105 OPTIONAL BENEFITS

¶6110 OPTIONAL EMPLOYEE LIFE AND OPTIONAL DEPENDANT LIFE INSURANCE PLANS

Optional life insurance, also called voluntary life insurance, is an inexpensive method for employees to purchase extra life insurance coverage. Optional life insurance is one-year renewable term insurance and is normally sold in "units" of $10,000, up to a specified maximum. The maximums typically range from $100,000 to $300,000. There will usually be a one- to two-page medical questionnaire to fill out, and if the employee, or dependent spouse passes this "medical", then insurance coverage will begin. If someone is declined by the insurance company, then that person has the right to appeal to the underwriters by providing additional medical evidence proving that the previous condition, causing the declination, has cleared up. This is no guarantee of acceptance, but it is an option for the person who has been declined.

Rates for optional insurance can be set up on a smoker/non-smoker basis, with non-smoker rates set at levels well below those of smokers. Rates can be set up on a male/female basis as well, where allowed by law. The rates are normally "age banded", which means that the insurance company charges an average rate for all people whose ages fall within that band. The bands are usually set up to charge the same rate for five consecutive years, although, on larger policies, there may be rates for each age. The individual rates paid go up as people age. For administration purposes, rates for all employees covered under an "optional life" policy can be set up to change, because of age, only once per year.

These optional policies have the advantage, for an employer, of offering a benefit to employees, which is totally paid for by the employees. They are inexpensive and can be paid for monthly by payroll deductions. Premiums paid are not tax deductible by an employee. Insurance companies may only underwrite an optional life benefit, except in the largest of policies, if they also underwrite the regular group life insurance benefit. Insurers may also want a minimum number of people signed up (i.e., ten), before issuing this benefit.

Optional life insurance, unlike other group life coverage, may include an exclusion for suicide for the first two years of coverage.

¶6115 OPTIONAL EMPLOYEE AND DEPENDANT ACCIDENTAL DEATH AND DISMEMBERMENT

Optional, or voluntary AD&D is a benefit which pays a lump sum of money to a beneficiary if the employee or the dependant, as the case may be, dies in an accident. There are also amounts, based on the total insurance purchased, which are paid in situations of accidental loss of, or loss of use of, a limb or an eye. Optional AD&D is usually set up by an employer as a 100 per cent employee-paid benefit. It is a very inexpensive benefit which is issued and promoted, more often by specialty AD&D insurers. The amounts of coverage are chosen by the employee, or the dependent spouse. The coverage is issued in "units" of $10,000 or $25,000 up to a specified maximum. The unit rate is normally the same for all ages. Medicals are not normally required.

The differences between insurer policies can be minor. Over the last few years, the AD&D market has been very competitive. Insurers in this business revise their benefits and their rates to be competitive with whoever else has quoted. AD&D still remains one of the most profitable benefits for insurers.

Some of the "add-ons" that are included in these policies are:

1. raising the spouse coverage to the same level as the employee coverage in the event of a common disaster, where both die at the same time from the same cause;

2. an education allowance for retraining paid to the spouse of a deceased employee;

3. occupational training for an employee who has lost a limb in an accident;

4. rehabilitation training for an employee who was accidentally injured and lost a limb;

5. repatriation of the body if an accidental death occurred overseas, or out of the province of residence;

6. a seatbelt clause which increases the benefit if there is a claim while the injured person was wearing a seatbelt.

Exclusions should be reviewed when comparing policies. No benefits are usually paid in the case of war, civil unrest, or participation in a riot. There may be other exclusions such as for self-inflicted injuries, or driving with "over the allowed legal limit" of alcohol in the blood.

¶6120 OTHER BENEFITS

¶6125 EXPATRIATE BENEFITS

Expatriate benefits, those for employees who have been transferred permanently to overseas posts, are not usually covered under standard Canadian group insurance contracts. Coverage under standard contracts is limited to employees and dependants who are covered by provincial Medicare. Coverage can be arranged for expatriates for health care, including replacement of most services covered by provincial Medicare, life insurance, short- and long-term disability through insurers such as Lloyds of London. Note that Lloyds policies can only be purchased through insurance brokers.

We will not go into the details of these coverages. Coverages are set up subject to being able to pass a medical, or can be set up with exclusions for whatever reason that coverage has been declined. Coverage can be expensive in comparison to Canadian policies. Life and disability coverages may be set up for a maximum of three years and may be non-renewable. That means that an "expat" will have to pass a medical to keep the coverage up at the end of the original policy terms. Dependants can also be covered for the medical insurance. Cost for the medical insurance alone, depending on deductibles, co-insurance factors and benefits covered, is currently in the $1,800 to $3,000 per person per year range, depending on the insurer, and the benefits covered. Life and disability coverage is dependent on amount, age, sex, occupation, and location of the person to be insured.

Large corporations, such as the oil giants, usually transfer their employees to their foreign subsidiaries, where coverage is arranged through their local subsidiaries' policies.

¶6130 SURVIVOR INCOME BENEFIT

Survivor income benefits (SIBs) have not become popular in Canada. SIB pays a contracted amount to a surviving spouse, and may pay a certain amount for each dependent child. The amount is paid out in regular payments, such as monthly. The advent of payment options under group life insurance benefits, has succeeded in making the SIB benefit a complicated alternative to protecting the financial interests of surviving families.

¶6135 EMPLOYEE/FAMILY ASSISTANCE PLANS

Employee/family assistance plans are programs that are set up to assist employees and their dependants with emotional or psychological problems. They also can provide assistance to employers who are trying to deal with the effects, in the workplace, of these problems, and the effects of drug and alcohol problems on their employees. These programs offer employers a ready-made solution to a myriad of problems that they may have with employees in the workplace. Employee assistance plans (EAPs), also called employee and family assistance plans (EFAPs) offer private and confidential counselling to employees and dependants. Employers only find out that the services have been used and how many times; the names or ID numbers are never released.

These programs are funded either on a monthly "premium" paying basis, or on an hourly rate. This rate is currently in the $85/hour range. Larger organizations can also hire their own EFAP counsellors on a full- or part-time basis. The use of "outside" EFAP counsellors is preferred by some employees, to satisfy their need for complete privacy. It is therefore appropriate for larger organizations to offer both "internal" and "external" counsellors to ensure the effectiveness of the programs. Smaller organizations will be adequately serviced by the "outside" providers. Most organizations implementing an EFAP report satisfaction with them, even though the "savings" to an organization of helping to solve an employee's personal problems may be hard to quantify.

EFAPs can be set up to cover just drug and alcohol problems, or, what is more common these days, to provide "blanket" coverage for many problem areas. Examples are: counselling for problems in the marriage, problems with children, problems with the death of a loved one, and stress. Employees with fewer personal problems might, in all likelihood, claim less on a sick leave or disability program, and thus reduce benefit claim costs in other areas. What these programs may not be able to fix is problems with employees caused by problems inherent to their employer organizations.

¶6140 GROUP LEGAL PLANS

Group legal plans have not yet become as popular in Canada as other benefits. Legal plans are set up to cover situations requiring legal counsel, such as buying or selling a house, getting a divorce, or for initial consultation on other matters. Legal plans are funded like group insurance plans, with the plan provider collecting premiums, keeping track of services provided and renewing the programs based on experience.

¶6145 GROUP HOME AND AUTO INSURANCE PLANS

Like legal plans, these have not yet taken hold in Canada, to the extent of other benefits, such as dental plans. These plans are not offered by life insurance companies, but through general insurance companies. There are different sets of rules and regulations that regulate the general insurance industry, and these benefits.

¶6150 GROUP REGISTERED RETIREMENT SAVINGS PLANS

Group registered retirement savings plans (RRSPs) are an excellent way of offering a benefit to employees without any, or with minimal, cost to an employer, other than some administration time. Group RRSPs can be set up directly through a life insurance company, with or without using an ABC, and with or without paying commissions. They can also be set up through banks or trust companies. Setting up an RRSP with an insurance company will have no effect on your group insurance rates.

¶6155 PENSION PLANS

Implementation of a pension plan will also have no effect on a group insurance program's rates, unless, as is the rare case, an LTD benefit program is set up to provide a payment, i.e., 3 to 5 per cent of pre-disability earnings, to the pension plan. The effect of disability claims, in this case, is not on the pension plan *per se*, but on the experience and rates of the LTD policy.

CHAPTER 7

¶7000 FUNDING THE BENEFITS

¶7005 INTRODUCTION

The six most common methods to fund a group insurance benefit in Canada are: fully-pooled; experience-rated; partially experience-rated; administrative-services-only (ASO); cost plus plans; and self-insurance. The following chapter describes how these methods differ.

¶7010 TYPES OF FUNDING

¶7015 FULLY-POOLED BENEFITS

A group insurance policyholder can "fully insure", or completely insure any benefit. This is often called the "fully-pooled" method of funding. It means that the policyholder pays whatever premium is charged by the insurance company. The premiums are put into a pot with other companies' premiums, and all claims and administration expenses come out of the pot. All renewals are based on how well the whole pool does. Each policyholder has no control and no real say as to where or how the premiums are allocated. In a "fully-insured" contract, the major cost control steps that can be taken are to add deductibles, reduce the percentage reimbursed by the insurer, or reduce benefits. The fully-insured method is used to fund benefits when the premiums are small. Hence, this method is used to fund group insurance benefits for smaller groups. Fully-insured policies are the norm for the smallest of groups, i.e., those under 15 to 20 employees. Even larger employers use the fully insured method to fund group life, AD&D, dependant group life, and long-term disability (LTD) policies. The best time to use this method of funding is when the premium of a group, over the course of a year or so, would not in total, be able to pay for all of the claims that might occur. In other words, if one person dies in an organization, could the organization pay that claim without difficulty? What about two claims? Or three or more? What if someone became disabled for life? Could the organization set aside, today, the amount of money needed to ensure that the claimant would receive benefits until age 65? What about two or more claimants?

¶7020 EXPERIENCE-RATED BENEFITS

The fully-insured method is one way of funding a benefit; "fully experience-rated" is another. With full experience-rating, the insurer works out each policyholder's premium rating, based solely on the policyholder's own past experience for the benefit. At renewal, the insurer takes the paid premium for the year and then allocates various expenses against it. In addition to the actual claim amounts there are separate costs or charges for each expense item. These are usually based on either a percentage of the premium, or a percentage of the claims. There are charges for paying the claims, for administration, for taxes, for commissions, for acquiring and setting up the policy, and for insurer profit or "contingencies". There are also requirements to fund reserves such as the "incurred but not reported (IBNR) reserve", and the "claims fluctuation reserve (CFR)". The IBNR is set up in case the policyholder cancels its policy. The IBNR's purpose is to pay for all of the outstanding claims that have not been submitted, or processed, and which still must be paid by the insurer. The CFR is set up as an account in which the insurer puts excess premium, if there is any, after the renewal has been calculated. The CFR is usually capped at 10 per cent of annual premium. It can be used by policyholders to "hide" extra cash away from the taxman, although there are limits as to how much can be held in a reserve. Insurance companies differ on the interest rates that they credit to these reserves. If marketing an experience-rated group policy, interest paid on reserves is an area which should be reviewed.

Experience-rating can be quite complicated. Why not just use a fully-insured method? The answer is "financial control". Fully-insured plans have all of the same charges and complications of experience-rated ones, except that you do not see them. In fully-insured policies, the insurance company sets all of the charges, and the rates, and normally does not give credit to any one policyholder directly, for any interest or investment earnings on the premiums. With experience-rated plans, you see all of the charges in the renewal statements. You know what percentage of claims or premium is going to be charged for each part of the retention before signing up for the policy. The retention charges can be compared with those of other insurers more accurately. Interest in experience-rated plans will be credited on the premium amounts put aside in the policy's reserves. If the policy is cancelled and there is money left in the reserves after all claims have been paid, the policyholder will receive the balance back as a refund. Why are not all benefits funded this way? The downside to full experience-rating is that if the insurance company does not collect enough premium for the year to pay the claims and the administration charges, etc., the policyholder will have that deficit added into the calculation for next year's renewal, unless the policyholder elects to pay it off earlier (either from cash, or with a transfer from the CFR). Fully-insured plans, on the other hand, do not accumulate deficits, but neither do they pay interest on, or refund, reserves.

Insurers usually suggest a minimum annual premium of $100,000 per benefit, or higher, to use full experience-rating. The reason is that the premium may have to support a number of large, unexpected claims over the course of the year. If a large deficit is run up and the organization cannot afford to pay it off or pay the higher rates needed for next year, financial problems may result. The organization could be forced to shop the market for another insurer and leave the deficit with the old insurer. No insurer wants to be stuck with deficits, so they try to protect themselves by limiting full experience-rating to those organizations with larger premiums. Actually, experience-rated benefits can be set up with an underwriting agreement in place, which can preclude the insurance company asking for, or receiving, any money from the policyholder to pay off accumulated deficits, at policy cancellation. Another reason that insurers do not like to underwrite fully experience-rated policies for smaller premium amounts is that there is more information to track and to report on than with a fully-insured policy, and the smaller premiums may not pay enough to warrant the extra expense.

¶7025 PARTIALLY EXPERIENCE-RATED PLANS

Many group insurance extended health care (EHC), dental and weekly indemnity (WI) policies, written today, fall into this category for funding. If the annual group insurance premium for these benefits is between $5,000 and $100,000, you can be quite certain that there is some form of partial experience-rating taking place, unless the benefits are underwritten on a cost plus arrangement. Partial experience-rating is a hybrid: a cross between fully-insured and full experience-rating. Its purpose is to provide some of the advantages of the fully-insured policy and some of the advantages of the experience-rated policy. Insurers like these policies because they can use a group's own experience to determine renewal rates, just like the fully experienced groups, yet they do not have to credit interest on the reserves, or track and report on a lot of calculations. And if a group cancels, the insurance company gets to keep whatever is left over in the IBNR reserve. (It also can get stuck with any deficits!) In addition, there is no requirement to fund a claims fluctuation reserve (CFR), which could be required under fully experience-rated contracts. The example of the renewal formula at ¶11,115, in Chapter 11, for Insurance Company B, shows a partially experience-rated plan.

In partially experienced-rated plans that run up deficits, unlike the fully-experienced plans, the deficits are not accumulated to be accounted for at the next renewal. In reality, this can be confusing, because the insurance company looks at the past experience to determine the next year's rates. Although there is not an amount built into the renewal rates "for deficit recovery", as there would be in fully experience-rated plans, there is certainly little latitude given to policyholders to negotiate their rates in partially experience-rated plans. In addition, if a policyholder has "good experience" in a partially experience-rated plan, over, say a year or more time period, renewal rates may not reflect that experience. For example, if the paid claims total, for a dental benefit, over each of the last three years was only 45 per cent, and the retention was 25 per cent, it is unlikely that the insurance company will offer a 35 or 40 per cent discount. A 5, 10 or perhaps 15 per cent discount might be offered. If a complaint to the group representative or underwriter is forceful enough, a 20 per cent discount on your last year's rates, at the renewal, might be obtained. But it is unlikely that the policyholder will receive the full discount, as calculated by the renewal formula. Renewals which are inconsistent, or which do not take good experience properly into account, call for a marketing of the policy.

Partial experience-rating is called by many different names in the insurance industry, among them, "prospective rating" and "retrospective rating", retrospective because one looks in retrospect at the experience to determine the renewal rates; prospective because the underwriter expects the rates to support the future (prospective) experience. My preference for the method's name is "partially experience-rated", because this describes the funding method using similar words to the other two methods previously discussed.

One problem with partial experience-rating is that the policyholder does not know how the retention is broken down into its component parts. Sometimes the actual "retention" percentage is not provided by the insurer to the policyholder. The insurer provides, instead, what is called a "break-even-loss ratio". A break-even-loss ratio is similar to "retention", but in reverse. The retention tells you what percentage of the premium dollar is taken off to provide the services. The break-even loss ratio tells what maximum percentage can be claimed in order for the policy to "break even". A ratio of 80 per cent means that you can claim up to 80 per cent of the premium dollar back in claims, before the insurance company puts the rates up. A total retention of 20 per cent of the premium dollar tells approximately the same thing.

¶7030 ADMINISTRATIVE SERVICES ONLY PLANS

Insurance companies will sometimes offer administrative services only (ASO) contracts to their group policyholders. With this funding method a policyholder pays an insurance company to provide only certain services. For example, if a group is large enough and has the systems to support it, it could hire someone to do all of the administration functions on the group plan, including those necessary to support the payment of claims. This group could then just hire the claims payment services of an insurance company, for a fee (expressed as either a flat charge per claim, or as a percentage of claims). The group could then save a portion of the "administration" percentage charged by the insurer and the "premium" taxes. The group may also decide not to set up any reserves such as the IBNR . If not having to pay the insurer administration charges results in a savings, and this savings is greater than the costs of doing the job internally, then there is a financial advantage to the policyholder, in going into an ASO arrangement. Insurance companies have minimum premium requirements that they recommend before offering these types of arrangements. Although the amounts differ between insurers, the minimum required annual benefit premium is typically in the $250,000 plus area. Specialty benefit providers may provide ASO type plans starting at the first premium dollar.

¶7035 COST PLUS PLANS

A cost plus plan is an arrangement where a benefit provider, or insurer, supplies benefit claims payment services to a group for a fee. This fee is usually expressed as a percentage of paid claims. A cost plus plan works like a bank account. The provider usually requires a deposit of two months of "premium" up front, and then suggests a monthly premium be paid thereafter. The amount required for the premium is negotiable between the group and the provider, but is generally based on the benefits covered under the plan. The plan wording, offered by benefit providers, is similar to the wording offered by insurance companies. At the end of the policy year, if there is any surplus, the group gets it back, either in cash, or as is more often the case, as a premium credit. On the other hand, if there is a deficit, the group may be required, under the terms of the underwriting contract, to pay it back to the benefit provider immediately.

These arrangements can be quite flexible in terms of what is covered and who is covered. Unlike a standard group insurance contract, which requires a minimum number of employees covered under the policy, or a minimum number of employees to set up a "class", cost plus arrangements can be set up to cover just the owner of the corporation, and if the owner wants, for reimbursement of 100 per cent of all claims. This method can also be quite useful to any employee who has high dental bills for such things as orthodontics. Since most "insured" orthodontic benefits only reimburse 50 per cent of the total claim amount, the employee is left paying the other 50 per cent. This other 50 per cent actually costs the employee more than that in pre-tax earnings. In order to make a dollar to pay the orthodontist, an employee in a 40 per cent tax bracket must earn approximately $1.40.

Employee benefit premiums, paid by an employer on behalf of an employee, are tax deductible by the employer. So are employee wages. Employee benefit premiums paid by an employer on an employee's behalf are not considered a taxable benefit to the employee, for federal tax purposes (or for provincial tax purposes, with the exception of Quebec). If an employer wishes to assist an employee in saving tax, the employer sets up the cost plus (dental) plan to pay 100 per cent of the cost of the (orthodontic) claim. The employer then reduces the employee's gross pay to compensate. The employee thereby saves the tax on his or her share of the cost, which would otherwise have had to be paid with after-tax dollars, if the cost plus plan was not in place. If the claim was for the owner of the company, the company will have to decide if it will pay the cost plus premium and not reduce the owner's income.

Now the tax department may not like this arrangement, and there may be some people somewhere who decide to protest this type of arrangement as being "tax avoidance". They should consider that some corporations pay higher premiums than others solely based on those groups' experience. The amounts that they pay and share with their employees may far exceed what is paid and deducted under this cost plus arrangement. So, the choice is to count all employer contributions to employee benefits as taxable, or none.

¶7040 SELF-INSURANCE

At present, self-insured benefits are not widespread in Canada. This is partially because the present benefits industry revolves around keeping the status quo. The insurance companies do not gain if people self-insure. Neither do the agents, brokers or consultants whose very livelihood depends on keeping these programs as complicated and as bureaucratic as possible. The actuarial profession makes its livelihood out of "consulting" to organizations and to governments on how "best" to structure and to fund benefits. The provincial governments gain their 2 per cent (plus) hidden tax on these benefits. It is in these organizations' best interests to keep a lid on and to discourage the concept of "self-insurance".

The *Income Tax Act* itself allows employers to deduct premiums for employee benefits. It also allows employers to pay certain benefits to employees directly, if the payment of these benefits is required by a union contract or an employment contract. Payments, such as reimbursements for employee benefit services, are not considered as taxable benefits in the hands of the employees in these two situations. Reimbursements (medical and dental) paid through policies of benefit providers, such as Blue Cross or insurance companies, are also not considered as taxable benefits in the hands of employees. The Act is not quite as clear when it comes to self-insurance, as to what must constitute an "employment contract". (See Revenue Canada Interpretation Bulletin 339R2 at ¶17,095.)

Why self-insure? The object of self-insurance is to save paying to the insurer retention costs and to save paying the premium tax. It has been argued that, for EHC and dental benefits, there is little insurance at all; one is only paying a fee to the insurance company to administer, adjudicate and pay the claims. Is this difficult for a smaller company? Under an insured contract, a high level of claims results in higher rates, and consequently more dollars paid in retention. Under a self-insured arrangement, when claims get higher, the group has some control over the "policy" administration expenses. Under both arrangements, the actual claims costs will be similar. The insurers argue that they offer experience in adjudicating claims, offer a third-party perspective, offer benefit plans in neat, ready-made policies, offer to track and administer the benefits, and offer the employer "someone to blame" when things go wrong. Benefit providers and insurance companies specialize in providing these services. But as long as there is an "employment" contract, or a union contract requiring the employer to provide benefits, then an employer can self-insure.

Interpretation Bulletin 339R2 does not specifically address the issue of self-insured plans, except with reference to "contract" and to union employees. Theoretically, one could argue that every employee hired has a form of contract with the employer, even if that contract is verbal. What is there to stop an employer from paying its employees' own health and dental claims, when there is no difference between contracts or policies from those of the "recognized" benefit suppliers and the employers? Unless there is an employment or union contract, or there is a policy issued by an insurer or benefit provider, benefit claims paid by an employer to an employee could be considered as taxable benefits to the employee. Is there any substantial difference between health and dental claims paid by an insurer or those paid directly by an employer who must pay them as part of an "employment contract"? After all, these two benefits, in particular, are recognized, even by the "experts", as being funded by a form of "dollar trading". A group can then theoretically pay these benefits through having a one-page contract letter for each employee qualifying for the benefit program. This should appease the tax department. As a minimum, an employer should have a written employment contract with the employees to provide health and or dental benefits. If unsure of how to handle the taxability issue, it would be advisable to check with Revenue Canada before proceeding with a self-insured plan.

¶7045 COMBINATION PLANS

It is possible to work with insurance companies and benefit providers to combine the above types of plan funding to suit specific needs. These plans are called "combined funding plans". For example, one could experience rate an EHC plan up to a maximum of $10,000 for any one claim. The funding can be set up to allocate any individual claim amount over the, say, $10,000 mark, to a "fully-insured" pool. The cost to do this might be 1.5 to 3 per cent of total EHC annual premium. The balance of the claims, under this amount, will be included in the experience-rated, or as the case may be, in the partially experience-rated portion of the benefit funding. What one is doing in this situation, is insuring the group's experience against high claims. Insurance companies and benefit providers can produce a myriad of combinations to suit specific requirements, depending on the size of the premium flow.

With the exception of the largest groups, self-insuring life, AD&D and LTD is not recommended. Medium-size groups may want to look into a combination of funding methods. Smaller groups will want to remain in an insured pool, as the potential claims payments, in a disaster situation, could place too high a burden on the financial resources of the group if it was self-insured.

¶7050 OTHER FUNDING ARRANGEMENTS

Other funding arrangements are available to larger groups (those paying $250,000 plus of annual premium per benefit). One is called a "Minimum Premium" plan. Used for EHC, dental and weekly indemnity (WI) benefits, this arrangement generally involves a group paying for all of its claims up to the "expected claims" level. The insurer still administers the policy and pays the claims which exceed the expected claims level. With this type of arrangement, the group only needs to fund its benefit "bank account" when the amount of money in the account is too low to cover claims. The advantages to this method are reduction of retention, and hence premium tax, and the elimination of any need for a Claims Fluctuation Reserve.

Another funding arrangement, available to larger groups, is called "stop loss". Generally used to put a cap on the possibility of a year in which there is an unexpected high level of total claims, this method is used by groups who self-insure group life benefits. A similar type of arrangement can be worked out for LTD, where the insurer only pays claims up to the two-year point. Thereafter, the policyholder itself will assume liability for them.

¶7055 CAPITATION PLANS

Although touted as a method of controlling claims, more than a funding method *per se*, "capitation" plans have been considered, both by insurers and benefit providers, as a method of funding benefits, especially EHC and dental plans. Capitation refers to placing "caps", or restrictions, on what is covered, the frequency of covered procedures and services, who can provide the services, and how the services are provided. In an industry that works very much on a pay-for-use basis, controlling the usage will control costs. On the other hand, benefits and services are also limited. Dental capitation has been tried in Canada by many life insurance companies and benefit providers. It has not been as widely accepted by the public, as was initially hoped by the insurance industry, basically because employees and their dependants did not like being told where they had to get their dental work done. Groups that offered capitation plans to their employees felt obliged to continue to offer the standard insured plans to employees who did not want to, or who could not see (due to their location) the dentists in the capitation network. The plans fell out of favour in many places.

There have been attempts, as well, to place "caps" onto medical service plans such as EHC. This works in the same manner as with dental. Only certain services, and certain drugs (i.e., generic drugs) are covered. This offers savings to groups, but has met with certain employee, and employer, resistance.

¶7060 FACTORS AFFECTING RATES

There are literally thousands of things that affect rates. Economic, social, legal, legislative and tax issues all affect rates in one way or another. This section will focus on the factors in which the policyholder and the insurer can have a direct effect.

¶7065 THE POOLING CONCEPT

The pooling concept is an integral part of the funding of most insurance policies. The concept is simple. An organization would like to cover all of its employees for life insurance. The management decides that coverage of two times annual earnings is what is needed. Because the company cannot afford the risk of paying a claim right away, it decides to put money away in a pot and combine this money with the money of other corporations wanting similar life insurance benefits for their employees. Claims and any administration costs come out of the pot. This is the way that "pooling" works. Group life, AD&D, dependant life, and LTD benefits, for all but the largest organizations, are pooled. Most small-to-medium-size organizations fund these benefits, by pooling.

What factors affect the pools? The biggest factor is the insurance company's own underwriting. If an insurer is not picky about the types of organizations that it takes on as clients, or about the past experience of these organizations, then eventually the pool will lose money and the rates will go up. Insurance companies, their underwriters, their group representatives and their agents are under constant pressure to put new business on the books. After a while, especially in a stagnant economy, the number of "good" prospects goes down, while the push to acquire business does not. This leads all concerned to look for ways to acquire the business, not for ways to see if an organization will be a good fit for the pool. Time pressures on underwriters also cause errors in calculations of rates. The accumulation of these underwriting "errors" can cause less money to be collected than is required to keep the pool on an even keel.

Poor claims adjudication can also cause more to be paid out than is necessary. An insurance company without proper claims services, including proper adjudication, will eventually lose money in its pools, causing rate increases. Poor investment practices or rates of return on reserves, such as the combined IBNR reserves, decrease income to the pool. Inefficient administration, and an overloaded top-end management structure will increase overall insurer expenses. These two insurer expenses can be charged to other corporate areas, such as the insurance pools, resulting in an overstated administration percentage charge levied against those pools. Inefficient systems, inefficient management, and poor planning all put pressure on the pools. Economic changes also cause pressure on the pools. A rise in interest rates can cause a decrease in the value of any bonds held by the insurer and allocated to the pool. Also, a downturn in the economy, and the resultant loss of jobs, causes an increase in the number of disability claims, many of which put additional pressure on the pools.

The other big factor affecting pools and pooled rates is called the "rate basis". Group life insurance and LTD rates are average rates based on the individual rates set for each age. The rates basis is also based on the sex of the individual at each age. Every five to ten years, insurers review the actual base rates that they charge for each age and sex, based on their experience. The insurers then change the individual rates as needed. The combination of the changed rates and the ones that did not change results in a new "rate basis". A new rate basis can cause overall increases or decreases in the average rates charged to group policyholders. Before changing insurers, it is important to ask when the new prospective insurers last had changes in their rate basis or when the insurers last had "pooled rate" revisions. If there have not been any revisions for a few years, prepare to hear about rate basis changes in a not-to-distant renewal.

¶7070 OTHER FACTORS AFFECTING RATES

1. *Type of business:* Heavy manual labour businesses have different claim histories than businesses that are white collar.

2. *Occupations:* Certain occupations have a higher incidence of claim than others.

3. *Locations:* The locations of your employees will affect certain rates. People in some areas of the country live longer, and rates can reflect this.

4. *Ages:* The older the average age of your group, the higher the average rates will be. A small group that hires one older individual may see a drastic effect on the life and disability renewal rates, as there will be a greater affect on the average than with a larger group.

5. *Sex:* Historically, females live longer, but are more often disabled. Therefore, the more females in your group, the lower the life insurance rate, but the higher the disability rates, all other things being equal.

6. *Unisex rates:* In areas where unisex rates are requested, the rates for males and females are averaged for each age. The results are that the average rates for life insurance for an all-male group will decrease, and they will increase for disability. The average rates for all-female groups will be the reverse.

7. *Taxation changes:* Any change in taxation will be immediately reflected in the rates; for example, if the "hidden" provincial tax is increased.

8. *Claims experience of the group:* The group's claims experience is one of the biggest factors on the rates. Having one, two or more people on prescription drugs for medical problems such as heart disease, Parkinson's disease, or diabetes, etc., can drive up the EHC rates, depending on group size, and past experience.

9. *Benefit design:* Having a so-called "Cadillac" plan, one which covers everything at 100 per cent with no deductibles, will increase the chances of paying higher rates, as more things are covered.

10. *Government cutbacks:* For people used to having everything paid for by the government, any cutbacks by that sector will put pressure on "Medicare supplement" group insurance benefits to pick up the difference. Insurers are often very willing to do this, for the "appropriate adjustment in the rates".

11. *Insurer experience:* An insurance company which experiences difficulties with one particular business in one location may extend this experience to others in that business sector. For example, if an insurer loses money on one meat packing plant, it will be less generous when quoting on the next one.

12. *Size of premium:* Volume discounts, or lower retention rates, are based on the size of the premiums; the larger the premium, the greater the "discount".

13. *Inflation:* Inflation causes the costs of administration and insurer overhead to rise, which in turn is reflected in the rates.

14. *Trend:* Medical practitioners and dentists are constantly finding new ways, better ways and hence more expensive ways to do procedures. This, plus "inflation" in the costs of these goods and services is known as the "trend".

15. *Hiring practices:* Hire poorly or hire well; rates will reflect hiring practices.

16. *Safety practices:* Safety pays by reducing the number of benefit claims.

17. *Corporate environment:* High stress environments lead to higher claims. Poor management leads to higher stress levels.

18. *Pre-employment medical examinations:* Can assist an organization to hire the most physically fit people. These medicals can become politically sensitive.

19. *Employee/Family Assistance Plans:* Offer counselling to employers, employees and dependants for a wide range of personal problem situations. Although difficult to quantify, organizations installing EFAPs have found that other benefit costs may drop and more importantly, individual productivity has generally increased for individuals using these services.

¶7075 PREMIUM PAYMENT

Premiums are normally due a month in advance. Insurance companies rarely produce and send the bills until past mid-month. So by the time a bill is received, there may not be enough time to review the bill, produce the cheque(s), get the proper signatures required, and mail the cheque to meet this "deadline". Insurance companies may be very generous in their approach to receipt date of premiums, in that they allow the practice of "late(r)" payment. Most insurance companies specify that a policyholder has 30 days from the due date (the beginning of the month of coverage) to pay the bill. They can technically refuse claims after the 30 days, and further more, could technically cancel the policy. Imagine the mess this would leave for an organization! Insurance companies may hold onto claim cheques if they have not received premiums for 30, 45 or 60 days from the due date, but they generally do not send out policy cancellation letters until the 90-day point. An interesting thing is that many of the group insurance and benefit providers do not charge interest, as other suppliers do, on overdue accounts! Some employers are constantly paying their premiums well after the due date. When this happens, I always wonder whether or not they have financial cash-flow problems, or are just trying to cream the last bit of interest in their corporate bank accounts from the due premiums.

¶7080 PREMIUM SHARING

There is not a "norm" for sharing premiums between the employer and the employees. Sharing premiums means splitting the total premium for the group insurance plan between the employees and the employer. From an employee perspective, having an employer pay the whole cost on a "Cadillac" plan would be the optimum situation. From some employers' perspectives, the reverse could be true. Insurance companies will not generally underwrite a group insurance program unless the employer contributes to the premium. This is because the insurers believe that if the employer has no financial interest in the plan, there will be less care taken in administration. On top of that, renewal rates are much harder to "sell" if employees pay for 100 per cent of the premium.

Insurance companies require that employers contribute to the premium. Some insurers do not stipulate what percentage must be contributed, except for one or two particular benefits, such as dental or EHC, and this percentage is typically 25 to 50 per cent. In contrast, some benefit providers do not require an employer to contribute, but life insurance companies generally do. Why do insurers think that employees should contribute? The answer is, they say, that employees who contribute will not take the plan for granted. Contributing employees will take more interest in claims and claims control. Most insurance companies and benefit providers are concerned that they receive the premiums, do not lose money on the account, and can sell the renewals without the plan going to market every year. It is more difficult to sell renewals, and rate increases, to employee pay-all group policyholders, as the employees must take the full brunt of any rate changes.

What positions do employers take concerning premium sharing? There is no standard answer. Many plans start off trying to have a 50/50 share between the employer and the employees. They have the employee share pay for, first, the LTD, then the WI, then the group life benefits. The reasoning behind this is that the disability programs (WI and LTD) can be set up so that employees receive "non-taxable" benefits if employees pay 100 per cent of the premium for these benefits. The concept is easier to sell to employees because of the perceived tax "advantage". No one likes to pay tax and offering a chance to "avoid" it is generally accepted by employees. Next, any premiums paid by an employer for the group life benefit are now considered by Revenue Canada as being a taxable benefit. Therefore, after having the employees' share pay for the disability benefits, have any balance of their share allocated to the group life benefit. This reduces, or removes the taxable benefit, as the employees will now pay the group life insurance premium. Any leftover share of the employees' percentage of premium share will then go to the other benefits, such as EHC and dental.

This scenario discriminates against single employees! Single employees pay the same premium rates for the life insurance and for the disability insurance benefits, as employees with dependants. Single employees and employees with dependants, who earn the same and who are in the same group insurance classifications, have the same benefit amounts. Hence the premium for these three benefits is the same, regardless of whether or not one is single or has dependants. However, the EHC and dental premiums for an employee with dependants is approximately 2.2 to 2.5 times the premium paid for a single employee. The bottom line result is that an employer can pay more money to a group insurance plan for employees with dependants than for single employees. The 50/50 split is much more difficult to provide in the case of single employees. To be more fair, the employer can provide the difference in cash or in some other benefit, but this is rarely done, because of its administrative complexity.

The 50/50 split is also difficult when an employee declines the EHC or dental benefit, due to being covered under a spouse's plan. This is called "declination due to duplicate coverage". In this case, the employer may not pay anything at all towards the employee's group insurance premiums, because the employee must pay the disability premiums to ensure the "non-taxable" status of those plans, and pay the life insurance premiums to avoid the premiums becoming taxable benefits. What is left? The AD&D premiums?

The best way to "split" premiums from an employee perspective, is to have a plan where the employer pays 100 per cent of the premiums. This is arguably the most tax-effective approach for employees, because it removes the necessity of paying their share of premiums with after-tax dollars. If a 100 per cent employer pay-all plan is not an option, have the employees pay for the LTD benefit, and then the WI benefit, keeping in mind the possible effects of the "all-source maximums" on the LTD benefit. If the federal and provincial governments decide to tax all employer premiums for the health and dental benefits, as they have threatened to do (and have done for provincial income tax purposes in Quebec), it will be time to review the possibility of dropping the EHC and dental plans as they would no longer be as tax effective from the perspective of many employees.

¶7085 HOW TO CALCULATE MONTHLY BILLED PREMIUMS FROM THE RATES

Benefit rates are expressed in the same way by all group insurers and benefit providers. The following provides examples of how to calculate monthly premiums for individuals from the rates.

1. *Group life insurance:* The rate is expressed as a rate per thousand dollars of insurance coverage per month. If an employee earns $24,000 per year, and the insurance coverage schedule is "two times annual earnings", then the amount of coverage will be (2 × $24,000 =) $48,000. If the coverage amount is not an even thousand, then the coverage amount is normally rounded up to the next highest thousand dollars of coverage.

If the life insurance rate is 25 cents per thousand, then the total cost for this employee's coverage will be (0.25 × 48,000 ÷ 1,000 =) $12.00 per month.

2. *AD&D (basic):* The rate, is expressed per thousand dollars of coverage per month. The monthly cost per employee is calculated in the same manner as the group life. In most cases, the AD&D schedule is the same as the life insurance schedule.

If the life insurance rate is 4 cents per thousand, then the total cost for the above employee's coverage will be (0.04 × $48,000 ÷ 1,000 =) $1.92 per month.

3. *Dependant life insurance:* This rate is expressed as a "unit" rate. This means that the rate is the same for the whole "dependant unit", regardless of whether there is, for example, just a spouse, a spouse and one child, a spouse and five children, or no spouse and five children.

If the rate for a dependant life is $3.50 per unit per month, then the total rate for each individual employee with qualified dependants will be $3.50 per month. The monthly premium for single employees with no children would be nil. (Single employees with dependent children can usually qualify for dependant coverage under most group insurance plans.)

4. *Long-term disability:* The LTD rate is expressed in two ways. The first and most common way to express the rate is per $100 of (calculated) benefit per month. If the employee earns $2,000 per month and the benefit percentage is 66.67 per cent (up to a maximum benefit of $2,500 per month), then the benefit would be ($2,000 × 0.6667 =) $1,333.40. If the rate per hundred dollars of benefit is 45 cents, then the total monthly cost of the benefit for this employee will be (0.45 × $1,333.40 ÷ 100 =) $6.00.

The second way of expressing an LTD rate is as a percentage of eligible payroll. To calculate this, take the total payroll for all eligible employees, and deduct the earnings which are cut off because of the maximum benefit (i.e., in the above schedule, the maximum benefit is $2,500 per month. That means that salaries over ($2,500 ÷ 2 × 3 =) $3,750 per month will not be included as eligible payroll). The result will be the total eligible payroll. The rate is expressed as a percentage of that eligible payroll. Following the above example, if we had ten employees all earning the same and covered for the maximum benefit level, the total eligible payroll would be ($2,500 × 10 =) $25,000. The total premium required per month is (from the above calculation, 10 × $6 =) $60.00. Expressed as a per cent of eligible payroll, the rate is (60 ÷ 25,000 =) 0.0024 per cent. The calculation of the cost for the above individual employee benefit is $2,500 × 0.0024 = $6.00

5. *Weekly indemnity:* The rate is expressed as a rate per $10 of benefit per month. To calculate the total monthly cost, first calculate the weekly benefit. In the above example, divide the annual earnings by 52 (weeks) to get the weekly earnings. Then multiply the weekly earnings times the benefit percentage, remembering that there is a maximum benefit allowed. The result will be the benefit amount for that employee. Multiply the benefit times the rate and then divide that result by ten to get the monthly premium.

In the above example, if the rate is $0.75 per $10 of benefit and the benefit percentage is 66.67 per cent, the monthly cost will be ($24,000 ÷ 52 × 0.6667 × 0.75 ÷ 10 =) $23.08 per month.

6. *Extended health care and dental:* (The rates for EHC and for dental are expressed in the same manner.) All rates are per month. Single employees have one monthly rate. Rates for employees with dependants can be expressed in two ways; as a "married" rate, and as a "dependant" rate. Many mistakes are made in confusing "dependant" with "married" rates. The dependant rate is for the dependant unit only. The married rate is obtained by adding the dependant rate and the single rate together. The married rate is usually between 2.2 and 2.5 times the single rate.

For example the single EHC rate is $18 per month. The EHC dependant rate is $21.60 per month. The married rate will be ($18 + $21.60 =) $39.60.

¶7090 INCURRED CLAIMS FORMULAS

¶7095 INTRODUCTION

The term "incurred claims" refers to the actual processed and paid claims amount plus an amount that the insurance company believes to be claimed but not yet processed and paid. Insurers use different formulas based on their experience with their own book of business. The following is a comparison of various incurred claim formulas used by insurers for extended health care and dental benefits. All "premium" figures refer to annual premium. An insurer may use different formulas for its various sized policyholders. The following are examples only.

¶7100 INCURRED CLAIMS FORMULAS COMPARISON CHART

Insurer	*EHC Formula*	*Dental Formula*
1.	25 per cent of premium	8 per cent of premium
2.	Hospital. First year: 10 per cent of paid claims Second + years 7.5 per cent of premium Other EHC First year: 15 per cent of paid claims Second + years: 23.3 per cent of paid claims	First year: 14.2 per cent of premium Second + years 4 per cent of paid claims
3.	25 per cent of higher of premium or paid claims	15 per cent of higher of premium or paid claims
4.	28 per cent of "expected" incurred claims	18 per cent of "expected" incurred claims
5.	First year: 30 per cent of paid claims Second + years = actual claims runoff	First year: 12 per cent of paid claims Second + years = actual claims runoff

¶7110 RETENTION CHARGES

¶7115 INTRODUCTION

The retention on a group insurance policy is the amount of the premium dollar charged by the insurance company for the following: to set up and administer the policy; to administer claims; to pay the taxes; to pay the commissions; and to make a profit. Retention formulas differ by insurer and by size of the account. The following is a representative comparison of the various retention charges provided by insurance companies for an account with a combined EHC and dental premium of $325,000.

¶7120 CHART OF RETENTION FORMULAS: INSURER COMPARISON

Insurer	*General Administration Charge*
1.	2.5 per cent of premium + $1,500
2.	2.5 per cent of premium + $3,200 + $3,350 first year only + $5,000 first year only + $ 115 first year only
3.	10.5 per cent including general administration, claims administration, risk and profit charges
4.	4.2 per cent of premium
5.	2.94 per cent of premium

Insurer		*Claims Administration Charge*
1.	EHC:	6 per cent of incurred claims
	Dental:	4 per cent of incurred claims
2.	EHC:	5 per cent of paid claims
	Dental:	5 per cent of paid claims
3.	EHC:	Included in Administration Charge
	Dental:	Include in Administration Charge
4.	EHC:	3.5 per cent of premium
	Dental:	3.5 per cent of Premium
5.	EHC:	4.12 per cent of paid claims
	Dental:	4.12 per cent of paid claims

Insurer	*Risk or Profit Charge*
1.	1 per cent of premium
2.	0 per cent
3.	1.5 per cent of premium
4.	2 per cent of premium
5.	1.69 per cent of premium

Insurer	*Taxes*
1.	2 per cent of premium
2.	2 per cent of premium
3.	2 per cent of premium
4.	2 per cent of premium
5.	0

Insurer	*Commissions*
1.	4.5 per cent of premium
2.	4.5 per cent of premium
3.	4.5 per cent of premium
4.	4.5 per cent of premium
5.	4.5 per cent of premium

CHAPTER 8

¶8000 THE MARKETING

¶8005 INTRODUCTION

The purpose of this chapter is to discuss how to prepare and present a group insurance plan for marketing. Whether a group has an existing plan or not, this chapter will discuss what is needed, how to obtain information, how to prepare the specifications, and what must be included. Chapter 9 will discuss how to compare the responses, how to draw up a short list, how to choose the best provider, and how to implement a new policy. The steps and suggestions are intended for the use of employers, associations, and unions who want to market their existing group plan, or who wish to purchase and install a plan from scratch. The steps and suggestions are also intended for the use of ABCs acting on behalf of a group.

It has historically been the job of agents, brokers and consultants to gather copies of policies, policy amendments, employee booklets, experience information, rate information, and employee data for marketing purposes. These have been combined with, in many cases, retyped clauses from master policies, and sent to the insurance companies and benefit providers as the specifications package. The job of insurer and provider group offices has been to sort through these specifications, look for missing information, and then, along with their underwriters, prepare lengthy proposals to return to the ABCs. The ABCs in turn, have had to sort through all of the responses, look for missing information, obtain clarifications, prepare spreadsheets, and then prepare reports for their clients. This historical approach involves many repetitive steps for all parties. The information, sample letters and the spreadsheet concept provided in this book can be used to combine many of these steps. The result will be a final report that is useful in terms of a group's bottom line and in terms of the preparation of a detailed comparison. Use of this method will also mean quicker turnaround time. For agents, brokers and consultants, use of standardized spreadsheets will enable all concerned to review and compare policy terms quickly and efficiently. If the spreadsheets are filled out by the insurers and providers themselves, the chance of ABC error will be reduced, the analysis of proposals would be quicker and fair, and informative comparative reports for the clients would be produced. The use of the spreadsheet concept will also enable groups to conduct marketing reviews on their own, if they have the resources and the time.

¶8010 WHO CAN MARKET A PLAN?

Anyone can ask a life insurance company directly for a group insurance quote. It is not necessary to be a licensed life insurance agent, broker or consultant to obtain a quote. However, the majority of plans historically have been marketed by ABCs. Some insurers and benefit providers require that quotes be obtained through ABCs if a group has under a certain number of employees. This minimum number may be as many as 20 or as few as three, depending on the insurer or benefit provider.

¶8015 WHERE TO OBTAIN A QUOTE

Life insurance companies that sell group insurance policies (not all do), have satellite offices called group sales offices, or group marketing offices. These are located in major centres across Canada. These offices are staffed by salaried (plus bonus) representatives whose job is to provide quotes to organizations and ABCs that request them. Group sales offices can, in many cases, sell group insurance policies on a "direct to the consumer" basis, but the majority of their business comes through agents, brokers and consultants. It is a group representative's job to assist you:

— by explaining their company's policy terms;

— by preparing group insurance proposals;

— in setting up and implementing policies;

— by making presentations at employee benefit meetings;

— by providing ongoing day-to-day service; and

— by providing training to group administrators and ABCs.

In terms of getting quotes and implementing a plan, the only thing that a group policyholder cannot do is collect group insurance commissions, unless someone in the policyholder's organization is licensed in the province to do so.

Some insurance companies are set up in such a way that their "small group" policies are only available through their own agents. "Small group policies", also called "packaged group policies", are designed for groups covering, typically, under 20 people. This number varies between the insurers and can sometimes be for groups with as few as three employees. Local group offices can advise you as to what their minimum numbers are for a "direct" (no commission) quote or for a quote through an insurance "broker". The group offices can also provide references for local ABCs.

It is important that contact be made with the group insurance sales or marketing office. Ask to speak with the group office manager or a group representative. Life insurance companies are large corporations with many divisions. Each division in itself may act as a separate company. The local group offices will provide assistance in obtaining a quote, or in directing smaller groups to the closest agency branch office able to quote on "small group" products.

¶8020 INTRODUCTION TO USING ABCs

In Canada, agents, brokers and consultants have controlled the group insurance market for decades. Consultants in particular, control the majority of the large business accounts, those over 50 employees. Consulting firms got their start by offering knowledge to employers about the inside workings of pension plans and group insurance plans. This knowledge was previously not made available by insurance companies, nor was it well understood by people outside of the industry. Life insurance agents were poorly trained in the mechanics of group insurance plans. Compared to today, there was little competition to the actuaries who started up and ran those first consulting firms. Part of a consultant's sales pitch then, was to ask the prospective client if he or she knew how much the insurance company was paying out in commissions to the agent or broker. The next questions were "What does one receive for those commission dollars and wouldn't it be better to have someone who is not held 'captive' to one insurer review the program for you?" So the presentation went. Offer a better service, or at least offer the perception of better service for the same, or less money and the world should beat a path to your door, shouldn't it?

The truth is that, in today's marketplace, the knowledge level of the consumer is much higher than it was even ten years ago. In addition, the overall knowledge level of agents and brokers has risen dramatically, partially in response to the pressure to keep clients against the attack of the major consulting firms. Consulting firms themselves have been under constant pressure to increase business and add to the bottom line. But in the recent recessionary business environment, these pressures have taken their toll. Major consulting firms have reduced staff and closed unprofitable offices. The combination of increased consumer knowledge, increased knowledge by the competitors (the agents and brokers) and a recessionary climate has caused more than one consulting firm to re-evaluate its business plan.

Despite this scenario, business continues to be conducted in the group insurance market much the same way that it has been done for years. There have been few attempts to market group insurance plans in any other way than through the traditional method of using ABCs.

Agents, brokers and consultants all operate in a similar manner. In the past, a consumer's first step, when looking for a group plan, was to appoint an ABC. This is still the first step for many organizations today. The ABC gathers the relevant information, which includes a copy of the master policy, copies of amendments, a copy of the employee booklet, the employee data and the experience information. Then the ABC draws up a set of specifications, which may or may not be reviewed by the client prior to mailing out to the various insurers on the ABC's list. The responses from the insurers are analyzed by the ABC and the best quotes are presented either in proposal format, report format, or through the use of spreadsheets. The client picks what is perceived as the best combination of products and services that suits its needs. The ABC then arranges to have the chosen insurer's representative come and sign up the new plan. It is not rocket science, to use the cliché. And, that 20 to 60 hours of work by the ABC, can result in thousands of dollars of income being paid out for his or her work. Those dollars come directly from the pockets of the policyholders and employees who pay those premiums!

Employees, who share premiums with the employer, will pay a share of the ABC's commission, on plans where commissions are payable. This can lead to an inequitable position for the employees, especially if employee contributions to the policy are split 50/50 with the employer. Employer contributions to a group insurance plan are tax deductible; employee contributions to premium, in most cases, are not (see Chapter 14, Taxation). Therefore, employees pay for the ABC commissions, which are built into their share of premiums, with after-tax dollars. In contrast, consulting fees are usually charged to and paid for by the employer.

¶8025 REASONS TO MARKET A PLAN

¶8030 INTRODUCTION

There are many reasons to market a group insurance plan, some of which are good, and some of which are not. It is not always in the best financial interest of the policyholder to market a plan solely because the rates have gone up, especially if the rates have gone up because the number and amounts of claims by a policyholder's employees have increased. The decision to go to market to change insurers should be made only after reviewing all of the financial implications, including the possible loss of reserves built up under the policy. There should be more than one reason to market a plan. Below are reasons which might cause an organization to go to market.

¶8035 MARKETING REASONS

¶8040 External Reasons

Problems Not Resolved with the Insurer

— Local insurer service problems.

— Insurer staff turnover.

— Personality conflicts with insurer representatives.

— Insurer uncaring attitude.

— Insurer bought out, or insolvent.

— Insurer promptness/efficiency.

— Insurer appears to operate without concern for your organization or industry.

— Insurer supports different political ideologies.

— Insurer closes local offices.

— Inadequate insurer communications.

— Inadequate insurer systems.

— Insurer ignores you (too big/too small).

— Insurer not keeping up with the global needs of your organization.

Product Problems

— Benefits not available.

— Inflexibility in product design.

— Low non-medical and medical maximum benefits.

— Restrictive policy terms and conditions.

— Restrictive policy definitions.

— Insurer withdraws product.

— Insurer tightens up or restricts previously available benefits.

— On-going insurer product administration errors.

Claim Problems

— Insurer refusal to pay claims without fair warning, or adequate explanation.
— Reduced insurer claims paying ability ratings.
— Poor claims turnaround time.
— On-going claim payment errors.

Policy Funding

— Pooled rate increases.
— Life insurance or LTD rate basis increases.
— Insurer retention increases.
— To release or re-evaluate policy reserves.
— Insufficient credit for good claims experience.

Tax Changes

— Changes to the ability to deduct employer premium payments.
— Changes to the "tax-free" nature of employer premium payments on behalf of employees.

¶8045 Internal Reasons to Market the Plan

— Budget restrictions.
— Change in business focus.
— Sale of corporate division.
— Addition of a division.
— Merger.
— To change the way that an organization is viewed internally and externally.
— Motivate and keep staff.
— Personnel changes/responsibility changes.
— Political.
— To increase benefits, or to add employees declined for coverage by present insurer.

Important Note: It is not always necessary to market a group insurance policy just to change an ABC. Contact the insurer's group office for recommendations if conflicts with an ABC cannot be resolved.

¶8050 WHEN IS THE BEST TIME TO MARKET THE PLAN?

A group insurance plan may be marketed at any time. The decision is that of the policyholder. Turnaround time for quotes is slowest around holidays and vacations. Competition among insurers for business is hottest from January to May and from mid-August to October. At other times, insurers may not be able to meet quote timing deadlines, or may have fulfilled their annual quotas (and thereby not need the business at that time).

Group insurance policies should be marketed no more frequently than once every two-and-a-half to three years. Insurance companies may decline to offer a quote if an organization becomes known as a "shopper", i.e., someone who goes out every year to look for the best rates. A reputation of this kind may do an organization a disservice in the long run.

A group insurance policy is called a "unilateral contract". What this means, in a nutshell, is that as long as the organization pays its premiums on time, as per the terms of the contract, the insurance company will pay the contracted claims. The organization, as the "policyholder", has only a few basic obligations to the insurer: pay the premiums on time, advise the insurer of any changes in the organization's employee or member data, and advise the insurer of any significant changes to the organization, i.e., buying another company or selling off part of the present company.

Premiums are paid on a month-to-month basis. Therefore, a policy can be cancelled or replaced at any time, although most organizations do so on an "account date" — usually the first day of the month. It is not necessary to wait until the policy anniversary date to change insurers!

Plans should be marketed, on average, every three to five years if the organization has under 500 employees or members. The general rule is that the more people covered, the less often it is generally necessary to market a plan. The reason is simple. Insurers offer more services, more funding options and a greater degree of flexibility to their larger clients.

¶8055 HOW MUCH TIME DOES A MARKETING TAKE?

The amount of time that a complete marketing will take depends on the following:

1. the size of the organization;
2. the complexity of the organization in terms of the number of divisions and policy schedules;
3. the number of benefits within the master policy(s);
4. the accuracy of the information that is provided to insurers;
5. the availability of information in the policyholder files;
6. the experience and knowledge of the policyholder's staff.

It typically takes a minimum of two months, from start to finish, to complete a marketing project. The number of hours required for a marketing will depend on the complexity of the policies and, more so, on the number of people that the organization "has to" get involved in making decisions. Typically, in an organization with under 500 employees, one person should be able to market the plan and, if necessary, install a new one in under 40 to 60 hours of total time using a spreadsheet format. In an organization with under 100 employees, the same person should be able to complete the whole project in under two days of work, far less if using the services of an ABC. Most of the time will be spent comparing the proposals that are received and clarifying missing information. Although the majority of the insurers provide proposals based on the specifications, there has been as of yet, no generally acceptable way to provide the proposals in an easy-to-compare format.

¶8060 ASSESSING AND ALLOCATING THE INTERNAL COSTS OF GROUP INSURANCE MARKETING

How much will it cost to market a group insurance policy? Some organizations have the personnel and the time to shop for the best group insurance programs on their own. Some are too busy with other things, or may have reduced staff to the point where it is not feasible to add another task to the already overloaded benefits person. The following is meant as a guide to determine the cost to an organization of marketing a group insurance policy.

The marketing costs will depend on the size and complexity of the employee group, and whether or not an ABC is assisting in the process. Costs will also depend on who within the organization does most of the work. There are a few ancillary charges for odds and ends, such as photocopying. Properly done, a group insurance policy marketing, for a small-to-medium-size organization (under 500 employees), should take a minimum of 20 hours and a maximum of 60 hours to complete from start to finish using current technology. (This assumes that only one policy is in effect, that there is only one subdivision, one location, and that all of the necessary information that the insurers need is on hand.)

Lost opportunity cost will vary depending on the size and complexity of the organization. It will also depend on who within the organization is in charge of the marketing. Having the sales manager take time off from his or her responsibilities to handle this may cost a big sale: the lost opportunity. On the other hand, the bookkeeper, controller, human resources manager or accountant may take on this responsibility as part of the normal functions of the position.

There should be no travel costs allocated to a marketing, unless it is imperative that various people at various locations within the organization be consulted prior to the start of this exercise. If this is the case, combining the trips with those made for other purposes will reduce costs.

The best and easiest way to "draw up specifications" is not to! ABCs for years have been wasting their time retyping the group insurance policies, almost word-for-word, getting them approved by the clients, and then sending them out to the insurers. Not only is this is a waste of time, but it increases the chances of an error or omission. There have been many cases of new insurance policies being installed and rates being charged based on incorrect specifications.

The best way to draw up specifications is to photocopy the present master policy and employee booklet, and send these out as part of the overall specifications package. Policies and booklets do not usually carry any copyright or photocopying permission wording, but it does not hurt to check for this. Be sure to include copies of all amendments to the policy and a copy of the most up-to-date employee booklet available. If there have been any revisions during the last three years, such as adding a deductible, changing the percentages reimbursed, or changing the schedule, these should also be included.

Telephone calls to insurance company group offices, if not local, will usually be accepted on a "collect" basis. Many insurers have toll-free, or 1-800 lines. Initial contacts can be made by fax. At the time of this writing, few, if any insurers can be contacted via E-mail or on the Internet. Initial contact costs should be minimal. You can always ask the insurance company to telephone you back on their "quarter".

Rent and utilities should not be a big factor in the calculation, as a marketing can be done from home if need be. Photocopying, supplies and material costs will also be minimal.

The costs of issuing and printing a new group insurance policy are paid for by the insurer as part of the general administration expenses allocated to a policy. The cost of printing employee booklets is also paid for by the insurer, unless, of course, the organization is self-insuring a benefit. If self-insuring or splitting the benefits up between two or more insurers, one insurer will usually include the self-insured benefit wording or the wording for the benefits underwritten by the other insurer, in the booklets. The other insurer may even pay a "pro-rata" share of the printing costs directly to the primary insurer, as their share of the printing costs. Any special printing, such as deluxe covers for the booklets will be an extra expense, whether or not an insured or self-insured plan is set up. Fancy booklet covers can be expensive. Remember that booklets are usually only glanced at by employees before being relegated to a back drawer, only to be brought out again in case of dire emergency, such as death or disability.

It is rarely necessary, unless you self-insure, to process any data for a marketing, other than to prepare an employee data list. If the payroll is run by a third party, you may have to pay for a copy of the employee data to be run off.

The cost of other communications, such as faxes and employee letters will be minimal. Communications with employees, about such things as informing them about a change of insurers, can be designed and printed by the new insurer(s) for little or no charge.

Holding employee meetings before putting the plan to market can be a costly venture. It can be as effective to ask for written comments from employees about the present programs, and to talk to the people who handle the administration of the policy internally within the organization, to gauge the acceptance of the present program design.

The cost of the presentations to the employees, after a review and marketing of the insurance program, can be minimized by holding the meetings over the lunch hour, or before or after working hours. Costs for presentations conducted by the insurer's representatives are included in the rates. It is usually not necessary to use and pay an ABC extra, to hold these meetings. There may be room rental and refreshment costs.

The following is an example of minimum and maximum cost factors to use when calculating your company's costs. Line 1 will be minimum cost; line 2 will be maximum cost.

Personnel Salaries:	*Your Cost*
1. Minimum time cost: 20 hours × $20/hour = $400	____
2. Maximum time cost: 60 hours × $20/hour = $1,200	____

¶8065 COSTS OF MARKETING A GROUP INSURANCE PLAN

The following can be used to discover the costs of group insurance marketing.

Expense Item	*Cost*	*Minimum*	*Maximum*
1. Personnel salaries	____	____	____
2. Personnel benefits	____	____	____
3. Lost opportunity cost	____	____	____
4. Travel	____	____	____
5. Drawing up the specifications	____	____	____
6. Photocopying	____	____	____
7. Postage	____	____	____
8. Telephone calls	____	____	____
9. Rent	____	____	____
10. Utilities	____	____	____
11. Printing and duplicating	____	____	____
12. Supplies and materials	____	____	____
13. Data processing	____	____	____
14. Employee communications	____	____	____
15. Employee meetings (optional)	____	____	____
16. Meeting room/refreshments	____	____	____
Totals:	____	____	____

¶8070 WHAT DO YOU NEED TO MARKET A PLAN?

Below is a list of the items that are needed to efficiently and effectively market a group insurance program. A copy of each item should be sent to each insurer and benefit provider. Make as many photocopies as required. It is not necessary to send the actual policies, amendments, letters etc. The copies should be sent along with an introductory letter, a request for alternative benefit quotes if required (see sample at ¶8120), and the *Specifications Questionnaire* (at ¶8130) to the group offices of the insurers and providers that handle the group's geographical area. If in doubt as to which office covers the territory, send the specifications package to the insurer/provider office nearest the group's location. If it is not the correct office, it will be forwarded. A list of insurer and provider local group offices is located in the appendices.

Include the following in the marketing package sent to each insurer and benefit provider.

1. Copy of the Master Policy(s).
2. Copies of all amendments to the Master Policy.
3. Copies of any Letters of Agreement for payment of claims outside of policy terms.
4. Copies of any union or association contract pages which mention group insurance benefits.
5. Copy of your employee data (see sample at ¶8155). This should include an identification number, the age (or date of birth), the sex, the marital status, the basic annual income, the occupation, and employment start date (if employees are not yet in the plan or are in the waiting period).
6. *Experience:* The paid premiums and paid claims per benefit for the last three years. This information must be current within the last three to four months before the date of the marketing.
7. *Rates:* The rates per benefit for the last three years. Include dates for which the rates were effective and any mid-year rate changes such as dental fee guide increases that happen off of the policy anniversary date.
8. *Specifications:* In most cases, it is necessary to enclose only a copy of the Master Policy plus all amendments, or an up-to-date employee booklet as your specifications. Check with your present insurers first to see about breaking any copyright laws. Most policies and employee booklets do not presently have restrictions on copying the contents. If there is a restriction, all the more reason to market the plan. Restrictions will mean that you will have to type up the major and minor benefit clauses and definitions from your policies to send as specifications.

9. *Agent of Record Letter:* Include this letter if an ABC is doing the marketing. Include with the letter the commission scale that has been negotiated. If the ABC is marketing the plan on a fee-for-service basis, state that the plan is to be quoted on a "net commission basis" only.

10. *Requests for Changes to the Plan Design:* Include any requests for plan changes on a separate page. For example, "Please include a quotation on increasing the group life insurance benefit to two times annual earnings", or "Please include a quotation on implementing a $100 single/$200 married deductible on the extended health care benefit".

Optional

11. Brochures and annual reports (important if you have a company listed on the stock exchange. Also important to show to the potential underwriters that you have a business "worth underwriting").

¶8075 STEPS TO MARKET A PLAN

¶8080 INTRODUCTION

The following is a list of the steps to take to market a group insurance plan. The first list of steps is for an organization that currently has a plan. The second is for an organization that does not currently have a plan. Whether or not there is a plan in force, first decide if an ABC is to be appointed to undertake the marketing. The ABC, or the organization requiring the quote, will then proceed with the following steps in turn.

¶8085 STEPS TO TAKE IF THERE IS A PLAN IN PLACE

1. Obtain a copy of the Master Policy and all policy amendments. If there is not a copy in the policyholder's files, then it can be obtained directly from the insurer or the benefit provider.

2. Obtain the last three years of experience broken down by benefit. Experience should be no older than three to four months from the current date. (Depending on the insurer, experience may not be available for groups of under 20 employees.) The experience must include the rates per benefit. Experience figures and rates must include the dates to which the figures and rates apply. These may have been included in the last three years' renewal letters from the ABC, or the insurer/benefit supplier. If the present insurer or ABC has not been regularly supplying these figures, use the sample letter to obtain them direct from the insurance company or benefit supplier. If there are employees off on short- or long-term disability, include the claims information as per the example. For employees off work on disability or on Workers' Compensation claim, note whether the present

insurer has approved their waiver-of-premium claims under the group life insurance benefit.

3. Compile an employee data list. Use the format included in this chapter. Alternatively, update, and use a copy of the last list supplied to the policyholder by the insurer. Another alternative is to update and use an employee list from the policyholder's own personnel records. Be sure to include all of the information suggested in the sample list (i.e., employee number, date of birth, marital status, annual, monthly or weekly earnings, occupation, date of employment if known, employee classification, province of residence). For employees whose occupation is "sales", indicate in a note what percentage of their income is based on commission. (Some insurers calculate additional rate loads for commissioned employees.) For all employees, overtime pay and bonuses are not usually included in the "earnings" figure.

4. Once the above have been compiled, review each benefit in turn to see if it meets or exceeds the organization's current needs. If the benefits do not meet the needs, compile a list of the changes that the organization would like to see implemented, if it is cost effective to do so. These "alternative benefit" requests can be attached to the specifications in a letter (see the sample included at ¶8130).

The plan is now prepared for the actual marketing. Once the above steps have been taken, proceed to the next steps:

5. Choose the insurers and benefit suppliers from whom the organization would like to see quotes. A list of the group offices for many of the suppliers is in the Appendices. Send the specifications to the addresses of the group offices who handle the organization's location. If it is not clear, call/fax one of their offices, or send the specifications to the office nearest the organization's location. (Note that not all insurers and providers operating in Canada are included in the Appendices.)

6. Photocopy enough copies of the Master Policy(s), plus amendments, and the employee booklet to send one to each insurer/benefit supplier.

7. Photocopy the employee data list, the experience/rates/disability claims lists, and the alternative benefit request letters, to send one copy of each to each insurer/benefit provider.

8. Photocopy enough copies of the spread sheets, if you are using them, to provide one to each insurer.

9. Photocopy enough copies of the *Specifications Questionnaire* (see sample included at ¶8130).

10. Prepare and make copies of the letter to accompany the specifications.

¶8090 CHECKLIST: STEPS TO TAKE IF THERE IS A PLAN IN PLACE

The policy is now ready to be marketed. The package sent to each insurer/supplier should include:

employee data list	☐
copy of policy(s)	☐
copy of policy amendments	☐
copy of experience/rate information	☐
copy of ongoing disability claims and group life waiver of premiuminformation	☐
copy of alternative benefit requests	☐
copy of specifications questionnaire	☐
copy of blank spreadsheets	☐
accompanying letter	☐

The specifications package may also include information (brochures, etc.) on the policyholder's organization.

¶8095 STEPS TO TAKE IF THERE IS NOT A PLAN CURRENTLY IN PLACE

If there is not a plan currently in place, the steps to take are identical to the ones above, except that experience/rate/disability claims information will obviously not be available, and thus need not be included in the specifications. This is unless the organization currently self-insures the benefits. (Omit steps 1, 2, and part of step 6 in ¶8085.)

For step 3 (in ¶8085), it will be necessary to ask the insurance companies/suppliers to quote on identical benefit schedules. Use the sample "Request for Proposals If There Is No Present Plan" included in this chapter at ¶8145.

Send the requests to the group offices of the insurers. A fair word of warning here: if the group is in the small group category with under 15 to 20 employees (depending on the insurer), the insurance company may only offer a quotation through one of its own agents. In this situation, it may not be possible to get a quote on a "net commission" basis, whether using an ABC or not.

¶8100 OBTAINING INFORMATION REQUIRED TO MARKET A GROUP INSURANCE PLAN

¶8105 SAMPLE LETTER FOR POLICYHOLDER USE: INFORMATION REQUIRED TO MARKET A GROUP INSURANCE POLICY

Use when requesting information directly from the insurer.

Your Corporate Letterhead

Date:_________

Mr./Ms. Group Representative
123 Somenice Street
Anytown, Province
Postal Code

Re: Group Policy Number(s)_______________

Dear Group Representative,

Our organization is currently conducting a review of our group benefit policies. Please provide us with the following information, per benefit, and the dates applicable, for the last three policy years: paid premium, paid claims, incurred claims, retention percentages, IBNR reserve formulas, and inflation factors. It would be appreciated if you would include the most up-to-date information available for our present policy year.

Also required is a list, if applicable, of current and pending long-term disability and group life waiver of premium claimants. We require the following information on each claimant: date of birth, sex, date of disability, reserve amount, net monthly claim amount, and cause of disability.

(Optional Paragraph) Please also forward copies of the Master Policy(s), all amendments and the latest employee booklet.

This information is required by (*date — two-week deadline*)__________. *Please (do not) send a copy of this information to our Agent of Record (name). Thank you.*

Yours truly,

Name, Title

¶8110 SAMPLE LETTER FOR ABC USE: INFORMATION REQUIRED TO MARKET A GROUP INSURANCE POLICY

Use when requesting information directly from the insurer.

Agent, Broker or Consultant Letterhead

Date:__________

Mr./Ms. Group Representative
123 Somenice Street
Anytown, Province
Postal Code

Re: Group Policy Number(s)_______________

Dear Group Representative,

We are currently conducting a review of the above group insurance policy(s) on behalf of our client (*client name*). Attached is an Agent of Record letter which includes our client's authorization to obtain information.

Please provide the following information, per benefit, for the last three policy years and the dates applicable: paid premium, paid claims, incurred claims, retention percentage, IBNR reserve formulas and inflation factors. If the current rates include commissions, provide a copy of the commission scale.

Also required is a list of current and pending long-term disability group life waiver of premium claimants. The following information is required for each claimant: date of birth, sex, date of disability, reserve amount, net monthly claim amount, and cause of disability.

(Optional paragraph #1) We also require copies of the Master Policy(s), all amendments, and the latest employee booklet.

(Optional Paragraph #2) Please provide copies of this information directly to our client, attention Mr./Ms_______________.

This information is required by (*date — two week deadline)*__________. *Any questions can be directed directly to the undersigned, or to my assistant (name). Thank you for your assistance.*

Yours truly,

Name, Title

¶8115 HOW TO PROVIDE RATES AND EXPERIENCE IN THE SPECIFICATIONS

The following is a suggested format in which to initially obtain rates and experience information from insurance companies. The same format can be used to provide experience and rates to insurance companies when requesting proposals. The same format should be used for each benefit. Rates should be stated as Single/Married when applicable.

Please provide the experience, per benefit, in this format.

Benefit: ________

Dates:	*Paid Premiums*	*Paid Claims*	*Rate(s)*
Day/Month/Year to Day/Month/Year	______	______	____
Day/Month/Year to Day/Month/Year	______	______	____
Day/Month/Year to Day/Month/Year	______	______	____
Day/Month/Year to Current Date (Within Three Months of today's date)	______	______	____

Note: EHC and dental rates are to be expressed as Single/Married.

Open Long-Term Disability Claims (if applicable)

Number	Sex	Date of Birth	Date of Disability	Benefit	Reserve	Nature of Disability
1.	__	_____	______	_____	_____	______
2.	__	_____	______	_____	_____	______
3. etc.						

Please note if the group life waiver of premium has been approved in each case.

¶8120 REQUESTS FOR BENEFIT CHANGES AND ALTERNATIVE BENEFIT QUOTES

Requests for alternatives in benefits, administration practices, funding, or costings should be addressed separately in the specifications. It is acceptable to request alternatives in the accompanying letter sent with the specifications.

The easiest way to make sure that your specifications are being met is to request that "All deviations from the specifications are to be detailed separately". This simple sentence can cut your comparison and analysis time in half. State this in the specifications or in the introductory letter which accompanies the specifications.

¶8125 EXAMPLE REQUEST FOR ALTERNATIVE BENEFIT QUOTATIONS

A page such as this should accompany the specifications when alternative benefit quotations are required.

Benefit Alternatives

Please quote on the following alternatives:

Group Life and Basic AD&D:	All Employees covered for two times annual earnings; your highest available non-medical maximum, EDB (extended disability benefit — waiver of premium on total disability) to age 65. Benefits reduce to one half at age 65 and cancel at age 70 or retirement.
Dependant Life:	Spouse $15,000; dependent child $7,500; child covered from birth to age 21/25 if a full-time student. Coverage extended for mentally and physically disabled children.
EHC:	As per present plan but include a $100 single / $200 family annual deductible.
Dental Alternative 1:	As per present plan but include a $100 single / $200 family annual deductible.
Alternative 2:	As per present plan but increase maximum on the orthodontics to $2,000.
Weekly Indemnity:	Please advise the effect on the other present plan rates if the weekly indemnity plan was dropped.

¶8130 QUESTIONS TO ACCOMPANY THE SPECIFICATIONS

Include this questionnaire with the specifications when marketing a plan, both when there is an existing plan, and when there is no existing plan.

QUESTIONNAIRE

Please answer the following applicable questions separately from the proposal.

Financial

1. Will all final quoted rates remain in effect for one year, unless the policy is amended? If the first year rates stay in force for more than 12 months, how long will they continue? What are the ramifications of the extension to the first renewal?

2. Will the rate basis(es) for the life insurance and for the LTD benefits be guaranteed for two or more years? What is the longest period for which the rate basis(es) can be guaranteed? What is the additional cost, if any?

3. Can you offer a cost plus arrangement to cover EHC and dental benefits which are not specified in the policy? What is the charge as a percentage of a claim?

4. Detail your incurred but not reported claims reserve formulas (IBNR) for all benefits. For how long will you guarantee these formulas?

5. Are any reserve formulas, such as claims fluctuation reserves, required in addition to the IBNR reserves? How often are all reserves re-evaluated?

6. Will excess premium be refunded after each renewal?

7. What deficit recovery formulas, if any, are used for each benefit?

8. If the policy is experience rated, what interest is credited on the IBNR reserves, the claims fluctuation reserves, cash flow and refunds? What interest is charged on negative cash flow and deficits? What were your interest rates on the above on the first day of last month?

9. Are the retention percentages for the health benefits based on the total premium for the EHC, WI and dental premiums combined?

10. If the policy cancels, how are surplus and deficits treated?

11. Provide three renewal examples for the EHC, the dental and the WI benefits (assume inflation is at 15 per cent for EHC, and at 2 per cent for dental):

(a) assume paid claims remain the same as the last complete policy year experience, as provided;

(b) assume paid claims for the last complete policy year, as provided, increase by 25 per cent;

(c) assume paid claims for the last complete policy year, as provided, decrease by 25 per cent.

Benefits

12. Detail separately all exclusions in your proposal which differ from the current program.

13. Detail overall maximum benefits, and maximum benefits available without evidence of insurability for: group life, AD&D, weekly indemnity, and LTD.

14. What is the per cent of premium charge, to "pool" all large EHC claims over $10,000?

15. Confirm that your definition of disability under the group life benefit, for waiver of premium, can be amended to match the definition of disability under the LTD benefit.

16. Which benefits are you willing to underwrite separately? If underwritten separately, what will be the effect (i.e., percentage increase or decrease) for each rate?

Service

17. From where will the EHC, dental, and short-term disability claims be paid? What is the average turnaround time per claim? What contingency plans are in place in case there is a postal or courier strike in the future?

18. Do you have public e-mail, toll-free telephone and fax numbers to your claims offices, your administration offices and to your group insurance office?

19. Detail the types of administration that you are able to offer on this account.

20. If enrolment in the group insurance policy is set up as a "condition of employment" for new employees, will you allow all new employees and dependants, including late enrolments, to join the plan without providing medical evidence, subject to back payment of premium?

21. If your organization is successful in underwriting only part of the benefits program, what amount will be credited if the other insurer/benefits provider prints the booklets?

22. Can our corporate logo be printed on the employee booklets? If so, is the cost included in the rates? If the booklets are printed by an outside company, what amount will be credited to the policy?

23. Can renewals be presented 45 days prior to rate changes?

24. Provide examples of all of the types of claims reports that are available at renewal. Detail any charges for these reports.

25. Can paid premium/paid claims experience be provided on a quarterly, or semi-annual basis? Is there a charge to do this?

26. Please provide your current claims paying ability rating as rated by Standard & Poors, A.M. Best and Moody's.

¶8135 SAMPLE LETTER FOR POLICYHOLDER USE: TO ACCOMPANY THE SPECIFICATIONS IF THERE IS A PRESENT PLAN

Your Corporate Letterhead
Date:________

Mr./Ms. Group Representative
ABC Group Office
ABC Insurance Company
111 That Street,
Big Town, Province
Postal Code

Re: Group Insurance Quotation

Dear Group Representative,

We are currently conducting a review of our group insurance program and invite you to quote based on the specifications. Our organization is involved in the business of____________. The organization was incorporated in (*year*) and currently has (*number of*) eligible employees. We have been with our present insurer(s) since (*year*).

Our reasons for marketing the plan are: (1) to test the competitiveness of the current program in terms of benefits, rates and retention; (2) to review the availability of alternative administration systems; (3) to compare the service capabilities of our present insurer with other insurers; and (4) to look into the ramifications of potential changes to the plan design.

Enclosed are the following: Copy of the Master Policy(s), (copies of all amendments), copy of the employee booklet, (three) years of experience and rate information, copy of the past and current rates plus dates applicable, employee data list, and an information brochure on our company.

All rates include (do not include) commissions. Please quote all rates on a "net commission basis". (Complete the enclosed spreadsheets as closely as possible. Mark all items not offered, or not applicable, as "N/A".) All deviations to the specifications should be detailed separately.

We require (*number of*) copies of the proposal and the spreadsheets. The deadline for submission of your proposal is (*date — allow three weeks). Submissions should be mailed or couriered. Questions should be addressed to the undersigned or (alternate person) at (telephone number).*

Yours truly,

Name, Title

¶8140 SAMPLE LETTER FOR ABC USE: TO ACCOMPANY THE SPECIFICATIONS IF THERE IS A PRESENT PLAN

ABC's Letterhead

Date________

Mr./Ms Group Representative
ABC Group Office
ABC Insurance Company
111 That Street
Big Town, Province
Postal Code

Re: Group Insurance Quotation

Dear Group Representative,

Our client, (*name of organization*), is presently reviewing its benefits program. We have been appointed to conduct a review of the group insurance policy and invite you to provide a quotation. Our client is involved in the business of __________. The organization was incorporated in (*year*) and currently employs (*number of*) people.

Our reasons for marketing the plan are: (1) to test the competitiveness of the current program in terms of benefits, rates and retention; (2) to review the availability of alternative administration systems; (3) to compare the service capabilities of our present insurer with other insurers; and (4) to look into the ramifications of potential changes to the plan design.

Enclosed are the following: Copy of the Master Policy(s), (copies of all amendments), copy of the employee booklet, (three) years of experience and rate information, copy of the past and current rates plus dates applicable, employee data list, an information brochure on our client's company, and a copy of the Agent of Record Letter.

All rates include (do not include) commissions, as per the attached scale. Please quote rates (with/without) the attached commission scale (or, Please quote all rates on a "net" commission basis). (Complete the enclosed spreadsheets as closely as is possible. Mark all items not offered, or not available, as "N/A".) All deviations to the specifications should be detailed separately.

We require (*number of*) copies of the proposal and the spreadsheets. The deadline for submission of your proposal is (*date — allow three weeks). Submissions should be mailed or couriered. Questions should be addressed to the undersigned or (alternate person) at (telephone number).*

Yours truly,

Name, Title

¶8145 REQUEST FOR PROPOSALS IF THERE IS NO PRESENT PLAN

The following example can be filled out and sent to insurance company group offices if a group insurance policy quotation is required and there is no present plan in force. Note that, depending on the size of the group, you may be required to deal through an agent of that insurance company, in order to obtain a quote from that insurer. The requirements differ between insurers. Small groups, particularly those under 20 employees, are the most affected.

The Request for Proposals should be accompanied by an explanatory introductory letter, the completed employee data list, the blank spreadsheets, and the *Specifications Questionnaire*.

Please provide a group insurance quotation based on the following:

Name of Company________________ Date of Incorporation ____________
Type of Business ________________ Number of Employees ____________
Present or Past Coverage: None____ Waiting Period for New Employees
Location(s) ____________________ ______ Months

Commission Scale: Waive waiting period at effective
Standard __________ or __________ date: Yes ___No ___

Benefits Required *Specifications*

1. Group Life and AD&D: Waiver of Premium to age 65
Benefits reduce to half at age 65 or ___

Benefits cancel at age 70 or Retirement

Coverage Schedule: All employees covered for
One times ______
Two times ______
or ______ times annual earnings
OR a level $______

Class A (identify by occupations) covered for
(amount)____________________
Occupations____________________

Class B (identify by occupations) covered for
(amount)____________________
Occupations____________________

Please quote your highest non-medical and medical maximums.

Benefits Required	*Specifications*
2. Dependant Group Life:	Spouse coverage: $2,000 ____ $5,000 ____ $10,000 ____ Other ____ Child coverage: half of the spouse amount ____ or ____ from Birth___, or Age 15 days___ to Age: 19___, or 21/25___ if a full-time student Please include coverage for mentally and physically handicapped children past age 21 ____________
3. Weekly Indemnity:	Per cent of Weekly Earnings: 60%___, 66.67%___, 70%___ Other___% Taxable Benefits: Yes___ No___ Non-taxable plans only available up to 66.67%. Benefits begin because of an Accident: 1st Day___or 4th Day___or 8th Day___or 15th Day___ or other ___ Option: Benefits Begin on the 1st Day of Hospitalization Yes___ No___ Benefits begin because of illness: 4th Day___or 8th Day___or 15th Day___ or other ___ Benefits continue for up to: 15 Weeks___ 17 Weeks___ 26 Weeks___ 52 Weeks___ 104 Weeks___ or other ___

Benefits Required	*Specifications*
Weekly Indemnity (cont'd.)	Maximum Benefit: please quote your highest non-medical and medical maximums or ___________ Names and occupations of any employees not covered for W.C.B. ____ ____ ____
4. Long-Term Disability	Per cent of Monthly Earnings: 60%___, 66.67%___, 70%___ other ___ Taxable benefits: Yes___ No___ Non-taxable plans only available up to 66.67%. Benefits are to coordinate with Weekly Indemnity benefits _______. Please quote your highest non-medical and medical maximums or _______. If Weekly Indemnity benefits are not taken, LTD benefits will begin after 15___, 17___, 26___, 52___, 104___ or ___ weeks CPP Offsets: Primary:____or Full: ____ Definition of Disability: Two years own occupation, any occupation thereafter to age 65 (preferred) or ______. All sources benefit maximum 85% of pre-disability gross earnings ___ or 85% of pre-disability net earnings ___ or other ___

Benefits Required	*Specifications*
5. Extended Health Care	Maximum benefit NIL ___ or ___
	Deductible: Nil___, or $25/$50___ or $50/$100___or other_______
	Coverage: Hospital:
	Semiprivate Room____or Private Room ____
	Co-insurance
	80%____or 90%____or 100%____ or other ___
	Prescription Drugs
	Co-insurance
	80%____or 90%____or 100%____ or other ___
	Extended Care
	Co-insurance
	80%____or 90%____or 100%____ or other ___

Extended care includes air ambulance, artificial limbs including replacements, and private duty nursing.

Paramedical Practitioners
Co-insurance

80%____or
90%____or
100%____ or other ___.

Maximum per practitioner per year:

$300____
$500____
Other____

Practitioners covered:

All ___ or ___

Benefits Required	*Specifications*
	Hearing aids: Yes____, or No ___ Orthopaedic shoes: Yes____, or No ___ Vision care: Yes____, or No ___ Maximum for vision care: $100____, or $150____, or other____
6. Dental	Deductible: Nil____, or $25/$50____, or $50/$100____, or other____ Benefits payable to current provincial fee guide limits or____. Coverage for Basic: Yes____, or No____ Basic co-insurance: 80%____, 90%____, or 100%____, or other Cover rebasing and relining of dentures in Basic: Yes____, No____ Cover root canals and gum disease in Basic____ or in Major______ Major coverage: Yes____, or No____ Major Co-insurance 50% or____ Basic and Major Combined Annual Maximum:

Benefits Required	*Specifications*
	$1,000____, or $1,500____, or $2,000____ other____
	Orthodontic coverage:
	Yes____, or No____
	Ortho. Co-insurance: 50% or____
	Ortho. Coverage for adults: Yes__, No__
	Ortho. Lifetime Maximum:
	$1,000____, or $1,500____, or $2,000____, or other____

---

7. Comments: ____

____

____

____

¶8150 SAMPLE LETTER FOR POLICYHOLDER USE: TO ACCOMPANY THE SPECIFICATIONS: IF THERE IS NO PRESENT PLAN

Your Corporate Letterhead

Date:__________

Mr./Ms Group Representative
ABC Group Office
ABC Insurance Company
111 That Street,
Big Town, Province
Postal Code

Re: Group Insurance Quotation

Dear Group Representative,

We are currently conducting a review of our group insurance requirements and invite you to quote based on the specifications. Our organization is involved in the business of__________. The organization was incorporated in ______, and currently does not have a policy in place. We would appreciate a quote (using the attached commission scale/net commissions).

Enclosed are the following: (1) set of specifications; (2) Employee Data List; and (3) an information brochure on our organization.

(Please complete the enclosed spreadsheets as closely as possible. Mark all items on the spreadsheets which are not covered, or not available, as "N/A".) Detail all deviations from the specifications separately. We require (*number of*) copies of the proposal (and the completed spreadsheets). We are conducting this review on our own, and we do not require agent, broker or consultant assistance. Questions should be addressed to the undersigned or (*alternate person*) at (*telephone number*). All responses should be mailed or couriered. The deadline for responses is_________.

Yours truly,

Name, Title

¶8155 SAMPLE EMPLOYEE DATA LIST

Employee Name	Employee Number	Age	D.O.B.	Date of Hire	Annual Earnings	Dependants' Coverage	Occupation	Class	Province of Residence
N/A	21		Feb. 1/60	June 1/78	$35,000	Yes	Accountant	A	Ont.

Eligibility: Only full-time, permanent employees, working a minimum of ___ hours per week, on average, are eligible, unless noted.

Comments: ______________________________

Notes on the Employee Data List

1. Use name or ID #; both are not necessary. Use ID #s when confidentiality is required.

2. Dependants' coverage is for EHC, dental, and dependant life. Note if an employee is not covered for one benefit, i.e., dental, but is covered for another, i.e., EHC.

3. Earnings need not be annual. They should be consistent i.e., all hourly, or all monthly. Note where it is not clear.

4. Use Age or Date of Birth (DOB), not both. Date of Birth will create more accurate rates.

5. Occupation should be as close as possible to the actual duties. Where someone does two jobs, i.e., President and Machinist, enter the occupation performed the majority of the time.

6. Class(ification) only needs to be filled in for policies that have different schedules of insurance for various occupational classes.

¶8160 PUTTING IT ALL TOGETHER

Remember to ask for mailed or couriered responses. This will allow more time to analyze the proposals and to make a short list. It will also save time in not having to sit down with every insurance company that sends a proposal. Asking the insurance company group offices to detail their proposals on spreadsheets (see ¶8170 and Appendices at ¶17,145) will also save time. Number the columns that the insurer is to fill in. When received, these completed spreadsheets can be glued together, and then photocopied, retyped or scanned. It is acceptable to ask the insurers and providers for more than one copy of the completed spreadsheets, their written proposals, answers to the questionnaire, and separately listed deviations (from the present plan). The number of copies required should be requested in the letter accompanying the specifications.

¶8165 MOST COMMON MARKETING ERRORS

The following lists the most common marketing and service errors:

1. Failure to obtain and provide all of the information required for marketing.

2. Failure to obtain up-to-date experience information (paid premiums, paid claims, rate histories, dates applicable).

3. Failure to obtain long-term disability open claims information.

4. Failure to obtain group life insurance waiver of premium claims information.

5. Failure to ensure that all life insurance waiver of premium claims, including for those claimants on Workers' Compensation have been applied for and approved.

6. Failure to include the most up-to-date employee data, including locations, salaries excluding overtime pay and bonuses, occupations, marital status, and dates of birth.

7. Failure to advise the current insurer that the case is out to market, and why.

8. Failure to study and ask questions about the group's particular business, and the needs of the group's employees.

9. Failure to properly set up eligibility wording in the group insurance plan.

10. Failure to make an in-depth comparison of the present and proposed policies prior to changing insurers.

11. Failure to be honest as to the reasons that the plan is being marketed.

12. Failure of all parties to keep in touch regularly after the "sale".

¶8170 SPREADSHEETS

¶8175 WHY USE SPREADSHEETS?

The group insurance industry involves a lot of routine and repetitive work. As much as insurers and providers like to think that their group products and services are unique, in fact they are very similar, especially in the basic schedules detailed in their policies. Group representatives and group administration personnel attached to sales offices can issue dozens of quotes a month. The quoting process is tedious, subject to a certain degree of error, and can take an inordinant amount of time in the insurer/provider offices. On the ABC and consumer end of the process, each insurer/provider's quote must be taken apart, analyzed and questioned because the quoting process has yet to be standardized within the insurance industry.

Use of a spreadsheet format when marketing group plans will promote standardized responses, and will enable ABCs and consumers to speed up comparisons, saving time, money, and effort for all concerned. It will also have the benefit of freeing up more time for the group office representatives and ABCs, allowing them to concentrate more on marketing their products and services and the servicing of their clients.

A spreadsheet format such as that in the Appendices at ¶17,150 can be designed to send to insurance companies and benefit providers. Having insurers fill in spreadsheets will save a great deal of time. The spreadsheets can be used for comparison purposes, and later, to present details to the client or to other members of a management team. Use of the completed spreadsheets can substitute for a more formal typed report. The spreadsheets can be very useful to the client after the presentation. They provide a handy method of reviewing the original plan's policy terms alongside of the other insurer/provider terms. This can prove useful when discussing future options and when addressing possible policy misinterpretations caused by a change in insurer/provider.

¶8180 HOW TO USE THE SPREADSHEETS

1. Send a copy of the blank spreadsheets, along with a copy of the Master Policy, all policy amendments, the experience and rate history, the employee data, the questionnaire, and the employee booklet to each insurer. Ask each quoting insurer to fill in the spreadsheets as closely as possible within the space limits allowed, and return the spreadsheets with the formal proposal. Mark or number which column the particular insurer should use.

2. Once the insurer spreadsheets and proposals have been returned to you, compare the rates for each benefit by preparing a set of rate spreadsheets using common volumes for each benefit. A comparison based on a

common volume is more accurate. Use the present plan design for the initial comparison.

3. Place the present insurer's rates and benefits in the far left-hand columns of the spreadsheets. Then insert the insurers' rates overall premiums and benefits to the spreadsheets, in the columns to the right of the "Present Insurer" column. This can be done manually, or, if a formal presentation is not that important, the cut and paste method works fine. Using spreadsheets, instead of the traditional insurer proposals, will reduce the amount of work required and increase the fairness of the comparison.

CHAPTER 9

¶9000 ANALYZING THE RESPONSES

¶9005 INTRODUCTION

Once all of the responses have been received, it will be necessary to review them for completeness and then to recalculate the spreadsheet rate pages using common or average volumes for each benefit. This is because each insurer and benefit provider uses a different method of calculating volumes. Two favourite methods of comparison, used by ABCs, are to calculate the average volume of all of the submissions by benefit, or to use the most common volume provided. If an insurer, or provider, sends in rates or volumes that are more than 25 to 30 per cent off of the averages, the underwriter may have made calculation, or typographical errors. It is good practice to ask an underwriter to check the calculations if there is too large a discrepancy.

¶9010 WHAT TO LOOK FOR IN THE PROPOSALS

(1) *Completeness:* How complete the spreadsheets and the proposals are will give you an immediate idea of how the policy will be treated on the local level. If there is not enough information in the proposals, or if the spreadsheets are not completed, telephone the group office and insist gently that the insurer's "assistance" in this area is required. Expect some insurers' proposals to be very sparse and to lack information. This is done

intentionally in order to get to "know you", and to keep the purchaser and the competition from doing a proper comparison.

(2) *Ability to offer the requested benefits and services:* Obviously, if an insurance company is not willing to underwrite a benefit such as LTD for an organization, then you should look for an insurer that does offer the benefits that you need. LTD is one of the benefits that is declined most often by insurers. It is a very important benefit. If an insurer will not quote a benefit, such as LTD, try to "mix and match" benefits between insurers, i.e., place the life and LTD benefits with one insurer, while placing the EHC and dental with another.

(3) *Quality of the response material:* Glossy brochures, and fancy say-nothing fact sheets which tell how much business an insurer has, are of little use in analyzing the quotes. They do tell, however, whether or not someone in that insurance company has money to spend on brochures. The question is, whose money is spent? What is important are examples of the reports that will be received. Also important are references from organizations within your area that use that insurer's services. Have the proposals and spreadsheets been returned completed, and legible, as per the request?

(4) *Obtaining missing information:* Do not be surprised if insurers telephone on the last day to request more time. Many people in the industry seem to work best in a crisis management setting. This includes many of the underwriters, the group offices and the ABCs. Also, do not be surprised if there is information missing in the material sent back. Insurer representatives may not be used to providing complete proposals or to filling out spreadsheets. To obtain missing information, telephone the group insurance office and ask to speak to the group office manager if the group representative is not available, or is not responding to the request.

(5) *The spreadsheets:* All insurance companies should be able to assist you in filling out the "benefits" portion of the spreadsheets which relate to their specific companies. Inexperienced group representatives may have trouble filling in the financial information, especially if your group has less than 15 to 20 employees. This is because financial information is not normally requested on the smaller policies. Much of it is available if you ask. If an insurance company does not provide the information in the format you require using excuses such as "We don't operate that way", it may be an early indication of the type of response that might be received for other requests in the future.

On the rate pages, be sure to take all of the insurer rates for each benefit and multiply them by the same (common) volumes. Otherwise the result will be an unfair comparison.

Confirm that all quoted rates are based on the same commission scale. On smaller "packaged" group insurance policies, especially for those groups under 15 to 20 employees, insurers may not be willing to quote on a "net commission basis", or may not be willing to quote using a commission scale other than its standard. In these cases, ask for a copy of the insurer's commission scale, and ask one of the insurer's representatives to assist in making a comparison of the effect on the rates of the various commission scales offered by the insurer/benefit providers.

¶9015 MAKING A SHORT LIST

Once the proposals are received and the spreadsheets compiled, it is time to narrow the search. This is done by reviewing the submissions, and picking three insurer/providers that best appear able to provide the benefits and services required.

¶9020 THE MOST IMPORTANT THINGS TO REVIEW

1. Did the insurance company quote on the benefits that you requested?
2. Were the spreadsheets and proposals complete?
3. Does the insurer offer high non-medical maximum benefits?
4. How does the insurer compare with the other insurers on the Ratings Agency charts?
5. Are the rates competitive?
6. Is the retention competitive?
7. Can the insurer offer the reports and other services that are needed?
8. Does the insurer reinvest in your local area? Is this important to your organization?
9. Does the insurer offer local service? Is this important to your organization?
10. Was the tone of the accompanying letters, and telephone responses appropriate?

(*Note:* Review the most up-to-date ratings that you can find. Be aware that some benefit providers may not be rated by the ratings agencies.)

You may find, especially with life insurance and disability benefits, that there may be a great range of rates to compare, but the benefits will be very similar. It is here that one can make the first preliminary cost comparison. The EHC, dental, and weekly indemnity (WI) benefits are more difficult to compare. It is necessary to look at what the quoted rates will produce in terms of annual premium, and then compare this against the paid claims for those benefits last year. Then do a quick renewal calculation using the formulas from Insurer A (as shown at ¶11,115 in Chapter 11, Renewals) with those figures. Include the insurer's own retention percentages and "incurred-but-not-reported" (IBNR) reserves. Low first-year rates will not necessarily save you money. They may cost you more money over a two-year period.

¶9025 CHECKLIST: WHAT TO LOOK FOR IN THE PROPOSALS

1. Completeness. ☐
2. Ability to offer the requested benefits and services. ☐
3. Completed questionnaire. ☐
4. Completed spreadsheets. ☐
5. Timeliness. ☐
6. Competitive rates. ☐
7. Ability to financially underwrite the benefits as requested. ☐
8. Availability of timely, informative claims reports. ☐
9. Availability of service personnel (local, if required). ☐
10. Quality of the response material. ☐

¶9030 HOW IMPORTANT ARE THE RATES?

The group life insurance, AD&D, dependant group life, and LTD benefits — the "pooled" benefits — should be compared first on the rates, and then on the benefit wording. They are usually so close in wording that they are often hard to tell apart. The rates for the extended health care and dental benefits should only be reviewed over a two-year period to see if they will produce enough premium to cover the total average claims for those benefits, as determined by the group's past claims experience. Weekly indemnity should be reviewed over a minimum three-year period, if possible. In other words, first-year quoted rates for WI, dental and for EHC should be viewed only in so far as they will support the experience of the group. Why would any insurance company quote rates which, when worked out using last year's experience, will lose money for the insurer? Rates are important, but the quoted rates for the experience rated benefits have to be reviewed to see if they will, at least, support the past two years of experience levels.

Make sure that all quoted rates include the same commission scale or are all quoted "net commission". This helps to ensure a more fair comparison. Commissions on larger policies can be added back in later to "net commission" quotes, if negotiated with and agreed to by the policyholder.

The questionnaire, which accompanies the specifications, asks quoting companies to provide sample second-year renewal calculations based on experience remaining the same as the last full policy year, increasing by 25 per cent, and decreasing by 25 per cent over the next year. These examples should also be compared along with the quoted rates. Comparison of these examples will give a better idea of whether or not each insurer/provider is just lowballing for the first year (with potential larger increases to come in the second year), than if slightly higher rates had been implemented initially.

¶9035 HOW IMPORTANT IS THE RETENTION?

Retention is an important area to review, especially for small-to-medium-sized organizations. The main focus area for these organizations should be the retention in the experience rated benefits, such as EHC, dental and WI. These benefits work like bank accounts, except with higher charges applied. Insurer charges make up the "retention". The retention is the percentage of the premium dollar that the insurance company takes to pay all of its expenses, to pay taxes, and to make a profit. The more the insurance company charges for its services, the more money it generally makes, and the more money is charged to the consumer. The retention is very important, even more so than the rates for the experience rated benefits. On the other hand, for the "pooled" (life and LTD) benefits provided to most small-to-medium-sized organizations, the retention really has a much less noticeable effect on the rates. Also, for the pooled benefits, the premiums, and the retention in terms of total dollars, are generally smaller than for the experience rated benefits.

¶9040 HOW IMPORTANT IS SERVICE?

The answer to this question is subjective in nature. What is service to you? To me, it means that there is someone there to answer my questions when I have them, to answer my telephone calls, not put me through to a machine and then start a never-ending game of "telephone tag". They should also talk my language. I want someone who can suggest answers to me before I ask the questions. I want someone who is local, because I like to support the local economy. I like an insurance company to have the most up-to-date systems so that they can adjudicate and pay the claims promptly. I like an insurance company to provide me with the reports necessary to do proper reviews and analysis of the benefit programs, including claims information. I like a friendly voice on the end of the telephone, someone who may not know all of the answers but at least knows where to look them up. I want to be informed of problem situations immediately. I like to be kept informed of any relevant, pending legislation, and recent court decisions, concerning benefits. I appreciate a once-per-month "check-up" call, from the insurer, just to see if everything is alright, or if there are any questions. I like public e-mail addresses, toll-free telephone and fax lines. To me this is worth something. To a policy administrator, this sort of service can be invaluable, just in terms of time saved in looking for answers.

¶9045 CALLING FOR PRESENTATIONS FROM THE SHORT LIST

Once you have made your decision and picked the best three of the contenders, telephone the finalist group offices and ask each of the group representatives to make a presentation on a certain day. Give them a couple of weeks' notice, unless a quicker implementation date is required. Group representatives will usually reprioritize everything else to make a "sale", so there should not be much of a problem in getting their attention. If the group representative cannot make your date and does not have a backup, you may want to question their position on the shortlist.

There may be some jostling for position by the group representatives for the best presentation time. The best position in which to present is last. The second-best is first. All presenters see the middle positions as the least favourable for making presentations.

¶9050 ANALYZING THE SHORT LIST PRESENTATIONS AND CHOOSING THE INSURER/PROVIDER

The finalist presentations are used to get a "feeling" for how an insurance company will treat a policyholder. A decision will have to be made based on the group representative's presentation, the style, the dress and most importantly, how well questions are answered. Presentations will range from the formal, with overheads and fancy slide shows, to those that prefer an informal question-and-answer session. Expect to see the traditional "suit and tie" look, the flamboyant look and perhaps even the casual look. Group representatives, who have done their homework about your organization, may try to dress to fit your group's style. Style of dress really does not tell much about the insurance company, but people who are alike are more likely to feel comfortable around one another.

The presenters should be able to answer the following questions. The answers may help to clarify certain facts that may not be answered in the proposals.

(1) Is the insurance company/benefit provider a stock or a mutual company? How will that affect the policy?

(2) What types of administration systems are offered?

(3) Where are the underwriting decisions made? Who does the underwriting?

(4) What kind of assistance does the insurer provide to protect the client against administrative errors?

(5) Can the insurer amend its policies to meet the organization's needs?

(6) Can the insurer meet special requests for reports and employee booklets?

(7) How many group insurance clients does the insurer service in the local area?

(8) What is the total group insurance premium serviced by the insurer's local group office?

(9) How do each of the insurer ratings agencies rate the insurer? If the insurer is not rated in the top category or has been recently downgraded, what are the reasons for this, what is being done to correct the situation and in what time frame?

The final decision is usually based on a combination of the facts and figures and on the group representatives' presentations.

¶9055 CHOOSING THE PROVIDER FROM THE SHORT LIST PRESENTERS

What to analyze:

Claims payment ratings: Is the insurer or provider more than financially solvent?

Type of company (stock or mutual company): Will this have an effect on the plan in the future?

Commitment to investment in your local area or province: Has the insurer made any local investments?

Technology: Has the insurer or provider kept up with your technological requirements?

The local representatives: Are they knowledgeable? Are they available? Do you get along with them?

Decision-making: Where are decisions made?

Ability to forgive errors: How does the insurer protect you from administration errors?

Administration fit: Can the insurer offer the type of administration system required? Can they amend their administration to fit your needs?

Policy working: Can they amend their policy wording to fit your needs?

Booklets: Can they provide special requests for employee booklets?

Rates: Are the rates too high, or too low in comparison to the competition?

Commissions: Did all quotes contain the same commission scale? Or, were all quotes net commission, if applicable?

Rate and rate basis guarantees: What is the insurer, or provider attitude towards guarantees?

CHAPTER 10

¶10,000 CHANGING INSURERS

¶10,005 INTRODUCTION

The program has been analyzed, the plan has been marketed, the short-list candidates have been interviewed, and a decision has been made to change insurers. What is the next step? First of all, review the following important points.

1. Before the decision is made to change insurers, make sure that a requote is obtained from the new insurer, (especially if there has been a change in the employee data since last quote), or if the insurer's proposal is stale-dated (proposals are valid for 30, 60 or 90 days, depending on the insurer). A change in employee data will occur if you have hired a new employee, terminated an employee, changed employee occupations, added or sold off a corporate division, or bought another company and placed those employees into the plan. n a small group of employees, hiring people older or younger than the average age used for the initial quote can radically affect the life insurance and long-term disability (LTD) rates. All insurers recalculate rates at the inception date of a policy, using current employee data. On a larger group, a variance of 5 per cent up or down, in the recalculated rates, from the original proposed rates may not be passed on by the insurer or provider. It may be reflected in the first renewal however.

2. Before cancelling the old group insurance policy, make sure that the new insurer's policy is approved. Get this in writing from the new

insurer, or the new insurer's representative. Make sure, as well, that the new insurer is going to honour all of its commitments and non-medical maximum benefits.

3. "Grandfathering" is a term which means that the new insurer will match all of the benefits and coverages available to all of the eligible employees and dependants under the old group policy. This is very important for the life insurance and LTD amounts. Above all, have it confirmed in writing that the old policy's coverage amounts will be matched by the new insurer. It may be too late after the old policy has been cancelled, to find out that one of your employees may lose coverage because he or she cannot pass a medical required by the new insurer.

4. The "not actively at work clause" is worthy of noting. At the date that the new policy is to come into effect, if an employee is on sick leave, even for the day, on Workers' Compensation, weekly indemnity (WI), LTD, or off on any other type of leave, benefits will not normally begin under the new insurer's policy until the employee returns to "actively at work" status. Employees on disability are not automatically covered for employer health care plans (EHC), dental or dependant life benefits under the new insurer, because they are not "actively at work" and do not qualify for benefits unless approved by the new insurer. Advise the new insurer before the date of the changeover of any employees in these situations. Also, write or fax a letter to the old insurer advising them that certain employees are still their responsibility for life insurance and LTD (see the sample letter at ¶10,025 below).

Group insurance policies are termed by law, unilateral contracts. This means that, subject to the policyholder paying the premiums, the insurer agrees to pay benefits under the terms of the policy. A policyholder is generally not under any obligation to the insurer to continue paying premiums or to keep a plan in force. Remember though, that the organization may have other obligations such as those to employees and their dependants. A 30-day notice is usually given to the old insurer before the start of the new insurer's policy. This notice is generally considered to be good practice because it gives everyone a chance to catch their breath and to prepare for the change. However, there are generally no penalties for not giving exactly 30 days' notice. Check with the insurer for its terms.

After the review of all of the proposals, and after the decision has been made to change insurers, ask the successful insurer's group representative, along with the ABC, if applicable, to meet with you. The insurer's representative will assist in the change. The last day that coverage is in effect under the old policy should coincide with the first day that the new policy is put into effect. There should be no gap between these dates, as any gap in coverage could jeopardize employee benefits.

¶10,010 NEW POLICY IMPLEMENTATION

Steps to Take

1. Choose new insurer.

2. Call new insurer group office and advise group representative.

3. Set up meeting with group representative to sign application prior to effective date.

4. Prepare new employee data list, or revise original list used in marketing the policy.

5. Obtain confirmation in writing from the group representative, that new insurer will accept policy, "grandfather" all old coverage levels, and issue all non-medical maximums as per the specifications.

6. Obtain confirmation in writing from the group representative, that people on any type of leave, or covered under termination of employment agreements, or currently off work on disability claim and still covered for EHC, dental and dependant life benefits, or who are retired, or who are directors of the organization and who are covered for benefits under the old policy, will be able to continue coverage.

7. Ask the group representative to recalculate and confirm the rates before signing the application.

8. Meet with group representative to sign application and finalize new policy details, and to confirm what and when claims reports are required.

9. Provide group representative with a company cheque for first month's premium.

10. Group representative meets with organization's policy administrator to review administration.

11. Write letter to old insurer cancelling old policy; group representative can assist.

12. Write letter to employees advising them of the change; group representative can assist.

13. Write and fax letter on last day old policy is in effect, to old insurer, advising it of all employees who are off sick or on disability. Old insurer will have to continue life and LTD coverage for these employees until they are able to return to work full time. Group representative can assist.

14. Review and revise draft policy and draft employee booklets.

15. Set up and hold employee meetings. Group representative can make the presentation(s).

16. Give benefit booklets to employees.

¶10,015 CHECKLIST: CHANGING INSURERS

The following is a checklist of the steps to take to change insurers.

1. Review current employee data with new insurer's representative. Compare the current data with the data provided for the original quote. ☐
2. Obtain new quote if there have been changes or if the new insurer's quote is out of date. Confirm inception rates. ☐
3. Get confirmation in writing from the new insurer that all coverages (with the exception agreed upon changes) will be "grandfathered". ☐
4. Get confirmation in writing from the new insurer that all employees on vacation, on approved leaves of absence, or on disability, with benefit coverage, will have coverage continued. ☐
5. Sign master application(s). ☐
6. Write cheque to the new insurer for the approximate first month's premium. ☐
7. Provide new insurer with a list of the employees eligible to go onto the new policy. This list should coincide closely with the list used for the quote. ☐
8. Provide new insurer with new enrolment cards, or new beneficiary change cards. If the policy is self-administered, keep the new cards in a safe, secure and fireproof place. ☐
9. Send the old insurer a list of those employees not actively at work on the date of the changeover, or on the first business day before the change date. Follow up with any additions on the next business day after the change. ☐
10. Give a copy of this list to the new insurer. ☐
11. Send a letter to the employees advising them of the change and the reasons for the change. ☐
12. Review new insurer's administration procedures. ☐
13. Arrange employee meetings to explain the plan(s). ☐
14. Confirm with the new insurer the new employee booklet wording and format. ☐
15. Review the new policy and employee booklet (draft) wording when sent by the insurer. ☐
16. Review experience on a quarterly or semi-annual basis. ☐

¶10,020 SAMPLE GROUP INSURANCE POLICY CANCELLATION LETTER

Corporate Letterhead

Date:________

ABC Life Insurance Company
123 Their Street
Anytown, Province
Postal Code

Re: Policy(s) # ______________

Dear Sirs,

Please cancel the above policy(ies) effective midnight (day, month, year). The reason for the cancellation is that we have been able to obtain (insert reason i.e., more favourable rates, more favourable retention, more favourable benefits, more suitable claims/administration services).

We will advise you of any employees not actively at work on the effective date of the new policy. Coverage for these employees is to remain in effect, for the (group life, accidental death, dependant life, weekly indemnity, and long-term disability) benefits until they return to actively-at-work status.

Thank you for your assistance.

Yours truly,

Name, Title

¶10,025 SAMPLE LETTER TO BE SENT LAST WORKING DAY A POLICY IS IN EFFECT

Corporate Letterhead

Date:_________

ABC Insurance Company
123 Their Street
Anytown, Province
Postal Code

Re: Policy(s) #____________________

Dear Sirs,

With reference to our previous correspondence dated__________, concerning the cancellation of the above policy, please be advised that the following employees are not actively at work as of the date of cancellation:

1. Employee Name.
2. Employee ID No.
3. Reason for Not-Actively-at-Work Status.

We understand that these employees will remain covered under the above policy number until they return to actively-at-work status. Please advise us of the administrative procedures to follow with respect to these employees.

Yours truly,

Name, Title

¶10,030 AFTER THE CHANGE

¶10,035 CHECKLIST: STEPS TO TAKE AFTER THE CHANGE OF INSURER

The following should be completed after you have changed insurers.

1. Review the draft insurance policy and draft employee booklets. ☐
2. Discuss the revisions to the drafts with insurer group representative. ☐
3. Read and confirm the following parts of the actual policy:
   - Summary pages. ☐
   - Eligibility wording. ☐
   - Non-medical and medical maximum benefits. ☐
   - Definition of disability for life waiver of premium and/or LTD. ☐
4. Set up time with the group representative to discuss changes to administration. ☐
5. Set up time for the group representative to hold employee meetings. ☐
6. Train a back-up administrator for your organization. ☐
7. Ask the insurer to provide you with any relevant information on changing legislation or insurance policy terms. ☐
8. Ask the insurer to provide you with the costs of any future insurer updates to policy terms as they become available. ☐
9. Request 45 days' advance notice of rate changes from the insurer. ☐

¶10,040 ANTICIPATING, ENCOUNTERING AND DEALING WITH PROBLEMS

Anticipating possible problems will enable you make contingency plans in advance. It is important to do as much homework as possible before any change is made. Choose the best available insurer when you market the plan. The best may or may not be the insurer with the lowest overall rates. The business environment can change.

Watch what the insurers promise, and watch what you promise. A new insurance company representative may be inexperienced and promise things that are not the insurer's policy, so get everything in writing. You, on the other hand, may have let the insurer know that one of your employees was going to retire before the effective date of the new policy, and then decided to keep the employee on staff. If the insurer has already calculated its rates before this happens, you may find that the insurer will want to pass on an increase at the inception date of the plan, after it has recalculated the rates.

Remember the old adage, "if something can go wrong, it will"? Dealing with experienced insurer representatives, dealing with financially stable insurers who have large books of business, and following proper procedures will reduce the chances of having problems.

Three problem areas that can be avoided in advance:

(1) Promising or negotiating benefits with or for employees before checking with the insurer on the availability and ramifications of the changes. This is especially important in situations where unions or employee associations are involved. In no circumstances should benefits be offered to employees, especially contract employees or subcontract employees, without first obtaining written permission from the insurers.

(2) Failure to advise insurers immediately of any changes in the employee census. Changes such as hiring new employees, employees going on sick leave, Workers' Compensation claims, and employees changing job status (i.e., going from temporary to full-time status) are all situations where the insurer must be advised. Advise the insurer in writing.

(3) Failure to make necessary changes to policies as soon as possible. The opportunity may not be there tomorrow.

Examples of "Big" Administration Problems

The following situations can potentially cause big (liability) problems especially if an employee dies or becomes disabled.

1. Premiums were not paid by the end of the policy's payment grace period.

2. Changed insurers; time passed. Administrator forgot to enrol an employee who was eligible.

3. Changed insurers; time passed. An employee forgot to submit claims which were incurred before the change to the new insurer. Old and new insurers refuse to pay the claim.

4. Beneficiary changes. The new signed beneficiary cards were lost or not submitted.

5. New employee hired, is eligible but not enrolled within the enrolment grace period.

6. Changed employee status from temporary to full-time; did not inform insurer.

7. Used a third party to do the plan administration and to collect premium; third party did not submit premium. Insurer refuses to pay.

8. Employees contribute to premium. Premiums are not put into a trust account. Employer goes bankrupt. Claims are not paid by the insurer for the period premium not paid.

9. Administrator forgot to put employee onto the plan. Employee cannot pass a medical. It is past the 30-day enrolment grace period. Employee declined for coverage by the insurer.

10. Administrator refuses to put an employee on the plan.

11. Administrator failed to get a refusal card signed by an employee, or administrator lost the refusal card.

12. Changed insurers; new insurer refuses to cover an employee for disability due to a medical condition. Employee loses LTD coverage.

CHAPTER 11

¶11,000 RENEWALS

¶11,005 FACTORS AFFECTING RENEWALS

¶11,010 A FAST CHECK OF A RENEWAL

To check that an extended health care (EHC) or a dental benefit's renewal is "in the ballpark", insert the policyholder's premiums, claims and retention information into Formula 1, provided later in this section (at ¶11,115). The result should be within 2 to 3 per cent, either way, of the renewal provided by the present insurer or benefit provider. If it isn't, ask the insurer or benefit provider for an explanation.

It is difficult to do a "fast check" of group life insurance or long-term disability (LTD) rates unless you have access to the actual rate basis and calculations used by the insurer. The only people who have access to these calculations work for the insurer. Even if your renewal rates are the same as last year's rates, ask the insurer for a complete explanation of the group life and LTD rates including an age/volume breakdown comparison showing the previous year's figures and the figures used for the latest renewal calculation.

¶11,015 Introduction

Negotiating a renewal with an insurer is much easier when you know how benefits are funded. If you are looking at a renewal for the first time, review Chapter 7, Funding the Benefits. A renewal depends on the size of the group, the type of benefit, the competitiveness of the insurance market, inflation, the insurer's rates of return on investments, the overall claims experience of the insurer's book of business, claims experience of the group, taxes, the commission scale and the percentage of the premium dollar (the retention) that the insurer is charging to provide the services.

¶11,020 Size

One primary fact about negotiating renewals is that the size of the group, in terms of the number of employees and the premium paid, affects rates. If the group has under 15 employees, many insurers use a "pooled" approach to review and to rate each policy in the pool. In other words, at the end of the policy year, the policy will be assigned whatever rate increases or decreases (the latter is a rarity) that the insurer assesses against the whole pool. If the insurer decides, after analysis, that the pool requires a 20 per cent increase, then all groups in that pool get that increase at their renewal dates. Pooled rates can also be increased for each policyholder in the pool on an individual basis. The insurer might do this if one policy in the pool has very large claims, or a history (i.e., over two or three years) of high claims. Insurance underwriters can, and will, increase the rates of even the smallest of groups in a pool on an individual basis, in an attempt to "put the rates at the appropriate level". In these cases, the size of the increase often forces the policyholder to search quickly for a new insurer. Most insurance companies do keep separate experience, per benefit, for all size groups, despite what they may tell you. "Experience" is the watchword for insurers these days. Most insurers request experience and rate information before issuing their best, or as they term it, their most appropriate rates. If the group is small, it may help for the policyholder to keep track of all benefits paid out on its own. This can be done by having all claim cheques returned by the insurer to the policyholder's administrator, before being given to the employees. A simple list of the total amount paid for each benefit, and the date received, will suffice. Paid premium information can be obtained from the monthly billing statements, as these statements usually split the the total premiums into premiums per benefit. Insurers do keep track of this information, but because of the sheer volume of small cases that they have on their books, they say that it would be very expensive to provide. Most insurers therefore, decline to provide it when asked, by saying, "Experience is not available on this size case".

The size of the group and the size of the premium determines the amount the insurer charges, or "retains", to provide a benefit. Basically the larger the premium, the larger the volume discount applied to the rates. This concept is similar to volume purchases of other products. Most underwriters have a scale which states what volume discount can be provided.

The scales are stated two different ways, either as changes to the retention percentage or as changes to the volume discount. In the former case, an insurer/provider will change the percentage of the premium dollar that it charges to set up the policy, provide administration and pay claims (the retention), as the total premium increases or decreases. For example, the insurer might charge 28 per cent of the premium dollar to provide the services if the premium is $2,000 per month. The charge might drop to 27 per cent of premium once the premium is $2,500 per month. Increasing the volume discount or decreasing the required retention can mean the same thing or have the same effect on the rates.

¶11,025 Competitiveness of the Insurance Market

Since the early 1970s, life insurance companies have been very aggressive in their attempts to procure new group insurance clients. The late 1970s and early 1980s often saw 15 to 20 per cent or more first-year savings for organizations shopping for better rates and service on their group insurance policies. There are over 150 life insurance companies operating in Canada today, all vying to serve a population of around 27 million people. Not all insurance companies sell group insurance policies. Employee benefits policies are generally only sold by life insurance companies and health benefit providers (who might specialize in one or two services). With the exception of policies such as group home and auto policies, general insurance companies do not underwrite the traditional "group life and health" insurance benefits. There are signs that insurance companies, by in large, are pulling in their horns.

Most insurance companies in the employee benefits market require their group offices to sell more business each year. This requirement exists despite whatever is happening to the economy, including recessions. Many insurers have now set up their local group offices as profit centres. Representatives are reimbursed, not only for new sales, but for keeping their own books of business profitable. Therefore, a representative who cuts the rates too much to obtain a new client, may end up showing a loss on that particular policy. The loss, in turn, affects the whole "book" of business and the group office's profitability bonus.

There are still bargains to be had in the marketplace. Insurance companies can have a "provide-at-cost" benefit. These "give-away" benefits are an inducement to keep the other benefits with that particular insurer. The last few years have seen huge percentage reductions in the rates offered for accidental death and dismemberment (AD&D). Rates, which ten years ago, were $0.04/$1,000 to $0.06/$1,000 of benefit, can often be obtained on the larger policies, for half of the old rate. In addition, AD&D benefits have been improved. Many life insurance rate bases have also been changed to reflect the fact that people are living longer. Group life insurance policy terms have been improved by some insurers. It is now possible to obtain benefits which were not available a few years ago, such as "living benefits®" (a particularly helpful benefit first introduced by Prudential (the Rock) which pays out a percentage of the group life amount to a terminally ill employee, while the employee is still alive). Sometimes a "bargain" can be in receiving better benefits at the same price, not just in receiving a better price.

Competitiveness in the life insurance business has been partially to blame for the failure of two large life insurers in the last couple of years. As employee benefits may be compromised if a group insurance plan is underwritten by an insurer that fails, it pays to keep a watchful eye on the claims-paying ability, as rated by rating agencies such as Standard and Poor, and A.M. Best, etc., of the insurers underwriting a group. Although Canadian life insurance companies have set up an organization, called Compcorp, to pay claims up to certain limits should a member company fail, there are limits to the amounts that can be claimed. Only life insurance companies belong to Compcorp; not-for-profit benefit providers do not belong. Coverage, under Compcorp, is limited to $200,000 for life insurance, including group life insurance; long-term disability is limited to $2,000 per month of benefit per employee. Group benefits are often higher than these limits, especially for higher paid employees. In addition, Compcorp has no assets of any size itself. The funding to cover benefits, in case of an insurer failure, is supplied by the other life insurance member companies, as required. To date, this has not caused a problem, however it may become one in the off-chance that more than one large life insurer fails within a short time of another. In comparison, the Canadian Deposit Insurance Corporation (CDIC), which provides services similar to Compcorp to the Canadian banking and trust industry, is backed by the federal government. CDIC ran huge deficits for many years. At least the life insurance industry has taken it upon itself to set up Compcorp, without waiting to be funded by the government! The insurers who failed did so because of a combination of reasons. Poor investment strategies, including overexposure to commercial real estate in their portfolios, and large, costly bureaucracies within the insurance companies, were as much, if not more, to blame for the failures than underwriting losses. There is little to no policyholder control over the expenses, or investments of the insurers. Because of this, it is very difficult for their clients to affect the way that the insurers, or benefit providers, conduct business.

¶11,030 Type of Benefit

Renewals are calculated on a benefit by benefit basis. Benefit costs are affected by situations external to the policy. For example, if the plan contains a dental benefit, and that benefit accounts for 40 per cent of the total cost of the benefits package, a 5 per cent increase in the provincial dental association's suggested fee guide can have a large impact on the total benefits cost. This will have an effect on a group which has frozen its benefits budget for the year. Renewals are affected by which benefits are in a policy. They are also influenced by external factors such as increases in the charges for health services, or increases in taxes.

Certain types of benefits are affected by inflationary factors. Inflation, or "trend" as some insurers call it, in the Medicare field, has been increasing at rates which far exceed the Consumer Price Index for the last four to five years. Consequently, rates for the extended health care benefit have risen to match. Insurance companies have no real control over this inflation. It is just passed on to the policyholders via increased rates. Trend is discussed further in the next section.

Rates for the group life and the long-term disability benefits are affected by the experience of the pools and the insurer's timing on re-evaluation of the rate bases.

¶11,035 Inflation and Trend

Insurance companies call inflation in health and dental benefits the "trend". Trend is another word for inflation. Canada's inflation index, the Consumer Price Index (CPI), is tied to Statistics Canada's basket of basic goods. This is the index factor that the public generally refers to when talking about inflation. The cost of medical goods and services however, is not included in Statistics Canada's basket. In addition, there has been a "trend", among certain medical practitioners, to find "better" and more expensive ways for the public to "utilize" their services. Because of these higher utilization costs, and the fact that the costs of medical goods and services were rising so dramatically in comparison to the CPI, insurance companies decided to call inflation "the trend". Trend is the result of higher utilization costs plus the rising costs of goods and services in the health care field.

The trend in extended health care benefits has been rising at a rate, depending on which insurer you want to believe, of between 15 and 23 per cent each year for the last four to five years. Is it any wonder that the public has become increasingly upset over these cost increases lately?

There are signs that these high-trend factors will continue for the next while. The recent Federal government revisions to increase the length of time that a drug manufacturer can have exclusive rights to manufacture a particular medication means that manufacturers will have longer to market their products without fear of competition based on price. There is a point in pricing, though, which will stop consumption of any product, except by the very rich. Inflation in Medicare may yet reach that point.

Trend factors vary between insurance companies. As shown to consumers, at renewal, they have sometimes been "adjusted" by underwriters, group representatives and ABCs, to make the renewal figures more palatable. Trend factors applied to dental policies in 1993 varied between 0 and 5 per cent between insurers. Trend factors applied to extended health care plan (EHC) renewals in 1993 varied between 15 and 23 per cent, depending on the insurer. Trend factors continue to be applied to group insurance policies today. Not only are policy renewals receiving trend increases, but, if the renewal is delayed after the policy year-end, either because of the insurer's renewal system, or because of negotiations between the policyholder and the insurer, the trend factor is often adjusted (increased) to compensate for the delay.

¶11,040 Insurer Claims Experience

Insurance companies continue to put pressure on their field employees to "sell, sell, sell". For every policy that is put on the books, the insurer must establish a reserve to pay claims. Insurers who put too much business on the books put a "strain on the reserves". Also, insurers who are constantly after as much new business as they can find, will also, almost by necessity, underwrite poorer than normal risks. An insurer who does this will almost certainly incur losses, unless it is very lucky.

Losses are eventually passed on to the policyholders in one way or another. If an organization switches insurers just before the new insurer passes these rate increases through to the policyholders, the next renewal may be higher than it might have been if the organization had stayed with the old insurer. Of course, a group policyholder is free to shop the market at any time if it feels that the increases are not its fault, or in insurance company language, if the rate changes are "not justified".

If the insurer is losing money in its "pools" or in its investments (i.e., too much exposure to commercial real estate), it can increase the rates to help offset the losses. An increase in pooled rates is a justifiable reason to shop around to test the competitiveness of any group's renewal.

¶11,045 The Group's Claims Experience

The biggest factor in determining the renewal rates (especially for the health and dental benefits) will be the group's own experience. The more that employees claim, the higher the group's rates will be next year. An organization that includes all of the bells and whistles in a benefit, will eventually have to pay the proverbial piper.

Extended health care and dental renewal rates, for most groups, are based almost exclusively on the previous year's experience. If the paid claims double in total from one year to the next, while the premium remains the same, you can expect a rate increase of similar magnitude at the renewal. On top of the potential doubling of the rate based on the experience, you will also find additional increases to account for the trend factors, and further increases to adjust the incurred-but-not-reported (IBNR) claim reserves.

On the other hand, if the experience shows a 50 per cent decline from one year to the next, you may expect a 50 per cent decrease in rates. The decrease will, of course, be tempered by the trend factor. Furthermore, with a drop in claims, there should be a release of the not required portions of the IBNR reserves. These amounts should be credited to the policy in terms of lower rates. Sometimes insurers are more willing to increase the IBNR reserves during rate increases, than they are willing to decrease them when rates decrease. Careful attention should be paid to the proper reflection of appropriate IBNR as well as other reserves' credits and debits at renewal.

With the exception of the largest groups (the fully experience rated policies), one or two group life insurance, AD&D, dependant life, voluntary life, voluntary AD&D or long-term disability claims should not cause an increase in the rates, for these (pooled) benefits. However, if the group experiences more claims than the average for the pool, an increase in the rates can be expected. The size of these rate increases are a judgment call for the underwriters. For "experience rated", EHC, dental and WI benefits, a group's experience can have a direct effect on the renewal, no matter what the size of the group.

If a group has lost, for whatever reason, an employee that had high claims, then that should also be pointed out to the underwriter. For example, if an employee had claimed $5,000 for last year, out of a total of $25,000 for the group as a whole last year, and that employee has now left the employer, the underwriter does not need to pay those claims during the next policy year. The $5,000 should be taken out of the experience when calculating the renewal rates. If the underwriter refuses to acknowledge this and take out these claims, then the organization has a valid reason to look for an insurer that will take the fact into consideration.

¶11,050 First Renewal: Timing and Reserves

The timing of the first renewal can affect the size of the increase or decrease in the renewal rates. This occurs when the insurer uses only nine months of actual claims, to determine the renewal. Claims fluctuate in terms of numbers during the year. In Canada, many, if not most, insurers find that their biggest claim period is from November to January. The least frequent period is during the summer months, due to vacations, fewer colds and flu, etc. If the first renewal takes its paid claims figure from the nine months of heavier claims, then the projection of paid claims for the year will be higher, and the renewal rates will be higher. On the other hand, if the first year renewal is calculated omitting the higher claims period, the first year renewal will probably be understated. Insurers who renew a benefit using a full 12 months of experience for the first renewal, have more accurate assessments of the experience, and can, thereby, generally set more accurate first renewal rates.

Also, at the first renewal, the insurance company will want to set up the IBNR reserve (the reserve set up to cover claims in case of cancellation of the policy). The IBNR calculation for the renewal is usually a percentage of the paid claims total for the policy, or a percentage of the paid premium, depending on the particular insurer's formula. The result can be a very large addition to the paid claims total, the sum of which will be used in the calculation of the renewal. Because of the addition of the IBNR, renewal rates, therefore, are adjusted with a much larger increase than there might have been, if there had been the same paid claims amount in a second or subsequent year. At the second and subsequent renewals, the insurance company would only need to make adjustments to the IBNR amount which was set up in the first policy year, if the IBNR was fully funded at the end of the policy year. But, the last policy year's IBNR is used on a continuous basis to pay claims, so, in effect, insurers have to set up a new IBNR at the end of each policy year.

¶11,055 Claims Reserves

All insurance companies set up reserves (including the IBNR reserves). IBNR reserves are set up to pay claims which occurred during the policy year, but which have yet to be submitted or processed by the insurer. They are also set up to pay claims in case a policy cancels and no more premium payments are made to the insurer. Any increase in a policyholder's premium rates will cause an increase in the amount required to fund these reserves for that policy. A decrease in premium for that same benefit, should cause a release of the excess premium still held in that reserve. The amount released should act as a credit on the renewal calculation.

On larger, fully experienced rated policies, insurance companies set up claims fluctuation reserves (CFRs) which hold, with interest paid, excess premiums. These excess premiums are used to smooth out the renewals from year to year. The CFRs can sometimes be used, by policyholders, to withhold money from their own corporate incomes, although this is rare, and there are limits as to the amounts that can be held. Amounts in excess of the limits should be refunded, to the policyholder, by the insurer/provider, and the amounts must then be accounted for as income by the group policyholder. Any amounts left over after a fully experience rated policy's cancellation and after the final accounting has been completed, should be returned to the policyholder.

¶11,060 Other Factors Which Will Affect Renewal Rates

The following are other factors which will affect group renewal rates:

1. The size of a group changes. The insurer compensates for the change by offering conservative rates. IBNR reserve credits may not be fully allocated, or in the case of an increased number of employees, may not be fully charged to a policyholder, (or the increase may be charged over two or more years).

2. Downsizing, by letting younger employees go, increases the average age of the group, increases the risk to the insurer, and hence, increases the rates.

3. Employee age. The rates charged for older employees, especially for group life, WI and LTD, are higher because the insurer's risk of paying a claim is greater. The older the average age, the higher the rates.

4. Downsizing decreases premium totals, and thereby reduces volume discounts and increases retention. Increasing the group size has the opposite effect.

5. High employee turnover can increase claims, unless there are longer eligibility waiting periods in place.

6. Changing the male/female percentages in the group. Women may live longer than men, statistically (and this is changing), but have a greater chance of becoming disabled. Therefore, the more women in a group, the lower the group life rate. The more men in a group, the lower the disability rates, assuming that the men and women compared are the same ages.

7. The insurer re-evaluates the "rate basis" — the actual internal rates used for each age and sex classification — which are in turn used to calculate the average rates. Changes in the rate basis have, in the past, occurred every eight to ten years for life insurance and long-term disability benefits. Expect these rate basis changes to happen more often in the future as insurers become able to evaluate more quickly. The insurer may also alter its occupation, industry or location rate basis loading factors.

8. The "location" increase/decrease. Where you live affects what you pay.

9. Changing the nature of the business, i.e., from a manufacturer to a distributor, will change job functions. This will affect occupational and industry loadings on the rates.

10. Trying to rate for the future by looking at the past: retrospective rating. Rating for the future is, at best, a calculated guess.

11. Credibility factors are changed by the insurer.

12. Over-inflating inflation. A quick survey of the insurers will show that there can be a significant difference in inflation, or trend, factors charged by each insurer on the same benefit lines.

13. The number, or amount of claims per benefit increases, or decreases. This is, generally, one of the biggest causes of EHC and dental rate changes.

14. A single, large, unexpected claim occurs. Depending on the benefit and the insurer, this may affect the rates.

15. Removing the ABC after re-evaluating corporate needs. Hiring an ABC and paying only for the services that are needed. Putting the plan on a "net commission" basis. Removing commissions, when ABC services are not required, should be immediately reflected in the policyholder's rates.

16. An employee/family assistance program is implemented.

17. Investment climate. The rates of return on the insurer's investments and reserves will affect the insurer's income, and hence the rates charged to the policyholders. Insurer accounting changes can also have an affect.

18. Insurance company failure. Group policies will obviously have to be replaced unless another insurer buys the failed insurer's book of business. The new insurer may not have the experience to handle the size and type of groups in the newly purchased book of business, or may have different ideas as to how the policies should be priced.

¶11,065 NEGOTIATING RENEWALS: RENEWAL COMPARISON

Insurance companies all have their own unique way of underwriting, both new policies, and renewals. The purpose of this section is to discuss the differences in the approaches between the insurers. Knowledge of the effect of the differences will give you an alternative point of view from which to discuss your renewal. Look at the two first-year renewal examples provided (at ¶11,115, pages 208 and 210).

¶11,070 Premium

The first item to notice is the accounting period. Some insurers use what is called a "delayed accounting" approach to underwriting renewals. These "delays" vary between insurers. Delays refer to the lag between the end of the experience period used to calculate the renewal, and the actual date that the new rates come into effect. It can mean that a renewal is not done until six weeks after the policy year-end, and rate changes occur six weeks after that. In other words, new rates come into effect three months after the policy year-end. Some insurers calculate the renewal after nine months of experience have passed, and their new rates come into effect at the policy's actual year-end, i.e., 12 months after last year's rates went into effect.

Paid premium is not the same as adjusted billed premium. The adjusted billed premium depends on the accounting period. An insurance company can use the actual paid premium from the first nine months of the policy year in its renewal calculations. This amount is grossed up (by dividing the nine months or premium by nine and then multiplying the result times 12) to provide an estimate of the whole year's total premium. The grossed-up premium figure is the adjusted billed premium. Use of the adjusted billed premium is less accurate than use of the actual premium figure for the 12 months of the policy year.

The use of the terms "paid premium" and "billed premium" should be reviewed carefully, at renewal and especially when marketing a policy. For example, if there has been a delay in remitting or processing the premium, the last month or maybe even two months' premium may not show on the experience report. The result may be nine months of claims, but only eight months of premium showing on the experience report. This will eventually come out in the wash over time, as they say, if the group remains with that insurer. ABCs should be aware that insurers, who want to make their groups look unattractive to the competition, when asked for experience statements, may provide an actual paid premium figure, which will show only premiums received, not premiums that are owed, billed, or paid but not yet processed. If 12 months of claims have been processed, but only ten or 11 months of premium, the resulting paid claims ratio will throw off other insurers' calculations and might cause some insurers to lose interest in providing a quote.

One difference between the approaches to premium figures in the examples, is that Insurance Company B has to guess what the premium is for the full 12 months, by grossing up the actual paid premium. This is a less accurate approach. Insurance Company A has a more accurate knowledge of paid premium and paid claims, for renewal purposes, especially for the first year. This accuracy is gained by the delay in accounting. However, the result of the delay is that insurer B will be able to adjust the rates earlier than A. Clients of B will get rate increases, or decreases, before clients of A. Furthermore, A must adjust the trend factors to account for the delay. (This adjustment is not shown in the example.) If applied, A's inflation factor would have been shown as (15 per cent times 15 divided by 12 months) = 18.75 per cent. Look at the premium figures in the examples again. For the purposes of the illustrations, both were set at $25,000. The premiums for insurer A are actual paid premiums. Those for B are actual for nine months and a best guess for the balance of the year. Insurer B uses an average of those nine months, times three, added to the actual first nine months' of premium, to determine the "adjusted" premium used in the calculation. The problem with this approach, especially in the first year, is that if the policyholder has fewer employees during those three months, then the final calculation, in effect, overstates what the premium would have been. The insurance companies argue that, if there are fewer employees due to seasonal layoff, a policyholder can end up with 12 months of claims anyway. Employees, who know that they are about to be laid off, run right to the dentist for their dental work and to the pharmacist to refill their prescriptions. The effect is a jump in the "normal" claims for that period. Whether or not it is equal to the amount that would be claimed if there were no layoff is debatable.

The use of billed premium to calculate renewals is an inaccurate way of showing the true paid premiums for the year as it may not reflect the actual premiums paid and owed. This is due to the fact that there can be changes in employee data, such as the number of employees on the plan that have not been processed and put onto the billing. This can be an advantage to the policyholder on a first renewal if the billed premium was for a greater number of employees than there actually were employed, such as would happen in the case with a recent layoff. It can also work the other way, where the billings actually show fewer employees than there actually are eligible, such as in the case of recent hirees not being processed onto the billing.

Why is this important? Will it not all wash out next year? We must not forget that the insurance companies turn the "paid loss ratios" into rate increases, or decreases, when calculating the renewal. This loss ratio is obtained by dividing the paid claims by the paid premium. Reduce the paid premium and you increase the percentage that the rates will increase, in most cases. In the worst case scenario, for the policyholder, if a rate decrease is called for, the rate decrease will not be as great as it should be. The end result is that the policyholder's organization, and its employees, if they are sharing premium, will pay higher rates! Will it wash out next year? The answer is yes, maybe. Much can change in the course of a year. The group can expand or contract in size, be bought out, decide to refocus, or decide to change insurers. If it changes insurers, unless there is an underwriting agreement in place (most policies do not have one), the policyholder will lose the incurred claims reserve when the policy cancels! There is not much to be gained by most consumers, in paying rates based on best-guess approaches, when there are alternatives which are more accurate.

¶11,075 Incurred Claims

The purpose of the incurred-but-not-reported (IBNR) claims reserve is to financially protect the insurance company in case of a policy cancellation, or in case the policyholder goes bankrupt. The chances are more likely that the former will happen than the latter. These reserves are set up to pay the claims that may have occurred, but are not yet claimed or processed while the policy was in force. Incurred claim formulas are expressed either as a percentage of paid premium, or as a percentage of paid claims. Both of the examples show the IBNR as a percentage of paid premium.

All IBNR formulas, used by insurers to determine amounts they may still owe to group policyholder employees, use a best-guess approach. Most insurers try to eliminate this guess work by basing their formulas on their experiences over their total books of business. Their resulting formulas are applied to almost all of their client groups (except ASO groups). Some insurers only use the formulas when calculating first-year renewals. For second and subsequent year renewals, they use the actual "claims run-off". The claims run-off is the total of the actual benefit's claims which were processed during, generally, the last six weeks to three months (depending on the benefit and the insurer) after the previous renewal date. Using actual "claims run-off" can be more accurate than using IBNR reserve formulas.

The incurred claims formula is important. The more premium required as a result of the formula, the higher your rates will be. Except for the largest of policies, no interest is credited by the insurer, to the IBNR account for the money that it holds in this reserve. In addition, should one cancel the policy, unless there is an underwriting agreement that says otherwise, any money remaining in the reserve after all claims have been paid becomes the property of the insurance company. The idea therefore, as a consumer, is to have the lowest percentage of the premium, or claims, put into this reserve, as is possible.

First year incurred formulas can differ from second and subsequent year renewals. In order to make a fair comparison between insurers, a minimum two years of claims should be reviewed. If you are comparing your present program against a proposed new insurer, you will be comparing your own (second year plus) formula, against the proposed insurer's first year formula. The amounts may differ significantly unless the present insurer and the proposed insurer both use the same formula for first and second plus years.

If the program is self-insured, there will be no need to establish a reserve for incurred claims. This is one of the reasons to self-insure. However, a group may decide to implement an IBNR reserve for a self-insured approach. Without one, there would be no protection for unpaid claims, in the event of the bankruptcy of the employer, or policyholder. The reserve, for a self-insured plan, should be placed in a trust account, especially if it is fully or partially funded with employee money.

Incurred claims in the second plus years, should take the previous year's IBNR reserve into consideration. This is an area which is sometimes overlooked. Once the first year reserve has been established, all that is necessary for future renewals, is to make adjustments to that reserve. These adjustments will be based on the most current year's premium or paid claims. These adjustments should be shown in the renewal calculations. If not, question why! Let us take a look at what this means. Assume that the first year renewal's calculation produced $7,500 as an IBNR reserve. The second year's calculation resulted in a reserve amount of $10,710. The recalculated reserve should not be the two added together. The new reserve will be $10,710, which is $7,500 plus ($10,710 – $7,500) = $3,210, the difference required to top up the reserve. So what is the difference? The difference is in how you look at the reserve. The second year difference is required because premiums increased and the formula is based on premiums. What happens if the second year premium had decreased below the initial $25,000? There should be an adjustment to that first year reserve that actually decreases the total amount held in the reserve. This is where the insurers sometimes fail to provide policyholders with the proper credits to the renewal rates.

The incurred claims formula is an area that is misunderstood by many people in the insurance business, especially certain ABCs. Its importance is often overlooked in the rush to provide a prospective new client with the "best" first year rates that can be shown.

Review the incurred claims formulas shown in Chapter 7, Funding the Benefits (at ¶7100, page 127). Now look at the example renewals presented later in this chapter. In the first-year renewal examples (on pages 208 and 210), "paid" premiums were $25,000, paid claims were $21,000. Insurer 1, from Chapter 7, charges 25 per cent of premium, or $6,250. Insurer 3 charges the higher of 25 per cent of premium, or 25 per cent of paid claims. In this case, Insurer B will charge $6,250, which is the higher amount. Insurer 5 charges 30 per cent of paid claims, or $6,300. We do not know Insurer 2's premium charge for hospital, because it did not provide it, and so cannot come up with an accurate charge for them. (Expect this sort of thing to happen. Insurers often fail to provide information which can be compared easily. This is often because they may second guess what you want, instead of trying to clarify it with you. It may also be because you are dealing with someone who is inexperienced, or that the insurer just does not want to be compared solely on the basis of a spreadsheet.) Insurer 4 also provides us with a formula which cannot readily be compared. We have no way of knowing what the "expected benefits" will be from year to year, because, on the smaller groups, it is based partially on the group's own experience, and partially on the average experience of the insurer's book of business.

Where does this lead us? The formulas in the examples have only a $500 difference in charge. Is it worth this "minor" difference? First of all, $500 over $25,000 is 2 per cent. This may not seem like much, but if it was my money, I would not be so willing to ignore it. A 2 per cent difference, in terms of larger premiums, means a larger dollar cost. On $50,000 of premium, the charge difference is $1,000; on $100,000, the difference amounts to $2,000, and so on. But look at what happens to the various calculated amounts if premiums stayed the same, but claims were $35,000 that year. Insurer 1 still charges $6,250. Insurer 3 now charges 25 per cent of $35,000, or $8,750. Insurer 5's charge will now be 30 per cent of $35,000, or $10,500!

Second year and other future renewals, are far more accurate in terms of where renewal rates should be set, than first year renewals. This is reflected in the fact that some insurers change their incurred formulas after that first renewal. Insurance companies, from time to time, do what they call "run-off studies". A run-off is comprised of the claims that are incurred during one year, but either not submitted, processed or paid by the insurer until after the policy year-end. A run-off study looks at these claims by benefit, for the entire book of business. These studies produce average amounts paid over set time periods. The actuaries then turn these figures into the "incurred" claims, or incurred-but-not-reported (IBNR), reserve formulas. These formulas are usually put in place for the insurers' book of business across the country. Except for the larger policies, it is rare to find an insurer who changes the formula by location. It is not so rare to find an insurer who is willing to set the incurred charge to equal the policy's actual runoff for the previous policy year. The latter is a more accurate method of establishing the reserve.

Can you negotiate with an insurance company to not set up an IBNR reserve? The answer, unless an insured plan covers only a few employees, is yes! It is possible to negotiate with many insurance companies towards calculation of the renewals without using an IBNR charge. The insurer will require the organization to sign an underwriting agreement which states that if the organization cancels the policy, it will reimburse the insurer for any claims that occurred prior to the cancellation but which had not been processed or paid. Is this a risky venture? Not if one considers that these agreements are usually only drawn up for the benefits that are, in effect, comparatively "risk free"; EHC, dental (and occasionally weekly indemnity). There will be a few outstanding claims for smaller amounts, such as prescription drugs, or perhaps a dental bill. The number of claims outstanding can be reduced by sending a letter to all covered employees, before a change of insurers, telling employees to submit their receipts into the old plan immediately. Is there a risk in removing the IBNR reserve? Yes, two in fact. The first is one where an employee has a large claim, which is not submitted in time before the group policy is changed to another insurer. For example an employee might have an out-of-country claim, which has been submitted to the insurer who underwrote a personal travel insurance policy for his last trip. The employee expects the claim to be paid by the travel policy, so does not put a claim in under the group insurance policy. The employee's organization in the meantime, changes group insurers. The claim is denied by the travel insurer two months later because the employee was found to have a pre-existing condition, which was excluded under that plan. (The claim was for an air ambulance and the total bill for everything was U.S.$15,000). If this claim was immediately submitted to the old insurer, and it fell within the time limit in the policy on submitting claims, then the old EHC group insurer would pay the claim, (assuming that out-of-country emergency was covered). With an underwriting agreement, the insurer would pay the claim and bill your organization for the amount and other outstanding claims subject to the terms of the agreement, plus service charges. Without an underwriting agreement, the IBNR reserve would cover the claim. If the claim was greater than the reserve, the insurance company would "eat the loss". If the claim was not submitted to the old insurer within the allotted time frames, and there was not an underwriting agreement in place, there is the potential that the claim would not be paid at all.

The second potential problem pertaining to the use of an underwriting agreement, can occur when a policyholder knows that it has a high number of outstanding claims and is considering changing insurers. Without an underwriting agreement, it can send in all of those claims to the old insurer immediately prior to the change, or shortly thereafter. Those claims are paid for by the IBNR and any loss is not billed to the policyholder. (In effect, these claims never show up in the experience, except as a loss for the old insurer. The new insurer will not know that they ever occurred.) If there is an underwriting agreement, then the employer can be billed for these claims. Of course the way to avoid this is to negotiate with the insurance company, when setting up the underwriting agreement, to not charge any late claims in the event of policy cancellation, (to "eat the loss", in other words).

¶11,080 Retention

Retention is the insurance company word for "How Much Do We Receive?" for providing our services. Literally it means, how much premium does the insurance company "retain". Insurers split retention into its component parts on larger accounts. The component parts making up the retention are identical, in terms of the services provided, on both smaller and larger policies. The difference is that on the smaller policies, the insurers do not show it broken down into its parts. They just provide the total retention as a percentage of premium or of claims.

Retention is comprised of the following: claims handling charges, administration charges, contingency charges, acquisition charges, taxes and commissions. These charges are generally shown as percentages of the premium, but there may be flat or level dollar charges for things such as the policy acquisition charge. Insurance companies express each of the charges in different ways. Because of these differences in approach, retention charges can be difficult to compare. The difficulty causes ABCs to sometimes overlook or to ignore the overall cost of the retention, in a policy, when comparing insurers. But these differences can have a substantial impact on the rates in the second plus years of the policy. In fact, for health, dental and WI policies, the retention is as important, if not more important, than the rates themselves!

Insurance companies occasionally increase the retention percentage that they charge for providing their services. An increase in retention is a proper reason to shop around to test the competitiveness of the insurer/provider's services.

Claims Handling Charges

Claims handling charges are what the insurance company charges to cover its costs of paying the claims. The charges include the costs of providing the claim forms, the cost of reviewing the claims, the cost of collecting missing information required to pay the claims, the cost of adjudicating the claims, the cost of the systems, the overhead costs, and the staffing costs. The claims handling charge is expressed in one of three ways: as a percentage of paid claims, as a percentage of incurred claims, or as a percentage of paid premium.

Administration Charges

Administration charges cover the cost of compiling and maintaining records, mailing statements and bills, issuing booklets, providing forms, providing reports, and answering written and phone enquiries. This charge is almost always expressed as a percentage of paid premium.

Contingency Charges

"Contingency" charges, in a retention formula, can mean several different things. It can be a portion of the premium, usually expressed as a percentage of premium, set aside to cover some contingency, such as a "catastrophic claim" (for example where several employees become ill overseas and require air medical evacuation. The cost can be in the tens of thousands of dollars). But in group retention formulas, a contingency reserve can mean "insurer profit". It is also sometimes referred to as a "risk" or "margin" charge. The profit charge can be between one and 3 per cent of premium, depending on the size of the group.

Taxes

There is a "hidden" tax in the retention formulas used by insurance companies. These taxes are usually 2 to 3 per cent of premium (except for Quebec, where the tax is currently 9 per cent of premium), depending on the province, and are paid to provincial governments. If the provincial governments increase this tax then the retention will increase and the rates will go up.

In some provinces, so-called "not-for-profit" health insurance benefit providers, such as Blue Cross, are not required to pay this tax, and therefore do not have to charge it to their clients. All life insurance companies have to pay the tax. At present, there are no federal taxes directly assessed on group insurance programs (see Chapter 14, Taxation).

Acquisition Charges

Acquisition charges are the costs to set up a new policy, or a new benefit for the policy. They cover the costs to issue the policy , the amendments, and the employee booklets. Some insurers may also include the amounts which they pay to their group representatives as sales bonuses, in the retention, although this is rare. Most insurers pay the bonuses from their marketing budgets. Acquisition charges differ between insurers. Some insurers say, up front, that they have acquisition charges, and they express these as flat dollar amounts. Others "hide" the charges in the administration costs. ABCs, sometimes, when negotiating with potential new insurers, ask the new insurers to waive acquisition charges. Insurance companies may sometimes do this if they are close on the rates and want to be more competitive. Acquisition charges are not universally waived, however.

Commission Charges

Commission charges can be a large component of the overall retention. Commission scales vary between the insurers, as do their subsequent effects on the rates. Up until the late 1970s, insurers paid what is now referred to as a "high/low" commission scale. This meant that the percentages paid as commissions were higher in the first year than they were in the following years. This was to reflect the fact that the majority of an ABC's work takes place in the first year, during the marketing of the policy. However, some ABCs took advantage of these schedules in order to keep getting the higher commission scale. They did this by convincing the policyholders that they had to shop the policy every year or two to obtain the best rates. What they did not say, was that the clients had as much chance of losing money because of the need to keep funding first year IBNR reserves, as they did of saving it by getting lower rates! In order to combat this tendency for ABCs to keep shopping the market, insurance companies started to introduce level commission scales. "Level commission" means that the insurer pays the same commission scale every year that the policy stays on the insurer's books. The level scale is not as high in the first policy year as the older high/low scales, but is higher in the second and subsequent years, and still produces a healthy income for those in the business. Although these scales are level, the actual break points, in the scales, for each level of premium, have remained the same for many years. Due to inflation, these premium break points have actually reduced the commissions paid, in "real" terms, resulting in small savings to the policyholders, all at the expense of the ABCs. A commission breakpoint is the level of premium at which the commission percentage paid reduces.

Another type of commission that is not generally documented in the retention statements, is the "conservation bonus". This is a bonus paid to an ABC as an incentive to keep the policy on the books with that insurer. The bonuses can either be expressed as a percentage of the premium, or as a percentage of the commission. In the latter case, the bonus can be paid based on just the one case by itself, or on the total commissions paid on all of the business that that ABC has with the specific insurer. These bonuses are rarely seen by the policyholders, but they do affect how ABCs look at any specific policy. The bonuses are an inducement to conserve the business on the books for the insurance company. It is obvious then that ABCs can be induced to maintain business with one insurer, when there may be better products or services on the market. This is especially true where the bonus scale increases every year that the policy stays with the insurer.

Is this bad? On the one hand, changing insurers can cause a policyholder to lose the IBNR, which is detrimental in most cases. On the other hand, staying with an insurer, without full knowledge of other products and services on the market, because the ABC may be unduly influenced by a bonus scale, is not the healthiest of situations either. This is one of the reasons to shop the market every three to five years or so. Review of the renewal process should be an integral part of any group insurance marketing. You will want to convince yourself, and your organization, that the plan is the best available which suits the organization's needs.

Credibility

This is one of the most misunderstood terms in the insurance industry. The concept of credibility means that a particular group insurance policy's experience can only be "believed" to a certain extent. For example, if we have ten groups, each having ten employees, and one of the employees in one of the groups dies, how should the renewal be treated to be fair to that one group? The choices are to: (1) increase just the one group's rate and leave everyone else the same; (2) increase all the groups' rates proportionally; or (3) review this one death in comparison to all of the insurer's experience and see how "credible" it is, over two, three or more years. So the insurance industry says, "How much credibility can we attach to that one death?" How does the experience of this one group compare to the experience in our overall book of policies? Credibility is a method of "smoothing" experience. The credibility formulas used by the insurers can change from year to year. The insurance companies are not generally requested to disclose their credibility formulas, so comparisons are rarely performed, except for the largest, experience rated cases.

Life insurance credibility is generally expressed as follows: "10 per cent credible after 500 life years", meaning that if there is a group of 5,000 employees who are insured for one year, then the insurance company would assess "all" life insurance claims occurring in that group in that year against the policy. A group of 5,000 employees would be 100 per cent credible.

EHC and dental credibility is typically expressed as being "100 per cent credible at 100 lives", meaning that if the group has 100 employees, all of the claims that occurred in that group's benefit will be assessed against that group's experience. At 100 employees, the experience, for those benefits, will not be adjusted by the average experience of other groups in the same size range. If there are only 33 employees, that group's experience, after three years, might be considered as "100 per cent credible" by some insurers. Confusing the matter even more, is the fact that insurers themselves have different definitions and formulas on how they calculate credibility, and what they mean by "pools" and "pooling". Credibility formulas are applied to certain groups within the pool in an attempt to compensate for the difference in sizes between the largest and smallest.

If the insurer's overall experience, in its "pools", is worse than the experience of a particular group in the pool, (see the example renewal formula for Insurance Company B later in the chapter, at ¶11,115), then the individual group with "good" experience will be affected by the poor experience of the group as a whole. The result is that the rates will go up even farther than they would if the one group's experience was "100 per cent credible"! If the group has a history of good claims experience being negatively affected by the rest of the groups in the "pool", it is a good reason to market the plan.

You may have noted in the example for Insurance Company B, a factor called "expected benefits". Insurance companies, for smaller premium accounts, put all of the premiums for all of the groups in the smaller group category, into the "pool". Claims and expenses, etc. come out of the pool. The reason for pooling is that smaller groups might have great difficulty in paying for rate increases if their employees had very high claims in any particular year. By pooling, an insurance company can smooth out the occasional large fluctuations that occur in group claims from time to time. This "smoothing out" can be very useful to a group that has high claims. It can also be detrimental to a group which has few or no claims. In the example of insurer B, this particular insurer has placed this group in a type of semi-pooling arrangement. Part of the experience that is charged against this group has come from the other groups in the pool. This method of funding is called partially experience rating. This smoothing out of the experience and the rates is also called "credibility". In the situation of Insurance Company B, we see an example of how pooling can actually work against the policyholder. In this situation, B's experience is better than the average experience for groups of this size as a whole. Therefore the insurance company increases the claims for this particular group so that they match the insurance company model. The policyholder loses as a result because the insurer, when doing the renewal, arbitrarily increases the actual claims. The result is higher renewal rates for the policyholder. Of course, this can work in reverse as well, with actual experience being worse than the pool, and the rate increases being lower than they would have been. It is preferable for organizations which more carefully control their programs and experience to reap the benefits of this care and receive the renewal rates obtained solely from their own experience.

If an insurance company tries to increase the EHC, dental or WI rates because of the "poorer" experience of their pools, a policyholder, or the ABC, should review the increases with the insurer's group representative. If the experience has been better than the pool for three years, and the rates have continued to increase, add your last three years of paid claims together, and divide it by sum of the last three years of paid premium. Work out the renewal using the formula used by Insurance Company A, but excluding the inflation factor. If the overall percentage is under 85 per cent, then you may, depending on the size of of your group, have a good case to ask the underwriters to take another look at the renewal. Underwriters, depending on their experience, realize that they have to be flexible in order to take care of their policyholders' needs. They sometimes will revise their initial rates if it is pointed out that the experience over a three-year period does not point to the size of their requested increase.

¶11,085 NEGOTIATING RENEWALS: PLOTS AND PLOYS

Insurers and ABCs are in business to make a profit. There is nothing wrong with making a profit, but policyholders want an insurer to make a reasonable profit. Policyholders do not want an insurer, ABC, or any other company for that matter, to make an exorbitant profit just from them! Even the "not-for-profit" benefit providers are in business to stay in business. Group insurance renewal costs can be at least partially controlled by paying attention to the following:

1. Many group insurance offices are "profit centres". Their representatives are reimbursed partially on renewing rates at the "correct rates". Group offices and group representatives, who are responsible for calculating renewals, can amend the renewal rates to provide themselves, or their offices, with an extra cushion. Having a good relationship with the representatives may help an organization to obtain the fairest rates. Shopping for quotes every three to five years will also tend to keep the rates more competitive.

2. Agents, brokers and consultants negotiate renewals for you, but if they are on a commission basis, the higher the rates, the more they make. If an organization is reimbursing the agent, broker or consultant on a fee for service basis, the more complicated that they make the renewal, the more they can charge, especially if they are on an hourly charge basis. Organizations should negotiate a firm package price to negotiate a renewal, if paying for ABC services on a fee-only basis.

3. Consultants, and sometimes agents or brokers, will occasionally charge fees and still collect commissions. This is acceptable if the commissions offset the fees. In no case should an ABC collect commissions without full disclosure to the policyholder.

4. As insurance companies and benefit providers have their own "lingo", it is often difficult to understand exactly what they are saying. When discussing the renewal with the ABC or group representative, it pays to have an understanding of the language, and a knowledge of how the benefits are rated.

5. Policyholders have a right to disclosure of what claims and what premiums were paid during the policy year. Occasionally, this is withheld by insurers or ABCs.

6. Policyholders have the option to appeal the renewal with the present insurers and benefit providers. Underwriters are generally willing to amend the renewal rates if they are provided with a reason to do so. These reasons can be as varied as the reasons to change the rates in the first place. Examples of valid reasons are recent changes in your employee

data, the resignation or retirement of an employee who had a history of high claims, the recovery from illness of an employee or dependant, a change in occupations of the employees, the implementation of an employee/family assistance program, a change in the hiring practices of the policyholder, the retirement of older employees, changing the numbers of males or females in the group, and the implementation of higher deductibles. There are many other reasons, including proving, by means of a competitive marketing, that the rates, or retention formulas are no longer competitive.

Remember that it may not be necessary to change providers just because one or two of the rates have gone up, or not been reduced as much as anticipated. All it may take is to provide the underwriter with a reason to review the initial renewal decision.

¶11,090 Information Needed to Calculate a Renewal

As a minimum, a renewal calculation requires specific information to be provided, as part of a renewal package: (1) paid premiums; (2) paid or cash claims; (3) incurred claims; (4) incurred but not reported claims reserve formulas; (5) retention percentages; (6) break-even formulas; (7) inflation or trend factors; (8) dates of the experience and rate information; and (9) rates. Renewal information is often provided to the ABC directly by the insurer. The ABC reviews, questions and renegotiates the rates on the policyholder's behalf. The ABC can also be at liberty to negotiate discounts on behalf of a group policyholder and, occasionally, insurers provide ABCs with the latitude to increase rates. If the ABC is inexperienced or wishes to hide facts, the information provided to the policyholder may not contain everything necessary to check the calculations. Renewal information is generally available directly from the insurance company's local group offices. Some offices have this information on hand, while others have to obtain it from their group underwriting departments. Any organization can obtain information directly from the insurer's group office, or at last resort, directly from the group underwriting department of the insurance company. The best route is to go through the group office. It is not necessary to go through the ABC, although (unless you direct them otherwise) the group office will contact the ABC to find out if there is a problem.

¶11,095 Renewal Checklist

The following renewal information should be provided by the insurance company, benefit provider, either directly to the policyholder, or to the policyholder through the agent, broker, or consultant. Depending on the size of the group, the insurers and providers may not release the information. The smallest groups usually receive the least amount of information.

1. Paid claims and paid premiums plus dates applicable for the previous policy year. ☐
2. Incurred claims for the previous year. ☐
3. Experience by employee classification. ☐
4. Rate comparison showing the previous year's and the proposed renewal rates plus the effective dates. ☐
5. Retention breakdown by benefit for EHC, dental and WI. ☐
6. Trend (or inflation), and utilization charges. ☐
7. Identification of pooled rate increases. ☐
8. Three-year experience history for WI. ☐
9. LTD open claims information. ☐
10. Life insurance and life insurance waiver of premium claims. ☐
11. Individual employee claim reports (may or may not be identifiable by name or number). ☐
12. Claim reports split by benefit procedures and claim type. ☐
13. Ideas on, and rates for, claims control or benefit enhancements. ☐
14. Details on any exceptionally large individual claims such as out-of-country claims. ☐
15. A nominal list of employees on the plan at the renewal calculation date. ☐
16. A volume/age comparison showing the previous year's and the current renewal data for life and LTD. ☐
17. A review of any financial agreements and their present appropriateness. ☐
18. Contact names and telephone/fax numbers. ☐
19. A minimum of 45 days, before the rate changes are implemented, in which to review and negotiate changes. ☐

If the insurer, benefit provider, agent, broker or consultant does not supply renewal information, use the following sample letter as a format to obtain it.

¶11,100 Sample Letter Used to Obtain Renewal Information for Use by Groups Not Using an ABC

Corporate Letterhead

Date:________

Mr./Ms. Group Representative
123 Somenice Street,
Anytown, Province
Postal Code

Re: Group Policy Number(s) ________

Dear Group Representative,

Our organization is currently conducting a review of our benefit program requirements. Please provide us with the following information per benefit and the dates applicable: paid premium, paid claims, incurred claims, retention percentage, IBNR reserve formulas and inflation factors. It would also assist us, if you could provide us with copies of claims reports per benefit, both by individual claimant, and by claim type. This information is required by (*date: two-week deadline*) ________.

Your truly

Name, Title

¶11,110 Renewal Formulas

Every insurance company, operating in Canada, has its own formula for renewing group insurance rates. These formulas often look like a witches brew; full of murky, seemingly unintelligible words and a hodgepodge of numbers. The underwriters and actuaries are partially to blame for the mess. When pressed for growth and profitability by senior management, in an industry where margins can be very thin, reinterpretations of numbers has become a fine art. As competition for business is still keen today, variations on these formulas continue to show up.

¶11,115 Renewal Examples

Renewal Formula 1 is the easiest and quickest method of checking a renewal. It can be used, at any time provided that the premiums, and the claims are provided for corresponding periods. It is especially useful to a policyholder for budget purposes. Renewal Formula 2, provided for comparison purposes, is more difficult to use for a quick comparison, because of its complexity.

Renewal Formula 1: Insurance Company A

To obtain the rate change:

$$\frac{\text{Incurred Claims (\#4)} \times \text{Trend (\#7)}}{\text{Premiums (\#1)} - [\text{Retention \% (\#5)} \times \text{Premiums (\#1)}]} = \text{Rate Change (\#7)}$$

Key		*Definition*
#1.	Premiums	Amount paid for the benefit over the year.
#2.	Cash claims	Amount paid out in cash by the insurer.
#3.	IBNR reserve	Amount thought to be claimed but not submitted.
#4.	Incurred claims	Total of cash claims (#2) plus IBNR (#3).
#5.	Retention	Total insurer expenses as a per cent of premium.
#6.	Trend	Inflation in the benefit coverage area.
#7.	Rate change	Percentage rates should be increased/decreased.

This is one of the least complicated renewal formulas. Let us review this formula with a step-by-step approach. If reviewing your own organization's renewal, obtain the above amounts from your insurance company or ABC. Remember that this formula is only used for health or dental benefits. The formula can be used for weekly indemnity (WI) benefits, except that there is no need to apply a "trend factor" (#6 above). WI is usually reviewed using total premiums and total claims for the last three policy years, instead of just one year's experience.

Step-by-Step Approach to Renewals: Insurance Company A

Step 1. Write down the annual paid premium for the benefit.

Step 2. Multiply the paid premium amount times the retention percentage. This will be your retention cost.

Step 3. Calculate the IBNR for the benefit from the IBNR formula, or obtain this figure from the insurer. If this is not available, ask the insurer for the "incurred claims" figure and subtract the cash claims from it. The result will be the IBNR reserve.

Step 4. Add the IBNR to the cash claims. This result will be the incurred claims figure.

Step 5. Subtract the retention cost, obtained in step 2 above, from the paid premium. The result will be the "net" (after insurer expenses) premium.

Step 6. Divide the incurred claims, obtained in step 4, by the net premium, obtained in step 5. The result will be the percentage rate change before the inflation (trend) factors are added.

Step 7. Multiply the inflation factor times 15 and then divide by 12, to account for the three-month delay after the policy year-end, and before the new rates go into effect (if the insurer uses a three-month delayed accounting method).

Step 8. Multiply the per cent rate change figure from step 6, times the adjusted inflation factor from step 7. The result will be the undiscounted percentage that will be applied to your old rates to obtain the renewal rates.

Example of a First Year Renewal: Insurance Company (A) EHC Benefit

Paid premium	$25,000
Paid claims	$21,000
IBNR	$ 6,250
Total paid claims + IBNR	$27,250
Incurred claims	$27,250
Retention (as percentage of premium)	22%
Retention (.22 × 25,000)	$ 5,500
Inflation (trend) factor	15%
Inflation factor adjusted (15% × 15 ÷ 12)	18.75

Calculation of rate change:

Renewal rate increase required is +65.94%

$$\frac{27{,}250 \times 1.1875}{25{,}000 - 5{,}500} = 165.94\%$$

Interpretation of the First Year Renewal Example: Insurance Company A

1. The insurance company is responsible for paying claims which occur during the policy year. Not all claims which happen, are submitted during that year. The insurer is still responsible for paying those claims, within certain time limits, and has to account for this when determining the renewal rate. Hence, the establishment of the IBNR reserve. (Set up of an underwriting agreement to have the policyholder fund any deficits at year-end, or at policy cancellation, may preclude the need for an IBNR.)

2. The IBNR is added to the actual paid claims for the policy year. The result is called the incurred claims.

3. Paid claims is defined as what has been submitted, processed and paid. It includes cheques that have been issued during the last policy year.

4. The inflation (trend) factor is the percentage the insurance company has determined that average claims will increase over the next year due to inflation. They calculate this figure by looking at previous years' increases and taking into consideration recent and announced changes to Medicare, the cost of prescription drugs etc.

5. The adjusted inflation accounts for the three-month delay, after policy year-end before making the new rates effective.

6. The retention percentage takes into consideration taxes, commissions, cost of administration, and cost of paying claims.

7. The insurance company has calculated, that if the renewal rates are increased by (165.94% – 100%) = 65.94%, it will "break even".

8. The insurance company will attempt to put in an increase of as close to 65.94 per cent as it thinks the policyholder organization will accept. In

many cases, group offices will use whatever marketing discounts are at their disposal, usually in the range of 5 to 15 per cent. The actual increase may, therefore, be lower than the calculated rate change percentage.

Example of a Second or Subsequent Year Renewal: Insurance Company A

Paid premium	$35,700
Paid claims	$24,150
IBNR	$10,710
IBNR (previous year)	$ 7,500

Adjustment to the IBNR ($10,710 – $7,500 = $3,210)

Incurred claims		= $(24,150 + 3,210)	= $27,360
Retention (as percentage of premium)		= 21%	
Retention (.21 × 35,700)		= $ 7,497	
Inflation (trend) factor		= 15%	
Adjusted inflation factor (15% × 15 ÷ 12)		= 18.75%	
Calculation of rate change:	Step 1.	$\frac{27,360}{35,700 - 7,497}$	= 97.01%
	Step 2.	97.01 × 1.1875	= 115.2%

The resulting increase in rates would be: (115.2 – 100 =) + 15.2% before insurer/provider marketing considerations (i.e., marketing discounts).

Interpretation of the Second Year Renewal Example: Insurance Company A

1. The IBNR reserve was recalculated as a percentage of paid premium as it was in the first year. The insurance company will subtract the previous year's IBNR from the current year IBNR The balance will be added to the paid claims figure to produce the incurred claims figure for this renewal.

2. The retention was reduced as a percentage of premium, from the previous year, due to the increase in premium.

3. For the purpose of the example, the inflation factor remained the same as the previous year. Inflation factors may vary from year to year.

Renewal Formula # 2: Insurer B

Example of a First Year Renewal Formula: Insurance Company B

Paid premium (Adjusted)	$25,000
Paid claims	$21,000
Incurred claims	$26,880
Inflation (trend) factor	1.177
Trended claims	$31,638
Expected benefits	$34,426
Pooling charge	$0
Margin	$0
Estimated expenses	$6,250
Required premium	$40,676
Renewal action	+ 62.7%

Key	*Definition*
1. Paid premium (adjusted)	Amount paid for the benefit for nine months, multiplied by 12 and divided by nine to approximate one year's premium.
2. Paid claims	Amount paid out in cash by the insurer.
3. Incurred claims	Paid claims plus amount thought to be claimed but not submitted (IBNR).
4. Inflation (trend) factor	Inflation in the benefit coverage area.
5. Trended claims	Incurred claims multiplied by the inflation (trend) factor. Notice that this trend factor is expressed differently than the example for insurance company A.

6. Expected benefits	The claims that the insurance company expects to pay out on a "typical" group of this size. This figure can only be calculated by the insurance company. It is based partially on what percentage of the actual paid claims the insurance company thinks is "credible", or real, for this group. The remaining is made up of what percentage of the claims for a typical group of this size the insurer thinks is "credible". In this case, 61 per cent credibility was given to the actual paid claims, while 39 per cent credibility was given to the typical group's experience.
7. Pooling charge	A charge, usually a percentage of premium, which can be used to offset any large claims. You are, in effect, insuring your insurance against any large claims. Here, this option had not been chosen, so the charge is nil.
8. Margin	Insurance company word for profit. In this example, the profit percentage is combined into the "estimated expenses".
9. Estimated expenses	Total insurer expenses as a per cent of premium. Another expression for "retention". Includes administration charges, claims payment charges, taxes, and commissions.
10. Required premium	Premium insurer thinks will be necessary for next year. Required premium is the sum of the expected benefits plus the pooling charge plus the margin plus the estimated expenses.
11. Renewal action	Percentage the current rates will be increased to pay next year's claims and expenses.

Step-by-Step to Renewals: Insurance Company B

Step 1. Insurance company B uses the total first nine months of the policy year's paid premium and grosses it up by, 12 divided by 9, to approximate the premium for the year.

Step 2. The premium is multiplied by the target loss ratio (similar to the break-even-loss-ratio) (75 per cent in this case) and then multiplied by the incurred claims factor (28 per cent of premium in this case).

Step 3. Multiply the incurred claims by the inflation factor to obtain what the insurance company believes will be the claims for the next year.

Step 4. Because this is a smaller group, the insurance company use a credibility formula to blend the trended claims to what they think will be typical for a group of this size. In this particular case, the insurance company has allocated 61 per cent credibility to the group's own experience, and 39 per cent credibility to what it thinks should be the average benefit. The resulting figure is called *expected benefits*. There is no way to verify whether or not the credibility formula is accurate. As a client of this insurer, you will have to believe that the insurer is giving you the best possible break.

Step 5. There are no pooling charges, or margin charges in the renewal, as shown. An example of a pooling charge would be if you wanted to insure your benefit against any large claims of over $10,000. For a fee, usually expressed as a percentage of premium, the insurance company will not charge your policy with any single claims over a set amount (i.e., over $10,000). Also, in this particular renewal, the insurer is not showing any "margin", or profit, charge.

Step 6. Estimated expenses is this insurer's term for retention. In the example, retention is 25 per cent of required premium. To obtain this figure, multiply the required premium by 0.25.

Step 7. Add the Expected Benefits, plus the pooling charge ($0), plus the margin ($0), plus the estimated expenses. The result will be the required premium.

Step 8. Divide the required premium by the adjusted premium. The result will be the percentage increase (or decrease as the case may be) to the current rates.

Other Formulas for Experience Rated Calculation Methods

[The following is taken from *A Course in Group Life & Health Insurance*, Part B, Appendix J, pages 311–313, 1985, and is reproduced with the permission of the Health Insurance Association of America, Washington, D.C.]

APPENDIX J

EXAMPLES OF EXPERIENCE RATED CALCULATION METHODS

Although various methods are used in developing the total amount of premium required with respect to any particular experience rated group, three general methods will be explored in this text. All three take into account each of the elements of the premium discussed in this chapter, namely, expected future claims; margin for higher than anticipated claims; expected future expenses; and the insurer's surplus objective.

For purposes of simplicity, expenses and contribution to surplus are often combined in the premium rate formula and are referred to by the term **"retention,"** which indicates amounts that will be retained by the insurer for items other than claims charged to the group. Retention can be broken down into constant and variable charges. "Constant retention" consists of charges which are independent of the size of the group's premium, such as a flat charge to provide for the establishment of records needed to pay claims for each group or for the drafting of an employee booklet. "Variable retention" applies to retention items which are related to the premium charged for the group, such as taxes and commissions. "Margin," in the following formula, refers to the margin for higher than anticipated claim results.

Desired Loss Ratio Method

The first general method for developing the required premium for groups eligible for experience refunds, known as the Desired Loss Ratio Method, is shown below:

$$\text{Required Premium} = \frac{\text{Expected Claims}}{1 - (\text{Margin \%}) - (\text{\% of Required Premium for Total Retention})}$$

In this equation, the numerator reflects the dollar amount of Expected Claims. The denominator represents the "desired loss ratio" e.g. the loss ratio needed to produce premiums adequate to cover claims, margin, expenses and the insurer's contribution to surplus or profit. This method develops the dollar amount of premium needed and is illustrated by the following example:

Assumptions:

Expected Claims	=	$200,000
Margin	=	7%
Total Retention	=	13%

Experience Rating Calculation:

$$\text{Required Premium} = \frac{\$200{,}000}{1-.07-.13} = \frac{\$200{,}000}{.80} = \$250{,}000$$

Each element of the premium may be separately identified as follows:

Expected Claims	=			$200,000
Margin	=	(.07) ($250,000)	=	17,500
Total Retention	=	(.13) ($250,000)	=	32,500
Required Premium				$250,000

INCURRED LOSS RATIO METHOD

A second method which derives the required rate increase directly is known as the Incurred Loss Ratio Method. The formula is demonstrated below.

$$\text{Required Premium Rate Increase} = \frac{(\text{Incurred Loss Ratio})\ (\text{Trend})\ (\text{Margin})}{1-\ (\%\ \text{of Required Premium for Total Retention})}$$

The Incurred Loss Ratio in the numerator reflects the ratio of total claims to total premiums during the previous rating period. By increasing this ratio by the expected trend, the insurer arrives at the loss ratio that can be expected to emerge in the coming rating period. A margin is added to the numerator to protect the insurer from higher than anticipated claims.

The denominator reflects the loss ratio needed for the group to break even e.g. the loss ratio required to produce premiums adequate to cover claims, expenses and the insurer's contribution to surplus or profit.

Dividing the expected loss ratio (numerator) by the loss ratio required to break even results in the required premium rate increase. This second method produces a percentage rate increase, whereas the first method develops the dollar amount of premium needed.

SPLIT RETENTION METHOD

The third general method also used for developing the required premium for groups eligible for experience refunds is:

Required Premium =Expected Claims + Margin + Constant Retention items
+ % Required Premium for Retention Items Based on Premiums

This may be written as:

$$\text{Required Premium} = \frac{\text{(Expected Claims) (1 + Margin \%) + Constant Retention, items}}{\text{1 – (\% of Required Premium for Retention items Based on Premiums)}}$$

In this method the retention is separated into constant and variable expenses. Constant expenses are reflected in the numerator and variable expenses are in the denominator. This formula produces the dollar amount of premium needed.

CHAPTER 12

¶12,000 YOUR RIGHTS

¶12,005 KNOW YOUR RIGHTS

Employers, employees, dependants, beneficiaries, agents, brokers, consultants and insurance companies all have responsibilities and "rights" under Canadian group insurance policies. Policies are legal "contracts", and as such are subject to contract law. Contracts spell out the "rights" and obligations of all parties. The purpose of this chapter is to briefly touch on those rights.

¶12,010 INSURER RIGHTS

As a party named in the group insurance contract, the insurance company has certain rights which are spelled out in that contract. Insurers have the following rights to:

1. Be provided with accurate information so that they can adequately assess the risks involved, assess the validity of claims, and set the rates appropriately.

2. Inspect group policyholders' payroll (and other) records to assess the eligibility of employees (this is usually specified in the policy).

3. Adjudicate claims as per the terms of their policies.

4. Underwrite and to decline business.

5. Decline to renew policies.

6. Sell all of, or a part of, their book of group clients to another benefit provider. A "book" of group insurance policies refers to a section or to a portfolio of policies.

7. Refuse to deal with a specific ABC (agent, broker, or consultant) and refuse to quote on any specific group.

8. Deal only in those locations which are allowed by law and in which proper services can be provided.

9. Change underwriting procedures, reserve formulas, interest credit formulas, retention formulas, benefit wording (with the signature of the president or CEO), underwriting guidelines, commission scales on future business, service procedures, service staff, and service locations.

10. Change internal administration procedures.

11. Invest the moneys in their pools as the insurers see fit (and as permitted by law).

12. Increase or decrease rates at any time (although rates have historically changed only at renewal or when a benefit is amended, or when there is an increase in Provincial Dental Association fee guides or taxes).

13. Decline coverage for any amount over the non-medical maximum coverages if the employee cannot pass medical underwriting approval.

14. Cancel benefits for employees who are "not actively at work", such as during a strike.

Insurers *do not* have the right to:

1. Change benefits or benefit wording in the middle of the policy year without the written permission of the policyholder, except as required by law.

2. Change an "Agent of Record" without the written permission of the policyholder (unless the agent represents only one insurer and the agent leaves the employ of the insurer).

3. Pay commissions to anyone other than to the Agent of Record; group representatives' bonuses and managers' overrides excepted.

4. Change the retention percentages charged in the middle of the policy year, unless agreed to in writing by the policyholder. Rate recalculations required as a result of changes in premium generated by an increase or decrease in total enrolment, the addition or deletion of a classification of employees, the addition or deletion of a benefit, the addition or deletion of an affiliated group under the eligibility clause of the policy, or a change in required premium taxes, would be exceptions.

5. Use specific policyholder reserves for anything other than what has been agreed to in the policy or in the underwriting agreement. The exception is in "pooled" situations where investments are (supposed to be) restricted by law.

6. Withhold from, or not supply employee booklets to the employer or group policyholder.

7. Release any personal and confidential employee information, including claims information, that is identifiable by employee. This is according to the recently revised Canadian Life and Health Insurance Association (CLHIA) guidelines, to which all life insurance companies (but not necessarily the "non-profit" benefit providers) are members (see Appendices at ¶17,050). There are situations, such as renewals, where it may be in the best interests of the "group as a whole" to have the employer or the ABC review all claims, including the identification of specific high claims users. This review would be for the purposes of identifying specific benefits that require claims control, and to identify areas of possible fraud. Anyone looking at this information would be subject to the privacy and confidentiality rules detailed in the CLHIA guidelines. However, technically, individual claims review is not allowed under those current guidelines except by the insurer's claims department.

¶12,015 POLICYHOLDER RIGHTS

Policyholders (or employers) have the right to the following:

1. Determine the design of the benefit program.

2. Determine which benefits are to be included, if this meets underwriting approval.

3. Determine the method of funding to be used, if this meets underwriting approval.

4. Determine the premium share between the employer and the employees.

5. Cancel the policy at any time and not replace it, unless specific employment contracts, union, or employee association agreements say otherwise. Employees will have to be advised immediately in order that they have the chance to convert their group life insurance benefits to personal life insurance policies.

6. Change insurers at any time, as long as no employee loses group life insurance coverage.

7. Change the premium sharing arrangement with the employees at any time.

8. Change the "Agent of Record" at any time. Smaller policyholders using a "captive" agent may only be able to change to another agent within that insurance company, if they wish to retain their policy with that specific insurer. All others can change at any time to whomever they wish. Commissions cannot be paid to people who are not licensed to receive commissions in the province where the group policyholder is located. (This is usually where the head office of the policyholder is located.)

9. Collect and remit the employee share of the premium.

10. Expect that the insurer will deliver the services and pay the claims as per the terms of the policy, any amendments, and anything promised verbally or specified in writing by the (salaried) insurance company representatives (not to be confused with the ABCs).

11. Receive and keep refunds of premium without refunding to the employees their share. Refunds may be accomplished in the form of a "premium holiday", where employees remain insured but are not required to contribute to premiums for a specified period.

12. Cancel or stop paying premiums for benefits when employees are not "actively at work", such as during a strike, except as required by law.

Policyholders (or employers) *do not* have the right to:

1. Cancel or change benefits without immediately informing the employees.

2. Cancel the policy without warning the employees.

3. Take money from employees to pay for premiums and then using the money for other purposes, or not remit it at all.

4. Deceive the employees into thinking that they have group insurance coverage when there is none in place.

5. Withhold premiums from the insurance company thereby jeopardizing employee coverage and causing suspension of claims.

6. Release or otherwise use any personal or confidential employee information in respect to any coverage, any claims information, or any specific claim, except to the insurance company that is underwriting the group insurance policy.

¶12,020 EMPLOYEE RIGHTS

Employees have the right to:

1. A say in the design of benefits for which they are paying (although this is rarely exercised and may not be legally enforceable).

2. Expect notification of any change to benefit wording within a reasonable time period, and preferably, before a change takes place.

3. Be provided with copies of a current employee booklet.

4. Expect the employer to make proper deductions and to remit the premiums in a timely manner so as not to jeopardize the policy or the claim payments.

5. Change their own revocable beneficiaries in the life insurance benefit at any time (not available in Quebec without the permission of the current beneficiary).

6. Expect that an employer is looking after the employees' best interests in terms of setting up coverage and handling the funding of the benefits in a judicious manner that represents the best interests of all concerned parties. (Note that this is rarely challenged by employees.)

7. Expect the employer to enroll employees on time so as not to cause a delay in the employee or dependant coverage, or the possible declination of that coverage. (This can be avoided if the policy is set up on a "condition of employment, backcharge" basis. The employer advises the insurer, in writing, that all future employees will have to join the group insurance plan. Declinations by new employees will not be allowed. The insurer agrees to cover, without medical examinations, all employees who might slip through the cracks, and not be enrolled on time, for whatever reason. Coverage is subject to payment of premiums back to the original date that the employee, or dependant would have been eligible. This is an excellent way to make sure that no one will miss enrolment.)

8. Privacy and confidentiality of all personal information and all information which pertains to their claims or the claims of their dependants. No information that is attributable to or identifiable with a specific employee can be released without the employee's, or the dependent spouse's, written permission.

9. Decline coverage, unless the policy's administration is set up by the employer, on a "condition of employment" basis. A refusal card must be signed and dated by the employee, and submitted to the insurer. Employees who decline coverage must be able to pass a medical evidence test for insurability, should they or their dependants subsequently wish to join the plan. The insurer retains the right to decline coverage for all employees and their dependants who refuse coverage.

Employees *do not* have the right to:

1. Jeopardize coverage for themselves, their dependants, or other employees by refusing to sign required group insurance documents, or by refusing or ignoring their duties in respect to the administration of the

group insurance plan. Employees who refuse to join benefits plans for religious reasons can do so upon providing evidence to the employer of the reasons for their objection, and by signing a refusal card. (Refusal cards must be signed in all cases where an employee refuses benefits.)

2. Amend a group insurance policy or tell other employees that it has been amended, when it has not.

¶12,025 DEPENDANT RIGHTS

Dependants covered under group insurance policies have few rights under those policies, particularly in terms of actual policy wording, coverage, the definition of "dependant", administration, rates and enrolment. Dependants are not usually named under group insurance policies as eligible classifications by themselves. Instead, they are defined in the policies as a sort of "attachment" to the coverage provided to employees. Unless specifically directed by the policyholder or by the terms of the group insurance policy wording, it is up to the employee to state on the group insurance enrolment form that there are dependants, and that coverage for dependants is required. Most policies allow employees to decline dependant coverage for EHC and dental benefits if the spouse is working and has coverage of his or her own. In order for an employee to be able to decline dependant coverage under these duplicate coverage circumstances, the policyholder's administrator should require proof of the dependant's alternate group insurance coverage, but this is administratively difficult to handle and to verify, and hence, is rarely done. In addition to the lack of ability to be able to affect the coverage in any way, dependents are not typically given the opportunity to name beneficiaries under the dependent life benefit. When an eligible dependant dies, the dependant life insurance benefit amount is paid to the employee.

Dependants themselves are usually only covered by and as a result, mostly concerned with the group life insurance, AD&D, dependant life, EHC and dental benefits. In divorce and separation situations, group insurance policies may allow coverage to remain in force for the separated or divorced spouses, and the eligible children, as long as the employee remains eligible under the policy. Group insurance policies usually allow only one "spouse" to be covered, in the event that the employee, subsequent to a separation or divorce, enters into another marriage or common-in-law relationship. In order to reduce the effect of the loss of group insurance coverage on dependants, especially on the dependent spouse, separation and divorce agreements should specify that individual life insurance policies be purchased to replace the lost coverage. Individual insurance policies are generally more expensive to buy than the employee's portion of a group insurance plan. The premiums for these individual policies would be paid for as per the terms of the separation or divorce agreements. Premium payments for the individual policies are the responsibility of the employee or the dependant, not the group policyholder.

Coverage for EHC and dental benefits, in divorce and separation situations, can be a complicated matter. Under the terms of most group insurance contracts, coverage ceases as soon as an employee, or a dependant, is no longer eligible under the terms of the policy. This means that coverage for a dependent spouse ceases as soon as the spouse no longer falls under the definition of a "spouse", or is no longer publicly represented as the spouse, in a case of common-law relationship. EHC and dental benefits can, therefore, stop as soon as the relationship ends, under the definitions in most policies. Complicating this matter, is that, unlike personal life insurance policies which are generally available to individuals, private EHC and dental coverage, equivalent to coverage available under group policies, is either not available, or at best, if available, is not necessarily offered at the same levels of coverage as offered under employees' group policies. If a dependent spouse loses benefits as a result of the breakdown of a relationship, it may be impossible to replace them outside of a group insurance policy. Individual coverage may not be available because the product does not exist, the person can not meet the underwriting medical requirements, or because the cost is prohibitive. Loss of coverage by a dependent spouse, as a result of a divorce or separation, is not usually handled through the group insurance contract, unless a specific request is made and agreed to by the insurer. If required under the terms of the divorce or separation agreement, dental claims are best paid for directly by the claimant and reimbursed directly by the spouse. In other words, it is best to keep the employee's group insurance policy out of the separation or divorce agreement. Insurers can, and will, decline coverage for an employee or a dependant who is no longer eligible.

Although dental claims may be paid directly by an employee to an ex-dependent spouse, coverage for EHC may be more difficult. Dental claims rarely exceed $2,500 per year per individual, and many plans are capped at less than that. Hence, a divorced or separated employee will have less problem paying these claims directly than the possible claims which could occur under an EHC benefit. Prescription drug costs, especially those for people requiring treatment for heart disease, or such things as Parkinson's disease, can be staggering. Artificial limbs are costly; private duty nursing costs can be well over $10,000 per year. It would be out of the financial ability of most employees to be able to directly reimburse these costs to a separated or divorced spouse. There is little option for the replacement of these coverages once they are lost, unless the divorced or separated spouse starts to work for an organization that has these benefits covered under its own group plan. Certainly, group policyholders do not want the responsibility of financially providing for ex-dependent spouses, nor should they be required to do so. There is no one answer here. Luckily, most group insurance contracts allow coverage for eligible dependent children regardless of separation or divorce agreements. Insurers generally allow eligible children to be covered under group insurance policies as long as the employee is allowed, by Revenue Canada, to use that particular child as a deduction on the employee's income tax.

With the exception of an employee living in Quebec, an employee can change the beneficiary on a group life insurance policy at any time, as long as the beneficiary is designated as "revocable". This means that an employee has the legal ability to make a change without asking for the beneficiary's permission. A dependant does not have a "right" to state who should be the beneficiary named by an employee, under a group life insurance policy. (In Quebec, an employee must obtain the permission of the present beneficiary in order to change beneficiaries.) Dependants do not have the right to ask a policyholder to provide any specific or identifiable claims information. Many policyholders will answer basic questions on eligibility and on benefit coverages, posed by dependants, but the policyholder is not required, per se, to provide these answers. A policyholder that provides wrong information to an individual employee, or to a dependant, may be called to correct any harm done by the provision of incorrect information.

Dependants do have the right to have all identifiable claims information kept strictly private and confidential, although this, in effect, is very difficult if claim forms are filled out, completed and signed by the policyholder's administrator. The claimant must rely on the integrity, and professionalism of the policyholder's administrator. In addition, claimants must rely on the policyholder's internal security systems, the security systems of the insurer and the security systems of the ABC to prevent release of this information.

The majority of the group insurance policies issued in Canada state that dependant coverage is only available to a dependent spouse of the opposite sex. It is doubtful that insurers will change their standard policies to include a same-sex spouse, unless requested by a policyholder, or unless required by a change in legislation.

¶12,030 ABC RIGHTS

ABCs who are not appointed by a policyholder to review a particular policy, have no rights whatsoever in terms of any particular policy. ABCs, appointed by a policyholder as Agent of Record, have the right to:

1. Request and inspect the overall premiums, claims and rate history per benefit of the policy. This can be requested directly from the insurer upon provision to the insurer of the policyholder's agreement, and the Agent of Record letter. Should the insurer refuse to provide this information, the ABC may ask the group policyholder to obtain this information directly from the insurer.

2. Request, inspect and clarify employee data information as required by insurers to provide competitive and accurate quotes.

3. Request clarification of the terms and conditions of the policy from the insurer, on behalf of the group policyholder.

4. Request assistance from an insurer, through the group office, in re-evaluating a particular claim (only if permission has been granted by both the group policyholder and the affected claimant to have access to the name or ID number of the claimant).

5. Request employee and dependant medical information on behalf of the insurer's underwriters; such information is to be sent in a sealed envelope directly to the insurer's underwriter and is not to be reviewed by the ABC.

6. Assist in the group insurance administrative functions of the policyholder only so far as requested by the policyholder, as allowed by the insurer, and as allowed by law.

7. Participate in the analysis of group insurance quotes only so far as is requested by a group policyholder.

An ABC *does not* have the right to:

1. Act on behalf of a group policyholder, in any capacity, unless requested by the group policyholder to do so.

2. Act on behalf of any particular insurer unless written permission from that insurer has first been obtained.

3. Misrepresent the requirements of any particular insurer.

4. Misinterpret, or intentionally misrepresent, the particular contractual terms of any insurer.

5. Intentionally fail to obtain a quote from any one particular insurer, if that insurer would normally be willing to provide a quotation through that particular ABC.

6. Divulge private and confidential information about a particular group insurance client, the individual employees or members covered under the policy, or any benefits and terms of the particular policy, unless

permission has first been granted by the group policyholder and any named or identifiable employees or dependants.

7. Withhold from the underwriters information about a group policyholder, its financial status, or its employees or members which, if otherwise known, would cause the underwriter to review its rating or to initially decline to quote. This includes advance knowledge of employee occupations, locations, and classifications. It also includes knowledge of past premium payment problems, policyholder inability to pay premiums, policyholder fraud, especially with respect to previous group insurance policies, past rate histories, past paid premium, and paid claim histories.

8. Interpret proposal or policy clauses on behalf of an insurer, when permission has not been granted, by that insurer.

9. Withhold from a potential client, the amount of experience and knowledge (the skill and competence level) that is required by the ABC to perform the marketing of a particular policy. In other words, the ABC should inform a potential client of the actual amount of experience that he or she has in respect to group insurance policy marketing, and service.

10. Withhold information about benefit terms, benefit interpretations or benefit financing alternatives, from a group policyholder or potential client, which would affect decisions made by the group policyholder concerning the group policy, its financing, and the policy's implementation.

11. Fail to disclose to the policyholder, the amount of all commissions paid on a particular policy, especially those that have a direct effect on policyholder rates.

12. Share commissions or payment in kind of any form or in any manner, with anyone who is not licensed by the province to accept commissions, or the payment in kind. It is not legal to share commissions with a policyholder, or a policyholder's representative, for any reason.

13. Solicit the employees for other insurance, without the policyholder's prior approval.

14. Hold employee meetings without the policyholder's knowledge or prior approval.

15. Accept and retain premiums. All premiums, including overpayments, should be immediately forwarded to the insurer, unless there is a third-party administration (TPA) contract in effect, and the insurer has acknowledged and agreed to the TPA collecting premiums.

16. Invest group insurance premiums on behalf of a policyholder.

17. Accept verbal policyholder requests concerning a policy, without requiring written confirmation.

18. Change the wording of a policy.

19. Make disparaging remarks about his or her competition.

20. Bribe a policyholder's, or an insurer's representative.

21. Misrepresent the limitations of a policy.

22. Withhold possible conflict of interest situations from a policyholder or from an insurer.

23. Disregard the terms of his or her agency, brokerage, or employment agreement.

24. Disregard human rights, or any other legislation.

25. Pay premiums on behalf of a policyholder in order to keep a policy in force.

¶12,035 ADVISING THE INSURER OF CHANGES IN THE POLICYHOLDER'S ORGANIZATION

Although it cannot exactly be termed a "right" of the insurer, a policyholder should make every attempt to inform the group insurer of any changes to the status of the policyholder's organization which could affect the status of the group insurance policy(s). The reason for this is that the policy is a "contract" and therefore subject to the provisions of contract law. Any changes to a contract must be agreed to by all concerned parties. The insurer's group office should be advised immediately of the following:

1. A change of name of the group policyholder.

2. A change in the directors or in the controlling interests of the owners.

3. A buyout or the takeover of another company by the policyholder.

4. The sale of a portion or of a specific division of the policyholder.

5. Any change of group insurance administrators.

6. Any change in the policyholder's executive management, especially those involved in the decision-making process with respect to the group insurance plan.

7. Any major change in the business focus of the policyholder, i.e., sending employees overseas or changing the nature of the business.

8. Any decision to change the self-insured benefits, such as sick-leave programs.

9. Any requests by associations or unions to change group insurance benefits. These should be submitted to the insurer's group office for approval prior to committing to the changes in writing in the association or union contracts.

Advise the insurer's administration department of any of the following changes. (These assume that the insurance company is handling the administration, not the employer, the association or the union, and that the policyholder is not using a "self-administration" arrangement.) The insurer should be advised of any changes prior to, or if not possible, at latest within 30 days of their occurrence, so as not to jeopardize coverage. When the insurer administers a policy, the insurer should be advised of the following changes:

1. Employee terminations.

2. New employees.

3. Changes in employment status, i.e., going from probationary to permanent employee status.

4. Changes of classification, i.e., getting a promotion to management and becoming eligible for a different level of insurance coverage.

5. Changes of dependant status, i.e., getting married, or divorced.

6. Errors in statistical information, i.e., dates of birth, Social Insurance Numbers of disability claimants, etc.

7. Changes in beneficiary nominations.

8. Employees who refuse coverage, by use of a refusal card.

When the policyholder, or a third party, administers the policy, then changes should always be made in writing, and they should be kept in the proper, dedicated files, so that any discrepancies can be verified.

¶12,040 WHEN NOT TO ADVISE THE INSURER

It is not usually necessary to advise an insurer of the following situations:

1. Changes in your Human Resources programming which do not affect the group insurance programs directly, such as the implementation of safety programs, an employee assistance plan, a pension, or a retirement savings plan arrangement.

2. Employees who are hired and who leave employment prior to the end of the benefit waiting period.

3. Age changes (unless required by the policy). These are usually calculated automatically by the insurance companies.

4. The addition of children for an employee who currently has "dependant coverage", unless required by a benefit schedule.

¶12,045 TO WHOM DO YOU COMPLAIN IF YOU HAVE A PROBLEM?

If you encounter a problem with any of the services or products offered through your insurance company, the first place to contact is the group office. If the problem is with a group representative, ask to speak to the group office manager. If the problem is with the group office manager, write a personal and confidential letter to the vice-president, group insurance, at the insurance company's head office, giving the facts, the dates and explaining the problem. If it is a problem with a specific claim, contact the section head of the area that is in question at the Health Claims office. If the problem is with the section head, contact the Health Claims office manager. If the problem is with the claims manager, write a personal and confidential letter to the vice-president, Health Claims, at the insurance company's head office, giving the facts, dates and explaining the problem.

Insurance companies in Canada, their employees and their representatives, generally go out of their way to be of assistance. As an industry, they have a lot of pride in the work they do. Every once in a while there will be a situation which seems to upset the balance. If the above people appear unwilling or unable to offer assistance, you may write to the president of the insurance company. A letter to the president will cause far more ripples than you might think.

Should you contact a lawyer? You may consult a lawyer at any time. Every effort should be made to try and find an answer to the problem, and the efforts can be directed to the insurance company. All inquiries should be followed up in writing. If someone in the insurance company tells you something, ask the person with whom you were speaking to confirm it in writing. You should also follow up telephone conversations in writing. Go all the way up the ladder if need be. If you are an employee and a claimant, start with your own company. Ask to speak to the manager of human resources and, if necessary, go up through the various levels of management, including the vice-president of finance, and even the president of the organization. If you are a policyholder, start with the ABC, if you have one, and then the group office. Work up the insurer chain of command, until you reach the top. If you have not received any satisfaction or feel more comfortable having a legal expert look into the problem for you, then consider obtaining the advice of a lawyer. As soon as a representative of the insurance company receives a letter from a lawyer, the insurance company generally has its own lawyers handle all correspondence and inquiries from that point. Whichever route you choose, all inquiries should be addressed, in writing, to the insurer prior to the claims notification time limitations taking effect.

4 TO WHOM DO YOU COMPLAIN IF YOU HAVE A PROBLEM?

CHAPTER 13

¶13,000 LEGAL RESPONSIBILITIES

¶13,005 INTRODUCTION

The following section is meant to be a brief introduction to the legal aspects involved in group insurance marketing. It is recommended that any specific questions and problems that you may have be referred to an expert in the field.

Legal responsibilities, in the field of group insurance and employee benefits, usually fall under the following categories: employee and dependant responsibilities, policyholder responsibilities, insurer responsibilities, and agent, broker and consultant responsibilities. Responsibilities are defined as who is to do what, where, how, for whom, in what circumstances, and at what time. Some of the responsibilities, such as benefit terms and definitions, are defined by means of a contract. Others are stated in laws, while still others are administrative in nature. All require the notion of trust. A group insurance policy is a legal contract called a "master policy". A group insurance policy, in contrast to an individual or personal policy, covers a number of people under one contract. There need not be any "insurable interest" between a group insurance policyholder and the employees, union or association members covered under the contract. This contrasts with an individual life insurance policy wherein a beneficiary usually has a financial tie to the life insured. In other words, there must be an insurable interest present between the insured and the beneficiary. (Exceptions to this would be insurance left to an estate to cover last expenses, insurance proceeds paid to charities, religious organizations, or to schools.) Underwriters of individual life insurance policies generally do not allow the purchase of insurance to cover people that you do not know. You cannot gamble, with insurance, on the lives of others.) All parties involved in group insurance policies have certain responsibilities to perform. There is an expectation that these responsibilities will be performed honestly, and to the best of one's ability. There is a trust and belief that all parties will perform their part in the formation of a group insurance policy because a policy is a contract, and as such, is subject to the laws established concerning contracts. A group life insurance policy is a unilateral contract. It is set up with the mutual assent of both parties involved: the insurance company, or benefit provider, and the group insurance purchaser, called the policyholder. The contract is termed unilateral because the obligation to pay the agreed upon benefits only falls on one of the parties. The payment of these benefits is subject to the group purchasing the contract or policy, paying the premiums on time, and advising the insurer or provider of changes in employee information or any other pertinent information as specified in the policy, such as changes to the status of the purchaser's corporate status.

A policy will normally be subject to the laws concerning contracts, such as validity, breach, effective date, termination, and who can accept or change the contract. A policy will stipulate the following:

— legal name(s) of the policyholder and the insurer or provider;

— effective date of the policy;

— effective date of coverage for employees and dependants *at* the policy inception date;

— effective date of coverage for employees and dependants *after* the inception date of the policy (the waiting period);

— termination clauses of the policy;

— termination of employee and dependant coverage;

— benefits to be covered;

— grace period for late premium payment;

— incontestability clause;

— reinstatement of coverage conditions;

— eligibility classifications;

— conversion (to a personal policy) privileges;

— claim limitations.

Policies are subject to consumer protection laws, human rights legislation, tax legislation and privacy legislation.

¶13,010 EMPLOYEE RESPONSIBILITIES

Employees, covered under group insurance contracts, have few responsibilities in terms of the policy *per se*. The employee has the right to nominate a beneficiary for a group life insurance, or an "optional (voluntary) group life" insurance, benefit. The employee will have the right in most cases to change the beneficiary at any time, unless the employee lives in Quebec, or unless the employee has nominated an irrevocable beneficiary. In these latter two situations, written consent of the previous beneficiary, unless deceased, is required to change a beneficiary. In all other provinces and most other situations, the employee may change the group life insurance beneficiary at any time. The group insurance administration manual, provided by the insurance company, normally provides examples of correct beneficiary nomination wording to suit the various situations allowed in each province.

The employee may be required to join the group insurance plan by the employer, or the policyholder, as a condition of being employed. The employee may also be required by the employer to pay a share of the premiums, but this is not stated in many group insurance contracts. Employees who are eligible, but who refuse to join the plan for personal reasons (i.e., religious), put the policyholder in an awkward position. Group insurance policies often stipulate that the eligibility is for "*all* permanent full-time employees". Allowing employees the option of joining complicates administration, increases the possibility of administrative error, can affect the renewal rates and can cause a disruption in employee morale, especially if there is a claim for an employee who has declined or refused coverage. In every case of refusal, an employee must be required to sign a "refusal card", and the insurer must be advised in writing. This lessens the possibility of future problems in the event of a claim for the person who refused the benefits.

If an employee is covered for extended health care and/or dental benefits under a spouse's plan, the group policyholder, and the insurer, may allow the employee to decline those benefits only, due to this "duplicate coverage". An employee is not covered for group life insurance, weekly indemnity, or long-term disability under a spouse's plan. An employee may be covered for dependant life, extended health care, dental, voluntary life insurance, or voluntary accidental death and dismemberment under a spousal plan.

Employees, members of associations, or union members are sometimes requested to work on committees which conduct surveys on benefits issues. Members of these groups most often work on behalf of the majority of the employees. To this extent, these members can be said to have certain responsibilities to represent the demands of other members of their groups. But these representatives generally do so in an advisory capacity, not a legal capacity.

¶13,015 DEPENDANT RESPONSIBILITIES

Dependants have little to do with the design or the administration of a group insurance program, despite the fact that they are often covered by it. Very rarely do employers consult with spouses when designing plans, or reviewing them. Dependants historically have had virtually no say in anything to do with the plans. The exception is that dependants can influence who is named as beneficiary under the group life contract, although, with perhaps the exception of Quebec, any employee who has nominated a (revocable) beneficiary can change his or her mind at any time. Dependants, if covered and eligible, can claim extended health care, dental and employee/family assistance program benefits. Employees may be required to sign claim forms for EHC, dental, and dependant life claims. When allowed by an insurer or a benefit provider, dependants may also sign the claim forms. By signing a claim form, the employee, or the dependant, is stating that the information on that claim form is correct, to the best of his or her knowledge.

¶13,020 EMPLOYER RESPONSIBILITIES AND ADMINISTRATION

Most group insurance policies state that a minimum percentage of eligible employees, usually 75 to 85 per cent, must join the plan in order that the policy remain in force. It is the employer's responsibility to ensure that employees are enrolled in the plan at the correct time. Should the percentage fall below the minimum stated in the policy, the insurer can cancel the policy. Alternatively, the group representative or another designated insurer representative, with the policyholder's consent, may resolicit the employees in an attempt to enrol more employees. Another approach to resolicitation would be to redefine the eligibility clauses in the policy to exclude those who declined prior to a specific date. Or, it is possible to redefine the eligibility to include only specific occupational classifications as of a specific date.

It is rare these days for group insurance policyholders to offer employees the chance to opt out of a plan, except in the case of association of employers, or association of individuals group plans. Employees who opt out tend to be the young and single. Their inclusion in the plan usually lowers the rates on all benefit lines; this is important to other employees, especially when they share the premiums with the employer. If a group insurance policyholder has a high turnover of employees, a possible solution to the minimum percentage enrolment problem is to implement a longer waiting period (i.e., six months or a year) before employees in that classification can become eligible for the plan.

There are more chances of administrative error by a policyholder whose policy has a long waiting period before new employees are eligible to join the plan. If an employee is not enrolled at the date of eligibility within the time period specified in the policy, the insurer can decline to cover the employee and the dependants for benefits, or have the employee and all of the dependants submit to medical examinations or pay late enrolment charges. Any medicals would have to be approved by the insurance company before coverage would be granted. This situation can become very tricky for the group policyholder, because it is the responsibility of the policyholder's administrator to make sure that employees are enrolled on time. One way for an administrator to make sure that an employee is enrolled on time is to have all full-time permanent employees, and any other classification of employee eligible under the policy, sign an enrolment card and beneficiary nominations on the date of hire. Historically, life insurance companies and benefit providers have been very generous in allowing backdating of enrolment for late enrolments, but this has been done outside of contract terms, and is done as a "special concession". Each situation is assessed by the insurance company on its own merit. Employers who are lax in their enrolment procedures, thereby jeopardizing new employee coverage, could be taken to task by the employee or the employee's estate.

Insurance companies offer group insurance policyholders various types of administration. Plans that are administered by the insurer are called "insurer administered", or "head office administered". Employer responsibilities with this type of administration are, basically, to have employees fill out enrolment cards, which in turn must be forwarded by the administrator to the insurer within the time limits allowed (they must usually be completed and sent to the insurer within 30 days from the date of eligibility). Employer administrators must also send in "change of beneficiary" cards, and depending on the type of claims administration, must complete and sign claim forms required by the insurer to determine eligibility. One of the most important things that an administrator must do is to send in the premiums on time, and within the "grace period" — usually within 30 days from the billing date. Group insurance premium payments are not usually given the 30, 60 and 90-day grace payment periods allowed by certain suppliers of other types of goods and services. Group insurance premiums must be paid on time in order not to jeopardize the coverage under the policy. Premiums are usually required, by insurers, to be paid in advance of the start of coverage period under any type of administration offered by an insurer.

Another popular type of administration offered by insurance companies is called "self-administration". In these situations, group policyholders keep all of the enrolment cards, beneficiary cards and other employee data, instead of sending these into the insurer. Self-administered plan policyholders are responsible for preparing their own billing statements and forwarding these once per month to the insurer, along with a cheque for the premiums. Larger groups find this type of administration easier to perform, because, as they keep all records, it is easier to keep track of changes, enrolments, deletions, etc. There is no time delay factor between sending these forms to an insurer and receiving confirmation that the forms have been received and processed. Self-administered plans put more responsibility on a policyholder, to ensure that everything is processed correctly and on time, that all beneficiary nominations are worded correctly, and that all records are kept strictly private and confidential. Employers not taking care in these areas could be subject to the legal ramifications of their errors.

Employers are responsible for immediately advising their insurers of any changes in the legal name, legal status as an organization, or changes in eligibility classifications within their organizations. Some insurers also require advice on any changes in the policyholder's "directors", especially if coverage is extended to these directors. Failure to advise the insurer can technically jeopardize coverage in the worst-case scenario, and delay claims payment in the best-case scenario.

A third type of administration is called "ASO", or Administrative Services Only. Under an ASO arrangement, a group policyholder only "hires" an insurance company to perform certain functions, which are defined in a contract. Usually, ASO contracts are only offered by insurers to very large organizations, but specialty benefit providers may offer an ASO arrangement to any size organization. Insurers or benefit providers are responsible, typically, to administer and pay the claims only. This is done on a "fee-for-service" basis, as a level amount per claim, or on a percentage of claim basis (i.e., the charge to adjudicate the claim, pay the claim, and issue the cheque might be 6 to 8 per cent of each claim). The group "insurer" or "provider" is in these cases, the employer. All responsibilities that would otherwise be the responsibility of an insurer or provider, other than actually providing the administrative function of paying the claims, falls on the employer, or group "policyholder". Under the ASO contract, the employer is responsible for all deficits in the funding of the benefit, unless alternate coverage, such as "stop-loss" has been arranged. Stop-loss coverage can be set up through insurers to pay either very large individual claims, or total claims over a pre-established amount.

ASO administration is similar to "cost-plus" arrangements. A cost-plus arrangement can be set up as a contract, with an insurer, but is more commonly set up as a method of paying ex-contractual claims under an insured policy. Ex-contractual benefit payments are paid, outside of the terms and conditions of a policy, with the consent of both the insurer and the policyholder. They are paid in situations where an employer wants a specific benefit paid for one employee, or classification of employees, on a one-time only basis. Policies or contracts can also be set up such that all claims are paid on a cost-plus basis. In both types of cost-plus arrangements, the insurer agrees to pay the claim for the cost of the claim itself, plus a stated per cent (typically 15 per cent). Claims paid on a one-time basis are not normally taken into consideration at renewal. Commissions to ABCs on one-shot, cost-plus claim payments, are also not normally paid.

Employers who are deducting money from employee paycheques to pay premiums for group insurance benefits, are responsible for the safety of the deductions and are responsible for submitting those premiums to the insurer or benefit providers.

Employers using self-insured plans are responsible for paying benefits to employees, as agreed to in a contract, union, or employee association agreement. In the rare case of employee contributions to self-insured plans, the employer is also responsible for safe-guarding these contributions (they should be in a trust account), applying them to the plan only, being fair when determining the premium split, and when determining the renewal rates.

¶13,025 INSURER RESPONSIBILITIES

Insurance companies are subject to heavy and complicated regulations, many of which were originally designed to cope with insurance products for individuals, and then subsequently massaged to use with group insurance plans. In order to stay within the intended practical nature of this book, we will keep this discussion focused on the basics. For a more detailed look at the legal responsibilities of the insurer, I suggest reviewing one of the books dedicated to this subject.

There are both federal and provincial regulations concerning the life insurance business. Basically, the provincial governments regulate insurance company "conduct" within their specific provinces, although both levels of government are primarily concerned with the financial soundness of the insurers themselves. Each province has a "Superintendent of Insurance", who is responsible for the administration of insurance laws within that province. The superintendent can be approached for clarification of insurance rules and regulations. Both provincial superintendents and the Canadian Life and Health Insurers Association (the CLHIA) have guidelines which are to be followed by insurers. Note that some benefit providers, who are not "insurers" *per se*, do not belong to the CLHIA. There is not a legislative requirement for insurers or benefit providers to belong to any industry association.

It is a responsibility of an insurer or a benefit provider to be fiscally responsible to its clients. Prudent investments are required to ensure that there will be enough money in reserve to pay future claims, especially life insurance and long-term disability claims. This means that not only must proper reserves be established, but also that the investments of these reserves, as well as the insurer's general funds, must be spread out to maximize investment, yet at the same time keep the risk level of the investments low. This means establishing a portfolio of investments that does not put all of its eggs in one basket, such as commercial real estate, or common stocks. A number of insurers have got into trouble over the last few years through poor investment management practices, the latest being the now defunct Confederation Life. At present, the public has to rely on government analysts to ensure that legislated guidelines are being adhered to by the insurers. Private corporate rating agencies also provide analysis of the overall financial status of the insurers, as they do for other corporations. Life insurance policyholders have little input into the overall operations, investment strategies, or cost reduction programs used by insurers, even in the case of "mutual" insurance companies. "Participating policyholders" of mutual life insurance companies (those who own "whole life" policies) are theoretically allowed to vote with rights similar to common stockholders of other types of companies, yet, as control is so widespread among the policyholders, they can rarely influence decisions.

In terms of group insurance marketing, insurance companies and benefit providers are required to abide by the terms and conditions set out within their contracts. They are also required to abide by the general aspects accorded to "contract law". Most problems with these contracts, for insurers, policyholders, and employees, occur because of varying interpretations of the specific terms and conditions within the contracts, usually in the areas of claims payment or eligibility. It is of paramount importance for all concerned parties, therefore, when setting up a policy, to ensure that there is a common understanding, confirmed in writing, of who is to be eligible, when, and if applicable, where they are to be eligible. The master policy is the primary medium in which the group policyholder must adequately define those who are to be covered, when the coverage is to begin and end, and where the employees are eligible to be covered. The "where" is particularly important for organizations whose employees are located in different provinces or countries. Some insurers are not licensed to provide benefits in all countries; others are unwilling to provide coverage to "overseas" employees, despite the trend in world trade to "globalization".

With respect to claims payment, life insurance payments are normally paid without incident, once eligibility and coverage have been confirmed. Problems can occur where there is suspicion of a crime, participation in a war, riot or civil commotion, or in the case of disappearances or suicide. Insurer treatment of disappearances is either referred to within the policy or there are laws on the books which state when benefits are to be paid. Unlike individual life insurance policies, many group life insurance policies do not have a (two-year coverage) restriction on payments in the case of suicide. There may be a restriction for suicide in voluntary life insurance benefits, however. Rather than tie up their time in courts, insurers sometimes pay any disputed amounts to the courts, in trust. The courts, then, determine if the claim is payable.

Disability claims, especially long-term disability claims, can be disputed as well. Huge amounts of money must be put aside in reserve to pay many of these claims. Disability claims that are "cut and dried", such as for diseases and conditions where there is little chance of full recovery documented, are normally paid without incident until the maximum time or age limits defined in the policy are reached. Problems occur with claims that are "borderline" or in a "grey area". These are claims where the actual affect of the disability on the individual is debatable. Some claims, such as those for back injuries, may not disable an employee for life, but may make it impossible for that employee to continue at his or her "own occupation". It is not up to the insurance company to provide any particular claimant with a job in another capacity, even if the insurance company has worked with the claimant and the employer to re-educate or to rehabilitate the claimant.

Insurance companies generally prefer to work out any disputes with their group insurance policyholders outside of court. Disputes can often be resolved by supplying the insurer with more information about the claim; especially information that fits the claims department format. For example, a claims department may require doctors to fill out specific claim forms; a simple doctor's note will not suffice. A policyholder, if there is a dispute, may elect to go up the corporate ladder of the insurer, to see if a more favourable resolution can be reached. When a policyholder or a claimant elects to use the legal system to come to a resolution of a claim, the local representatives of the insurer and those at the head office level are usually required by corporate policy to put their side of the case into the hands of their own legal staff. The claim then goes through the legal system, which has its own attendant delays.

Organizations that self-insure benefits are responsible for the payment of those claims. They are also responsible for administration of the benefits and for the resolution of disputed claims on those benefits. In situations where both self-insured and insured benefits are available to employees, the insurer is only responsible for the insured benefits (or the payment of claims under an ASO arrangement).

¶13,030 AGENT, BROKER AND CONSULTANT RESPONSIBILITIES

Agents, brokers and consultants (ABCs) are regulated by specific laws which concern the legal interpretation of "agency". In the majority of group insurance contracts, the agent, broker or consultant is not named in the contract or the policy. However, in cases where the ABC is hired by the policyholder to be the administrator of the plan, the ABC may be mentioned in the contract. Third-party administration, as this arrangement is called, can be accomplished through use of a contract between the ABC and the policyholder directly.

Although there are a few courses and certificate programs available (see Appendices at ¶17,020, Courses to Take), the consumer may encounter some difficulty in determining whether an ABC has the qualifications necessary to do a proper, effective, and cost-efficient job. At present, there are no universally accepted accreditations that will inform the consumer that the ABC chosen has the qualifications and experience necessary to do the best job. There is, as a result, no universally accepted code of ethics or moral conduct which can be applied to any of those offering advice on employee benefit matters. Actuaries, Chartered Life Underwriters, Fellows of the Life Management Institute, lawyers and accountants all have codes of ethics which apply to their areas, but none are specifically targeted at benefit consulting. If a particular ABC does a poor job or provides poor or deceitful information to clients or to insurers, there is no real comeback on them through the benefits industry. Indeed, if someone wished to become a benefits consultant and decided not to take commissions, in other words to work for fees only, even the local Superintendent of Insurance has little or no jurisdiction over this person.

However, any ABC is subject to "tort liability". In other words, if an ABC makes an error that causes either an insurer or a client financial loss, that ABC may be required to make financial restitution to the organization or individual that is harmed. Most of these types of errors fall into the "errors and omissions" (E. & O.) category: acts of error or negligence, which are deemed to be the ABC's fault. ABCs can purchase E. & O. business insurance policies that limit or cover the amount of financial loss for which an ABC might be responsible.

ABCs must be warranted (authorized) by an insurance company to undertake a contract on the insurer's behalf. With group insurance contracts, an ABC might shop the market for a particular client's group insurance contract, but it is often the group representative for the insurance company who signs the master policy application as a witness. On any group insurance contract, especially one for a smaller group, an ABC can be given that authority by the insurer. Neither the group insurance policyholder, nor the ABC, should cancel a policy that is about to be replaced until such time as the new underwriter(s) has approved in writing the new policy, and has grandfathered all existing coverages, especially for the life insurance and disability benefits.

An ABC owes a fiduciary relationship to the insurer. In fact, the ABC acts as an agent of the insurance company in fiduciary matters, according to the terms of the *Uniform Life Insurance Act*. Some ABCs say that their clients come first, but not according to the laws of agency in this regard. Agents, and those acting as agents, are required to hand over all monies collected for and owed to the insurer, to divulge any "secret" profits made through the agency relationship, to account for all monies owed to the insurer on a particular case, and to obey all laws and reasonable instructions provided by the insurer. An agent also owes the insurer a duty of loyalty and one of good faith, although this is rarely required by insurers in practical terms. The group insurance market is very competitive. Agents, in particular those that have been in business for two or more years, or who are not being financed by an insurer or who are required to stick only to their sponsoring companies products and services, may get to know their own company's products and services in detail, but they may be limited in their ability to offer their group insurance clients the most appropriate product or service available. Requiring agents to deal only with their own sponsoring companies allows group insurance brokers and consultants, who shop the market for the best selections of products and services, a very large competitive edge.

Because of the competitiveness of the group insurance marketplace during the 1970s, 1980s, and early 1990s, there has been constant pressure from insurers onto their own staff to increase their market share, to increase profits, and to grow larger. This pressure has been very good for the consumers, and has been especially good for the ABCs who have been involved in marketing group insurance products, because rates and retentions have been "shaved to the bone" by the insurers in order to attain their goals. ABCs have won because their commissions scales have not been lowered, except by the industry trend to go with "level" commission scales, although level scales actually pay out more in commissions over the long run, in comparison to the older "high/low" scales. Rising rates have meant rising revenues, via commissions, for the ABCs. The current desire of consumers, to lower group insurance expenses, has received only cursory mention from many ABCs. The ABC has little control over actual insurer expenses, or over the claims, or over the retention. The ABC can provide a service in marketing a group's plan and seeking the most competitive quote. The ABC has little control over much else, including actual rates charged by the insurers. The ABC can control, within certain limits, the commission scale paid by the insurers, can be a source of information and can act as an intermediary between the insurer and the policyholder. It is not much use for a consumer to blame an ABC over rising rates, unless of course, the ABC does not have the experience and is not offering to provide the information and services required by the particular client.

CHAPTER 14

¶14,000 TAXATION

¶14,005 INTRODUCTION

This chapter is a brief introduction to the common taxation considerations involved in setting up and marketing group insurance policies. It is not intended to be the ultimate interpretation of the *Income Tax Act*. Specific questions or problems should be addressed directly to Revenue Canada or to an expert in this field. Revenue Canada Income Tax Interpretation Bulletins relating to group insurance plans are included in the Appendices at ¶17,065.

Taxation in the area of group insurance policies generally falls into the following categories: employer and employee tax paid on premiums; employer and employee tax paid on benefits; the deduction of paid premium from corporate income; and the deduction of paid premium from personal income. At the present time, premiums paid by an employer for a group insurance program are tax deductible by that corporation. Premiums paid towards a group insurance program by an employee are not tax deductible. However, an employee who pays premiums into a "taxable" group disability policy, and who receives a claim cheque, can deduct the amount of the premiums paid from the claim amount when determining income tax for the year.

A "taxable" group disability policy (either weekly indemnity or long-term disability) is one in which the employer contributes (technically as low as one cent a year) to the premium for that benefit. Revenue Canada allows a disability benefit to be "non-taxable" when received, if employees pay 100 per cent of the premium for that benefit.

Employer contributions to the group life insurance benefit's premium for an employee are considered a taxable benefit to the employee. Prior to the 1994 Federal Budget, only premiums paid by the employer for group life insurance amounts over $25,000 were considered a taxable benefit for federal income tax purposes. Quebec is the only province that considers employer premiums paid to a group insurance program as a taxable benefit for provincial income tax purposes.

¶14,010 TAXATION OF HEALTH CARE BENEFITS

Currently, extended health care and dental benefits are not included in employee income as taxable benefits unless there is not a contracted plan, an insured plan or a union agreement in place. Premiums paid by an employer on behalf of employees for these benefits are also not taxable benefits to employees. These issues continue to be brought up by successive governments as a possible additional source of tax revenue. But bureaucrats and politicians who bring up this subject do not understand how these benefits are funded.

Should the premiums paid by the employer for these health benefits be considered as taxable benefits? The answer is simply no. The reason is that an insurance company takes a big portion of the premium dollar as "retention". On the smallest groups, the retention is up to 35 per cent of premium. That means the insurance company will only pay 65 cents back on the dollar, on average, to these groups, without putting up the rates. If an employer contribution was considered as taxable income to the employee, belonging to a group health insurance plan would make little financial sense to that employee. First of all, if the employee pays 50 per cent of the premium with after tax dollars, and then has to treat the employer portion as a taxable benefit, and the plan loses up to 35 per cent to the insurance company in the retention, where are the savings or the benefits to the employee? What about those people who never claim? They might be far better off to drop out of the plan and to invest the money that they would pay in premiums and in extra tax. If, however, the employer is paying, for example, 50 per cent or more of the premium, and this is not considered a taxable benefit, as is the case at present, the case for keeping an EHC, or dental plan, makes more financial sense to the employee. The conclusion has to be that taxing employer contributions to premium will effectively put an end to health and dental policies as they exist today, due to the fact that the policies lose their tax effectiveness for the employees.

¶14,015 THE HIDDEN TAX

Provincial governments assess a "hidden" tax on all group insurance premiums. It is called hidden because most people are not aware that they are paying it. This tax is paid as a percentage of the total premium per benefit. It is calculated, collected and remitted by the insurance company. The insurer in turn, charges the tax as a percentage of premium. The tax is typically included in the retention. The tax percentage varies between provinces, with 2 per cent of premium, historically, being the norm. Newfoundland and Quebec presently charge higher than 2 per cent. There is no income tax credit allowed for employee contributions to the group insurance premium tax. The group policyholder can write off, from (corporate) income taxes, its portion of the premiums, including the policyholder amount allocated to premium tax.

Some provinces allow "non-profit" benefit providers, such as Blue Cross, not to charge or to collect and remit this tax. All life insurance companies, however, must include the tax in the retention. This occasionally causes the "non-profits" to have an advantage in underwriting group health and dental plans. Non-profits must charge the tax on group life and disability benefits, if they are in that market. There has been a push by certain provinces to have all benefit providers, including the non-profits, charge this tax on all benefits. This would have the effect of evening out the competitive edge that is currently allowed by some provinces to the non-profits. The downside is that non-profits can be the only providers that have "head offices" in that province. These non-profits may also handle the government programs for seniors and for those on social assistance. To tax these plans would, in effect, tax the government. Having non-profits charge tax on plans that they underwrite for private industry would serve to even up the playing field with the insurers.

¶14,020 EMPLOYER DEDUCTIONS

Premiums paid by an employer for group life insurance, accidental death and dismemberment, dependant life insurance, weekly indemnity, long-term disability, survivor income, extended health care, dental and employee assistance plans are tax deductible by the employer as a business expense.

An employer is allowed to pay up to $10,000 as a death benefit to an employee's family outside the group insurance plan. This is also allowed as a employer deduction by Revenue Canada. The amount paid to the family is treated as a life insurance benefit, and as such, is not taxable upon receipt (see Appendices at ¶17,110 for the section of the *Income Tax Act* dealing with this matter).

Employers may also deduct expenses incurred and claims paid out under self-insured employee group insurance plans. (Refer to Revenue Canada Interpretation Bulletin 339-R2 in the Appendices, at ¶17,095.)

¶14,025 EMPLOYEE DEDUCTIONS

Generally, employees pay for their share of group insurance premiums with after-tax dollars. The employee share of premium is not tax deductible by the employee for any benefit, with one exception. Employees who claim for disability under a group disability benefit (either short-term or long-term, which is underwritten as a "taxable" plan, one in which the employee only partially contributes to the premium for that specific benefit), may deduct the amount of premiums that they paid from the benefit payment total, for income tax purposes. Employee contributions to premium for any other benefit are not tax deductible. However, should an employee's total health care expenses, including group health and dental premiums, in a particular tax year either equal $1,614, or exceed 3 per cent of net income (in 1994), then those premiums may be considered as a tax deduction.

¶14,030 TAXATION OF BENEFITS

Group insurance benefits received by employees currently are not taxable to employees, with the exception of weekly indemnity and long-term disability benefits paid under "taxable" plans. Disability benefits are only taxable if the employer has contributed to the premium for that specific benefit and the insurer has set it up as a "taxable" benefit. It is possible to set up a non-taxable weekly indemnity benefit and a taxable long-term disability benefit or vice versa.

Life insurance benefit amounts, paid to the beneficiary, are also not taxable. Tax must be paid on the interest earned by the life insurance proceeds after the date of death.

¶14,035 TAXATION OF EMPLOYER CONTRIBUTIONS TO PREMIUM

Currently, only the premium paid by an employer towards an employee's group life insurance and a group dependant life insurance benefit are considered by Revenue Canada to be a taxable benefit to the employee. Prior to 1993, this was true only for the dependant life benefit, and amounts of employer-paid employee life insurance premiums over $25,000.

The federal Goods and Services Tax (GST), currently at 7 per cent, must be paid on agent, broker and consulting charges, but it is not assessed on commissions. Consulting charges and the associated GST are usually paid by the employer. In Quebec, rules respecting agents and consulting fees are the same as for the GST.

All provinces differ in respect to whether or not they charge provincial sales tax on consulting fees.

CHAPTER 15

¶15,000 ETHICS AND GROUP INSURANCE MARKETING

The purpose of this chapter is to provide an introduction to the scope of the subject of ethics in business, particularly in the area of group insurance plan marketing. Because this scope is so large, it is not possible to do more than scratch the surface, even if we try to limit the subject to group insurance. The study of ethics involves more than the study of rules, regulations, and laws. The study involves more than what is right and what is wrong. It involves processes such as moral reasoning and moral action. More recently, the study of ethics and its practical uses, especially in terms of its use in business, has been termed the study of practical ethics. Included in this chapter is a list of group insurance marketing practical ethical issues. Following these issues are lists of questions that might be considered when trying to solve moral issues especially those that are pertinent to group insurance marketing. The intent of these questions is to assist individuals, agents, brokers and consultants (the ABCs), policyholders, insurers and benefit providers in the decision making process.

Ethics is an area of business education that has much room for study. Some people believe that ethics and business are poor partners. Others believe that the whole subject of business ethics is an oxymoron! Many people leave the study of ethics to others, yet everyone has opinions and beliefs on what is right or wrong. Canadians, historically, have turned to lawyers and politicians to make the rules by which we all live. Yet, as many lawyers and other "professionals" will tell you, they are not required to study ethics during their degree programs, with the exception of a course on what is right or wrong in their particular professional practice. Most business degrees do not require extensive study in ethics or offer more than a cursory course in the subject. As an industry, insurance is highly regulated, yet the professionals that run the companies are mostly self-regulated. The insurance industry is highly regulated in terms of what kind of investments it can make, what types of disclosure it must make, and how its accounting must be done. Yet, like most other industries, the insurance industry does not require its employees, or its sponsored ABCs, to participate in any course strictly on ethics. In fact, many business professionals have not studied the very basics of what constitutes "ethical" business behaviour. For example, does corporate profit come before the good of the overall community, or before the rights of the individual? The employee benefits industry, like other industries, employs professionals who play a wide range of roles in the planning, control, management and success of their organizations and the industry as a whole. The benefits industry relies on the concept of trust as a prime motivation for the purchase of its products and services. Corporations, associations, unions, and their members pay for benefits which amount to, in many cases, a promise to pay at some time in the future. The employee benefits industry is controlled by people in recognized professions, and because of this, the subject of professional ethics has to be seen as strongly connected to the industry's ability to compete profitably and to prosper.

When considering many basic questions in ethics, it is important to review and to come to an understanding of what is often called the "big picture". How do we describe this big picture in terms of ethics and especially in terms of business ethics? First of all, we have to ask ourselves what we consider to be the most important things in our lives. Whatever we, as individuals or groups, hold to be the most valuable, will affect the decisions we make and how we set our priorities. Because some of these things overlap one other, we have to prioritize them. At the same time, it is necessary to put a value on the things that we are trying to compare, in order that the comparisons be fair. Along the way we must consider the following questions: how do we determine what is right or wrong? What takes priority and what does not? Who defines value? What is our duty? What are the consequences of action and inaction? Who really has the moral expertise to determine these answers? What are the rights, obligations and responsibilities of others? What are our obligations and responsibilities as individuals, as employees, as business owners, as professionals, as citizens of the community, as citizens of the state, and as citizens of the world? In addition, there are questions as to how things are to be determined and who is to make that determination. There are questions as to who is to teach these moral issues, and how and when they are to be taught. Who has the power to determine what is ultimately right or wrong, and who gives them the power to make the decisions? How is power to be allocated and how is it to be controlled? What "first principles" are necessary in order for us to make moral judgments? On what assumptions do we base these first principles? Are these assumptions sound and logical? There are very few people in the employee benefits industry, or many other industries for that matter, who are willing or able to contemplate these questions. Most prefer a quick bottom line solution which can be arrived at without fuss by reference to a law or a rule. But rules and laws tend to be inflexible. As circumstances and situations change, this inflexibility can lead to problems, more laws and rules, and a growing bureaucracy to handle them.

A report entitled *Towards a Canadian Research Strategy for Applied Ethics: A Report, by the Canadian Federation of the Humanities*, written by Michael McDonald, was submitted to the Social Science and Humanities Research Council in May 1989. It outlined the scope of research that had been done to date, in Canada, in the area of practical ethics. In addition, the report published the names of researchers who were then active in the field, and also listed publications that were germane to the subject and which had a Canadian perspective. This report, along with a book entitled *Business Ethics in Canada*, (second edition), edited by D.C. Poff and W.J. Waluchow (Prentice-Hall Canada, Inc., Scarborough, Ontario, 1991) are recommended to those who wish to study the subject area in greater detail.

¶15,005 PRACTICAL ETHICAL ISSUES IN GROUP INSURANCE MARKETING

The following are areas which contain ethical issues and considerations. The list is by no means exhaustive. Comments are suggestions only and are intended to maintain the degree of trust that is necessary for the employee benefits industry and its member employees to continue to prosper.

¶15,010 PRIVACY AND CONFIDENTIALITY

Employee information should be kept strictly private and confidential. This includes policy enrolment cards, payroll records, billing statements, certificates of insurance coverage, employee booklets that state exact benefit amounts, annual insurer lists and all completed claim forms and follow-up correspondence. All employer and policyholder files and records should be kept locked up and be made accessible only to the manager of human resources, and staff who must deal directly with a claim. No records are to be seen by or released to anyone without written authorization from any identified individuals, and the policyholder's representative.

Insurers and benefit providers must ensure that individual claimants are provided with the utmost in security precautions which will assist in keeping the records strictly private. Third-party administrators and third-party claims payers must also ensure that their records are kept private and confidential. Any person involved with the records must protect the confidentiality of the records and not discuss the information with anyone outside of that specific administration or claims department.

Agents, brokers and consultants who require information to market a benefits plan, or who are asked to act as an intermediary on behalf of a group policyholder, or a member of the benefits plan, must obtain specific written agreement from any identifiable claimants or members of the plans before receiving or acting on such information. Agents, brokers and consultants should keep all employee records and copies of any correspondence identifying employees or claimants safe and secure, preferably locked up. Files should not be left open and accessible on desks.

Names, Social Insurance Numbers, and identifiable employee ID numbers should be left out of employee lists during a group insurance plan marketing. These should also be left out of claims listings and experience reports, unless there is suspicion of fraud. If fraud is suspected, the insurer or benefit provider should have the right of conducting the investigation. If a plan is self-insured, it may be necessary to hire outside auditors or investigators. Any outside people brought in for investigative or audit purposes should be required to provide confirmation that all information pertinent to individual claims will be kept confidential.

Under no circumstances should people not directly involved with the files, or the claims information, be allowed access to the files.

¶15,015 BENEFIT DESIGN AND FUNDING

Unilateral decisions concerning the implementation, or cancellation, of employee benefit plans or benefits are not recommended methods of action. Adequate time must be allowed for the input of all eligible employees or members, and their dependent spouses, if applicable. Employee surveys should be used on a regular basis to ensure that plans fit the needs of the employees and their dependants. Benefits should be subsequently added, dropped, or amended as the need arises.

Overall plan and benefit funding should be reviewed on an annual basis to ensure that the most appropriate funding method is being used.

Employee contributions to premium should be reviewed on an annual basis to ensure that the agreed upon premium share is maintained, and that the employee share is being used in the most tax-effective method to benefit the employees.

Premium overpayments and funds taken back into policyholder revenue from claims fluctuation or incurred but not reported (IBNR) reserves should be credited back to employees in direct proportion to the employee share of premiums. All claim reserves should be reviewed annually to ensure that proper credits and debits have been allocated.

Deductibles and co-insurance factors should be reviewed annually to ensure that they adequately reflect the impact of inflation on both the benefit coverage and the premiums charged.

Annual maximum benefits under the employer health care (EHC), and dental benefits should be reviewed annually to ensure that they adequately reflect the needs of the employees and their dependants.

Non-medical and medical weekly indemnity (WI) and long-term disability (LTD) maximum benefits should be reviewed annually to ensure that they reflect the needs of the employees and that they are adequate to maintain the same percentages of coverage for all eligible employees.

Life insurance medical and non-medical maximums should also be reviewed annually to ensure that all eligible employees can be fully covered under the same schedule.

Benefit plan designs should be compared to those of other organizations in the policyholder's geographic area and industry.

Employers should allocate rate changes fairly between the employees and the employer.

Benefit design and funding should be considered as part of the overall compensation package. Employee share of premiums should be set within the employees' ability to pay.

Group life insurance and disability benefits are rated based on the average age, incomes and the occupations of the employees. Overall average rates should not be overly influenced by small sub-groups of higher risk, older aged, higher income employees.

¶15,020 APPOINTING AGENTS, BROKERS AND CONSULTANTS

Appoint the best available person who has the experience, the knowledge and the time to do the job. Appointments should only be made after careful analysis of the ABC's qualifications, references, and desire to provide a complete, thorough, accurate, detailed and timely service.

Only one ABC or ABC team should be appointed to review a group insurance program. ABCs should only be appointed after careful analysis of the needs of the organization.

Compensation for ABC services should be reviewed before a project begins and before the ABC is appointed. Commission scales should be negotiated in advance and be confirmed in writing with the ABC and the insurer(s). No hidden commissions should be paid to ABCs. When using commissions to offset fees, maximum fees and maximum commissions allowed should be confirmed in advance. Fee-only projects should state maximum fees to be charged for project completion. All sundry fees, not covered in the initial project, should be stated and confirmed in advance. Policyholders must ensure that complete and up-to-date information is available to the ABC before asking for a firm price.

ABCs using sub-consultants should state in advance who is in charge of the project, and who is providing the back-up, or sub-consulting assistance. Projects contracted on an hourly fee basis should be charged the sub-consultant rate for the hours worked by the sub-consultant, and not the full consultant rate.

¶15,025 MARKETING INFORMATION

Information provided by all parties should be truthful and accurate. Dates should correspond with the appropriate experience and rate periods. All deviations should be noted. Premiums should be clearly identified as paid, billed or adjusted. Claims should be clearly identified as paid, or incurred. In all cases, premium and claims information should be provided in the format requested. Experience and rate information, used for group insurance marketing purposes, is not to be older than three months. Rate changes, as a result of amendments, should be identified and the effective dates noted.

There should be no attempt to hide pertinent facts on a particular policy or benefit. There should be no attempt to disguise experience or claims information. Information on all open and pending LTD claims, together with information on all life insurance waiver of premium claims, is to be provided where requested. Names and other identifying information of individual claimants is not to be included in marketing packages.

Employee data should include all employees or members currently covered, and all employees and members currently in the waiting period. Employees in the policy waiting period should be identified. Employees or members who have declined coverage or benefits should be identified, but not be identifiable by name or any type of ID number.

Employee data sheets should be complete. Names and any type of identifying numbers should not be included.

There should be no attempt at deception concerning the benefits to be covered, the internal benefit wording, the method of benefit funding, the consequences of good or poor experience on the pooled rates. The actual amount of benefit that will be received, in every situation, should be emphasized. Increases or decreases in the retention or in a rate basis should be identified as such.

¶15,030 PROPOSAL ANALYSIS

All insurers and providers should be identified on the spread sheets. All declinations should be identified along with their reasons. Any deviations from the specifications and from the present benefits should be identified and discussed.

— Missing information should be obtained.

— A minimum of 10 working days should be provided to the insurers and benefit providers to submit their quotations.

— Benefits should be compared before rates.

— References should be checked.

— Presentations should be timely.

— Proposals should include all information necessary to complete a spread sheet analysis.

— Proposals occasionally contain errors; any blatant deviations from the specifications or from the average rates shown by other insurers and providers should be confirmed prior to their implementation and preferably prior to the figures and data being entered onto the spreadsheets.

— Assessments should be accurate.

— Opinions should be identified as such.

— Recommendations should be adequately reasoned.

— Recommendations should include an assessment of the financial strength of the insurer or the provider.

— Recommendations should identify insurer and policyholder administrative strengths and weaknesses.

— Recommendations should identify insurer and policyholder systems strengths and weaknesses.

— Recommendations should include insurer and provider service strengths and weaknesses.

— Recommendations should include insurer and provider personnel strengths and weaknesses.

— Recommendations should be made with candour.

Unless there is an underlying fundamental problem, the present insurer or benefit provider should be given the opportunity to review its current rates and benefit wording, in light of the comparison, and before a change of insurer is made. The policyholder, together with the ABC if applicable, should make the decision whether or not it is appropriate to show the present insurer the spread sheet analysis, prior to a change.

¶15,035 ETHICAL SITUATIONS AND PROBLEM ANALYSIS

The following questions may be of assistance should a question of ethical concern occur. The questions are by no means exhaustive. They are meant only as brief introduction to the complexities of the subject of business ethics. Examples of situations or problems that need analysis, both from a management and from an individual point of view are: the addition of a benefit, the deletion of a benefit, a change in a benefit, a change in financing a benefit, implementing a plan, hiring an ABC, changing an ABC, wrongdoing, disloyalty, failure to disclose information, favouritism, etc.

¶15,040 Part I — What Is the Situation or Problem and Who Should Be Involved?

1. Situation or problem description: ____________________
2. Who has this problem: ____________________
3. Is this an individual's problem? ____________________
4. Is this a corporate, or group problem? ____________________
5. Is this a community problem? ____________________
6. Is this a state problem? ____________________
7. Is this a global problem? ____________________
8. Is this a combination of the above (#3 to #7) problems? __________
9. Is this a current problem? ____________________
10. Is this a possible future problem?. ____________________
11. Has this been a problem in the past? ____________________

12. For how long has this problem existed? ______
13. For how long is this problem anticipated to exist? ______
14. Why has this problem occurred? ______
15. Why will this problem continue to occur? ______
16. How can this problem be fixed? ______
17. How can this problem be prevented in the future? ______
18. What do we need to fix this problem? ______
19. What are the alternative methods of fixing this problem? ______
20. Who is able to fix this problem? ______
21. Who else should be involved? ______
22. What can others add to the discussion or solution? ______
23. What other agendas do these people have? ______
24. What other agendas do we have? ______
25. What priority should this problem's solution have? ______
26. What methods of analysis are available? ______
27. How accurate are the methods of analysis? ______
28. Are there others in similar situations? ______
29. Will specific assistance offered by others conflict with anything? ______
30. Do others have the time available to assist us? ______
31. What is the direct monetary cost of the problem or the situation? ______
32. What is the lost opportunity cost of the problem or situation? ______
33. What are the direct and indirect costs of the solution? ______
34. What are the potential costs of ignoring the problem or situation? ______
35. Do we want to correct the situation or problem? ______

¶15,045 Part II — Laws, Rules, Duties and Obligations

1. Is there a health or safety issue involved? ______
2. Would any decisions be affected by health and safety issues? ______
3. Was a current law or rule directly broken? ______
4. Will the valuation methods break any laws or rules? ______
5. Do current laws or rules need clarification? ______
6. Has the situation changed since the law or rule was written? ______
7. What is the review process regarding the appropriateness of the law or rule? ______
8. Is there an adequate education process in place? ______
9. What are the duties of the individuals involved? ______
10. What are the duties of the groups involved? ______
11. What are the duties of the corporations involved? ______
12. What are the individual's obligations to the parties involved? ______
13. What are the group's obligations to the parties involved? ______
14. What are the corporate obligations to the parties involved? ______
15. What are the community obligations to the parties involved? ______
16. What are the state obligations to the parties involved? ______
17. What are the global obligations to the parties involved? ______
18. Are there other social obligations? ______
19. Do any of these obligations conflict with each other? ______

¶15,050 Part III — Commitments, Limitations, Credibility, Experience, Honesty and Favouritism

1. What are the individual's commitments to the group? ____________
2. What are the group's commitments to the individual? ____________
3. What are the community's commitments to the individual? ________
4. What are the community's commitments to the group? ____________
5. What are the state's commitments to the individual? ____________
6. What are the state's commitments to the group? ________________
7. What are the state's commitments to the community? ____________
8. Do any of the commitments conflict? ________________________
9. What are the limitations on the individual? ___________________
10. What are the limitations on the group? _______________________
11. What are the limitations on the community? __________________
12. What are the limitations on the state? _______________________
13. Are there any global limitations? ___________________________
14. Who do the limitations affect? _____________________________
15. Why were the limitations originally imposed? _________________
16. Are the limitations still necessary? _________________________
17. Are the limitations still adequate? __________________________
18. Are the limitations easily communicated and understood? ________
19. Are the limitations taught to all parties? ____________________
20. Do any of the limitations conflict? _________________________
21. Do all parties involved have credibility? _____________________
22. What are the implications of a lack of credibility? ____________
23. Do all parties involved have experience? _____________________
24. What are the implications of a lack of experience? ____________
25. Do all parties involved act in an honest manner? ______________
26. What are the implications on all parties of a lack of honesty? _____

27. Was favouritism towards the individual involved? ____________

28. Was favouritism towards the group involved? ________________

29. Was favouritism towards the community or state involved? ________

30. What are the effects of the favouritism? ____________________

¶15,055 Part IV — Rewards, Fairness and Consequences

1. What are the rewards to the individual of the action or inaction? ____________
2. What are the rewards to the group of the action or inaction? ______
3. What are the rewards to the corporation of the action or inaction? ____________
4. What are the rewards to the community of the action or inaction? ____________
5. What are the rewards to the state of the action or inaction? ______
6. Are the rewards fair to the individual? ____________
7. Are the rewards fair to the group? ____________
8. Are the rewards fair to the corporation? ____________
9. Are the rewards fair to the community? ____________
10. Are the rewards fair to the state? ____________
11. Are the rewards fair to the global community? ____________
12. What are the consequences of the individual's action or inaction? ____________
13. What are the consequences of the group's action or inaction? ______
14. What are the consequences of the corporation's action or inaction? ____________
15. What are the consequences of the community's action or inaction? ____________
16. What are the consequences of the state's action or inaction? ______
17. What conflicts occur as a result of the consequences? ____________

¶15,060 Part V—Professionals, the Sales Process, and Conflict of Interest

1. Is a professional person, or group involved? ______
2. Does the professional specialize in the problem area? ______
3. What proof is there that the professional has kept up to date in the problem area? ______
4. Is there general agreement as to adequacy of the comparison methods employed? ______
5. Were the specifications and instructions adequate? ______
6. Was there adherence to the specifications and instructions? ______
7. Is a specific and quantifiable level of knowledge required to do the project? ______
8. What specific methods of conduct are required to do the project? ______
9. Were the methods of conduct appropriate for the project? ______
10. Were the methods of conduct used during all phases of the project? ______
11. What sales methods were used to obtain the project? ______
12. Did the sales methods provide full disclosure of pertinent facts to all parties? ______
13. Were all pertinent facts discussed with all parties? ______
14. What were the pertinent facts for the sales process? ______
15. Was the project sold or bought on the basis of need? ______
16. Was the project sold or bought on the basis of buying a dream? ______
17. Name all things necessary to make the dream a reality. ______
18. Was the project bought or sold on the basis of fear versus comfort? ______
19. Was the project bought or sold on the basis of something being right or wrong? ______
20. Was the project bought or sold for the most appropriate reasons? ______

21. Did the sales process involve advertising? ____________________
22. Was the advertising deceptive? ____________________
23. Does the agent, broker or consultant have fiduciary responsibilities for the project? ____________________
24. To whom and in what order do these responsibilities fall? ________
25. What process was followed in choosing the agent, broker, or consultant? ____________________
26. Did the process for choosing the ABC examine all pertinent facts? ____________________
27. Was the process for choosing the ABC fair? ____________________
28. Was there a conflict of interest between any of the individuals or parties involved? ____________________
29. Did the conflict of interest have an impact on the possible results and were the results fair? ____________________
30. Did all individuals and parties present all facts honestly and upfront? ____________________
31. Did friendship affect the decision making process? ____________________

¶15,065 Part VI — Facts, Assumptions, Results, Decisions, Limitations

1. Were all necessary facts presented by all parties? ____________
2. Were the facts presented in a completely understandable manner? ____________
3. Were all necessary facts and names kept private and confidential? ____________
4. Were any facts intentionally held back? ____________
5. Were all assumptions agreed to by all parties? ____________
6. Were all facts and assumptions presented independent of outside influence? ____________
7. Was the research used to justify the results preformed independent of outside influence? ____________
8. Did an obligation for cooperation affect the results or the decisions? ____________
9. Did administration procedures adversely affect the results or decisions? ____________
10. Did personal opinion have an effect on the results and decisions? ____________
11. Did the results and decisions recognize the effect of the opinions? ____________
12. Were the results and decisions presented promptly and on time? ____________
13. What part did timing play in the results and decisions? ____________
14. What limits were imposed in the process and the decisions? ____________
15. Were limits adequately defined and named? ____________
16. What effects did the limits have on the process and the decisions? ____________
17. Were all objections to the process and the decisions adequately argued? ____________
18. Were all objectors to the process and the decisions heard? ____________

19. What conflicts were there between objectors, objections and objectives? ____________
20. What conciliation was reached between objectors, objections and objectives? ____________
21. What extent did bluffing play for all parties in the process and the decisions? ____________
22. What extent did lying play for all parties in the process and in the decisions? ____________
23. What extent did "passing the buck" play in the process and the decisions? ____________
24. What extent did whistle blowing play in the process and the decisions? ____________
25. What extent did bribery or extortion play in the process and the decisions? ____________
26. Were individual, group, corporate, community, or state rights placed at the forefront? ____________
27. Was corporate or individual social performance part of the issue? ____________
28. Was equality between individuals or between groups part of the issue? How? ____________
29. Were human rights part of the issue? ____________
30. Were corporate, individual or group rights part of the issue? How? ____________
31. Was corporate or group indoctrination part of the issue? How? ____
32. Was bottom-line-mentality part of the issue? How? ____________
33. Was financial speculation part of the issue? How? ____________
34. Was tax effectiveness versus tax evasion part of the issue? How? ____________
35. Was currency or investment control part of the issue? How? ______
36. Was corporate profit put before all else? ____________
37. Was personal gain put before all else? ____________

¶15,070 Part VII — Making Decisions and Finding Solutions

1. Have all of the facts been gathered? ____________
2. Have all of the facts been analyzed? ____________
3. Has the follow-up been completed? ____________
4. Has everything been documented? ____________
5. Has a back-up of the documentation been completed? ____________
6. Has the situation and its ramifications been discussed with those who need to know? ____________
7. What type of solution is required by the individual? ____________
8. What type of solution is required by the group? ____________
9. What type of solution is required by the corporation? ____________
10. What type of solution is required by the community? ____________
11. What type of solution is required by the state? ____________
12. What types of solutions are required or permitted by law? ____________
13. Is a balance required between various solutions and all of the parties? ____________
14. Is a balance necessary and has it been attained or maintained? ____________
15. Does the proposed solution fit the needs of the individual? ____________
16. Does the proposed solution fit the needs of the group? ____________
17. Does the proposed solution fit the needs of the corporation? ____________
18. Does the proposed solution fit the needs of the community? ____________
19. Does the proposed solution fit the needs of the state? ____________
20. Does the proposed solution fit the needs of the global community? ____________
21. Will the proposed solution(s) break any laws? ____________
22. Is punishment or re-education required? ____________
23. What have others historically recommended as punishment or re-education? ____________
24. Have past recommendations been effective and fair? ____________

25. Will past recommendations suffice in this situation? __________

26. What specific punishment or re-education will be undertaken? ____

27. When will the punishment or re-education take place? __________

28. Are there extenuating circumstances which might temper any decisions? ____

29. Is the situation appropriate for leniency? __________________

30. How can the situation be best used to be fair to all concerned? ____

Like many other business practices, business ethics requires an interdisciplinary approach to find the most appropriate solutions. Posing a solution for a particular ethical problem not only involves the corporation or group, but also must involve the individuals within the corporation and the individuals within the community and the state. The consequences of inaction, inappropriate action, incomplete action, overpriced action, non-action, immoral action, amoral action, undignified action, and overvalued action all cross the boundaries between the individual, the group, the corporation, the community, the state, and now, the world. Whereas illegal action may be specifically dealt with, or dismissed through existing legal systems, there are many grey areas in the law that complicate these systems and their solutions to the problems. These grey areas are caused by changing times, changing attitudes, changing virtues and inadequately reflected consequences. In addition, the concept of fairness is variable and fluctuating. The definition of fairness often seems controlled by those who have the power and the money. Concepts of right and wrong, together with how they are to be measured or valued, ebbs and flows between lawyers, politicians, community leaders, business leaders, church leaders, educators, and philosophers. Individual human rights, the rights of the corporation, the rights of the family, the rights of the community, and the rights of the state all attempt to live together. Corporate profit objectives, state income objectives and the income objectives of individuals also attempt to live together, under similar sets of ethical guidelines. Yet corporations, communities, states and individuals are different categories of entities who operate with different motives, for different purposes, and under different laws. Reward and punishment are valued and treated in different ways for each of these categories. This different treatment can lead to uncertainty and can destroy trust between the various categories. Sticking to the rules, honouring commitments and acting for mutual advantage are often voiced as concrete ethical guidelines for business. Do these constitute the first principles of ethical business conduct? Do they always constitute socially responsible behaviour? The employee benefits industry is, by and large, self-regulating. Should someone in the industry fail to perform or fail to act in the best interests of the client, there is rarely more than a slap on the wrist applied, or at worst, the suspension of a licence to collect commissions, or the loss of Agent of Record status. When a policyholder intentionally deceives an insurer, there are generally few, if any, repercussions to the policyholder or the individual involved, with the exception of, perhaps, a declination to renew a policy. Should more rules be set up in an attempt to control every possible action, or do we have too many rules and regulations already? Can these rules predict all of the consequences of specific actions? In business, does one have to bother with what is ethical and what is not? Whatever the answer, the repercussions will affect our attitudes not only to group insurance marketing, but to the very way that we structure and conduct our lives and our business.

CHAPTER 16

¶16,000 LOOKING AHEAD

Where is the Canadian group insurance industry headed? Part of the answer depends on what the government (a.k.a. the people) ends up doing with Medicare. If the trend continues, for the government to divest itself of the expense of paying for every and all types of medical problems, then there will be a growing demand for private insurers to take over where the government leaves off. Who will pay for these expenses? Within ten years, the federal government should be well out of debt, as long as the government forces the Bank of Canada to keep interest rates low. To do this, the government will have to keep fighting the pressures and misinformation flow produced by the international currency traders. High interest rates on the accumulated debt will be replaced with lower interest rates, which by itself, will put a huge dent in the national debt total. If current taxation rates continue, there should be enough money for social programs, including Medicare. This assumes that the government takes a more moderate approach when considering future high risk corporate and Third World loan guarantees. If the government succeeds in getting a handle on the debt, it can continue to provide Medicare services. If not, private insurers may be given the opportunity to cover those services that have been divested by the Public Sector.

There is a real chance that borders between countries will become virtually meaningless, especially between Canada, the U.S.A. and Mexico. This trend is partly due to advances in how people manage information; it affects how people view themselves, their government, and their government services. One of the major problems that Canadians have with politics south of the border is the Americans' lack of universal Medicare. Give the U.S. basic Medicare, reduce Medicare in Canada to more basic services, and you have a neat stepping-stone to further ties with the United States. Canada has the natural resources that will assure future U.S. requirements; Quebec might establish a more independent type of state government; the railways might go; and north-south trade routes may become more stable than east-west routes. If this is the scenario (and is it such a longshot?), then Canadian group insurance companies will have to compete head-to-head with the huge, established U.S. insurers. This is not news to many Canadian life insurance companies; they already have substantial U.S. assets. At least one major Canadian life insurance company already has approximately 60 per cent of its assets invested outside of Canada! Life insurance companies lobbied hard for free trade. They wanted the ability to move capital around globally, and not just be restricted to operating in this country.

There will be fewer insurers, of course. At present, Canada has a huge surplus of life insurance companies. There are far too many companies, and too many ABCs chasing too little business. Ask most life insurance agents who have been in business for a few years, whether they would come into the business if they had to start now. There are over 150 life insurance companies operating in Canada, for approximately 27 million people. How many companies are in Japan, which has ten times the population? Less than ten! There will be many Canadian life insurance companies merging in the next decade. There would be more, and they would merge more quickly were it not for the large number of mutual life insurance companies. In mutual life companies, the policyholders "own" the companies. They will be tough to contact and to convince that mergers make sense. But when the trend starts, thousands of insurance company personnel will be made redundant.

Banks will join the group insurance fray. Group life insurance is a natural adjunct to the advanced payroll systems that they offer to their clients. The banks will initially seek the easy-to-offer, and to underwrite business such as accidental death, dependant life, optional life, optional accidental death and dismemberment, and term-life insurance policies. Banks have the financial ability to purchase insurance companies and benefit providers. Acquisition will be the easiest route for the banks to follow to gain a foothold into the health care, dental and disability markets. Unlike the life insurers, who have had problems with their recent attempts to get into the banking and trust business, the banks have the resources to buy large and profitable insurers, and their all-important systems. More insurers will come up with the "for sale" signs out front, as the U.S. corporate rating agencies, which must have been somewhat embarrassed by the timing of their downgrading of the failing Confederation Life, take a harsher look at the industry. Downgraded insurers will be easy pickings for the banks, assuming that deregulation of the former "pillars" of the financial community has had enough time to filter down through the system to enable them to make these purchases.

Until the purchases and the mergers happen and the chaos settles down, insurer margins will continue to be very tight. One major Canadian insurer has recently hiked its retention on some group insurance plans by 5 per cent. Others may follow. Combine tighter margins with decreases in government services and lower overall rates of return on investments, and you will see higher premiums. Higher premiums, a more educated buying public, and higher retention charges will put pressure on insurers to lower commission scales. Commission scales in the U.S. are much lower than they are in Canada, basically because of their higher premium payments. This will happen here. In future, a more educated buying public may find that it can deal directly with the insurance companies, and save on paying commissions and the high consulting fees now charged by the ABCs.

Dealing directly with insurers will be made more easy, especially for group insurance quotes, via the "electronic highways". Obtaining quotes will be accomplished electronically. Copies of the policy, experience, rates and employee data will be transmitted electronically to any number of insurance companies, along with instructions for alternative quotes. The insurers will be able to electronically process their quotes and transmit them back to your organization within a couple of days, complete with spreadsheets. You are left to pick the winner and contact the insurer to set up the policy. The technology is here now. The industry is waiting for someone to start the stampede.

Electronic underwriting, advanced electronic education, and electronic purchases, combined with the pressure of the banks getting into the life insurance business, will mean the demise of the life insurance agency system as we know it. The career life insurance agent today has to know an incredible number of products, as well as taxation, accounting, funding, investing, and how to deal with people. An agent has one of the most complex jobs that there is in the financial marketplace, yet the old reputation of the shyster, door-to-door salesman still haunts the industry. Talk to the clerk in the bank that you trust your money to and ask for advice on investment decisions. How does it feel to talk to a relatively inexperienced person about your family's and your own financial future? What products does this person know well? Yet many people still think that someone who brings home low wages from a bank or trust company is a better person to deal with than a life insurance agent. Is it sad to think that the agent, who, historically, has come to your house, in your time, at his or her own expense, to personally see that you and your family are looked after, may be replaced by a computerized underwriter?

The "alphabet" group benefit consulting houses will survive, but in a much different form. Huge downtown offices are not as useful in today's electronic world. A consultant can literally work out of the car or out of a suitcase, from anywhere in the world. The need for an expensive location with high overhead, in a downtown location, will be reduced. Want to hold a meeting with clients? Book a meeting room in a hotel. Need to meet with your associates? Do it over the telephone. The alphabet houses will survive, but only because the have spread out into other human resource areas and have globalized. Those that have not, or will not, will die off.

New players will join the group insurance and employee benefits field. More accountants and lawyers will join with actuaries to offer consulting services. Individual ABCs will continue to serve in local specialty markets aided by the technological jumps that allow work to be completed at home, or in other places with low overhead.

The workforce is changing, with the huge companies of the past becoming extinct. Employees will work as consultants do now, independently, and with the ability to write off employment expenses. With the trend to individuals setting themselves up as companies, or as self-employed persons, the tax system will have to be re-evaluated in order to offset the self-employed person's ability to write off expenses. The present insurer emphasis, of offering their least expensive group insurance rates to corporations and to unions, will change as more people work for themselves and out of their homes. A greater emphasis will be put on the association of individuals type of group plans because these are better suited to underwrite individual entrepreneurs. The present tax system will be modified into a far less complicated user-pay system. On everything purchased, including services, and every time that a dollar changes hands (even from one bank account to another), a level tax will be assessed. The majority of our current taxes, including income taxes and GST could be replaced by this system. This will result in the demise of group health and dental insurance plans as we know them, because the tax advantage for installing them will be gone. Imagine the consequences of doing away with all taxes that now exist and implementing a system that generates income every time a dollar moves in the economy. The number of jobs that are currently tied to the present tax system is enormous. That is why there is such a great desire by those holding tax-related jobs, to keep the huge complicated mess we currently have. The same goes for our present pension and insurance schemes. The people who create the complexity make it more and more complex, thereby keeping themselves employed.

Demographics show that a large group of people will surge into the retirement years within the next decade. These people will continue to work (probably more in part-time roles than full time) because they will still want to make a contribution. And opportunities to contribute will be there. Group insurance plans will have to change reduction and cancellation clauses to accommodate the older workforce. Average life expectancy will continue to increase, barring the calamities of new diseases or natural disasters. This will result in a drop in life insurance rates. It will also mean that annuities will cost more. Continuing benefits beyond age 65 will also cause LTD rates to increase.

Insurance companies will be "leaner and meaner" than they are now. The life insurance industry is just starting to slim down the way that the trust companies have had to do, and the banks before them. Insurers who survive will be in the global marketplace, both by offering products, and through investment in those areas. Insurer management will examine and implement all of next year's "management system of the day" fads. Total Quality Management will be mixed with benchmarking, re-engineering, and new management effectiveness systems. Electronic data interchange will be combined with the use of stored and new information to achieve business goals and to market an organization's value. Management will still be involved in cost reduction strategies, performance measurement, detection of fraud, implementing and maintaining corporate goals, as well as disaster recovery plans. The public's views on the necessity for "privacy" may change, as personal information continues to be accumulated by computers. People will still buy insurance against disasters. And the world will still require people to sell and service the policies.

In the interim, people in the benefits area will continue as they have for the last 40 years, by revising old products, offering various methods of financing benefits, and by offering new "money saving" ways to ease administration chores. With approximately 40 per cent of households now having a form of "home" office or home-based business, will traditional group insurance plans through employers and unions be as prevalent ten years from now? Traditional plans do not usually allow contract employees to be eligible. This will cause a demand to purchase benefits through association of individuals type plans. And these plans will be purchased over your home computer lines through your financial institution of choice.

The following are other issues that will affect, or are currently affecting, insurance companies, benefit providers, and people involved in the benefits industry.

— Changes in the public health care system.

— Changes in the private health care system.

— Consideration of a two- or three-tier health care system.

— Insurer and provider corporate financial ratings.

— Industry consolidation and fewer insurers.

— Tighter margins.

— Higher premiums caused by inflation and trend issues in the health care field.

— The aging of the population.

— Lower commissions.

— Restructured fees.

— Direct purchases from insurers.

— Revamping of the current insurer agency system.

— Re-evaluating the agent's home and business sales call.

— Revamping of the "alphabet" consulting houses.

— New players: accountants, lawyers joining the actuaries.

— Technological jumps.

— A corporate move towards self-insurance and risk co-operatives.

— Reductions in tax incentives for employee benefits.

— The changing workforce; changing needs.

— The effect of retired employees on group insurance benefits and rates.

— The impact of global economics.

— Revised capital management and asset quality.

— ISO 9000 and similar quality control requirements.

— Fraud detection.

— New cost reduction strategies.

— Changes in evaluating financing information.

— Use of stored information to achieve new business goals.

— Electronic data interchange.

— Implementing and maintaining disaster recovery plans.

— Replacement of amalgam fillings due to mercury content.

Future financial service industries will remain viable for as long as people and economies continue to trade money for goods and services. Insurers and benefit providers will amalgamate and specialize. To date, Canadian life insurers have not, for the most part, expanded their services beyond the financial services area. They do not control food stuffs, entertainment, brand names, patents or technology. The life insurers have not registered any patents in the last 25 years, nor will one see copyright protection on much, if any, of their policies or services. Instead, they continue to sell peace of mind and consumer confidence through conservative investment strategies, detailed standards, accurate methods of financial measurement, heavy corporate structure, industry positioning and trust.

The employee benefits industry believes that small changes and refinements can have huge effects. The benefits industry continues to promote people from inside the industry. This can have the benefit of maintaining the comfortable status quo, but it can also have the effect of reducing the ability to produce new ideas and services. The Canadian life insurance industry, including the area of group insurance, is mature and crowded. Future industry growth will be fuelled by acquisitions and by further involvement in the global business community.

¶17,000 APPENDICES

¶17,005 GLOSSARY

[The following *Glossary of Group Insurance and Related Terms* is reproduced with the permission of Metropolitan Life Insurance Company. It contains some amendments by the author (within square brackets), as well as deletions (marked by three asterisks) which were not pertinent to this book.]

This Glossary has been prepared for the general information of sales agents, consultants, brokers, and other individuals working in the field of group life and health insurance. Metropolitan, its employees and agents, [CCH Canadian and the author] assume no liability whatsoever for the accuracy of any of the definitions contained in this Glossary, or for reliance by any person on any of the definitions.

The definitions in contracts, quotes and other such material will govern in any specific case.

FOREWORD

The definitions for terms contained in this Glossary were not composed specifically for this production, but rather drawn from numerous published sources. It is, therefore, acknowledged that more precise definitions may exist, and that interpretations plus usage of terms will change through time.

* * *

A

A & H. *Refer to* **Accident and Health**

Accident and Health

A general term applied to all group coverages, except group life insurance, which pertains to accidents and illnesses of employees and dependants. The Insurance Industry's new general term is Health Insurance and means disability, medical and dental.

Accident Insurance

A form of health insurance against loss by accidental bodily injury (an injury sustained as the result of an accident).

Accidental Death and Dismemberment Benefits

A lump sum payment is assured if the insured dies as the result of an accident, within a specified period. Usually the same sum is paid on the accidental loss of both limbs, hand and foot or the sight of both eyes.

Accidental Death Benefit

A lump sum payment upon the loss of life of an insured person due to the direct cause of an accident.

Accidental Means

An unforeseen unexpected, unintended cause of an accident. Both the cause and the result of what happened must be accidental.

Accounting, Short Method. *Refer to* **Self-Administration**

Accumulation Period

The maximum length of time an individual has to incur covered expenses which satisfy a required deductible.

* * *

Acquisition Cost. *Refer to* **Cost, Acquisition**

Actively-at-Work-Requirement

A form of individual evidence of insurability, since the insured's health must be at least sound enough to be actively at work at the usual place of employment on the date the insurance takes effect. Since this definition is impractical for dependants, there is usually a requirement that if the dependant is confined in a hospital on the date the insurance would otherwise become effective, the effective date of insurance will be deferred until release from the hospital.

Actuary

An accredited, professionally trained person in insurance mathematics, who calculates rates, reserves, dividends and other valuations as well as makes statistical studies and reports.

AD&D. *Refer to* **Accidental Death and Dismemberment**

Addition

A person who becomes insured subsequent to the effective date of the group policy.

Additional Provisions

Provisions in addition to the insuring and benefit provisions, and to the uniform provisions which define and limit the coverage.

Administration

The handling of all functions related to the operation of the group insurance plan once it becomes effective. The claim function may or may not be included.

Administration, Home Office. *Refer to* **Head Office Administration**

Administration Manual

A manual of instructions provided to the policyholder by the insurance company, or administrator, which outlines and explains those duties required of the plan to assure the successful operation of the group insurance program.

Administration, Third-Party. *Refer to* **Third-Party Administration**

Administrative Services Only

Plans which do not require the underwriting services of the in surer. Instead, the only services required are administrative services, in particular, claim paying services. There is no premium to be paid and no premium tax. The client may open a bank account and direct the bank to accept cheques written against the account by authorized individuals of the insurance company, or administrator.

Administrator

The individual or company responsible for administrating a group insurance contract. This may include services such as accounting, certificate issuance and claims settlement.

Advance Expense Adjustment Factor

A factor applied in a group life rate calculation in recognition of the variation in expenses by size of case.

Advance Payment. *Refer to* **Deposit Premium**

Adverse Selection

The tendency of persons with poorer than average health expectations to apply for or continue insurance to a greater extent than do persons with average or better health expectations.

Affiliate

A corporation of which a majority of the capital stock is owned or controlled by any or all of the stockholders, directors or officers of another corporation, who also own or control a majority of the stock of such other corporation.

Age, Attained. *Refer to* **Attained Age**

Age Distribution

A distribution of either eligible or insured employees under a group plan by the rate, based on either their Insurance Year of Birth, their Attained Age or Year of Birth.

Age Limits

Minimum or maximum age limits for the insuring of individuals under insurance contracts.

Age, Misstatement of. *Refer to* **Misstatement of Age**

Age Reduction

A reduction in the amount of insurance on an individual who attains a specified age.

Aggregate Amount (Limit)

The maximum sum for which an insurer is liable for any single loss series of losses, as outlined within the contract.

Aggregate Limit Clause

Under this clause (used in noncancellable policies), the company promises to pay up to a total of 15 months, two years, five years or every ten years for an aggregate of all disabilities. When the total payments for all of the insured's disabilities reach the aggregate limit, the policy expires.

Agreement, Commission. *Refer to* **Commission Agreement**

Agreement, Single Case. *Refer to* **Single Case Agreement**

Agreement, Trust. *Refer to* **Trust Agreement**

Air Trip Insurance. *Refer to* **Travel Accident Policies**

* * *

Allocated Benefits

Payments (in some policies) for specified services which are limited to maximum specified amounts.

Allowable Expense

Any necessary, reasonable, or customary item of expense which is covered, at least in part, by one or more of the plans under which an individual is insured.

Amendment

A formal document changing the provisions of the group contract and agreed to jointly by authorized representatives of the insurer and the policyholder.

* * *

Amount, Aggregate (Limit). *Refer to* **Aggregate Amount (Limit)**

Analysis, Experience. *Refer to* **Experience Analysis**

Anniversary

Used to refer to a specific date following the effective date of the master contract for renewal action, such as rate determination and dividend calculation.

Anniversary, Policy. *Refer to* **Policy Anniversary**

Announcement Material

Written communications that are used to enroll and explain a group insurance program.

Annual Statement

The yearly report, provided by insurers to provincial and federal authorities, showing assets and liabilities, receipts and disbursements, and other financial data.

Antiselection

Employees selecting coverage in a manner that is beneficial to themselves and detrimental to the plan as a whole.

Applicant, Late. *Refer to* **Late Applicant**

Application, Employee Group

The employee application provides the pertinent data regarding each employee. In addition it may also allow for authorization of payroll deductions, beneficiary designations, waiver of contributory coverages (where permitted).

Application, Final. *Refer to* **Final Application**

Application, Group Master. *Refer to* **Group Master Application**

Appointment of Beneficiary. *Refer to* **Beneficiary, Appointment of**

Appropriateness of Care

In this context, the term is used to describe the proper setting for delivery of medical care, e.g., an acute care hospital, an extended care facility, etc.

A & S Group Benefits. *Refer to* **Benefits, Group Accident and Sickness Insurance**

ASO. *Refer to* **Administrative Services Only. (Plans and Contracts)**

Assignment

Group life insurance may not be assigned under the usual group insurance plan provisions. However, hospital and dental benefits may be assigned to providers.

Association Group Plans

Health insurance plans designed for members of a professional association or trade association. Members may be protected under a group policy or by individual franchise policies.

* * *

Assurance

This term which today is synonymous with "Insurance" is more commonly used in Canada and Great Britain.

Attained Age

The age attained at one's last birthday which does not change until the next birthday.

Authorization to Pay Benefits

A provision in a medical benefits claim form, by which the insured authorizes the insurance company to pay any benefits directly to the provider of care on whose charges the claim is based.

Automatic Reinsurance

A type of reinsurance in which the insurer must cede and the reinsuring company must accept all risks within certain contractually defined areas. The reinsuring company undertakes in advance to grant reinsurance to the extent specified in the agreement in every case where the ceding company accepts the application and retains its own limit.

Automatic Restoration Provision

A policy provision for automatic annual reinstatement of used benefits under major medical plans with lifetime maximums. Benefits reinstated annually are limited to the lesser of a stated amount or the unrestored portion of the original maximum.

Average Factor

The application of a percent to the premium received. Arrived at by relating the estimated commission to be paid to the estimated premium to be received. Usually adjusted to actual at end of commission year.

Average Premium Rate

The rate per $1,000 of Group Life or, Health Insurance that is determined by dividing the total premium (modified by various adjustment factors) by the total volume of insurance in force.

B

Baby Group. *Refer to* **Small Group**

Back Charge

A charge made to a policyholder on a current billing statement for premium due for an insured whose insurance became effective at an earlier date.

Bad Debts

The amount of income lost to a provider because of failure of patients to pay amounts owed. These amounts are recovered by increasing rates of charge paying patients by a proportional amount.

Bank Plans

This type of plan has many forms but the most common is one which insures the depositor for the amount of his savings account, but with some upper limit.

Bargaining, Collective. *Refer to* **Collective Bargaining**

Base Plan

Any basic medical care plan that provides limited first-dollar hospital, surgical or medical benefits, as contrasted with major medical benefit plans which provide comprehensive hospital, surgical and medical benefits.

Basic Compensation

The basic salary or wages paid to an employee, excluding overtime, bonuses and other forms of additional compensation. It may or may not include commission income. Basic compensation is often used as a means of establishing an employee's benefits and contributions.

Basic Group Life Tables, Canadian. *Refer to* **Canadian Basic Group Life Tables**

Basic Life Coverage

Refers to a base life insurance plan to which optional/Voluntary Life Coverage may be added.

Basic Schedule of Operations

A standard schedule on which the procedures, benefit amounts and premium rates of all other schedules are based. An insurer may offer a variety of base schedules and offer various multiples of these base schedules.

Beneficiary

The person(s) designated by an insured to receive Group Life and/or Accidental Death Benefits upon the death of the insured.

Beneficiary, Appointment of

The employee may nominate a beneficiary to receive the insurance proceeds and has the right to change the beneficiary subject to any legal restrictions which apply [i.e., Quebec regulations differ].

Beneficiary, Change of

Subject to the law, employees may change their designated beneficiary(ies). This is commonly done by submitting a written request which may be a form provided for this specific purpose.

Beneficiary, Contingent. *Refer to* **Contingent Beneficiary**

Beneficiary, Designated. *Refer to* **Designated Beneficiary**

Beneficiary, Irrevocable. *Refer to* **Irrevocable Beneficiary**

Beneficiary, Joint. *Refer to* **Joint Beneficiary**

Beneficiary, Primary. *Refer to* **Primary Beneficiary**

Benefit

The amount payable by the insurance company to a claimant, assignee, or beneficiary when the insured suffers a loss covered by the policy.

Benefit, Accidental Death. *Refer to* **Accidental Death Benefit**

Benefit, Daily. *Refer to* **Daily Benefit**

Benefit, Disability. *Refer to* **Disability Benefit**

Benefit, Extended Death. *Refer to* **Extended Death Benefit**

Benefit Formula

A formula or rule for determining the amount of benefit payable under each contingency covered by a group insurance contract. The formula frequently takes into account salary and employment [classification or] category at the time the loss is incurred.

Benefit, Maximum. *Refer to* **Maximum Benefit**

[Benefit Provider]

[An organization that provides group benefits and services, such as EHC and Dental. The organization may or may not be an insurance company, and may or may not operate "for profit". See also **Non-Profit Insurers**.]

Benefit Waiting Period

The period of time which must elapse before someone is eligible for benefits under a group insurance contract.

Benefits, Authorization to Pay. *Refer to* **Authorization to Pay Benefits**

Benefits, Extended. *Refer to* **Extended Benefits**

Benefits, Group Life Insurance

Group life insurance is based upon the one year term plan. It is pure life insurance coverage and contains no savings element. The benefit provided is a lump sum payable to the beneficiary named by the employee upon the death of the employee from any cause whatsoever.

Benefits, Maternity. *Refer to* **Maternity Benefits**

Billing, Level Premium. *Refer to* **Level Premium Billing**

Billing, Monthly Adjustment. *Refer to* **Monthly Adjustment Billing**

Billing, Premium Notice. *Refer to* **Premium Notice Billing**

Billings

An initial billing statement will contain a list of each employee covered, and the corresponding premium for that employee. Subsequent billings are usually prepared monthly.

Binder Premium. *Refer to* **Advance Payment**

Blanket Insurance

A class of group insurance that covers loss arising from specific hazards incidental to, or defined by reference to, a particular activity or activities.

Blanket Policy

A contract between an insurer and a policyholder which provides for combining all major and minor coverages in a single master group policy. This type is in contrast to issuing an individual master group policy for each major coverage with riders for the minor coverges attached to the applicable major policy.

Blue Cross

An independent nonprofit membership corporation providing protection against insurable health care costs.

Booklet — Certificate

Many carriers distribute booklets to individuals insured under a master contract. These summarize policy provisions, coverages and limitations provided to each insured member of a group insurance plan. In some instances this booklet replaces any additional certificate cards.

Broker

A term generally used to describe one who places business with more than one company, and who has no exclusive contract requiring that all his business first be offered to a single company.

Business, Community-Rated. *Refer to* **Community Rated Business and to Pooling**

Business, Fully-Pooled *Refer to* **Community-Rated Business and to Pooling**.

C

Call, Service. *Refer to* **Service Call**

Call, Service Renewal. *Refer to* **Service Renewal Call**

[**Canada Pension Plan Disability Offsets**. *Refer to* **CPP Disability Offsets** and **Full CPP Disability Offsets**]

Canadian Basic Group Life Tables

Tables which have been constructed by the Canadian Institute of Actuaries provide rates of mortality for male lives and female lives separately and also for male lives and female lives combined.

Canadian Institute of Actuaries

An organization of individuals who have passed the required examinations and have become Associates in the Institute. The Institute provides continuing education and development programs, promotes and publishes actuarial research, and enforces a professional code of ethical conduct for its members.

Canadian Life & Health Insurance Association

An association of most of the life and health insurance companies in Canada. It conducts research on insurance issues and promotes the best interests of the insurance industry. It is the primary source of information about the life and health insurance industry in Canada.

Cancellable Contract

A contract of accident and sickness insurance that may be terminated by the policyholder or insurer at any time. The fact that the contract is cancel able must be stated in the contract and usually provides that the insurer must give the policyholder ten days' notice by registered mail and the policyholder give the insurer notice by registered mail.

Capitation. *Refer to* **Dental Capitation Plans**

Capitation Plans, Dental. *Refer to* **Dental Capitation Plans**

Card, Change in Classification. *Refer to* **Change in Classification Card**

Card, Change of Dependants. *Refer to* **Change of Dependants Card**

Card, Enrollment. *Refer to* **Enrollment Card**

Card, ID (Identification). *Refer to* **ID Card**

Card, Record. *Refer to* **Record Card**

Card, Refusal. *Refer to* **Waiver Card**

Card Register. *Refer to* **Record Card**

Card, Waiver. *Refer to* **Waiver Card**

Cards, Certificate. *Refer to* **Certificate Cards**

Care, Appropriateness of. *Refer to* **Appropriateness of Care**

Care, Extended Health. *Refer to* **Extended Medical Expense**

Care, Home Health. *Refer to* **Home Health Care**

Carrier

The party (insurer) to the group contract who agrees to underwrite (carry the risk) and provide certain types of coverage and service.

Carve-Out

The term often used when referring to an **Integrated Plan**.

Case

An expression used to refer to the group plan of a policyholder in its entirety.

Cash Claims. *Refer to* **Claims, Cash**

Casualty Insurance

Such lines of insurance as automobile, liability, aviation, bonding and theft.

[**CEBS**. *Refer to* **International Foundation of Employee Benefit Plans**]

Cede

To effect re-insurance. See **Re-insurance**.

Census Data

Statistical information such as age, sex, income, insurance classification, or dependent status on persons eligible for or insured under a group policy which is used to determine premium rates or benefits.

Certificate — Booklet. *Refer to* **Booklet-Certificate**

Certificate Cards

The insurer may issue certificate cards to the covered employees, in a form convenient for insertion in a wallet. The certificate mentions the name of the employee, the benefits for which he or she and (eventually) any dependants are covered, and a capsule summary of the amount of coverage.

Certificate Holder

The insured person under a group plan.

Certificate Rider

A document which amends and or supplements the certificate of insurance.

Chance Fluctuation. *Refer to* **Statistical Fluctuation**

Change in Classification Card

From time to time an employee will change his/her insurance classification and in that case a change in classification card is filled out in order that the coverage can be changed and the appropriate charge made thereafter. This may happen because of a change in salary or because of a change in position, etc.

Change of Beneficiary. *Refer to* **Beneficiary, Change of**

Change of Dependants Card

When a single employee marries, or when a married employee becomes single because of the death or divorce of a spouse without children, a change of dependants card is filled out to advise the insurance company of this change in status.

Charge, Conversion. *Refer to* **Conversion Charge**

Charged, Claims. *Refer to* **Claims Charged**

[**Chartered Life Underwriter (CLU)**. *Refer to* **Life Underwriters Association of Canada**]

Child

Refers to a child who is supported solely by the insured and permanently living in the home of which the insured is the head; a child who is legally adopted and a stepchild who lives in the insured's home.

Child, Handicapped

Specific provision in contract for the continuing coverage of child dependants regardless of age if handicapped and unable to provide for themselves.

Claim

A demand to the insurer by the insured person for the payment of benefits under a policy.

Claimant

Plan beneficiary exercising his/ her right to receive benefits.

Claim, Closed

A claim under which all apparent benefits have been paid.

Claim Cost Control

Efforts made by an insurer both inside and outside its own organization to restrain and direct claim payments so that health insurance premium dollars are used as efficiently as possible.

Claim Lag

The time interval between incurred date of a claim and its submission to the insurer for payment; also used to mean the time between claim incurral and payment (cheque or draft issue or redemption).

Claim List

A list of claims paid under a plan or coverage for a specified time period, which includes such information as identification of the covered person, cause of the claim, and kind and amount of charges paid.

Claim Manual

The manual supplied to the administrator of the group plan by the insurer which describes the procedures to follow in processing a claim. It is usually part of the administration manual.

Claim Payment, Draft Book. *Refer to* **Draft Book Claim Payment**.

Claim Reserves

Must be held by an insurance company to cover the liability which has been incurred by reason of carrying the risk to a certain point of time. Even though the risk may be discontinued at that point, claims may still be due under the terms of the contract and other claims may not be reported until after the actual date of termination of the contract. The claim reserve must be sufficient to meet all such claims which are properly payable even though they may not be reported at the precise time of cancellation.

Claims, Cash

Cash disbursed, drafts redeemed, or drafts drawn for the settlement of group insurance claims.

Claims Charged

Denotes amount of claim dollars actually charged to a group policy. If pooling or claim averaging is used to stabilize a group's experience during a single contract period, the claim expense "charged" to the group's premium in that single year may be more or less than the group's actual incurred claims.

Claims, Co-ordination of Benefits

The policy will specify how benefits will be calculated if the claimant is insured under several group contracts against the same event.

Claims Examinations

The policy will specify that the insurance company has the right at its own expense to make an independent medical examination if it so requires in order to determine whether a claim is valid.

Claims Fluctuation Reserve

The insurance company attempts to set its premium rate at such a level that after deducting claims incurred and the company's retention, the balance is likely to be positive, leaving available a cash amount which, after reserves have been set up, may be refunded to the policyholder. The reserve is held to the credit of the policyholder and used only to cover any negative results which may occur in future experience.

Claims Incurred

This is the total of claims paid for the period plus changes in the reserves held for incurred but unreported, unsettled, or continuing claims. It represents the estimate of the total liability created in the policy year by the plan of benefits in effect for that policy year.

Claims, Incurred But Unpaid

Incurred claims which have not been paid as of some specified date (may include both reported and unreported claims).

Claims, Notice and Proof

The policy will specify time limits for giving notice, and then proof of claim. It also specifies the manner in which the proof of loss must be submitted.

Claims, Paid

Most insurers define paid claims as those benefit cheques dated within the policy year. Other insurers count only those cheques issued which cleared the bank during the policy period. Although some other definitions do exist, these two are the most common.

Claims, Payment of

The policy will specify to whom benefits are payable and whether there are alternative methods of settlement.

Claims, Pooled. *Refer to* **Pooled Claims**

Claims, Recurring Disability. *Refer to* **Recurring Disability**

Claims, Time of Payment

The policy will specify under what conditions and when a claim will be paid.

Class

The category into which an insured is placed in the schedule of insurance in order to determine the amount of eligible coverage under the policy.

Classes of Persons

Group insurance is a form of insurance which is designed to insure classes of persons rather than specific individuals. The lives insured are not named or otherwise identified as individuals, they are defined as members of a class. From time to time different persons will be insured under the contract but the terms of the contract remain the same. The names of the persons insured are usually never mentioned in the contract of insurance.

Classification, Change in Card. *Refer to* **Change in Classification Card**

Classification of Employees

In reviewing the group plan, the underwriter will look for a precise definition of the employees who are eligible, a precise determination of when new employees become covered for benefits and a precise definition of the various classes in the schedule of insurance. The underwriter will check to see that the employees have been enrolled and classified precisely according to the schedule of insurance which will appear in the master policy.

Clause, Incontestable. *Refer to* **Incontestable clause**

Clerical Error Provision

A policy provision that an eligible person, who submits proper written request for coverage, shall not be denied same because of the policyholder's failure (due to clerical error) to give proper notice to the insurer.

Closed Groups

A closed group is one where there are no new entrants. In such a case the persons covered gradually dwindle in number and eventually the group falls below an acceptable size. This is not a permanent plan of group insurance and is therefore not acceptable. Furthermore, several of the basic requirements for a group are usually not present.

Closed Panel Plan

A service approach to the provision of group legal insurance in which a limited number of lawyers provide legal services to members of the plan. The lawyers agree to accept a predetermined schedule of fees from the plan as full payment for the services. (It is also applicable to a limited number of physicians or dentists who provide dental services to members of a plan).

COB. *Refer to* **Co-ordination of Benefits**

Co-insurance

A provision in an accident and sickness contract by which the insurer and insured share, in a specific ratio, the covered losses under a policy. For example, the insurer may reimburse the insured for 80 per cent of covered expenses, the insured paying the remaining 20 per cent of such expenses.

Co-insurance Factor

When there is a coinsurance factor, the plan reimburses only a percentage of the incurred expenses, the rest being the responsibility of the employee.

Collateral Dependants

Persons made eligible for dependant coverage under a group contract by expansion of the definition of eligible dependants usually found therein. Such may include parents, grandparents, brothers, sisters, or grandchildren of the employee, or his wife, who live with the employee and depend upon him for the major portion of their support.

Collective Bargaining

A negotiation between organized labour and employer(s) on matters such as wages, hours, working conditions and health and welfare programs.

Combined Policy. *Refer to* **Blanket Policy and Package Policy**

Combining for Commissions

The premiums for all coverages under a particular case or piece of business are combined when entering a commission scale rather than entering separately for certain coverages (e.g., Group Life, Weekly Indemnity, Hospital or Major Medical Benefits).

Combining for Experience

The process of combining the premiums and claims of two or more coverages for experience rating purposes.

Commission

The percent of premium paid by an insurer to a duly licensed agent or broker who sells the insurance to a policyholder.

Commission Agreement

The contract issued to parties entitled to receive commissions either on a particular group case (single case agreement) or all group cases (blanket arrangement) they sell. It explains the amount of commissions payable, the period payable, on what premium they will be computed and the requirements to be fulfilled in order to be entitled to such commission.

Commission, High-Low Scale

A commission scale providing for the payment of a high first year commission and lower renewal commissions.

Commission, Level Scale

A commission scale which applies the same commission rates to the premium each year, regardless of the policy year. (Contrast with **Commission, High-Low Scale**).

Commission on Transferred Business

Generally an agent will not be paid the regular first year and renewal commission but instead a flat rate of commission.

Commissions, Point-In-Scale

Used in cases where top-of-scale is not authorized. This method is primarily used when new business is submitted within six months from the time when top-of-scale commissions were last paid and is characterized by beginning at that point in the commissions scale last reached and then proceeding down the scale.

Community-Rated Business

The renewal underwriting process does not always take into account the specific client experience. Another kind of renewal underwriting is based on the "fully pooled" or "community-rated" concept. This is particularly appropriate for small groups where, from a statistical point of view two or even three years' experience is not really indicative of the claim trend.

Community Rating

Refers to the practice of grouping all insured groups in a given [geographic] area for experience purposes, thus basing the costs on the general experience and level of costs in the area. It is rarely used in Group insurance; more often it is associated with prepayment plans such as Blue Cross. Insurance carriers rate by individual case experience, or where smaller risks are involved, by pools that are not geographical in nature.

Commuted Value

The single sum which represents the present worth, or equivalent value, of a stipulated number of installments payable at fixed future dates. The commuted value is computed on the basis of a given rate of interest. Often called "discounted value".

Company, Parent. *Refer to* **Parent Company**

Compensation, Basic. *Refer to* **Basic Compensation**

* * *

Composite Rates

When different rates are combined to arrive at an average, the result is termed a "composite rate". A good example is the "dependent rate", which makes no distinction between workers who have one child or a dozen.

Comprehensive Health Coverage. *Refer to* **Extended Health Care**

Confining Sickness

Sickness which confines the insured to his or her home which is usually defined to include hospital and sanitorium.

Conservation

The attempt by an insurer to prevent the lapse of a policy or its transfer to another insurer.

Consultant

A person or firm specializing in the design, sale, and service of employee benefit plans, usually representing the policyholder in placing insurance coverage with an insurer. Compensation is provided either by commissions from the insurer or by the policyholder on a fee-for-service basis, or a combination thereof.

Contingency Reserve

A reserve established to share among all policyholders the cost to the insurer of unpredictable, catastrophic losses.

Contingent Beneficiary

The person(s) or party legally entitled to the proceeds of an insurance policy upon death of the insured if the primary beneficiary does not survive the insured.

Contingent Event

An event, which, in a particular situation, may or may not occur.

Continued Protection. *Refer to* **Waiver of Premium**

Contract

A binding agreement between two or more parties for the doing or not doing of certain things. A contract of insurance is embodied in a written document usually called the policy. The chief requirements for the formation of a valid contract are (1) parties having legal capacity to contract, (2) mutual assent of the parties to a promise, or set of promises, generally consisting of an offer made by one party and an acceptance thereof by the other, (3) a valuable consideration, (4) the absence of any statute or other rule making the contract void, and (5) the absence of fraud or misrepresentation by either party.

Contract, Insurance. *Refer to* **Policy**

Contract, Master. *Refer to* **Master Contract**

Contributions

That part of the insurance premium paid by either the policyholder or the insured, or both.

Contributory

Group people use "contributory" to designate those situations where the insured individual pays or "contributes" part of the premium. The alternative is "noncontributory", meaning employer-pay-all.

Convalescent Hospital

An institution which provides recuperative care and which is qualified to participate and is eligible to receive payments under and in accordance with the provisions of the Provincial Hospital act and which:

- is operated in accordance with the applicable laws of the jurisdiction in which it is located
- has a licensed Doctor and Registered Nurses (RN) in attendance 24 hours a day
- is regularly engaged in providing room and board and skilled nursing care of sick or injured persons during the convalescent stage of a sickness or injury
- maintains a daily record of each patient under the care of a Doctor.

Conversion

Group Life laws require that benefits lost upon termination be "convertible" into individual Life Insurance, without evidence of good health.

Conversion Charge

A charge made by a Group Department for credit to the Individual insurance Department whenever group life insurance is converted. This charge, which is charged directly to the case involved, is made because experience has shown that the average mortality on individual policies issued as conversions of group insurance is excessive.

Co-ordination of Benefits — Claims. *Refer to* **Claims, Co-ordination of Benefits**

Corridor Deductible

A fixed amount which the insured must pay out of his own pocket above the benefits payable under the base plan before supplemental benefits are payable.

Cost, Acquisition

The [. . .] additional start-up costs to the insurer of placing new business in force.

Cost Containment

The control of the overall cost of health care services within the health care delivery system. Costs are contained when the value of the resources committed to an activity are not considered to be excessive.

Cost, Direct. *Refer to* **Direct Cost**

Cost, Gross. *Refer to* **Gross Cost**

Cost Plus

An insurance arrangement whereby a policyholder is charged the amount of claims paid plus the insurer's retention. Generally, no claim reserves are held by the insurer under this arrangement.

Counter Signature

The signature of an authorized representative of an insurer validating an insurance contract.

Cover

Means an insurance contract.

Coverage

(1) The aggregate or risks insured by a contract of insurance.

(2) A major classification of benefits provided by a group policy (ie. term life, weekly indemnity, major medical).

(3) the amount of insurance or benefit stated in the group policy for which an insured is eligible.

Coverage, Basic Life. *Refer to* **Basic Life Coverage**

Coverage, Comprehensive Health. *Refer to* **Extended Health Care**

Coverage, Twenty-Four Hour. *Refer to* **Twenty-Four Hour Coverage**

Covered Charges

Charges for medical care or supplies which, if incurred by an insured or other covered person, create a liability for the insurance under terms of a group policy.

Covered Medical Expenses

Not all expenses incurred in connection with a sickness or an accident are covered under A&S insurance policies in general. Covered expenses are enumerated. Excluded items and benefit limited are specified in every policy.

Covered Person

Any person entitled to benefits under a group policy (insured or covered dependant).

[**CPP Disability Offsets** *Refer to* **Primary CPP Offsets** and **Full CPP Offsets**]

Credibility

The degree of belief that can be given to actual loss experience compared with anticipated loss experience.

Credibility Factors

Numerical values expressing the degree of credibility assigned to observed samples of actual claims experience for experience rating or analysis.

Creditors' Disability

Insurance issued in conjunction with indebtedness that provides for the payment of loan instalments while the borrower is disabled.

Creditor Group Health Insurance

That form of insurance under which a borrower of money or purchaser of goods is indemnified in connection with a specific loan or credit transaction against loss of time resulting from an accident or illness.

Creditor Group Life Insurance

That form of group life insurance insuring lives of a group of persons who have become indebted to a creditor under agreements to repay their indebtness according to a fixed plan; the main purpose being to liquidate the indebtness of the debtor in the event of death prior to the repayment of the indebtness.

Criteria

Predetermined elements of health care against which the necessity, appropriateness or quality of health services may be compared. For example, criteria for appropriate diagnosis of a urinary tract infection may be performance of urine culture and urinalysis. Often used synonymously with guidelines.

Cross Experience Rating. *Refer to* **Combining for Experience**

Cutbacks

Refers to a reduction in group life insurance for an insured at a specified older age, usually at retirement. This device is used to keep life insurance coverage costs within reason. Generally, the cutback is a specified percentage, reduction in the face amount of insurance each year, beginning at age 65 and until coverage drops to a minimum amount.

D

Daily Benefit

A specified maximum amount payable for room and board charges under a hospital or major medical benefits policy.

Data, Census. *Refer to* **Census Data**

Date, Due. *Refer to* **Due Date**

Date, Eligibility. *Refer to* **Eligibility Date**

Date, Par. *Refer to* **Par Date**

DCPs. *Refer to* **Dental Capitation Plans**

Death Benefit, Accidental. *Refer to* **Accidental Death Benefit**

Declination

The rejection of an application for insurance by the insurer.

Decrease

The amount of coverage reduction because of a change in' classification due to attainment of a specified age, demotion, salary decrease, etc., as provided by the master policy.

Deductible

The amount of covered expenses that must be incurred and paid by the insured before benefits become payable by the insurer.

Deductible, Family. *Refer to* **Family Deductible**

Deductible, Integrated. *Refer to* **Integrated Deductible**

Deductions, Pay. *Refer to* **Pay Deductions**

Defensive Medicine

Physicians have increased the use of laboratory tests, hospital admissions and extended lengths of stays in hospitals when necessary as a protection measure against malpractice suits.

Deferred Premium

An arrangement by which the grace period during which premiums may be paid is extended beyond the usual 30 days.

Delayed Coverage for Newborns

Because of a higher incidence of mortality in newborn children, it is customary not to cover children until they are at least 14 days of age. However, coverage could start right from day one, subject to a suitable extra premium.

Dental Capitation Plans

In general, capitation dental plans provide for defined types of dental services to be delivered by a closed panel of selected dentists for a fixed annual per capita fee. The fee, which is usually paid monthly, does not vary with the amount of services provided.

Dental Care, Managed. *Refer to* **Managed Dental Care**

Dental Care Plans, Prepaid. *Refer to* **Dental Capitation Plans**

Dental Plans

Extent of benefits varies by contract. Coverage typically helps to pay for preventive and maintenance services and major restorative procedures such as crowns, bridges, dentures, braces and orthodontic services.

Dependant

An insured's spouse, not legally separated from the insured, and unmarried child(ren) who meet certain eligibility requirements, and who are not otherwise insured under the same group policy. The precise definition of a dependent varies by insurer.

Dependant, Insured. *Refer to* **Insured Dependant**

Dependant Life

This is Life Insurance issued on the spouse and children of an insured employee.

Dependants, Change of Card. *Refer to* **Change of Dependants Card**

Dependants, Collateral. *Refer to* **Collateral Dependants**

Dependants, Sponsored. *Refer to* **Sponsored Dependants**

Deposit Liability

Under Minimum Premium arrangements, this refers to the Policyholders' liability to deposit funds into a special account from which the insurer is authorized to pay claims.

Deposit Premium

The premium deposit paid by a prospective policyholder when an application is made for a group insurance policy. It is usually equal, at least, to the first month's estimated premium and is applied toward the actual premium when billed.

Description, Job. *Refer to* **Job Description**

Designated Beneficiary

The person(s) or party designated by the insured to receive the proceeds of an insurance policy upon death of the insured.

Diagnosis

The art and scheme of determining the nature and cause of a disease, and of differentiating among diseases.

Direct Claim Payment

A method of paying claims where by the insured individuals deal directly with the insurance company rather than submitting claims through the group policyholder.

Direct Cost

Acquisition and administration costs directly attributable to particular group cases which exclude any share of overhead expenses.

Disability

A physical or mental condition that makes an insured person incapable of performing one or more duties of his or her occupation.

Disability Benefit

A payment which arises because of the total and/or permanent disability of an insured; a provision added to a policy which provides for a waiver of premium in case of total and permanent disability.

Disability, Creditors'. *Refer to* **Creditors' Disability**

Disability Income Insurance

These plans pay a periodic cash amount, for example, 70 per cent of normal earnings. Short-term plans begin benefits the first day off work, or soon after, and continue payments for a limited number of weeks. Long-term plans normally start benefits three to six months after the onset of disability and continue payments for a stated term or to a stipulated age.

Disability, Long-Term. *Refer to* **Long-Term Disability**

Disability, Partial. *Refer to* **Partial Disability**

Disability, Period of. *Refer to* **Period of Disability**

Disability, Permanent and Total. *Refer to* **Permanent and Total Disability**

Disability, Recurring. *Refer to* **Recurring Disability**

Disability, Total. *Refer to* **Total Disability**

Disabled Life Reserve

Funds reserved for payment of known and/or potential claims on lives of currently disabled insureds.

Disablement

The occurrence of an event (injury or sickness) which results in disability.

Dismemberment

The accidental loss of limb or sight.

Dismemberment Insurance

A form of insurance that provides payment in case of loss by bodily injury of one or more body members (such as hands or feet) or the sight of one or both eyes.

Distribution

The segregation of all insureds (prospective or in-force) under a group insurance plan by age, sex, location, income, dependency status and benefit class for the purpose of computing gross premium rates.

Distribution, Age. *Refer to* **Age Distribution**

Distribution, Sex. *Refer to* **Sex Distribution**

Dividend

The portion of the premiums collected which the insured, issuing group policies on a participating basis, returns to a policyholder after taking into account the claims incurred, expense charges, risk charges, and changes in contingency reserves.

Dividend, Policy. *Refer to* **Policy Dividend**

Double Indemnity

An additional payment offered for injury or death occurring in a prescribed manner (e.g., accidental death on a common carrier).

Draft Book Claim Payment

A method of claim settlement whereby the policyholder is authorized by the insurer to settle claims and to issue drafts on the insurer in direct payment.

D & U. *Refer to* **Due and Unpaid Premium**

Dual Choice

[A Dental Capitation Plan which] offers individuals covered by the group contract, the dual choice of either obtaining dental care under the Dental Capitation program, or under the traditional "fee for service" arrangement.

Due and Unpaid Premium

Premium due an insurer which has not been received as of some specified date.

Due Date

The date premiums become due on a case. Also called Premium Due Date.

Duplication of Coverage

It exists when an insured is covered under two or more policies for the same exposure to loss. Non-duplication provisions are utilized to control this situation, especially when such double coverage results in over insurance.

E

Earned Premium

That part of the premium for which coverage (protection) has already been provided and which the insurer has, therefore, "earned".

Earnings Schedule

A type of schedule of insurance whereby insureds are classified by wage or salary and the insurance benefits (type and amount) vary by earnings classes.

[**EDB**. *Refer to* **Extended Death Benefit**]

Effective Date

The date a policy becomes effective. If the hour is not specified, the effective time is 12:01 a.m. on the appropriate date.

Effective Date Adjustment Factor

A factor used in a group life rate calculation that modifies the total premium which is based on attained ages to give an approximate total premium based on ages nearest birthday. This factor simplifies what would otherwise be a labourious calculation.

[**EHC**. *Refer to* **Extended Health Care**]

Elective Indemnities

If the insured suffers an accidental injury resulting in a sprain, dislocation fracture or amputation of fingers or toes, insured may elect to receive a lump sum in accordance with the policy schedule in place of any regular income payments provided.

Eligible Group

A group of persons eligible, under insurance laws and company underwriting practices, to be insured under a group policy; usually includes individual employer groups, multiple-employer groups, labour union groups, creditor-debtor groups and certain association groups.

Eligibility

The provisions of the group policy which state requirements that the members of the group must satisfy to become insured with respect to themselves or their dependants.

Eligibility Date

The date on which a member of an insured group becomes eligible to apply for insurance.

Eligibility Period

The period of time following the eligibility date (usually 31 days) during which a member of an insured group is eligible to apply for insurance without evidence of insurability.

Eligible Employees

Those employees who have met the eligibility requirements for insurance set forth in the group policy.

Elimination Period. *Refer to* **Qualification Period**

EME. *Refer to* **Extended Medical Expense**

Employee Benefit Program

A program through which various benefits are offered to employees by their employer to cover such contingencies as medical expenses, disability income, retirement and death, usually paid for wholly or in part by the employer. Such benefits frequently are referred to as "fringe benefits" because they are separate from wages and salaries.

Employee Census

Data, such as age, sex, occupation, earnings and dependency status, relating to the insured persons under a group policy.

[**Employee Data Card**. *Refer to* **Record Card**]

Employee-Pay-All-Plan

One in which the insureds (employees) pay the entire premium. Thus, the policyholder does not contribute at all.

Employees, Classification of. *Refer to* **Classification of Employees**

Employees, Eligible. *Refer to* **Eligible Employees**

Employer-Pay-All-Plan

One in which the employer (policyholder) pays the entire premium.

Employment, Rehabilitative. *Refer to* **Rehabilitative Employment**

Endorsement

The changing of provisions in a policy or certificate of insurance by means of an official entry over the signature of an officer of an insurer on the policy or certificate itself.

Enrollment Card

A document signed by an eligible person as notice of his desire to participate in the group insurance plan. In a contributory case, this card also provides an employer with authorization to deduct contribution from an employee's pay. If group life and accidental death and dismemberment coverage is involved, the card usually includes the beneficiary's name and relationship.

Enrollment (Solicitation)

The process of explaining the proposed group insurance plan to the eligibles and assisting them in the proper completion of their enrollment cards.

Estimate, Retention. *Refer to* **Retention Estimate**

Evaluation, Initial. *Refer to* **Initial Evaluation**

Evaluation, Vocational. *Refer to* **Vocational Evaluation**

Event, Contingent. *Refer to* **Contingent Event**

Evidence of Insurability

Proof presented through written statements on an application from and/or through a medical examination, that an individual is eligible for a certain type [or level] of insurance coverage. This form is required for eligibles who do not enroll during the open enrollment period (generally 31 days) who apply for reinstatement after having previously withdrawn from the plan; who apply for reinstatement after having received an overall maximum benefit or who apply for excess amounts of group life insurance. [The form is also required for individuals requesting levels of insurance benefits over the non-medical limits.]

Examination, Medical. **Medical Examination**

Examinations, Claims. *Refer to* **Claims Examinations**

Excess Amounts of Life Insurance

An amount of life insurance offered a certain class in excess of the amount normally allowed, based upon the total life volume developed for the case. This excess amount of life insurance is usually medically underwritten.

Exclusions

A standard feature of every contract issued by every company is the list of items not covered.

Expectancy, Life. *Refer to* **Life Expectancy**

Expected Mortality

The number of deaths expected to occur in a given group within a specified time period; usually expressed as a ratio of expected death claim payments to premium.

Expense, Allowable. *Refer to* **Allowable Expense**

Expense, Extended Medical. *Refer to* **Extended Medical Expense**

Expense, Hospital Insurance. *Refer to* **Hospital Expense Insurance**

Expense Loading

That portion of group insurance premium required to cover acquisition and administration costs.

Expense, Major Medical Insurance. *Refer to* **Extended Medical Expense**

Expense, Out-of-Pocket. *Refer to* **Out-of-Pocket Expense**

Expense Ratio

The ratio of expenses to earned premiums.

Expense, Supplementary Major Medical. *Refer to* **Extended Health Care**

Experience

Refers to the premium-claim history of a given risk. The larger the risk, the more valid the ratio of claims to premiums. Generally, used to calculate renewal rates.

Experience Analysis

Any statistical analysis of experience for all or any segment of the group business such as a line or a territory; any group of cases, coverages, or benefits; or any single case, coverage or benefit. It may include single or multiple experience periods, analysis of past and projection of future trends, plus various descriptive or inferential statistics.

Experience, Combining for. *Refer to* **Combining for Experience**

Experience Rated Premium Rates

Premium rates for a group coverage which are based, wholly or partially, on the past claims experience of the group to which they will apply.

Experience Rating

The process of determining the premium rate for a group risk wholly or partially, on the basis of that risk experience.

Experience Refund

The amount of premium returned by an insurer to a group policyholder when the financial experience of the particular group (or the experience refund class to which the group belongs) has been more favourable than anticipated in the premiums collected from the group (a **Dividend**).

Exposure

The state of being exposed to the chance of loss. The extent of exposure to loss as measured by participation in a group, ratio of female lives to total lives, amounts at risk, etc.

Extended Benefits

The extension of certain benefits under specific conditions, beyond the termination of an insured's participation in a plan or the termination of the master policy.

Extended Death Benefit

A provision in a group life contract which states that if the insured is to totally and continuously disabled from the date the policyholder stops paying the premium for the insured's insurance until the date of the insured's death, the insurer will pay the amount of insurance in force on the insured's life at the date of cessation of premium payments provided that death occurs (a) within one year of the date of cessation of premium payments, and (b) prior to insured's 65th birthday. [Occasionally referred to as an Extended Disability Benefit. EDB is similar to Temporary Disability Benefits under personal life insurance policies.]

Extended Health Care

[This term refers to benefits offered under a group policy, which are supplementary to benefits provided by **Medicare**, sometimes referred to as Medicare Supplement benefits, or "Major Medical".]

Extended Insurance

The extension of benefits under certain conditions beyond the termination date of insurance.

Extended Medical Expense

This term refers to a medical plan that has a deductible and/or reimburses covered expenses at some percentage less than 100 per cent. These plans are in addition to the Provincial Plan coverage. . . . You may sometimes hear this type of plan referred to as "Major Medical".

F

Facility of Payment

A facility of payment clause based on insurance law allows the insurer to pay an amount not exceeding $2,000 to (a) a relative by blood or connection by marriage of the person (or group person) insured, and (b) any person appearing to be entitled to it by reason of having incurred expense for the maintenance, medical attendance or burial of the person (or group person) insured or to have a claim against the estate of the person (or group person) insured in relation thereto. The clause is subject always to the rights of any assignee.

Factor, Advance Expense Adjustment. *Refer to* **Advance Expense Adjustment Factor**

Factor, Average. *Refer to* **Average Factor**

Factor, Co-insurance. *Refer to* **Co-insurance Factor**

Factor, Effective Date Adjustment. *Refer to* **Effective Date Adjustment Factor**

Factor, Loading. *Refer to* **Loading Factor**

Factors, Credibility. *Refer to* **Credibility Factors**

Family Deductible

A type of deductible which may be satisfied by the combined expenses of all covered family members rather than a single family member; may also be used to refer to a deductible provision whereby after two or three family members have satisfied individual deductibles, no further deductible is applied to any family member in that deductible period.

Fee-for-Service

Method of charging whereby a physician or other practitioner bills for each visit or service rendered. Under this system, expenditures increase not only if the fees themselves increase but also if more units of service are charged for, or more expensive services are substituted for less expensive ones. [A term also used by insurance consultants to designate how they are paid.]

Fee, Policy. *Refer to* **Policy Fee**

Fee Schedule

Maximum dollar or unit allowances for health services which apply under a specific contract.

Fees, Service. *Refer to* **Service Fees**

Female

When used in the group insurance business it refers to the percentage of (a) females in a group case and/or (b) coverage on female lives.

* * *

Final Application

The application which is made part of the group policy after it has been signed by the policyholder upon receipt of the policy formally establishing the risk.

Firm Quotation

A group insurance quotation which provides guaranteed issue rates rather than estimated rates which are subject to recalculation based on the enrollment census.

Flat Schedule

A type of schedule of insurance under which everyone is insured for the same benefit(s) regardless of salary, position, or other circumstances.

Fluctuation, Chance. *Refer to* **Statistical Fluctuation**

Fluctuation, Reserve Claims. *Refer to* **Claims Fluctuation Reserve**

Fluctuation, Statistical. *Refer to* **Statistical Fluctuation**

Form, Hospital Admission. *Refer to* **Hospital Admission Form**

Formula, Benefit. *Refer to* **Benefit Formula**

Formula, Reduction. *Refer to* **Reduction Formula**

Fraternal Society

A social organization that provides insurance for its members.

Frequency, Premium. *Refer to* **Premium Frequency**

[Full CPP Offset]

[Offset used in LTD policies, usually in Small Groups. The insurer subtracts all of the CPP money paid to a disability claimant, including amounts paid on behalf of dependent children, from the LTD amount paid by the insurer. The sum total of all amounts paid by CPP plus the amounts paid by the insurer are combined in the calculation of the LTD benefit percentage paid.]

Full Disability. *Refer to* **Fully Disabled**

Fully Disabled

Inability to do your job due to bodily injury or disease.

Fully-Pooled Business. *Refer to* **Pooling**

* * *

G

G.A.A.P. *Refer to* **Generally Accepted Accounting Principles**

Gain, Investment. *Refer to* **Investment Gain**

Gain or Loss Report

A financial report which shows underwriting and investment gain or loss and the elements thereof for a particular case, a group of cases, or for an entire line of group business.

* * *

Generally Accepted Accounting Principles

Principles of accounting and reporting business results developed by the American Institute of Certified Public Accountants.

General Provisions. *Refer to* **Additional Provisions**

Going-In Rate. *Refer to* **Initial Rate**. Also a premium rate quoted in a group insurance proposal.

Grace Period

A specified time after a premium payment is due within which the policyholder may make such payment, and during which the protection of the policy continues.

Gross Cost

The cost of an insurance program over a specified period of time (e.g., a policy year) before taking dividends, rate credits, etc., into consideration.

Gross Premium

The contracted premium (manual plus any loadings) before applying any discounts.

Group

A number of people classed together by some common factor such as place of employment, occupation, membership in an association, etc.

Group A & S Benefits. *Refer to* **Benefits, Group Accident and Sickness Insurance**

Group Accident and Sickness Insurance Benefits. *Refer to* **Benefits, Group Accident and Sickness Insurance**

Group, Baby. *Refer to* **[Small] Group**

Group Case

Expression used to refer to the group plan of a policyholder in its entirety as a collective unit.

Group Contract. *Refer to* **Master Policy**

Group, Creditor Health Insurance. *Refer to* **Creditor Group Health Insurance**

Group, Eligible. *Refer to* **Eligible Group**

Group Employee Applications. *Refer to* **Applications, Employee Group**

Group Insurance

Insurance issued, usually without medical examination, on a group of people under a master contract. It is usually issued to an employer for the benefit of employees. The individual members of the group hold certificates as evidence of their insurance.

Group Insurance Applications. *Refer to* **Applications, Employee Group**

Group Life, Basic Canadian Tables. *Refer to* **Canadian Basic Group Life Tables**

Group Life Insurance Benefits. *Refer to* **Benefits, Group Life Insurance**

Group Life Insurance In-force

The sum of the face amounts of group life insurance certificates outstanding at a given time; includes all employee and dependant insurance life exposed whether or not a specific premium is charged therefore.

Group Life Insured

A person whose life is insured under a contract of group insurance, excluding a contract of group A & S insurance, and upon whom a right is conferred by the contract, but not including a person who is insured thereunder as a person dependent upon or related to the group life insured.

Group Master Application

Sets out the details of the plan so that a good description can be written into the plan's announcement to employees.

Group, Multiple-Employer. *Refer to* **Multiple-Employer Group**

Group Permanent Life Insurance

Level premium life insurance issued on a group basis and containing cash values and paid-up values, in contrast to group term life insurance. [Rarely seen in Canada.]

Group Policyholder

The legal entity to whom the master policy is issued.

* * *

Group Representative

A salaried employee of the insurer whose principal tasks are to assist agents and brokers in developing and soliciting prospects for group insurance and to install and service group contracts.

Group, Small. *Refer to* **Small Group**

Groups, Closed. *Refer to* **Closed Groups**

* * *

Guaranteed Renewable Policies

A contract provision in which the insurance company must renew the policy, but premiums may be raised by class. This means that the increase applies to all policyholders in a particular group, rather than to one individual policyholder.

H

Handicapped Child. *Refer to* **Child, Handicapped**

Hazard

The measure of risk assumed by an insurer. It can involve physical, moral or financial elements.

Hazard, Moral. *Refer to* **Moral Hazard**

Head Office Administration

Method of administration under which the insurer maintains the basic insurance records pertaining to the persons covered. The policyholder reports the changes which have occurred and the insurer prepares and sends a premium statement to the policyholder for all premiums due.

Health and Accident. *Refer to* **Accident and Health**

Health Care, Extended. *Refer to* **Extended Medical Expense**

Health Coverage, Comprehensive. *Refer to* **Extended Medical Expense**

Health Insurance

Insurance providing for the payment of benefits as a result of sickness or injury, includes various types of insurance such as accident insurance, disability income replacement insurance, medical expense insurance, accidental death insurance and dismemberment insurance. Often includes government hospital-medical plans.

Health Insurance Association of America

This is an association of more than 300 insurance companies in the U.S. and Canada. Its purpose is to help its member companies promote and develop voluntary health insurance to protect people from loss of income and the other financial burdens resulting from sickness or injury.

Health Insurance, Creditor Group. *Refer to* **Creditor Group Health Insurance**

Health Maintenance Organizations

A modern name for what in the past has been known variously as a prepaid group practice program, a foundation for medical care, and a local independent practice program. It is an organized health care system that accepts the responsibility to provide, or otherwise assure, the delivery of health services. Premiums are prepaid on a monthly or annual basis.

HIAA. *Refer to* **Health Insurance Association of America**

High-Low Commission Scale. *Refer to* **Commission, High-Low Scale**

HMO. *Refer to* **Health Maintenance Organizations**

Holistic Medicine

A trend in medicine which emphasizes that the system must extend its focus beyond solely the physical aspects of disease or the particular organ in question. It is concerned with the whole person and the interrelationships between the emotional, social, spiritual as well as physical implications of disease and health.

Home Health Care

Health Services rendered in the home to aged, disabled sick, or convalescent individuals who do not need institutional care. The most common types of home care are the visiting nurses service, speech, physical, occupational and rehabilitation therapy. These services are provided by home health agencies, hospitals, or other community organizations.

Home Office Administration. *Refer to* **Head Office Administration**

Home Office Administration Claims. *Refer to* **Total Claims Administration**

Hospital

A facility which is legally licensed and provides a broad range of 24 hour a day medical and surgical services for sick and injured persons by or under the supervision of a staff of Doctors and provides 24-hour-a-day nursing care by, or under the direction of a nurse.

Hospital Admission Form

A form used to implement a hospital admission plan. It normally provides for advance certification of insurance and benefits by the policyholder, authorization for release of information by the hospital and assignment of benefits to the hospital by the insured and a section which may be used by the hospital to submit a claim to the insurer.

Hospital Admission Plan

A plan used to facilitate admission of persons covered by group medical care insurance to hospitals and to assure the prompt payment of applicable insurance benefits to hospitals.

Hospital, Convalescent. *Refer to* **Convalescent Hospital**

Hospital Expense Insurance

Insurance that provides specific benefits for hospital room and board and prescribed hospital service during hospital confinement which are not covered by government hospital plans [i.e., semi-private or private room].

Hospital Indemnity

A form of health insurance that provides a stipulated daily, weekly, or monthly indemnity during hospital confinement.

HSM

Abbreviation for Hospital-Surgical-Medical Benefits.

I

IBNR (Reserves). *Refer to* **Incurred But Not Reported Claim Reserves**

ICA. *Refer to* **international Claim Association**

ID Card

[Identification (ID) or wallet certificate cards are provided by insurers to group policyholders and their employees to identify coverage policy and certificate numbers.]

Impaired Risk. *Refer to* **Substandard Risk**

Income, Disability Insurance. *Refer to* **Disability Income Insurance**

Income, Loss of Insurance. *Refer to* **Disability income insurance**

Incontestable Clause

The provision in a group life and/or health insurance policy which prevents the insurance company from disputing the validity of: (a) an insurance policy once it has been in force for a specified period of time (e.g., two years) — as long as premiums are paid and (b) an individual's insurance, on the basis of statements made by the individual in connection with insurability at the time of application for the coverage, once the insurance has been in force for two years during the individual's lifetime.

Incontestability

A provision in the law that a contract providing accident and/or sickness insurance benefits which, together with renewals thereof, has been in effect continuously for two years is incontestable, except for fraud or misstatement of age, with respect to a failure to disclose or a misrepresentation of a fact relevant to the insurance, with respect to a person insured or a group person insured as the case may be.

Increase

An increase in benefits which becomes effective for an insured or a group of insureds as a result of a change in class (e.g., due to a wage or salary increase or occupational Promotion).

Incurred But Not Reported Claim Reserves (IBNR)

These reserves represent an estimation of claims actually incurred in the policy year but not settled as of the end of the policy year. They may be established as a function of premiums earned, claims paid, or benefits in force, using average factors, or in exceptionally large cases they may be the result of a detailed study of that particular policyholder's actual claims. Reserves for known pending claims, generally restricted to Life and AD & D are added to these claim reserves.

Incurred But Unpaid Claims. *Refer to* **Claims, Incurred But Unpaid**

Incurred, Claims. *Refer to* **Claims incurred**

Indemnity

To make good a loss.

Indemnity, Double. *Refer to* **Double indemnity**

Indemnity, Hospital. *Refer to* **Hospital Indemnity**

Indemnity, Multiple. *Refer to* **Multiple indemnity**

Individual Insurance

A contract of insurance made with an individual called the policyholder or the insured, which normally covers such individual and in certain instances, members of his or her family. [Also called Personal Insurance]

Inforce

The total outstanding volume of insurance in-force on the lives of covered employees at any given time. Measured in terms of cases, lives, amount (volume) of insurance, or premium.

Initial Deposit

The premium deposit paid by the employer when an application is completed for a group insurance policy. It is usually equal, at least, to the 1st month's premium and is applied as such when the actual premium for the 1st premium frequency is calculated.

Initial Evaluation

The first major step conducted by a rehabilitation specialist following case referral, usually consisting of an insured, employer and sometimes physician contact. Medical, psychological, social, vocational, educational and economic factors are explored to ascertain the feasibility of and appropriate courses of action to accomplish rehabilitation.

Initial Premium. *Refer to* **Initial Deposit**

Initial Rate

A premium rate which is effective on the effective date of a new group policy.

Inside Limits

The upper benefit limits that cannot be exceeded as stated within the group policy.

Inspection Reports

Investigative reports by a commercial inspection agency to check the finances, apparent health, and the stability of a group prospect's business operation, especially important in underwriting small group risks. Similar inspection reports are ordered selectively in the underwriting of individual policies.

Installation

The process of assisting a policyholder to set up the administrative practices essential to the proper handling of records, reports, claims, changes, conversions, ordering of supplies, who to contact when and how, hospital admissions, certification of eligibility etc., under a group insurance plan.

Insurability

Refers to the physical, moral, occupational and financial status of a risk and acceptability to the insurer.

Insurability, Evidence of. *Refer to* **Evidence of Insurability**

Insurable Interest

The interest of an insured or beneficiary who may suffer loss from a peril insured against.

Insurance

For all licensing and regulation purposes under the insurance act, the term "insurance" means: the undertaking by one person to indemnify another person against loss or liability for loss in respect of a certain rise or peril to which the object of the insurance may be exposed, or to pay a sum of money or other thing of value upon the happening of a certain event. In the A & S part of the act, as regards contracts, "insurance" means: accident insurance, sickness insurance or accident and sickness insurance.

Insurance, Accident. *Refer to* **Accident Insurance**

Insurance Age

Generally, for insurance purposes a person's age changes six months following his or her last birthday. For this reason, an individual's date of birth rather than year of birth is required by application forms or insurance enrollment documents.

Insurance, Casualty. *Refer to* **Casualty insurance**

Insurance Class [Classification]

A classification of insured persons (described in a group policy) which determines the types and amounts of insurance for which they are eligible under the policy.

Insurance Contract. *Refer to* **Policy**

Insurance, Creditor Group Health. *Refer to* **Creditor Group Health Insurance**

Insurance Exposure. *Refer to* **Exposure Insurance**

Insurance, Group. *Refer to* **Group Insurance**

Insurance, Group Life Creditor. *Refer to* **Group Life Creditor Insurance**

Insurance, Group Life (in-force). *Refer to* **Group Life Insurance In-force**

Insurance, Health. *Refer to* **Health insurance**

Insurance, Individual. *Refer to* **Individual Insurance**

Insurance, Joint. *Refer to* **Joint Insurance**

Insurance, Key-man Health. *Refer to* **Key-man Health Insurance**

Insurance Month

A period commencing on the (e.g., 1st, 10th) day of any calendar month and ending on the (1st, 9th) day of the next succeeding calendar month.

Insurance, Nonoccupational. *Refer to* **Nonoccupational insurance**

Insurance, Sickness. *Refer to* **Sickness insurance**

Insurance, Weekly Indemnity. *Refer to* **Weekly Indemnity insurance**

Insurance Year of Birth

The year of birth for an individual insured under a group insurance plan which reflects the insurance age of the individual on any policy anniversary.

Insured Dependant

Refers to your spouse or unmarried child with exceptions as outlined within the group policy.

Insured Person

A person employed and paid for services by the policyholder on a full-time basis and who qualifies as an insured under the Policy.

Insurer

The party of the insurance contract who promises to pay losses or benefits. Also, any corporation licensed to furnish insurance to the public.

Insurers, Non-Profit. *Refer to* **Non-Profit Insurers**

Insuring Clause

A clause which defines and describes the scope of the coverage provided and the limits of indemnification.

Integrated Deductible

A fixed amount or the sum of the benefits paid under a base medical care plan, whichever is greater, which must be exceeded before supplemental major medical benefits are payable.

Integration

co-ordination of the disability income insurance benefits with other disability income benefits, such as Canada and Quebec Pension Plans.

Intentional Injury

An injury resulting from an intentional act or that could be expected to result from an intentional act. Intentional self-inflicted injuries are not covered by an accident policy because they are not an accident.

Interest, Insurable. *Refer to* **Insurable Interest**

International Claim Association

A national organization which provides services in the field of group health insurance.

International Foundation of Employee Benefit Plans

A membership organization, its sole purpose the education of and exchange of information between, people who are responsible for the operation of employee benefit programs. Those attaining the Certified Employee Benefit Specialist [CEBG] designation are eligible for membership in this society.

Investment Gain

Profit or gain from earnings on invested funds (as distinguished from underwriting gain).

Irrevocable Beneficiary

A beneficiary whose designation as such by the insured may not be changed without his/her consent.

J

Job Description

A detailed description of the duties, tasks and requirements of the insured's pre-disability job, including specific physical and mental qualifications for performance. This is an important evaluative tool in analyzing the insured's potential to return to the job and for ascertaining transferable skills.

Joint Beneficiary

Person or persons legally entitled to share in the proceeds of an insurance policy.

Joint Insurance

The joint underwriting of a group insurance risk by two or more carriers sharing the premiums, claims and expenses on an agreed percentage basis. One company usually handles the administration, and the policy is usually on special forms naming each insurer.

K

Key-Man Health Insurance

A group plan designed to protect essential employees against the loss of income resulting from disability.

L

Lag, Claim. *Refer to* **Claim Lag**

Lag Run

A computer listing of claims (usually summarized by benefit or coverage) for which drafts have been issued or redeemed, by claim incurred dates or periods.

Lapse

Termination of a policy upon the policyholder's failure to pay the premium within the time allowed.

Lapsed Policy

A group master contract that has automatically expired, as provided by its terms, due to non-payment of premium.

Late Applicant

An eligible who applies for insurance after the normal 31 days open enrollment period. Evidence of Insurability is not required during the 31 day period but is required for a late applicant.

Late Entrant. *Refer to* **Late Applicant**

Length of Service Schedule

A schedule of insurance under which employees are insured for an amount based upon the length of time the employee has worked for the employer.

Length of Stay

The length of an inpatient's stay in a hospital or other health facility. It is one measure of use of health facilities, reported as an average number of days spent in a facility per admission or discharges. It is calculated as follows: total number of days in the facility for all discharges and deaths occurring during a period divided by the number of discharges and deaths occurring during the same period. In concurrent review an appropriate length of stay may be assigned each patient upon admission. Average length of stay vary and are measured for people with various ages, specific diagnosis, or sources of payment.

Level Commission Scale. *Refer to* **Commission, Level (Scale)**

Level Plan (Life Schedule)

A group life policy that provides a flat schedule of benefits as opposed to a graded schedule where different benefits are offered to different classes of people. In a level plan, everyone receives the same benefits, regardless of salary or position.

Level Premium Billing

A method of premium billing which allows the policyholder to pay a certain set amount of premium on each due date during the policy year, based upon an estimated annual premium with an adjustment at the end of the policy year for the changes in coverage that have occurred during the policy year.

Liability, Deposit. *Refer to* **Deposit Liability**

License

Certification, issued by Provincial Department of Insurance, that an individual is qualified to solicit insurance applications for the period covered. Usually issued for a period of one year, renewable on application without necessity of the individual's periodic repetition of the original qualifying requirements.

Life, Basic Coverage. *Refer to* **Basic Life Coverage**

Life, Dependant. *Refer to* **Dependant Life**

Life, Disabled Reserve. *Refer to* **Disabled Life Reserve**

Life Expectancy

The average number of years of life remaining for persons of a given age according to a particular mortality table.

Life Insurance, Excess Amounts of. *Refer to* **Excess Amounts of Life Insurance**

Life Insurance, Group Benefits. *Refer to* **Benefits, Group Life Insurance**

Life Insurance Marketing and Research Association (LIMRA)

This is a nonprofit, industry — supported corporation dedicated to serve the public, and life and health insurance companies, in areas such as, industry research, information dissemination, consulting services, and training. Its headquarters are in Hartford, Connecticut.

Life Insured. *Refer to* **Group Life Insured**

Life Limit

The maximum amount of life insurance which is offered to a benefit class, or classes of employees under a group insurance plan, as developed by the total life volume for the case or by statutory regulation.

Life Office Management Association (LOMA)

An international association founded in 1924. Through education, training, research, and information sharing, LOMA is dedicated to promoting management excellence in leading life and health insurance companies and other financial institutions. It is also responsible for the FLMI insurance education Program.

Life Underwriters Association of Canada

This Canadian organization works through local groups of life insurance agents to sponsor sales congresses and seminars, promote high ethical standards, participate in community service projects, and support public policies in the interest of their members. [It is responsible for the basic life insurance agents training course (LUATC) and the advanced CLU training program and designation.]

Limitation, No Pre-Existing Conditions. *Refer to* **No Pre-Existing Conditions Limitation**

Limitations. *Refer to* **Exclusions**

Limited Policy

One that covers only specified accidents or sicknesses.

Limit, Life. *Refer to* **Life Limit**

Limits

The maximum amount of insurance an insurer will write on one risk. The maximum and minimum ages above and below which an insurer will not issue or offer restricted coverage.

LIMRA. *Refer to* **Life Insurance Marketing and Research Association**

List, Claim. *Refer to* **Claim List**

Loading, Expense. *Refer to* **Expense Loading**

Loading Factor

The amount added to the net premium rate determined for a group insurance plan to cover an excess age group, hazardous industry, large percentage of unskilled employees, or adverse experience.

LOMA. *Refer to* **Life Office Management Association**

Long-Term Disability

It provides income protection in the event of time lost due to sickness or accident of long term nature. Generally monthly payments commence after a specified waiting period and continue while the employee remains disabled usually up to age 65 [in Canada].

Loss

The amount of insurance or benefit for which the insurer becomes liable on the happening of the event insured against.

Loss-of-Income Insurance. *Refer to* **Disability Income Insurance**

Loss-of-Time Insurance. *Refer to* **Disability Income Insurance**

Loss Ratio

The ratio of claims to premiums. It may be calculated in several different ways, e.g., using paid premiums or earned premiums versus paid claims with or without changes in claim reserves.

Loss, Wage Insurance. *Refer to* **Disability Income Insurance**

LTD. *Refer to* **Long Term Disability**

LUAC. *Refer to* **Life Underwriters Association of Canada**

M

MAAPAL. *Refer to* **Metropolitan Advance Award Policyholder Account Liability**

Major Medical

Metropolitan term for "Extended Medical Expense".

Major Medical Expense Insurance. *Refer to* **Extended Medical Expense**

Major Medical Expense, Supplementary. *Refer to* **Extended Medical Expense**

Malingering

The practice of feigning illness or inability to work in order to collect insurance benefits.

Managed Dental Care [*See* **Dental Capitation Plans**].

Manual, Administration. *Refer to* **Administration Manual**

Manual, Claim. *Refer to* **Claim Manual**

Manual Rate

The premium rate developed for,a group coverage from the insurers standard rate tables, usually contained in its rate manual or underwriting manual.

Margin, Risk. *Refer to* **Risk Margin**

Master Application, Group. *Refer to* **Group Master Application**

Master Policy. *Refer to* **Master Contract**

Master Contract

The single or combined policy issued to the policyholder setting forth the provisions of his group insurance plan. The insureds are then issued booklets/certificates.

Material, Announcement. *Refer to* **Announcement Material**

Maternity Benefits

Benefits payable for hospital expenses arising out of a pregnancy and resulting childbirth, abortion or miscarriage.

Maximum Benefit

The maximum amount any one individual may receive under an insurance contract.

Maximum Benefit Period

The maximum period for which the benefit payments are made.

Medical Examination

The examination given by a qualified physician to determine the insurability of the applicant. May be used in group insurance when an application is submitted later than a prescribed period, the applicant has previously withdrawn voluntarily from the plan, the applicant is applying for an excess (ie, an amount beyond the insurer's non-medical maximum) of life insurance or the applicant is applying for the reinstatement of a previously received maximum benefit.

Medical Expense Period

Usually the period from January 1st to December 31st.

Medical, Major Expense Insurance. *Refer to* **Extended Medical Expense**

Medicare

This is the most common term used in reference to the Provincial Government Plans that cover hospital ward care, hospital services and doctor's fees in and out of hospital.

Medicine, Defensive. *Refer to* **Defensive Medicine**

Medicine, Holistic. *Refer to* **Holistic Medicine**

Medicine, Preventive. *Refer to* **Preventive Medicine**

Medicine, Wholistic. *Refer to* **Holistic Medicine**

* * *

Minimum Premium Plan

A combination approach to funding an insurance plan which is aimed primarily at premium tax savings. The employer self-funds a fixed per cent (e.g., 90 per cent) of the estimated monthly claims and the insurance company insures the excess.

Misrepresentation

A false statement as to a past or present material fact, made in an application for insurance, that induces an insurer to issue a policy it would not otherwise have issued.

Misstatement of Age

The declaration by an employee of an age that is lesser or greater than his/her actual age.

Month, Insurance. *Refer to* **Insurance Month**

Monthly Adjustment Billing

A method of premium billing where the policyholder is billed on each premium due date for the insurance coverage on the actual number of persons covered by the group insurance plan.

Monthly Statement

A statement sent by Group Administration to the policyholder on all Home Office administered cases which reflects the previous in-force, current in-force, premium adjustments and premium due. On a monthly case it serves as the bill. On other than a monthly case it serves as the bill and as an interim statement of liability.

Moral Hazard

An element of risk selection considered by an insurer in underwriting evidence of insurability applications for group insurance. It refers to the potential risk associated with an applicant's habits, his surroundings, mode of life and general reputation.

Morbidity

The incidence and severity of sicknesses and accidents in a well-defined class or classes of persons.

Morbidity Table

A statistical table showing the average number of illnesses (and sometimes accidents) befalling a large group of persons.

Mortality

The death rate at each age as determined from prior experience. A mortality study (table) shows the probability of death and survival at each age for a credible unit of population.

Multiple-Employer Group

Employees of two or more employers covered under one master contract (eg. trade associations of employers in the same industry, union members who work for more than one employer).

Multiple Employer Trust

A trust formed to provide group insurance benefits for employees of companies that band together with the expectation that the coverage rate for each participating firm will be lower than if they had separate policies.

Multiple Indemnity

A provision under which the principal sum will be multiplied by 100, 200, 300 or more percent in case of death from certain types of accidents.

Mutual Company

An insurance company whose management is directed by a board of directors elected by the policyholders.

N

NAAP. *Refer to* **Net Annual Average Premium**

* * *

NALU. *Refer to* **National Association of Life Underwriters**

* * *

National Association of Life Underwriters

This U.S. organization works through local groups of life insurance agents to sponsor sales congresses and seminars, promote high ethical standards, participate in community service projects, and support public policies in the interest of their members.

Net Annual Average Premium

The average annual cost per $1,000 of insurance for each employee insured under that policy. This cost has been reduced to reflect any dividends paid during the policy year in question.

Net Cost

In group insurance it equals claims & expenses & reserves. The determining factor in Net Cost is not premium but mostly claims even though to some extent expenses are a direct function of premiums and the contingency reserve charge may depend somewhat on premiums.

Net Premium

Paid or earned premium (after discounts).

Net Premium Rate

The portion of the premium rate developed for a group insurance coverage, which is designed to provide for expected claims, including female loading but not including industry, age, unskilled labor or area loading, or application of reduction factors, nor increases or decreases due to experience.

Newborns, Delayed Coverage For. *Refer to* **Delayed Coverage for Newborns**

New Business

For new cases, it represents the increase in force resulting from the sale of insurance coverages to a new policyholder. Normally commissions and production credit are allowed.

New Business (Existing Case)

For additional business on existing cases it represents the increase in inforce resulting from the extension of coverage, addition of coverages, or the increase in coverages purchased by an existing policyholder for which, in most instances, new commissions and production credit are allowed, subject to an insurer's production rules.

No Loss/No Gain

In group insurance, an agreement by a carrier that benefits paid under the previous carrier's plan will not be diminished.

Non-Cancellable Policy

A contract provision in which the insurance company can neither cancel coverage nor vary the premiums rate specified in the contract. Policies specify, at the time of purchase, the length of time the coverage is noncancellable and guaranteed renewable.

Non-Confining Sickness

Illness which prevents the insured person from working but which does not confine him/her to a hospital or to his/her home.

Non-Contributory

A term used to describe a group insurance plan under which the policyholder pays the entire cost.

Non-Contributory Plan. *Refer to* **Employee-Pay-All Plan**

Non-Disabling Injury

One which requires medical care but does not result in a loss of time from work.

Non-Duplication Provision

Stipulates that insured shall be ineligible to collect for charges under a group plan if the charges are reimbursed under his or her spouses group plan.

[Non-Evidence Maximum]

[The maximum benefit available without providing evidence of insurability.]

Non-Insurance. *Refer to* **Self-Insurance**

Non-Occupational Insurance

Insurance that does not provide benefits for an accident or sickness arising out of a person's employment.

Non-Profit Insurers

Bodies organized under provincial laws to provide hospital, medical or dental insurance on a co-operative basis. They are exempt from certain types of taxes.

No Pre-Existing Conditions Limitation

Grants the insured coverage for expenses incurred while insured resulting from conditions existing prior to the date insured. See **Pre-Existing Conditions Limitation.**

Normal Underwriting Maximum

Represents the limit of exposure on a single insured for life or medical care. That is to say, it defines the recommended maximum amount of a single claim that can feasibly be charged to an account's premium during a single year. A pooling charge is "automatically" paid in lieu of having claims above the NUM impact on experience.

Notice and Proof — Claims. *Refer to* **Claims, Notice and Proof**

NUM. *Refer to* **Normal Underwriting Maximum**

O

Obstetrical Benefits

Reimbursement for a surgeon's charges incurred due to a surgical procedure in connection with pregnancy.

Occupational Classifications

The grouping together of occupations into classes having approximately the same degree of hazard. Each insurance company issues a manual of such classes.

Occupational Hazard

A hazard inherent in the insured's line of work. Degree of danger of incurring an accidental injury or sickness in the line of work.

Occupational Injury

An injury arising out of or in the course of, employment.

Occupational Schedule

A schedule of insurance under which persons are insured for an amount based upon their job classification.

Occupational Therapy

A program of prescribed activities emphasizing co-ordination and mastery, designed to assist the insured to regain independence particularly in the Activities of Daily Living (ADL).

Open Enrollment Period

A time period during which uninsured employees (with respect to themselves or their dependants) may obtain insurance under an existing group plan without presenting evidence of insurability.

Operations, Basic Schedule of. *Refer to* **Basic Schedule of Operation**

Optional Modes of Settlement

The right of the insured, or under certain circumstances the beneficiary, to elect to receive the proceeds of a life insurance policy in one of a number of ways other than a lump sum.

Options, Settlement. *Refer to* **Settlement Options**

Organizations, Health Maintenance. *Refer to* **Health Maintenance Organizations**

Organizations, Preferred Provider. *Refer to* **Preferred Provider Organizations**

Orthotics

A specialized field, relating to orthopaedic appliances, braces and other devices used to support weight, align, prevent or correct deformities, or improve the function of movable parts of the body.

Other Insurance Clause

A clause in an insurance contract stating the effect thereon of the presence of other insurance.

O & U. *Refer to* **Reserves**

Out-of-Pocket Expense

Those medical expenses which an insured is required to pay because they are not covered under the group contract.

[Overall Maximum]

[The maximum benefit available, usually only after the underwriters have approved amounts over the **Non-Evidence Maximum Benefit**.]

Overdue Premium. *Refer to* **Due and Unpaid Premium**

Overinsurance

Insurance exceeding in amount the probable loss to which it applies. This serious problem is controlled in group medical care coverages by the contractual use of non-duplication of benefits provision.

Overriding Commission

A commission paid to general agents or agency Commission managers in addition to the commission paid the soliciting agent or broker.

Overwrite. *Refer to* **Overriding Commission**

P

Package Plan

A Plan consisting of several coverages each of which must be elected by the eligibles. The entire package must be either accepted or rejected by the individuals eligible.

Packaging. *Refer to* **Package Plan**

Paid, Claims. *Refer to* **Claims Paid**

Par Date

This is an arbitrary date, usually the mean point of the grace period (i.e., the 15th of the month). Often, premium received, prior to the par date receives an interest credit towards retention expenses while premium paid after the par date normally incurs an interest charge.

Parent Company

A company which controls other companies (subsidiaries). When employees of a parent company and its subsidiaries have group insurance with a common insurer, the parent company is usually the group policyholder with whom the insurer does business (sends billings etc.)

Partial Disability

A benefit sometimes found in disability income policies providing payment of reduced monthly income in the event the insured cannot work full-time or is prevented from performing one or more important daily duties pertaining to his/her occupation.

Partial Payment

A payment to a claimant where it is expected other payments will be made before the claim can be considered as closed.

Participation

The number of insureds covered under the group plan in relation to the total number eligible to be covered, usually pressed as a percentage.

Participation Percentage. *Refer to* **Percentage Participation**

Past Financial Experience. *Refer to* **Transferred Business**

Past Service Cost

The actuarial value (single sum) of the past service benefits as of the effective date of the establishment of the plan, or at the date of the latest liberalization.

Pay Deductions

For successful operation of a group insurance plan, the employer must agree to deduct the employee's contributions from his pay and remit this in a single sum, together with the employer's contribution, to the insurance company on the premium due date. This is a fundamental principle of group insurance.

Payment of Claim. *Refer to* **Claims, Payment of**

Payment, Partial. *Refer to* **Partial Payment**

Payments, Advance. *Refer to* **Deposit Premium**

Payments Direct Claim. *Refer to* **Direct Claim payment**

Payor, Third-Party. *Refer to* **Third-Party Payor**

Payroll Deduction

The amount taken from the employee's earnings with his/her consent, as contribution toward the cost of the group insurance plan.

PCS. *Refer to* **Pharmaceutical Card System**

Peer Review System

A mechanism used by Future Focus Health Systems, Ltd. to provide assurance that quality dental care is delivered in an efficient manner and that any deviations from normal modes of practice are discovered and corrected.

Pending Claim

A claim which has been reported but on which final action has not yet been taken.

Percentage Participation

A provision in a health insurance contract that the insurer and insured will share covered losses in agreed proportion.

Period, Accumulation. *Refer to* **Accumulation Period**

Period, Benefit Waiting. *Refer to* **Benefit Waiting Period**

Period, Eligibility. *Refer to* **Eligibility Period**

Period of Disability

The period during which an employee is prevented from performing the usual duties of his occupation or employment or a dependant from performing the normal activities of a healthy person of the same age or sex. More than one cause (accident or sickness) may be present during or contribute to a single period of disability.

Permanent and Total Disability

A disability that will presumably last for the insured's lifetime and prevents engagement in any occupation for which the insured is reasonably fitted.

Person, Covered. *Refer to* **Covered Person**

Personal Health Statement

A general health questionnaire completed by an applicant for coverage under a group insurance plan.

[Personal Insurance. *Refer to* **Individual Insurance]**

Persons, Classes of. *Refer to* **Classes of Persons**

Pharmaceutical Card System

One of the third party claim administrators used by Metropolitan for the payment of drug claims on cases where an insured employee can obtain a drug directly from a PCS participating pharmacy at a predetermined and nominal co-payment costs such as .35.

Physical Hazard

That type of hazard which arises from the physical characteristics of an individual (e.g., impediments of hearing or sight). It may exist because of a current condition, past medical history or physical condition present at birth.

Physical Impairment

A physical defect that makes an applicant a below-average risk.

Plan Administrator

The person appointed by the insured (employer or sponsor) to administer a group insurance plan.

Plan, Base. *Refer to* **Base Plan**

Plan, Closed Panel. *Refer to* **Closed Panel Plan**

Plan, Employee-Pay-All. *Refer to* **Employee-Pay-All-Plan**

Plan, Employer-Pay-All. *Refer to* **Employer-Pay-All-Plan**

Plan, Noncontributory. *Refer to* **Noncontributory Plan**

Plan, Trusteed Group Insurance. *Refer to* **Trusteed Group Insurance Plan**

Plan, Union Sponsored. *Refer to* **Union Sponsored Plan**

Plans, Bank. *Refer to* **Bank Plans**

Plans, Dental. *Refer to* **Dental Plans**

Plans, Service-Type. *Refer to* **Service-Type Plans**

Point-In-Scale Commissions. *Refer to* **Commissions, Point-In-Scale**

Policy

The legal document issued by the insurer to the insured which outlines the conditions and terms of the insurance. Also called the contract.

Policy Anniversary

The annual date which separates the experience under a group policy between one period of time and the next for dividend and retroactive rate purposes, the periods of time normally being twelve consecutive months.

Policy, Blanket. *Refer to* **Blanket Policy**

Policy, Combined. *Refer to* **Blanket Policy**

Policy Constant

The factor that is added to the total premium in a group life rate calculation in recognition of the minimum expense loading associated with any case regardless of the size of the risk. This factor amounts to $.20 per thousand of insurance multiplied by the number of thousands of insurance but in no event to exceed $8.00.

Policy Dividend

A refund to the policyholder each year of a portion of the premium based on the company's experience and anticipated costs. Policy dividends are not guaranteed but depend on mortality and morbidity experience, investment earnings, expenses and other factors and may be increased or decreased at the discretion of the insurer.

Policy Fee

An amount sometimes charged in addition to the first premium as a fee for issuance of the policy (e.g., group health conversion policies).

Policyholder

The owner of a policy.

Policyholder, Group. *Refer to* **Group Policyholder**

Policy, Lapsed. *Refer to* **Lapsed Policy**

Policy, Limited. *Refer to* **Limited Policy**

Policy, Master. *Refer to* **Master Contract**

Policy, Non-Cancellable. *Refer to* **Non-Cancellable Policy**

Policy Term

That period for which the policy is written.

Policy, Travel Accident. *Refer to* **Travel Accident Policy**

Policy Year

The period of time that elapses between policy anniversaries, as specified in the policy.

Pooled. *Refer to* **Community-Rated Business and to Pooling**

Pooled Claims

Claims applicable to pooled risk which are excluded from individual case experience rating.

Pooling

The combining of all premiums, claims, expenses, etc., for certain size cases (e.g., all cases involving ten but less than 50 insureds), types of coverage (e.g., all AD&D business), or excess classes (e.g., amounts of group life insurance that are medically examined or are in excess of normal limits) in order to spread the risk. See also Community-Rated Business and Community Rating.

Pooling Charges

These are automatic charges against premium in lieu of charging single large claim amounts against premium in years of adverse experience. They operate to reduce individual exposures (i.e., an amount of a life claim above the account's normal under-writing maximum).

PPO. *Refer to* **Preferred Provider Organizations**

Pre-Existing Condition

Any physical and/or mental condition or conditions that existed prior to the effective date of coverage under a contract.

Pre-Existing Conditions Limitation

A restriction on payments on those charges directly resulting from an accident or illness for which the insured received care or treatment within a specified period of time (e.g., three months) prior to the date of coverage.

Preferred Provider Organizations

A mechanism for purchasing group health care services. A panel or network of suppliers (physicians, dentists or hospitals) form an organization and agree to provide services to a consumer group at a fixed fee which tends to be less than prevailing rates. In exchange for this agreement, the providers expect preferred and simplified claims handling procedures and an increased market share, as the sponsor's benefit plan is restructured to provide members with incentives to use participants' services.

Pregnancy, Complications of. *Refer to* **Complications of Pregnancy**

Premium

The amount paid to the insurer for the insurance protection.

Premium, Average Rate. *Refer to* **Average Premium Rate**

Premium, Binder. *Refer to* **Advance Payment**

Premium, Deferred. *Refer to* **Deferred Premium**

Premium, Deposit. *Refer to* **Deposit Premium**

Premium, Due and Unpaid. *Refer to* **Due and Unpaid Premium**

Premium, Due Date. *Refer to* **Due Date**

Premium Earned

This is the total premium the consumer is liable to pay based on the rates and volumes inforce during the period.

Premium Frequency

The number of times premiums are payable in a policy year. For example, a policy on which premiums are paid on a monthly basis is said to have a monthly premium frequency.

Premium, Gross. *Refer to* **Gross Premium**

Premium, Initial. *Refer to* **Initial Deposit**

Premium, Net. *Refer to* **Net Premium**

Premium Notice Billing

The premium statement requesting the policyholder to pay a premium on a particular due date. The insurer may enclose a premium remittance card which should be returned with the policyholder's cheque.

Premium, Overdue. *Refer to* **Due and Unpaid Premium**

Premium Paid

That portion of earned premium actually paid and receipted during the policy year.

Premium Rate

The price of a unit of coverage or benefit.

Premium Refund

Premium returned to a policyholder (usually because of favorable experience; ie. an experience rating refund).

Premium, Retrospective Agreement. *Refer to* **Retrospective Premium Agreement**

Premium Statement

The bill prepared by the insurer and sent to the policyholder for each premium due on a group plan administered by the insurer; or the report submitted to the insurer as of each premium due date by a policyholder whose group plan is on a self-administered basis.

Premium, Step-Rate. *Refer to* **Step-Rate Premium**

Premium Tax

As assessment levied by a Provincial Government on the Net Premium income collected in a particular Province by an insurer.

Premium, Unearned. *Refer to* **Unearned Premium**

Prepaid Dental Care Plans. *Refer to* **Dental Capitation Programs**

Prescription Period

The period of time within which certain acts with respect to a claim must be done.

Preventive Medicine

Care directed at preventing disease or its consequences, including immunization, early detection and inhibiting further deterioration. Promotion of health through improving the environment or altering behaviours, especially by health education, have gained prominence in this field.

Primary Beneficiary

The first person(s) designated to receive proceeds of an insurance policy upon death of the insured.

[**Primary CPP Offsets**]

[Standard offset on a group LTD policy which subtracts the amount paid by Canada Pension Plan's (CPP) disability benefit, on behalf of the disabled person only, from the amount paid by the insurer. CPP disability amounts paid for dependent children are not used as "primary" offsets. See also **Full CPP Offsets**.]

Principal Sum

The payment specified in the policy. Normally the amount paid for accidental death, dismemberment or loss of sight. A fixed or definite amount payable for a specified loss. Sometimes called "Capital Sum".

Probationary Period

The length of time a person must wait from the date of entry into an eligible class or application for coverage to the date insurance is effective. Also referred to as the Service Period or Waiting Period.

Professional Association Plans

Plans designed for associations of lawyers, doctors, dentists, and other professions and written on a group or franchise basis.

Profit, Underwriting. *Refer to* **Underwriting Profit**

Proof of Loss

Documentary evidence required by an insurer to prove a valid claim exists. In group life insurance, it usually consists of a completed claim form and proof of death (death certificate or acceptable substitute); in group medical care insurance, it usually consists of a completed claim form and itemized medical bills.

Proposal

A quotation submitted to a prospective group insurance policyholder by the insurance company through an agent, broker or group representative. This quotation outlines the benefits available under the proposed plan and the costs to both employer and employee.

Prospective Rating

A method of renewal rating that adjusts the rates for the coming policy year in accordance with such factors as known credible past experience, insurance industry and insurance company trends, general business trends (e.g., inflation, deflation) current manual rates, etc.

Prosthetics

A specialized field relating to the design and use of an artificial substitute for a missing body part such as an arm, leg or eye.

Provincial Government Plans. *Refer to* **Medicare**

Provision

A part (clause, sentence, paragraph, etc.) of a group insurance contract which describes or explains a feature, benefit, condition, requirement, etc., of the insurance protection afforded by the contract.

Provision, Automatic Restoration. *Refer to* **Automatic Restoration Provision**

Provision, Clerical Error. *Refer to* **Clerical Error Provision**.

Provisions, Standard. *Refer to* **Standard Provisions**

Provisions, Statutory. *Refer to* **Standard Provisions**

Q

Qualification Period

The period of time whether for short or long term disability during which the employee must be totally disabled before commencement of benefits.

Quotation

The offer to a prospective policyholder to underwrite specified insurance benefits at quoted premium rates. The quoted premium rates may be firm or estimates subject to recalculation based on enrollment.

Quotation, Firm. *Refer to* **Firm Quotation**

R

Rate, Average Premium. *Refer to* **Average Premium Rate**

Rate, Initial. *Refer to* **Initial Rate**

Rate, Manual. *Refer to* **Manual Rate**

Rate, Net Premium. *Refer to* **Net Premium Rate**

Rate, Premium. *Refer to* **Premium Rate**

Rate, Table. *Refer to* **Table Rate**

Rates, Composite. *Refer to* **Composite Rate**

Rates, Experience Rates Premium. *Refer to* **Experience Rated Premium Rates**

Rating, Community. *Refer to* **Community Rating**

Rating, Cross-Experience. *Refer to* **Combining for Experience**

Rating, Experience. *Refer to* **Experience Rating**

Rating, Prospective. *Refer to* **Prospective Rating**

Rating, Renewal. *Refer to* **Renewal Rating**

Rating, Retrospective. *Refer to* **Retrospective Rating**

Ratio, Expense. *Refer to* **Expense Ratio**

Ratio, Loss. *Refer to* **Loss Ratio**

R & C. *Refer to* **Reasonable and Customary**

Reasonable and Customary

This term refers to limiting benefit payments to fees which are reasonable and representative for the service rendered, under the circumstances rendered, by the physician rendered. The term is used extensively in the U.S. but seldom in Canada.

Record Card

A card used by the insurer and/or the administrator of the plan to show the person insured, his coverages and amounts of insurance, beneficiary, and any other information necessary to successfully administer the group plan. [Also called an Employee Data Card.]

Recurrence Clause

A clause specifying a period of time during which the recurrence of a condition is considered as being a continuation of the condition.

Recurring Disability

An important provision in the group insurance plan covering the situation where an employee, having been disabled and having recovered, again becomes disabled from the same or related disability. In such event such later period of disability shall be treated as a continuation of the previous period of disability unless the employee has completely recovered from the previous disability and was continuously actively working for the employer for a stipulated minimum period after termination of the previous disability.

Reduction, Age. *Refer to* **Age Reduction**

Reduction Formula

This is used to keep Life insurance rates at a reasonable level. Where there is substantial coverage on older and retired workers an attempt is normally made starting at age 65 to reduce the amount of Group Life insurance by 500/0 or more.

Reduction of Benefit

Automatic reduction in coverage under certain specified conditions e.g., the monthly benefits may be reduced to 50 per cent while the insured ceases to be fully and gainfully employed away from home or after the insured has reached age 60, 65, etc.

Refund, Experience. *Refer to* **Experience Refund**

Refund, Premium. *Refer to* **Premium Refund**

Refusal Card. *Refer to* **Waiver Card**

Register Card. *Refer to* **Record Card**

Rehabilitation

Refers to a provision in many long-term disability (LTD) plans that enables the insured claimant to receive at least partial benefits while undergoing retraining and seeking new employment.

Rehabilitation Specialist

Usually a rehabilitation professional affiliated with the group insurer's rehabilitation program who is directly involved in facilitating rehabilitation of disabled individuals.

Rehabilitative Employment

Any occupation or work for compensation or profit approved by the Insurer and undertaken by the insured while unable to work on a full-time basis usually in conjunction with a LTD plan.

Reimbursement

Medical & Dental Care Insurance are on a reimbursement basis; that is, benefits are based on actual charges made, and no more.

Reimbursement Policy

A policy which provides benefits for actual expense incurred by the insured, subject to a maximum amount.

Reinstate

To place inforce again, without the usual probationary or service period, an individual's group insurance which for some reason has terminated; or, to place inforce again a group contract which has terminated.

Reinstatement

The revival of a contract which has lapsed. In Group Insurance, a provision allowing portions of the maximum benefit exhausted in prior claims to be reinstated following a specified period during which no benefits are payable.

Reinsurance

The acceptance by one or more insurers, called reinsurers of a portion of the risk underwritten by another insurer who has contracted for the entire coverage.

Reinsurance, Automatic. *Refer to* **Automatic Reinsurance**

Renewable, Guaranteed Policies. *Refer to* **Guaranteed Renewable Policies**

Renewal

An offer and acceptance of a premium for a new policy term.

Renewal Date

The annual date on which the present policy is scheduled to be reviewed for experience.

Renewal Rating

The review given by the insurance company of the premium rates that have been used for the group plan. It is a process of reviewing premium paid, claims and expenses, employee age and benefit distribution to determine the necessity of changing billing rates.

Requirement, Active-at-Work. *Refer to* **Actively-at-Work Requirement**

Reserve

A sum set aside by an insurance company as a liability to fulfill future obligations.

Reserve, Claim Fluctuation. *Refer to* **Claims Fluctuation Reserve**

Reserve, Contingency. *Refer to* **Contingency Reserve**

Reserve, Disabled Life. *Refer to* **Disabled Life Reserve**

Reserves

In Group Insurance, reserves are normally two types (1) claim reserves and (2) special (or contingency) reserves. Claim reserves are for claims which have occurred but not yet been reported or which are unsettled or continuing (open) in nature. [Also called] Open and Unreported (O&U) Claim Reserves. They are most often referred to in the marketplace as "Incurred But Not Reported" (IBNR) reserves. Special reserves are used to accomplish specific goals. They include premium stabilization reserves, rate reduction reserves, special risk reserves, retired life insurance reserves, etc. . . .

Reserves, Claim (IBNR). *Refer to* **Incurred But Not Recorded Claim Reserves**

Resolicitation

A campaign conducted to enroll persons in an existing group insurance plan who are eligible to participate in but not covered for insurance. Evidence of insurability may or may not be required.

Retention

That portion of the premium retained by the insurer for expenses, contingencies and profits or contribution to surplus.

Retrospective Premium Agreement

A formal binding agreement from the policyholder to pay the insurer for deficits which are incurred as a result of the insurer's agreement to continue coverage at a rate level which eliminates any margin for claim fluctuation.

Retrospective Rating

A method of experience rating that adjusts the final premium of a risk in accordance with the experience of that risk during the term of the policy for which the premium is paid.

Revision

Change in benefits, terms or conditions of a group case.

Rider

An amendment which modifies the terms of the group contract or certificates of insurance. It may increase or decrease benefits, waiver a condition or coverage, or in any other way amend the original contract.

Rider, Certificate. *Refer to* **Certificate Rider**

Risk

The probable amount of loss foreseen by an insurer in issuing a contract.

Renewal, Request for Data. *Refer to* **Request for Renewal Data**

Renewal Service Call

A periodic visit made by a representative of the insurance company to the policyholder. The purpose of the call is to discuss the group plan and render any service that appears necessary.

Renewal Underwriting

The review of the financial experience of a group case and the establishment of the renewal premium rates and terms under which the insurance may be continued.

Report, Gain or Loss. *Refer to* **Gain or Loss Report**

Representation

Statements made by an applicant on the application that he or she represents as being substantially true to the best of his or her knowledge and belief, but which are not warranted as exact in every detail.

Representative, Group. *Refer to* **Group Representative**

Retention Estimate

A projection of estimated expenses on a particular group insurance case.

Retroactive Rate Credit

The portion of the premiums which the insurer, issuing group policies on a nonparticipating basis, returns to a policyholder after taking into account the claims incurred, expense charges, risk charges, changes in reserves and profit.

Risk Charge

The portion of a group insurer's retention intended to be used for any of the following: (1) to spread the cost of catastrophic or epidemic losses over all groups (2) to pay certain claims which may be "pooled" and not charged against the experience of a particular group, (3) to cover the experience deficits arising on the poorer risks in a given class, (4) to provide a contribution to the insurer's general surplus as protection against major losses affecting its entire group business.

Risk, Impaired. *Refer to* **Substandard Risk**

Risk Margin

That portion of the insurer's retention other than for expenses; i.e., risk and other contingency charges and profits.

Risk, Substandard. *Refer to* **Substandard Risk**

Risk, Target. *Refer to* **Target Risk**

Run, Lag. *Refer to* **Lag Run**

S

SAP. *Refer to* **Simplified Accounting Procedure**

Scale, High-Low Commission. *Refer to* **Commission, High-Low Scale**

Scale, Level Commission. *Refer to* **Commission, Level Scale**

Schedule, Earnings. *Refer to* **Earnings Schedule**

Schedule, Fee. *Refer to* **Fee Schedule**

Schedule, Flat

Refer, to Flat Schedule.

Schedule, Length of Service. *Refer to* **Length of Service Schedule**

Schedule, Occupational. *Refer to* **Occupational Schedule**

Schedule of Insurance

A list of the amounts of insurance for each coverage according to predetermined classifications for each person which have been decided upon by the policyholder and insurer.

Selection, Adverse. *Refer to* **Adverse Selection**

Self-Accounting. *Refer to* **Self-Administration**

Self-Administration

The policyholder maintains all records regarding the insureds covered under the group insurance plan. The employer prepares the premium statement for each payment date and submits it with a cheque to the insurance company. The insurance company has the contractible prerogative to audit the policyholder's records.

Self-Insurance

A special fund, such as a mutual benefit association or health and welfare fund, established by an employer or employee group, or a combination of the two which directly assumes the functions, responsibilities and liabilities of an insurer. This non-insurer directly provides rather than purchases insurance coverage.

Semi-Private

Medical-expense insurance generally provides payment for a semi-private hospital room.

Service Call

A visit made by a representative of the insurer to the policyholder. The purpose of the visit is to discuss the group plan and its administration and to render any service that appears necessary.

Service, Fee-for. *Refer to* **Fee-for-Service**

Service Fees

Special compensation usually granted to consultants and/or brokers who directly perform many of the functions of a group representative and/or Home Office (e.g., they prepare specifications, prepare and present proposals, handle solicitations and enrollments, prepare announcement materials, install the case, handle all service calls, do certain calculations, handle all renewals, etc.) Commissions paid to the servicing agent after the vested commissions have ceased.

Service-Type Plans

Plans which provide their benefits in the form of services rendered rather than cash benefits (e.g., Blue Cross, Blue Shield, Dental Service Corporations).

Settlement, Optional Modes of. *Refer to* **Optional Modes of Settlement**

Settlement Options

The provisions (stated or intended) in insurance contracts through the use of which an insured or the beneficiary can direct the distribution of the proceeds in other than a lump sum payment.

Sex Distribution

A distribution of covered insureds by their sex. From this distribution it is determined whether special consideration must be given to the rate because of the number of females/males to total eligibles to be covered in the plan.

Sickness

Illness not arising from accident or injury. Usually the sickness causing disability must be contracted by the insured while the policy is in effect. Some policies require that the sickness need only manifest itself while the policy is in effect.

Sickness Insurance

A form of health insurance providing benefits for loss resulting from illness or disease.

Simplified Accounting. *Refer to* **Self-Administration**

Simplified Accounting Procedure

Arrangement under which the policyholder performs practically all of the clerical and billing operations, rather than [the insurer]. The insurance records of each employee are maintained exclusively by the policyholder.

Single Case Agreement

An agreement with an agent or broker specifying commissions which will be paid under a particular contract.

Skills, Transferable. *Refer to* **Transferable Skills**

Small Group

The insurance available to employee groups of usually from two to 50 lives. The schedules, coverages and limitations vary by insurer.

Society of Actuaries

An organization of individuals who have passed the required examinations and have become Fellows in the society. The Society provides continuing education and development programs, promotes and publishes actuarial research, and enforces a professional code of ethical conduct for its members.

Solicitation (Enrollment). *Refer to* **Enrollment**

Specialist, Rehabilitation. *Refer to* **Rehabilitation Specialist**

Specifications

A detailed professional listing of the qualifications of a certain group of individuals (e.g., type of risk, complete census date, contributions, past experience if a transferred case), and the coverages (types, amounts, schedules) and services (self-administration, draft book claims level commissions) which they will require usually provided by consultants/brokers when soliciting competitive from insurers.

Sponsored Dependants. *Refer to* **Collateral Dependants**

Spouse

(a) The person to whom you are lawfully married, or (b) if there is no such person as described in (a) a person [usually] of the opposite sex who has been cohabiting and residing with you [usually] for a continuous period of at least one year, and has been publicly represented by you as your spouse.

Standard Provisions

A set of policy provisions prescribed by provincial laws setting forth certain rights and obligations of both the insured and the company under an insurance policy.

Statement, Annual. *Refer to* **Annual Statement**

Statement, Monthly. *Refer to* **Monthly Statement**

Statement of Health [*See also* **Evidence of Insurability**]

This is the form used to establish the insurability of an applicant who did not enroll when first eligible or who re-enrolls. It asks specific questions about recent treatment and requests authorization to check further with hospitals and attending physicians. A statement of health may also be necessary to obtain amounts of insurance in excess of pre-determined non-evidence amounts.

Statement, Personal Health. *Refer to* **Personal Health Statement**

Statement, Premium. *Refer to* **Premium Statement**

Statistical Fluctuation

A result which deviates from that expected on the basis of an event's true probability or likelihood.

Statutory Provisions. *Refer to* **Standard Provisions**

Stay, Length of. *Refer to* **Length of Stay**

[**STD**]

[Short-term disability plan, also called Weekly Indemnity. See **Disability Income Insurance**.]

Step-Rate Premium

Premium rates for a single unit of group insurance (e.g., $10,000 or $25,000 life) scheduled according to age, sex, occupation or other classification of individual insureds; most often used in employee pay-all group life policies and most often found in five-year age bands.

Stock Company

An insurance company owned by stockholders who elect a board of directors to direct the company's management.

Stop-Loss Provisions

In group insurance, provisions that determine (in advance) the amount of insurance claims in excess of which the policyholder is not charged. A premium is levied for this limitation of risk.

Subrogation

The acquiring by the insurer of the insured's rights against third parties for the indemnification of a loss to the extent that the insurer pays the loss.

Subsidiary

A corporation of which a majority of the capital stock is owned or controlled by another corporation, called the "parent company".

Substandard Risk

A risk that cannot meet the normal health requirements of a standard insurance policy. Protection is provided in consideration of a waiver, a special policy form, or a higher premium charge. Substandard risks may include hazardous sports or occupations.

Supplementary Major Medical Expense. *Refer to* **Extended Health Care**

Surplus

The amount by which the value of an insurer's assets exceed its liabilities.

Surgical Schedule

A list of cash allowances which are payable for various types of surgery, with the respective maximum amounts payable based upon the severity of the operations. The stipulated maximum usually covers all professional fees involved (e.g., surgeon, anaesthetist fees).

T

Table, Morbidity. *Refer to* **Morbidity Tables**

Table Rate

A rate as selected from a premium rate table.

Tables, Canadian Basic Group Life. *Refer to* **Canadian Basic Group Life Tables**

Tabular Claim Charges

To the extent that a group is too small to have all actual claims charged to their premium (those claims below the pooling level, on any one insured) artificial claims must be substituted. The purpose of tabular claim charges is to "average out" over a number of years the paid claims (below the pooling level) for the group. Tabular claim charges are usually determined by adding a percentage (creditability factor) of the actual claims experienced to a percentage (inverse of creditability factor) of the average claim amount expected, plus any pooling charges.

Target Risk

A large premium risk that attracts unusually keen competition among insurers, agents or brokers.

* * *

Tax, Premium. *Refer to* **Premium Tax**

* * *

Termination

An employee who terminates employment or withdraws from the protection of the group plan offered by this employer.

Therapy, Occupational. *Refer to* **Occupational Therapy**

Third-Party Administration

The method of administration under which a third party (such as a professional insurance administrator or a broker) maintains all records regarding the person covered under the group insurance plan. The third party administrator may also pay claims using the draft book system.

Third-Party Payor

Any organization, public or private, that pays or insures health or medical expenses on behalf of beneficiaries or recipients (e.g., Blue Cross and Blue Shield, Commercial insurance companies). The individual generally pays a premium for such coverage in all private and some public programs. The organization then pays bills on his behalf; such payments are called third-party payments and are distinguished by the separation between the individual receiving the service (the first party), the individual or institution providing it (the second party) and the organization paying for it (the third party).

* * *

Ticket Insurance

Accident only protection which is issued in conjunction with a ticket for transportation on a common carrier.

Time Limit

The period of time in which a notice of claim or proof of a loss must be filed.

Time, Loss of Insurance. *Refer to* **Disability Income Insurance**

Time of Payment-Claims. *Refer to* **Claims, Time of Payment**

Total Disability

Refers to the inability to perform all of the duties of one's regular occupation or the duties of any occupation for which the individual may become fitted due, to education, training or experience.

Trade Association Groups

Those made up of many employers in the same industry. Group policies cover the members of the trade association and their employees and dependants.

Transferable Skills

The skills an insured has acquired through occupational or vocational endeavors which may be applied with minimal training in another occupation which can be performed within prescribed physical or mental limitations.

Transferred Business

Underwriters sometimes use this term to refer to premium and claims information while a group has been insured with another carrier. This is referred to most often as "past financial experience."

Transferred Business, Commissions on. *Refer to* **Commissions on Transferred Business**

Travel Accident Policies

Limited contracts covering only accidents while an insured person is travelling (e.g., on business of his employer away from his usual place of business).

Trust Agreement

A legal document which establishes a trust fund, makes provisions as to how the trust fund shall be allocated and appoints and defines the duties, responsibilities and liabilities of the trustees.

Trustee

A person appointed by a trust agreement to administer a trust fund. In group insurance it would be an individual (usually one of several) designated to administer a fund for purposes which include the purchase of group insurance.

Trusteed Group Insurance Plan

A policy issued to the trustees of a fund established by a formal trust agreement covering employees subject to a collective bargaining agreement, or employees of two or more employers who are participants of the trust agreement. A trust arrangement can also be used on a voluntary basis to cover persons who are members of an association or employees of a particular employer.

Turn Over

The term is used in a restricted sense to mean the ratio of employees who leave employment during a given year to the total of all employees at the beginning of such year.

Twenty-Four Hour Coverage

Insurance providing benefits for an accident or sickness incurred either on the job or off the job.

U

UCR. *Refer to* **Usual, Customary and Reasonable**

[**UI**. *Refer to* **Unemployment Insurance**]

Unallocated Benefit

A reimbursement provision, usually for miscellaneous hospital and medical expenses, which does not specify how much will be paid for each type of treatment, examination, dressing or the like, but only sets a maximum which will be paid for all such treatments.

Underwriting

The process by which an insurer determines whether or not and on what basis it will accept an application for insurance.

Underwriting Profit

An insurer's profit from its insurance operations as distinguished from its investment earnings on group term insurance; it is calculated by deducting claims, expenses, and reserve contributions from earned premium.

Underwriting, Renewal. *Refer to* **Renewal Underwriting**

Unearned Premium

That portion of a premium for which the protection of the policy has not yet been given.

[**Unemployment Insurance**]

[A federal government-sponsored plan which provides benefits to contributing employees who lose their jobs. UI also provides a form of short-term disability benefit to contributing employees who are not covered by other short-term disability plans.]

Union Sponsored Plan

A benefit program developed through a union's initiative. The funds to finance the benefits are usually paid out of a trust fund which receives its income from (1) employer contributions, (2) employer and union member contributions, or (3) union members alone.

Uninsured Plans

Provide health or short-term disability benefits, often administered by an insurance company. Because they're not insured, benefits are not guaranteed.

Usual, Customary and Reasonable

Health insurance plans that pay a physician's full charge if it does not exceed his usual charge, does not exceed the amount customarily charged for the service by other physicians in the area or it is otherwise reasonable.

Utilization

The extent to which a given group uses a specified service in a specific period of time. Usually expressed as the number of services used per year per 100 or per 1,000 persons eligible for the service, but utilization rates may be expressed in other types of ratios.

V

Value, Commuted. *Refer to* **Commuted Value**

Vocational Evaluation

A professional analysis of the insured's work potential, integrating information about physical capabilities, mental aptitudes, interests, personality, motivation, transferable skills and environmental considerations.

W

Wage Loss Insurance. *Refer to* **Disability Income Insurance**

Waiting Period. *Refer to* **Probationary Period**

Waiting Period, Benefit. *Refer to* **Benefit Waiting Period**

Waiver

An agreement attached to a policy which exempts from coverage certain disabilities [or risks]normally covered by the policy.

Waiver Card

A card used when an eligible [person] wishes to surrender his right to enroll in a group insurance program. [Also called a Refusal Card (see **Waiver Card**.]

Waiver of Premium

A provision that under certain conditions a person's insurance will be kept in full force by the insured without further payment of premiums. It is used most often in the event of permanent and total disability.

Weekly Indemnity Insurance. *Refer to* **Disability Income Insurance**]

Wholistic Medicine. *Refer to* **Holistic Medicine**

[**WI**. *Refer to* **Weekly Indemnity Insurance**]

Worker's Compensation Act

A statute imposing liability on employers to pay benefits and furnish care to employees injured, and to pay benefits to dependants of employees killed, in the course of and because of their employment.

Y

Year of Birth, Insurance. *Refer to* **Insurance Year of Birth**

Yearly Renewal Term (YRT)

Life insurance where the premium rate is recalculated each year based on attained age. YRT is used almost exclusively for group insurance.

YMPE

Year's Maximum Pensionable Earnings.

¶17,010 ORGANIZATIONS TO JOIN

Organization	Meetings	Seminars	Publications	Open to Public or Insurance Trade only
Canadian Benefits and Pension Conference (C.B.P.C.) Local Chapter	Yes	Yes	Newsletters	Public and Trade
C.E.B.S				Public and Trade
Human Resources Association Local Chapters	Yes	Yes	Yes	Public and Trade
Life Underwriters Association Local Chapters	Yes	Yes	Yes	Trade only
Health Insurance Association of America	Three/year	Health Insurance Information Available to the Public		Trade only
Life Office Management Association (LOMA)	Not Locally	Yes	Yes, textbooks Workbooks	Trade only
National Association of Life Underwriters (NAHU)	Annual	Annual	Yes	Trade only
National Association of Health Underwriters	Not Locally	Annual		Trade only
International Claim Association	Not Locally	Annual	Newsletter	Trade only
Association of Life Insurance Counsel (ALIC)	Not Locally	Annual	No	Trade only (legal)
Society of Actuaries	Not Locally	Four/year	Yes	Trade only (actuarial)

¶17,015 INSURANCE ASSOCIATIONS

1. Canadian Institute of Actuaries	360 Albert Street, Suite 820, Ottawa, Ontario K1R 7X7 Telephone: (613) 236-8196 Fax: (613) 233-4552
2. Canadian Life and Health Insurance Association	1 Queen Street East, Suite 1700, Toronto, Ontario M5C 2X9. Telephone: (416) 1-800-268-8099 (English); (416) 1-800-361-8070 (French)
3. Independent Life Insurance Brokers of Canada,	2175 Sheppard Avenue East, Suite 110, Willowdale, Ontario M2J 1W8. Telephone: (416) 491-9747 Fax: (416) 491-1670
4. Insurance Bureau of Canada,	181 University Avenue, 13th Floor Toronto, Ontario M5H 3M7. Telephone: (416) 362-2031 Toll-free: 1-800-387-2880 Fax: (416) 361-5952
5. Insurance Institute of Canada	18 King Street East, 6th Floor Toronto, Ontario M5C 1C4. Telephone: (416) 362-8586 Fax: (416) 362-1126
6. Life Underwriters Association of Canada,	41 Lesmill Road, North York, Ontario M3B 2T3. Telephone: (416) 444-5251 Fax: (416) 444-8031
7. Health Insurance Association of America	1025 Connecticut Avenue N.W., Suite 1200f]Washington, D.C. 20036- 3998 Telephone: (202) 824-1600 Fax: (202) 824-1800
8. Life Insurance Marketing Research Association (LIMRA International)	P.O. Box 208 Hartford, Connecticut 05141-0033 Telephone: (203) 677-0033 Fax: (203) 674-4249
9. Life Office Management Association (LOMA)	5770 Powers Ferry Road N.W. Atlanta, Georgia 30327 Telephone: (404) 951-1770 Fax: (404) 984-0441
10. National Association of Health Underwriters (NAHU)	1000 Connecticut Avenue N.W., Suite 810 Washington, D.C. 20036 Telephone: (202) 223-5533 Fax: (202) 785-2274

11. National Association of Life Underwriters (NALU)	1922 F Street N.W. Washington, D.C. 20006 Telephone: (202) 331-6005 Fax: (202) 331-2179
12. Society of Actuaries	475 North Martingale Road, Suite 800 Schaumberg, Illinois 60173-2226 (708) 706-3500 (708) 706-3599

¶17,020 COURSES TO TAKE

Course	Contact Address	Designation	Number of Courses	Comments
C.E.B.S.	2261 Lake Shore Blvd. West Suite SPH12, Etobicoke, Ontario M8V 3X1 Telephone: (416) 253-7434 Fax: (416) 253-9745	C.E.B.S.	10	Available to the public and the trade; university level; by correspondence
Chartered Life Underwriter	Life Underwriters Association of Canada 41 Lesmill Road, North York, Ontario M3B 2T3	C.L.U.	10	Available to the trade
Life Management Institute		F.L.M.I.	10	"
Society of Actuaries		F.S.A	10	
Health Insurance Association of America				
National Association of Health Underwriters		NAHU		
National Association of Life Underwriters		NALU	10	

¶17,025 SUGGESTED READINGS

1. *Mercer Handbook of Canadian Pension and Welfare Plans*, by Laurence E. Howard, 10th edition, CCH Canadian Limited, North York, Ontario M3C 1Z5.

2. *Employee Benefits in Canada*, by Guy A. Jobin *et al.*, The International Foundation of Employee Benefit Plans, P.O. Box 69, Brookfield, Wisconsin 53008-0069. Telephone: (414) 786-6700, or 2261 Lake Shore Blvd. West, Suite SPH12, Etobicoke, Ontario M8V 3X1. Telephone: (416) 253-7434; Fax (416) 253-9745.

3. *Benefits Canada* (magazine), published by Maclean Hunter Limited, 777 Bay Street, Toronto, Ontario M5W 1A7. Telephone (416) 596-5000.

4. *Benefits and Pensions Monitor* (magazine), published by Powershift Communications Inc., 235 Yorkland Blvd., 3rd Floor, North York, Ontario M2J 4Y8. Telephone (416) 494-1066.

5. *Canadian HR Reporter* (newspaper), published by MPL Communications Inc., 133 Richmond Street West, Toronto, Ontario M5H 3M8. Telephone (416) 869-1177.

6. *Canadian Life and Health Insurance Law*, by Harriett E. Jones, published by the Life Management Institute (LOMA), Atlanta, Georgia, 1992.

7. A Course in Group Life & Health Insurance, Part B, by the Health Insurance Association of America, Washington, D.C., 1985.

8. *Employee Benefits Programs: Management, Planning & Control*, by Ernest J.E. Griffes, 2nd Edition, Business One Irwin, 1990,

9. *Life Insurance Laws of Canada*, by Bruce R. MacDonald, Life Underwriters Association of Canada, North York, Ontario, 1989.

10. *Elements of Group Insurance*, by George N. Watson and Bernard Ouimet, Life Underwriters Association of Canada, North York, Ontario, 1989.

11. Selected chapters from *The Handbook of Employee Benefits: Design, Funding and Administration*, by Jerry S. Rosenbloom, Dow Jones-Irwin, Homewood, Illinois, 1988.

12. *Employee Benefit Plans: A Glossary of Terms*, 6th edition, edited by June M. Lehmen, International Foundation of Employee Benefit Plans, Brookfield, Wisconsin, 1987.

13. CCH Canadian Employment Benefits and Pension Guide Reports, CCH Canadian, North York, Ontario.

¶17,030 GOVERNMENT TELEPHONE NUMBERS: BENEFIT ISSUES AND PROGRAMS

Federal:		
	Reference Canada-All Departments and Programs	1-800-667-3355
	Statistics Canada — Publications Order Line	1-800-267-6677
	Office of the Superintendent of Financial Institutions	(613) 990-7788
	Canada Labour Relations Board	(613) 996-9466
	Information Commission of Canada	1-800-267-0441
	Privacy Commissioner	1-800-267-0441

Provincial Governments:	**General Telephone Numbers: Regular**	**Fax**
Alberta	(403) 427-2711	n/a
British Columbia	(604) 660-2421	n/a
Manitoba	(204) 945-3744	n/a
New Brunswick	(506) 453-2525	n/a
Newfoundland	(709) 729-2300	n/a
Nova Scotia	(902) 424-5200	(902) 425-3026
Ontario	(416) 326-1234	n/a
Prince Edward Island	(902) 368-4000	(902) 368-5544
Quebec	(418) 643-1344	n/a
Saskatchewan	(306) 787-0222	n/a
Yukon	(403) 667-5811	(403) 667-3518
Northwest Territories	(403) 920-3888	(403) 920-4218

Provincial Health Care:	**General Telephone Numbers: Regular**	**Fax**
Alberta	(403) 427-1432	n/a
British Columbia	(604) 952-3166	n/a
Manitoba	(204) 786-7282	(204) 945-4564
New Brunswick	(506) 453-2536	(506) 453-3963
Newfoundland	(709) 722-6980	(709) 722-6980
Nova Scotia	(902) 424-4310	n/a
Ontario	(416) 327-4327	(416) 327-4266
Prince Edward Island	(902) 368-4064	(902) 838-2050
Quebec	(418) 643-3380	n/a
Saskatchewan	(306) 787-3251	n/a
Yukon	(403) 667-5209	n/a
Northwest Territories	(403) 873-7039	(403) 920-4969

Provincial Pension Authorities:	**General Telephone Numbers: Regular**	**Fax**
Alberta	(403) 427-7105	(403) 421-1652
British Columbia	(604) 775-1266	(604) 660-6517
Manitoba	(204) 945-2740	(204) 948-2375
New Brunswick	(506) 453-2055	(506) 453-3806
Newfoundland	(709) 729-3931	(709) 729-2070
Nova Scotia	(902) 424-8915	(902) 424-0602
Ontario	(416) 314-0626	(416) 314-0620

Prince Edward Island	(902) 368-4564	(902) 368-5283
Quebec	(418) 643-8302	n/a
Saskatchewan	(306) 787-7650	(306) 787-2208
Yukon	n/a	n/a
Northwest Territories	n/a	n/a

Provincial Workers' Compensation Boards:	**General Telephone Numbers: Regular**	**Fax**
Alberta	(403) 498-4000	(403) 422-0972
British Columbia	(604) 273-2266	(604) 276-3151
Manitoba	(204) 786-5471	(204) 786-4610
New Brunswick	(506) 632-2200	(506) 632-2226
Newfoundland	(709) 778-1000	(709) 738-1714
Nova Scotia	(902) 424-8440	(902) 424-0509
Ontario	(416) 927-4135	(416) 927-5141
Prince Edward Island	(902) 368-5680	(902) 368-5696
Quebec	(418) 646-3171	(418) 643-2236
Saskatchewan	(306) 787-4370	(306) 787-0213
Yukon	(403) 667-5645	(403) 668-2079
Northwest Territories	(403) 920-3888	(403) 873-4596

Provincial Employment Standards:	**General Telephone Numbers: Regular**	**Fax**
Alberta	(403) 427-3731	n/a
British Columbia	(604) 660-4000	(604) 356-1886
Manitoba	(204) 945-3352	n/a
New Brunswick	(506) 453-2725	n/a
Newfoundland	(709) 729-2742	n/a
Nova Scotia	(902) 424-4311	(902) 424-3239
Ontario	(416) 326-7160	(416) 326-7061
Prince Edward Island	(902) 368-5550	(902) 368-5526
Quebec	(418) 643-8742	(418) 643-5132
Saskatchewan	(306) 787-2438	(306) 787-4780
Yukon Labour Services	(403) 667-5944	n/a
Northwest Territories	(403) 873-7486	n/a

Provincial Occupational/Worker Health and Safety:	**General Telephone Numbers: Regular**	**Fax**
Alberta	(403) 427-6941	(403) 427-5698
British Columbia (WCB)	(603) 273-2266	n/a
Manitoba	(204) 945-3446	(204) 945-4556
New Brunswick	(506) 453-2467	(506) 453-7982
Newfoundland	(709) 729-5548	n/a
Nova Scotia	(902) 424-4328	(902) 424-3239
Ontario	(416) 975-9728	(416) 975-9775
Prince Edward Island	(902) 368-5470	(902) 368-5544
Quebec	(418) 643-5850	(418) 643-2236
Saskatchewan	(306) 787-4496	(306) 787-2208
Yukon	(403) 667-5450	n/a
Northwest Territories	(403) 873-7468	n/a
Canadian Centre for Occupational Health and Safety	1-800-263-8466	(905) 572-4500

¶17,035 LIST OF INSURANCE COMPANIES AND BENEFIT PROVIDERS

Abbey Life
Aetna Canada
American Home
Blue Cross Life
Canada Life
Co-operators
Crown Life
Empire Life
Equitable Life
Great West Life
Laurentian Imperial
London Life
Manulife Financial
Maritime Life
Metropolitan Life
Mutual Group
Mutual of Omaha
National Life
New York Life
North American Life
Norwich Union
Paul Revere Life Insurance
Prudential Insurance of America (the Rock)
Royal Life
Standard Life
Sunlife Assurance Company
Toronto Mutual Life
Transamerica Life
Wawanesa Mutual Life
Zurich Life

The following is a partial list of firms, other than life insurance companies, providing benefits in Canada. Some of these are so called "not-for-profit" companies such as Blue Cross. These organizations provide a variety of services for specific benefits. At the time of this printing, some provinces were still not charging premium tax on premiums paid to these not-for-profit organizations. The current trend, however, is for provinces to extend the tax (approximately 2 or 3 per cent of premiums depending on the province) to both the profit and not-for-profit organizations who provide these benefits. If your organization's head office is located in a province where not-for-profits are not required to charge premium tax, there may be a (2 or 3 per cent) savings on your health and dental plans by placing these benefits with a not-for-profit organization. A tax savings may not necessarily mean an overall savings, better service, or better systems.

List of Not-for-Profit Benefit Providers

Alberta Dental Service Corporation
Blue Cross Atlantic Canada
Green Shield Canada
Group Medical Services (Saskatchewan Blue Cross)
Liberty Health (formerly Ontario Blue Cross)
M.S.A. (Blue Cross British Columbia)
M.S.I. (Saskatchewan Blue Cross)
Maritime Medical
Quebec Hospital Service Corporation (Quebec Blue Cross)

TABLE / TABLEAU

MAXIMUM MONTHLY RATES FOR NEW BENEFITS
TAUX MENSUELS MAXIMUM POUR LES NOUVELLES PRESTATIONS

Year / Année	Retirement Pension (1) / Pension de retraite	Disability Pension / Pension d'invalidité	Survivor's Pension / Pension de survivant (3) Under 65 / Moins de 65 (A)	Survivor's Under 65 / Moins de 65 (B)	Survivor's 65 and over / 65 et plus (A)	Survivor's 65 and over / 65 et plus (B)	Orphan & Child's Benefits (4) / Prestations d'orphelin et d'enfant (A)	Orphan & Child's (B)	Death Benefit / Prestation de décès	Combined Pensions / Pensions combinées Ret./Surv. / Ret./Surv. (1)	Combined Disb./Surv. / Inv./Surv.
	$	$	$	$	$	$	$	$	$	$	$
1967	19.97 (2)	–	–	–	–	–	–	–	–	–	–
1968	30.58 (2)	–	64.82	–	62.92	–	25.50	12.75	510.00	104.85	–
1969	41.62 (2)	–	65.85	66.12	63.75	64.18	26.01	13.01	520.00	106.25	–
1970	53.26 (2)	106.43 (2)	67.15	67.17	65.00	65.03	26.53 (5)	13.27 (5)	530.00	108.33	108.33
1971	65.33 (2)	109.88	68.47	68.50	66.25	66.30	27.06	13.53	540.00	110.42	110.42
1972	77.81 (2)	111.98	69.79	69.84	67.50	67.58	27.60	13.80	550.00	112.50	112.50
1973	90.71 (2)	114.09	71.12	71.18	68.75	68.85	28.15	14.08	560.00	114.58	114.58
1974	109.60 (2)	125.95	79.86	80.25	73.75	74.39	33.76	16.88	660.00	122.92	122.92
1975	134.97 (2)	139.35	88.31	88.76	81.67	81.42	37.27	18.64	740.00	136.10	136.10
1976	154.86	157.59	99.51	98.20	92.92	90.81	41.44	20.72	830.00	154.85	154.85
1977	173.61	175.05	109.94	107.68	104.17	100.54	44.84	22.42	930.00	173.60	173.60
1978	194.44	194.02	121.11	118.18	116.66	111.98	48.19	–	1,040.00	194.44	194.44
1979	218.06	216.06	134.28	131.99	130.84	127.16	52.51	–	1,170.00	218.06	218.06
1980	244.44	240.58	148.92	146.38	146.66	142.61	57.25	–	1,310.00	244.44	244.44
1981	274.31	268.64	165.78	163.65	164.59	161.18	62.91	–	1,470.00	274.31	274.31
1982	307.65	301.42	186.05	186.20	184.59	184.83	70.68	–	1,650.00	307.65	307.65
1983	345.15	337.46	208.03	206.89	207.09	205.27	76.60	–	1,850.00	345.15	345.15
1984	387.50	374.50	229.18	221.98	232.50	220.97	83.87	–	2,080.00	387.50	387.50
1985	435.42	414.13	250.84	239.27	261.25	242.73	87.56	–	2,340.00	435.42	435.42
1986	486.11	455.64	273.35	260.88	291.67	271.70	91.06	–	2,580.00	486.10	486.10
1987	521.52	634.09	290.36	284.56	312.91	303.62	94.79	–	2,590.00	521.52	764.47
1988	543.06	660.94	302.61	303.14	325.84	326.68	98.96	–	2,650.00	543.06	796.70
1989	556.25	681.23	311.61	315.02	333.75	339.20	103.02	–	2,770.00	556.25	820.29
1990	577.08	709.52	324.37	326.57	346.25	349.77	107.96	–	2,890.00	577.08	853.79
1991	604.86	743.64	339.96	339.93	362.92	362.87	113.14	–	3,050.00	604.86	894.85
1992	636.11	783.89	358.24	359.68	381.67	383.96	154.70	–	3,220.00	636.11	942.92
1993	667.36	812.85	372.11	364.69	400.42	388.54	157.48	–	3,340.00	667.36	979.69
1994	694.44	839.09	384.59	379.19	416.66	408.02	160.47	–	3,440.00	694.44	1,012.70
1995	713.19	854.74	392.24	386.51	427.91	418.75	161.27	–	3,490.00	713.19	1,033.04

(1) Maximum amount paid to a person who retires at age 65. / Montant maximum versé à une personne qui prend sa retraite à 65 ans.
(2) Maximum amount for December. / Montant maximum pour décembre.
(3) Col. (A) Pension begins in year of death, col. (B) Contributor dies in December—pension begins in January.
Col. (A) La pension commence l'année du décès, col. (B) Le cotisant décède en décembre – la pension commence en janvier.
(4) Col. (A) For first four children up to 1977; from 1978 each child receives equal amount, col. (B) For additional child.
Col. (A) Pour quatre premiers enfants jusqu'à 1977; de 1978 montant égal pour chaque enfant, col. (B) Pour enfant additionnel.
(5) Disabled contributor's child's benefit started in 1970. / La prestation d'enfant de cotisant invalide a commencé en 1970.

TABLE / TABLEAU

DATA RELATED TO CALCULATION OF CONTRIBUTIONS AND BENEFITS
DONNÉES RELATIVES AU CALCUL DES COTISATIONS ET DES PRESTATIONS

Year / Année	Maximum Pensionable Earnings / Maximum de gains admissibles	Year's Basic Exemption / Exemption de base annuelle	Maximum Contributory Earnings / Maximum des gains cotisables	Maximum Employee's or Employer's Contribution / Cotisation maximale de l'employé ou de l'employeur: Rate / Taux	Amount / Montant	Maximum Self-employed Contribution / Cotisation maximale du travailleur autonome: Rate / Taux	Amount / Montant	Flat Rate / Taux uniforme: Survivor's / Survivant	Disability / Invalidité	Maximum Retirement Pension Base / Base maximale de la pension de retraite
	$	$	$	%	$	%	$	$	$	$
1966	5,000	600	4,400	1.8	79.20	3.6	158.40	–	–	–
1967	5,000	600	4,400	1.8	79.20	3.6	158.40	–	–	–
1968	5,100	600	4,500	1.8	81.00	3.6	162.00	–	–	104.17
1969	5,200	600	4,600	1.8	82.80	3.6	165.60	25.50	–	104.86
1970	5,300	600	4,700	1.8	84.60	3.6	169.20	26.01	–	106.25
1971	5,400	600	4,800	1.8	86.40	3.6	172.80	26.53	26.53	108.33
1972	5,500	600	4,900	1.8	88.20	3.6	176.40	27.06	27.06	110.42
1973	5,600	600	5,000	1.8	90.00	3.6	180.00	27.60	27.60	112.50
1974	6,600	700	5,900	1.8	106.20	3.6	212.40	28.15	28.15	114.58
1975	7,400	700	6,700	1.8	120.60	3.6	241.20	33.76	33.76	122.92
1976	8,300	800	7,500	1.8	135.00	3.6	270.00	37.27	37.27	136.11
1977	9,300	900	8,400	1.8	151.20	3.6	302.40	41.44	41.44	154.86
1978	10,400	1,000	9,400	1.8	169.20	3.6	338.40	44.84	44.84	173.61
1979	11,700	1,100	10,600	1.8	190.80	3.6	381.60	48.19	48.19	194.44
1980	13,100	1,300	11,800	1.8	212.40	3.6	424.80	52.51	52.51	218.06
1981	14,700	1,400	13,300	1.8	239.40	3.6	478.80	57.25	57.25	244.44
1982	16,500	1,600	14,900	1.8	268.20	3.6	536.40	62.91	62.91	274.31
1983	18,500	1,800	16,700	1.8	300.60	3.6	601.20	70.68	70.68	307.65
1984	20,800	2,000	18,800	1.8	338.40	3.6	676.80	78.60	78.60	345.15
1985	23,400	2,300	21,100	1.8	379.80	3.6	759.60	83.87	83.87	387.50
1986	25,800	2,500	23,300	1.8	419.40	3.6	838.80	87.56	87.56	435.42
1987	25,900	2,500	23,400	1.9	444.60	3.8	889.20	91.06	91.06	486.11
1988	26,500	2,600	23,900	2.0	478.00	4.0	956.00	94.79	242.95	521.52
1989	27,700	2,700	25,000	2.1	525.00	4.2	1,050.00	98.96	253.64	543.06
1990	28,900	2,800	26,100	2.2	574.20	4.4	1,148.40	103.02	264.04	556.25
1991	30,500	3,000	27,500	2.3	632.50	4.6	1,265.00	107.96	276.71	577.08
1992	32,200	3,200	29,000	2.4	696.00	4.8	1,392.00	113.14	289.99	604.86
1993	33,400	3,300	30,100	2.5	752.50	5.0	1,505.00	119.70	306.81	636.11
1994	34,400	3,400	31,000	2.6	806.00	5.2	1,612.00	121.85	312.33	667.36
1995	34,900	3,400	31,500	2.7	850.50	5.4	1,701.00	124.17	318.26	694.44
								124.79	319.85	713.19

AMOUNTS OF BENEFITS PAYABLE UNDER THE CANADA PENSION PLAN — 1995

TABLE 1 — RETIREMENT PENSION PAYABLE IN 1995

Percentage of Yearly Maximum Pensionable Earnings	25%	40%	50%	60%	75%	80%	100%
Monthly pension at age 65 ($)	178.30	285.28	356.60	427.91	534.89	570.55	713.19

When the pension is payable in a month other than the month of the 65th anniversary of the beneficiary the above amounts are reduced or raised by ½ of 1% as the case may be for each month between the starting of the pension and the 65th anniversary. The adjustment
cannot be more than 30%

TABLE 2 — DISABILITY PENSION PAYABLE IN 1995

Percentage of Yearly Maximum Pensionable Earnings	25%	40%	50%	60%	75%	80%	100%
Monthly pension ($)	453.58	533.81	587.30	640.78	721.02	747.76	854.74

TABLE 3 — SURVIVING SPOUSE'S PENSION — PAYABLE IN 1995 (Death of Contributor in 1995)

Percentage of Yearly Maximum Pensionable Earnings	25%	40%	50%	60%	75%	80%	100%
Monthly pension by the age of surviving spouse ($)							
less than 65	191.65	231.77	258.52	285.26	325.37	338.75	392.24
65 and more	106.98	171.17	213.96	256.75	320.93	342.33	427.91

TABLE 4 — DEATH BENEFITS PAYABLE IN 1995

Percentage of Yearly Maximum Pensionable Earnings	25%	40%	50%	60%	75%	80%	100%
Lump-sum payment ($)	1,069.80	1,711.68	2,139.60	2,567.46	3,209.34	3,423.30	3,490.00

NOTE: The above tables present approximately monthly pension amounts payable to persons who start receiving a pension in 1995, and whose percentage of Yearly Maximum Pensionable Earnings since 1966 had been as shown at the top of each column.

AMOUNTS OF BENEFITS PAYABLE UNDER THE QUEBEC PENSION PLAN — 1995

RETIREMENT PENSION PAYABLE IN 1995

Percentage of Yearly Maximum Pensionable Earnings	25%	40%	50%	60%	75%	80%	100%
Monthly pension at age 65 ($)	178.30	285.28	356.60	427.91	534.89	570.55	713.19

When the pension is payable in a month other than the month of the 65th anniversary of the beneficiary, the above amounts are reduced or raised by ½ of 1% as the case may be for each month between the starting of the pension and the 65th anniversary. The adjustment cannot be more than 30%.

DISABILITY PENSION PAYABLE IN 1995

Percentage of Yearly Maximum Pensionable Earnings	25%	40%	50%	60%	75%	80%	100%
Monthly pension ($)	451.99	532.22	585.71	639.19	719.43	746.17	853.15

SURVIVING SPOUSE'S PENSION — PAYABLE IN 1995 (Death in 1995)

Percentage of Yearly Maximum Pensionable Earnings	25%	40%	50%	60%	75%	80%	100%
Monthly pension by the age of surviving spouse: ($)							
less than 45 (without child)	148.38	188.50	215.25	241.99	282.10	295.48	348.97
less than 45 (with child)	362.37	402.49	429.24	455.98	496.09	509.47	562.96
45 to 54	385.12	425.24	451.99	478.73	518.84	532.22	585.71
55 to 65	466.45	506.57	533.32	560.06	600.17	613.55	667.04
65 and more	106.98	171.17	213.96	256.75	320.93	342.33	427.91

DEATH BENEFITS PAYABLE IN 1995 (Death in 1995)

Percentage of Yearly Maximum Pensionable Earnings	25%	40%	50%	60%	75%	80%	100%
Lump-sum payment ($)	1069.80	1711.68	2139.60	2567.46	3209.34	3423.30	3490.00

NOTE: The pension amounts contained in the four tables represent the pension payable in 1995 to the extent that the contributor (pensioner, disabled or deceased) realized in each year of his assessable period the maximum proportion of allowable gains at the top of each column. The pension for orphans and children of disabled contributors remains the same at $50.95 per child per month.

¶17,045 FINANCIAL INSTITUTIONS RANKINGS

[Reprinted by permission of *Canadian Business* magazine ©1995.]

1 to 50

FINANCE 100

Assets rank '94		Assets ($MIL)	Assets % CHANGE	Revenue ($MIL)	Revenue % CHANGE	Net Income ($MIL)	Net Income RANK	Net Income % CHANGE	Return on assets	Year-end
1	Royal Bank of Canada	173,079.0	4.9	13,434.0	14.2	1,169.0	4	289.7	0.7	Oct-94
2	Canadian Imperial Bank of Commerce	151,053.0	6.9	11,214.0	3.4	890.0	5	21.9	0.6	Oct-94
3	Bank of Montreal	138,175.0	18.2	5,196.0	6.9	825.0	6	16.4	0.6	Oct-94
4	Bank of Nova Scotia	132,928.0	24.8	9,376.0	12.7	482.0	8	-32.5	0.4	Oct-94
5	Toronto-Dominion Bank	99,759.0	17.3	6,993.0	10.6	683.0	7	148.4	0.7	Oct-94
6	Conféd. des caisses pop. et d'écon. Desjardins	77,000.0	31.4	8,633.2	40.4	338.0	9	17.1	0.4	Dec-94
7	Sun Life Assurance Co. of Canada	60,521.8	35.4	9,965.6	20.5	304.5	10	101.6	0.5	Dec-94
8	CT Financial Services Inc.	49,036.0	6.3	3,846.0	1.1	222.0	13	33.7	0.5	Dec-94
9	Caisse de dépôt et placement du Québec	44,860.0	-4.8	2,883.0	-27.7	2,900.0	1	-62.3	6.5	Dec-94
10	National Bank of Canada	44,774.0	4.8	1,800.0	10.4	217.0	14	24.0	0.5	Oct-94
11	Manulife Financial	40,227.2	4.5	8,142.7	9.1	280.9	11	49.9	0.7	Dec-94
12	Canada Trust[1]	39,359.0	4.7	3,121.0	-1.0	154.0	18	41.3	0.4	Dec-94
13	Power Financial Corp.	30,453.0	6.8	6,656.4	14.3	273.1	12	36.2	0.9	Dec-94
14	Bank of Canada	30,049.7	3.5	1,704.9	-3.0	1,495.7	3	-3.6	5.0	Dec-94
15	Great-West Lifeco Inc.	27,172.2	7.3	6,068.3	15.0	209.8	15	21.1	0.8	Dec-94
16	Bank of Montreal Mortgage Corp.	26,569.2	12.8	1,927.4	-4.2	36.9	40	-11.7	0.1	Oct-94
17	Canada Life Assurance Co.	24,898.0	0.0	2,913.3	5.1	111.6	23	-18.8	0.4	Dec-94
18	Ontario Municipal Employees Retirement Board	21,167.0	3.8	2,725.0	3.3	2,079.0	2	-0.7	9.8	Dec-94
19	Trilon Financial Corp.	19,178.0	1.7	5,026.0	9.2	58.0	30	-	0.3	Dec-94
20	Mutual Group[2]	18,907.0	14.2	3,754.0	-0.6	155.0	17	24.0	0.8	Dec-94
21	RBC Dominion Securities Ltd.	18,375.2	30.4	1,029.2	25.6	133.3	20	31.4	0.7	Sep-94
22	Montreal Trustco Inc.	18,044.3	61.9	1,434.6	21.9	3.5	76	-	0.0	Dec-94
23	London Insurance Group	17,816.0	7.3	4,647.0	10.0	121.0	21	-8.3	0.7	Dec-94
24	Hongkong Bank of Canada	16,021.2	18.5	1,050.0	10.4	85.9	24	35.8	0.5	Oct-94
25	National Trustco Inc.	15,887.9	0.4	1,365.9	-8.3	57.7	31	21.3	0.4	Oct-94
26	London Life Insurance Co.	13,972.0	7.5	3,733.0	11.5	83.0	26	0.0	0.6	Dec-94
27	Canada Mortgage & Housing Corp.	13,824.7	17.0	1,309.5	5.9	-93.5	98	-	-0.7	Dec-94
28	Laurentian Bank of Canada	10,467.5	8.3	837.3	-2.2	13.2	55	-63.0	0.1	Oct-94
29	Export Development Corp.	9,375.0	2.4	864.0	23.6	171.0	16	317.1	1.8	Dec-94
30	North American Life Assurance Co.	9,280.4	4.1	1,953.0	34.6	-17.4	91	-	-0.2	Dec-94
31	Desjardins-Laurentian Life Group	8,857.6	7.8	2,471.5	-0.5	43.8	35	-31.7	0.5	Dec-94
32	Alberta Treasury Branches	8,125.7	5.3	276.5	2.1	24.5	48	34.2	0.3	Mar-94
33	Crown Life Insurance Co.	6,745.7	-9.7	1,486.8	-7.4	36.2	41	429.9	0.5	Dec-94
34	Industrial-Alliance Life Insurance Co.	6,700.0	3.1	1,686.0	5.4	51.1	32	87.7	0.8	Dec-94
35	General Motors Acceptance Corp. of Canada Ltd.	6,587.1	10.8	1,017.1	22.5	41.1	36	93.0	0.6	Dec-94
36	Metropolitan Life Insurance Co.	6,209.8	5.6	1,344.6	4.8	81.3	27	397.3	1.3	Dec-94
37	Hees International Bancorp Inc.	5,469.2	2.1	449.1	18.9	112.1	22	67.2	2.0	Dec-94
38	Prudential Insurance Co. of America	4,903.6	3.8	1,239.1	-2.7	7.5	64	884.9	0.2	Dec-94
39	Société de l'assurance automobile du Québec	4,798.9	-4.4	572.5	14.3	-115.3	99	-	-2.4	Dec-94
40	Imperial Life Assurance Co. of Canada	4,752.1	3.5	690.4	0.8	1.7	82	-94.8	0.0	Dec-94
41	Insurance Corp. of British Columbia	4,353.4	11.2	2,163.7	6.0	140.9	19	-9.7	3.2	Dec-94
42	Richardson Greenshields of Canada Ltd.	4,263.7	3.8	449.6	4.0	31.5	44	-17.4	0.7	Dec-94
43	Citibank Canada	4,210.8	-18.9	463.5	20.6	-40.9	95	-	-1.0	Dec-94
44	General Electric Capital Canada Inc.	4,165.4	36.6	912.9	51.1	50.2	33	180.0	1.2	Dec-94
45	Vancouver City Savings Credit Union	4,083.7	7.6	345.4	9.3	21.2	51	0.8	0.5	Dec-94
46	Crédit Suisse Canada	3,698.6	-2.3	171.6	5.1	2.0	81	9,925.0	0.1	Dec-94
47	Household Financial Corp. Ltd.	3,212.7	·7.3	339.4	-6.4	-15.2	90	-	-0.5	Dec-94
48	Midland Walwyn Inc.	3,087.9	63.7	480.8	-3.1	33.0	42	-47.7	1.1	Dec-94
49	E-L Financial Corp. Ltd.	3,029.9	2.9	812.1	-11.2	41.1	37	-1.4	1.4	Dec-94
50	Federal Business Development Bank	3,022.2	9.3	295.3	-8.4	4.1	73	-	0.1	Mar-94

Footnotes

1. Formerly Canada Trustco Mortgage Co.
2. Formerly Mutual Life Assurance Co. of Canada

51 to 100 PERFORMANCE 500

FINANCE 100

Assets rank '94		Assets ($MIL)	Assets % CHANGE	Revenue ($MIL)	Revenue % CHANGE	Net Income ($MIL)	Net Income RANK	Net Income % CHANGE	Return on assets	Year-end
51	Maritime Life Assurance Co.	2,676.3	2.3	670.0	1.3	20.9	52	26.0	0.8	Dec-94
52	First Marathon Inc.	2,572.1	80.0	160.5	-14.4	25.2	47	-66.0	1.0	Dec-94
53	BC Central Credit Union	2,370.3	12.0	125.8	0.9	7.4	65	21.8	0.3	Dec-94
54	Crédit Lyonnais Canada	2,360.6	-0.3	130.1	11.9	0.0	86	-	-	Dec-94
55	Royal Insurance Co. of Canada	2,218.0	16.8	1,004.6	11.4	37.1	39	-25.5	1.7	Dec-94
56	Fairfax Financial Holdings Ltd.	2,173.4	81.1	634.9	84.6	38.1	38	14.3	1.8	Dec-94
57	Banque Nationale de Paris (Canada)	2,157.5	-4.0	130.5	-13.7	-30.4	94	-	-1.4	Oct-94
58	Aetna Life Insurance Co. of Canada	2,138.6	-2.6	536.9	-11.7	8.2	63	-	0.4	Dec-94
59	Province of Ontario Savings Office	2,084.6	0.8	116.5	-16.3	8.9	59	-18.9	0.4	Mar-94
60	Gentra Inc.	2,083.0	-33.7	217.0	-85.1	-19.0	92	-	-0.9	Dec-94
61	Union Bank of Switzerland (Canada)	2,040.8	3.1	211.5	26.0	3.5	74	-37.2	0.2	Dec-94
62	Zurich Canada	1,991.9	5.2	1,016.8	-2.5	-43.4	96	-	-2.2	Dec-94
63	National Westminster Bank of Canada	1,875.9	14.7	78.9	16.9	-13.8	89	-	-0.7	Oct-94
64	Investors Group Inc.	1,865,9	-4.4	543.2	7.4	84.6	25	20.3	4.5	Dec-94
65	General Accident Assurance Co. of Canada[1]	1,789.5	-0.8	913.0	-13.9	-71.9	97	-	-4.0	Dec-94
66	National Life Assurance Co. of Canada	1,756.1	2.2	420.5	-14.4	8.9	60	-12.1	0.5	Dec-94
67	Bank of Tokyo Canada	1,558.6	-2.7	87.8	-1.1	-2.6	87	-	-0.2	Oct-94
68	Alberta Mortgage and Housing Corp.	1,453.9	-	2,770.1	1,680.8	-137.9	100	-	-9.5	Mar-94
69	Surrey Metro Savings Credit Union	1,449.1	17.1	116.7	4.5	10.4	57	0.2	0.7	Dec-94
70	Sears Acceptance Co. Inc.	1,404.1	-2.5	340.7	23.9	70.0	29	10.5	5.0	Dec-94
71	Banca Commerciale Italiana of Canada	1,400.3	5.6	90.6	2.6	-6.7	88	-	-0.5	Dec-94
72	Deutsche Bank (Canada)	1,389.7	5.7	92.0	5.7	4.9	71	-29.7	0.4	Dec-94
73	Avco Financial Services Canada Ltd.	1,346.2	10.4	260.8	4.8	28.7	46	25.0	2.1	Dec-94
74	Empire Life Insurance Co.	1,338.0	0.5	320.4	12.2	22.4	50	16.1	1.7	Dec-94
75	Economical Group	1,302.0	4.4	693.6	2.9	29.6	45	129.9	2.3	Dec-94
76	Groupe SGF[2]	1,300.8	8.9	579.5	4.9	72.8	28	-	5.6	Dec-94
77	Richmond Savings Credit Union	1,271.3	9.2	99.7	7.3	7.3	66	20.8	0.6	Dec-94
78	Credit Union Central of Ontario	1,248.0	-1.3	92.1	-1.8	3.5	75	5,247.7	0.3	Dec-94
79	Seaboard Life Insurance Co.	1,223.1	0.3	318.0	7.2	5.7	68	-32.2	0.5	Dec-94
80	ING Canada	1,197.0	10.6	723.2	13.3	48.2	34	-11.4	4.0	Dec-94
81	Municipal Bankers Corp. (1931) Ltd.	1,192.9	-4.3	108.4	-9.9	0.8	85	-	0.1	Oct-94
82	Continental Canada Group	1,143.9	10.2	498.3	8.9	23.5	49	-34.9	2.1	Dec-94
83	SSQ Société d'assurance-vie inc.	1,117.0	2.7	406.2	-2.7	10.5	56	66.3	0.9	Dec-94
84	Co-operators Life Insurance Co.	1,084.4	4.6	313.3	1.7	8.5	61	79.8	0.8	Dec-94
85	Co-operative Trust Co. of Canada	1,078.9	0.7	96.0	-8.2	2.7	80	-3.8	0.3	Dec-94
86	Agriculture Financial Services Corp.[3]	1,077.8	-15.0	606.2	-5.5	32.3	43	-56.1	3.0	Mar-94
87	Fuji Bank Canada	1,057.0	-5.8	65.3	-7.0	-21.0	93	-	-2.0	Oct-94
88	BT Bank of Canada	951.9	-27.4	19.7	-6.0	15.8	54	-6.9	1.7	Dec-94
89	Canadian General Insurance Group	951.8	3.5	443.7	1.5	3.4	77	-83.6	0.4	Dec-94
90	Dresdner Bank Canada	929.1	39.2	13.9	15.2	4.3	72	110.9	0.5	Dec-94
91	Sakura Bank (Canada)	910.7	12.9	42.6	2.9	1.6	83	-	0.2	Oct-94
92	Republic National Bank of New York (Canada)	888.1	17.9	24.4	2.1	7.3	67	48.2	0.8	Dec-94
93	Industrial Bank of Japan (Canada)	862.9	10.9	46.0	-5.4	1.4	84	-	0.2	Oct-94
94	NN Life Insurance Co. of Canada	857.5	-4.8	225.0	-3.3	9.5	58	13.5	1.1	Dec-94
95	Manitoba Public Insurance Corp.	846.5	2.1	383.2	-0.9	8.3	62	361.3	1.0	Oct-94
96	Civil Service Co-operative Credit Society Ltd.	828.8	1.3	59.3	-3.8	3.4	78	-14.0	0.4	Dec-94
97	Dominion of Canada General Insurance Co.	805.0	-5.3	429.4	-15.5	16.2	53	-10.0	2.0	Dec-94
98	Equitable Life Insurance Co. of Canada	784.0	-5.4	106.4	-13.0	5.5	69	-59.2	0.7	Dec-94
99	Boreal Assurances Inc.	730.8	3.8	515.5	15.0	3.2	79	-78.1	0.4	Dec-94
100	Canadian Western Bank	706.3	18.2	57.6	12.9	5.0	70	175.2	0.7	Oct-94

Footnotes

1. Amalgamation of General Accident Assurance Co. of Canada and General Accident Indemnity Co.
2. Formerly Société Générale de Financement du Québec
3. Formerly Alberta Agricultural Development Corp.

¶17,050 CLHIA PRIVACY GUIDELINES*

March 1993

CLHIA
RIGHT TO PRIVACY GUIDELINES

FOREWORD

In providing life and health insurance to Canadians, insurance companies require significant amounts of detailed information about individuals. This information, much of which can be regarded as "personal", is required both for risk evaluation and for claim adjudication under both individual and group contracts. Indeed, it could be said that personal information is the principal raw material for the life and health insurance process.

In recognition of this fact, and of the potentially sensitive nature of such information, insurance companies must adhere closely to strict rules governing the protection of the confidential information they hold.

These Guidelines set a minimum standard. Insurance companies may adopt these Guidelines or may develop their own guidelines which are at least as protective as these minimum standards.

1. SCOPE & PURPOSE OF GUIDELINES

These Guidelines apply to the collection, verification, possession, protection, use and disclosure of personal information acquired by a life and health insurance company in the course of its Canadian operations.

2. DEFINITIONS

"company": means a life and health insurance company and includes its life and health insurance subsidiaries and benefit plan administration subsidiaries.

"personal information": means any information relating to an identified or identifiable individual, including, but not limited to health and financial information.

3. COLLECTION LIMITATION

Only lawful means will be used to collect personal information. To the extent appropriate:

a) such personal information will be obtained directly from the individual, and,

* Reprinted with the permission of the Canadian Life and Health Association Inc.

- 2 -

b) prior to collecting such information from any other source, the individual concerned will be notified or his/her written authorization obtained.

Parts (a) and (b) of this section do not apply to information supplied to the company by a group plan sponsor for the purpose of risk evaluation, administering a group plan or claims adjudication.

4. DATA QUALITY

Every reasonable effort will be made to ensure that personal information obtained by the company is:

a) pertinent to the effective conduct of the company's business;

b) as accurate and complete as possible consistent with the purpose(s) for which it was obtained.

5. PURPOSE SPECIFICATION

The purpose(s) for which personal information is collected from an individual will be specified on or before the collection of information, and any change of purpose will be communicated to the individual.

6. USE AND DISCLOSURE

Personal information will not be disclosed or used for purposes other than those specified to the individual in accordance with Section #5, except:

i) with the consent of the individual concerned; or
ii) where required by law; or
iii) where reasonably necessary, to determine eligibility for an insurance benefit or, to protect the interests of the company against criminal activity, fraud, and material misrepresentation in connection with an insurance contract; or
iv) in the discharge of public duty.

- 3 -

7. INDIVIDUAL ACCESS TO INFORMATION

Each company will adopt a general policy of openness about the company's practices and policies with respect to the use and protection of personal information. In particular:

a) Upon appropriate identification and written request satisfactory to the company, an individual will be advised of personal information about him/her retained in the company's records. A company may charge a reasonable administration fee to supply the information. Some medical information may be made available only through the individual's designated physician.

b) Where information cannot be disclosed to the individual, he/she will be given the reasons for not disclosing information.

c) An individual may clarify or correct erroneous personal information retained by the company.

Incorrect or incomplete information will be amended and differences as to the correctness of the information will be noted.

8. COMPLIANCE AND COMPLAINT RESOLUTION

In order to ensure compliance with the protection of privacy guidelines each company will:

a) designate an officer to receive complaints;

b) establish procedures for receiving and resolving complaints.

Individuals dissatisfied with the complaint resolution of a company can contact the office of the insurance regulators in their province.

9. SECURITY SAFEGUARDS

Personal information will be considered confidential, and comprehensive safeguards will be established by the company to protect that confidentiality.

A company will take the necessary measures to ensure that all employees of the company are required to conform to the company's applicable privacy guidelines.

All agents, brokers, plan sponsors and other persons or organizations acting for or on behalf of the company will be required to comply with the guidelines.

(Adopted March 10, 1993)

* * * * *

re054

¶17,055 NAMES AND ADDRESSES OF INSURANCE COMPANY GROUP OFFICES

Company	Territory Covered By Office	Address, Contact Numbers
Alberta Dental Service Corporation (Dental benefits only)	Alberta British Columbia Saskatchewan (organizations with Alberta head offices)	4th Floor 10508 82nd Avenue Edmonton, Alberta T6E 6H2 Tel.: (403) 433-3330 Fax: (403) 439-4301 Toll-Free Tel.: 1-800-232-1997
American International American Home Group (A.I.G.) AD&D and Special Risk	Montreal	2000 McGill College Avenue Suite 1200 Montreal, Quebec H3A EH3 Tel.: (514) 842-0603 Fax: (514) 987-5357 Toll-Free 1-800-361-7211 (Quebec, Ontario) Toll-Free 1-800-361-4657 (Atlantic Canada)
	Toronto	145 Wellington Street West Toronto, Ontario M5J 1H8 Tel.: (416) 596-3000 Fax: (416) 596-4067 Toll-Free 1-800-387-4426 (Quebec and Ontario) Toll-Free 1-800-387-4481 (rest of Canada)
	Western Canada	666 Burrard Street Suite 1100 Vancouver, B.C. V6C 1T2 Tel.: (604) 691-2904 Fax: (604) 691-2939 Toll-Free 1-800-663-0231
Blue Cross (Alberta)	Alberta Edmonton	10009 108 Street Edmonton, Alberta T5J 3C5 Tel.: (403) 498-8500 Fax: (403) 498-8989
	Calgary	Main Floor, Norcen Tower 715 5 Avenue S.W. Calgary, Alberta T2P 2X6 Tel.: (403) 265-6258 Fax: (403) 266 5644
	Fort McMurray	22 Morrison Centre 9914 Morrison Street Fort McMurray, Alberta T9H 4A4 Tel.: (403) 790-9053 Fax: (403) 791-6999
	Grande Prairie	101A, 10712 100 Street Grande Prairie, Alberta T8V 3X8 Tel.: (403) 532-3505 Fax: (403) 539-0455

Company	Territory Covered By Office	Address, Contact Numbers
Blue Cross (Alberta)	Lethbridge	470 Chancery Court 220 4 Street South Lethbridge, Alberta T1J 4J7 Tel.: (403) 328-6081 Fax: (403) 327-9823
	Medicine Hat	21, 419 3 Street S.E. Medicine Hat, Alberta T1A 0G9 Tel.: (403) 529-5550 Fax: (403) 527-3798
	Red Deer	152 Riverside Office Plaza 4919 59 Street Red Deer, Alberta T4N 6C9 Tel.: (403) 343-7008 Fax: (403) 340-1098
Blue Cross (Atlantic Canada)	New Brunswick Bathurst	Habourview Place Suite 200, 375 Main Street Bathurst, New Brunswick E2A 3Z4 Tel.: (506) 546-5222 Fax: (506) 546-4225
	Fredericton	136 Prospect Street Fredericton, N.B. E3B 3C1 Tel.: (506) 452-8581 Fax: (506) 444-9239
	Moncton	644 Main Street Moncton, New Brunswick E1C 1E2 Tel.: (506) 853-1811 Fax: (506) 853-4651
	St. John	110 Crown Street St. John, New Brunswick E2L 2X7 Tel.: (506) 634-6811 Fax: (506) 634-7329
	Newfoundland	66 Kenmount Road Suite 304, Woodgate Bldg. St. John's, Newfoundland A1B 3V7 Tel.: (709) 739-8810 Fax: (709) 726-4719
	Nova Scotia	1874 Brunswick Street Halifax, Nova Scotia B3J 2G7 Tel.: (902) 422-4420 Fax: (902) 422-7754
	Prince Edward Island	Shops of St. Avards 15 St. Peters Road Charlottetown, P.E.I. C1A 5N1 Tel.: (902) 368-8620 Fax: (902) 566-1785
Blue Cross (Head Office)	Manitoba	100A Polo Park Centre 1485 Portage Avenue Winnipeg, Manitoba R3G 0W4 Mailing Address: P.O. Box 1046 Winnipeg, Manitoba R3C 2X7 Tel.: (204) 775-0151 Fax: (204) 786-5965

Company	Territory Covered By Office	Address, Contact Numbers
Canada Life	British Columbia	Suite 2620 1066 West Hastings Street Vancouver, B.C. V6E 3X1 Tel.: (604) 689-1574 Fax: (604) 669-2180
	Alberta Calgary	Suite 3850 Bankers Hall East Tower 855 2nd Street S.W. Calgary, Alberta T2P 4J8 Tel.: (403) 266-8921 Fax: (403) 265-3584
	Edmonton	Canada Trust Tower Suite 440 101014 103 Avenue 4th Floor Edmonton, Alberta T5J 0H8 Tel.: (403) 424-0499 Fax: (403) 428-6887
	Manitoba	Suite 1135, One Lombard Place Winnipeg, Manitoba R3B 0X3 Tel.: (204) 949-6385 Fax: (204) 942-4446
	Ontario Hamilton	Suite 504, Commerce Place One King Street West Hamilton, Ontario L8P 1A4 Tel.: (905) 528-7573 Fax: (905) 528-6438
	Ottawa	1600 Carling Avenue Suite 660 Ottawa, Ontario K1Z 8R7 Tel.: (613) 729-1741 Fax: (613) 729-2597
	Toronto	5255 Yonge Street Suite 901 North York, Ontario M2N 6P4 Tel.: (416) 512-1211 Fax: (416) 512-1222
	Toronto-Consultants only	120 Adelaide Street W. Suite 401 Toronto, Ontario M5H 1T2 Tel.: (416) 947-0216 Fax: (416) 947-9522
	Windsor	Bank of Commerce Bldg. Suite 600, 100 Ouellette Avenue Windsor, Ontario N6A 6T3 Tel.: (519) 258-88114 Fax: (519) 252-70685
	Quebec Montreal	630 René Levesque Blvd. W. Suite 1900 Montreal, Quebec H3B 4V5 Tel.: (514) 878-9401 Fax: (514) 878-4257

Company	Territory Covered By Office	Address, Contact Numbers
Canada Life	Quebec City	Bureau 402, 1305 Boul. Lebourgneuf Quebec, Quebec G2K 2E4 Tel.: (418) 624-1993 Fax: (418) 624-1996
	New Brunswick	One Brunswick Square Suite 1105 St. John, New Brunswick E2L 4V1 Tel.: (506) 648-0055 Fax: (506) 632-4023
	Nova Scotia	Purdy's Wharf Tower 2 Suite 1704 Halifax, Nova Scotia B3J 3R7 Tel.: (902) 364-6465 Fax: (902) 423-8169
The Co-operators	Alberta	202 E, Heritage Square 8500 MacLeod Trail S.E. Calgary, Alberta T2H 0M6 Tel.: (403) 221-7130 Fax: (403) 221-7106
	Atlantic Canada	200 Commercial Street P.O. Box 890, Moncton New Brunswick E1C 8N9 Tel.: (506) 853-1323 Fax: (506) 853-1270
	British Columbia	Suite 103, 1001 West Broadway Vancouver, B.C. V6H 4B2 Tel.: (604) 736-6694 Fax: (604) 736-4081
	Manitoba/Saskatchewan	1920 College Avenue Regina, Sask. S4P 1C4 Tel.: (306) 347-6567 Fax: (306) 347-6801
	Ontario Guelph	Priory Square Guelph, Ontario N1H 6P8 Tel.: (519) 824-4400 Fax: (519) 824-0599
	Toronto	5600 Cancross Street P.O. Box 527, Station A Mississauga, Ontario L5A 3A4 Tel.: (905) 890-4214 Fax: (905) 890-4202
Crown Life	Alberta, Southern	205 5th Avenue S.W. Suite 1770 Calgary, Alberta T2P 2V7 Tel.: (403) 269-6126 Fax: (403) 237-7870 Toll-Free Tel.: 1-800-661-9543
	Alberta, Northern	10205 101 Street Suite 1904 Edmonton, Alberta T5J 2Z2 Tel.: (403) 424-3005 Fax: (403) 424-3153 Toll-Free Tel.: 1-800-403-7914

Company	Territory Covered By Office	Address, Contact Numbers
Crown Life	British Columbia	1500 W. Georgia Street Suite 1300 Vancouver, B.C. V6G 2Z5 Tel.: (604) 682-1484 Fax: (604) 683-2503 Toll-Free Tel.: 1-800-663-0234
	Manitoba Saskatchewan	Reed Stenhouse Building 2201 11th Avenue Suite 602 Regina, Sask. S4P 0J8 Tel.: (306) 791-3280 Fax: (306) 522-8113
	New Brunswick Newfoundland Nova Scotia Prince Edward Island	Park Lane Terraces 5657 Spring Garden Road Halifax, Nova Scotia B3J 3R4 Tel.: (902) 422-0712 Fax: (902) 422-1642
	Ontario	4100 Yonge Street Suite 402 Willowdale, Ontario M2P 2C3 Tel.: (416) 733-1525 Fax: (416) 733-0825 Toll-Free Tel.: 1-800-387-0960
	Quebec	2201 University Street Room 1470 Montreal, Quebec H3A 1C9 Tel.: (514) 282-1900 Fax: (514) 282-0168 Toll-Free Tel.: 1-800-361-4871
Empire Life (Groups Over 20)	Alberta British Columbia	1185 West Georgia Street Vancouver, B.C. V6E 4E6 Tel.: (604) 687-2643 Fax: (604) 687-7790
Empire Life	Ontario Hamilton	Suite 1025, 135 James Street South Hamilton, Ontario L8P 2Z6 Tel.: (905) 525-0437 Fax: (905) 522-2838
	Kingston	200, 920 Princess Street Kingston, Ontario Tel.: (613) 548-8883 Fax: (613) 548-3094
	London	Suite 404 171 Queens Avenue London, Ontario N6A 5J7 Tel.: (519) 438-1751 Fax: (519) 438-8389
	Toronto	Suite 701, 2550 Victoria Park Avenue Toronto, Ontario M2J 5A9 Tel.: (416) 494-6830 Fax: (416) 494-7691

Company	Territory Covered By Office	Address, Contact Numbers
Empire Life	Quebec New Brunswick Newfoundland Nova Scotia Prince Edward Island	Suite 1206 630 Sherbrooke Street West West Tower Montreal, Quebec H3A 1B9 Tel.: (514) 842-0003 Fax: (514) 842-4752

(Quotes for groups under 20 employees can be obtained by ABCs through Empire Life's Regional Marketing Centres located in most major centres.)

Company	Territory Covered By Office	Address, Contact Numbers
Equitable Life Group Marketing	Alberta, Southern	Suite 206, 5809 MacLeod Trail S. Calgary, Alberta T2H 0J1 Tel.: (403) 259-3392 Fax (403) 252-8998
	Alberta, Northern	Suite 1907, 10060 Jasper Avenue Scotia Place, Esso Tower Edmonton, Alberta T5J 3R8 Tel.: (403) 425-6622 Fax: (403) 424-4496
	British Columbia	Suite 320, 1500 W. Georgia Street Vancouver, B.C. V6G 2Z6 Tel.: (604) 685-7935 Fax: (604) 685-5974
	Ontario Hamilton	Suite 3830 Century 21, 100 Main St. E., Hamilton, Ontario N6A 5P6 Tel.: (905) 527-4185 Fax: (905) 527-2625
	London/Windsor	Suite 252 Pall Mall St., Suite 302 London, Ontario N6A 5P6 fTel.: (519) 433-0196 Fax: (519) 642-7674 Toll-Free Tel.: 1-800-263-5559
	Mississauga	Suite 103, 2077 Dundas St. E. Mississauga, Ontario, L4X 1M2 Tel.: (905) 238-8293 Fax: (905) 238-8295
Great West Life	Toronto, Willowdale	Suite 401, 2 Lansing Square Willowdale, Ontario M2J 4P8 Tel.: (416) 492-2810 Fax: (416) 492-9330
	Waterloo	Uni-Park I, 175 Columbia St. W. Waterloo, Ontario N2L 5Z5 Tel.: (519) 746-5611 Fax: (519) 746-5308 Toll-Free Tel.: 1-800-387-1704
	Alberta, Northern	Suite 610, Canada Trust Tower 10104 103 Avenue Edmonton, Alberta T5J 0H8 Tel.: (403) 428-1021 Fax: (403) 429-2809
	Alberta, Southern	Suite 2800, 500 4th Avenue S.W. Calgary, Alberta T2P 2V6 Tel.: (403) 262-9880 Fax: (403) 266-2427

Company	Territory Covered By Office	Address, Contact Numbers
Great West Life	British Columbia	Suite 1510, 1177 West Hastings St. Vancouver, B.C. V6E 3Y9 Tel.: (604) 688-3591 Fax: (604) 688-9762
	Atlantic Canada	Purdy's Warf, Tower II Suite 1407, 1969 Upper Water Street Halifax, Nova Scotia B3J 3R7 Tel.: (902) 429-8653 Fax: (902) 429-0998
	Quebec Montreal	Suite 900, Place Montreal Trust 1800 McGill College Avenue Montreal, Quebec H3A 3J6 Tel.: (514) 845-1532 Fax: (514) 845-5819
	Quebec City	Tour de la Cité Local 800 8iẽme étage 2600 boul Laurier Ste Foy, Quebec G1V 4W2 Tel.: (418) 650-4238 Fax: (418) 453-3037
	Manitoba	1C 100 Osborne Street N. Winnipeg, Manitoba R3C 1V3 Tel.: (204) 946-7850 Fax: (204) 946-8916
	Ontario Southwestern	Suite 825, 1 King Street W. Hamilton, Ontario L8P 1A4 Tel.: (416) 525-2920 Fax: (416) 525-9070
	Ottawa	Suite 520, 1600 Carling Avenue Ottawa, Ontario K1Z 8R7 Tel.: (613) 725-1123 Fax: (613) 728-2971
	Toronto	14th Floor, 200 King Street W. Toronto, Ontario M5H 3T4 Tel.: (416) 979-5652 Fax: (416) 979-8531 or 979-1166
	Saskatchewan	Suite 600, Royal Bank Bldg. 2010 11th Avenue Regina, Saskatchewan S4P 0J3 Tel.: (306) 525-2729 Fax: (306) 352-9474

(Small groups may obtain quotes through Great West Life's Individual Agency Offices located in most major centres.)

Company	Territory Covered By Office	Address, Contact Numbers
Green Shield	Alberta Brritish Columbia Manitoba Saskatchewan	777 West Broadway Suite 702 Vancouver, B.C. V5Z 4J7 Tel.: (604) 872-4443 Fax: (604) 873-2414

Company	Territory Covered By Office	Address, Contact Numbers
Green Shield	New Brunswick Newfoundland Nova Scotia P.E.I.	1959 Upper Water Street Suite 1502 Purdy's Warf, Tower 1 Halifax, Nova Scotia B3J 3N2 Tel.: (902) 422-5800 Fax: (902) 422-6242
	Ontario London	195 Dufferin Avenue Suite 317 London, Ontario N6A 1K7 Tel.: (519) 673-4410 Fax: (519) Toll-Free Tel.: 1-800-265-4429
	North York	5001 Yonge Street Suite 1600 North York, Ontario M2N 6P5 Tel.: (416) 221-7001 Fax: (416) 221-0350 Toll-Free Tel.: 1-800-268-6613
	Windsor	285 Giles Blvd. P.O. Box 1606 Windsor, Ontario N9A 6W1 Tel.: (519) 255-1133 Fax: (519) Toll-Free Tel.: 1-800-265-5615
Group Medical Services (Blue Cross)	Saskatchewan	1992 Hamilton Street Regina, Sask. S4P 2C6 Tel.: (306) 352-7638 Fax: (306) 525-3825
Industrial Alliance Insurance Company	Quebec Montreal	Unit 235, 680 Sherbrooke Street Montreal, Quebec H3A 2S6 Tel.: (514) 499-3750 Fax: (514) 284-2655 Toll-Free Tel.: 1-800-363-3540
	Quebec City	1080 Saint-Louis Road Sillery, Quebec G1X 4G5 Tel.: (418) 650-1821 Fax: (418) 650-1824 Toll-Free Tel.: 1-800-463-7274
	Ontario	160 Eglinton Avenue East 6th Floor Toronto, Ontario M4P 3B5 Tel.: (416) 487-4730 Fax: (416) 487-7457 Toll-Free Tel.: 1-800-268-8882
Laurentian/Imperial	Alberta Manitoba Saskatchewan	Suite 1960, 205 5th Avenue S.W. Calgary, Alberta T2P 2V7 Tel.: (403) 261-4900 Fax: (403) 265-1653 Toll-Free Tel.: 1-800-661-8666

Company	Territory Covered By Office	Address, Contact Numbers
Laurentian/Imperial	British Columbia	Suite 434, 4720 Kingsway Metrotower II Burnaby, B.C. V5H 4N2 Tel.: (604) 436-1664 Fax: (604) 431-0526 Toll-Free Tel.: 1-800-667-6267
	New Brunswick Newfoundland Nova Scotia Prince Edward Island	Suite 1160, 99 Wyse Road Dartmouth, Nova Scotia B3A 4S5 Tel.: (902) 466-8881 Fax: (902) 466-4074 Toll-Free Tel.: 1-800-567-8881
	Ontario Ottawa	1525 Carling Avenue Suite 405 Ottawa, Ontario K1Z 8R9 Tel.: (613) 761-9216 Fax: (613) 761-9652
	Toronto	Suite 610, 214 King Street West Toronto, Ontario M5H 3S6 Tel.: (416) 977-4792 Fax: (416) 977-3535 Toll-Free Tel.: 1-800-263-1810
	Other than Toronto and Ottawa areas	Suite 410, 1 West Pearce Street Richmond Hill, Ontario L4B 3K3 Tel.: (905) 771-2236 Fax: (905) 771-2237 Toll-Free Tel.: 1800-561-0999
	Quebec Montreal	Suite 2104, 800 Victoria Square Stock Exchange Tower Montreal, Quebec H4Z 1C8 Tel.: (514) 392-7552 Fax: (514) 392-6959 Toll-Free Tel.: 1-800-361-8936
	Quebec City	Suite 201, 2960 Laurier Blvd. Ste-Foy, Quebec G1V 4S1 Tel.: (418) 654-3439 Fax: (418) 654-9582 Toll-Free Tel.: 1-800-561-1506
Liberty Health (Head Office)	Ontario	150 Ferrand Drive Toronto, Ontario M3C 1H6 Tel.: (416) 429-2661 Fax: (416) 429-1363
	Kitchener	Suite 512, 22 Frederick Street Kitchener, Ontario N2H 6M8 Tel.: (519) 578-7340 Fax: (519) 578-4322 Toll-Free Tel.: 1-800-265-2306
	London	Unit 3, 151 Pine Valley Blvd. London, Ontario N6K 3T6 Tel.: (519) 668-0050 Fax: (519) 668-2311 Toll-Free Tel.: 1-800-265-1880

Company	Territory Covered By Office	Address, Contact Numbers
Liberty Health	Nepean	Suite 360, 117 Centrepointe Drive Nepean, Ontario K2G 5X3 Tel.: (613) 224-2444 Fax: (613) 224-8356 Toll-Free Tel.: 1-800-267-1270
	Sudbury	Suite 107, 888 Regent Street Sudbury, Ontario PE3 6C6 Tel.: (705) 675-3401 Fax: (705) 675-3982 Toll-Free Tel.: 1-800-461-3315
	Thunder Bay	Suite 707, 34 Cumberland Street Thunder Bay, Ontario P7A 4L3 Tel.: (807) 345-0918 Fax: (807) 345-2758 Toll-Free Tel.: 1-800-265-8828
	Toronto	Suite 120, 2005 Sheppard Avenue E. Willowdale, Ontario M2J 5B4 Tel.: (416) 502-3200 Fax: (416) 490-9167 Toll-Free Tel.: 1-800-461-1060
Lloyds of London (through ABCs only) (out of country and expatriot coverage)		33 Yonge Street Suite 420 Toronto, Ontario M5E 1S9 Available through William J. Sutton & Co. Ltd. Tel.: (416) 366-2223 Fax: (416) 366-4608 Toll-Free Tel.: 1-800-461-3292
London Life	Alberta Calgary	Suite 680, 717 7th Avenue S.W. Calgary, Alberta T2P 0Z4 Tel.: (403) 261-4680
	Edmonton	Suite 801, 1001 Centre, Edmonton Edmonton, Alberta T5J 3W6 Tel.: (403) 428-8560 Fax: (403) 429-1894
	British Columbia Vancouver	Suite 200, 815 West Hastings Vancouver, B.C. V6C 3E4 Tel.: (604) 685-9281
	Victoria	Suite 370, 4243 Glanford Victoria, B.C. V8Z 4B8 Tel.: (604) 727-3337 Fax: (604) 727-2031
	Manitoba	Suite 315, 175 Hargrave Street Winnipeg, Manitoba R3C 3R8 Tel.: (204) 949-1714 Fax: (204) 944-0894
	New Brunswick/P.E.I. Moncton	814 Main Street Moncton, New Brunswick E1C 1G1 Tel.: (506) 853-6115
	Saint John	40 Charlotte Saint John, New Brunswick E2L 2H6 Tel.: (506) 634-8805 Fax: (506) 634-0614

Company	Territory Covered By Office	Address, Contact Numbers
London Life	Newfoundland Nova Scotia	111 Ilsley Avenue Dartmouth, Nova Scotia B3B 1S8 Tel.: (902) 468-7443 Fax: (902) 468-2754
	Ontario Burlington	3410 South Service Road Burlington, Ontario L7N 3T2 Tel.: (905) 639-3431
	London	Suite 308, 700 Richmond London, Ontario N6A 5C7 Tel.: (519) 432-6315
	Ottawa	Suite 1860, 112 Kent Street Ottawa, Ontario K1P 5P2 Tel.: (613) 236-9677
	Toronto	2 County Court Blvd Suite 205 Brampton, Ontario L6W 3W8 Tel.: (905) 452-8800
	Toronto National Accounts	40 University Avenue Toronto, Ontario M5J 1T1 Tel.: (416) 977-8737
	Windsor	880 Ouellette Avenue Windsor, Ontario N9A 1C7 Tel.: (519) 353-1167
	Quebec Montreal	2075 University Montreal, Quebec H3A 1T9 Tel.: (514) 849-1393
	Saskatchewan Regina	Suite 410, 2100 Broad Street Regina, Saskatchewan S4P 3W4 Tel.: (306) 352-1753
	Saskatoon	Suite 980, 606 Spadina Crescent E. Saskatoon, Saskatchewan S7K 0C4 Tel.: (306) 244-8440

(Quotes for groups under 400 employees are not available to brokers, but are available through London Life agents.)

Company	Territory Covered By Office	Address, Contact Numbers
Manulife Financial	Alberta, Northern	Suite 2220, 10180 101 Street Edmonton, Alberta T5J 3S4 Tel.: (403) 421-1151 Fax: (403) 421-1273
	Alberta, Southern Manitoba, Sask. Thunder Bay N.E. Ontario	Suite 400, 808 4th Avenue S.W. Calgary, Alberta T2P 3E8 Tel.: (403) 265-1111 Fax: (403) 265-1284
	Atlantic Canada	Suite 1540, 1801 Hollis Street Halifax, Nova Scotia B3J 3N4 Tel.: (902) 420-1115 Fax: (902) 423-5274
	British Columbia	Suite 406, 111 West Georgia Street Vancouver, B.C. V6E 4M3 Tel.: (604) 689-5525 Fax: (604) 689-0052 or 684-6152

Company	Territory Covered By Office	Address, Contact Numbers
Manulife Financial	Ontario Hamilton	Suite 675, 110 King Street W. Hamilton, Ontario L8P 4S6 Tel.: (905) 528-4277 Fax: (905) 546-0623
	Kitchener/Waterloo	Suite 202, 1 Blue Springs Drive Waterloo, Ontario N2J 4M1 Tel.: (519) 746-1221 Fax: (519) 746-0807
	Ottawa	Suite 600, 1525 Carling Avenue Ottawa, Ontario K1Z 8R9 Tel.: (613) 724-3022 Fax: (613) 724-3098
	Toronto	Suite 305, 2 Lansing Square Willowdale, Ontario H2J 4P8 Tel.: (416) 496-1602 Fax: (416) 496-1555
	Ontario Windsor	Suite 807, 500 Ouellette Avenue Windsor, Ontario N9A 1B3 Tel.: (519) 258-2230 Fax: (519) 258-6977
	Quebec Montreal	Suite 500, 2000 Mansfield Street Montreal, Quebec H3A 2Z2 Tel.: (514) 288-1515 Fax: (514) 288-5355

(For groups of under 20 employees, quotes are available through Manulife offices, located in most major centres.

Note: At the time of this writing, Manulife Financial had purchased the group insurance block of business from (the former) Confederation Life. According to sources at Manulife, the group policies originally sold by Confederation Life would continue to be serviced through the former Confederation Life group offices. The addresses of the Confederation Life group offices have been excluded from this list, as that company no longer exists as a separate entity.)

Company	Territory Covered By Office	Address, Contact Numbers
Maritime Life	Alberta British Columbia Manitoba Saskatchewan	Box 49108 Suite 2323, #3 Bentall Centre Vancouver, B.C. V7X 1G4 Tel.: (604) 689-1429 Fax: (604) 688-2140
	New Brunswick Newfoundland Nova Scotia P.E.I.	2701 Dutch Village Road Halifax, Nova Scotia B3L 4G6 Tel.: (902) 453-4300 Fax: (902)
	Ontario Toronto	20 Eglinton Avenue West Suite 2000 Toronto, Ontario M4R 2G6 Tel.: (416) 482-8666 Fax: (416) 482-2857
	Quebec Montreal	220 University Avenue Suite 1700 Montreal, Quebec H3A 2A5 Tel.: (514) 288-9014 Fax: (514) 288-7496

Company	Territory Covered By Office	Address, Contact Numbers
Maritime Medical Care Incorporated	New Brunswick Nova Scotia Prince Edward Island	7 Spectacle Lake Drive Dartmouth, Nova Scotia Mailing Address P.O. Box 2200, Halifax Nova Scotia, B3J 3C6 Tel.: (902) 468-9700 Fax: (902) 468-8115
Medical Services Association (M.S.A.) (Head Office) (B.C. Blue Cross)	British Columbia	2025 West Broadway P.O. Box 9300 Vancouver, B.C. V6B 6M1 Tel.: (603) 737-5700 Fax: (603) 737-5619
Medical Services Inc. (M.S.I.) (Head Office) (Saskatchewan Blue Cross)	Saskatchewan, Northern	516 Second Avenue North Saskatoon, Sask. S7K 3T2 Mailing Address P.O. Box 4030 Saskatoon, Sask. S7K 3T2 Tel.: (306) 244-1192 Fax: (306) 652-5751
Metropolitan Life	Alberta	Bow Valley Square 1 Suite 1270, 202 6th Avenue S.W. Calgary, Alberta T2P 2R9 Tel.: (403) 233-9444 Fax: (403) 262-5819
	Saskatchewan, Southern	2550 12th Avenue Regina, Sask. S4P 3X1 Tel.: (306) 525-5025 Fax: (306) 525-2124
	British Columbia	One Bentall Centre Suite 1020, 505 Burrard Street Vancouver, B.C. V7X 1M5 Tel.: (604) 689-3660 Fax: (604) 689-1249
	Ontario Ottawa	99 Bank Street Suite 737 Ottawa, Ontario K1P 5A3 Tel.: (613) 560-6991 Fax: (613) 560-7555
	Toronto	One University Avenue Suite 1800 Toronto, Ontario M5J 2P3 Tel.: (416) 862-5200 Fax: (416) 862-5217
	Quebec Montreal	L'Edifice Strathcona 770 ouest, rue Sherbrooke Bureau 225 Montreal, Quebec H3A 1G1 Tel.: (514) 499-3500 Fax: (514) 499-0773
Mutual Life	Alberta, Northern Saskatchewan, Northern	1312 Oxford Tower 10235 101 Street Edmonton, Alberta T5J 3J8 Tel.: (403) 428-0420 Fax: (403) 429-1652

Company	Territory Covered By Office	Address, Contact Numbers
Mutual Life	Alberta, Southern Saskatchewan, Southern	715 5th Avenue S.W. Suite 420 Calgary, Alberta T5J 3J8 Tel.: (403) 266-2069 Fax: (403) 269-4985
	British Columbia	1188 West Georgia Street Suite 1750 Vancouver, B.C. V6E 4A2 Tel.: (604) 689-1494 Fax: (604) 689-7820
	Manitoba, Ontario Thunder Bay	1661 Portage Avenue Suite 689 Winnipeg, Manitoba R3J 3T5 Tel.: (204) 783-1653 Fax: (204) 774-8710
	New Brunswick Nova Scotia P.E.I.	2000 Barrington Street Suite 1002 Halifax, N.S. B3J 3K1 Tel.: (902) 420-1944 Fax: (902) 422-5685
	Newfoundland	16 Forest Road St. John's, Newfoundland AIC 2B9 Tel.: (709) 576-6243 Fax: (709) 576-8941
	Ontario Hamilton	224 James Street Hamilton, Ontario L8P 3A9 Tel.: (905) 528-4267 Fax: (905) 527-6626
	London	380 Wellington Street Suite 801 London, Ontario N6A 5B5 Tel.: (519) 433-8655 Fax: (519) 433-7894
	Ottawa	Dow's Lake Court 875 Carling Avenue Ottawa, Ontario K1S 5P1 Tel.: (613) 725-6033 Fax: (613) 236-6075
	Toronto	Box 2426, Yonge-Eglinton Centre 2300 Yonge Street Suite 402 Toronto, Ontario M4P 1E4 Tel.: (416) 483-3870 Fax: (416) 487-3117
	Sudbury Sault Ste. Marie Timmins, North Bay	38 Cedar Street Sudbury, Ontario P3E 1A4 Tel.: (705) 674-2114 Fax: (705) 674-7243
	Waterloo	Allen Square Building 180 King Street South Suite 220 Waterloo, Ontario N2J 1P8 Tel.: (519) 888-3983 Fax: (519) 888-3870

Company	Territory Covered By Office	Address, Contact Numbers
Mutual Life	Quebec	1555 Peel Street Suite 1000 Montreal, Quebec H3A 1X6 Tel.: (514) 282-1655 Fax: (514) 282-9911
Mutual of Omaha	Ontario	500 University Avenue Toronto, Ontario M5G 1V8 Tel.: (416) 598-4321 Fax: (416) 586-0161
	Alberta Manitoba Saskatchewan	Southland Towers, Suite 1000 10655 Southport Road S.W. Calgary, Alberta T2W 4Y1 Tel.: (403) 271-3939 Fax: (403) 278-5149
	British Columbia	500–555 West 8th Avenue Vancouver, B.C. V5Z 1C6 Tel.: (604) 872-4802 Fax: (403) 872-0852
	Quebec New Brunswick Newfoundland Nova Scotia P.E.I.	50 Cremazie Blvd. W., 6th Floor Montreal, Quebec H2P 2T3 Tel.: (514) 385-7167 Fax: (514) 384-3411
National Life	Alberta Manitoba Saskatchewan	140 4th Avenue S.W. Suite 1740 Calgary, Alberta T2P 0H3 Tel.: (403) 233-8290 Fax: (403) 237-5865 Toll-Free Tel.: 1-800-668-8270
	British Columbia	1095 W. Pender Street Suite 1740 Vancouver, B.C. V6E 2M7 Tel.: (604) 689-0388 Fax: (604) 689-0537
	Ontario, Southern	Suite 900, 522 University Avenue Toronto, Ontario M5G 1Y7 Tel.: (416) 585-8854 Fax: (416) 598-5131 Toll-Free Tel.: 1-800-668-8270
	Ontario, Northern Ottawa New Brunswick Newfoundland Nova Scotia Prince Edward Island	Varette Building 130 Albert Street Suite 1407 Ottawa, Ontario K1P 5G4 Tel.: (613) 236-4769 Fax: (613) 236-5311
	Quebec	1800 McGill College Avenue Suite 820 Montreal, Quebec H3A 3J6 Tel.: (514) 284-3466 Fax: (514) 284-1994 Toll-Free Tel.: 1-800-263-3466

Company	Territory Covered By Office	Address, Contact Numbers
~~North American Life~~ Taken over by Manulife	Alberta, Northern	Suite 1100, 10104 103 Avenue Edmonton, Alberta T5J 0H8 Tel.: (403) 423-0177 Fax: (403) 425-9203
	Alberta, Southern	Suite 2311, 855 2nd Avenue S.W. Calgary, Alberta T2P 4J8 Tel.: (403) 262-4181 Fax: (403) 265-6326
	Atlantic Canada	Suite 600 North American Life Centre 1770 Market Street Halifax, Nova Scotia B3J 3M3 Tel.: (902) 423-3550 Fax: (902) 425-5097
	British Columbia	Suite 1503, 666 Burrard Street Vancouver, B.C. V6C 3C4 Tel.: (604) 891-5230 Fax: (604) 891-5205
	Manitoba	Suite 1502, 363 Broadway Winnipeg, Manitoba R3C 3N9 Tel.: (204) 944-8762 Fax: (204) 949-9158
	Ontario Western	Suite 303, 285 King Street London, Ontario N6B 3M6 Tel.: (519) 434-4558 Fax: (519) 667-2170
	Toronto	Suite 1102, 5700 Yonge Street North York, Ontario M2M 4K2 Tel.: (416) 226-6440 Fax: (416) 226-4630
	Quebec Montreal	1501 McGill College Avenue Suite 1203 Montreal, Quebec H3A 3M7 Tel.: (514) 845-2122 Fax: (514) 849-0565
Paul Revere	Alberta, Northern	Suite 480, 10665 Jasper Avenue Edmonton, Alberta T5J 3S9 Tel.: (403) 428-0736 Fax: (403) 425-7561
	Alberta, Southern	Suite 730, 840 6th Avenue S.W. Calgary, Alberta T2P 3E5 Tel.: (403) 262-4659 Fax: (403) 265-3064
	Ontario Southwestern	Suite 170 B, 140 Fullerton Street London, Ontario N6A 5P2 Tel.: (519) 679-9735 Fax: (519) 679-4010
	Toronto	Suite 830, 3210 Front Street W. Toronto, Ontario M5V 3B6 Tel.: (416) 971-9124 Fax: (416) 971-9504

Company	Territory Covered By Office	Address, Contact Numbers
Paul Revere	Quebec Montreal	Suite 2100, 1002 Sherbrooke St. W. Montreal, Quebec H3A 2L6 Tel.: (514) 679-9735 Fax: (514) 679-4010
Prudential Insurance Company of America	Alberta, Northern	Suite 1430, 10020 101A Avenue Edmonton, Alberta T5J 3G2 Tel.: (403) 425-1886 Fax: (403) 425-9711 Toll-Free Tel.: 1-800-803-6328
	Alberta, Southern	Suite 2140, 255 5th Avenue S.W. Calgary, Alberta T2P 3G6 Tel.: (403) 531-1480 Fax: (403) 531-1477
	British Columbia	5000 Kingsway Plaza 501 4980 Kingsway Burnaby, B.C. V5H 4K7 Tel.: (604) 436-0054 Fax: (604) 436-1060
	Ontario Northern	Suite 606, Station Tower 421 Bay Street Sault Ste. Marie, Ontario P6A 1X3 Tel.: (705) 254-6667 Fax: (705) 254-6940
	Southwestern	Unit 4, 2480 Homer Watson Blvd. Kitchener, Ontario N2G 3W5 Tel.: (519) 895-2112 Fax: (519) 895-2092
	Toronto	Suite 320, 33 Yonge Street Toronto, Ontario M5E 1G4 Tel.: (416) 361-0691 Fax: (416) 361-6316
	Quebec Montreal	12th Floor, 1080 Beaver Hall Hill Montreal, Quebec H2Z 1S8 Tel.: (514) 878-9721 Fax: (514) 878-4607
	Quebec Hospital Service Ass'n (Quebec Blue Cross)	550 Sherbrooke Ave. W. Montreal, Quebec H3A 1B9 Tel.: (514) 286-8400 Fax: (514) 286-8475
Seaboard Life Special Marketing Division Offices (AD&D specialty)	British Columbia	2165 W. Broadway P.O. Box 5900, Vancouver B.C. V6B 5H6 Tel.: (604) 734-1667 Fax: (604) 734-9286
	Alberta Manitoba Saskatchewan	Suite 1000, 777 8th Avenue S.W. Calgary, Alberta T2P 3R5 Tel.: (403) 266-7582 Fax: (403) 265-3346
	Ontario Atlantic Canada Quebec	201, 2235 Sheppard Avenue E. Willowdale, Ontario M2J 5B5 Tel.: (416) 498-8319 Fax: (416) 498-9892

Company	Territory Covered By Office	Address, Contact Numbers
S.O.S International Assistance (Travel Assistance Overseas Medical Assistance, Political Evacuation Plans)	Canada	Case postale/ P.O. Box 466 Place Bonaventure Montreal, Quebec H5A 1C1 Tel.: (514) 874-7674 Fax: (514) 874-1620 Toll-Free Tel.: 1-800-363-0263
Standard Life	Alberta Northern	The Standard Life Building 639–5th Avenue South West Calgary, Alberta T2P 0M9 Tel.: (403) 531-1100 Fax: (403) 531-1149
	Southern	The Standard Life Centre 10405 Jaspar Avenue Suite 1200 Edmonton, Alberta T5J 3N4 Tel.: (403) 944-0660 Fax: (403) 425-8810
	British Columbia	The Standard Life Building 625 Howe Street Suite 900 Vancouver, B.C. V6C 2T6 Tel.: (604) 664-8030 Fax: (604) 664-8033
	Manitoba	330 Portage Avenue Suite 1200 Winnipeg, Man. R3C 0C4 Tel.: (204) 949-2580 Fax: (204) 956-2530
	New Brunswick Newfoundland Nova Scotia P.E.I.	1791 Barrington Street Suite 1800 Halifax, Nova Scotia B3J 3L1 Tel.: (902) 423-8888 Fax: (902) 423-7083
	Quebec Sillery	Complexe Standard Life 1126 chemin Saint-Louis Bureau 150 Sillary, Quebec G1S 1E5 Tel.: (418) 684-2400 Fax: (418) 681-7164
	Montreal	Place du Canada 1010 de la Gauchetière Street West Suite 1750 Montreal, Quebec H3B 4N9 Tel.: (514) 877-4242 Fax: (514) 877-0272
	Ontario Ottawa	The Standard Life Building 275 Slater Street Suite 1200 Ottawa, Ontario K1P 5H9 Tel.: (613) 237-4222 Fax: (613) 230-3404

Company	Territory Covered By Office	Address, Contact Numbers
Standard Life	Toronto	Standard Life Ass. Co. 5255 Yonge Street Suite 610 North York, Ontario M2N 6P4 Tel.: (416) 218-5300 Fax: (416) 218-5325
	Ontario Hamilton	Standard Life Centre 120 King Street West Suite 220 Hamilton, Ontario L8P 4V2 Tel.: (905) 528-0601 Fax: (905) 546-5279
	London	Standard Life Ass. Co. 285 King Street Suite 200 London, Ontario N6B 3M6 Tel.: (519) 672-6063 Fax: (519) 672-3148
	Manitoba Winnipeg	Standard Life Ass. Co. 330 Portage Avenue Winnipeg, Manitoba R3C 0C4 Tel.: (204) 949-2580 Fax: (204) 956-2530
Sun Life Assurance Company	Alberta, Northern B.C., Northeastern Saskatchewan, Northern	Suite 1360, Sun Life Place 10123 99 Street Edmonton, Alberta T5J 3H1 Tel.: (403) 429-9015 Fax: (403) 425-9155
	Alberta, Southern Saskatchewan, Southern	Suite 1250, 140 4th Avenue S.W. Calgary, Alberta T2P 3N3 Tel.: (403) 266-8959 Fax: (403) 233-0529
	British Columbia	Suite 700, Sun Life Plaza 1100 Melville Place Vancouver, B.C. V6E 4A6 Tel.: (604) 689-9578 Fax: (604) 681-0684
	Manitoba, Northwestern Ontario	Suite 1130, 330 St. Mary Avenue Winnipeg, Manitoba R3C 3Z5 Tel.: (204) 942-6501 Fax: (204) 942-2087
	New Brunswick Newfoundland Nova Scotia P.E.I.	Suite 501, CIBC Bldg. 1809 Barrington Street P.O. Box 1620 Halifax, Nova Scotia B3J 2Y9 Tel.: (902) 422-1621 Fax: (902) 423-0445
	Ontario Ottawa	Suite 401, Pebb Bldg. 2197 Riverside Drive Ottawa, Ontario K1H 7X3 Tel.: (613) 523-9134 Fax: (613) 521-5205

Company	Territory Covered By Office	Address, Contact Numbers
Sun Life Assurance Company	Southwestern	Suite 203, 200 James Street S. Hamilton, Ontario L8P 3A9 Tel.: (416) 525-6291 Fax: (416) 528-8384
	Toronto	225 King Street West 7th Floor Toronto, Ontario M5V 3C5 Tel.: (416) 408-8880 Fax: (416) 595-1675
	Quebec Montreal	Immeuble Sun Life Suite 1160, 1155 rue Metcalfe Montreal, Quebec H3C 3G5 Tel.: (514) 866-6411 Fax: (514) 866-1863

(Quotes for groups with under 20 employees are available only through Sun Life agents. Sun Life Assurance Company Branch offices are located in most major centres.)

Company	Territory Covered By Office	Address, Contact Numbers
Zurich Life	Alberta Calgary	933 17th Avenue S.W. Suite 504 Calgary, Alberta T2T 5R6 Tel.: (403) 244-7533 Fax: (403) 244-7697
	Edmonton	10109 106 Street Suite 1203 Edmonton, Alberta T5J 3L7Tel.: (403) 423-2259
	British Columbia Kelowna	Suite 108, 565 Bernard Avenue Kelowna, B.C. V1Y 6N9 Tel.: (604) 861-3214 Fax: (604) 861-5006
	Vancouver	Suite 1850, 401 West Georgia Street Vancouver, B.C. V6B 5A1
	Manitoba	363 Broadway Avenue Suite 1020 Winnipeg, Manitoba R3C 3N9 Tel.: (204) 942-2588 Fax: (204) 944-8690
	New Brunswick Nova Scotia Newfoundland Prince Edward Island	Suite 430, 33 Alderney Drive Dartmouth, Nova Scotia B2Y 2N4 Tel.: (902) 464-5433 Fax: (902) 463-5974
	Ontario Burlington	Suite 203, 3027 Harvester Road Burlington, Ontario L7N 3G7 Tel.: (905) 632-6592 Fax: (905) 632-5629

Company	Territory Covered By Office	Address, Contact Numbers
Zurich Life	London	Suite 1508, 148 Fullarton Street London, Ontario N6A 5P3 Tel.: (519) 433-2849 Fax: (519) 433-2850
	Ottawa	Suite 702, 1565 Carling Avenue Ottawa, Ontario K1Z 8R1 Tel.: (613) 725-1177 Fax: (613) 725-0590
	Pickering	Suite 208, 1550 Kingston Road Pickering, Ontario K1Z 8R1 Tel.: (905) 420-2411 Fax: (905) 420-3171
	Toronto	Suite 2100, 4950 Yonge Street Toronto, Ontario M2N 6K1 Tel.: (416) 733-4524 Fax: (416) 733-2878
	Quebec Montreal	Suite 900 5100 Sherbrooke Street E. Montreal, Quebec H1V 3R9 Tel.: (514) 254-1414 Fax: (514) 254-0153
	Quebec City	Suite 950, 2635 Hochelaga Boulevard Ste-Foy, Quebec G1V 4W2 Tel.: (418) 654-1070 Fax: (418) 654-1128
	Saskatchewan	Suite 1202, 2500 Victoria Avenue Regina, Saskatchewan S4P 3X2 Tel.: (306) 757-8596 Fax: (306) 359-7010

¶17,060 BENEFITS AND UNDERWRITING MINIMUMS

The following are benefits and underwriting minimums offered by insurers and benefit providers.

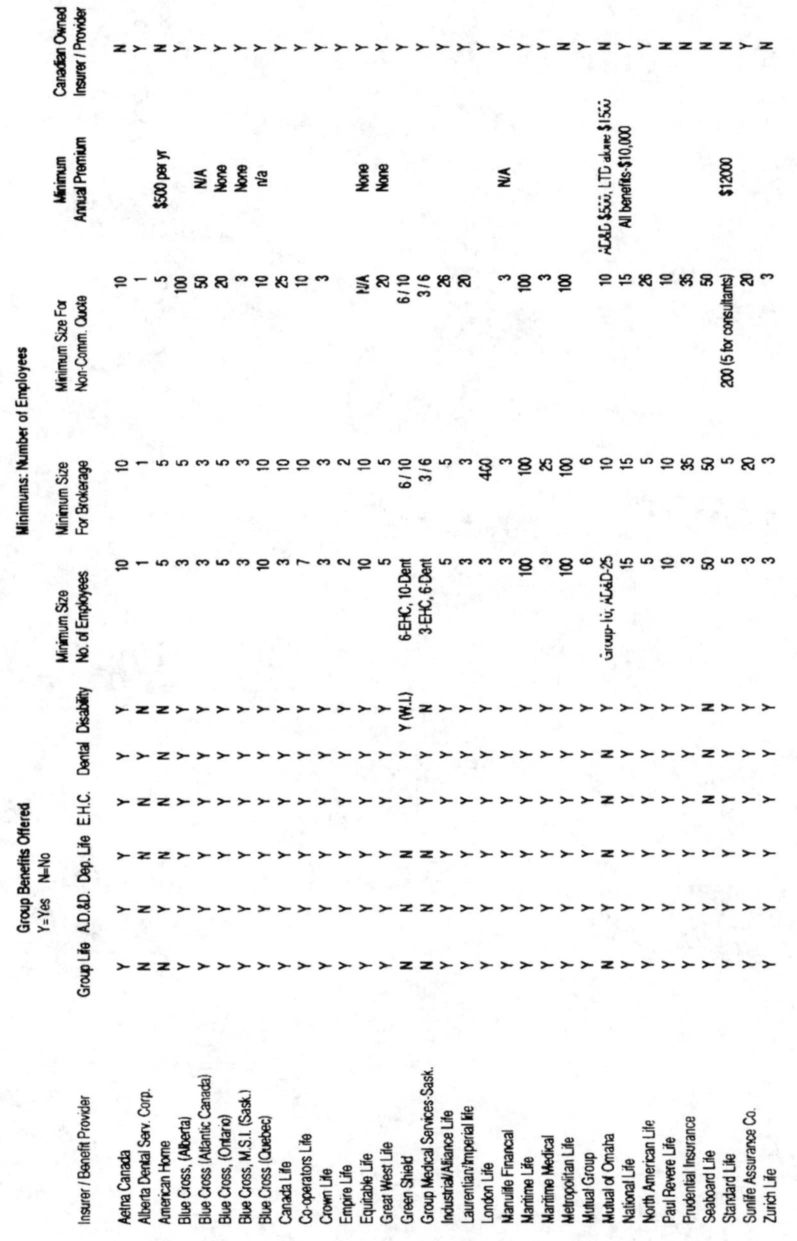

Insurer / Benefit Provider	Group Benefits Offered Y=Yes N=No						Minimums: Number of Employees				
	Group Life	A.D.&D.	Dep. Life	E.H.C.	Dental	Disability	Minimum Size No. of Employees	Minimum Size For Brokerage	Minimum Size For Non-Comm. Quote	Minimum Annual Premium	Canadian Owned Insurer / Provider
Aetna Canada	Y	Y	Y	Y	Y	Y	10	10	10		N
Alberta Dental Serv. Corp.	N	N	N	N	Y	N	1	1	1		Y
American Home	N	Y	N	N	N	N	5	5	5	$500 per yr	N
Blue Cross, (Alberta)	Y	Y	Y	Y	Y	Y	3	5	100		Y
Blue Cross (Atlantic Canada)	Y	Y	Y	Y	Y	Y	3	3	50	N/A	Y
Blue Cross, (Ontario)	Y	Y	Y	Y	Y	Y	5	5	20	None	Y
Blue Cross, M.S.I. (Sask.)	Y	Y	Y	Y	Y	Y	3	3	3	None	Y
Blue Cross (Quebec)	Y	Y	Y	Y	Y	Y	10	10	10	n/a	Y
Canada Life	Y	Y	Y	Y	Y	Y	3	10	25		Y
Co-operators Life	Y	Y	Y	Y	Y	Y	7	10	10		Y
Crown Life	Y	Y	Y	Y	Y	Y	3	3	3		Y
Empire Life	Y	Y	Y	Y	Y	Y	2	2			Y
Equitable Life	Y	Y	Y	Y	Y	Y	10	10	N/A	None	Y
Great West Life	Y	Y	Y	Y	Y	Y	5	5	20	None	Y
Green Shield	N	N	N	Y	Y	Y (W.I.)	6-EHC, 10-Dent	6 / 10	6 / 10		Y
Group Medical Services-Sask.	N	N	N	Y	Y	N	3-EHC, 6-Dent	3 / 6	3 / 6		Y
Industrial/Alliance Life	Y	Y	Y	Y	Y	Y	5	5	26		Y
Laurentian/Imperial life	Y	Y	Y	Y	Y	Y	3	3	20		Y
London Life	Y	Y	Y	Y	Y	Y	3	400			Y
Manulife Financal	Y	Y	Y	Y	Y	Y	3	3	3	N/A	Y
Maritime Life	Y	Y	Y	Y	Y	Y	100	100	100		Y
Maritime Medical	Y	Y	Y	Y	Y	Y	3	25	3		Y
Metropolitan Life	Y	Y	Y	Y	Y	Y	100	100	100		N
Mutual Group	Y	Y	Y	Y	Y	Y	6	6			Y
Mutual of Omaha	N	Y	N	N	N	Y	Group-10, AD&D-25	10	10	AD&D $500, LTD alone $1500	N
National Life	Y	Y	Y	Y	Y	Y	15	15	15	All benefits-$10,000	Y
North American Life	Y	Y	Y	Y	Y	Y	5	5	26		Y
Paul Revere Life	Y	Y	Y	Y	Y	Y	10	10	10		N
Prudential Insurance	Y	Y	Y	Y	Y	Y	3	35	35		N
Seaboard Life	Y	Y	Y	N	N	N	50	50	50		N
Standard Life	Y	Y	Y	Y	Y	Y	5	5	200 (5 for consultants)	$12000	N
Sunlife Assurance Co.	Y	Y	Y	Y	Y	Y	3	20	20		Y
Zurich Life	Y	Y	Y	Y	Y	Y	3	3	3		N

Notes:
Minimum Group Size is the minimum number of employees required for a group quote.
Minimum Group Size For Brokerage is the minimum number of employees required to quote to brokers.
Minimum For Non-Comm. Quote is the minimum number of employees required for a quote without commissions.
All insurers and benefit providers have the right to change benefits offered and their minimums at any time.

¶17,065 REVENUE CANADA INTERPRETATION BULLETINS

Notes to Appendix on Revenue Canada Interpretation Bulletins

The following tax Interpretation Bulletins are included because of their relevancy to group life, health and disability insurance plans. Also included are Interpretation Bulletins on the subject of life insurance, which are referred to by human resources, accounting and insurance professionals, among others. The object of including these other bulletins is to provide a centralized source of reference and to provide readers in other countries with more insight into the regulatory situation in Canada.

Interpretation Bulletins pertaining to the subject of group insurance benefits include:

- IT-85R2: Health and Welfare Trusts for Employees (¶17,070).
- IT-202R2: Employees' or Workers' Compensation (¶17,075).
- IT-227R: Group Term Insurance Premiums (¶17,080).
- IT-247: Employer's Contribution to Pensioners' Premiums under Provincial Medical and Hospital Services Plans (¶17,085).
- IT-301: Death Benefits — Qualifying Payments (¶17,090).
- IT-339R2: Meaning of "Private Health Services Plan" (¶17,095).
- IT-428: Wage Loss Replacement Plans (¶17,100).
- IT-519R: Medical Expense and Disability Tax Credits and Attendant Care Expense Deduction (¶17,105).

Although not included in this book, the following tax Interpretation Bulletins, available from Revenue Canada, will be important to other areas of employee benefits such as life insurance, pension plans, retirement plans, profit sharing plans, and employer payments to employees for the use of personal vehicles.

Life Insurance Benefits, Not Just Group Insurance

- IT-87R: Policyholders' Income from Life Insurance Policies.
- IT-140R3: Buy-Sell Agreements.
- IT-223: Overhead Expense Insurance vs. Income Insurance.
- IT-309R2: Expense of Borrowing Money — Life Insurance Premiums.
- IT-342R: Trusts — Income Payable to Beneficiaries.
- IT-355R2: Interest on Loans to Buy Life Insurance Policies and Annuity Contracts, and Interest on Policy Loans.

- IT-381R2: Trusts — Deduction of Amounts Paid or Payable to Beneficiaries and Flow-through Taxable Gains to Beneficiaries.
- IT-394R: Preferred Beneficiary Election.
- IT-416R3: Valuation of Shares of a Corporation Receiving Life Insurance Proceeds on Death of a Shareholder.

Retirement Benefits

- IT-76R2: Exempt Portion of Pension When Employee Has Been a Non-Resident.
- IT-105: Administrative Costs of Pension Plans.
- IT-124R6: Contributions to Registered Retirement Savings Plans.
- IT-320R2: Registered Retirement Savings Plans — Qualified Investments.
- IT-337R2: Retiring Allowances.
- IT-408R: Life Insurance Policies as Investments of RRSPs and DPSPs.
- IT-415R: Deregistration of RRSPs.
- IT-499R: Superannuation or Pension Benefits.
- IT-500: Registered Retirement Savings Plans (maturing after June 29, 1978) — Death of Annuitant after June 29, 1978.
- IT-517: Pension Tax Credit.

Profit Sharing Plans and Payments from an Employer to an Employee

- IT-196R2: Payments by Employer to Employee.
- IT-280: Employees' Profit Sharing Plans — Payments Computed by Reference to Profits.
- IT-281R2: Elections on Single Payments from a Deferred Profit Sharing Plan.
- IT-363R2: Deferred Profit Sharing Plans — Deductibility of Contributions and Taxation of Amounts Received by a Beneficiary.
- IT-379: Employees Profit Sharing Plans — Allocations to Beneficiaries.

Other Employee Benefits

- IT-63R4: Benefits, Including Standby Charge for an Automobile from the Personal Use of a Motor Vehicle Supplied by an Employer.
- IT-113R3: Benefits to Employees — Stock Options.

¶17,070 IT-85R2 — Health and Welfare Trusts for Employees

[IT-85R2 — Health and Welfare Trusts for Employees is dated July 31, 1986.]

Reference. Paragraph 6(1)(*a*) and section 104 (also subsections 6(4), 12.2(3), 12.2(4) and 12.2(7), paragraphs 6(1)(*f*), 56(1)(*d*) and 56(1)(*d*.1), 60(*a*), 110(8)(*a*) and subparagraphs 148(9)(*c*)(vii) and 148(9)(*c*)(ix); also section 19 of the *Income Tax Application Rules, 1971* (ITAR)).

This bulletin replaces and cancels IT-85R, dated January 20, 1975. Proposals contained in the Notice of Ways and Means Motion of June 11, 1986 are not considered in this release.

1. The general thrust of paragraph 6(1)(*a*) is to include in employment income the value of all benefits received or enjoyed in respect of an employee's employment. However, there are a number of specific exceptions many of which can be described as benefits relating to the health and welfare of the employee. In some cases, the scope of the excepted benefits and applicable tax treatment are well established by other provisions of the Act, (e.g., registered pension funds or plans, deferred profit sharing plans, supplementary unemployment benefit plans, the standby charge for the use of an employer's automobile, employee benefit plans and employee trusts). The treatment to be accorded to the other exceptions can be less clear, particularly when the benefits form part of an omnibus health and welfare program administered by an employer. The purpose of this bulletin is to describe the tax treatment accorded to an employee health and welfare benefit program that is administered by an employer through a trust arrangement and that is restricted to

(a) a group sickness or accident insurance plan (see 2 below),

(b) a private health services plan,

(c) a group term life insurance policy, or

(d) any combination of (a) to (c).

2. Paragraph 6(1)(*f*) sets out the treatment of periodic receipts related to loss of income from employment under three types of insurance plans to which the employer had made a contribution. These types of plans are sickness or accident, disability and income maintenance (also known as salary continuation). In the absence of any statutory definition, the Department generally accepts that an employer's contribution to any of the three types of plans will be a contribution to a "group sickness or accident insurance plan" as described in subparagraph 6(1)(*a*)(i), provided that the particular plan is a "group" plan and an insured plan. This

is based on the assumption that a "disability" resulting in loss of employment income would almost invariably arise from sickness or an accident and that an "income maintenance" payment would likely arise from loss of employment income due to sickness or an accident if not lay off (the latter reason justifying an exception under subparagraph 6(1)(*a*)(i) as a supplementary unemployment benefit plan). There may be situations where these assumptions will prove invalid but, subject to this caveat, 1(a) above may also be read as a "group disability insurance plan" or "a group income maintenance insurance plan that is not a supplementary unemployment benefit plan".

Employee Benefit Plans and Employee Trusts

3. Employee benefit plans are broadly defined in subsection 248(1) and can encompass health and welfare arrangements. However, funds or plans described in 1(a) to (d) above are specifically excluded in the definition and are thus accorded the tax treatment outlined in this bulletin. Health and welfare arrangements not described in 1(a) to (d) above (e.g., those not based on insurance) may be employee benefit plans or, less likely, employee trusts subject to the tax consequences outlined in IT-502.

4. Where part of a single plan could be regarded as a plan described in 1(a) to (d) above and another part as an employee benefit plan or an employee trust, the combined plan will be given employee benefit plan or employee trust treatment in respect of the timing and amounts of both the employer's expense deductions and the employee's receipt of benefits under the plan. However, if contributions, income and disbursements of the part of the plan that is described in 1(a) to (d) above are separately identified and accounted for, the tax treatment outlined in this bulletin will apply to that part of the plan.

Meaning of Health and Welfare Trust

5. Health and welfare benefits for employees are sometimes provided through a trust arrangement under which the trustees (usually with equal representation from the employer or employer's group and the employees or their union) receive the contributions from the employer(s), and in some cases from employees, to provide such health and welfare benefits as have been agreed to between the employer and the employees. If the benefit programs adopted are limited to those described in 1(a) to (d) above and the arrangement meets the conditions set out in 6 and 7 below, the trust arrangement is referred to in this bulletin as a health and welfare trust.

6. To qualify for treatment as a health and welfare trust the funds of the trust cannot revert to the employer or be used for any purpose other than providing health and welfare benefits for which the contributions

are made. In addition, the employer's contributions to the fund must not exceed the amounts required to provide these benefits. Furthermore, the payments by the employer cannot be made on a voluntary or gratuitous basis. They must be enforceable by the trustees should the employer decide not to make the payments required. The type of trust arrangement envisaged is one where the trustee or trustees act independently of the employer as opposed to the type of arrangement initiated unilaterally by an employer who has control over the use of the funds whether or not there are employee contributions. Employer control over the use of funds of a trust (with or without an external trustee) would occur where the beneficiaries of the trust have no claim against the trustees or the fund except by or through the employer.

7. With the exception of a private health services plan, two or more employees must be covered by the plan. Where a partnership seeks to provide health and welfare benefits for both the employees and the partners by means of a trust, two distinctly separate health and welfare trusts (one for the partners and one for the employees) must be set up to ensure that the funds of each are at all times identifiable and that cross-subsidization between the plans will not occur. The exception in subparagraph 6(1)(*a*)(i) will of course not apply to such a trust established for the partners.

Tax Implications to Employer

8. To the extent that they are reasonable and laid out to earn income from business or property, contributions to a health and welfare trust by an employer using the accrual method of computing income are deductible in the taxation year in which the legal obligation to make the contributions arose.

Tax Implications to Employee

9. An employee does not receive or enjoy a benefit at the time the employer makes a contribution to a health and welfare trust. However, subject to 10 below, the tax consequences to an employee arising from benefits provided under such a trust are as follows:

Group Sickness or Accident Insurance Plans

(a) Where a group sickness or accident insurance plan provides that benefits are to be paid by the insurer directly to the employee, the premium paid by the trustees to the insurer for the employee's coverage will not result in a benefit to be included in the employee's income.

(b) Where this type of group sickness or accident insurance plan existed before June 19, 1971 and the requirements of section 19 of the ITAR are met (see IT-54, "Wage Loss Replacement Plans"), the benefits paid to an employee by the trustees or the insurers under such a plan in consequence of an event happening before 1974 will not result in a taxable benefit to the employee. Where these requirements are not met and in all cases of payments for events happening after 1973, the wage loss replacement benefits will be taxable under paragraph 6(1)(*f*) (see IT-428, "Wage Loss Replacement Plans").

Private Health Services Plans (defined in paragraph 110(8)(a))

(c)Payment by the trustees of all or part of the employee's premium to a private health services plan does not give rise to a taxable benefit to the employee. Benefits provided to an employee under a private health services plan are also not subject to tax.

Group Term Life Insurance

(d) Payment by the trustees of a premium under a group term life insurance policy will not result in a taxable benefit to the employee unless the aggregate amount of the employee's coverage under one or more group term life insurance policies exceeds $25,000 (see IT-227R, "Group Term Life Insurance Premiums"). The provisions of section 12.2 which tax accrued amounts under a life insurance policy do not apply since a group term life insurance policy will be an exempt policy for that purpose.

(e) Where a group term life insurance policy provides for a lump sum payment to the employee's estate or a named beneficiary, the receipt of the payment directly from the insurer is not included in the recipient's income.

(f) Certain group term life insurance policies provide beneficiaries thereunder with an option to take periodic payments in lieu of the lump sum payment and others provide only for periodic payments to beneficiaries. Prior to the introduction of the accrual rules in section 12.2 for 1983 and subsequent taxation years, benefits thus paid by the insurer to a beneficiary, whether as a result of exercising the option or by the terms of the policy, were annuity payments that were income of the recipient (paragraph 56(1)(*d*)) who deducted the capital element of the annuity payment (paragraph 60(*a*) of the Act and Part III of the Regulations).

(g) For the 1983 and subsequent taxation years, paragraphs 56(1)(*d*) and 60(*a*) continue to apply to a beneficiary who is a holder and annuitant under an annuity contract if subsection 12.2(3) does not apply because of the exceptions in paragraphs 12.2(3)(*c*) to (*e*) or the application of subsection 12.2(7). Generally speaking, this will occur where the annuity contract

(i) is a prescribed annuity contract as defined in Regulation 304,

(ii) was acquired before December 2, 1982 under which annuity payments commenced before December 2, 1982,

(iii) is an annuity contract that was received as proceeds of a group term life insurance policy which was itself neither an annuity contract nor acquired after December 1, 1982, or

(iv) was acquired before December 2, 1982, can never be surrendered and in respect of which the terms and conditions have not been changed

and is not the subject of an election under subsection 12.2(4).

(h) For annuity contracts other than ones described in (g) above, the annuitant is required by subsection 12.2(3) for the 1983 and subsequent taxation years to include in income accrued amounts on every "third anniversary" of the contract. In addition, in any year that does not include a "third anniversary", paragraph 56(1)(*d*.1) requires the inclusion of amounts in respect of annuity payments received during the year under the contract. As an alternative to the application of subsection 12.2(3) and paragraph 56(1)(*d*.1), the annuitant may elect under subsection 12.2(4) (before annuity payments commence) to include accrued amounts on an annual basis. In each instance, the issuer will provide the annuitant with a T-5 information slip indicating the amount of income to be reported in respect of the annuity contract.

Shared Contributions

10. In 9 above the trustees are assumed to be receiving contributions only from the employer to pay for the cost of benefits under the trust plan. However, the trustees may also receive employee contributions to pay a part of the cost of the benefits being provided under the plan. If the plan does not clearly establish that the trustee must use the employee contributions to pay all or some part of the cost of a specific benefit, then it will be assumed that each benefit under the plan is being paid out of both the employer and the employee contributions. If the benefit in question is otherwise taxable to the employee, then in these circumstances a part of it is non-taxable. The non-taxable part is that proportion of the benefit received by the employee for the year that the total of employee contributions received by the trustees in the year is of the aggregate of the employer and employee contributions received by the trustees in the year. The above treatment will not apply if the benefit must be reported as income according to paragraph 6(1)(*f*) (see 9(b) above). However, the employee's contributions to plans referred to in

9(b) may be deductible for tax purposes from benefits received from the plan. See IT-428 for details.

Taxation of Trust

11. A trust which invests some of the contributions received and earns investment income, or has incidental income (other than contributions from employers and employees which are not included in computing income of the trust), is subject to tax under section 104 on the amount of such "trust income" remaining after the deductions discussed in 12 below. Where gross income (i.e., the aggregate of its income from all sources) exceeds $500 in the taxation year (and in certain other circumstances indicated on the form), the trustee is required to file form T3 (Trust Information Return and Income Tax Return).

12. In computing trust income subject to tax, the trust is allowed to deduct, to the extent of the gross trust income, the following expenses, premiums and benefits it paid, and in the following order:

(a) expenses incurred in earning the investment or other income of the trust,

(b) expenses related to the normal operation of the trust including those incurred in the collection of and accounting for contributions to the trust, in reviewing and acquiring insurance plans and other benefits and for fees paid to a management company to administer the trusts, except to the extent that such expenses are expressly not allowed under the Act,

(c) premiums and benefits payable out of trust income of the current year pursuant to paragraph 104(6)(*b*). Benefits that are paid out of proceeds of an insurance policy do not qualify. Other benefits paid are normally regarded as having been paid first out of trust income of the year. However, premiums and benefits that would not otherwise be taxable in the hands of the employee by virtue of paragraph 6(1)(*a*) may be treated at the trustee's discretion as having been paid out of prior year's funds or current year's employer's contributions, to the extent that they are available, to avoid the application of subsection 104(13).

The remainder of the income of the trust is subject to income tax under section 122 of the Act. As an *inter vivos* trust, the taxation year of the trust coincides with the calendar year.

13. For administrative simplicity, payments of taxable benefits by the trustee to or on behalf of employees are to be reported on Form T4A by the trustee and not on the T3 Supplementary. Information on the completion of Form T4A is contained in the "Employer's and Trustee's Guide". Although the trustee is required to withhold income tax from taxable

benefits paid to employees, these amounts will not be subject to either Canada Pension Plan contributions or unemployment insurance premiums when paid by the trustee.

14. Although actuarial studies of the trust may recommend the establishment of "contingency reserves" to meet its future obligations, transfers to such reserves are not deductible for tax purposes by the trust.

Setting up a Plan

15. There is no formal registration procedure for a health and welfare trust and no requirement that the trust agreement be submitted to the Department for approval prior to the implementation of the plan. However, the advice of the District Taxation Office may be requested where there is any doubt as to the acceptability of the trust agreement as a health and welfare trust. Full particulars of the arrangement including a copy of all pertinent documents should accompany the request.

¶17,075 IT-202R2 — Employees' or Workers' Compensation

[IT-202R2 — Employees' or Workers' Compensation is dated September 19, 1985.]

Reference: Paragraph 56(1)(*v*) and subparagraph 110(1)(*f*)(ii) (also subsection 5(1).)

This bulletin cancels and replaces IT-202R dated July 14, 1980 and IT-202R2 Special Release dated December 29, 1980.

1. In this bulletin

(a) "compensation board" includes any employees' or workers' compensation board or commission in any province or territory of Canada, and

(b) "compensation" refers to the amount of an award, as adjudicated by a compensation board, which a worker or his or her dependants will receive as a result of the worker having suffered illness, injury or death in the performance of his or her duties of employment and includes any such compensation to which entitlement is provided under the *Government Employees Compensation Act* or any employees' or workers' compensation Act or Ordinance of a province or territory of Canada.

2. Prior to 1982, the amount of compensation that was received in a taxation year by any person (other than as the employer or former employer of the person in respect of whom the amount was paid) was excluded from income by virtue of paragraph 81(1)(*h*), which paragraph was repealed applicable to the 1982 and subsequent taxation years. The

main income tax effect of the repeal of paragraph 81(1)(*h*), and other amendments to the Act, is that compensation received, while continuing to be non-taxable, is now included in income of the person who receives it. The amount of compensation received in a taxation year is therefore relevant in determining

(a) the extent to which the recipient thereof may be claimed as a dependant by another taxpayer, and

(b) the amount that is the aggregate of the family net income for purposes of the child tax credit.

Inclusion in Income

3. For 1982 and subsequent taxation years, the amount of compensation received in a taxation year by any person is, by virtue of paragraph 56(1)(*v*), required to be included in computing that person's income for the year.

4. For the purpose of paragraph 56(1)(*v*) the amount of compensation may be received either from a compensation board or from the employer or former employer of the person entitled thereto. An employee may, under the terms of an employment contract or collective agreement, or by reason of being granted injury leave with pay under the *Financial Administration Act*, be entitled to receive salary or wages during a period in which the employee is also entitled to compensation. Where, in these circumstances, the employee receives no payment from a compensation board, the amount received from his or her employer, to the extent that it does not exceed the compensation amount, will be included in the employee's income for the year, as compensation, under paragraph 56(1)(*v*). The excess, if any, will be included in the employee's income under subsection 5(1).

Deduction in Computing Taxable Income

5. For 1982 and subsequent taxation years, any compensation received by a taxpayer in a taxation year, that was included in the taxpayer's income under paragraph 56(1)(*v*), may, by virtue of subparagraph 110(1)(*f*)(ii), be deducted in computing the taxpayer's taxable income for the year, except any such compensation received by the taxpayer as the employer or former employer of the person in respect of whom the compensation was paid.

Payments Received by Employers

6. Any amount received by an employer from a compensation board, or remitted by the employee to the employer, or any other amount paid to an employer in reimbursement of salary or wages paid by employer is included, without exception, in computing the employer's income.

Loans or Advances

7. Where it can be established that an employee received a loan or advance from his or her employer which is to be repaid from future payments of compensation, the loan or advance constitutes neither income to the employee nor deductible expense to the employer. However, when the compensation is paid and is received by the employee, it will be treated in accordance with 3 and 5 above. The amount received by the employer from or on behalf of the employee in repayment of the loan or advance will not constitute income to the employer.

¶17,080 IT-227R — Group Term Life Insurance Premiums

[*IT-227R — Group Term Life Insurance Premiums is dated May 26, 1980.*]

Reference. Subsection 6(4) (also subsection 6(5) and paragraph 6(1)(*a*).)

[This bulletin cancels and replaces Interpretation Bulletin IT-227 dated June 9, 1975.]

1. This bulletin explains the application of subsection 6(4) which includes in the income of an officer, employee, former officer or former employee (hereinafter referred to as an employee) a part of the premium of certain group term life insurance policies.

2. Paragraph 6(1)(*a*) specifically excludes premiums paid by an employer under a group term life insurance policy from the benefits taxable under that paragraph, and there is no provision in the Act to include in an employee's income premiums paid by one or more employers or former employers under one or more group term life insurance policies where the total insurance coverage on the taxpayer's life is $25,000 or less. However, subsection 6(4) provides that where an employee is insured at any time in his taxation year for an amount in excess of $25,000 under one or more group term life insurance policies, part of any premiums paid by his employer(s) or former employer(s) is included in his income as income from an officer or employment. The method for calculating the amount to be included in income is outlined in paragraphs (*a*) to (*c*) of subsection 6(4). Sample calculations are set out in paragraphs 16 to 18 of this bulletin.

*3. The phrase "group term life insurance policy" is defined in subsection 248(1) as a group life insurance policy under which no amount is payable as a result of the contributions made to or under the policy by the employer except in the event of the death or disability of the employee. An employees' group life insurance policy is a policy whereby the lives of

* As amended by Special Release, November 10, 1980, effective May 26, 1980.

employees are insured severally under a single contract between the insurer and an employer contracting with the insurer. The Department accepts as a life insurance policy any policy of insurance where one of the risks covered is the death of the person insured but not an insurance policy which covers death only by reason of accident.

4. The calculation under subsection 6(4) takes into account any premium, premium refund or dividend in respect of the policy year ending in the taxation year of the employee, even though part or all of any of those items may have been paid or payable in another policy year or another taxation year. Ordinarily, the policy year is a twelve-month period, but subsection 6(5) provides for a shorter period to be the "policy year"where, for example, a group policy is terminated during a taxation year prior to its anniversary date in that year and the policy year is considered to have ended. Again, if a policy is a new one which has no anniversary date in the taxation year, subsection 6(5) provides that the policy year is from the date of issue of the policy to the end of the taxation year. In this case, the calculation takes into account only the premium payable for that period; any experience rating refund or dividend payable, being based on the full policy year, is considered not to be applicable, even *pro rata*, to any period forming part of that year. Where the group coverage is transferred from one insurance company to another before the end of a policy year, two calculations are required: one to the date of termination of the old policy, and one from the date of issue of the new policy.

5. Certain "paid-up" group life insurance certificates, where the whole premium is paid in the first policy year, may qualify as group term life insurance policies which are subject to the exception in paragraph 6(1)(*a*) and the provisions of subsection 6(4). In computing the benefit under subsection 6(4), the premium to purchase such a policy would be included in the "total premium payable on account of life insurance under the policy in respect of the policy year ending in the year", under paragraph 6(4)(*a*) in the year it was paid, notwithstanding that the premium could be considered to be in respect of the first policy year and all subsequent years until the employee dies.

6. The part of a premium, premium refund or dividend under an employees' group policy that is taken into account for the purposes of paragraph 6(4)(*a*) is limited to the part paid in respect of "life insurance" (as defined in 3 above). Accordingly any part that relates to long-term disability or accident and sickness benefits is excluded. Again where, because of the employer's contributions, a benefit (e.g., a cash surrender value) is payable under a policy other than upon the death or disability of the employee, the whole premium paid for the policy is excluded since it is not then a term life insurance policy within the meaning of subsection 248(1).

7. In some cases, the employer may be the beneficiary of part or all of the coverage on an employee's life. If so, the relevant portion of the coverage and, if applicable, of the premiums, premium refunds or dividends is excluded from the calculation under paragraph 6(4)(*a*). However, the portion of the premiums applicable to the coverage on which the employer is the beneficiary in these cases is not an allowable business expense of the employer.

8. The phrase "the number of days in that period" in paragraph 6(4)(*a*) refers to the number of days in the calendar year that the employee is covered under the policy for more than $25,000. Where he is covered for $25,000 or less (or not at all) for part of the year, but for more than $25,000 for another part of the year, an apportionment, on a daily basis, should be made in that part of the calculation governed by paragraph 6(4)(*a*). Where the employee is covered for part or all of the year for more than $25,000 and the amount of that excess has changed at some time in the year, a complete calculation must be made under subsection 6(4) for each excess amount, with an apportionment being made under paragraph 6(4)(*a*) in each case, based on the number of days to which the specific excess applies and as if there were no excess for the remainder of the year; the sum of the amounts so calculated is to be included in income under this subsection. The example in 18 below illustrates this kind of calculation. Where there is excess coverage for part of the year with no change in the amount, only a single calculation is required.

9. In determining the "amount of life insurance in effect" at any given time, referred to in paragraph 6(4)(*a*), all benefits provided by a group term life insurance policy should be taken into account, whether payable on a periodic basis such as survivor income benefits, or in a lump sum. Thus the commuted value of any survivor benefits payable is added to the amount of any lump sum payable on death in calculating the "amount of life insurance in effect".

10. The "mean", or average, total term life insurance in effect under the policy, also referred to in paragraph 6(4)(*a*), is based only on the amounts in force at the beginning and end of the policy year. Any fluctuation in total coverage between those two dates is disregarded and no apportionment is required.

11. The amount of premium paid by the employee that is to be apportioned under paragraph 6(4)(*c*) is the amount he pays in his taxation year for the period during which his coverage is in excess of $25,000; this is determined on the basis of what, factually, he pays in respect of the group term life insurance policy. However, for the 1974 and subsequent taxation years where an employee reimburses the employer for all or part of the

premium for the coverage in excess of $25,000, his benefit under subsection 6(4) is reduced accordingly.

Multiple Policies

12. An employee may be covered under two or more group term life insurance policies for each of which his employer pays part or all of the premiums. If, for one of those policies, the separate calculation required by paragraph 6(4)(*d*) shows that the part of the employee's contributions as determined under paragraph 6(4)(*c*) exceeds the amount determined pursuant to paragraph 6(4)(*b*), that excess is not taken into account to reduce the amount to be included in the employee's income because of the other policies.

13. Where an employee is covered under more than one group term life insurance policy for which his employer pays part or all of the premiums, a separate computation must be made in respect of each policy, with the $25,000 "exemption" being apportioned among the policies pursuant to paragraph 6(4)(*e*).

14. A difficulty arises where the amount of the employee's coverage under one or more of the policies changes, since there is no one figure under each policy upon which to base an apportionment. The Department will accept the computation of a level amount of coverage under each policy, using the weighted average (based on months of coverage) of the varying amounts in force under the policy during the year, or any other reasonable method proposed.

15. A group insurance policy of any kind for which no part of the premiums is payable by the employer is ignored for the purposes of paragraphs 6(4)(*d*) and (*e*).

Examples

16. The two examples below show the calculations required first, before and after 1974 where the employee's premium is in respect of his total coverage under the policy and, second, for 1974 and subsequent taxation years where the employee's premium is specifically in respect of his excess coverage.

17. In an uncomplicated case where the employee's coverage is, say $40,000 throughout the year and the mean total amount of term life insurance under the group policy is, say, $1,250,000, the two calculations under subsection 6(4) would be as follows:

Total premium for policy year (say)	$ 8,000
Less: Experience rating refund (say)	1,000
Net premium cost for policy year	$ 7,000

Average cost per $1,000 of insurance

$7,000 × $\left(\frac{\$1,000}{\$1,250,000}\right)$ .... $ 5.60

Amount of employee's excess coverage
($40,000 - $25,000) .... $ 15,000

Amount to be included in employee's income if no premium paid by him

$\left(\$15,000 \times \frac{\$5.60}{\$1,000}\right)$ $84.00

(i) Premium for Total Coverage

If employee paid, say, $50 in respect of his total coverage, the deductible portion is

$\left(\$50 \times \frac{\$15,000}{\$40,000}\right)$ $18.75

Amount to be included in employee's income
($84.00 - $18.75) .... $ 65.25

(ii) Premium for Excess Coverage, 1974 and Subsequent Taxation Years

If employee paid, say, $50 in respect of his excess coverage, the amount to be included in his income is ($84.00 - $50.00) $ 34.00

18. To illustrate a more complicated situation assume:

(a) the mean total amount of life insurance in effect under the policy in the policy year was $1,250,000.00;

(b) the total premium for the policy year was $8,000;

(c) the experience rating refund for the policy year was $1,000;

(d) an employee ("the taxpayer") was covered under the above group policy (but under no other group policy) during his taxation year as follows:

for 90 days at $20,000
180 $50,000
95 $75,000 and

(e) during his taxation year, the employee paid personally the following amounts in respect of this insurance:

for period of $20,000 coverage — $15
$50,000 — $50
$75,000 — $40

Calculation of the amount that is to be included in the employee's income is as follows:

(A) First calculation: Period of $50,000 coverage

Paragraph 6(4)(*a*)

Total premium for policy year	$ 8,000	
Less: experience rating refund	1,000	
Net premium cost for policy year	$ 7,000	
Premium cost for this period $\left(\$7{,}000 \times \frac{180}{365}\right)$	$3,452.05	
Average cost per $1,000 of insurance for this period $\left(\$3{,}452.05 \times \frac{\$1{,}000}{\$1{,}250{,}000}\right)$	2.76164	

Paragraph 6(4)(*b*)

Amount of excess coverage for this period ($50,000 - $25,000)	$ 25,000	
Average cost of insurance per paragraph 6(4)(a)	$2.76164	
Amount to be included in employee's income in respect of this period if no premium paid by him $\left(\$25{,}000 \times \frac{\$2.76164}{\$1{,}000}\right)$		$69.04

(i) Premium for Total Coverage

Paragraph 6(4)(*a*)

If employee paid, say, $50 in respect of his total coverage for this period, the deductible portion is $\left(\$50 \times \frac{\$25{,}000}{\$50{,}000}\right)$	$25.00	
Amount to be included in employee's income		$ 44.04

(ii) Premium for Excess Coverage — 1974 and Subsequent Taxation Years

If employee paid, say, $50 in respect of his excess coverage for this period, the amount to be included in his income is ($69.04 — $50)		$ 19.04

(B) Second calculation: period of $75,000 coverage

Paragraph 6(4)(*a*)

Total premium for policy year	$ 8,000	

Less: experience rating refund	1,000	
	$ 7,000	
Premium cost for this period		
$\left(\$7{,}000 \times \frac{95}{365}\right)$	$1,821.92	
Average cost per $1,000 of insurance for this period		
$\left(\$1{,}821.92 \times \frac{\$1{,}000}{\$1{,}250{,}000}\right)$	$1.4575	

Paragraph 6(4)(*b*)

Amount of excess coverage for this period	$ 50,000	
Average cost of insurance per paragraph 6(4)(a)	$ 1.4575	
Amount to be included in employee's income in respect of this period if no premium paid by him		
$\left(\$50{,}000 \times \frac{\$1.4575}{\$1{,}000}\right)$		$72.88

(i) Premium for Total Coverage

Paragraph 6(4)(*c*)

If employee paid, say, $40 in respect of his total coverage for this period, the deductible portion is		
$\left(\$40 \times \frac{\$50{,}000}{\$75{,}000}\right)$	$26.66	
Amount to be included in employee's income		$ 46.22

(ii) Premium for Excess Coverage — 1974 and Subsequent Taxation Years

If employee paid, say, $40 in respect of his excess coverage for this period, the amount to be included in his income is ($72.88 - $40)		$ 32.88
Total amount to be included in employee's income, (calculations (A) and (B)) if his payments in both periods were in respect of his total average		$ 90.26
Total amount to be included in employee's income, for 1974 and subsequent taxation years (calculations (A) and (B)) if his payments in both periods were in respect of his excess coverage		$ 51.92

¶17,080

¶17,085 IT-247R — Employers' Contribution to Pensioners' Premiums under Provincial Medical and Hospital Services Plans

[*IT-247R — Employers' Contribution to Pensioners' Premiums under Provincial Medical and Hospital Services Plans is dated August 25, 1975.*]

Reference: Subparagraph 56(1)(*a*)(i) (also subsection 6(3)).

1. A former employer may pay contributions or premiums on behalf of a pensioner to a provincial hospital and medical care insurance plan. For the purpose of this bulletin "pensioner" includes early retirees and disabled pensioners who have severed all employer-employee relationships with the person making the contributions.

2. Where these amounts are paid on account of an obligation arising out of an agreement made by the former employer with the former employee (or with a union on his behalf) immediately prior to, during or immediately after the former period of employment, they are taxable under paragraph 6(3)(*b*).

3. Where paragraph 6(3)(*b*) does not apply, the amounts are considered to be "superannuation or pension benefits" whether they are paid out of the former employer's pension funds or from his general funds (i.e., sources other than a superannuation or pension fund or plan), and as such are subject to tax in the hands of the pensioner pursuant to paragraph 56(1)(*a*). However, this treatment in respect of payments from general funds will only be applied to payments that are made in respect of former employees who became pensioners on or after the date of this bulletin.

4. A pensioner who is no longer required to contribute to a provincial hospital and medical insurance plan may receive amounts from his former employer equivalent to the premium or portion thereof that was being paid on his behalf. These are generally subject to tax in the manner described in paragraphs 2 and 3 above.

5. Where these contributions or premiums are taxable in the hands of a pensioner, they will be deductible to the employer as an allowable outlay or expense for the purpose of gaining or producing income pursuant to paragraph 18(1)(*a*).

¶17,090 IT-301R — Death Benefits — Qualifying Payments

[*IT-301R — Death Benefits — Qualifying Payments is dated April 6, 1976.*]

Reference: Subparagraph 56(1)(*a*)(iii) (also paragraph 61(2)(*c*)).

1. The term "death benefit" as used in subparagraph 56(1)(*a*)(iii) and paragraph 61(2)(*c*) of the Act is defined in subsection 248(1) to mean the gross amounts received in a taxation year by any person upon or after the death of an employee in recognition of his service in an office or employment minus the deductions permitted by that subsection. The "qualifying" or "non-qualifying" payments discussed in paragraphs 2 and 3 below are not all-inclusive. In paragraph 2 the payments are the gross amounts received before the deductions specified in subsection 248(1). Such deductions are discussed in Interpretation Bulletin IT-237 entitled "Death Benefits — Calculation".

Qualifying Payments

2. The following payments are regarded as death benefits:

(*a*) Payments in recognition of the employee's service even though the payments continue for a long time on a periodic basis, or for the lifetime of the recipient, if they were made under an employer's fund or plan that is distinctly separate from a superannuation or pension fund or plan.

(*b*) Payments in recognition of service of an employee who dies prior to retirement that represent a settlement of his accumulated sick leave credits to which the employee was entitled under the terms of his employment.

Non-Qualifying Payments

3. The following are not regarded as death benefits and therefore are not subject to the reduction under subsection 248(1) of the amount to be included in income under other provisions of the Act.

(*a*) A payment received out of a superannuation or pension fund or plan upon or after the death of an officer or employee.

(*b*) Where an employee dies prior to retirement, a payment in respect of accumulated vacation leave not taken by him before his death.

(*c*) A death benefit paid under the Canada or Quebec Pension Plan.

(*d*) A payment representing deferred employment income that would have been taxable in the employee's hands under subsection 6(3) if he had not died.

Taxation of Death Benefits

4. Subparagraph 56(1)(*a*)(iii) brings into a recipient's income death benefits (the net amount) received in the year. However, a payment or payments received as death benefits in the year of death or within one year after that year entitle a recipient who is not an estate or trust (see Interpretation Bulletin No. IT-245) to claim the deduction under subsection 61(1) in respect of the purchase of an income-averaging annuity contract.

Public Servants of the Federal Government

5. Under Part II of the *Public Service Superannuation Act*, public servants of the Federal Government make contributions to the Public Service "Supplementary Death Benefit" Plan for which a specific account is established separate from the Superannuation Plan. Since this plan is in substance a group term life insurance plan, contributions thereto are not deductible in computing income nor are the benefits payable thereunder income as death benefits or otherwise.

Superannuation or Pension Benefit

6. As provided in subsection 248(1), a superannuation or pension benefit includes any amount received out of or under a superannuation or pension fund or plan. This specific provision is considered to override the definition of a death benefit in subsection 248(1); thus payments from such funds or plans cannot qualify as death benefits in any circumstances.

¶17,095 IT-339R2 — Meaning of "Private Health Services Plan"

[*IT-339R2 — Meaning of "Private Health Services Plan" is dated August 8, 1989.]*

Reference: Subsection 248(1) (also paragraphs 6(1)(*a*), 18(1)(*a*) and 118.2(2)(*q*) and 118.2(3)(*b*)).

Application

The provisions discussed below are effective for the 1988 and subsequent taxation years. For taxation years prior to 1988, refer to Interpretation Bulletin IT-339R dated June 1, 1983.

Summary

This bulletin discusses the meaning of a "private health services plan" and describes some of the arrangements for covering the cost of medical and hospital care under such a plan. It also discusses the tax status of contributions made to such a plan by an employer on behalf of an employee and the circumstances under which the premium costs incurred by an employee qualify as medical expenses for purposes of the medical expense tax credit.

Discussion and Interpretation

Contributions made by an employer to or under a private health services plan on behalf of an employee are excluded from the employee's income from an office or employment by virtue of subparagraph 6(1)(*a*)(i). On the other hand, an amount paid by an employee as a premium, contribution or other consideration to a private health services plan qualifies as a medical expense for purposes of the medical expense tax credit by virtue of paragraph 118.2(2)(*q*). The amounts so paid must be for one or more of

(a) the employee,

(b) the employee's spouse, and

(c) any member of the employee's household with whom the employee is connected by blood relationship, marriage or adoption.

For further comments on the medical expense tax credit see the current version of IT-519.

For purposes of the Act, a "private health services plan" is defined in subsection 248(1).

2. The contracts of insurance and medical or hospital care insurance plans referred to in paragraphs (*a*) and (*b*) of the definition in subsection 248(1) of "private health services plan" include contracts or plans that are either in whole or in part in respect of dental care and expenses.

3. A private health services plan qualifying under paragraphs (*a*) or (*b*) of the definition in subsection 248(1) is a plan in the nature of insurance. In this respect the plan must contain the following basic elements:

(a) an undertaking by one person,

(b) to indemnify another person,

(c) for an agreed consideration,

(d) from a loss or liability in respect of an event,

(e) the happening of which is uncertain.

4. Coverage under a plan must be in respect of hospital care or expense or medical care or expense which normally would otherwise have qualified as a medical expense under the provisions of subsection 118.2(2) in the determination of the medical expense tax credit (see IT-519).

5. If the agreed consideration is in the form of cash premiums, they usually relate closely to the coverage provided by the plan and are based on computations involving actuarial or similar studies. Plans involving contracts of insurance in an arm's length situation normally contain the basic elements outlined in 3 above.

6. In a "cost plus" plan an employer contracts with a trusteed plan or insurance company for the provision of indemnification of employees' claims on defined risks under the plan. The employer promises to reimburse the cost of such claims plus an administration fee to the plan or insurance company. The employee's contract of employment requires the employer to reimburse the plan or insurance company for proper claims (filed by the employee) paid, and a contract exists between the employee and the trusteed plan or insurance company in which the latter agrees to

indemnify the employee for claims on the defined risks so long as the employment contract is in good standing. Provided that the risks to be indemnified are those described in paragraphs (*a*) and (*b*) of the definition of "private health services plan" in subsection 248(1), such a plan qualifies as a private health services plan.

7. An arrangement where an employer reimburses its employees for the cost of medical or hospital care may come within the definition of private health services plan. This occurs where the employer is obligated under the employment contract to reimburse such expenses incurred by the employees or their dependants. The consideration given by the employee is considered to be the employee's covenants as found in the collective agreement or in the contract of service.

8. Medical and hospital insurance plans offered by Blue Cross and various life insurers, for example, are considered private health services plans within the meaning of subsection 248(1). In addition, the Group Surgical Medical Insurance Plan covering federal government employees qualifies as a private health services plan within the meaning of subsection 248(1). Therefore, payments made by an individual under any such plan qualify as medical expenses by virtue of paragraph 118.2(2)(*q*).

9. Private health services plan premiums, contributions or other consideration paid for by the employer are not included as medical expenses of the employee under paragraph 118.2(2)(*q*) by virtue of paragraph 118.2(3)(*b*) and are not employee benefits (see 1 above). They are however, business outlays or expenses of the employer for purposes of paragraph 18(1)(*a*). On the other hand, contributions or premiums qualify as medical expenses under paragraph 118.2(2)(*q*) where they are paid directly by the employee, or are paid by the employer out of deductions from the employee's pay. The amounts so paid must be for one or more of

(a) the employee,

(b) the employee's spouse, and

(c) any member of the employee's household with whom the employee is connected by blood relationship, marriage or adoption.

¶17,100 IT-428 — Wage Loss Replacement Plans

[*IT-428 — Wage Loss Replacement Plans is dated April 30, 1979.*]

Reference: Paragraph 6(1)(*f*) (also paragraph 6(1)(*a*) of the Act and section 19 of the *Income Tax Application Rules, 1971* (ITAR)).

1. Paragraph 6(1)(*f*) provides that, for 1972 and subsequent taxation years, amounts received on a periodic basis by an employee or an ex-employee as compensation for loss of income from an office or employment, that were payable under a sickness, accident, disability or income

maintenance insurance plan (in this bulletin referred to as a "wage loss replacement plan") to which the employer made a contribution, are to be included in income, but subject to a reduction as specified in that paragraph for contributions made by the employee to the plan after 1967. Before 1972, such amounts received by a taxpayer were not included in income.

2. Paragraph 6(1)(*f*) does not apply to a self-employed person inasmuch as any amount received by such person in the way of an income maintenance payment would not be compensation for loss of income from an office or employment. With regard to "overhead expense insurance" and "income insurance" of a self-employed person, see Interpretation Bulletin IT-223.

Exemption for Plans Established before June 19, 1971

3. Transitional provisions in section 19 of the *Income Tax Application Rules, 1971* stipulate that amounts that would otherwise be included in income under paragraph 6(1)(*f*) are to be excluded if they were received pursuant to a plan that existed on June 18, 1971 and were in consequence of an event that occurred prior to 1974. Comments on these transitional provisions, particularly with regard to admissible and non-admissible changes in pre-June 19, 1971 plans, appear in IT-54. It is to be noted that, for 1974 and subsequent taxation years, the exemption in section 19 of the ITAR is applicable only if amounts received by a taxpayer are attributable to an event occurring before 1974. In this context, the word "event" has reference to the thing that caused the disability. In the case of an accident, for example, although the effect on the taxpayer's health may not have become noticeable or serious until 1974 or a later year, the "event" would have occurred before 1974 if the accident took place before 1974 and the later disability was directly attributable to the accident. Similarly, in the case of a degenerative disease such as muscular dystrophy, the "event" is the onset of the disease however much later the incapacity occurs. On the other hand, a recurring disease, such as a seasonal allergy or chronic tonsillitis, would qualify as an "event" only for the particular period of one attack.

4. For an illustration of the calculations involved where both paragraph 6(1)(*f*) of the Act and section 19 of the ITAR apply to a particular taxpayer, in different taxation years, see 25 below.

Meaning of a "Wage Loss Replacement Plan"

5. In the Department's view, a plan to which paragraph 6(1)(*f*) applies is any arrangement, however it is styled, between an employer and employees, or between an employer and a group or association of employees, under which provision is made for indemnification of an employee, by means of benefits payable on a periodic basis, if an employee

suffers a loss of employment income as a consequence of sickness, maternity or accident. This arrangement may be formal in nature, as evidenced by a contract negotiated between an employer and employees, or it may be informal, arising from an understanding on the part of the employees, that wage loss replacement benefits would be made available to them by the employer. Where the arrangement involves a contract of insurance with an insurance company, the insurance contract becomes part of the plan but does not constitute the plan itself.

6. Where it is apparent that a plan was instituted with the intention or for the purpose of providing wage loss replacement benefits, the assumption will be that it is a plan to which paragraph 6(1)(*f*) applies unless the contrary can be established. Such a plan will be considered to exist where, for example, payments under the plan are to commence only when sick leave credits are exhausted or where benefits are subject to reduction by the amount of any wages or wage loss replacement benefits payable under other plans. A supplementary unemployment benefit plan, as defined in subsection 145(1), is not considered to be a plan to which paragraph 6(1)(*f*) applies.

7. A plan for purposes of paragraph 6(1)(*f*) of the Act and section 19 of the ITAR must be an "insurance" plan. Those provisions are not applicable, therefore, to uninsured employee benefits such as continuing wage or salary payments based on sick leave debits, which payments are included in income under paragraph 6(1)(*a*). It is to be noted that, while a plan must involve insurance, it is not necessary that there be a contract of insurance with an insurance company. If, however, insurance is not provided by an insurance company, the plan must be one that is based on insurance principles, i.e., funds must be accumulated, normally in the hands of trustees or in a trust account, that are calculated to be sufficient to meet anticipated claims. If the arrangement merely consists of an unfunded contingency reserve on the part of the employer, it would not be an insurance plan.

8. An employer may contribute to separate plans for different classes or groups of employees. For example, there may be one plan for clerical staff and another plan for administrative staff. Each plan will be recognized as a separate plan. In other circumstances, an employer may have one plan that provides for short-term sickness benefits and another plan that provides for long-term disability benefits. Each such plan normally would be considered a separate plan for all purposes but, if desired, they may be treated as one plan provided they comply with the following conditions:

(a) the same classes of employees are entitled to participate in both plans, and

(b) the premiums or other cost of each plan is shared in the same ratio by the employer and the employees.

9. An association of employers, or a health and welfare trust that is organized and managed by or on behalf of both employers and employees in a certain industry, may establish a plan with an insurer that is available to all employer-members. In these circumstances, if there is one insurance contract between the insurer and the association of employers or the health and welfare trust and the contract was entered into after June 19, 1971, there is considered to be one plan. Where employees contribute to the cost of benefits provided by a health and welfare trust, see paragraph 6 of IT-85R regarding the amount that may qualify as an employee's contribution for purposes of subparagraph 6(1)(*f*)(v). For plans that existed prior to June 19, 1971, see paragraph 7 of IT-54.

10. Where the nature of employment in a particular industry is such that it is usual for employees to change employers frequently (e.g. the construction industry) and the continuity of wage loss replacement benefits can be assured only if such benefits are provided under a plan administered by a union or a similar association of employees rather than directly by the various employers, the arrangement between the participating employers and the organization representing the employees is viewed as a single wage loss replacement plan.

Lump-sum Payments

11. If a lump-sum payment is made in lieu of periodic payments, that amount will be considered to be income under paragraph 6(1)(*f*).

12. Some contracts of employment may provide for payment of periodic benefits to employees in respect of loss of income due to disability and may also provide that employees will receive a lump-sum payment on retirement, resignation or death based on the value of unused sick leave credits accumulated under that plan. Even though these separate arrangements may be jointly funded by employer-employee contributions, it is the position of the Department that such lump-sum payments are not a periodic payment under a wage loss replacement plan to which paragraph 6(1)(*f*) applies but are taxable in the employee's hands by subsections 5(1) and 6(3) as remuneration received by them pursuant to their contract of employment. To the extent that a part of the lump sum payment has been funded by employee contributions not deducted by the employee under subparagraph 6(1)(*f*)(v) in computing the portion of amounts taxable under paragraph 6(1)(*f*), the accumulated employee contributions in respect thereof (but not any interest credited thereon) would represent a return of capital to employees and need not be included as part of the taxable lump sum payment.

Employee's Contribution

13. Employee contributions that are deductible under subparagraph 6(1)(*f*)(v), are restricted to those that were made to the particular plan from which the benefits were received. Thus, if an employee changes employment and becomes a beneficiary under the plans of the new employer, the employee may not deduct the contributions made during the previous employment from benefits received from the new employer's plan. For this purpose, a change in employment is not considered to take place where an unincorporated business is incorporated or where there has been a merger or amalgamation. Also, the continuity of an existing plan is generally not affected by internal alterations in the plan, such as a change in insurer or an improvement in benefits. However, for purposes of section 19 of ITAR, an increase in benefits after June 18, 1971, in a pre-June 19, 1971 plan may be viewed as the creation of a new plan as indicated in paragraph 4 of IT-54. On the other hand, where an employee, because of a promotion or job reclassification, is moved from one of his employer's plans to another, such as a move from the "general" plan to the "executive" plan, contributions to the former plan would not be deductible in respect of benefits received from the latter plan.

Employer's Contributions

14. For benefits received by an employee under a wage loss replacement plan to be subject to tax in his hands under paragraph 6(1)(*f*), the plan must be one to which the employer has made a contribution out of his own funds. An employer does not make such a contribution to a plan if he merely deducts an amount from an employee's gross salary or wages and remits the amount on the employee's behalf to an insurer. In these circumstances, the employee's remuneration for tax purposes is not reduced by the amount withheld and remitted by the employer to the insurer. Where the employer has made an actual contribution to a plan, paragraph 6(1)(*a*) provides that it is not to be included in the income of the employees if the plan is a "group sickness or accident insurance plan". It is considered that this exemption in paragraph 6(1)(*a*) applies to any of the three types of plans mentioned in paragraph 60(1)(*f*), provided that they are group plans.

15. If an employer should have a plan that is in part a wage loss replacement plan and in part a plan that provides for other types of benefits, the employer must be prepared to identify that part of any premiums paid by him, or other contribution by him to the plan, that relates to the other types of benefits included in the plan and, similarly, the part of the employees' contributions, if any, that relate to the wage loss replacement part of the plan. This information is required to determine whether the wage loss replacement plan is one to which the employer has contrib-

uted and the relevant amount of an employee's contribution for purposes of subparagraph 6(1)(*f*)(v).

Employee-Pay-All Plans

16. An employee-pay-all plan is a plan the entire premium cost of which is paid by one or more employees. Except as indicated under 21 below, benefits out of such a plan are not taxable even if they are paid in consequence of an event occurring after 1973, because an employee-pay-all plan is not a plan within the meaning of paragraph 6(1)(*f*).

17. It is a question of fact whether or not an employee-pay-all plan exists and the onus is generally on the employer to prove the existence of such a plan. It should be emphasized that the Department will not accept a retroactive change to the tax status of a plan. For example, an employer cannot change the tax status of a plan by adding at year end to employees' income the employer contributions to a wage loss replacement plan that would normally be considered to be non-taxable benefits. On the other hand, where an employee-pay-all plan does, in fact, exist and it provides for the employer to pay the employee's premiums to the plan and to account for them in the manner of wages or salary, the result is as though the premiums had been withheld from the employee's wages or salary. That is, the plan maintains its status as an employee-pay-all plan if the plan provided for such an arrangement at the time the payment was made.

18. If, under a wage loss replacement plan, the employer makes contributions for some employees, but not all, the plan will not be considered to be an employee-pay-all plan even for those employees who must make all contributions themselves. It is the Department's view that all payments out of a wage loss replacement plan to which the employer has contributed are subject to the provisions of paragraph 6(1)(*f*) regardless of the fact that the employer's contributions may be on account of specific employees only.

19. Where the terms of a plan clearly establish that it is intended to be an employee-pay-all plan, the plan will be recognized as such even though the employer makes a contribution to it on behalf of an employee during an elimination period (i.e. the period after the disability but before the first payment from the plan becomes due). During this period normally there would be no salary or wages from which the contribution could be deducted. Any amount so contributed by an employer should be reported as remuneration of the employee on whose behalf it was contributed in order to maintain the employee-pay-all character of the plan.

20. Where an employer pays, on behalf of an employee, the premium under a non-group plan that is

(a) a sickness or accident insurance plan,

(b) a disability insurance plan, or

(c) an income maintenance insurance plan,

the payment of the premium is regarded as a taxable benefit to the employee. The payment by the employer is not viewed as a "contribution" by the employer under the plan, and paragraph 6(1)(*f*) does not apply to subject to tax in the employee's hands any benefits received by him pursuant to the plan.

21. Whether or not the benefits an employee receives under a plan are required to be included in his income is governed both by the type of plan in effect at the time of the event that gave rise to them and any changes in the plan subsequent to that time. When a pre-June 19, 1971 plan, or an employee-pay-all plan, is changed and becomes a new taxable plan, an employee who was receiving benefits at the time of the change may continue to receive them tax-free thereafter but only in the amount and for the period specified in the plan as it was before the change. Where the new taxable plan provides any increase in benefits, whether by increases in amounts or through extension of the benefit period, the additional benefits must be included in income since they flow from the new taxable plan. Where an employee is receiving benefits under a taxable plan at a time when it is converted to a new employee-pay-all plan, the benefits he continues to receive subsequent to the date of conversion, to the extent that they were provided for in the old plan, will remain of an income nature because they continue to flow from the old taxable plan.

Claimant's Survivors

22. If the payment of wage loss replacement benefits should continue after the death of an employee who was receiving such benefits, paragraph 6(1)(*f*) is not applicable to such benefits paid to the widow or other dependent for the reason that the amounts received do not relate to a loss of income from an office or employment of the recipient. Such payments, however, may be viewed as being received in recognition of the deceased employee's service in an office or employment and be included in income as a death benefit if they exceed the exemption provided in subsection 248(1).

Information Returns

23. Paragraph 200(2)(*f*) of the *Income Tax Regulations* stipulates that every person who makes payments pursuant to a wage loss replacement plan is required to file a Form T4A information return. The law does not require that income tax be deducted from such payments.

U.I.C. Employee Premium Rebate

24. A wage loss replacement plan may qualify the employer for a reduction in unemployment insurance premiums under subsection 64(4) of the *Unemployment Insurance Act, 1971*. This subsection also provides

that five-twelfths of any such reduction must be used by the employer for the benefit of his employees. The benefit may be conferred directly by the employer, indirectly through an employees health and welfare trust or in any other manner, but it will only be tax-free in an employee's hands if it is conferred in the form of a benefit specifically exempt from taxation by paragraph 6(1)(*a*).

Computation of Benefit

25. The following is an example of the computation of the amount of payments received under a wage loss replacement plan that is included in income pursuant to paragraph 6(1)(*f*):

Assume:

(a) Employee's contributions (in addition to employer's contributions)

Year	*Amounts*	*Cumulative balance*
1968-71	$ 110 per annum	$ 440
1972	120	560
1973	140	700
1974	140	840
1975	140	980
1976	140	1,120
1977	160	1,280

(b) payments received

1972	$ 200	$ 200
1973	300	500
1974	240	740
1975	1,000	1,740
1976	100	1,840
1977	1,000	2,840

(c) The plan was in existence prior to June 19, 1971 and remains unchanged.

(d) The payments received out of the plan in 1974, 1975, 1976 and 1977 are as a result of events occuring after 1973.

Amount Included In Income:

1972 and 1973 —

none of the payments received are income because of section 19 of the ITAR

1974 — lesser of:

(a) payments received in 1974.... $ 240

(b) aggregate of payments received after 1971	$ 740		
less: aggregate of contributions made after 1967	840	NIL	
amount to be included under paragraph 6(1)(*f*)			NIL
1975 — lesser of:			
(a) payments received in 1975....		$1,000	
(b) payments received in 1975 ...	$1,740		
less: aggregate of contributions made after 1967	980	760	
amount to be included under paragraph 6(1)(*f*)			$ 760
1976 — lesser of:			
(a) payments received in 1976....		$ 100	
(b) payments received in 1976 ...	$ 100		
less: contributions made in 1976	140	NIL	
amount to be included under paragraph 6(1)(*f*)			NIL
1977 — lesser of:			
(a) payments received in 1977....		$1,000	
(b) payments received since the most recent year during which a benefit was taxable under this provision (1975) ..	$1,100		
less: contributions made since 1975	300	800	
amount to be included under paragraph 6(1)(*f*)			$ 800

¶17,105 IT-519R — Medical Expense and Disability Tax Credits and Attendant Care Expense Deduction

[*IT-519R — Medical Expense and Disability Tax Credits and Attendant Care Expense Deduction is dated February 20, 1995.*]

Reference: Sections 64, 118.2, 118.3 and 118.4 of the *Income Tax Act* (also sections 64.1, 118, 118.7 and 118.8; subsections 6(16), 110.4(2), 117(2) and 117(7) and paragraph 117.1(1)(*b*) of the Act and section 5700 of the Income Tax Regulations.

Application

This bulletin cancels and replaces Interpretation Bulletin IT-519 dated March 31, 1989. Unless otherwise indicated, the provisions outlined below have been in effect since at least the 1992 taxation year.

Summary

An individual may claim a non-refundable tax credit for medical expenses (referred to in this bulletin as the "medical expense tax credit") when calculating Part I tax payable. The amount of the medical expense tax credit is determined by multiplying the lowest personal tax rate percentage (17% in 1994) by the amount of qualifying medical expenses in excess of certain minimum amounts.

An individual who has a severe and prolonged mental or physical impairment as certified by a medical doctor or optometrist may claim a non-refundable "disability tax credit" when calculating Part I tax payable. The amount of the disability tax credit is determined by multiplying the lowest personal tax rate percentage by $4,233 (for 1994). In addition, the unused portion of the individual's disability tax credit may be transferred to the individual's spouse or to a "supporting individual".

Individuals with a disability entitling them to the disability tax credit may also claim, under certain conditions, a deduction for amounts paid for attendant care enabling them to earn certain types of income. The maximum amount that may be claimed as a deduction is $5,000.

When a medical expense or disability tax credit relates to a non-resident or a part-year resident, please refer to the current versions of Interpretation Bulletin IT-171, *Non-Resident Individuals — Computation of Taxable Income Earned in Canada and Non-Refundable Tax Credits*, or Interpretation Bulletin IT-193, *Part-Year Residents — Computation of Taxable Income and Non-Refundable Tax Credits.*

Discussion and Interpretation

1. The topics covered in this bulletin are as follows:

Severe and Prolonged Impairment

2. Subsection 118.4(1) of the *Income Tax Act* contains a set of rules that define certain terms for purposes of the section 118.3 disability tax credit and also for some section 118.2 medical expense tax credit claims. There will be subsequent references back to this paragraph (and to 3 below), when applicable. Subsection 118.4(1) provides the following rules:

(a) An impairment is prolonged when it has lasted, or may reasonably be expected to last, for a continuous period of at least 12 months.

(b) An individual's ability to perform a basic activity of daily living is markedly restricted only when, all or substantially all of the time, even with therapy and the use of appropriate devices and medication, the individual is blind or is unable (or requires an inordinate amount of time) to perform such an activity.

(c) A basic activity of daily living in relation to an individual means:

(i) perceiving, thinking and remembering;

(ii) feeding and dressing oneself;

(iii) speaking so as to be understood, in a quiet setting, by another person familiar with the individual;

(iv) hearing so as to understand, in a quiet setting, by another person familiar with the individual;

(v) eliminating (bowel or bladder functions); or

(vi) walking.

(d) No other activity including working, housekeeping or a social or recreational activity is considered a basic activity of daily living.

In addition to blindness, examples of other disabling conditions that could satisfy the rules discussed above are severe cardio-respiratory failure, severe mental impairment, profound bilateral deafness, and functional impairment of the neuro- or musculo-skeletal systems.

3. Subsection 118.3(4) provides that Revenue Canada may obtain the advice of Health Canada (now Human Resources Development Canada) as to whether the individual has a severe and prolonged impairment that markedly restricts his or her ability to perform a basic activity of daily living. Subsection 118.3(4) also stipulates that any person who is referred to in subsection 118.3(1) or 118.3(2) shall, at the written request of Health Canada (now Human Resources Development Canada), provide that department with information about the individual's impairment, and how he or she is affected by the impairment. This gives Health Canada (now Human Resources Development Canada) the authority to request, from the individual with the impairment, from a supporting individual who claims the credit, or from the certifying doctor or optometrist, more information to determine if the individual with the impairment is entitled to the credit.

References to Medical Professionals

4. This bulletin uses the terms "medical doctor", "medical practitioner", as well as various other terms to describe individuals involved in the medical profession, in a way that is consistent with the terms found in the *Income Tax Act*. The term "medical doctor" is used in section 118.3 for purposes of the disability tax credit. Section 118.2, on the other hand, uses the term "medical practitioner" for purposes of the medical expense tax credit. "Medical practitioner" encompasses a broad range of individuals in the medical profession including medical doctors (see 5 below).

5. For purposes of the medical expense and disability tax credits under sections 118.2 and 118.3, subsection 118.4(2) provides that a reference to a medical practitioner, dentist, pharmacist, nurse or optometrist

means a person who is authorized to practice as such according to the following laws:

(a) for a service rendered to an individual, the laws of the jurisdiction in which the service is rendered;

(b) for a certificate issued for an individual, the laws of the jurisdiction in which the individual resides or of a province; and

(c) for a prescription issued to an individual, the laws of the jurisdiction in which the individual resides, of a province or of the jurisdiction in which the prescription is filled.

Medical practitioners authorized to practice in accordance with the above laws can include (depending on the applicable province or jurisdiction, as the case may be) the following:

(i) an osteopath;

(ii) a chiropractor;

(iii) a naturopath;

(iv) a therapeutist (or therapist);

(v) a physiotherapist;

(vi) a chiropodist (or podiatrist);

(vii) a Christian Science practitioner;

(viii) a psychoanalyst who is a member of the Canadian Institute of Psychoanalysis or a member of the Quebec Association of Jungian Psychoanalysts;

(ix) a psychologist;

(x) a qualified speech-language pathologist or audiologist such as, for example, a person who is certified as such by The Canadian Association of Speech-Language Pathologists and Audiologists ("CASLPA") or a provincial affiliate of that organization;

(xi) an occupational therapist who is a member of the Canadian Institute of Occupational Therapists;

(xii) an acupuncturist; and

(xiii) a dietician.

Additionally, a "nurse" includes a practical nurse whose full-time occupation is nursing as well as a Christian Science nurse authorized to practice according to the relevant laws referred to in subsection 118.4(2).

Disability Tax Credit

6. Subsection 118.3(1) provides the formula for determining the disability tax credit for an individual who has a severe and prolonged mental or

physical impairment (for the sake of brevity, referred to in this bulletin as the "disabled person"). Under the formula, the disability tax credit for a particular year is determined by taking a fixed amount (which will increase from one taxation year to the next each time there is an annual indexation adjustment) and multiplying that amount by the lowest tax rate percentage referred to in subsection 117(2). For 1994, the disability tax credit is 17% of $4,233 = $720. For a taxation year other than 1994, the fixed amount and the lowest tax rate percentage can be found in the T1 General income tax return for that year.

7. Subsection 118.3(1) also requires that the effects of the disabled person's severe and prolonged mental or physical impairment be such that his or her ability to perform a basic activity of daily living is markedly restricted. This must be certified in prescribed form by a medical doctor, or where the impairment is an impairment of sight, a medical doctor or an optometrist. Form T2201, *Disability Tax Credit Certificate*, is to be used for this purpose and filed with the disabled person's income tax return. The Department may not require that a new Form T2201 be filed for each year after the first year for which the form is filed — for further particulars, see the T1 General income tax return and guide. See 2 above regarding the meanings of "prolonged", "basic activity of daily living" and "markedly restricted". See also 3 above.

8. Under certain circumstances, the unused portion of the disability tax credit of a disabled person who is resident in Canada at any time in the year may be transferred under subsection 118.3(2) to another individual (the "supporting individual") who supports the disabled person. Such a transfer may be made if one of the following occurs:

(a) The supporting individual has claimed a personal tax credit for the disabled person

(i) under paragraph 118(1)(*b*) (an equivalent-to-spouse tax credit); or

(ii) under paragraph 118(1)(*d*) (a dependant tax credit), if the disabled person is the supporting individual's child or grandchild.

(b) The supporting individual could have claimed a personal tax credit described in (a) above (where the disabled person is the supporting individual's parent, grandparent, child or grandchild) if the supporting individual were not married and the disabled person had no income for the year and had reached the age of 18 before the end of the year.

9. The amount of disability tax credit that may be transferred to and claimed by the supporting individual under subsection 118.3(2) is the excess of the amount that the disabled person may claim for the year as a disability tax credit under subsection 118.3(1) over the disabled person's

Part I tax payable determined before deducting any tax credits except the personal, age and pension tax credits under section 118 and the tax credit under section 118.7 for unemployment insurance premiums and for Canada and Quebec Pension Plans contributions. When more than one individual is entitled under subsection 118.3(2) to deduct a tax credit transferred from the same disabled person for a taxation year, subsection 118.3(3) limits the total of all such deductions for that year to the maximum amount that could be claimed by one individual for that year if that individual were the only one entitled to use subsection 118.3(2) to claim a tax credit transferred from that disabled person. If the individuals fail to agree on the portions to be claimed, the Minister may fix the portions.

10. There is also a provision, section 118.8, which allows (subject to certain limitations) one spouse to transfer to the other spouse certain unused tax credits, including the unused portion of the transferring spouse's disability tax credit (if any). More information is available at "Line 326 — Amounts transferred from your spouse" in the T1 General income tax return and guide. If a disabled person's spouse claims any non-refundable tax credit in the year for the disabled person under section 118 or 118.8 (i.e., any personal tax credit for the disabled person or any tax credit transferred from the disabled person), a third person will not be entitled to a subsection 118.3(2) transfer of a disability tax credit from the disabled person for the same year, even if that third person qualifies as a "supporting individual" of the disabled person. For taxation years after 1992, the extended meaning of "spouse" in paragraph 252(4)(a) is applicable.

11. Neither the disability tax credit outlined in 6 above nor the transfer of the disability tax credit outlined in 8 to 10 above may be claimed if the cost of nursing home care or remuneration for an attendant (subject to one exception, mentioned in 29 below) for the disabled person is included as a qualifying medical expense under section 118.2 in calculating a medical expense tax credit of the disabled person or of any other person.

Medical Expense Tax Credit

12. Any individual may deduct a medical expense tax credit determined by the formula under subsection 118.2(1). Under the formula, assuming there is no adjustment as described in 18 below, the allowable portion of the qualifying medical expenses claimed is the portion of those expenses that exceeds the lesser of the following two amounts: a fixed amount ($1,614 for 1994 — this will increase in subsequent years each time there is an annual indexation adjustment), or 3% of the individual's net income for the year. The allowable portion of the expenses is multiplied by the lowest tax rate percentage for the year (17% for 1994) to determine the medical expense tax credit. For example, assume that an individual,

whose net income for 1994 is $50,000, claims $5,000 of qualifying medical expenses. Since 3% of $50,000 = $1,500 is less than the 1994 fixed amount of $1,614, the individual's medical expense tax credit is 17% of ($5,000 - $1,500) = $595. For a taxation year other than 1994, the fixed amount and lowest tax rate percentage can be obtained from the T1 General income tax return for that year. Forward averaged amounts included in taxable income under subsection 110.4(2) do not form part of an individual's net income upon which the 3% calculation is based.

13. To qualify for the medical expense tax credit, the medical expenses must have been paid or deemed to have been paid (see 66 below) by either the individual or his or her legal representative for qualifying medical expenses as provided for in subsection 118.2(2) (see 21 below). Furthermore, the medical expenses used in calculating a medical expense tax credit for a particular taxation year:

(a) must have been paid within any 12-month period ending in the calendar year, unless the individual died in the year; in which case, the medical expenses must have been paid within any 24-month period that includes the date of death (see 19 and 20 below);

(b) must be proven by filing supporting receipts (see 68 below);

(c) must not have been used in calculating a previous year's medical expense tax credit; and

(d) must not have been reimbursed or be reimbursable (see 67 below).

14. An individual's qualifying medical expenses are not restricted to those incurred or paid in Canada but they must have been paid on behalf of the individual, the individual's spouse or a dependant of the individual. The word "patient" is used in the law and throughout this bulletin to refer to the individual or to the individual's spouse or dependant, as the case may be, on whose behalf the individual's qualifying medical expenses are paid.

15. For purposes of the medical expense tax credit, a person qualifies as a "dependant" of the individual for a particular taxation year if the following conditions are met:

(a) The person must be the child, grandchild, parent, grandparent, brother, sister, uncle, aunt, niece or nephew of the individual or of the individual's spouse.

(b) The person must be dependent on the individual for support at some time in the year.

(c) The person must be a resident of Canada at some time in the year. This residence requirement does not apply if the person is the child or grandchild of the individual or of the individual's spouse.

For a taxation year prior to the 1993 year, the individual could claim the medical expenses of a dependant only if the individual could claim a section 118 personal tax credit for the dependant (the individual would not have been entitled to such a tax credit, for example, if the dependant's net income had been too high; see, however, 18 below).

16. If a medical expense was incurred in one year on behalf of a spouse or dependant but is not paid until the following year at a time when such person is no longer a spouse or a dependant, the expense can nevertheless qualify in the year of payment since the person referred to is only required to have been a spouse or a dependant at the time the expense was incurred.

17. An individual may use the medical expenses of a spouse or a separated spouse regardless of that spouse's income in the taxation year. A receipt in the name of a husband or wife is considered acceptable for a medical expense of either, and the amount of that expense may be used by either, as agreed between them.

18. Commencing in the 1993 year, an adjustment must be made to the individual's medical expense tax credit if the medical expenses claimed include those paid on behalf of a "dependant" (the term "dependant" is explained in 15 above and does not include the individual's spouse) and the dependant has net income for the year which exceeds the "basic personal amount". (The basic personal amount is the base for calculating the paragraph 118(1)(*c*) individual tax credit. It is $6,456 for 1994 and will increase in subsequent years each time there is an annual indexation adjustment.) In the situation described above, there are two ways of calculating the adjustment. The first way is to follow the formula in subsection 118.2(1), which provides that the medical expense tax credit, as calculated in the manner described in 12 above, must be reduced by 68% of the excess of the dependant's net income over the basic personal amount. In the example in 12 above, in which the individual has net income for 1994 of $50,000 and claims qualifying medical expenses for that year of $5,000, the individual's medical expense tax credit would generally be 17% of ($5,000 - $1,500) = $595. Assume also, however, that the $5,000 in medical expenses claimed by the individual includes $4,000 paid on behalf of a dependant whose net income is $7,000. The formula in subsection 118.2(1) requires that the $595 tax credit be reduced by 68% of ($7,000 - $6,456) = $370. The reduced medical expense tax credit would therefore be $595 - $370 = $225. The second way of calculating the adjustment is to reduce the qualifying medical expenses claimed by four times the excess of the dependant's net income over the basic personal amount. In the above example, the reduction to the qualifying medical expenses claimed would be 4 × ($7,000 - $6,456) = $2,176. The individual's medical expense tax credit would therefore be calculated as 17% of ($5,000 - $1,500 - $2,176) =

$225. Using the latter method makes it easier to determine whether it is to the individual's benefit to claim the medical expenses paid on behalf of the dependant. In the above example, if the dependant's net income was $8,000 instead of $7,000, the reduction to the medical expenses claimed would be 4 × ($8,000 - $6,456) = $6,176. Since this reduction would be more than the $4,000 expenses paid on behalf of the dependant, it would not be to the individual's benefit to claim those expenses.

For taxation years prior to 1993, if the dependant had net income that was high enough to prevent the individual from claiming a section 118 personal tax credit for the dependant (see 15 above), subsection 117(7) nevertheless allowed the individual to claim the medical expenses paid on behalf of the dependant as long as the individual added to his or her tax otherwise payable (i.e., in calculating the "basic federal tax" on the T1 General income tax return) 68% of the excess of the dependant's net income over the basic personal amount.

Option on Death of Individual

19. Whereas a living individual may include only medical expenses paid or deemed to have been paid within any 12-month period ending in the calendar year, in the case of a deceased individual, subsection 118.2(1) permits the inclusion of expenses paid within any 24-month period that includes the date of death.

20. If the legal representative of a deceased individual has filed a return for the year of death and has subsequently (but within the time period specified for a deceased individual in 19 above) paid additional medical expenses, an adjustment in qualifying medical expenses and in the medical expense tax credit will be made, if requested, to reflect such payments.

Qualifying Medical Expenses

21. Subsection 118.2(2) describes in detail the types of medical expenses that may qualify for the medical expense tax credit. Some of these expenses are described in the following paragraphs.

Payments to Medical Practitioners, Hospitals, etc.

22. Paragraph 118.2(2)(*a*) allows an individual to include, as a qualifying medical expense, an amount paid to a medical practitioner, dentist or nurse or a public or licensed private hospital for medical or dental services provided to the patient (for the meaning of "patient", see 14 above). The rules for determining whether a person is a medical practitioner, dentist or nurse for purposes of the medical expense tax credit are discussed in (a) to (c) of 5 above. Also shown in 5 above is a list of certain types of medical practitioners that (depending on the applicable province or jurisdiction) may meet these rules. Although some of the medical practitioners in that

list are not doctors, the Department considers that their fees can qualify as being "for medical services", for purposes of a claim under paragraph 118.2(2)(*a*), to the extent that the fees are for diagnostic, therapeutic or rehabilitative services.

23. Payments made to partnerships, societies and associations for medical services rendered by their employees or partners are qualifying medical expenses as long as the person who provided the service is a medical practitioner, dentist or nurse authorized to practice in accordance with the laws discussed in 5(a) to (c) above. For example, the Arthritis Society employs physiotherapists to provide medical services to persons suffering from arthritis and rheumatism. Payments made to that society for the services of such employees are qualifying medical expenses. Other similar organizations are the Victorian Order of Nurses and The Canadian Red Cross Society Home Maker Services. Payments qualify only to the extent that they are for the period when the patient is at home. Payments for a period when the nurse is simply looking after a home and children when the patient is in hospital or otherwise away from home do not qualify since these would be personal or living expenses. In some instances, such as that of the Canadian Mothercraft Society, the visiting worker instead of the society may give the receipts but, if the worker can be regarded as being a practical nurse, those receipts will be accepted.

24. If there is doubt as to whether an institution is a licensed private hospital (see 22 above), a Revenue Canada tax services office should be contacted for an opinion on the matter. Individuals should not rely on the name of the institution, since some hospitals do not have the word "hospital" in their official title. Possession of a municipal licence to carry on business does not necessarily qualify the institution. However, if the institution possesses a municipal licence designating it as a "hospital", subject to its meeting and maintaining standards set by local health, building and fire authorities, the institution may qualify as a hospital for income tax purposes.

25. When an institution is situated in another country and there is doubt as to whether it qualifies for purposes of the Act, the individual should obtain full particulars of the state or other licence under which it operates. The individual should also obtain details of the professional qualifications of the medical staff in attendance and of the medical or remedial care given to the patient to whom the expense relates. Doubtful cases may be referred, with full particulars, to any Revenue Canada tax services office.

Care of Individual with Mental or Physical Impairment

26. Paragraph 118.2(2)(*b*) allows an individual to include, as a qualifying medical expense, remuneration paid for one full-time attendant upon,

or the cost of full-time care in a nursing home (see 33 below) of, a patient who has a severe and prolonged mental or physical impairment (see 2 and 3 above). The patient on whose behalf these medical expenses are paid must be a disabled person for whom a disability tax credit could be claimed (i.e., either by the disabled person or by some other person, in accordance with the rules outlined earlier in this bulletin) for the taxation year in which these medical expenses were incurred if it were not for the rule described in 29 below. Also, for purposes of the medical expense tax credit, paragraph 118.2(2)(*b*) provides that, at the time the remuneration is paid, the full-time attendant cannot be under 18 years of age or be the individual's spouse.

27. Paragraph 118.2(2)(*b*.1) allows an individual to include, as a qualifying medical expense, remuneration paid for attendant care in Canada of a patient who has a severe and prolonged mental or physical impairment (see 2 and 3 above). The claim for these expenses cannot be more than $5,000 ($10,000 if the patient died in the year). At the time the remuneration is paid, the attendant must not be under 18 years of age or be the individual's spouse. The patient must be a disabled person for whom a disability tax credit can be claimed (i.e., either by the disabled person or by another person) for the taxation year in which the attendant care is given. The individual must file receipts (see 68 below), issued by the payee, for payment of remuneration for the attendant care. If the payee is an individual, such receipts should include that individual's social insurance number. It should be noted that remuneration paid for the attendant care of the patient cannot be claimed under paragraph 118.2(2)(*b*.1) if, for the taxation year in which that remuneration is paid, a section 63 child care expense deduction or a section 64 attendant care expense deduction (see 69 to 72 below) is claimed for the patient or if medical expenses paid on behalf of the patient are claimed (for purposes of calculating a medical expense tax credit) under paragraph 118.2(2)(*b*) as described above or under one of the provisions described in 30 to 33 below. While most claims under paragraph 118.2(2)(*b*.1) will be for a part-time attendant, a full-time attendant could also be claimed under that provision (as long as the above-mentioned dollar limit is observed) in order not to prevent a claim for the disability tax credit (see 29 below).

28. Note that only amounts for salary or remuneration that are actually paid will qualify as medical expenses under paragraph 118.2(2)(*b*) or (*b*.1). Imputed salary or remuneration will not qualify since no actual payment is made.

29. As noted in 11 above, when an individual includes, as a qualifying medical expense, remuneration for an attendant or the cost of nursing home care for a patient, neither that individual nor any other person may claim the disability tax credit or its transfer referred to in 6 and 8 to 10

above for that patient. As an exception to this rule, the disability tax credit can still be claimed if remuneration for an attendant is claimed under paragraph 118.2(2)(*b*.1), which is subject to a dollar limit (see 27 above). Also, when attendant care expenses are included as qualifying medical expenses under any provision in subsection 118.2(2) for purposes of the medical expense tax credit, the same expenses cannot be deducted under section 64 (see 69 to 72 below) when determining the patient's income.

Care in a Self-Contained Domestic Establishment

30. An individual may include, as a qualifying medical expense, remuneration paid for a full-time attendant for a patient in a self-contained domestic establishment in which the patient lives, provided that the following conditions in paragraph 118.2(2)(*c*) are met:

(a) A medical practitioner certifies that, because of mental or physical infirmity, the patient is, and will likely continue for a prolonged period of indefinite duration to be, dependent on others for personal needs and care and, as a result, requires a full-time attendant.

(b) At the time the remuneration is paid, the attendant is neither the individual's spouse nor under 18 years of age.

(c) Receipts for payments to the attendant must be issued by the payee and include, if the payee is an individual, his or her social insurance number.

Note that only amounts for salary or remuneration that are actually paid will qualify as medical expenses under paragraph 118.2(2)(*c*). Imputed salary or remuneration will not qualify since no actual payment is made.

Care Due to Lack of Normal Mental Capacity

31. Amounts that the individual has paid for the cost of full-time care in a nursing home (see 33 below) for a patient qualify under paragraph 118.2(2)(*d*) as medical expenses if the patient, due to lack of normal mental capacity, is and apparently will continue to be dependent upon others for personal needs and care. Receipts from the nursing home and a certificate from a medical practitioner are required to support a claim for an expenditure of this nature (see 68 below).

Care in an Institution

32. The costs paid for the care, or the care and training, of a patient at a school, institution or other place will qualify under paragraph 118.2(2)(*e*) as a medical expense when an appropriately qualified person has certified that patient to be a person who, by reason of a physical or mental impairment, requires the equipment, facilities or personnel specially provided by that place. For purposes of paragraph 118.2(2)(*e*),

"other place" includes an out-patient clinic and also includes a nursing home (see 33 below). An "appropriately qualified person" includes a medical practitioner as well as any other person who has been given the required certification powers under provincial or federal law. A patient (e.g., a dependant) suffering from a behavioral problem arising out of a mental or physical impairment or suffering from a learning disability, including dyslexia, who attends a school that specializes in the care and training of persons who have the same type of problem or disability is considered to qualify under paragraph 118.2(2)(*e*), and the expenses paid for the patient are qualifying medical expenses even though some part of the expenses could be construed as being tuition fees (see *Rannelli v. MNR*, 91 DTC 816, [1991] 2 CTC 2040, (TCC)). A patient suffering from an addiction to drugs or alcohol can also qualify under paragraph 118.2(2)(*e*). Consequently, when all the conditions of that paragraph, as discussed above, are met, the expenses paid for the care of the patient in a detoxification clinic qualify as medical expenses. Fees paid for a stop-smoking course or program are not considered to qualify as medical expenses under paragraph 118.2(2)(*e*) unless, in an exceptional case, such a course or program is part of a patient's medical treatment that is required because of a serious health deterioration problem and that is both prescribed and monitored by a medical practitioner.

33. There is no requirement that a nursing home or a detoxification clinic be a public or licensed private hospital. The fact that the name of a residential establishment sometimes includes the word "school" or "nursery" will not affect the determination of whether it qualifies as a nursing home. While the care need not be full time, it must be stressed that equipment, facilities or personnel specially provided by the nursing home (or other place described in 32 above) must be specifically tailored for the care of persons suffering from the physical or mental impairment in question and that the other conditions set out in 32 above must be met, for the fees to qualify as medical expenses under paragraph 118.2(2)(*e*). However, if a claim is made for nursing home care under paragraph 118.2(2)(*e*), see 29 above.

Transportation and Travel Expenses of Patient and Accompanying Individual

34. An amount paid for transportation of a patient by ambulance to or from a public or licensed private hospital qualifies as a medical expense under paragraph 118.2(2)(*f*).

35. Under paragraph 118.2(2)(*g*), an amount paid to a person engaged in the business of providing transportation services can qualify as a medical expense to the extent that the amount relates to transporting a patient between the locality where the patient lives and a location which is at least

40 kilometres away in order for the patient to receive medical services at that location. In order for such an amount to qualify under paragraph 118.2(2)(*g*), it must be paid under the following circumstances:

(a) Substantially equivalent medical services are unavailable within the patient's locality.

(b) The patient takes a reasonably direct travel route.

(c) It is reasonable, in the circumstances, for the patient to travel to that place for the medical services.

If a person engaged in the business of providing transportation services is not readily available, subsection 118.2(4) instead allows as a qualifying medical expense under paragraph 118.2(2)(*g*) reasonable expenses incurred for the use of a vehicle (see 37 below) for transporting the patient provided that the above rules and circumstances are otherwise fulfilled. For this purpose, the term "vehicle" means any type of conveyance used to transport the patient by land, water or air including a vehicle owned by the individual claiming the expenses, the patient or a family member.

If expenses for transporting the patient are being claimed under paragraph 118.2(2)(*g*) as described above, that provision also allows the same kind of expenses for transporting one individual who accompanies the patient provided that a medical practitioner has certified that the patient is incapable of travelling without an attendant.

36. Paragraph 118.2(2)(*h*) refers to travel expenses other than those referred to in paragraph 118.2(2)(*g*) (discussed in 35 above). Paragraph 118.2(2)(*h*) provides that an individual may include, as qualifying medical expenses, such other reasonable travel expenses (see 37 below) for a patient to obtain medical services if the patient travels to a place that is at least 80 kilometres away from the locality where he or she dwells to get the medical services, and provided the following other conditions are also all met:

(a) Substantially equivalent medical services are unavailable within the patient's locality.

(b) The patient takes a reasonably direct travel route.

(c) It is reasonable, in the circumstances, for the patient to travel to that place for the medical services.

The individual claiming travel expenses for the patient under paragraph 118.2(2)(*h*) may also claim, under the same paragraph, the same kinds of travel expenses (i.e., reasonable travel expenses other than those referred to in paragraph 118.2(2)(*g*)) for one individual to accompany the patient as long as the patient has been certified by a medical practitioner as being incapable of travelling without an attendant.

37. In determining reasonable expenses incurred for the use of a vehicle as noted in 35 above, no amount may be included for capital cost allowance on the vehicle. "Other reasonable travel expenses" in 36 above refers to amounts expended for meals and accommodation for a patient and, where applicable, for an accompanying individual. The individual claiming the medical expense tax credit for these expenses must substantiate them with receipts (see 68 below). Furthermore, the onus is on the individual to demonstrate that the expenses qualify. For example, the individual may have to show that an amount paid for lodging is necessary as a result of the distance travelled, or the condition of the patient for travel, and not solely for the sake of convenience.

Artificial Limbs, Aids and Other Devices and Equipment

38. By virtue of paragraph 118.2(2)(*i*), qualifying medical expenses include the purchase price or, where applicable, the rental charge or other expenses (e.g., maintenance, repairs, supplies) related to the following:

(a) an artificial limb;

(b) an iron lung (see 39 below);

(c) a rocking bed for poliomyelitis victims;

(d) a wheelchair;

(e) crutches;

(f) a spinal brace (see 40 below);

(g) a brace for a limb (see 40 and 41 below);

(h) an ileostomy or a colostomy pad (see 42 below);

(i) a truss for a hernia;

(j) an artificial eye;

(k) a laryngeal speaking aid (see 43 below);

(l) an aid to hearing (see 44 and 45 below); and

(m) an artificial kidney machine (see 46 to 50 below).

39. The term "iron lung" in 38 above includes a portable chest respirator that performs the same function in substantially the same manner as the appliance ordinarily thought of as an iron lung. That term is also accepted as including a machine for supplying air (possibly in combination with oxygen or medication) to the lungs under pressure, for therapeutic use.

40. The term "spinal brace" in 38 above includes a spinal support. A "brace for a limb" (see 38 above) does not necessarily have to be some-

thing of a rigid nature, although at least one of the functions of the brace must be to impart some degree of rigidity to the limb which is being braced. Accordingly, that phrase is considered to include woven or elasticized stockings where these are of a kind that are carefully fitted to measurement or are made to measure.

41. When a brace for a limb (see 38 above) is necessarily built into a boot or shoe in order to permit a person to walk, the brace will be considered to include the boot or shoe.

42. "Ileostomy or colostomy pads" (see 38 above) include pouches and adhesives used for the same purpose.

43. A "laryngeal speaking aid" (see 38 above) is an electronic type of instrument that assists a person to produce speech sounds. An artificial larynx or a similar type of speaking aid for a person who would otherwise be deprived of an effective speech capability may also qualify for purposes of the medical expense tax credit. Qualifying expenses related to these devices may include the cost of batteries, maintenance, repairs or replacements.

44. In addition to the more usual hearing aid devices, an "aid to hearing" (see 38 above) includes:

(a) a device that produces extra-loud audible signals such as a bell, horn or buzzer;

(b) a device to permit the volume adjustment of telephone equipment above normal levels;

(c) a bone-conduction telephone receiver; and

(d) a "Cochlear" implant, which consists of a series of electrodes surgically placed in the sensory organ of a person who is profoundly deaf and for whom traditional hearing aids are not feasible.

45. When a hearing aid is incorporated into the frame of a pair of eyeglasses, both the hearing aid and the eyeglass frame qualify under paragraph 118.2(2)(*i*). The phrase "an aid to hearing" includes the batteries that are required for that purpose, and repairs. A listening device that is acquired to alleviate a hearing impairment by eliminating or reducing sound distortions for the purpose of listening to television programs, movies, concerts, business conferences or similar events, is also considered to qualify as an "aid to hearing" under paragraph 118.2(2)(*i*).

46. Qualifying medical expenses relating to an "artificial kidney machine" (see 38 above) include the costs of alterations to a home or the upgrading of the home's existing electrical or plumbing systems, provided that these costs are reasonable in the circumstances and are necessary for the installation of the machine. In addition to providing receipts to sub-

stantiate such costs, the individual should provide a certificate from the official at the hospital who authorized the installation of the artificial kidney machine stating that such expenditures were required to enable the hospital to install the equipment (see 68 below).

47. When an artificial kidney machine is installed at the individual's residence, the following costs, to the extent that they are reasonable, may also be included as qualifying medical expenses under paragraph 118.2(2)(*i*):

(a) repairs, maintenance, and supplies for the machine;

(b) water and electricity to operate the machine (see 48 below); and

(c) the costs of housing the machine (i.e., municipal taxes, insurance, heating, lighting, and maintenance and repairs, but not including capital cost allowance or mortgage interest) or the portion of rent that is attributable to the room where the machine is kept (see 48 and 49 below).

48. If it is not possible to determine the actual amount of one of the costs of operating or housing an artificial kidney machine, as referred to in 47(b) or (c) above, it will be necessary to allocate a reasonable proportion of the total amount of that particular cost for the whole home (e.g., the total insurance or the total heating cost) in order to determine the portion that qualifies as a medical expense pertaining to the articicial kidney machine. However, no portion of a cost should be claimed if that cost cannot reasonably be considered to relate to the operation or housing of the machine. Thus, for example, a repair expense for another part of the home would not qualify. When an actual cost of operating or housing the machine can be determined, this actual cost must be used when determining the total which qualifies as a medical expense (e.g., the amount of municipal taxes attributable to an addition to the home that houses the machine when such an amount can be ascertained from the property tax bill, or the cost of lighting repairs in the room where the machine is kept).

49. In determining the portion of rent that qualifies as a medical expense for purposes of 47(c) above, the amount must be based on actual rent paid and not on the rental value of the room in a home that is owned.

50. Necessary and unavoidable costs of transporting supplies for the artificial kidney machine may be included as qualifying medical expenses when the supplier will not deliver, as long as all of these conditions are met:

(a) The distance from the patient's residence to the nearest supply depot is at least 40 kilometres.

(b) The means of transportation is the least expensive available that is suitable in the circumstances.

(c) The quantity of supplies obtained is adequate for a reasonable period of time.

Products Required Because of Incontinence

51. The cost of diapers, disposable briefs, catheters, catheter trays, tubing or other products required by the patient because of incontinence caused by illness, injury or affliction are qualified medical expenses under paragraph 118.2(2)(*i*.1).

Eyeglasses

52. The cost of eyeglasses that qualifies as a medical expense under paragraph 118.2(2)(*j*) includes the cost of both the frames and lenses. The phrase "other devices for the treatment or correction of a defect of vision" in paragraph 118.2(2)(*j*) includes contact lenses. In all cases, a medical practitioner (oculist or ophthalmologist) or an optometrist must prescribe the item.

Oxygen Tents

53. The cost of buying or renting an oxygen tent or other equipment necessary to administer oxygen for medical purposes (including, for example, oxygen face masks, tanks containing oxygen under pressure, etc.) qualifies as a medical expense under paragraph 118.2(2)(*k*).

Guide and Hearing-Ear Dogs and Other Animals

54. The costs of acquiring and the care and maintenance (including food and veterinary care) of an animal qualify as medical expenses under paragraph 118.2(2)(*l*) as long as certain conditions are met. These costs must be paid on behalf of a patient who is blind, profoundly deaf or who has a severe and prolonged impairment (see 2 and 3 above) that markedly restricts the use of the patient's arms or legs. The animal must be specially trained to assist a patient in coping with his or her impairment and the animal must be provided by a person or organization one of whose main purposes is the training of animals for this purpose. The patient's reasonable travel expenses incurred for the purpose of attendance at, and reasonable board and lodging expenses incurred for the purpose of full-time attendance at, a school, institution or other facility that trains persons with the same kind of impairment in the handling of such animals will also qualify as medical expenses.

Bone Marrow or Organ Transplants

55. Reasonable expenses, including legal fees and insurance premiums, paid to locate a compatible bone marrow or organ transplant donor for a patient and to arrange for the transplant, qualify as medical expenses under paragraph 118.2(2)(*l*.1). Reasonable travel, board and lodging expenses (other than expenses described in paragraphs 118.2(2)(*g*) and

(*h*) as discussed in 35 to 37 above) paid for the donor and the patient, in respect of the transplant, also qualify under paragraph 118.2(2)(*l*.1) as do any such expenses in respect of the transplant that are paid for one other person who accompanies the donor and for one other person who accompanies the patient.

Renovations and Alterations to a Dwelling

56. In the case of an individual who lacks normal physical development or who has a severe and prolonged (see 2(a) above) mobility impairment, reasonable expenses relating to renovations or alterations to the individual's dwelling can be claimed as medical expenses under paragraph 118.2(2)(*l*.2). To qualify, these expenses must be paid to enable the individual to gain access to the dwelling or be mobile and functional within it. Included in this category are reasonable expenses for necessary structural changes, such as:

(a) the purchase and installation of outdoor or indoor ramps where stairways impede the individual's mobility;

(b) the enlarging of halls and doorways to allow the individual access to the various rooms of the dwelling; and

(c) the lowering of kitchen or bathroom cabinets to allow the individual access to them.

The types of structural changes that could be eligible are not restricted to the above examples. "Reasonable expenses" pertaining to a particular structural change may include payments to an architect or a contractor.

Rehabilitative Therapy

57. Amounts paid for reasonable expenses relating to rehabilitative therapy, including training in lip reading or sign language, incurred to adjust for the patient's hearing or speech loss qualify as medical expenses under paragraph 118.2(2)(*l*.3).

Devices and Equipment Prescribed by Regulation

58. By virtue of paragraph 118.2(2)(*m*), the list of devices and equipment which qualify for purposes of the medical expense tax credit has been expanded by means of the Income Tax Regulations (the Regulations), which are amended from time to time by order-in-council. An amount paid for a device or equipment cannot be claimed under paragraph 118.2(2)(*m*) unless the device or equipment:

(a) is prescribed by the Regulations;

(b) is for the patient's use as prescribed by a medical practitioner;

(c) is not described in any of the other paragraphs of subsection 118.2(2); and

(d) meets any conditions contained in the Regulations as to its use or as to the reason for its acquisition. Part LVII (section 5700) of the Regulations, *Medical Devices and Equipment*, contains the list of prescribed devices and equipment for purposes of paragraph 118.2(2)(*m*) and sets out the conditions as to their use and reasons for their acquisition (see the Appendix to this bulletin).

Preventive, Diagnostic and Other Treatments

59. A person suffering from diabetes is allowed to include as a qualifying medical expense the cost of insulin, under paragraph 118.2(2)(*k*), or substitutes, under paragraph 118.2(2)(*n*), as prescribed by a medical practitioner. When such a person has to take sugar-content tests using test-tapes or test tablets and a medical practitioner has prescribed this diagnostic procedure, the tapes or tablets qualify as devices or equipment under paragraph 118.2(2)(*m*) and Part LVII of the Regulations (see 58 above and item (s) of the Appendix). On the other hand, the cost of various kinds of scales, which diabetics frequently use for weighing themselves or their food, is not a qualifying medical expense.

60. Qualifying medical expenses under paragraph 118.2(2)(*o*) include the cost of laboratory, radiological and other diagnostic procedures or services, with necessary interpretations, for maintaining health, preventing disease or assisting in the diagnosis or treatment of any injury, illness or disability of the patient, as prescribed by a medical practitioner or dentist.

61. Payments made for acupuncture treatments are a qualified medical expense under paragraph 118.2(2)(*a*) only when the payments are made to a medical practitioner.

Drugs, Medicaments and Other Preparations or Substances

62. For purposes of calculating the medical expense tax credit, there are two categories of drugs, medicaments or other preparations or substances (other than those included in the account of a medical practitioner or hospital) the cost of which may qualify as medical expenses:

(a) the substances, mentioned in paragraph 118.2(2)(*k*) (insulin, oxygen and, for pernicious anaemia, liver extract and vitamin B12) which, for purposes of this paragraph, a medical practitioner must have prescribed, but which a pharmacy or any other type of store may sell without a written prescription; and

(b) the drugs (and other items), referred to in paragraph 118.2(2)(*n*), which a medical practitioner or dentist must have prescribed, and which must be purchased from a pharmacist who has recorded the prescription in a prescription record.

63. Birth control pills which a medical practitioner has prescribed are considered to qualify under paragraph 118.2(2)(*n*) if a pharmacist has recorded the prescription.

Dentures

64. Frequently, a denture is prescribed and fitted by a dentist, even though it may have been made in a dental laboratory, and the payment qualifies under paragraph 118.2(2)(*a*) as an amount paid to a dentist. However, paragraph 118.2(2)(*p*) specifically provides that amounts paid for the patient to a dental mechanic, who is authorized under the laws of a province to make or repair dentures or to otherwise carry on the business of a dental mechanic, also qualify as medical expenses.

Premiums to Private Health Services Plan

65. Paragraph 118.2(2)(*q*) provides that any premium that the individual or his or her legal representative has paid to a private health services plan for that individual, the individual's spouse or a member of the household with whom the individual is connected by blood relationship, marriage or adoption (see the current version of Interpretation Bulletin IT-339, *Meaning of "Private Health Services Plan"*) mmay be included as a qualifying medical expense. However, premiums paid to provincial medical or hospitalization insurance plans cannot be included.

Medical Expenses Paid or Deemed to Have Been Paid

66. As indicated in 13 above, a medical expense cannot qualify for the medical expense tax credit unless it has actually been paid or is deemed to have been paid by the individual claiming the credit or by the individual's legal representative. Any reference throughout this bulletin to the "cost" of a particular medical expense is subject to this rule. Medical expenses paid or provided for by an employer but included in the employee's income are deemed by paragraph 118.2(3)(*a*) to have been paid by the employee and, therefore, can be claimed by the employee (assuming they otherwise qualify) for purposes of the medical expense tax credit under subsection 118.2(1). The employee is deemed to have paid such expenses at the time the employer paid or provided them.

Expenses That Do Not Qualify

67. Paragraph 118.2(3)(*b*) provides that qualifying medical expenses of an individual do not include any expense for which the individual, the patient or the legal representative of either such person has been, or is entitled to be, reimbursed except to the extent that the amount is required to be included in income and cannot be deducted in computing taxable income. Thus, for example, an amount reimbursed under a public or private medical, dental or hospitalization plan would not qualify for purposes of

the medical expense tax credit. Similarly, an amount reimbursed by an employer and not included in the employee's income would not qualify.

Receipts

68. Proper receipts must support all amounts claimed as qualifying medical expenses (including travel expenses commented on in 35 to 37 above). A receipt should indicate the purpose of the payment, the date of the payment, the patient for whom the payment was made and, if applicable, the medical practitioner or dentist who prescribed the purchase or gave the service. A cancelled cheque is not acceptable as a substitute for a proper receipt. If required forms, receipts or other supporting documents are not filed with the return of income, such as when the return is electronically filed ("E-filed"), they should nevertheless be retained and readily available as the Department has the authority, under subsection 220(2.1) of the Act, to subsequently request them as proof of the claims being made or in support of the information being reported.

Attendant Care Expense Deduction in Computing Income

69. Section 64 provides for a deduction, in computing income for the year, for attendant care expenses. This deduction can be claimed only by a disabled person who qualifies for the disability tax credit for the year in accordance with the rules discussed in 6 and 7 above. If the disability tax credit is claimed under the rules discussed in 8 to 10 above by a supporting person or spouse rather than by the disabled person, only the disabled person may claim the section 64 attendant care expense deduction. Under section 64, the disabled person can deduct the amounts he or she has paid in the year for attendant care provided in Canada to enable him or her to earn any of the types of income mentioned in 70(b) below. An amount cannot qualify for the deduction if it was paid to an attendant who, at the time of the payment, was under 18 years of age or was the disabled person's spouse. The total amount of the deduction allowed for the year is subject to the limitation described in 70 below. An attendant care payment cannot be deducted under section 64 when calculating income if it was claimed (for any taxation year) by the disabled person or another person as a medical expense for purposes of the section 118.2 medical expense tax credit (see 29 above). A disabled person claiming a section 64 attendant care expense deduction should file prescribed Form T929, *Attendant Care Expenses*, with his or her income tax return for the year. Note, however, that the T929 form may not be submitted with a return filed under subsections 70(2), 104(23) or 150(4) (these are separate returns filed for a deceased taxpayer in respect of certain types of income) or with a return filed under paragraph 128(2)(*e*) (this is a return filed for a bankrupt person). Attendant care payments claimed under section 64 must be supported by receipts (see 68 above). Each receipt must be issued by the

payee and, if the payee is an individual, must show his or her social insurance number.

70. The attendant care expense deduction that a taxpayer (disabled person) may claim for the year under section 64 is limited to the least of these three amounts:

(a) the total of all attendant care payments that meet all the rules described in 69 above, paid by the taxpayer in the year to enable him or her to be employed, carry on a business (alone or as an active partner in a partnership), take a training course for which a training allowance was received under the *National Training Act* or carry on research or similar work for which a grant was received, less any reimbursements or other assistance (other than prescribed assistance or amounts included in income and not deductible in calculating taxable income) which the taxpayer received or is entitled to receive for the amounts paid;

(b) two thirds of the total of all amounts included in calculating the taxpayer's income from employment (including stock options and other employment benefits), carrying on a business (alone or as an active partner in a partnership), taxable training allowances (received under the *National Training Act*), scholarships, fellowships, bursaries, prizes and research grants; and

(c) $5,000.

71. Section 64.1 provides a special rule for an individual who is absent from Canada for all or part of the year but is nevertheless a resident of Canada for tax purposes while absent (either because of residential ties with Canada or because he or she is deemed to be resident in Canada under section 250). For the period of the individual's absence, section 64.1 removes two of the requirements that would otherwise have to be met under section 64 for purposes of the attendant care expense deduction:

(a) the requirement that the attendant care be provided "in Canada"; and

(b) the requirement that the attendant payee's social insurance number appear on the receipt (this requirement remains, of course, if the attendant is a resident of Canada for tax purposes).

Therefore, if the individual is a disabled person, he or she can claim the attendant care expense deduction for attendant care provided outside Canada, assuming all the other requirements of section 64 (as discussed in 69 and 70 above) are met.

72. When determining income from employment in 70(b) above, subsection 6(16) should be kept in mind. Because of that subsection, benefits or allowances (not in excess of a reasonable amount) provided by an

employer that relate to either of the following are not to be included when determining employment income:

(a) transportation to and from work, including parking near the work location, for an employee who is blind or who has a severe and prolonged mobility impairment that markedly restricts the employee's ability to perform a basic activity of daily living (e.g., walking); or

(b) an attendant to assist the employee in performing the duties assigned if the employee has a severe and prolonged mental or physical impairment which markedly restricts his or her ability to perform a basic activity of daily living.

The rules contained in subsection 118.4(1) regarding the meanings of "prolonged", "markedly restricted" and "basic activity of daily living", which are described in 2 and 3 above, apply for purposes of the rules in subsection 6(16).

APPENDIX (see 58 above)

Part LVII of the Regulations — Prescribed Medical Devices and Equipment

For the purpose of paragraph 118.2(2)(*m*), the following devices and equipment are prescribed under section 5700 of the Income Tax Regulations and, therefore, an amount paid for any such device or equipment that is prescribed for the patient's use by a medical practitioner qualifies as a medical expense, subject to the conditions described below:

(a) A wig made to order for an individual who has suffered abnormal hair loss because of disease, medical treatment or accident.

(b) A needle or syringe designed to be used for the purpose of giving an injection.

(c) A device or equipment, including a replacement part, designed exclusively for use by an individual suffering from a severe chronic respiratory ailment or a severe chronic immune system disregulation, but not including an air conditioner, humidifier, dehumidifier, heat pump or heat or air exchanger.

(c.1) An air or water filter or purifier for use by an individual who is suffering from a severe chronic respiratory ailment or a severe chronic immune system disregulation to cope with or overcome that ailment or disregulation.

(c.2) An electric or sealed combustion furnace acquired to replace a furnace that is neither an electric furnace nor a sealed combustion furnace, when the replacement is necessary solely because of an individual's severe chronic respiratory ailment or a severe chronic immune system disregulation.

(d) A device or equipment designed to pace or monitor the heart of an individual who suffers from heart disease.

(e) An orthopaedic shoe or boot or an insert for a shoe or boot made to order for an individual, in accordance with a prescription, to overcome a physical disability.

(f) A power-operated guided chair installation, for an individual, that is designed to be used solely in a stairway.

(g) A mechanical device or equipment designed to assist an individual to enter or leave a bathtub or shower or to get on or off a toilet.

(h) A hospital bed, including any attachments to the bed prescribed for the patient.

(i) A device designed to assist an individual in walking, when the individual has a mobility impairment.

(j) An external breast prosthesis that is required because of a mastectomy.

(k) A teletypewriter or similar device, including a telephone ringing indicator, that enables an individual who is deaf or mute to make and receive telephone calls. (This will include visual ringing indicators such as flashing lights, as well as acoustic couplers, and teletypewriters providing either printed or visual display screen communications. The individual may be required to provide a certificate from a medical practitioner to establish that such equipment was obtained to mitigate the effects of a hearing or speech disability. Additional equipment and accessories provided to others in order to make telephone communications possible between those other persons and the individual who is deaf or mute may also qualify.)

(l) An optical scanner or similar device designed to enable an individual who is blind to read print.

(m) A power-operated lift or transportation equipment designed exclusively for use by, or for, an individual who is disabled to allow the individual access to different areas of a building or to assist the individual in gaining access to a vehicle or to place the individual's wheelchair in or on a vehicle.

(n) A device designed exclusively to enable an individual who has a mobility impairment to operate a vehicle.

(o) A device or equipment, including a synthetic speech system, braille printer and large print-on-screen device, designed exclusively for use by an individual who is blind, in operating a computer.

(p) An electronic speech synthesizer that enables an individual who is mute to communicate by using a portable keyboard.

(q) A device to decode special television signals to permit the script of a program to be visually displayed.

(q.1) A visual or vibratory signalling device, including a visual fire alarm indicator, for an individual who has a hearing impairment.

(r) A device designed to be attached to an infant diagnosed as being prone to sudden infant death syndrome in order to sound an alarm if the infant ceases to breathe.

(s) An infusion pump, including disposable peripherals, used to treat diabetes or a device designed to enable an individual with diabetes to measure blood sugar level.

(t) An electronic or computerized environmental control system designed exclusively for the use of an individual who has a severe and prolonged mobility restriction.

(u) An extremity pump or elastic support hose designed exclusively to relieve swelling caused by chronic lymphedema.

(v) An inductive coupling osteogenesis stimulator for treating non-union of fractures or aiding in bone fusion.

Explanation of Changes

Introduction

The purpose of the *Explanation of Changes* is to give the reasons for the revisions to an interpretation bulletin. It outlines revisions that we have made as a result of changes to the law, as well as changes reflecting new or revised departmental interpretations.

Overview

This bulletin discusses the medical expense tax credit and the disability tax credit, both of which are non-refundable tax credits that directly reduce the amount of income tax payable. We have revised the bulletin primarily to reflect amendments to the *Income Tax Act* resulting from Bills C-28 (1990), C-18 (1991), C-80 (1992), C-92 (1993) and C-27 (1994) and Amendments to Income Tax Regulations, P.C. 1990-2491 and P.C. 1994-271, regarding these tax credits. We have also added a discussion, at the end of the bulletin, on the attendant care expense deduction, which is a deduction in calculating income. The comments in the bulletin are not affected by proposed legislation as of January 25, 1995.

Legislative and Other Changes

New ¶2 (former ¶6) reflects a Bill C-18 amendment to subsection 118.4(1), which took effect for the 1991 and subsequent taxation years.

The amendment added rules to establish what is and is not a basic activity of daily living and to specify the circumstances under which an impairment is considered to markedly restrict an individual's ability to perform such an activity, for purposes of the disability tax credit and (in some cases) the medical expense tax credit.

New ¶3 deals with subsection 118.3(4), which was added to the law in 1991 under Bill C-18, to give Health Canada (now Human Resources Development Canada) the authority to request additional information to determine if an individual is entitled to the disability tax credit.

The first part of new ¶5 (former ¶3) has been amended to reflect subsection 118.4(2) as found in the Revised Statutes of Canada, 1985 (5th Supplement).

New ¶5(v) adds, to the list of medical practitioners, a physiotherapist (which is used in an example in ¶17).

New ¶5(viii) (former ¶3(vii)) is modified to add, as psychoanalysts, members of the Quebec Association of Jungian Psychoanalysts.

New ¶5(x) (former ¶15) is added to the bulletin to include, in the list of medical practitioners, qualified speech-language pathologists and audiologists and to indicate the Department's recognition of persons certified as such by The Canadian Association of Speech-Language Pathologists and Audiologists or a provincial affiliate of that organization.

New ¶s 5(xi), (xii) and (xiii) were added to the bulletin to include, in the list of medical practitioners, occupational therapists, acupuncturists and dieticians who are authorized to practice under the laws of a province.

New ¶7 reflects a Bill C-18 amendment to subsection 118.3(1), effective for the 1991 and subsequent taxation years, which added the requirement, for purposes of the disability tax credit, that the disabled person's ability to perform a basic activity of daily living be markedly restricted.

New ¶8(b) (former ¶7(b)) is expanded to reflect a Bill C-27 amendment to subsection 118.3(2) which took effect for the 1993 and subsequent taxation years to ensure that, when a parent supports more than one disabled child, the parent will be able to claim the unused portion of each child's disability tax credit, which otherwise might have been prevented by the fact that the equivalent-to-spouse tax credit can never be claimed for more than one child, and that the dependant tax credit for dependants under 18 years of age was replaced by the child tax benefit under Bill C-80.

New ¶10 provides more information on the transfer of the unused portion of a spouse's disability tax credit, than was covered in the last sentence of former ¶7. New ¶10 also reflects a Bill C-18 amendment to subsection 118.3(2), which took effect for the 1988 and subsequent taxation years. This amendment prevents a supporting person from claiming the unused portion of a disabled dependant's disability tax credit if the disabled person's spouse claims certain tax credits for the disabled person. The last sentence of new 10 refers to paragraph 252(4)(*a*), which was added to the Act as a result of Bill C-92.

New ¶12 (first sentence of former ¶8) has been expanded to give an example of the calculation to be done using the formula under subsection 118.2(1) for the medical expense tax credit. The last sentence of former ¶8 has been moved to the Summary, and former ¶11 is now the last sentence of new ¶12.

New ¶14 (first sentence of former ¶9) is the paragraph that now gives the explanation of the term "patient". This term was previously explained in the last sentence of former ¶20.

New ¶15 gives the meaning of "dependant" as provided for in subsection 118(6), which is used for purposes of the medical expense tax credit. This results from a Bill C-80 amendment to paragraph 118.2(2)(*a*), which took effect for the 1993 and subsequent taxation years and which is related to the amendment reflected in new ¶18.

New ¶18 (former ¶10) is modified to reflect a Bill C-80 amendment to subsection 118.2(1), which took effect for the 1993 and subsequent taxation years. This amendment requires that an adjustment, which is illustrated in new ¶18 by an example, must be made when calculating a medical expense tax credit if medical expenses are claimed on behalf of a "dependant" who has a certain amount of net income. This adjustment replaces the "notch provision" in subsection 117(7), which was repealed under Bill C-80 for the 1993 and subsequent taxation years as a result of the simultaneous replacement of the dependant tax credit for dependants under 18 years of age by the child tax benefit.

New ¶22 clarifies that "medical services" for purposes of paragraph 118.2(2)(*a*) include diagnostic, therapeutic and rehabilitative services.

New ¶26 (former ¶20) reflects an amendment to paragraph 118.2(2)(*b*) which resulted from Bill C-18 and which took effect for expenses incurred after 1990. The amendment to paragraph 118.2(2)(*b*) added new conditions to those that must be met for remuneration paid for one full-time attendant or the cost of full-time care in a nursing home of a patient to qualify as a medical expense.

New ¶27 reflects a Bill C-18 amendment which added paragraph 118.2(2)(*b*.1), which took effect for expenses incurred after 1990. Remuneration for a part-time (or full-time) attendant can qualify under paragraph 118.2(2)(*b*.1), subject to a dollar limit, if certain conditions are met.

New ¶28 (last sentence of former ¶21) expands on the salary or remuneration that can qualify as a medical expense.

New ¶29 (former ¶19) reflects Bill C-18 and Bill C-92 amendments to subsections 118.3(1) and (2), respectively, both of which took effect for the 1991 and subsequent taxation years. Because of these amendments, a disability tax credit would not be prevented by a medical expense tax credit claim for remuneration paid to a part-time (or full-time) attendant if that claim is made under paragraph 118.2(2)(*b*.1). New ¶29 now also indicates that when attendant care expenses are included as qualifying medical expenses, they cannot be deducted under the section 64 attendant care expense deduction, which was introduced into the Act as a result of Bill C-18.

New ¶30 (former ¶21) reflects Bill C-18 amendments to paragraph 118.2(2)(*c*), which took effect for expenses incurred after 1990. These amendments have changed the wording of subparagraphs 118.2(2)(*c*)(ii) and (iii) to parallel, where applicable, the wording of paragraph 118.2(2)(*b*.1).

New ¶32 (former ¶23) adds learning disabilities, including dyslexia (because of the *Ranelli* court case), as well as an addiction to drugs or alcohol, as impairments for which expenses paid for the care, or for the care and training, at a school, institution or other place can qualify as medical expenses under paragraph 118.2(2)(*e*). Also added to new ¶32 is an indication that an out-patient clinic or a detoxification clinic can qualify as an "other place" for purposes of paragraph 118.2(2)(*e*). A final addition is the Department's position that fees paid for stop-smoking courses generally do not qualify for purposes of this provision.

New ¶33 (former ¶24) is modified to reflect a revised departmental interpretation regarding care in an institution, for purposes of paragraph 118.2(2)(*e*). The Department's revised position is that such care does not have to be full-time to qualify, as long as equipment, facilities or personnel are specially provided by the institution for the care of patients suffering from the same handicap as the one suffered by the patient for whom the medical expenses are claimed (and the other conditions of paragraph 118.2(2)(*e*) are met).

New ¶36 (former ¶26) is modified to reflect a Bill C-18 amendment to paragraph 118.2(2)(*h*), which applies for the 1988 and subsequent taxation years. This amendment ensures that a patient may be entitled to claim travelling expenses under that provision even when he or she travels alone.

New ¶38 (former ¶28) now refers to "the purchase price or, where applicable, the rental charge or other expenses (e.g., maintenance, repairs, supplies) related to" any device or equipment listed in paragraph 118.2(2)(*i*) (such devices and equipment being discussed in new ¶s 39 to 50).

New ¶s 38 and 42 (former ¶s 28 and 32) no longer refer to cloth diapers and other items required by a patient's incontinence. These items are now discussed in new ¶51.

New ¶44 (former ¶34) is expanded to add, as an "aid to hearing", a "Cochlear" implant.

New ¶51 (second sentence of former ¶32) discusses products required by reason of incontinence. Such products were moved from paragraph 118.2(2)(*i*) to new paragraph 118.2(2)(*i*.1), and their list expanded, as a result of Bill C-18, for expenses incurred after 1990.

New ¶54 (former ¶43) is modified to reflect Bill C-18 amendments to paragraph 118.2(2)(*l*), which took effect for expenses incurred after 1990. As a result of these amendments, this provision applies for all animals specially trained to assist disabled individuals, and the provision was also extended to permit expenses for individuals who have a severe and prolonged impairment that markedly restricts the use of their arms or legs.

New ¶55 discusses paragraph 118.2(2)(*l*.1), which was added to the Act as a result of Bill C-28. This provision allows certain expenses relating to a bone marrow or organ transplant as medical expenses.

New ¶56 discusses paragraph 118.2(2)(*l*.2), which was added to the Act under Bill C-28 and amended, for expenses incurred after 1990, under Bill C-18. This provision allows, as medical expenses, certain renovations or alterations to a dwelling to accomodate an individual who lacks normal physical development or who has a severe and prolonged mobility impairment.

New ¶57 discusses paragraph 118.2(2)(*l*.3), which was added to the Act under Bill C-92. This provision, which took effect for the 1992 and subsequent taxation years, allows certain rehabilitative therapy expenses relating to a person's speech or hearing loss as medical expenses.

New ¶58 (former ¶44) is modified to reflect a Bill C-18 amendment to paragraph 118.2(2)(*m*), which took effect on December 17, 1991. This amendment increases the scope of the Regulations by allowing the Governor in Council to stipulate not only what kind of devices or equipment, but also what they must be used or purchased for, in order to qualify as medical expenses.

New ¶67 (former ¶53) is modified to reflect a Bill C-92 amendment to paragraph 118.2(3)(*b*), which took effect for the 1992 and subsequent taxation years. The amendment ensures that the treatment of a reimbursement of a medical expense will also apply to a reimbursement received by the patient (if the patient is not the taxpayer who would otherwise be claiming the medical expense) or by the patient's legal representative. The amendment also ensures that a reimbursed expense, to the extent that it is included in computing income under Part I and deductible in computing taxable income, will not qualify as a medical expense for purposes of the medical expense tax credit.

New ¶68 (former ¶54) is expanded to discuss the retention of tax receipts and forms by a taxpayer when they are not filed with the return.

New ¶s 69 to 72 have been added to the bulletin to discuss the section 64 attendant care expense deduction, which was added to the Act under Bill C-28 and amended in 1991 under Bill C-18, as well as related provisions that were added to the Act under Bills C-28 and C-18. The section 64 attendant care expense deduction, which is available to a disabled person who qualifies for the section 118.3 disability tax credit, is a deduction (in calculating income) that is allowed for certain attendant care expenses paid to enable the disabled person to earn certain income related to his or her work, training or research.

All the modifications to items in the *Appendix* are contained in *Amendments to the Income Tax Regulations*, P.C. 1990-2491 or P.C. 1994-271.

Item (c) of the Appendix is modified to add a severe chronic immune system disregulation as a reason to acquire a device or equipment of the type dealt with in this item and to add other devices that do not qualify as medical expenses.

Items (c.1) and (c.2) of the Appendix describe items that were added to section 5700 of the Regulations by P.C. 1994-271, applicable after December 16, 1991.

Item (i) of the Appendix is modified to add, as a condition, that the individual must have a mobility impairment.

Item (m) of the Appendix is modified to add a reference to transportation equipment as equipment that can qualify under that item.

Item (q) of the Appendix is modified to replace, in the English version, the words "the vocal portion of the signal" by "the script of a program".

Item (q.1) of the Appendix describes items that were added to section 5700 of the Regulations by P.C. 1994-271, applicable to the 1992 and subsequent taxation years.

Item (s) of the Appendix is modified to add a specific device used in the treatment of diabetes.

Items (t), (u) and (v) of the Appendix describe items that were added to section 5700 of the Regulations by P.C. 1990-2491.

In addition, we have made other wording changes throughout the bulletin, and have reordered some paragraphs to clarify the bulletin and improve its cohesiveness.

¶17,110 DEATH BENEFIT — TAX TREATMENT

Subparagraph 56(1)(*a*)(iii) and subsection 248(1) of the federal *Income Tax Act*, reproduced below, allow employers to pay up to a $10,000 tax-free death benefit.

Subdivision d — Other Sources of Income

SECTION 56: Amounts to be included in income for year.

(1) Without restricting the generality of section 3, there shall be included in computing the income of a taxpayer for a taxation year,

◀ 56(1)(a) ▶

(a) Pension benefits, unemployment insurance benefits, etc. — any amount received by the taxpayer in the year as, on account or in lieu of payment of, or in satisfaction of,

* * *

(iii) a death benefit,

* * *

SECTION 248: [Interpretation].

◀ 248(1) ▶

(1) Definitions. In this Act.

* * *

"death benefit" — "death benefit" means the total of all amounts received by a taxpayer in a taxation year on or after the death of an employee in recognition of the employee's service in an office or employment minus

(*a*) where the taxpayer is the only person who has received such an amount and who is a surviving spouse of the employee (which person is, in this definition, referred to as the "surviving spouse"), the lesser of

(i) the total of all amounts so received by the taxpayer in the year, and

(ii) the amount, if any, by which $10,000 exceeds the total of all amounts received by the taxpayer in preceding taxation years on or after the death of the employee in recognition of the employee's service in an office or employment, or

(*b*) where the taxpayer is not the surviving spouse of the employee, the lesser of

(i) the total of all amounts so received by the taxpayer in the year, and

(ii) that proportion of

(A) the amount, if any, by which $10,000 exceeds the total of all amounts received by the surviving spouse of the employee at any time on or after the death of the employee in recognition of the employee's service in an office or employment

that

(B) the amount described in subparagraph (i)

is of

(C) the total of all amounts received by all taxpayers other than the surviving spouse of the employee at any time on or after the death of the employee in recognition of the employee's service in an office or employment;

* * *

¶17,115 NOTES ON THE RATING AGENCIES AND THEIR COMPARISONS

The following section of the appendices provides some information on the rating agencies and their comparison of the life insurance companies. Note that not all companies are rated by all rating agencies. Not-for-profit benefit suppliers are often excluded in these comparisons. In addition, the ratings published by the agencies may be out of date soon after they are published, due to changing situations at each insurer. Please pay attention to the dates of publication whenever reviewing a particular rating. You may also wish to contact any of the rating agencies directly for more up-to-date information on any particular insurer or benefit supplier.

There are many rating agencies, such as A.M. Best Company, Duff & Phelps Credit Rating Co., Moody's Investor Services and Standard & Poor's Ratings Group, providing services and information to the public. Some information is available from the rating agencies on-line through organizations such as CompuServe, for a fee.

Included in this section is a Rating Agency Comparison Chart (see ¶17,120), which provides an outline of four of the rating agencies; an explanation of the ratings (¶17,125); a comparison chart of insurers operating in Canada (¶17,130); and Standard & Poor's Claims Paying Ability Ratings (¶17,140), which also includes the ratings of many U.S. insurers. A ratings chart from Duff & Phelps Credit Rating Co., comparing that firm's ratings with Standard & Poor's and Moody's Investors Services, was to have been included; however, Moody's Investors Services has declined permission to include the chart in this text.

Readers should note that ratings are subject to review and change. Listed below are the addresses, telephone and fax numbers of the major ratings agencies.

A.M. Best Company
Ambest Road
Oldwick, New Jersey 08858
Tel.: (908) 439-2200
Fax: (908) 439-3027

Duff & Phelps Credit Rating Co.
55 East Monroe Street,
Suite 3500
Chicago, Illinois 60603
Tel.: (312) 368-3157
Fax: (312) 368-4064

Moody's Canada Inc.
BCE Place, 181 Bay Street
Suite 1610
P.O. Box 753
Toronto, Ontario M5J 2T3
Tel.: (416) 214-1644
Fax: (416) 216-2020

Standard & Poor's Ratings Group
Suite 2750, P.O. Box 486
2 First Canadian Place
130 King Street West
Toronto, Ontario M5X 1E5
Tel.: (416) 364-8580
Fax: (416) 364-5336

Stone & Cox Limited
111 Peter Street, Suite 202
Toronto, Ontario M5V 2H1
Tel.: (416) 599-0772
Fax: (416) 599-0867

TRAC Insurance Services Ltd.
133 Richmond Street W., Suite 600
Toronto, Ontario M5H 2L3
Tel.: (416) 363-8266
Fax: (416) 363-2673
Toll-Free: 1-800-263-8722

¶17,120 LIMRA RATING AGENCY COMPARISON CHART*

Rating Agency Comparison Chart

RATING FIRM	FOCUS	REVIEW FREQUENCY	MAJOR USERS	KEY FINANCIAL AREAS	QUALITATIVE FACTORS	REPORTS INCLUDE:
A.M. Best Co. Inc.	Overall company performance to evaluate relative financial strength and ability to meet contractual obligations	• Published at least annually • Periodic rating monitors • Quarterly updates	• Sales force • Consumers • Other insurers • Banks	• Leverage • Liquidity • Profitability • Also concerned with reserves, investments, reinsurance, and diversification	• Management • Spread of risk • Size • Diversification • Asset quality • Reinsurance • Reserves	• Summary of items found in major financial statements • Discussion of company history, ownership, and management
Duff & Phelps Credit Rating Co.	Long-term solvency and liquidity; closely allied to credit analysis Asset/liability management practices	• Published at least annually • Quarterly updates	• Investors • Investment bankers • Other insurers • Sales force	• Leverage • Operating efficiency • Profitability	• Economic fundamentals of principal lines • Asset/liability management • Operating results • Competition • Management • Corporate relationships	• Key ratios listed • Reason for rating • Fundamentals • Operating results • Asset/liability considerations
Moody's Investors Service, Inc.	Long-term performance to evaluate relative financial strength and ability to meet contractual obligations; focus on pension and annuity writers	Periodic updates/confirmations; at least annually	• GIC brokers • Pension plan trustees • Structured-settlement advisors • Investors • Other insurers • Banks • Sales force	• Capital adequacy • Profitability • Also concerned with asset quality, asset/liability management and liquidity	• Strengths/weaknesses • Fundamentals • Risks • Management • Relationships with parent, subsidiaries, and affiliates	• Opinion highlights key factors • Strengths/opportunities • Weaknesses/risks • Fundamentals • Management • Financials
Standard & Poor's Corp.	Prospective assessment of insurer's financial capacity, tailored to insurer's principal lines of business and markets; also attempt to get at true earnings	Periodic updates/confirmations; at least annually	• Investors • Other insurers • Banks • Sales force • Consumers	• Capitalization • Return on assets • Also concerned with investments, liquidity, expenses, lapses, and claims	• Management • Operating effectiveness • Risk tolerance • Strategy • Performance projections	Includes financial summary in five areas: • Business review • Operating statistics • Investment performance • Investment portfolio • Capital and liquidity statistics

This information has been taken from the Life Insurance Marketing and Research Association's (LIMRA) brochure entitled "A Producer's Guide to Life Insurer Ratings" and has been reprinted with the express written permission of LIMRA. July 1994

* Reproduced with the permission of Manulife Financial and the Life Insurance Marketing and Research Association, Inc. (LIMRA® International).

¶17,125 INDEPENDENT RATING AGENCY RATING CLASSIFICATIONS*

Independent Rating Agency Rating Classifications

Ratings by A.M. Best

RATING CLASSIFICATIONS:	
A++ *A+*	**Superior.** Assigned to companies which, in our opinion, have achieved superior overall performance when compared to the standards established by the A.M. Best Company. A++ and A+ (Superior) companies have a very strong ability to meet their obligations to policyholders over a long period of time.
A *A-*	**Excellent.** Assigned to companies which, in our opinion, have achieved excellent overall performance when compared to the standards established by the A.M. Best Company. A and A- (Excellent) companies have a strong ability to meet their obligations to policyholders over a long period of time.
B++ *B+*	**Very Good.** Assigned to companies which, in our opinion, have achieved a very good overall performance when compared to the standards established by the A.M. Best Company. B++ and B+ (Very Good) companies have a strong ability to meet their obligations to policyholders, but their financial strength may be susceptible to unfavorable changes in underwriting or economic conditions.
B *B-*	**Good.** Assigned to companies which, in our opinion, have achieved good overall performance when compared to the standards established by the A.M. Best Company. B and B- (Good) companies generally have an adequate ability to meet their obligations to policyholders, but their financial strength is susceptible to unfavorable changes in underwriting or economic conditions.
C++ *C+*	**Fair.** Assigned to companies which, in our opinion, have achieved fair overall performance when compared to the standards established by the A.M. Best Company. C++ and C+ (Fair) companies generally have a reasonable ability to meet their obligations to policyholders, but their financial strength is vulnerable to unfavorable changes in underwriting or economic conditions.
C *C-*	**Marginal.** Assigned to companies which, in our opinion, have achieved marginal overall performance when compared to the standards established by the A.M. Best Company. C and C- (Marginal) companies have a current ability to meet their obligations to policyholders, but their financial strength is very vulnerable to unfavorable changes in underwriting or economic conditions.
D	**Below Minimum Standards.** Assigned to companies which meet our minimum size and experience requirements, but do not meet the minimum standards established by the A.M. Best Company for a Best's Rating of "C-." Note: This rating category was formerly the NA-7 (Below Minimum Standards) Rating "Not Assigned" category.
E	**Under State Supervision.** Assigned to companies which are placed by a state insurance regulatory authority under any form of supervision, control or restraint, such as conservatorship or rehabilitation, but does not include liquidation. May be assigned to a company under a cease and desist order issued by a regulator from a state other than its state of domicile. Note: This rating category was formerly the NA-10 (Under State Supervision) Rating "Not Assigned" category.
F	**In Liquidation.** Assigned to companies which have been placed under an order of liquidation or have voluntarily agreed to liquidate. Note: This is a new rating category in 1992 to distinguish between companies under state regulatory supervision (E) and those in the process of liquidation.
Watch List	Indicates the company is under close surveillance because it has experienced a downward trend in its current financial performance or may be exposed to a possible legal, financial or market situation which could adversely affect its performance.

Ratings by Moody's**

FINANCIAL STRENGTH RATINGS:	
	Rating Symbols Moody's rating symbols for Insurance Financial Strength Ratings are identical to those used to show the credit quality of bonds. These rating gradations provide investors with a simple system to measure an insurance company's ability to meet its senior policyholder claims and obligations. Ratings gradations are broken down into nine distinct symbols, each symbol representig a group of ratings in which the quality characteristics are broadly the same. These symbols, which comprise two distinct rating groups, range from that used to designate the greatest financial strength (i.e. highest investment quality) to that denoting the least financial strength (i.e., lowest investment quality). Numeric modifiers are used to refer to the ranking within the group—one being the highest and three being the lowest. However, the financial strength of companies within a generic rating symbol (Aa, for example) is broadly the same.
Aaa	Insurance companies rated Aaa offer exceptional financial security. While the financial strength of these companies is likely to change, such changes as can be visualized are most unlikely to impair their fundamentally strong position.
Aa	Insurance companies rated Aa offer excellent financial security. Together with the Aaa group they constitute what are generally know as high grade companies. They are rated lower than Aaa companies because long-term risks appear somewhat larger.
A	Insurance companies rated A offer good financial security. However, elements may be present which suggest a susceptibility to impairment sometime in the future.
Baa	Insurance companies rated Baa offer adequate financial security. However, certain protective elements may be lacking or may be characteristically unreliable over any great length of time.
Ba	Insurance companies rated Ba offer questionable financial security. Often the ability of these companies to meet policyholder obligations may be very moderate and thereby not well safeguarded in the future.
B	Insurance companies rated B offer poor financial security. Assurance of punctual payment of policyholder obligations over any long period of time is small.
Caa	Insurance companies rated Caa offer very poor financial security. They may be in default on their policyholder obligations or there may be present elements of danger with respect to punctual payments of policyholder obligations and claims.
Ca	Insurance companies rated Ca offer extremely poor financial security. Such companies are often in default on their policyholder obligations or have other marked shortcomings.
C	Insurance companies rated C are the lowest rated class of insurance company and can be regarded as having extremely poor prospects of ever offering financial security.
	Note: Moody's applies numerical modifiers 1, 2, and 3 in each rating classification: the modifier 1 indicates that the security ranks in the higher end of its generic rating category; the modifier 2 indicates a mid-range ranking and the modifier 3 indicates that the issue ranks in the lower end of its generic rating category.

*** Reprinted with the permission of A.M. Best Company Inc., Duff & Phelps Credit Rating Co., Moody's Investors Service Inc., Standard & Poor's Ratings Group and Manulife Financial. Manulife Financial put together the comparison. Note that ratings are subject to review and change. See ¶17,115 for addresses and telephone numbers of major ratings agencies.**

**** See *Note* on page 470.**

Ratings by Duff & Phelps

CLAIMS PAYING ABILITY RATINGS:	
AAA	Highest claims paying ability. Risk factors are negligible.
AA+ AA AA-	Very high claims paying ability. Protection factors are strong. Risk is modest, but may vary slightly over time due to economic and/or underwriting conditions.
A+ A A-	High claims paying ability. Protection factors are average and there is an expectation of variability in risk over time due to economic and/or underwriting conditions.
BBB+ BBB BBB-	Adequate claims paying ability. Protection factors are average. However, there is considerable variability in risk over time due to economic and/or underwriting conditions.
BB+ BB BB-	Uncertain claims paying ability and less than investment grade quality. However, the company is deemed likely to meet these obligations when due. Protection factors will vary widely with changes in economic and/or underwriting conditions.
B+ B B-	Possessing risk that policyholder and contractholder obligations will not be paid when due. Protection factors will vary widely with changes in economic and underwriting conditions or company fortunes.
CCC	There is substantial risk that policyholder and contractholder obligations will not be paid when due. Company has been or is likely to be placed under state insurance department supervision.
DD	Company is under an order of liquidation.

Ratings by Standard & Poor's

SECURE RANGE: AAA TO BBB-	
AAA	Superior financial security on an absolute and relative basis. Capacity to meet policyholder obligations is overwhelming under a variety of economic and underwriting conditions.
AA+ AA AA-	Excellent financial security. Capacity to meet policyholder obligations is strong under a variety of economic and underwriting conditions.
A+ A A-	Good financial security, but capacity to meet policyholder obligations is somewhat susceptible to adverse economic and underwriting conditions.
BBB+ BBB BBB-	Adequate financial security, but capacity to meet policy holder obligations is susceptible to adverse economic and underwriting conditions.
VULNERABLE RANGE: BB+ TO CCC	
BB+ BB BB-	Financial security may be adequate, but capacity to meet policyholder obligations, particularly with respect to long-term or "long-tail" policies, is vulnerable to adverse economic and underwriting conditions.
B+ B B-	Vulnerable financial security. Currently able to meet policyholder obligations, but capacity to meet policyholder obligations is particularly vulnerable to adverse economic and underwriting conditions.
CCC	Extremely vulnerable financial security. Continued capacity to meet policyholder obligations is highly questionable unless favorable economic and underwriting conditions prevail.
R	Regulatory action. As of the date indicated, the insurer is under supervision of insurance regulators following rehabilitation, receivership, liquidation, or any other action that reflects regulatory concern about the insurer's financial condition. Information on this status is provided by the National Association of Insurance Commissioners and other regulatory bodies. Although believed to be accurate, this information is not guaranteed. The R rating does not apply to insurers subject only to non-financial actions, such as market conduct violations.
Watch List	Ratings appear on CreditWatch where an event or deviation from an expected trend occurs, and additional information is necessary to evaluate the current rating. A rating decision is normally made within 120 days unless pending the outcome of a specific event. Ratings may change without appearing on CreditWatch.

Note: **Moody's Investors Services Inc. Financial Strength Ratings disclaimer states as follows:**

Moody's Insurance Financial Strength Ratings

Moody's insurance Financial Strength Ratings are opinions of the ability of insurance companies to repay punctually senior policyholder claims and obligations. Specific obligations are considered unrated unless individually rated because the standing of a particular insurance obligation would depend on an assessment of its relative standing under those laws governing both the obligation and the insurance company. It is important to note that Moody's makes no representation that rated insurance company obligations are exempt from registration under the U.S. Securities Act of 1933 or issued in conformity with any other applicable law or regulation. Nor does Moody's represent that any specific insurance company obligation is legally enforceable or a valid senior obligation of a rated issuer.

Insurance Financial Strength Ratings shown in connection with property/casualty groups represent the ratings of individual companies within those groups, as displayed in Moody's insurance industry ratings list. The rating of an individual property/casualty company may be based on the benefit of its participation in an intercompany pooling agreement. Pooling agreements may or may not provide for continuation of inforce policyholder obligation by pool members in the event that the property/casualty insurer is sold to a third party or otherwise removed from the pooling agreement. Moody's assumes in these ratings that the pooling agreement will not be modified by the members of the pool to reduce the benefits of pool participation, and that the insurer will remain in the pool. Moody's makes no representation or warranty that such pooling agreement will not be modified over time, nor does Moody's opine on the probability that the rated entity may be sold or otherwise removed from the pooling agreement.

¶17,130 COMPETITIVE RATING SUMMARY*

The following is a list of selected life insurance competitors and their ratings from all major rating agencies.

Company	Duff & Phelps	S & P	A.M. Best	Moody's
Aetna Life***	AA	A+	A	Aa3
Allstate Life**	—	AA+	A+	Aa3
American General	AAA	AAA	A++	Aa3
Canada Life	AAA	AAA	A++	Aa2
Colonia Life	—	—	A-	—
Commercial Union	—	—	—	—
Crown Life	—	BBB+	A–	Ba1 **
Equitable Life (Canada)	—	—	—	—
Great West Life	AAA	AAA	A++	Aa2
Imperial Life	—	—	A	—
Industrial/Alliance	—	—	A	—
John Hancock	AAA	AA+	A++	Aa2
Laurier Life	—	—	—	—
London Life	—	AAA	A++	Aa2
Manulife Financial	AAA	AA+	A++	Aa3
Maritime Life	—	—	A+	—
Metropolitan Life***	AAA	AA	A+	Aa1
Mutual Group	—	AA+	A++	Aa2
NN Life of Canada	—	—	A	—
National Life	—	—	A	A1
North American Life	—	A	A–	Baa1
Prudential of America***	AA	AA-	A	Aa3
Seaboard Life	—	—	A	—
Standard Life (UK)***	—	AAA	—	Aaa
Sun Life	AAA	AAA	A++	Aa2 **
Transamerica Life***	AA+	AA+	A+	Aa3
UNUM Life**	—	AA+	A++	Aa2

Source: Rating Agencies, April 1995. Reproduced with the permission of Duff & Phelps Credit Rating Company, Standard & Poor's Ratings Group, A.M. Best Company, Moody's Investor Service and Manulife Financial. Manulife Financial put together the comparison.

* *Note:* Ratings are subject to review and change. For telephone numbers and addresses of major ratings agencies see ¶17,115.

** See notes on page 472.

*** Parent company rating

** Moody's Investors Services Inc. has included the following notes to its ratings:

Ba1 rating for Crown Life is under review for possible upgrading.

Aa2 rating for Sun Life Assurance Company of Canada, foreign currency insurance financial strength rating.

¶17,140 CLAIMS PAYING ABILITY RATINGS*

CLAIMS-PAYING ABILITY

INSURER	RATING	RATING DATE	FORMER RATING
20th Century Insurance Co.	CCC	Se09,94	B
21st Century Casualty Co.	CCC	Se09.94	B
Aachen Reinsurance Co.	AA	Oc21,94	
Aegon USA Group	AA+	Jy16,90	
Aetna Casualty & Surety Co. Group	A+	Au23.94	AA-
Aetna Excess & Surplus Lines Insurance Co	A+	Au23,94	AA-
Aetna Life Insurance & Annuity Co.	AA	Au23,94	AAA
Aetna Life Insurance Co.	A+	Fe09,94	AA-
Aetna Life Insurance Co of America	A+	Au23,94	AA-
Aetna Life Insurance Co of Illinois	A+	Fe09.94	AA-
Aetna Lloyd's of Texas Insurance Co.	A+	Au23,94	AA-
Aid Association for Lutherans	AAA	Mr27,91	
AIG Life Insurance Co	AAA	De16,91	
Alexander Hamilton Life Insurance Co of America	AA	De28,90	
All American Life Insurance Co	AA+	Au21,91	
ALLIED Group Intercompany Pool	A+	My24,93	A
Allstate County Mutual Insurance Co	AA	Jn08,93	AA-
Allstate Indemnity Co	AA	Jn08,93	AA-
Allstate Insurance Co	AA	Jn08,93	AA-
Allstate Life Insurance Co.	AA+	Oc13,92	AAA
Allstate Life Insurance Co of New York	AA+	Oc13,92	AAA
Allstate Property & Casualty Insurance Co	AA	Jn08,93	AA-
Allstate Reinsurance Co Ltd.	AA	Oc06,93	
Allstate Texas Lloyd's	AA	Jn08,93	AA-
AMBAC Indemnity Corp	AAA	Ja01,74	
American Bankers Insurance Co of FL	A+	Ja04,94	A-
American Bankers Life Assurance Co. of FL	A+	Ja05,94	
American Crown Life Insurance Co	BBB+	Se09,94	A+
American Foundation Life Insurance Co	AA	No15,93	
American General Life & Accident Insurance Co	AAA	No08,91	
American General Life Insurance Co	AAA	Jy12,91	
American General Life Insurance Co. of New York	AAA	Jy24,91	
American International Group Intercompany Pool	AAA	Mr28,83	
American International Life Assurance Co of New York	AAA	De16,91	
American International Specialty Lines Insurance Co	AAA	Jn13,94	
American Life & Casualty Insurance Co	A-	Se29,94	A
American Life Insurance Co.	AAA	Mr31,86	
American Life Insurance Co. of NY	AA-	De23,93	
American Loan Guarantee Assn	AAA	Se18,87	
American Maturity Life Insurance Co	AAA	De07,94	
American Mayflower Life Insurance Co of New York	AA+	Se24,91	
American Re-Insurance Co.	AA	Mr18,94	AA-
American Road Insurance Co (The)	A+	Ja23,95	A
American Security Insurance Group	AA-	Mr02,94	AA
American Skandia Life Assurance Corp	BBB+	Ja06,95	BBB
American States Insurance Co. of TX	AA	My27,92	AA+
American States Intercompany Pool	AA	My27,92	AA+
American States Lloyd's Insurance Co.	AA	My27,92	AA+
American United Life Insurance Co	AA-	No19,91	
Americas Insurance Co	A-	Ja11,93	
Amerin Guaranty Corp	AA	Se10,92	
Ameritas Bankers Assurance Co	AA	Jy08,91	
Ameritas Life Insurance Corp.	AA	Jy08,91	
Ameritas Variable Life Insurance Co	AA	Jy08,91	
Anchor National Life Insurance Co	AA	Se27,91	
Argonaut Intercompany Pool	AA+	Jn14,94	AA
Arkansas Blue Cross & Blue Shield	A+	Fe20,92	
Asset Guaranty Insurance Co	AA	Au02,93	
Associated Insurance Companies, Inc.	A+	De09,91	AA-
Assurances Generales de France (AGF)	AA	Ap12,94	AAA
Attorneys' Liability Assurance Society (Bermuda) Ltd	AA	Au23,94	AA-
Attorneys' Liability Assurance Society Inc	AA	Au23,94	AA-
Ausa Life Insurance Co	AA+	No15,93	
Australian Mutual Provident Society	AAA	Au01,94	
AXA Belgium S A.	AA	Ap12,94	AA+
AXA Domestic Life Group	AA	Ap12,94	AA+
AXA Domestic Non-Life Group	AA	Ap12,94	AA+
AXA Group	AA	Ap12,94	AA+
AXA Insurance Co., Ltd	AA	Ap12,94	AA+
AXA Marine & Aviation Insurance (U.K.) Ltd.	AA	Ap12,94	AA+
AXA Reassurance S.A.	AA	Ap12,94	AA+
AXA Reinsurance Co.	AA	Ap12,94	AA+
AXA Reinsurance U K. PLC	AA	Ap12,94	AA+
Baltica Forsikring A/S	BBB	No21,94	BBB-
Baltimore Life Insurance Co.	A+	Jy16,91	
Bankers Security Life Insurance Society	A+	Se26,90	A
Berkshire Hathaway Insurance Group	AAA	My11,94	
Berkshire Life Insurance Co.	AA	Ap27,92	
Blue Cross & Blue Shield of Florida	A+	Mr20,91	
Blue Cross & Blue Shield of Illinois	AA	Jy20,92	
Blue Cross & Blue Shield of Minnesota	AA-	Oc24,91	
Blue Cross & Blue Shield of Nebraska	A+	No17,94	
Blue Cross & Blue Shield of Texas Inc.	A	Mr20,91	
Blue Cross & Blue Shield of Virginia	AA-	Oc08,92	
Business Men's Assurance Co. of America	AA	Ja09,92	
C.M. Life Insurance Co.	AA-	Ap23,91	
California Housing Loan Insurance Fund	A+	Fe13,89	
Canada Life Assurance Co. (The)	AAA	My19,88	
Canada Life Insurance Co. of America	AAA	Jy18,90	
Canada Life Insurance Co. of New York	AAA	Jy18,90	
Capital Guaranty Insurance Co.	AAA	No14,86	
Capital Markets Assurance Corp	AAA	Ja26,88	
Capital Mortgage Reinsurance Co.	AA	Fe07,94	
Capital Mortgage Reinsurance Co. (Bermuda)	AA-	Ap13,94	
Capital Reinsurance Co.	AAA	Fe11,88	
Capitol Bankers Life Insurance Co.	A	No04,94	AA
Central Life Assurance Co.	A+	Ap20,93	A
Central National Life Insurance Co of Omaha (The)	AA	Oc01,91	
Centre Reinsurance (Bermuda) Ltd & Related Entities	AA	Fe13,92	
Chicago Title & Trust Insurance Co Group	A-	No10,92	
Chiyoda Fire & Marine Insurance Co. (Europe) Ltd.	A	Fe15,94	
Chiyoda Fire & Marine Insurance Co., Ltd	AA+	Mr08,94	AAA
Chubb Custom Insurance Co	AAA	Au16,91	
Chubb Group	AAA	Ap08,85	
Chubb Insurance Co. of Europe	AAA	Oc09,92	
Chubb Insurance Co. of New Jersey	AAA	Au16,91	
Chubb LifeAmerica Group	AAA	Au28,92	AA+
Chubb Lloyd's Insurance Co. of Texas	AAA	Au16,91	
Cincinnati Insurance Co.	AA+	De30,8J	
Citizens Insurance Co. of America	AA-	Mr10,95	AA
Clarendon Insurance Group	BBB+	Se01,93	BBB
Clerical, Medical & General Life Assurance Society	AA-	Fe21,95	
CNA Intercompany Pool	AA-	Se02,93	AA
College Life Insurance Co. of America	A	Ja03,95	
Colonial Life & Accident Insurance Co.	AA-	Mr17,94	NR
Colonial Mutual Life Assurance Society Ltd	A+	Ja31,95	
Colonial Penn Property/Casualty Insurance Group	A-	My27,94	BBB+
Columbus Life Insurance Co.	AAA	Jn21,94	AA
Combined Insurance Co. of America	AA	No03,94	
Combined Life Insurance Co. of NY	AA	No03,94	
Commercial Union Australian Mortgage Insurance Corp.	AA-	Oc01,94	
Commonwealth Insurance Co.	A-	Oc12,93	
Commonwealth Land Title & Transamerica Title Insurance Cos.	A	No21,94	
Commonwealth Life Insurance Co.	AAA	Se22,86	
Commonwealth Mortgage Assurance Co	AA	My18,87	AA-
Compagnie Generale de Reassurance de Monte-Carlo	AA	Ap12,94	AA+
Confederation Life Insurance & Annuity Co.	R	Au12.94	BBB+

APRIL 1995

* Reprinted with the permission of Standard & Poor's Ratings Group.

STANDARD & POOR'S RATINGS HANDBOOK

INSURER	RATING	RATING DATE	FORMER RATING
Confederation Life Insurance Co.	R	Au12.94	BBB+
Connecticut General Life Insurance Co	AA	De22.94	AA+
Connecticut Mutual Life Insurance Co	AA-	No22.89	AA+
Connie Lee Insurance Co.	AAA	De20.88	
Constitution Reinsurance Corp	AA	Mr10.94	
Continental Assurance Co. Intercompany Pool	AA+	Ja07.91	AAA
Continental Intercompany Pool	A-	Oc04.94	AA-
Coregis Insurance Group	A	Se07.94	
Crown America Life Insurance Co	AA-	Mr02.94	A+
Crown Life Insurance Co.	BBB+	Se09.94	A+
Crum & Forster Insurance (CFI)	A	Jy01.94	
Dai-Tokyo Fire & Marine Insurance Co Ltd.	AA+	Mr08.94	AAA
Dowa Fire & Marine Insurance Co . Ltd	AA	Oc29.87	
Eagle Star Insurance Co . Ltd	A+	Jy11.94	AA-
Eagle Star Life Assurance Co., Ltd	A+	Jy11.94	AA-
Eisen und Stahl Ruckversicherungs AG	AA-	Fe01.93	AA
Empire General Life Assurance Corp	AA	Fe23.93	
Empire Insurance Intercompany Pool	A	De17.90	
Employers Reinsurance Corp.	AAA	De24.92	
Employers Reinsurance International A/S	A+	Ja06.94	
Enhance Reinsurance Co	AAA	No04.86	
Equitable Life Assurance Society (The)	AA	Se27.93	
Equitable Life Assurance Society of the U S	A+	Jy27.92	A
Equitable Life Insurance Co of Iowa	AA	My26.92	AA-
Equitable of Colorado Inc	A+	De17.93	
Equitable Variable Life Insurance Co	A+	Jy27.92	A
Essex Insurance Co Group	A-	Jy26.93	
Europaeiske Rejseforsikring A/S	A-	Au18.93	
European Reinsurance Co of Zurich	AAA	Jn04.86	
Evanston Insurance Group	A-	Au07.92	
Executive Life Insurance Co., CA	R	Au20.92	CC
Executive Re Intercompany Pool	A+	Ja10.95	A
Farmers Insurance Co. of Arizona	A+	Mr10.95	AA
Farmers Insurance Co. of Columbus (OH)	A+	Mr10.95	AA
Farmers Insurance Co. of Idaho	A+	Mr10.95	AA
Farmers Insurance Co. of WA	A+	Mr10.95	AA
Farmers Insurance Exchange Intercompany Pool	A+	Mr10.95	AA
Fidelity & Guaranty Life Insurance Co	BBB+	Mr01.91	A
Fidelity Bankers Life Insurance Co.	R	Au20.92	CC
Fidelity Standard Life Insurance Co	AA-	Oc29.92	
Financial Guaranty Insurance Co.	AAA	No11.84	
Financial Security Assurance (U K) Ltd.	AAA	My16.94	
Financial Security Assurance Inc	AAA	Au31.85	
Financial Security Assurance International Inc	AAA	Se27.88	
Financial Security Assurance of Oklahoma Inc	AAA	Se27 88	
Fireman's Fund Intercompany Pool	AA	Jn08.93	AA+
First Ameritas Life Insurance Corp of NY	AA	No08.94	
First Capital Life Insurance Co	R	Au20.92	C
First Central National Life Insurance Co of New York (The)	AA	De20.91	
First Colony Life Insurance Co	AA+	De22.89	
First GNA Life Insurance Co. of New York	AA	Se19.93	AA-
First Liberty Insurance Co	AA	Jy24.92	AA+
First Penn-Pacific Life Insurance Co.	AA-	Ja30.92	
First Reliance Standard Life Insurance Co.	A-	Au01.91	
First SAFECO National Life Insurance Co. of New York	AA	Jy17.91	
First Transamerica Life Insurance Co	AA+	Ja17.91	
First UNUM Life Insurance Co.	AA	Ja31.95	AA+
Ford Life Insurance Co	A+	Mr07.95	AA
Forestview Mortgage Insurance Co	AAA	Oc27.94	
Forethought Life Insurance Co.	A	De16.92	
Fortis Life & Health Insurance Group	AA	Ap14.92	
Franklin Life Insurance Co.	AA	Fe07.95	AA+
Frankona Reinsurance Co	AA	De22.93	NR
Frontier Insurance Co.	A+	Jy19.94	A
GAN Life & Pensions PLC	A-	No17.93	
GEICO Casualty Co.	AAA	Jy18.91	
GEICO General Insurance Co.	AAA	Jy18.91	
GEICO Indemnity Insurance Co.	AAA	Jy18.91	
General Accident Fire & Life Assurance Corp PLC	AA-	Fe04.92	AA
General Accident Insurance Co. of America Intercompany Pool	AA-	Mr07.95	AA+
General American Life Insurance Co.	AA-	Jy21.92	AA
General Casualty of Wisconsin Intercompany Pool	AA	Au05.94	NR
General Electric Capital Assurance Co.	AA	Ap14.94	BBB
General Electric Mortgage Insurance Corp	AAA	My12.86	
General Electric Mortgage Insurance Corp. NC	AA	Mr11.85	
General Electric Residential Mortgage Insurance Corp of NC	AAA	My12.86	
General Reinsurance Corp	AAA	No29.84	
GIO General Ltd	A	Jy09.92	
GIO Insurances Ltd.	A	Jy09.92	
Gjensidige Skadeforsikring	AA-	No03.89	
Globe Life & Accident Insurance Co	AAA	Se15.89	
Golden Rule Insurance Co	AA-	Ja06.92	
Government Employees Insurance Co.	AAA	Fe04.85	
Great Northern Insured Annuity Corp	AA	Se19.93	AA-
Great Southern Life Insurance Co	A	Au07.90	
Great-West Life & Annuity Insurance Co (U.S.)	AAA	No27.90	
Great-West Life Assurance Co.	AAA	Oc27.86	
Guardian Insurance & Annuity Co. (The)	AAA	Jn13.90	
Guardian Life Insurance Co of America	AAA	Jn08.90	
Guardian Reinsurance Co	BBB	De09.94	
Gulf Life Insurance Co.	AAA	No08.91	
Hannover Reinsurance Co	AA+	Fe01.93	AAA
Hanover Insurance Co.	AA-	Mr10.95	AA
Hanover Lloyd's Insurance Co	AA-	Mr10.95	AA
Hartford Intercompany Pool	AAA	Au01.83	
Hartford Life & Accident Insurance Co	AAA	Jy17.91	
Hartford Life Insurance Co	AAA	Jy02.85	
Hawaiian Insurance & Guaranty Co	BB+	Au10.94	BB
Hawkeye-Security Insurance Co Intercompany Pool	AA-	Mr07.95	AA+
Health Care Group	A	Jy30.91	
Healthcare Underwriters Mutual Insurance Co	A-	My10.94	
Home Insurance Intercompany Pool	BB-	Fe24.95	BB
Horace Mann Insurance Co.	AA-	Jn29.92	
Horace Mann Life Insurance Co.	AA-	Jn29.92	
IASD Health Services Corp.	AA-	No30.94	
Industrial Indemnity Group	A+	My10.94	
Integrity Life Insurance Co	A	Au10.93	A+
Inter-State Assurance Co	AA-	De10.90	
International Business & Mercantile Reassurance Co.	AA+	Jy17.91	
International Insurance Co. of Hannover Ltd	A	Fe02.94	
International Life Investors Insurance Co.	AA+	Au22.91	
Investors Life Insurance Co. of Nebraska	AA+	My04.92	
Irish Life Assurance PLC	AA-	De06.90	
ITT Hartford International Life Reassurance Corp.	AAA	Oc18.94	
ITT Hartford Life & Annuity Insurance Co.	AAA	Jy17.91	
ITT London & Edinburgh Insurance Co., Ltd.	AA	Mr07.94	AA-
Jackson National Life Insurance Co.	AA	Jn25.92	
Jefferson-Pilot Life Insurance Co	AAA	My29.91	
John Alden Life Insurance Co.	A+	Au31.94	
John Alden Life Insurance Co. of NY	A+	No17.94	
John Deere Property Casualty Insurance Group	AA	Jy06.92	AA+
John Hancock Mutual Life Insurance Co	AA+	Mr03.95	AAA
John Hancock Variable Life Insurance Co.	AA+	Mr03.95	AAA
Kansas City Life Insurance Co	AA	Mr08.93	
Kemper Europe Reassurances S.A.	A	Se16.94	
Kemper National Insurance Companies Intercompany Pool	AA-	Ap15.91	AA
Kemper Reinsurance Co	A	Au02.94	A+

APRIL 1995

CLAIMS-PAYING ABILITY

INSURER	RATING	RATING DATE	FORMER RATING
Kemper Reinsurance London Ltd.	A	Au02.94	A+
Kentucky Central Life Insurance Co.	R	Fe16.93	BB
Keyport Life Insurance Co.	AA-	Ja27.94	A+
Knights of Columbus	AAA	De23.91	
L'Union des Assurances de Paris	AA	Ap12.94	AAA
Legal & General Assurance Society Ltd (Long-Term Fund)	AAA	Ja27.88	
Legion Insurance Co.	A	Oc17.91	
Leucadia Life Insurance Group	A	Jn01.94	
Lexington Insurance Co	AAA	Jn03.92	
Liberty Life Assurance Co of Boston	AA	Ja19.95	AA-
Liberty Mutual Intercompany Pool	AA	Jy24.92	AA+
Liberty National Life Insurance Co	AAA	Se15.89	
Life Insurance Co of GA	AAA	Au26.91	
Life Insurance Co of Virgina	AA	Ap13.89	
Life of Maryland Inc	A+	Jy16.91	
Lincoln National Life Insurance Co.	AA-	Oc03.91	AA+
Lincoln Security Life Insurance Co	AA-	Au21.91	
LM Insurance Co	AA	Jy24.92	AA+
London Life Insurance Co	AAA	Mr19.92	
Lutheran Brotherhood	AAA	No09.90	
Lutheran Brotherhood Variable Insurance Products Co.	AAA	Jn14.91	
Lyndon Insurance Group (Life/Health Div.)	AA-	Ap26.91	
Lyndon Insurance Group (Property/Casualty Div.)	AA-	Ap26.91	A+
Manufacturers Life Insurance Co. (The)	AA+	Oc21.94	AAA
Manufacturers Life Insurance Co (USA) (The)	AA+	Oc21.94	AAA
Manufacturers Life Insurance Co. of America (The)	AA+	Oc21.94	AAA
Massachusetts Bay Insurance Co	AA-	Mr10.95	AA
Massachusetts Mutual Life Insurance Co	AAA	Jn28.94	AA+
MBIA Assurance S A	AAA	No26.91	
MBIA Insurance Corp of Illinois	AAA	My14.85	
Medical Protective Co.	AA	My07.93	
Meiji Mutual Life Insurance Co	AA+	Mr08.94	AAA
Mercantile & General Reinsurance Co of America	A	Se13.94	AA-
Mercantile & General Reinsurance Co PLC	A	Se13.94	AA-
Merrill Lynch Life Insurance Co	AA-	Jn05.91	
Metropolitan Insurance & Annuity Co	AA+	Jy15.94	AAA
Metropolitan Life Insurance Co	AA+	Jy15.94	AAA
Metropolitan Property & Casualty Insurance Group	AA	Au21.91	
MGIC Mortgage Insurance Corp	AAA	My15.87	
MGICA (1992) Ltd	AA-	Se16.94	AA
Mid-Century Insurance Co of Texas	A+	Mr10.95	AA
Midland National Life Insurance Co.	AA+	De31.91	
Minnesota Mutual Life Insurance Co	AA+	Se24.91	AAA
Mitsui Marine & Fire Insurance Co. Ltd	AAA	No07.89	
ML Life Insurance Co of NY	AA-	Jn05.91	
MLC Life Ltd	AAA	Mr03.94	
MML Bay State Life Insurance Co.	AAA	Jn28.94	AA+
MML Pension Insurance Co.	AAA	Jn28.94	AA+
Mortgage Guaranty Insurance Corp.	AA+	Oc05.94	AA
Munich Reinsurance Co AG	AAA	Jn24.91	
Municipal Bond Insurance Assn.	AAA	Jn15.74	
Municipal Bond Investors Assurance Corp	AAA	Ja06.87	
Mutual Life Assurance Co. of Canada (The)	AA+	De05.94	AAA
Mutual Life Insurance Co of N.Y.	A	Ja30.95	A+
Mutual of America Life Insurance Co	AA+	Jn12.91	AA
Mutual of Omaha Insurance Co.	AA	Au24.92	
Mutual Trust Life Insurance Co	AA-	My02.94	
NAC Reinsurance Corp	AA-	Jn18.92	
National Home Life Assurance Co	AA	Oc20.89	
National Integrity Life Insurance Co	A	Au10.93	A+
National Life Insurance Co (VT)	AA-	Mr31.92	A+
National Provident Institution	A	Au16.93	
National Reinsurance Corp.	AA+	Ja06.95	
National Western Life Insurance Co.	A+	Jn23.94	
Nationwide Life Insurance Co	AAA	De14.88	
Nationwide Mutual Insurance Intercompany Pool	AA+	Jn18.93	AA
New England Mutual Life Insurance Co	A+	No10.94	AA-
New England Variable Life Insurance Co.	A+	No10.94	AA-
New York Life Insurance & Annuity Corp.	AAA	Fe13.91	
New York Life Insurance Co.	AAA	Oc30.86	
Nichido Fire & Marine Insurance Co. Ltd.	AA+	Mr08.94	AAA
Nippon Fire & Marine Insurance Co.	AA+	Mr08.94	AAA
North American Life Assurance Co.	A	No04.94	AA
North American Reinsurance Corp.	AAA	Jn04.86	
North American Security Life Insurance Co	A	No04.94	AA
North Pacific Insurance Co.	AA-	Mr07.95	AA+
Northbrook Excess & Surplus Insurance Co.	AA	Jn08.93	AA-
Northbrook Indemnity Co.	AA	Jn08.93	AA-
Northbrook National Insurance Co.	AA	Jn08.93	AA-
Northbrook Property & Casualty Insurance Co.	AA	Jn08.93	AA-
Northern Life Insurance Co.	AA-	Jy08.91	
Northwestern Mutual Life Insurance Co	AAA	Jn03.87	
Northwestern National Life Insurance Co.	A+	Au26.93	A
Northwestern Pacific Indemnity Co.	AAA	Au16.91	
Norwich Union Life Insurance Society	AA-	Se28.94	
Ohio Casualty Insurance Co. Intercompany Pool	AA-	Mr20.91	
Ohio National Life Assurance Corp	AA	Jn25.91	
Ohio National Life Insurance Co. (The)	AA	Jn25.91	
Old American Insurance Co.	A+	Mr08.93	
Old Line Life Insurance Co. of America (The)	AA+	De10.91	
Old Republic General Insurance Group	AA+	Au03.89	
Old Republic Title Insurance Group	A+	Se16.93	
Oregon Automobile Insurance Co.	AA-	Mr07.95	AA+
Orion Capital Insurance Group	A	Se14.93	A-
Pacific Guardian Life Insurance Co., Ltd.	AA+	Mr08.94	AAA
Pacific Mutual Life Insurance Co.	AA+	Oc03.91	AAA
Painewebber Life Insurance Co.	A-	Fe23.94	
Paragon Life Insurance Co.	AA-	Jy21.92	AA
Paul Revere Life Insurance Co.	AA-	No07.94	AA
Paul Revere Protective Life Insurance Co.	AA-	No07.94	AA
Paul Revere Variable Annuity Insurance Co.	AA-	No07.94	AA
Pearl Assurance PLC (General Insurance Fund)	AAA	No17.93	
Pearl Assurance PLC (Long-term Fund)	AAA	Au05.93	
Pelstate Insurance Group	R	Au20.92	B
Penn Insurance & Annuity Corp.	AA-	Fe23.94	A+
Penn Mutual Life Insurance Co.	AA-	Fe23.94	A+
Peoples Security Life Insurance Co.	AAA	Se22.86	
PHICO Insurance Co.	A	Oc05.94	
PHL Variable Insurance Co.	AA-	Oc20.94	
Phoenix American Life Insurance Co.	AA-	Jn30.92	AA
Phoenix Home Life Mutual Insurance Co.	AA-	Jn30.92	
Phoenix Life Insurance Co.	AA-	Oc20.94	
Physicians Insurance Exchange	A-	Au19.94	
Physicians Life Insurance Co.	AA-	Jn03.93	
Physicians Mutual Insurance Co.	AA-	Jn03.93	
PMI Mortgage Insurance Co.	AA+	Oc27.94	AAA
Pohjola Insurance Co., Ltd.	A-	Ja18.95	BBB+
Previasa S.A.	BBB+	Jy11.94	
Primerica Life Insurance Co.	AA	Jn27.90	A+
Principal Mutual Life Insurance Co.	AA+	Se24.91	AAA
Principal National Life Insurance Co.	AA+	Se24.91	
Protective Life Insurance Co.	AA	Oc11.89	
Provident Life & Accident Insurance Co	A+	Oc06.94	AA-
Provident Mutual Life Insurance Co of Philadelphia	AA-	Jy17.92	AA
Provident National Assurance Co.	A+	Oc06.94	AA-
Providentmutual Life & Annuity Co. of America	AA-	Jn09.93	
PRUCO Life Insurance Co.	AA-	De22.94	AA
PRUCO Life Insurance Co. of Illinois	AA-	De22.94	AA
PRUCO Life Insurance Co. of New Jersey	AA-	De22.94	AA
PRUCO Life Insurance Co. of Texas	AA-	De22.94	AA

STANDARD & POOR'S RATINGS HANDBOOK

INSURER	RATING	RATING DATE	FORMER RATING
Prudential Insurance Co. of America	AA-	De22.94	AA
Prudential Property & Casualty Insurance Co. of Indiana	AA-	De22.94	AA
Prudential Reinsurance Co.	A	Ja21.94	AA
PXRE Reinsurance Co.	A-	Ja19.95	
QBE Insurance and Reinsurance (Europe) Ltd.	A	Ja14.94	
QBE Insurance Group Ltd.	A	Ja14.94	
QBE International Insurance Ltd.	A	Ja14.94	
Re Capital Reinsurance Corp.	A	Se02.93	
Reale Riassicurazioni S.p.A.	BBB+	Oc24.94	
Reliance Insurance Co. Intercompany Pool	A	No05.93	BBB+
Reliance Standard Life Insurance Co.	A-	De29.89	
Republic Mortgage Insurance Co of NC	AA	Jy07.94	
Republic Mortgage Insurance Co.	AA	Mr28.83	
Royal Indemnity Co. Intercompany Pool	A	Mr03.95	A-
Royal Insurance PLC	A	Fe28.95	A-
SAFECO Insurance Co. Intercompany Pool	AAA	Au26.85	
SAFECO Life Insurance Co.	AA	Jy17.91	
SAFECO National Life Insurance Co.	AA	Jy17.91	
San Francisco Reinsurance Co.	A+	Au01.91	
Savings Bank Life Insurance (MA)	AA-	Ja03.92	
Scottish Equitable PLC	AA-	Au25.94	
Scottish Life Assurance Co.	A+	Oc14.93	
Scottish Provident Institution	AA+	Jn05.91	
Seaboard Surety Co.	AA	Ja22.91	
Security Benefit Life Insurance Co.	AA-	My28.93	A+
Security Equity Life Insurance Co.	AA-	My20.94	A+
Security First Life Insurance Co.	AA-	Mr19.92	
Security Life of Denver Insurance Co.	AAA	Fe12.87	
Security Mutual Life Insurance Co. of NY	A+	Oc05.92	AA-
Security-Connecticut Life Insurance Co.	AA-	Au15.91	
Selective Insurance Co. of America Intercompany Pool	A	De07.88	
Sirius International Insurance Corp.	A+	Ja13.93	
Skandia America Reinsurance Corp.	BBB	No09.92	A
Skandia Insurance Co., Ltd.	BBB+	De30.94	
Skandia International Insurance Corp.	BBB+	De30.94	BBB
SMA Life Assurance Co.	A+	Mr10.95	AA
Southland Life Insurance Co.	AAA	Au26.91	
Southwestern Life Insurance Co.	B+	Ja27.95	BB+
Sphere Drake Insurance PLC	BBB	Se03.93	
St. Paul Fire & Casualty Insurance Co. (The)	AAA	Jn27.91	
St. Paul Fire & Marine Insurance Co. Intercompany Pool	AAA	Mr28.83	
St. Paul Guardian Insurance Co. (The)	AAA	Jn27.91	
St. Paul Indemnity Insurance Co.	AAA	Jn27.91	
St. Paul Insurance Co. (The)	AAA	Jn27.91	
St. Paul Insurance Co. of Illinois	AAA	Jn27.91	
St. Paul Insurance Co. of North Dakota	AAA	Jn27.91	
St. Paul International Insurance Co.	AAA	De20.93	BBB
St. Paul Lloyd's	AAA	Jn27.91	
St. Paul Mercury Insurance Co.	AAA	Jn27.91	
St. Paul Property & Casualty Insurance Co.	AAA	Jn27.91	
St. Paul Reinsurance Co., Ltd.	AAA	Oc04.93	BBB
Standard Insurance Co. (OR)	AA-	Ja28.92	
Standard Life Assurance Co. (The)	AAA	No26.90	
State Farm Group	AAA	Oc31.94	
State Farm Life Insurance Co.	AAA	Mr20.91	
State Government Insurance Commission South Australia	AA	Jy27.92	
State Mutual Life Assurance Co. of America	A+	Mr10.95	AA
Sumitomo Marine & Fire Insurance Co., Ltd.	AAA	Oc21.87	
Sun Alliance & London Insurance PLC & Related Entities	AA-	Ja13.93	AA
Sun Life Assurance Co. of Canada	AAA	Au28.86	
Sun Life Assurance Co. of Canada (U.S.)	AAA	Ja16.90	
Sun Life Insurance & Annuity Co. of New York	AAA	My13.91	
Sun Life Insurance Co. of America	AA	Ap13.89	A+
Sunset Life Insurance Co. of America	AA	Mr08.93	
Superior National Insurance Co.	BBB	Fe28.95	
Swiss Reinsurance Co.	AAA	Jn04.86	
Sydney Reinsurance Co., Ltd.	A	Ja14.94	
Teachers Insurance & Annuity Assn.	AAA	No01.90	
Teachers Insurance Co.	AA-	Jn29.92	
Texas Pacific Indemnity Co.	AAA	Au16.91	
TIG Insurance Group	AA-	Ja13.89	
TMG Life Insurance Co.	AA+	De05.94	AAA
Tokio Marine & Fire Insurance Co., Ltd.	AAA	Au26.91	
Transamerica Life Insurance & Annuity Co.	AA+	De05.89	
Transamerica Occidental Life Insurance Co.	AA+	De22.88	
Travelers Indemnity Intercompany Pool	AA-	Mr30.92	AA
Travelers Insurance Co.	A+	Oc05.90	AA-
Travelers Life & Annuity Co.	A+	Oc05.90	AA-
Trenwick America Reinsurance Corp.	A	De29.92	
Triad Guaranty Insurance Co.	AA-	No18.93	
Trygg-Hansa Insurance Co., Ltd.	A+	Se20.94	AA
Union Central Life Insurance Co. (The)	A+	No17.93	A
Union Labor Life Insurance Co.	BBB+	Oc09.92	BBB
Union Reinsurance Co.	AA-	Ja11.94	
Unionamerica Insurance Company, Ltd.	A-	No04.94	
United American Insurance Co.	AAA	Se15.89	
United Guaranty Residential Insurance Co.	AAA	My12.86	
United Investors Life Insurance Co.	AAA	Ja03.92	
United of Omaha Life Insurance Co.	AA	Au24.92	
United Services Automobile Assn.	AAA	Se16.88	
United Services Life Insurance Co.	A+	Se26.90	A
United States Fidelity & Guaranty Co.	A-	Fe23.94	BBB+
United States Life Insurance Company in the City of New York	AA+	Fe20.92	
UNUM Life Insurance Co. of America	AA	Ja31.95	AA+
USAA Casualty Insurance Co.	AAA	Jn28.91	
USAA General Indemnity Co.	AAA	Jn28.91	
USAA Life Insurance Co.	AAA	Oc30.91	
USG Annuity & Life Co.	AA	My26.92	AA-
Variable Annuity Life Insurance Co.	AAA	Ap15.92	AA+
Verex Assurance Inc.	BBB-	Jn03.88	A
Veritas Reinsurance Co. Ltd.	BBB	Oc21.94	
Veritus Inc. (d/b/a Blue Cross of Western PA)	AA-	Jn07.91	AA
Westchester Specialty Group (WSG)	A	Jy08.94	
Western and Southern Life Insurance Co. (The)	AAA	Au26.91	
Western National Life Insurance Co.	A+	Ja08.92	A-
Western Reserve Life Assurance Co. of Ohio	AA+	Au23.91	
Western-Southern Life Assurance Co.	AAA	Au26.91	
Winterthur Swiss Insurance Co.	AAA	My27.86	
Wisconsin Mortgage Assurance Corp.	AA	Fe22.85	
Woodmen of the World and/or Omaha Woodmen Life Ins. Society	AA	Mr01.94	
Xerox Financial Life Insurance Co.	A	Au03.94	A+
Xerox Financial Services Life Insurance Co.	A	Au03.94	A+
Yasuda Fire & Marine Insurance Co., Ltd.	AAA	Jy01.87	
Zenith National Insurance Group Intercompany Pool	AA-	De30.88	
Zurich American Insurance Intercompany Pool	AAA	Jn03.92	
Zurich American Life Insurance Co.	AA-	Au01.91	
Zurich Insurance Co.	AAA	Mr15.84	
Zurich International (Bermuda) Ltd.	AA	Fe13.92	
Zurich Reinsurance Centre Inc.	AA-	Oc05.93	

¶17,145 HOW TO USE THE SPREADSHEETS

The spreadsheets are designed to be filled out on an item-by-item basis. If a benefit is not applicable, or if the insurance company will not or cannot quote a benefit, indicate this by marking “N/A” at the particular line. Similarly, if a portion of a specific benefit does not apply, indicate by marking an “N/A” next to the item. Should two or more classifications of employees be covered for different scheduled amounts, note on the spreadsheets, or in the accompanying letter, that a photocopy of the blank spreadsheet page, containing the particular benefit, should be used for each classification. For example, Class A is covered for a 75 per cent of monthly earnings, taxable LTD plan, while Class B is covered for a 66.67 per cent non-taxable LTD plan. A separate spreadsheet page should be used, and clearly marked as to which class it applies, for each classification.

To protect the insurers/providers, the ABCs and the consumers, note that the spreadsheet pages are subject to Errors and Omissions. The spreadsheets and their contents are intended as illustrations only. In the event of a discrepancy, the terms and conditions of the actual group insurance, or provider, policy will apply.

The Premium/Rate Comparison charts (nos. 1 and 2) are examples of how to set up proper rate comparisons. No. 1 shows the present plan comparison for a group of 100 employees. No. 2 shows a present plan premium/rate comparison for a group of 25 employees. Note the use of common volumes for each benefit.

When conducting a group insurance marketing project where benefit variations are required, use spreadsheets similar to the ones used for the present plan. Title the benefit variation spreadsheets “Proposed Plan(s)”. Use common volumes for the proposed plans premium/rate comparison.

¶17,150 EMPLOYEE BENEFITS SPREADSHEET COMPARISON PAGES

1. Rate Comparison page: Example 1 for a group with 100 employees.
2. Rate Comparison page: Example 2 for a group with 25 employees.
3. Group Life Insurance Benefit.
4. Group Employee Voluntary Life Insurance Benefit.
5. Basic AD&D, page 1: Benefits.
6. Basic AD&D, page 2: Benefits.
7. Group Voluntary AD&D, page 1: Benefits.
8. Group Voluntary AD&D, page 2: Benefits.
9. Group Dependant Life Insurance Benefit.
10. Group Dependant Voluntary Life Insurance Benefit.
11. Group LTD Benefit, page 1: Schedule, all-source maximum, elimination/waiting periods.
12. Group LTD Benefit, page 2: Maximum, residual, partial, re-employment benefits, offsets.
13. Group LTD Benefit, page 3: Pre-existing conditions, exclusions.
14. Weekly Indemnity Benefit, page 1: Schedule, reductions, premium waiver, definition.
15. Weekly Indemnity Benefit, page 2: Maximum, benefit start, benefit duration.
16. Weekly Indemnity Benefit, page 3: Rehabilitation, offsets, exclusions.
17. Weekly Indemnity Benefit, page 4: Pre-existing conditions, UI and LTD integration.
18. EHC, page 1: Deductibles, co-insurance, maximum, surviving dependants' coverage.
19. EHC, page 2: Home province hospital.
20. EHC, page 3: Convalescent hospital deductibles, co-insurance.
21. EHC, page 4: Convalescent hospital maximum, coverage, exclusions.
22. EHC, page 5: Prescription drugs deductibles, co-insurance.

23. EHC, page 6: Prescription drugs coverage, exclusions.
24. EHC, page 7: Other coverage — deductibles, co-insurance.
25. EHC, page 8: Other coverage — ambulance, nursing, artificial limbs, casts, mammary prosthesis.
26. EHC, page 9: Other coverage — blood, oxygen, dental, bra, hearing aids, orthopaedic shoes, wigs.
27. EHC, page 10: Other coverage — stockings, eye exams, vision care.
28. EHC, page 11: Paramedical practitioners deductibles, co-insurance, maximums.
29. EHC, page 12: Paramedical practictioners, x-rays, acupuncture, chiropractors, masseurs, naturopaths, osteopaths.
30. EHC, page 13: Paramedical practitioners, psychologists, physiotherapists, speech therapists, other.
31. EHC, page 14: Out-of-country referrals, deductibles, co-insurance.
32. EHC, page 15: Out-of-country referrals, maximums, exclusions.
33. EHC, page 16: Out-of-country emergencies/travel health deductibles.
34. EHC, page 17: Out-of-country emergencies/travel health co-insurance, hospital, maximum.
35. EHC, page 18: Out-of-country emergencies/travel health administration, doctors, ambulance.
36. EHC, page 19: Out-of-country emergencies/travel health, return flight, cash, luggage, etc.
37. EHC, page 20: Other medical benefits, decompression chambers.
38. Political Evacuation and Kidnapping/Extortion Insurance.
39. Dental Benefit, page 1: Overall Deductibles and Maximum Benefits.
40. Dental Benefit, page 2: Overall benefits, percentages reimbursed.
41. Dental Benefit, page 3: Basic benefits — exams, x-rays, cleaning, emergencies, anaesthesia.
42. Dental Benefit, page 4: Basic benefits — fluoride, fillings, extractions, hygiene, sealants.
43. Dental Benefit, page 5: Root canals, gum disease.
44. Dental Benefit, page 6: Other basic, and basic benefit exclusions.

45. Dental Benefit, page 7: Relining, rebasing and repairs to dentures.
46. Dental Benefit, page 8: Major dental benefits deductibles, co-insurance, benefits.
47. Dental Benefit, page 9: Orthodontic benefits and overall dental benefit exclusions.
48. Basic AD&D Benefit, page 1: Benefits.
49. Basic AD&D Benefit, page 2: Benefits.
50. Group Voluntary AD&D Benefit, page 1: Eligibility, maximums.
51. Group Voluntary AD&D Benefit, page 2: Benefits.
52. Group Insurance Claims Information, page 1: All benefits: Office locations, claims reports.
53. Group Insurance Claims Information, page 2: All benefits: Report types, turnaround times, comments.
54. Group Insurance Service and Administration, page 1: Systems, booklets, access numbers.
55. Group Insurance Service and Administration, page 2: Office locations, representatives, insurer information.
56. Group Insurance Financial Information, page 1: Break-even loss ratios, trend factors, IBNR formulas.
57. Group Insurance Financial Information, page 2: IBNR (Life Insurance) formula, credibility formulas.
58. Group Insurance Financial Information, page 3: Retention charges for EHC and dental.
59. Group Insurance Financial Information, page 4: Retention charges for WI, LTD, and life insurance.
60. Group Insurance Financial Information, page 5: Pooling levels and interest formulas.
61. Group Insurance Financial Information, page 6: Rate basis and rate guarantees, dental fee guide.
62. Group Insurance Financial Information, page 7: Alternate financing cost-plus, experience rating, EFAPs.
63. Group Insurance Financial Information, page 8: Alternate financing ASO charges, stop-loss.

1. Rate Comparison: Example 1 (100 employees)

Premium/Rate Comparison: Present Plan   Employee Classifications Covered: All   Example 1: For a Group of 100 Employees

	A	B	D	E	G	H	J	K	M	N	P	Q	S	T	V	W
1			Present													
2			Insurer		Insurer A		Insurer B		Insurer C		Insurer D		Insurer E		Insurer F	
3	Benefit	Volume	Rate	Monthly Cost	Rate	Monthly Cost	Rate	Monthly Cost	Rate	Monthly Cost	Rate	Monthly Cost	Rate	Monthly Cost	Rate	Monthly Cost
4																
5	Life Insurance	4500	0.28	$1,260.00	0.26	$1,170.00	0.25	$1,125.00	0.31	$1,395.00	0.29	$1,305.00	N/A	$0.00	N/A	$0.00
6	Dependent Life	40	2.50	$100.00	3.00	$120.00	1.75	$70.00	2.25	$90.00	2.84	$113.60	N/A	$0.00	N/A	$0.00
7	Long Term Disability	1250	0.75	$937.50	0.86	$1,075.00	0.98	$1,225.00	0.79	$987.50	0.73	$912.50	N/A	$0.00	N/A	$0.00
8	AD&D	4500	0.04	$180.00	0.045	$202.50	0.055	$247.50	0.038	$171.00	0.5	$2,250.00	N/A	$0.00	N/A	$0.00
9																
10	Weekly Indemnity	2884.62	0.62	$1,788.46	0.55	$1,586.54	0.74	$2,134.62	0.65	$1,875.00	0.49	$1,413.46	N/A	$0.00	N/A	$0.00
11	Extended Health Care (Single)	40	$18.20	$728.00	19.25	$770.00	20.89	$835.60	22.69	$907.60	26.87	$1,074.80	19.22	$768.80	N/A	$0.00
12	Extended Health Care (Family)	60	$40.04	$2,402.40	42.35	$2,541.00	45.75	$2,745.00	54.46	$3,267.60	59.11	$3,546.60	41.49	$2,489.40	N/A	$0.00
13																
14	Travel Plan (Single)	40	Included	$0.00	Included	$0.00	Included	$0.00	2.51	$100.40	Included	$0.00	1.75	$70.00	N/A	$0.00
15	Travel Plan (Family)	60	Included	$0.00	Included	$0.00	Included	$0.00	5.25	$315.00	Included	$0.00	3.85	$231.00	N/A	$0.00
16																
17	Dental (Single)	40	$26.80	$1,072.00	19.80	$792.00	26.49	$1,059.60	28.33	$1,133.20	25	$1,000.00	24.9	$996.00		Cost Plus 15%
18	Dental (Family)	60	$58.96	$3,537.60	43.56	$2,613.60	58.28	$3,496.80	67.99	$4,079.40	55.12	$3,307.20	55.6	$3,336.00		Cost Plus 15%
19																
20	Monthly Cost E.H.C. + Dent+WI+ Trav.			$9,528.46		$8,303.14		$10,271.62		$11,678.20		$10,342.06		$7,891.20		$0.00
21																
22	Monthly Cost (Life+AD/D+D L. +L.T.D.)			$2,477.50		$2,567.50		$2,667.50		$2,643.50		$4,581.10		$0.00		$0.00
23																
24	Total Monthly Cost			$12,005.96		$10,870.64		$12,939.12		$14,321.70		$14,923.16		$7,891.20		Cost Plus 8%
25	Total Annual Cost			$144,071.57		$130,447.69		$155,269.43		$171,860.44		$179,077.97		$94,694.40		Cost Plus 8%
26																
27																
28																
29																
30																
31																
32																
33																
34																
35																
36																
37	Notes:															
38	Life Insurance and A.D.& D. Volumes are expressed in $1,000's.															
39	Long Term Disability Volumes are expressed in $100's.															
40	Weekly Indemnity Volumes are expressed in $10's.															
41	Dependent Life Volumes are expressed in number of Family Units.															

The contents of this report are for comparison purposes only. The terms and conditions of the actual policy apply in the event of a discrepancy. CONFIDENTIAL

2. Rate Comparison: Example 2 (25 employees)

Premium/Rate Comparison: Present Plan Employee Classifications Covered: All Example 2: For a Group of 25 Employees

	A	B	D	E	G	H	J	K	M	N	P	Q	S	T	V	W
1			Present													
2			Insurer		Insurer A		Insurer B		Insurer C		Insurer D		Insurer E		Insurer F	
3	Benefit	Volume	Rate	Monthly Cost	Rate	Monthly Cost	Rate	Monthly Cost	Rate	Monthly Cost	Rate	Monthly Cost	Rate	Monthly Cost	Rate	Monthly Cost
4	Life Insurance	1125	0.28	$315.00	0.26	$292.50	0.25	$281.25	0.31	$348.75	0.29	$326.25	N/A	$0.00	N/A	$0.00
5	Dependent Life	10	2.50	$25.00	3.00	$30.00	1.75	$17.50	2.25	$22.50	2.84	$28.40	N/A	$0.00	N/A	$0.00
6	Long Term Disability	312.5	0.75	$234.38	0.86	$268.75	0.98	$306.25	0.79	$246.88	0.73	$228.13	N/A	$0.00	N/A	$0.00
7	AD&D	1125	0.04	$45.00	0.045	$50.63	0.055	$61.88	0.038	$42.75	0.5	$562.50	N/A	$0.00	N/A	$0.00
8																
9	Weekly Indemnity	721.154	0.62	$447.12	0.55	$396.63	0.74	$533.65	0.65	$468.75	0.49	$353.37	N/A	$0.00	N/A	$0.00
10	Extended Health Care (Single)	10	$18.20	$182.00	19.25	$192.50	20.89	$208.90	22.69	$226.90	26.87	$268.70	19.22	$192.20	N/A	$0.00
11	Extended Health Care (Family)	15	$40.04	$600.60	42.35	$635.25	45.75	$686.25	54.46	$816.90	59.11	$886.65	41.49	$622.35	N/A	$0.00
12																
13	Travel Plan (Single)	10	Included	$0.00	Included	$0.00	Included	$0.00	2.51	$25.10	Included	$0.00	1.75	$17.50	N/A	$0.00
14	Travel Plan (Family)	15	Included	$0.00	Included	$0.00	Included	$0.00	5.25	$78.75	Included	$0.00	3.85	$57.75	N/A	$0.00
15																
16	Dental (Single)	10	$26.80	$268.00	19.80	$198.00	26.49	$264.90	28.33	$283.30	25	$250.00	24.9	$249.00		Cost Plus 15%
17	Dental (Family)	15	$58.96	$884.40	43.56	$653.40	58.28	$874.20	67.99	$1,019.85	55.12	$826.80	55.6	$834.00		Cost Plus 15%
18																
19	Monthly Cost E.H.C. + Dent+WI+ Trav			$2,382.12		$2,075.78		$2,567.90		$2,919.55		$2,585.52		$1,972.80		$0.00
20																
21	Monthly Cost (Life+AD/D+D L. +L.T.D.)			$619.38		$641.88		$666.88		$660.88		$1,145.28		$0.00		$0.00
22																
23	Total Monthly Cost			$3,001.49		$2,717.66		$3,234.78		$3,580.43		$3,730.79		$1,972.80		Cost Plus 8%
24	Total Annual Cost			$36,017.89		$32,611.92		$38,817.35		$42,965.10		$44,769.49		$23,673.60		Cost Plus 8%
25																
26																
27																
28																
29																
30																
31																
32																
33																
34																
35																
36																
37	Notes:															
38	Life Insurance and A.D.& D. Volumes are expressed in $1,000's.															
39	Long Term Disability Volumes are expressed in $100's.															
40	Weekly Indemnity Volumes are expressed in $10's.															
41	Dependent Life Volumes are expressed in number of Family Units.															

The contents of this report are for comparison purposes only. The terms and conditions of the actual policy apply in the event of a discrepancy. CONFIDENTIAL

3. Group Life Insurance Benefit

GROUP LIFE INSURANCE BENEFIT

A	A	C	E	G	I	K	M	O
1	**Benefit Terms**	**Present Insurer**	**Insurer A**	**Insurer B**	**Insurer C**	**Insurer D**	**Insurer E**	**Example**
2								
3	Class A Schedule							2 Times Ann. Earnings
4								To Next Highest $1,000
5	Class B Schedule							1.5 X Ann. Earnings
6								To Next Highest $1,000
7	Class C Schedule							N/A
8								
9	Class D Schedule							N/A
10								
11	Coverage Reductions							Half At Age 65
12	Age							Cancel At Age 70
13	Retirement							Cancel At Retirement
14								
15	Conversion Privilege							Yes
16								
17	Waiver of Premium on							
18	Total Disability							Yes
19	Waiver Maximum Age							Age 65
20								
21	Living Benefit ®							No
22								
23	Overall Maximum							
24	Benefit							$250,000
25	Maximum Benefit							
26	Without a Medical							$150,000
27								
28	Will New Insurer							
29	Continue Coverage							
30	Without Medicals?							N/A
31								
32	Location of Claims Office							Toronto
33								
34	Other							
35								
36								
37								
38								
39								
40								

The contents of this report are for comparison purposes only. The terms and conditions of the actual policy apply in the event of a discrepency. CONFIDENTIAL

4. Group Employee Voluntary Life Insurance Benefit

GROUP EMPLOYEE VOLUNTARY LIFE INSURANCE BENEFIT

A	A	C	E	G	I	K	M	O
1	**Benefit Terms**	**Present Insurer**	**Insurer A**	**Insurer B**	**Insurer C**	**Insurer D**	**Insurer E**	**Example**
2								
3	Class A Schedule							Offered
4								
5	Class B Schedule							Offered
6								
7	Class C Schedule							N/A
8								
9	Class D Schedule							N/A
10								
11	Insurance Unit Amount							$10,000
12								
13	Coverage Reductions:							
14	Age							Cancel At Age 65
15	Retirement							Cancel At Retirement
16								
17	Conversion Privilege							Yes
18								
19	Waiver of Premium on							
20	Total Disability							Yes
21	Waiver Maximum Age							Age 65
22								
23	Living Benefit ®							No
24								
25	Overall Maximum							
26	Benefit							$200,000
27	Maximum Benefit							
28	Without a Medical							$0
29								
30	Will New Insurer							
31	Continue Coverage							
32	Without Medicals?							N/A
33								
34	Location of Claims Office							Toronto
35								
36	Other							
37								
38								
39								
40								

The contents of this report are for comparison purposes only. The terms and conditions of the actual policy apply in the event of any discrepency. Confidential.

5. Basic AD&D, page 1: Benefits.

BASIC ACCIDENTAL DEATH AND DISMEMBERMENT: Page. 1 Benefits

A	A	B	C	D	E	F	G	H	I	J	K	L	M	N	O
1	**Benefit Terms**		**Present Insurer**		**Insurer A**		**Insurer B**		**Insurer C**		**Insurer D**		**Insurer E**		**Example**
2															
3	Basic Accidental Death														
4	and Dismemberment														
5															
6	Class A Schedule														2 x Annual Earnings
7															To Next Highest $1000
8	Class B Schedule														1.5 x Annual Earnings
9															To Next Highest $1000
10	Class C Schedule														N/A
11															
12	Class D Schedule														N/A
13															
14	Coverage Reductions														
15	Age														Cancel At Age 65
16	Retirement														Cancel At Retirement
17															
18	Conversion Privilege														No
19															
20	Waiver of Premium														
21	On Total Disability														Yes
22	Waiver Maximum Age														Age 65
23															
24	Overall Maximum														
25	Benefit														$250,000
26															
27	Time Restriction For														
28	Dismemberment Loss														One Year
29															
30	Loss Includes														
31	"Loss Of Use Of "														Yes
32															
33	Claims Office Location														Toronto
34															
35	Comments														
36															
37															
38															
39															
40															

The contents of this report are for comparison purposes only. The terms and conditions of the actual policy apply in the event of any discrepancy. Confidential.

6. Basic AD&D, page 2: Benefits.

BASIC ACCIDENTAL DEATH AND DISMEMBERMENT: Page. 2 Benefits

A	A	B	C	D	E	F	G	H	I	J	K	L	M	N	O
1	**Benefit Terms**		**Present Insurer**		**Insurer A**		**Insurer B**		**Insurer C**		**Insurer D**		**Insurer E**		**Example**
2															
3	Basic AD&D Benefits														
4															
5	Benefits: Paid For Loss Of														
6	Life														2 x Annual Earnings
7	Both Hands														2 x Annual Earnings
8	Both Feet														2 x Annual Earnings
9	Both Eyes														2 x Annual Earnings
10	One Hand And One Foot														2 x Annual Earnings
11	One Hand And One Eye														2 x Annual Earnings
12	Speech And Hearing														2 x Annual Earnings
13															
14	One Hand														1 x Annual Earnings
15	One Foot														1 x Annual Earnings
16	One Eye														1 x Annual Earnings
17	One Leg														1 x Annual Earnings
18	One Arm														1 x Annual Earnings
19															
20	Speech Or Hearing														50% of Annual Earning
21	Four Fingers On One Hand														50% of Annual Earning
22	Thumb And Index Finger														
23	On One Hand														50% of Annual Earning
24	All Toes On One Foot														25% of Annual Earning
25	Hearing In One Ear														25% of Annual Earning
26															
27	Paralysis Benefit														
28	Quadraplegia														4 x Annual Earnings
29															
30	Paraplegia														2 x Annual Earnings
31															
32	Hemiplegia														2 x Annual Earnings
33															
34	Other														
35															
36															
37	Exclusions														
38	Self-Inflicted Injury Or Death														Not Covered
39	War, Civil Insurrection, Riot														Not Covered
40	Other														

The contents of this report are for comparison purposes only. The terms and conditions of the actual policy apply in the event of any discrepency. Confidential.

7. Group Voluntary AD&D, page 1: Benefits.

GROUP VOLUNTARY ACCIDENTAL DEATH AND DISMEMBERMENT: Page. 1 Benefits

A	A	B	C	D	E	F	G	H	I	J	K	L	M	N	O
1	**Benefit Terms**		**Present Insurer**		**Insurer A**		**Insurer B**		**Insurer C**		**Insurer D**		**Insurer E**		**Example**
2															
3	Class A Eligible														Yes
4															
5	Class B Eligible														Yes
6															
7	Class C Eligible														N/A
8															
9	Class D Eligible														N/A
10															
11	Insurance Unit Amount														$10,000
12	Level Amount														N/A
13															
14	Spouse Coverage														Spouses Eligible
15															
16	Optional Family Cover														Yes
17	Spouse and No Children														Yes
18	Spouse and Children														Yes
19	Dependent Child Only														Yes
20															
21	Coverage Reductions														
22	Age														Cancel At Age 65
23	Retirement														Cancel at Retirement
24															
25	Maximum Age For														
26	Dependent Children														21
27															
28	Conversion Privilege														
29															
30	Waiver of Premium on														
31	Total Disability														Yes
32	Waiver Maximum Age														65
33															
34	Overall Maximum Benefit														$250,000
35															
36	Overall Common														
37	Disaster Maximum														$1,000,000
38															
39															
40															

The contents of this report are for comparison purposes only. The terms and conditions of the actual policy apply in the event of any discrepency. Confidential.

8. Group Voluntary AD&D, page 2: Benefits.

GROUP VOLUNTARY ACCIDENTAL DEATH AND DISMEMBERMENT: Page. 2 Benefits

A	A	C	E	G	I	K	M	O
1	**Benefit Terms**	**Present Insurer**	**Insurer A**	**Insurer B**	**Insurer C**	**Insurer D**	**Insurer E**	**Example**
2								
3	Voluntary AD&D Benefits							
4								
5	Will New Insurer Continue							
6	Coverage Without							
7	A Medical?							Yes
8								
9	Claims Office Location							Toronto
10								
11	24-Hour Per Day Cover							Yes
12								
13	Child Benefit Continued							
14	For Physically and							
15	Mentally Handicapped							
16	Children (Past Child							
17	Maximum Age)							Yes, Past Age 21
18								
19	Time Restriction For Loss							One Year
20								
21	Other Benefits							
22								
23								
24								
25								
26								
27								
28								
29								
30	Exclusions							
31	War							Excluded
32	Riot, Civil Commotion							Excluded
33	Self-Inflicted Injury							Excluded
34								
35								
36								
37								
38								
39								
40								

The contents of this report are for comparison purposes only. The terms and conditions of the actual policy apply in the event of any discrepency. Confidential.

9. Group Dependant Life Insurance Benefit

GROUP DEPENDENT LIFE INSURANCE BENEFIT

A	A	B	C	D	E	F	G	H	I	J	K	L	M	N	O
1	**Benefit Terms**		**Present Insurer**		**Insurer A**		**Insurer B**		**Insurer C**		**Insurer D**		**Insurer E**		**Example**
2															
3	Class A Schedule														Covered
4															
5	Class B Schedule														Covered
6															
7	Class C Schedule														N/A
8															
9	Class D Schedule														N/A
10															
11	Spouse Coverage														$10,000
12	Child Coverage														$5,000
13															
14	Minimum Age For Child														Aged 24 Hours
15	Maximum Age For Child														Age 21
16	Maximum Age: Students														Age 25
17															
18	Extension of Child Cover														
19	For Mentally, Physically														
20	Challenged Children?														Yes, After Age 21
21															
22	Conversion Privilege														
23	For Spouse														Yes
24	For Children														No
25															
26	Common-Law Coverage														
27	After What Time?														One Year Cohabitation
28															
29	Waiver of Premium														
30	On Employee's														
31	Total Disability														Yes
32	Waiver Maximum Age														Age 65
33															
34	Living Benefit ®														No
35															
36	Will New Insurer														
37	Continue Coverage														
38	Without Medicals?														N/A
39															
40	Location of Claims Office														Toronto

The contents of this report are for comparison purposes only. The terms and conditions of the actual policy apply in the event of any discrepancy. Confidential.

10. Group Dependant Voluntary Life Insurance Benefit

GROUP DEPENDENT VOLUNTARY LIFE INSURANCE

A	A	B	C	D	E	F	G	H	I	J	K	L	M	N	O
1	**Benefit Terms**		**Present Insurer**		**Insurer A**		**Insurer B**		**Insurer C**		**Insurer D**		**Insurer E**		**Example**
2															
3	Class A Schedule														Offered
4															
5	Class B Schedule														Offered
6															
7	Class C Schedule														N/A
8															
9	Class D Schedule														N/A
10															
11	Spouse Coverage														Yes
12															
13	Dependent Child														
14	Coverage														No
15															
16	Insurance Unit Amount														$10,000
17															
18	Coverage Reductions:														
19	Age														Cancel At Age 65
20	Retirement														Cancel At Retirement
21															
22	Conversion Privilege														
23	For Spouse														Yes
24	For Children														N/A
25															
26	Waiver of Premium														
27	On Employee's														
28	Total Disability														Yes
29	Waiver Maximum Age														Age 65
30															
31	Living Benefit ®														No
32															
33	Overall Maximum														
34	Benefit														$200,000
35	Maximum Benefit														
36	Without a Medical														$0
37															
38	Will New Insurer														
39	Continue Coverage														
40	Without Medicals?														N/A

The contents of this report are for comparison purposes only. The terms and conditions of the actual policy apply in the event of any discrepency. Confidential.

11. Group LTD Benefit, page 1: Schedule, All-Source Maximum, Elimination/Waiting Periods

GROUP LONG TERM DISABILITY INSURANCE BENEFIT Page. 1

A	A	B	C	D	E	F	G	H	I	J	K	L	M	N	O
1	**Benefit Terms**		**Present Insurer**		**Insurer A**		**Insurer B**		**Insurer C**		**Insurer D**		**Insurer E**		**Example**
2															
3	Class A Schedule														66.67 % of Monthly
4															Earnings
5	Class B Schedule														Same as Class A
6															
7	Class C Schedule														N/A
8															
9	Class D Schedule														N/A
10															
11	Coverage Reductions:														
12	Age														Cancel at Age 65
13	Retirement														Cancel At Retirement
14															
15	Maximum Age														Age 65
16															
17	Definition of Disability														
18															
19															
20															
21	Waiver of Premium														
22	While Disabled?														Yes
23	Date Waiver Starts														Date of Disability
24															
25	Benefits Taxable?														No. 100% Employee
26															Paid Benefit
27	All-Source Maximum														
28	Benefit														Yes
29															
30	% of Pre-Disability														
31	Gross Earnings														N/A
32															
33	% of Pre-Disability														
34	Net Earnings														85%
35															
36	Waiting Period For														
37	New Employees														3 Months
38															
39	Benefit Elimination														
40	Period														17 Weeks

The contents of this report are for comparison purposes only. The terms and conditions of the actual policy apply in the event of any discrepency. Confidential.

12. Group LTD Benefit, page 2: Maximum, Residual, Partial, Re-employment Benefits, Offsets

GROUP LONG TERM DISABILITY INSURANCE BENEFIT Page. 2

A	A	C	E	G	I	K	M	O
1	**Benefit Terms**	**Present Insurer**	**Insurer A**	**Insurer B**	**Insurer C**	**Insurer D**	**Insurer E**	**Example**
2								
3	Rehabilitation Benefit							No
4	Amount							
5								
6	Rehabilitation Expenses							Yes
7	Amount							
8								
9	Residual Disability							No
10	Benefit Amount							
11								
12	Partial Disability							No
13	Benefit Amount							
14	Date Awarded							
15								
16	Re-Employment							
17	Allowance							Yes
18	Paid To Employer?							Yes
19	Amount							Three Months of Benefit
20								
21	Offsets From							
22	LTD Benefit Paid							
23								
24	Workers Compensation							Yes
25								
26	Canada Pension Plan							Yes
27	Primary CPP Offsets							Yes
28	Full CPP Offsets							
29								
30	Subrogation Offset							Yes
31								
32	Other Offsets							
33								
34								
35								
36								
37								
38	Will new insurer							
39	continue coverage							
40	without coverage							

The contents of this report are for comparison purposes only. The terms and conditions of the actual policy apply in the event of any discrepency. Confidential.

13. Group LTD Benefit, page 3: Pre-existing Conditions, Exclusions

GROUP LONG TERM DISABILITY INSURANCE BENEFIT Page. 3

A	A	B	C	D	E	F	G	H	I	J	K	L	M	N	O
1	**Benefit Terms**		**Present Insurer**		**Insurer A**		**Insurer B**		**Insurer C**		**Insurer D**		**Insurer E**		**Example**
2															
3	Exclusions														
4	War/Riot/Civil Commotion														Yes
5	While Committing A Crime														Yes
6	Blood Alcohol Over .08%														Not Specified
7	Self-Inflicted Injuries														Yes
8	Working For														
9	Another Employer														Yes
10															
11	Disability Caused By														
12	Mental And Nervous														Must Be In An Approved
13	Conditions														Rehab. Program
14															
15	Disability Caused by														Must Be In An Approved
16	Drug Or Alcohol Abuse														Rehab. Program
17															
18	Other Exclusions														
19															
20															
21															
22	Conversion Privilege														No
23	Without A Medical?														N/A
24	Without A New Job?														N/A
25															
26	Pre-Existing Conditions														
27	Clause														Yes
28	Can Clause Be Waived?														Yes for + 5% on Rate
29	Clause Terms														Past Medical Problem
30															Not On-Going = 3 Month
31															On-Going = 12 Months
32															
33	Location Of Claims Office														Toronto
34	Location of Rehabilitation														
35	Counsellor														Montreal
36															
37	Comments														
38															
39															
40															

The contents of this report are for comparison purposes only. The terms and conditions of the actual policy apply in the event of any discrepency. Confidential.

14. Weekly Indemnity Benefit, page 1: Schedule, reductions, premium waiver, definition

WEEKLY INDEMNITY BENEFIT: Page. 1

	A	B	C	D	E	F	G	H	I	J	K	L	M	N	O
1	Benefit Terms		Present Insurer		Insurer A		Insurer B		Insurer C		Insurer D		Insurer E		Example
2															
3	Class A Schedule														66.67% of Monthly
4															Earnings
5	Class B Schedule														Same as Class A
6															
7	Class C Schedule														N/A
8															
9	Class D Schedule														N/A
10															
11	Coverage Reductions:														Continues After Age 70
12	Age														Maximum 17 Weeks
13	Retirement														Cancels At Retirement
14															
15	Maximum Age														Age 75
16															
17	Conversion Privilege														No
18	Without a Medical?														N/A
19	Without a New Job?														N/A
20															
21	Waiver of Premium														
22	While Disabled?														No
23	Date Waiver Starts														N/A
24															
25	Benefits Taxable?														No. 100% Employee
26															Paid
27	All-Source Maximum														
28	Benefit														No
29															
30	% of Pre-Disability														
31	Gross Earnings														N/A
32															
33	% of Pre-Disability														
34	Net Earnings														N/A
35															
36	Waiting Period For														
37	New Employees														3 Months
38															
39	Definition of Disability														Unable To Perform
40															Own Occupation

The contents of this report are for comparison purposes only. The terms and conditions of the actual policy apply in the event of any discrepancy. Confidential.

15. Weekly Indemnity Benefit, page 2: Maximum, benefit start, benefit duration

WEEKLY INDEMNITY BENEFIT: Page. 2

A	A	B	C	D	E	F	G	H	I	J	K	L	M	N	O
1	**Benefit Terms**		**Present Insurer**		**Insurer A**		**Insurer B**		**Insurer C**		**Insurer D**		**Insurer E**		**Example**
2															
3	Overall Maximum														
4	Benefit														$850/Week
5	Maximum Benefit														
6	Without A Medical														$600/Week
7															
8	Class A														
9	Benefits Begin														
10	After _ Days of Accident														1st Day
11	After _ Days of Sickness														8th Day
12	1st Day Hospital														Yes
13	Maximum Number														
14	Days/Weeks														17 Weeks
15															
16	Class B														
17	Benefits Begin														
18	After _ Days Accident														1st Day
19	After _ Days Sickness														8th Day
20	1st Day Hospital														No
21	Maximum Number														
22	Days/Weeks														17 Weeks
23															
24	Class C														N/A
25	Benefits Begin														
26	After _ Days Accident														
27	After _ Days Sickness														
28	1st Day Hospital														
29	Maximum Number														
30	Days/Weeks														
31															
32	Class D														N/A
33	Benefits Begin														
34	After _ Days Accident														
35	After _ Days Sickness														
36	1st Day Hospital														
37	Maximum Number														
38	Days/Weeks														
39															
40															

The contents of this report are for comparison purposes only. The terms and conditions of the actual policy apply in the event of any discrepency. Confidential.

16. Weekly Indemnity Benefit, page 3: Rehabilitation, offsets, exclusions

WEEKLY INDEMNITY BENEFIT: Page. 3

A	A	B	C	D	E	F	G	H	I	J	K	L	M	N	O
1	Benefit Terms		Present Insurer		Insurer A		Insurer B		Insurer C		Insurer D		Insurer E		Example
2															
3	Rehabilitation Benefit														
4	Amount														N/A
5															
6	Rehabilitation Expenses														
7	Amount														N/A
8															
9	24 Hour Coverage														Yes
10															
11	Employees Covered While														
12	On The Job?														No
13															
14	Offsets From														
15	Benefit Paid														
16															
17	Workers Compensation														Yes
18															
19	Canada Pension Plan														Yes
20															
21	Subrogation Offset														Yes
22															
23	Other Offsets														
24															
25															
26															
27	Exclusions														
28	War/Riot/Civil Commotion														Yes
29	While Committing A Crime														Yes
30	Blood Alcohol Over .08%														Yes
31	Self-Inflicted Injuries														Yes
32	Working For														
33	Another Employer														Yes
34	Other														
35															
36															
37															
38	Will New Insurer														
39	Continue Coverage														
40	Without Medicals?														Yes

The contents of this report are for comparison purposes only. The terms and conditions of the actual policy apply in the event of any discrepency. Confidential.

17. Weekly Indemnity Benefit, page 4: Pre-existing conditions, UI and LTD integration

WEEKLY INDEMNITY BENEFIT: Page. 4

A	A	B	C	D	E	F	G	H	I	J	K	L	M	N	O
1	**Benefit Terms**		**Present Insurer**		**Insurer A**		**Insurer B**		**Insurer C**		**Insurer D**		**Insurer E**		**Example**
2															
3	Pre-Existing Conditions														
4	Clause														No
5	Can Clause Be Waived?														
6	Terms														N/A
7															
8	Location of Claims Office														Toronto
9	Location of Rehabilitation														
10	Counsellor														Toronto
11															
12	Can Rehabilitation Start														
13	While On W.I.?														Yes, If Claim Is Going
14															Long Term
15	Does Plan Qualify For														
16	U.I.C. Premium Rate														
17	Reduction?														Yes
18	Has U.I.C. Rate Reduction														
19	Been Applied For?														Yes
20															
21	Does W.I. Plan Integrate														
22	With The L.T.D. Plan?														Yes, With No Gaps
23															
24	Other														
25															
26															
27															
28															
29															
30	Comments														
31															
32															
33															
34															
35															
36															
37															
38															
39															
40															

The contents of this report are for comparison purposes only. The terms and conditions of the actual policy apply in the event of any discrepency. Confidential.

18. EHC, page 1: Deductibles, co-insurance, maximum, surviving dependants' coverage

EXTENDED HEALTH CARE BENEFIT: Page. 1 Overall Deductibles and Overall Maximum Benefits

A	A	B	C	D	E	F	G	H	I	J	K	L	M	N	O
1	**Benefit Terms**		**Present Insurer**		**Insurer A**		**Insurer B**		**Insurer C**		**Insurer D**		**Insurer E**		**Example**
2															
3	Class A Covered														Yes
4	Class A Deductible														Yes
5	Single														$50.00
6	Dependent														
7	Family														$100.00
8															
9	Class B Covered														Yes
10	Class B Deductible														Yes
11	Single														$100.00
12	Dependent														
13	Family														$200.00
14															
15	Class C Covered														N/A
16	Class C Deductible														
17	Single														
18	Dependent														
19	Family														
20															
21	Class D Covered														N/A
22	Class D Deductible														
23	Single														
24	Dependent														
25	Family														
26															
27	Overall Contract Maximum														No Maximum
28	Overall Annual Maximum														No Maximum
29	Overall Individual Maximum														Lifetime $1 Million
30															
31	Policy Year From/To														Jan. 1st to Dec. 31st
32															
33	Surviving Dependants														
34	Coverage														Yes
35	Premiums Waived														Yes
36	Maximum Time														2 Years
37															
38															
39															
40															

The contents of this report are for comparison purposes only. The terms and conditions of the actual policy apply in the event of any discrepency. Confidential.

19. EHC, page 2: Home province hospital

EXTENDED HEALTH CARE BENEFIT: Page. 2 Home Province Hospital

A	A	B	C	D	E	F	G	H	I	J	K	L	M	N	O
1	**Benefit Terms**		**Present Insurer**		**Insurer A**		**Insurer B**		**Insurer C**		**Insurer D**		**Insurer E**		**Example**
2															
3	Home Province Hospital														
4															
5	Hospital Room Covered														Yes
6	Private														No
7	Semi-Private														Yes
8	Private When Ordered														
9	By A Doctor														N/A
10															
11	Overall Deductible Applied														
12	Class A														No
13	Class B														Yes
14	Class C														N/A
15	Class D														N/A
16															
17	Percentage Reimbursed														
18	Class A														100%
19	Class B														80%
20	Class C														N/A
21	Class D														N/A
22															
23	Admittance Charges														
24	Covered														Yes
25	Utilization Charges														
26	Covered														Yes
27															
28	Maximum Number Of Days														No Maximum
29	Maximum Amount Per Day														No Maximum
30															
31	Other														
32															
33															
34															
35															
36															
37															
38															
39															
40															

The contents of this report are for comparison purposes only. The terms and conditions of the actual policy apply in the event of any discrepency. Confidential.

20. EHC, page 3: Convalescent hospital deductibles, co-insurance

EXTENDED HEALTH CARE BENEFIT: Page. 3 Convalescent Hospital Coverage

A	A	C	E	G	I	K	M	O
1	**Benefit Terms**	**Present Insurer**	**Insurer A**	**Insurer B**	**Insurer C**	**Insurer D**	**Insurer E**	**Example**
2								
3	Convalescent Hospital							
4								
5	Class A Covered							Yes
6								
7	Class A Deductible							
8	Single							Not Separate From
9	Dependent							Overall Maximum
10	Family							Deductible
11								
12	Class B Covered							Yes
13								
14	Class B Deductible							
15	Single							Not Separate From
16	Dependent							Overall Maximum
17	Family							Deductible
18								
19	Class C Covered							N/A
20								
21	Class C Deductible							
22	Single							
23	Dependent							
24	Family							
25								
26	Class D Covered							N/A
27								
28	Class D Deductible							
29	Single							
30	Dependent							
31	Family							
32								
33	Percentage Reimbursed							
34	Class A							100%
35	Class B							80%
36	Class C							N/A
37	Class D							N/A
38								
39								
40								

The contents of this report are for comparison purposes only. The terms and conditions of the actual policy apply in the event of any discrepency. Confidential.

21. EHC, page 4: Convalescent hospital maximum, coverage, exclusions

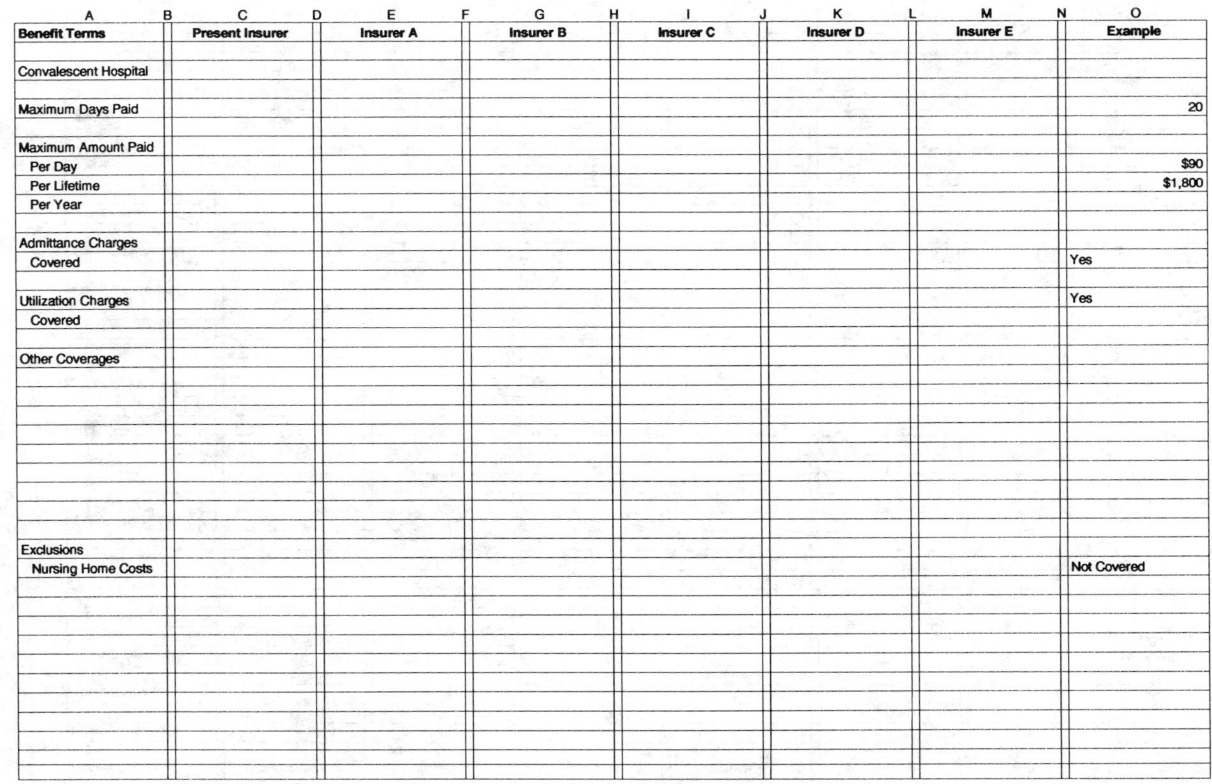

EXTENDED HEALTH CARE BENEFIT: Page. 4 Convalescent Hospital Coverage

	A	B	C	D	E	F	G	H	I	J	K	L	M	N	O
1	**Benefit Terms**		**Present Insurer**		**Insurer A**		**Insurer B**		**Insurer C**		**Insurer D**		**Insurer E**		**Example**
2															
3	Convalescent Hospital														
4															
5	Maximum Days Paid														20
6															
7	Maximum Amount Paid														
8	Per Day														$90
9	Per Lifetime														$1,800
10	Per Year														
11															
12	Admittance Charges														
13	Covered														Yes
14															
15	Utilization Charges														Yes
16	Covered														
17															
18	Other Coverages														
19															
20															
21															
22															
23															
24															
25															
26															
27															
28	Exclusions														
29	Nursing Home Costs														Not Covered
30															
31															
32															
33															
34															
35															
36															
37															
38															
39															
40															

The contents of this report are for comparison purposes only. The terms and conditions of the actual policy apply in the event of any discrepency. Confidential.

22. EHC, page 5: Prescription drugs deductibles, co-insurance

EXTENDED HEALTH CARE BENEFIT: Page. 5 Prescription Drugs Coverage

A	A	B	C	D	E	F	G	H	I	J	K	L	M	N	O
1	**Benefit Terms**		**Present Insurer**		**Insurer A**		**Insurer B**		**Insurer C**		**Insurer D**		**Insurer E**		**Example**
2															
3	Prescription Drugs														
4															
5	Class A Covered														Yes
6															
7	Class A Deductible														Not Separate From
8	Single														Overall Maximum
9	Dependent														Deductible
10	Family														
11															
12	Class B Covered														Yes
13															
14	Class B Deductible														Not Separate From
15	Single														Overall Maximum
16	Dependent														Deductible
17	Family														
18															
19	Class C Covered														N/A
20															
21	Class C Deductible														
22	Single														
23	Dependent														
24	Family														
25															
26	Class D Covered														N/A
27															
28	Class D Deductible														
29	Single														
30	Dependent														
31	Family														
32															
33	Percentage Reimbursed														
34	Class A														100%
35	Class B														80%
36	Class C														N/A
37	Class D														N/A
38															
39															
40															

The contents of this report are for comparison purposes only. The terms and conditions of the actual policy apply in the event of any discrepency. Confidential.

23. EHC, page 6: Prescription drugs coverage, exclusions

EXTENDED HEALTH CARE BENEFIT: Page. 6 Prescription Drugs Coverage

A	A	C	E	G	I	K	M	O
1	**Benefit Terms**	**Present Insurer**	**Insurer A**	**Insurer B**	**Insurer C**	**Insurer D**	**Insurer E**	**Example**
2								
3	Prescription Drugs							
4								
5	Maximum Benefit							
6	Per Year							No Maximum
7	Per Lifetime							Overall Ben. $1,000,000
8								
9	Drug Coverage Definition							
10	Prescription Drugs Only							Yes
11	Any Prescribed Drug							
12	Only Generic Drugs							
13	Only Selected Drugs							
14	Life-Sustaining Drugs-							
15	Non-Prescription							Yes
16								
17	Contraceptives Covered							
18	Birth Control Pills							Yes
19	I.U.D.'s							Yes
20	Other Contraceptives							No
21								
22	Diabetic Supplies							Yes
23	Insulin							Yes
24								
25	Colostomy Supplies							Yes
26								
27	Exclusions							
28	Patent Drugs							Excluded
29	Proprietary Drugs							Excluded
30	Baby Foods, Formulas							Excluded
31	Cough Medicine							Excluded
32	Minerals, Proteins							Excluded
33	Vitamins							Excluded
34	Collagen Treatments							Excluded
35	Anti-Obesity							
36	Treatments							Excluded
37	Charges to Administer							
38	Drugs							Excluded
39	Injectable Drugs							Excluded
40	Other							

The contents of this report are for comparison purposes only. The terms and conditions of the actual policy apply in the event of any discrepency. Confidential.

24. EHC, page 7: Other coverage — deductibles, co-insurance

EXTENDED HEALTH CARE BENEFIT: Page. 7 Other Coverage

A	A	B	C	D	E	F	G	H	I	J	K	L	M	N	O
1	**Benefit Terms**		**Present Insurer**		**Insurer A**		**Insurer B**		**Insurer C**		**Insurer D**		**Insurer E**		**Example**
2															
3	Other Benefits Coverage														
4															
5	Class A Covered														Yes
6															
7	Class A Deductible														Not Separate From
8	Single														Overall Maximum
9	Dependent														Deductible
10	Family														
11															
12	Class B Covered														Yes
13															
14	Class B Deductible														Not Separate From
15	Single														Overall Maximum
16	Dependent														Deductible
17	Family														
18															
19	Class C Covered														N/A
20															
21	Class C Deductible														
22	Single														
23	Dependent														
24	Family														
25															
26	Class D Covered														N/A
27															
28	Class D Deductible														
29	Single														
30	Dependent														
31	Family														
32															
33	Percentage Reimbursed														
34	Class A														100%
35	Class B														80%
36	Class C														N/A
37	Class D														N/A
38															
39															
40															

The contents of this report are for comparison purposes only. The terms and conditions of the actual policy apply in the event of any discrepency. Confidential.

25. EHC, page 8: Other coverage — ambulance, nursing, artificial limbs, casts, mammary prosthesis

EXTENDED HEALTH CARE BENEFIT: Page. 8 Other Coverage

A	A	C	E	G	I	K	M	O
1	**Benefit Terms**	**Present Insurer**	**Insurer A**	**Insurer B**	**Insurer C**	**Insurer D**	**Insurer E**	**Example**
2								
3	Maximum Benefit							
4	Per Year							
5	Per Lifetime							$1,000,000
6								
7	Ambulance Covered							Yes
8	Local							Yes
9	Inter-City in Province							Yes
10	Inter-City Next Province							Yes
11	Air Ambulance							Yes
12	Other Transport: Taxi							No
13	Other Transport: Other							No
14								
15	Private Duty Nurses							
16	Covered							Yes
17	Maximum Benefit							$10,000/Three Years
18	Per Day							
19	Per Year							
20	Per Lifetime							
21								
22	Casts, Splints Covered							Yes
23	Braces Covered							Yes
24	Trusses Covered							Yes
25	Crutches Covered							Yes
26								
27	Artificial Limbs and Eyes							
28	Covered							Yes
29	Replacements							
30	Covered							Yes
31	Repairs Covered							Yes
32	Maximum Benefit							overall $1,000,000
33	Myoelectric Limbs							
34	Covered							No
35	Myoelectric Maximum							N/A
36								
37	Mammary Prosthesis							
38	Covered							Yes
39	Maximum Benefit							Two per Benefit Year
40								

The contents of this report are for comparison purposes only. The terms and conditions of the actual policy apply in the event of any discrepency. Confidential.

26. EHC: page 9: Other coverage — blood, oxygen, dental, bra, hearing aids, orthopaedic shoes, wigs

EXTENDED HEALTH CARE BENEFIT: Page. 9 Other Coverage

A	A	B	C	D	E	F	G	H	I	J	K	L	M	N	O
1	**Benefit Terms**		**Present Insurer**		**Insurer A**		**Insurer B**		**Insurer C**		**Insurer D**		**Insurer E**		**Example**
2															
3	Other Coverage														
4															
5	Radiotherapy Covered														Yes
6															
7	Coagulotherapy														Yes
8															
9	Laboratory Tests														Yes
10	Covered In Doctor's														
11	Offices														No
12	Covered In														
13	Pharmacies														No
14															
15	Oxygen Covered														Yes
16	Plasma and Blood														Yes
17															
18	Accidental Dental														
19	Coverage														Yes
20	Natural Teeth														Yes
21	Bridges, Dentures														No
22	Maximum Benefit														No Maximum
23	Maximum Timeframe														6 Months
24															
25	Surgical Bra Covered														Yes
26	Maximum														2 Per Year
27															
28	Hearing Aids Covered														Yes
29	Maximum Benefit														$250.00
30	Timeframe														Every 3 Years
31															
32	Orthopaedic Shoes														Yes
33	Maximum Benefit														One Pair
34	Timeframe														Year
35															
36	Wigs Covered After														
37	Chemotherapy														No
38	Maximum Benefit														N/A
39	Timeframe														N/A
40															

The contents of this report are for comparison purposes only. The terms and conditions of the actual policy apply in the event of any discrepency. Confidential.

27. EHC, page 10: Other coverage — stockings, eye exams, vision care

EXTENDED HEALTH CARE BENEFIT: Page. 10 Other Coverage

A	A	B	C	D	E	F	G	H	I	J	K	L	M	N	O
1	**Benefit Terms**		**Present Insurer**		**Insurer A**		**Insurer B**		**Insurer C**		**Insurer D**		**Insurer E**		**Example**
2															
3	Other Coverage														
4															
5	Surgical Stockings														Yes
6	Maximum														Two Pair
7	Timeframe														Year
8															
9	Eye Exams Covered														Yes
10	Adult Maximum														$25
11	Adult Timeframe														Per Two Years
12	Child Maximum														$25
13	Child Timeframe														Per One Year
14															
15	Eye Glasses Covered														Yes
16	Adult Maximum														$200
17	Adult Timeframe														Per Two Years
18	Child Maximum														$200
19	Child Maximum														Per One Year
20															
21	Contact Lenses Covered														Yes
22	Adult Maximum														$200
23	Adult Timeframe														Per Two Years
24	Child Maximum														$200
25	Child Timeframe														Per One Year
26															
27	Contact Lenses As A														
28	Result Of Eye Surgery														N/A
29															
30	Overall Maximum														$200
31	Timeframe Adults														Per Two Years
32	Timeframe Child														Per One Year
33															
34	Preferred Price Purchase														
35	Program For Glasses														Yes
36															
37															
38															
39															
40															

The contents of this report are for comparison purposes only. The terms and conditions of the actual policy apply in the event of any discrepency. Confidential.

28. EHC, page 11: Paramedical practitioners deductibles, co-insurance, maximums

EXTENDED HEALTH CARE BENEFIT: Page. 11 Paramedical Practitioners

A	A	C	E	G	I	K	M	O
1	**Benefit Terms**	**Present Insurer**	**Insurer A**	**Insurer B**	**Insurer C**	**Insurer D**	**Insurer E**	**Example**
2								
3	Paramedical Practitioners							
4								
5	Class A Covered							Yes
6								
7	Class A Deductible							Not Separate From
8	Single							Overall Maximum
9	Dependent							Deductible
10	Family							
11								
12	Class B Covered							Yes
13								
14	Class B Deductible							Not Separate From
15	Single							Overall Maximum
16	Dependent							Deductible
17	Family							
18								
19	Class C Covered							N/A
20								
21	Class C Deductible							
22	Single							
23	Dependent							
24	Family							
25								
26	Class D Covered							N/A
27								
28	Class D Deductible							
29	Single							
30	Dependent							
31	Family							
32								
33	Percentage Reimbursed							
34	Class A							100%
35	Class B							80%
36	Class C							N/A
37	Class D							N/A
38								
39	Overall Maximum							$500 Per Practitioner
40	Maximum Timeframe							Per Year

The contents of this report are for comparison purposes only. The terms and conditions of the actual policy apply in the event of any discrepency. Confidential.

29. EHC, page 12: Paramedical practitioners, x-rays, acupuncture, chiropractors, masseurs, naturopaths, osteopaths

EXTENDED HEALTH CARE BENEFIT: Page. 12 Paramedical Practitioners

A	A	B	C	D	E	F	G	H	I	J	K	L	M	N	O
1	**Benefit Terms**		**Present Insurer**		**Insurer A**		**Insurer B**		**Insurer C**		**Insurer D**		**Insurer E**		**Example**
2															
3	Paramed. Practitioners														
4															
5	Paramedical X-Rays														
6	Covered														Yes
7	Maximum														One Per Practitioner
8	Timeframe														Per Year
9															
10	Acupuncturists														No
11	Maximum														
12	Timeframe														
13															
14	Christian Science														
15	Practitioners														No
16	Maximum														
17	Timeframe														
18															
19	Chiropodists														Yes
20	Maximum														$500
21	Timeframe														Per Year
22															
23	Chiropractors														Yes
24	Maximum														$500
25	Timeframe														Per Year
26															
27	Masseurs														Yes
28	Maximum														$500
29	Timeframe														Per Year
30															
31	Naturopaths														Yes
32	Maximum														$500
33	Timeframe														Per Year
34															
35	Osteopaths														Yes
36	Maximum														$500
37	Timeframe														Per Year
38															
39															
40															

The contents of this report are for comparison purposes only. The terms and conditions of the actual policy apply in the event of any discrepency. Confidential.

30. EHC, page 13: Paramedical practitioners, psychologists, physiotherapists, speech therapists, other

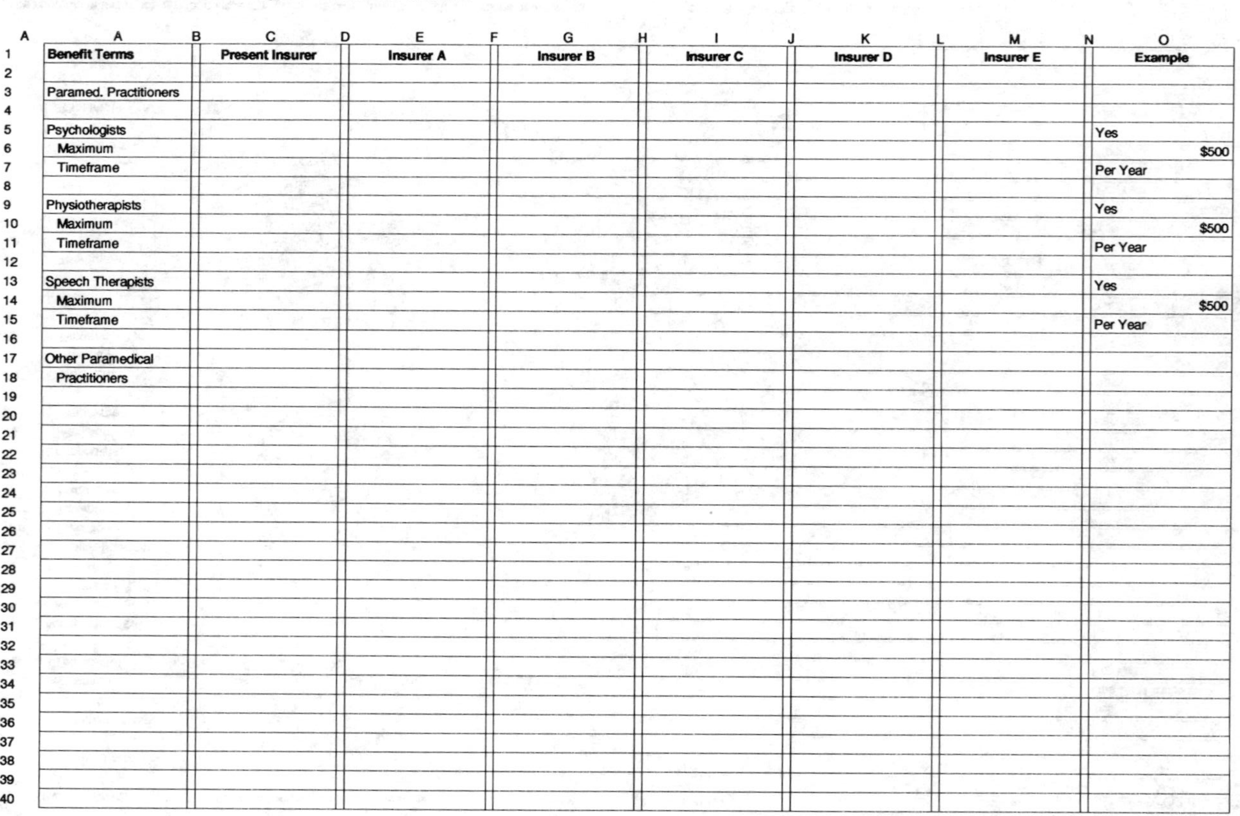

EXTENDED HEALTH CARE BENEFIT: Page. 13 Paramedical Practitioners

A	A	C	E	G	I	K	M	O
1	Benefit Terms	Present Insurer	Insurer A	Insurer B	Insurer C	Insurer D	Insurer E	Example
2								
3	Paramed. Practitioners							
4								
5	Psychologists							Yes
6	Maximum							$500
7	Timeframe							Per Year
8								
9	Physiotherapists							Yes
10	Maximum							$500
11	Timeframe							Per Year
12								
13	Speech Therapists							Yes
14	Maximum							$500
15	Timeframe							Per Year
16								
17	Other Paramedical							
18	Practitioners							
19								
20								
21								
22								
23								
24								
25								
26								
27								
28								
29								
30								
31								
32								
33								
34								
35								
36								
37								
38								
39								
40								

The contents of this report are for comparison purposes only. The terms and conditions of the actual policy apply in the event of any discrepancy. Confidential.

31. EHC, page 14: Out-of-country referrals, deductibles, co-insurance

EXTENDED HEALTH CARE BENEFIT: Page.14 Out-of-Country Referrals

A	A	C	E	G	I	K	M	O
1	**Benefit Terms**	**Present Insurer**	**Insurer A**	**Insurer B**	**Insurer C**	**Insurer D**	**Insurer E**	**Insurer F**
2								
3	Out-of-Country Referrals							
4	From Canadian Doctors							
5	Covered							Yes
6								
7	Class A Covered							Yes
8								
9	Class A Deductible							Not Separate From
10	Single							Overall Maximum
11	Dependent							Deductible
12	Family							
13								
14	Class B Covered							Yes
15								
16	Class B Deductible							Not Separate From
17	Single							Overall Maximum
18	Dependent							Deductible
19	Family							
20								
21	Class C Covered							N/A
22								
23	Class C Deductible							
24	Single							
25	Dependent							
26	Family							
27								
28	Class D Covered							N/A
29								
30	Class D Deductible							
31	Single							
32	Dependent							
33	Family							
34								
35	Percentage Reimbursed							
36	Class A							100%
37	Class B							80%
38	Class C							N/A
39	Class D							N/A
40								

The contents of this report are for comparison purposes only. The terms and conditions of the actual policy apply in the event of any discrepency. Confidential.

32. EHC, page 15: Out-of-country referrals, maximums, exclusions

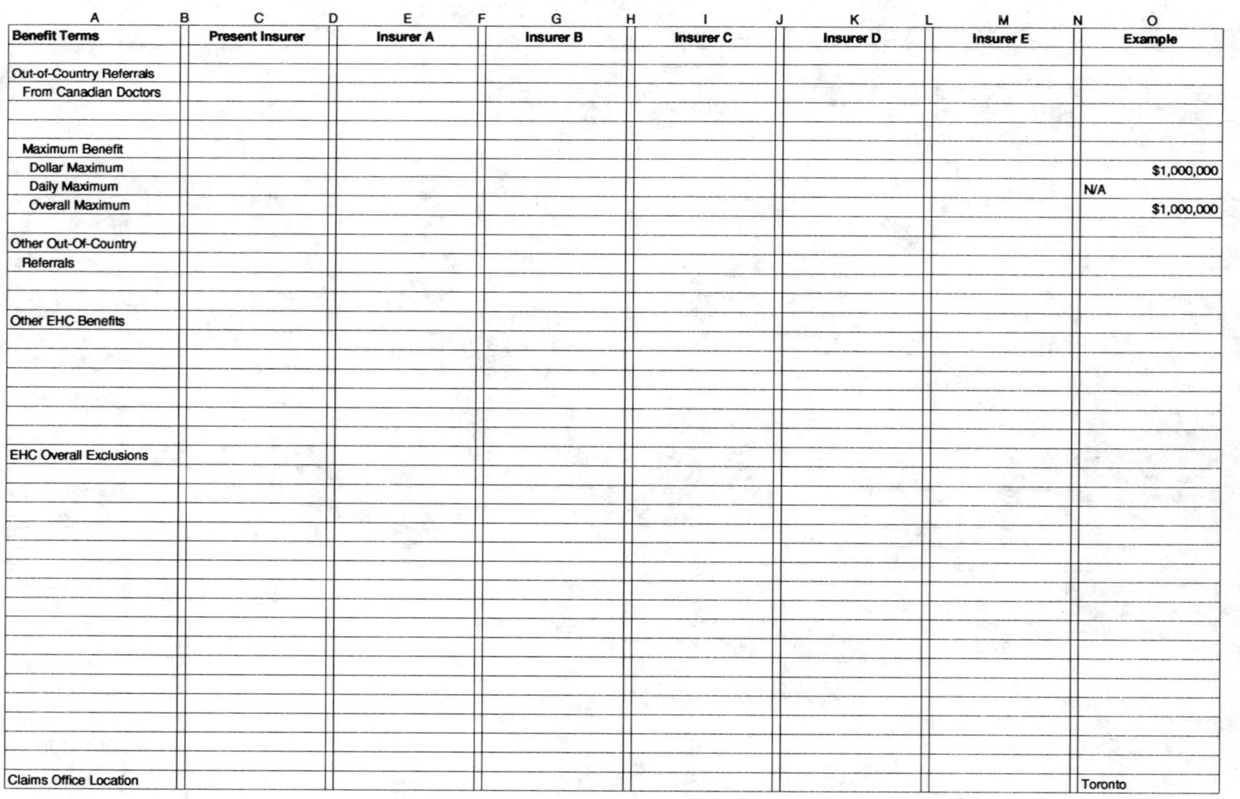

EXTENDED HEALTH CARE BENEFIT: Page. 15 Out-Of-Country-Referrals and Other Extended Health Care Benefits

A	A	C	E	G	I	K	M	O
1	**Benefit Terms**	**Present Insurer**	**Insurer A**	**Insurer B**	**Insurer C**	**Insurer D**	**Insurer E**	**Example**
2								
3	Out-of-Country Referrals							
4	From Canadian Doctors							
5								
6								
7	Maximum Benefit							
8	Dollar Maximum							$1,000,000
9	Daily Maximum							N/A
10	Overall Maximum							$1,000,000
11								
12	Other Out-Of-Country							
13	Referrals							
14								
15								
16	Other EHC Benefits							
17								
18								
19								
20								
21								
22								
23	EHC Overall Exclusions							
24								
25								
26								
27								
28								
29								
30								
31								
32								
33								
34								
35								
36								
37								
38								
39								
40	Claims Office Location							Toronto

The contents of this report are for comparison purposes only. The terms and conditions of the actual policy apply in the event of any discrepency. Confidential.

33. EHC, page 16: Out-of-country emergencies/travel health deductibles

EXTENDED HEALTH CARE BENEFIT: Page. 16 Out-of-Country Emergency Coverage/Travel Health Insurance

A	A	B	C	D	E	F	G	H	I	J	K	L	M	N	O
1	**Benefit Terms**		**Present Insurer**		**Insurer A**		**Insurer B**		**Insurer C**		**Insurer D**		**Insurer E**		**Example**
2															
3	Out-of-Country														
4	Emergency Coverage														
5															
6	Covered														Yes
7	Covered As A Separate														
8	Benefit From E.H.C.														No
9	Included In E.H.C.														Yes
10															
11	Class A Covered														Yes
12															
13	Class A Deductible														Not Separate From
14	Single														Overall Maximum
15	Dependent														Deductible
16	Family														
17															
18	Class B Covered														Yes
19															
20	Class B Deductible														Not Separate From
21	Single														Overall Maximum
22	Dependent														Deductible
23	Family														
24															
25	Class C Covered														N/A
26															
27	Class C Deductible														
28	Single														
29	Dependent														
30	Family														
31															
32	Class D Covered														N/A
33															
34	Class D Deductible														
35	Single														
36	Dependent														
37	Family														
38															
39															
40															

The contents of this report are for comparison purposes only. The terms and conditions of the actual policy apply in the event of any discrepency. Confidential.

34. EHC, page 17: Out-of-country emergencies/travel health co-insurance, hospital, maximum

EXTENDED HEALTH CARE BENEFIT: Page. 17 Out-Of-Country Emergency Coverage/Travel Health Insurance

	A	B	C	D	E	F	G	H	I	J	K	L	M	N	O
1	**Benefit Terms**		**Present Insurer**		**Insurer A**		**Insurer B**		**Insurer C**		**Insurer D**		**Insurer E**		**Example**
2															
3	Out-Of-Country														
4	Emergency Coverage														
5															
6	Percentage Reimbursed														
7	Class A														100%
8	Class B														80%
9	Class C														N/A
10	Class D														N/A
11															
12	Maximum Benefits														
13	Overall Lifetime														$1,000,000
14	Overall Per Trip														N/A
15	Overall Per Day														No Maximum
16	Overall Per Person														$1,000,000
17															
18	Maximum Number of														
19	Days Covered														No Maximum
20															
21	Benefits Paid After														
22	Prov. Medicare Pays														Yes
23															
24	Must Travellers Be														
25	Covered By Provincial														
26	Medicare?														Yes
27															
28	Emergency Benefits														
29															
30	Hospital Covered														Yes
31	Ward Room														Yes
32	Semi-private Room														Yes
33	Private Room														No
34															
35	Admittance Charges														
36	Covered														Yes
37															
38															
39															
40															

The contents of this report are for comparison purposes only. The terms and conditions of the actual policy apply in the event of any discrepancy. Confidential.

35. EHC, page 18: Out-of-country emergencies/travel health administration, doctors, ambulance

EXTENDED HEALTH CARE BENEFIT: Page. 18 Out-Of-Country Emergency Coverage/Travel Health Insurance

A	A	B	C	D	E	F	G	H	I	J	K	L	M	N	O
1	**Benefit Terms**		**Present Insurer**		**Insurer A**		**Insurer B**		**Insurer C**		**Insurer D**		**Insurer E**		**Example**
2															
3	Out-Of-Country														
4	Emergency Coverage														
5															
6	Administration Charges														
7	Covered														Yes
8															
9	Doctors' Services														Yes
10	Covered														
11															
12	Surgeons' Services														
13	Covered														Yes
14															
15	Specialists' Services														
16	Covered														Yes
17															
18	Prescription Drugs														
19	Covered														Yes
20															
21	Local Ambulance														Yes
22	Covered														
23															
24	Air Ambulance Covered														Yes
25															
26	Other Emergency														
27	Transport Covered														No
28	Taxis														
29	Water Taxis														
30	Other														
31															
32	Medical Evacuation														
33	To Canada														Yes, If Medically
34															Required
35	Maximum Number of														
36	Commercial Airline														
37	Seats Paid														N/A
38															
39	Health Care Attendent														
40	Covered														Yes; Not A Relative

The contents of this report are for comparison purposes only. The terms and conditions of the actual policy apply in the event of any discrepency. Confidential.

36. EHC, page 19: Out-of-country emergencies/travel health, return flight, cash, luggage, etc.

EXTENDED HEALTH CARE BENEFIT: Page. 19 Out-of-Country Emergency Coverage/Travel Health Insurance

A	A	B	C	D	E	F	G	H	I	J	K	L	M	N	O
1	**Benefit Terms**		**Present Insurer**		**Insurer A**		**Insurer B**		**Insurer C**		**Insurer D**		**Insurer E**		**Example**
2															
3	Out-of-Country														
4	Emergency Coverage														
5															
6	Return Flight For														
7	Dependants Covered														No
8	Maximum														N/A
9															
10	Emergency Cash														
11	Assistance														No
12	Maximum Amount														N/A
13															
14	Loss Of Luggage														No
15	Covered														
16	Maximum Amount														N/A
17															
18	Airfare For A Relative														
19	To Visit Hospitalized														
20	Person														No
21	Maximum Benefit														N/A
22	Limitations														
23															
24	Repatriation Of The Body														
25	Covered														Yes
26	Maximum Benefit														$2,500
27															
28	Travel Assistance														
29	Program Covered														Yes
30															
31	Covered Separately														No
32															
33	Covered In E.H.C.														
34	Benefit														Yes
35															(Expatriates Covered
36	Other Benefits														Separately)
37															
38	Exclusions														
39															
40															

The contents of this report are for comparison purposes only. The terms and conditions of the actual policy apply in the event of any discrepency. Confidential.

37. EHC, page 20: Other medical benefits, decompression chambers

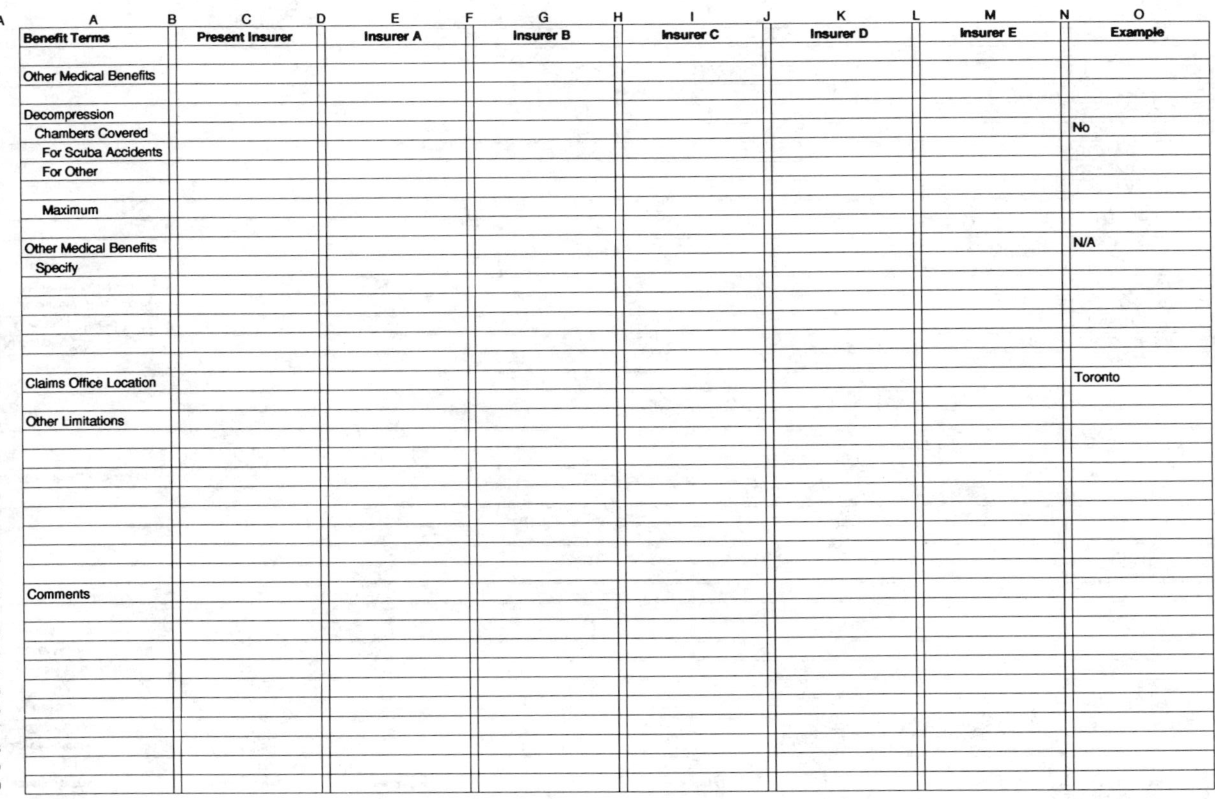

EXTENDED HEALTH CARE BENEFIT: Page. 20 Other Medical Benefits

A	A	B	C	D	E	F	G	H	I	J	K	L	M	N	O
1	**Benefit Terms**		**Present Insurer**		**Insurer A**		**Insurer B**		**Insurer C**		**Insurer D**		**Insurer E**		**Example**
2															
3	Other Medical Benefits														
4															
5	Decompression														
6	Chambers Covered														No
7	For Scuba Accidents														
8	For Other														
9															
10	Maximum														
11															
12	Other Medical Benefits														N/A
13	Specify														
14															
15															
16															
17															
18															
19	Claims Office Location														Toronto
20															
21	Other Limitations														
22															
23															
24															
25															
26															
27															
28															
29															
30	Comments														
31															
32															
33															
34															
35															
36															
37															
38															
39															
40															

The contents of this report are for comparison purposes only. The terms and conditions of the actual policy apply in the event of any discrepancy. Confidential.

38. Political Evacuation and Kidnapping/Extortion Insurance

POLITICAL EVACUATION AND KIDNAPPING/EXTORTION INSURANCE

A	A	C	E	G	I	K	M	O
1	**Benefit Terms**	**Present Insurer**	**Insurer A**	**Insurer B**	**Insurer C**	**Insurer D**	**Insurer E**	**Example**
2								
3	Out-of-Country							
4	Political Evacuation							Paid By Employer
5	Coverage							Separate Policy
6								
7	Political Evac. Offered							Provided
8	Dollar Maximum Benefit							
9	Benefit Terms							
10								
11								
12								
13								
14								
15								
16								
17	Political Evac. Limitations							
18								
19								
20								
21								
22								
23								
24	Kidnapping/Extortion							Yes, for overseas
25	Coverage Offered							Projects
26	Maximum Coverage in $							$10,000,000.00
27	Maximum Number (Days)							6 Months
28	Valid Locations							Far East
29								
30								
31								
32	Exclusions							Country A
33								Country B
34								Country C
35								
36	Other							
37								
38								
39								
40								

The contents of this report are for comparison purposes only. The terms and conditions of the actual policy apply in the event of any discrepency. Confidential.

39. Dental Benefit, page 1: Overall deductibles and maximum benefits

DENTAL BENEFIT: Page. 1 Overall Deductibles and Maximum Benefits

A	A	B	C	D	E	F	G	H	I	J	K	L	M	N	O
1	**Benefit Terms**		**Present Insurer**		**Insurer A**		**Insurer B**		**Insurer C**		**Insurer D**		**Insurer E**		**Example**
2															
3	Dental Benefits														
4															
5	Class A Covered														Yes
6	Class A Deductible														
7	Single														$50
8	Dependent														
9	Family														$100
10															
11	Class B Covered														Yes
12	Class B Deductible														
13	Single														$100
14	Dependent														
15	Family														$200
16															
17	Class C Covered														N/A
18	Class C Deductible														
19	Single														
20	Dependent														
21	Family														
22															
23	Class D Covered														N/A
24	Class D Deductible														
25	Single														
26	Dependent														
27	Family														
28															
29	Maximums														
30	Basic Benefits Max.														
31	Preventative Max.														
32	Diagnostic Max.														
33	Major Benefits Max.														
34	Crowns Max.														
35	Bridges Max.														
36	Dentures Max.														
37	Basic + Major Max.														$1,500 Per Year
38	Orthodontics Max.														$1,500
39	Timeframe														Per Person Lifetime
40	First Year Benefit Max.														$750

The contents of this report are for comparison purposes only. The terms and conditions of the actual policy apply in the event of any discrepancy. Confidential.

40. Dental Benefit, page 2: Overall benefits, percentages reimbursed

DENTAL BENEFIT: Page.2 Overall Benefits Percentages Reimbursed

A	A	C	E	G	I	K	M	O
1	**Benefit Terms**	**Present Insurer**	**Insurer A**	**Insurer B**	**Insurer C**	**Insurer D**	**Insurer E**	**Example**
2								
3	Predetermination Max.							$300.00
4								
5	Percentage Reimbursed							
6	Basic Coverage							
7	Class A Basic %							100%
8	Class B Basic %							100%
9	Class C Basic %							N/A
10	Class D Basic %							N/A
11	Major Coverage							
12	Class A Major %							50%
13	Class B Major %							50%
14	Class C Major %							N/A
15	Class D Major %							N/A
16	Orthodontic Coverage							
17	Class A Ortho. %							50%
18	Class B Ortho. %							N/A
19	Class C Ortho. %							N/A
20	Class D Ortho. %							N/A
21								
22	Dental Fee Guide							
23	Current							Yes; All Classes
24	Year							
25								
26	Surviving Dependants							
27	Coverage							Yes
28	Premiums Waived							Yes
29	Maximum Time							24 months
30								
31	Comments							
32								
33								
34								
35								
36								
37								
38								
39								
40								

The contents of this report are for comparison purposes only. The terms and conditions of the actual policy apply in the event of any discrepency. Confidential.

41. Dental Benefit, page 3: Basic benefits — exams, x-rays, cleaning, emergencies, anaesthesia

DENTAL BENEFIT: Page. 3 Basic Benefits

A	A	B	C	D	E	F	G	H	I	J	K	L	M	N	O
1	**Benefit Terms**		**Present Insurer**		**Insurer A**		**Insurer B**		**Insurer C**		**Insurer D**		**Insurer E**		**Example**
2															
3	Basic Dental Benefits														
4															
5	Complete Oral Exam														Yes
6	Maximum														Once
7	Timeframe														Per 36 months
8	Recall Exam														Yes
9	Maximum														Once
10	Timeframe														Per 6 Months
11	Specific Exam														Yes
12	Maximum														No Maximum
13	Timeframe														
14	Emergency Exam														Yes
15	Maximum														No Maximum
16	Timeframe														
17															
18	Complete X-Rays														Yes
19	Maximum														Once
20	Timeframe														Per 36 months
21	Specific X-Rays														Yes
22	Maximum														No Maximum
23	Timeframe														
24	Regular Bite-Wing X-Rays														Yes
25	Maximum														No Maximum
26	Timeframe														
27															
28	Consultations Covered														Yes, With Other Dentists
29															
30	Teeth Cleaning														Yes
31	(Prophylaxes)														
32	Number of Units														Two
33	Timeframe														Per 6 Months
34															
35	Emergency Palliative														
36	Services Covered														Yes
37															
38	Anaesthesia Covered														Yes
39															
40															

The contents of this report are for comparison purposes only. The terms and conditions of the actual policy apply in the event of any discrepency. Confidential.

42. Dental Benefit, page 4: Basic benefits — fluoride, fillings, extractions, hygiene, sealants,

DENTAL BENEFIT: Page. 4 Basic Benefits

A	A	B	C	D	E	F	G	H	I	J	K	L	M	N	O
1	**Benefit Terms**		**Present Insurer**		**Insurer A**		**Insurer B**		**Insurer C**		**Insurer D**		**Insurer E**		**Example**
2															
3	Basic Dental Benefits														
4															
5	Space Maintainers For														
6	Missing Primary Teeth														Yes
7															
8	Topical Fluoride														
9	Treatment For Adults														No
10	Maximum														
11	Treatment For Children														No
12	Maximum														
13															
14	Oral Hygiene Instruction														No
15	Maximum														
16	Timeframe														
17															
18	Pit And Fissure Sealants														No
19	Maximum														
20	Timeframe														
21															
22	Fillings Covered														Yes
23															
24	Extractions Covered														
25	Regular Extractions														Yes
26	Impacted Extractions														Yes
27															
28	Surgery Covered														Yes
29															
30															
31															
32															
33															
34															
35															
36															
37															
38															
39															
40															

The contents of this report are for comparison purposes only. The terms and conditions of the actual policy apply in the event of any discrepency. Confidential.

43. Dental Benefit, page 5: Root canals, gum disease

DENTAL BENEFIT: Page. 5 Root Canals (Endodontics) and Gum Disease (Periodontics)

A	A	C	E	G	I	K	M	O
1	**Benefit Terms**	**Present Insurer**	**Insurer A**	**Insurer B**	**Insurer C**	**Insurer D**	**Insurer E**	**Example**
2								
3	Root Canals							
4	(Endodontics) Covered							Yes
5								
6	Classes Covered							Classes A & B
7								
8	Covered Under Basic							Yes
9	Covered Under Major							
10								
11	Deductible Applied							Yes-Overall Deductible
12								
13	Percentage Reimbursed							100% For Classes A & B
14								
15	Benefit Maximum							Overall Maximum
16	Timeframe							
17								
18	Gum Disease							
19	(Periodontics) Covered							Yes
20								
21	Classes Covered							Classes A & B
22	Covered Under Basic							Yes
23	Covered Under Major							
24								
25	Deductible Applied							Yes-Overall Deductible
26								
27	Percentage Reimbursed							100% For Classes A & B
28								
29	Benefit Maximum							Overall Maximum
30	Timeframe							
31								
32	Endo. And Periodontics							
33	Exclusions							
34								
35								
36								
37								
38								
39								
40								

The contents of this report are for comparison purposes only. The terms and conditions of the actual policy apply in the event of any discrepency. Confidential.

44. Dental Benefit, page 6: Other basic, and basic benefit exclusions

DENTAL BENEFIT: Page.6 Other Basic Benefits and Basic Benefit Exclusions

	A	C	E	G	I	K	M	O
1	**Benefit Terms**	**Present Insurer**	**Insurer A**	**Insurer B**	**Insurer C**	**Insurer D**	**Insurer E**	**Example**
2								
3	Other Basic Benefits							
4								
5	Pre-Formed Stainless							
6	Steel Crowns							Yes
7	Maximum							No Maximum
8	Timeframe							
9								
10	Implants Covered							No
11	Maximum							
12	Timeframe							
13								
14	Transplants Covered							No
15	Maximum							
16	Timeframe							
17								
18	Repositioning Of							
19	The Jaw Covered							No
20	Maximum							
21	Timeframe							
22								
23	Other Basic Coverage							
24								
25								
26								
27								
28								
29								
30								
31								
32								
33	Basic Benefits Exclusions							
34								
35								
36								
37								
38								
39								
40								

The contents of this report are for comparison purposes only. The terms and conditions of the actual policy apply in the event of any discrepency. Confidential.

45. Dental Benefit, page 7: Relining, rebasing and repairs to dentures

DENTAL BENEFIT: Page. 7 Rebasing, Relining, and Repairs to Dentures

A	A	B	C	D	E	F	G	H	I	J	K	L	M	N	O
1	**Benefit Terms**		**Present Insurer**		**Insurer A**		**Insurer B**		**Insurer C**		**Insurer D**		**Insurer E**		**Example**
2															
3	Dental Benefit: Dentures														
4	Rebasing, Relining														
5	and Repairs														
6															
7	Denture Relining														
8	Classes Covered														A, and B
9	Covered Under Basic														Yes
10	Covered Under Major														
11	Deductible Applied														Yes-Overall Deductible
12	Percentage Reimbursed														100% For Classes A & B
13															
14	Benefit Maximum														Included In Overall Max.
15	Timeframe														
16															
17	Dental Rebasing														
18	Classes Covered														A and B
19	Covered Under Basic														Yes
20	Covered Under Major														
21	Deductible Applied														Yes-Overall Deductible
22	Percentage Reimbursed														100% For Classes A & B
23															
24	Benefit Maximum														Included In Overall Max.
25	Timeframe														
26															
27	Denture Repairs														
28	Classes Covered														A and B
29	Covered Under Basic														Yes
30	Covered Under Major														
31	Deductible Applied														Yes-Overall Deductible
32	Percentage Reimbursed														100% For Classes A & B
33															
34	Benefit Maximum														Included In Overall Max.
35	Timeframe														Per Year
36															
37	Rebasing, Relining														
38	And Repairs to Dentures														
39	Exclusions														
40															

The contents of this report are for comparison purposes only. The terms and conditions of the actual policy apply in the event of any discrepency. Confidential.

46. Dental Benefit, page 8: Major dental benefits deductibles, co-insurance, benefits

DENTAL BENEFIT: Page. 8 Major Dental Benefits

A	A	C	E	G	I	K	M	O
1	**Benefit Terms**	**Present Insurer**	**Insurer A**	**Insurer B**	**Insurer C**	**Insurer D**	**Insurer E**	**Example**
2								
3	Major Dental Benefit							
4	Crowns, Bridges, Dentures							
5								
6	Classes Covered							Classes A & B
7	Deductible Applied							Yes-Overall Maximum
8	Percentage Reimbursed							Classes A & B - 50%
9								
10	Inlays Covered							Yes
11	Onlays covered							Yes
12								
13	Crowns Covered							Yes
14	Crown Repairs Covered							Yes
15								
16	Dentures Covered							
17	(Prosthodontics)							Yes
18	Maximum							One Set
19	Timeframe							Per Five Years
20								
21	Denture Replacements							Yes
22	Maximum							One Set
23	Timeframe							Per Five Years
24								
25	Bridge Replacements							Yes
26	Maximum							One Set
27	Timeframe							Per Five Years
28								
29	Waiting Period For							
30	Prosthodontics							Yes
31	Timeframe							Twelve Months
32								
33	Exclusions: Major Dental							
34	Lost or Stolen							
35	Bridges, Dentures							Excluded
36	Missing Tooth Exclusion							No
37								
38								
39								
40								

The contents of this report are for comparison purposes only. The terms and conditions of the actual policy apply in the event of any discrepency. Confidential.

47. Dental Benefit, page 9: Orthodontic benefits and overall dental benefit exclusions

DENTAL BENEFIT: Page.9 Orthodontic Benefits and Overall Dental Benefit Exclusions

A	A	B	C	D	E	F	G	H	I	J	K	L	M	N	O
1	**Benefit Terms**		**Present Insurer**		**Insurer A**		**Insurer B**		**Insurer C**		**Insurer D**		**Insurer E**		**Example**
2															
3	Orthodontic Benefits														
4															
5	Classes Covered														
6															
7	Deductible Applied														Yes, Overall Deduct.
8	Percentage Reimbursed														50%
9															
10	Orthodontics Coverage														
11	Adults Covered														No
12	Children Covered														Yes
13	Child Minimum Age														Five
14	Child Maximum Age														Nineteen
15															
16	Other Orthodontic Benefits														
17															
18															
19	Orthodontic Exclusions														
20															
21															
22															
23	Dental Benefit														
24	Overall Exclusions														
25	Cosmetic Purposes														Excluded
26	T.M.J. Services														Excluded
27															
28															
29	Other Exclusions														
30															
31															
32															
33	Comments														
34															
35															
36															
37															
38															
39															
40															

The contents of this report are for comparison purposes only. The terms and conditions of the actual policy apply in the event of any discrepancy. Confidential.

48. Basic AD&D Benefit, page 1: Benefits

BASIC ACCIDENTAL DEATH AND DISMEMBERMENT: Page. 1 Benefits

A	A	B	C	D	E	F	G	H	I	J	K	L	M	N	O
1	**Benefit Terms**		**Present Insurer**		**Insurer A**		**Insurer B**		**Insurer C**		**Insurer D**		**Insurer E**		**Example**
2															
3	Basic Accidental Death														
4	and Dismemberment														
5															
6	Class A Schedule														2 x Annual Earnings
7															To Next Highest $1000
8	Class B Schedule														1.5 x Annual Earnings
9															To Next Highest $1000
10	Class C Schedule														N/A
11															
12	Class D Schedule														N/A
13															
14	Coverage Reductions:														
15	Age														Cancel At Age 65
16	Retirement														Cancel At Retirement
17															
18	Conversion Priviledge														No
19															
20	Waiver of Premium														
21	On Total Disability														Yes
22	Waiver Maximum Age														Age 65
23															
24	Overall Maximum														
25	Benefit														$250,000
26															
27	Time Restriction For														
28	Dismemberment Loss														One Year
29															
30	Loss Includes														
31	"Loss Of Use Of "														Yes
32															
33	Claims Office Location														Toronto
34															
35	Comments														
36															
37															
38															
39															
40															

The contents of this report are for comparison purposes only. The terms and conditions of the actual policy apply in the event of any discrepency. Confidential.

49. Basic AD&D Benefit, page 2: Benefits

BASIC ACCIDENTAL DEATH AND DISMEMBERMENT: Page. 2 Benefits

A	A	B	C	D	E	F	G	H	I	J	K	L	M	N	O
1	**Benefit Terms**		**Present Insurer**		**Insurer A**		**Insurer B**		**Insurer C**		**Insurer D**		**Insurer E**		**Example**
2															
3	Basic AD&D Benefits														
4															
5	Benefits: Paid For Loss Of														
6	Life														2 x Annual Earnings
7	Both Hands														2 x Annual Earnings
8	Both Feet														2 x Annual Earnings
9	Both Eyes														2 x Annual Earnings
10	One Hand And One Foot														2 x Annual Earnings
11	One Hand And One Eye														2 x Annual Earnings
12	Speech And Hearing														2 x Annual Earnings
13															
14	One Hand														1 x Annual Earnings
15	One Foot														1 x Annual Earnings
16	One Eye														1 x Annual Earnings
17	One Leg														1 x Annual Earnings
18	One Arm														1 x Annual Earnings
19															
20	Speech Or Hearing														50% of Annual Earnings
21	Four Fingers On One Hand														50% of Annual Earnings
22	Thumb And Index Finger														
23	On One hand														50% of Annual Earnings
24	All Toes On One Foot														25% of Annual Earnings
25	Hearing In One Ear														25% of Annual Earnings
26															
27	Paralysis Benefit														
28	Quadraplegia														4 x Annual Earnings
29															
30	Paraplegia														2 x Annual Earnings
31															
32	Hemiplegia														2 x Annual Earnings
33															
34	Other														
35															
36															
37	Exclusions														
38	Self-Inflicted Injury or Death														Not Covered
39	War, Civil Insurrection, Riot														Not Covered
40	Other														

The contents of this report are for comparison purposes only. The terms and conditions of the actual policy apply in the event of any discrepency. Confidential.

50. Group Voluntary AD&D Benefit, page 1: Eligibility, maximums

GROUP VOLUNTARY ACCIDENTAL DEATH AND DISMEMBERMENT: Page. 1 Benefits

	A	C	E	G	I	K	M	O
1	**Benefit Terms**	**Present Insurer**	**Insurer A**	**Insurer B**	**Insurer C**	**Insurer D**	**Insurer E**	**Example**
2								
3	Class A Eligible							Yes
4								
5	Class B Eligible							Yes
6								
7	Class C Eligible							N/A
8								
9	Class D Eligible							N/A
10								
11	Insurance Unit Amount							$10,000
12	Level Amount							N/A
13								
14	Spouse Coverage							Spouses Eligible
15								
16	Optional Family Cover							Yes
17	Spouse and No Children							Yes
18	Spouse and Children							Yes
19	Dependent Child Only							Yes
20								
21	Coverage Reductions:							
22	Age							Cancel at 65
23	Retirement							Cancel at Retirement
24								
25	Maximum Age For							
26	Dependent Children							21
27								
28	Conversion Priviledge							No
29								
30	Waiver of Premium on							
31	Total Disability							Yes
32	Waiver Maximum Age							65
33								
34	Overall Maximum Benefit							$250,000
35								
36	Overall Common							
37	Disaster Maximum							$1,000,000
38								
39								
40								

The contents of this report are for comparison purposes only. The terms and conditions of the actual policy apply in the event of any discrepency. Confidential.

51. Group Voluntary AD&D Benefit, page 2: Benefits

GROUP VOLUNTARY ACCIDENTAL DEATH AND DISMEMBERMENT: Page. 2 Benefits

A	A	C	E	G	I	K	M	O
1	**Benefit Terms**	**Present Insurer**	**Insurer A**	**Insurer B**	**Insurer C**	**Insurer D**	**Insurer E**	**Example**
2								
3	Voluntary AD&D Benefits							
4								
5	Will New Insurer Continue							
6	Coverage Without							
7	A Medical?							Yes
8								
9	Claims Office Location							Toronto
10								
11	24 Hour Per Day Cover							Yes
12								
13	Child Benefit Continued							
14	For Physically and							
15	Mentally Handicapped							
16	Children (Past Child							
17	Maximum Age)							Yes, Past Age 21
18								
19	Time Restriction For Loss							One Year
20								
21	Other Benefits							
22								
23								
24								
25								
26								
27								
28								
29								
30	Exclusions							
31	War							Excluded
32	Riot, Civil Commotion							Excluded
33	Self-Inflicted Injury							Excluded
34								
35								
36								
37								
38								
39								
40								

The contents of this report are for comparison purposes only. The terms and conditions of the actual policy apply in the event of any discrepency. Confidential.

52. Group Insurance Claims Information, page 1: All benefits: Office locations, claims reports

GROUP INSURANCE CLAIMS INFORMATION: Page. 1 All Benefits

A	A	C	E	G	I	K	M	O
1	**All Benefits**	**Present Insurer**	**Insurer A**	**Insurer B**	**Insurer C**	**Insurer D**	**Insurer E**	**Example**
2								
3	Service and Claims							
4	Information							
5								
6	Claims Office Locations							
7	Life Insurance							Toronto
8	Dependent Life							Toronto
9	Voluntary Life							Toronto
10	Voluntary Dep. Life							Toronto
11								
12	Basic A.D.& D.							Toronto
13	Voluntary A.D.& D.							Toronto
14	Voluntary Dep. A.D.& D.							Toronto
15								
16	Long Term Disability							Toronto
17	Weekly Indemnity							Toronto
18								
19	Extended Health Care							Toronto
20	Out-of-Country Emergency							Toronto
21								
22	Dental							Toronto
23								
24	Other							
25								
26	Rehabilitation Office							Toronto
27								
28	Claims Reports							
29	Available Monthly							No
30	Available Quarterly							Yes
31	Available Semi-Annually							Yes
32	Available Annually							Yes
33								
34	Report Costs							
35	Monthly Reports							N/A
36	Quarterly Reports							$250
37	Semi-Annual Reports							No Charge
38	Annual Reports							No Charge
39								
40								

The contents of this report are for comparison purposes only. The terms and conditions of the actual policy apply in the event of any discrepency. Confidential.

53. Group Insurance Claims Information, page 2: All benefits: Report types, turnaround times, comments

GROUP INSURANCE CLAIMS INFORMATION: Page. 2 All Benefits

A	A	B	C	D	E	F	G	H	I	J	K	L	M	N	O
1	**Benefit Terms**		**Present Insurer**		**Insurer A**		**Insurer B**		**Insurer C**		**Insurer D**		**Insurer E**		**Example**
2															
3	Do Claims Reports														
4	Break Out Claims By:														
5	Benefit Type														Yes
6	Individual Claiment														Yes
7	Claim														No
8	Procedure														No
9	Prescription Drug?														No
10															
11	Claims Turnaround Times														
12	On Average														
13	Extended Health Care														3.5 Days
14	Dental														2.5 Days
15	Weekly Indemnity														4 Days
16															
17	Claims: Other														
18															
19															
20															
21															
22															
23															
24															
25															
26															
27															
28															
29															
30	Comments														
31															
32															
33															
34															
35															
36															
37															
38															
39															
40															

The contents of this report are for comparison purposes only. The terms and conditions of the actual policy apply in the event of any discrepency. Confidential.

54. Group Insurance Service and Administration, page 1: Systems, booklets, access numbers

GROUP INSURANCE SERVICE AND ADMINISTRATION: Page. 1 All Benefits

A	A	B	C	D	E	F	G	H	I	J	K	L	M	N	O
1	**Group Service**		**Present Insurer**		**Insurer A**		**Insurer B**		**Insurer C**		**Insurer D**		**Insurer E**		**Example**
2	**And Administration**														
3															
4	Administration														
5															
6	Insurer Administration														
7	Available														Yes
8															
9	Self-Administration														Yes
10	Available														
11															
12	Self-Administration														
13	Software Available														Yes
14	Software Cost														$250
15															
16	Direct Computer Link														
17	Available To:														
18	Claims System														No
19	Administration System														No
20	E-Mail Access														No
21	Internet Access														No
22															
23	Toll-Free Phone Numbers														
24	To Group Office														Yes
25	To Administration Dept.														Yes
26	To Claims Dept.														Yes
27	To Rehabilitation Dept.														No
28															
29	Contract Turnaround Time														Two Weeks
30	Booklet Turnaround Time														Two Weeks
31															
32	Employee Booklets														
33	Insurer Supplied														Yes
34	Cost														Included
35	Reimbursement Amount														
36	If Booklets Printed														
37	By An Outside Publisher														$250/Three Year Supply
38	Customized Booklet														
39	Available														Yes
40	Cost														At Insurer Cost

The contents of this report are for comparison purposes only. The terms and conditions of the actual policy apply in the event of any discrepency. Confidential.

55. Group Insurance Service and Administration, page 2: Office locations, representatives, insurer information

GROUP INSURANCE SERVICE AND ADMINISTRATION: Page. 2 All Benefits

A	A	B	C	D	E	F	G	H	I	J	K	L	M	N	O
1	**Benefit Terms**		**Present Insurer**		**Insurer A**		**Insurer B**		**Insurer C**		**Insurer D**		**Insurer E**		**Example**
2															
3	Service														
4															
5	Group Office Location														Toronto
6	Number Of Group Reps. In														
7	Local Office														5
8	Name Of Representative														
9	To Handle Account														H.E. Good
10	Representative's Year's														
11	Of Experience														8
12	Name Of Back-Up Rep.														I. M. Bright
13	Back-Up's Experience														
14	In Years														15
15	Group Office's Total Block														
16	Of Business In Premium $														$12,000,000
17															
18	Do Local Group Rep.'s														
19	Have Underwriting Authority?														Yes
20															
21	Are Local Group Rep.'s														
22	Paid On Profitability?														Yes
23															
24	Do Local Group Rep.'s														
25	Calculate The Renewals?														Yes
26															
27	Insurer Head Office Location														Toronto
28															
29	In Which Countries Does The														
30	Insurer Operate?														Canada, U.S.A., Britain
31															
32	How Much Has The Insurer														
33	Invested Locally in $														$50,000,000 in Buildings
34															
35	Canadian Owned Insurer?														Yes
36															
37	Will Insurer Back Up														
38	Administration Errors?														Depends On Situation
39															
40															

The contents of this report are for comparison purposes only. The terms and conditions of the actual policy apply in the event of any discrepency. Confidential.

56. Group Insurance Financial Information, page 1: Break-even loss ratios, trend factors, IBNR formulas

GROUP INSURANCE FINANCIAL INFORMATION: Page. 1 All Benefits

A	A	B	C	D	E	F	G	H	I	J	K	L	M	N	O
1	**Financial Information**		**Present Insurer**		**Insurer A**		**Insurer B**		**Insurer C**		**Insurer D**		**Insurer E**		**Example**
2															
3	Breakeven Loss Ratios														
4	Extended Health Care														86%
5	Dental														87.5%
6	Weekly Indemnity														85%
7	Long Term Disability														N/A; Pooled
8	Life Insurance														N/A; Pooled
9															
10	Current Trend Factors														
11	Extended Health Care														17%
12	Dental														2%
13	Average Trend Factors														
14	At Jan. 1st For														
15	Last Three Years														
16	Extended Health Care														21%
17	Dental														4.5%
18															
19	I.B.N.R. Reserve														
20	Formulas														
21	Extended Health Care														1st Year = 30% Paid Claims
22															2nd+ Years = Actual Runoff
23															
24															
25	Dental														1st Year + 12% Paid Claims
26															2nd + Years = Actual Runnoff
27															
28															
29															
30	Weekly Indemnity														1st Year = 35% Paid Premium
31															2nd + Years = Actual Runoff
32															
33															
34															
35															
36	Long Term Disability														N/A; Pooled
37															
38															
39															
40															

The contents of this report are for comparison purposes only. The terms and conditions of the actual policy apply in the event of any discrepency. Confidential.

57. Group Insurance Financial Information, page 2: IBNR (life insurance) formula, credibility formulas

GROUP INSURANCE FINANCIAL INFORMATION: Page. 2 All Benefits

	A	B	C	D	E	F	G	H	I	J	K	L	M	N	O
1	**Financial Information**		**Present Insurer**		**Insurer A**		**Insurer B**		**Insurer C**		**Insurer D**		**Insurer E**		**Example**
2															
3	I.B.N.R. Reserve Formulas														
4	Life Insurance														N/A; Pooled
5															
6															
7															
8															
9															
10	Credibility Formulas														
11	Extended Health Care														100% Of Paid Claims
12															
13															
14	Dental														100% Of Paid Claims
15															
16															
17	Weekly Indemnity														50% Of Paid Claims
18															100% Credible After
19															Three Years
20															
21	Life Insurance														10% Credible After 500
22															Life years
23															
24	Dependent Life														N/A
25															
26															
27	A.D.& D.														N/A
28															
29															
30	Long Term Disability														10% Credible After
31															500 Life Years
32															
33	Other														
34															
35															
36															
37															
38															
39															
40															

The contents of this report are for comparison purposes only. The terms and conditions of the actual policy apply in the event of any discrepency. Confidential.

58. Group Insurance Financial Information, page 3: Retention charges for EHC and dental

GROUP INSURANCE FINANCIAL INFORMATION: Page. 3 Retention Charges for EHC and Dental

A	A	B	C	D	E	F	G	H	I	J	K	L	M	N	O
1	**Financial Information**		**Present Insurer**		**Insurer A**		**Insurer B**		**Insurer C**		**Insurer D**		**Insurer E**		**Example**
2															
3	Retention Charges														
4															
5	Extended Health Care														
6															
7	General Administration														4.5% Of Paid Premium
8															
9	Claims Administration														3.75% Of Paid Premium
10															
11	Risk And Profit Charges														2% Of Paid Premium
12															
13	Commission														4.5% Of Premium
14															
15	Taxes														2% Of Premium
16															
17	Other														
18															
19	Dental Acquisition														
20															
21	General Administration														4.5% Of Paid Premium
22															
23	Claims Administration														3% Of Paid Premium
24															
25	Risk And Profit Charges														2% Of Paid premium
26															
27	Commission														4.5% Of Premium
28															
29	Taxes														2% Of Premium
30															
31	Other Acquisition														
32															
33															
34															
35	Comments														
36															
37															
38															
39															
40															

The contents of this report are for comparison purposes only. The terms and conditions of the actual policy apply in the event of any discrepency. Confidential.

59. Group Insurance Financial Information, page 4: Retention charges for WI, LTD, and life insurance

GROUP INSURANCE FINANCIAL INFORMATION: Page. 4 Retention Charges for Weekly Indemnity, Group Life Insurance and Long Term Disability

A	A	B	C	D	E	F	G	H	I	J	K	L	M	N	O
1	**Financial Information**		**Present Insurer**		**Insurer A**		**Insurer B**		**Insurer C**		**Insurer D**		**Insurer E**		**Example**
2															
3	Weekly Indemnity														
4															
5	General Administration														4.5% Of Paid Premium
6	Claims Administration														2.75% Of Paid Premium
7															
8	Risk And Profit Charges														2% Of Paid Premium
9															
10	Commission														
11															
12	Taxes														
13															
14	Other														
15															
16	Long Term Disability														N/A; Pooled
17															
18	General Administration														
19	Claims Administration														
20															
21	Risk And Profit Charges														
22															
23	Commission														15%
24															
25	Taxes														2% Of Premium
26															
27	Other Acquisition														
28															
29	Life Insurance														N/A; Pooled
30															
31	General Administration														
32	Claims Administration														
33															
34	Risk And Profit Charges														
35															
36	Commission														10%
37															
38	Taxes														2% Of Premium
39															
40	Other Acquisition														

The contents of this report are for comparison purposes only. The terms and conditions of the actual policy apply in the event of any discrepency. Confidential.

60. Group Insurance Financial Information, page 5: Pooling levels and interest formulas

GROUP INSURANCE FINANCIAL INFORMATION: Page. 5 Pooling Levels for the E.H.C. Benefit and All Benefit Interest Formulas

	A	C	E	G	I	K	M	O
1	**Financial Information**	**Present Insurer**	**Insurer A**	**Insurer B**	**Insurer C**	**Insurer D**	**Insurer E**	**Example**
2								
3	Pooling Levels For							
4	Large EHC Claims							
5								
6	Extended Health Care							Claims Over $10,000
7	Cost							2% Of E.H.C. Premium
8								
9	Private Duty Nurse							N/A
10	Cost							Claims Limited To
11								$10,000 Per 3 years
12	Out-of-Country Claims							Claims Over $10,000
13	Cost							2.5% Of Premium
14								
15	Other							
16	Cost							
17								
18	Interest Formulas							
19								
20	Paid On Cash Flow							Average True Savings
21								Acount Rate For Year
22	Today's Rate/Date							2.5%
23								
24	Charged On Cash Flow							Average True Savings
25								Account Rate For Year
26	Today's Rate/Date							2.5%
27								
28	Paid On I.B.N.R. Reserves							Equals Average Yield
29								Of 364 Day T-Bills
30	Today's Rate/Date							4%
31								
32	Paid On Claims							Equals Average Yield
33	Fluctuation Reserves							Of 364 Day T-Bills
34								
35	Today's Rate/Date							4%
36								
37	Charged On The Deficit							Equals Average Yield
38								Of 364 Day T-Bills
39	Today's Rate/Date							4%
40								

The contents of this report are for comparison purposes only. The terms and conditions of the actual policy apply in the event of any discrepency. Confidential.

61. Group Insurance Financial Information, page 6: Rate basis and rate guarantees, dental fee guide

GROUP INSURANCE FINANCIAL INFORMATION: Page. 6 Rate Guarantees, Rate Basis Guarantees And Dental Fee Guide Increases

A	A	B	C	D	E	F	G	H	I	J	K	L	M	N	O
1	**Financial Information**		**Present Insurer**		**Insurer A**		**Insurer B**		**Insurer C**		**Insurer D**		**Insurer E**		**Example**
2															
3	Rate Basis Guarantees														
4	Life Insurance														Yes
5	Timeframe														Three Years
6	Long Term Disability														Yes
7	Timeframe														Three Years
8															
9	Rate Guarantees														
10	First Year														
11	Life Insurance														15 months
12	A.D.& D.														15 months
13	Dependent Life														15 Months
14	Long Term Disabilty														15 Months
15	Extended health Care														15 Months
16	Dental														15 Months
17	Weekly Indemnity														15 Months
18	Other														
19															
20	All First Year Rates														15 months
21															
22	Prov. Dental Fee Guide														
23	Increases Occur:														
24	At Renewal														No
25	At Date New Fee														
26	Guide Is Effective														Yes; Usually Jan. 1st.
27															
28															
29															
30	Comments														
31															
32															
33															
34															
35															
36															
37															
38															
39															
40															

The contents of this report are for comparison purposes only. The terms and conditions of the actual policy apply in the event of any discrepency. Confidential.

62. Group Insurance Financial Information, page 7: Alternate financing, cost-plus, experience rating, EFAPs

GROUP INSURANCE FINANCIAL INFORMATION: Page. 7 Alternate Financing

A	A	B	C	D	E	F	G	H	I	J	K	L	M	N	O
1	**Financial Information**		**Present Insurer**		**Insurer A**		**Insurer B**		**Insurer C**		**Insurer D**		**Insurer E**		**Example**
2															
3	Alternate Financing														
4															
5	Cost-Plus Available On														
6	Extended Health Care														Yes
7	Cost														Cost Plus 15%
8	Dental														Yes
9	Cost														Cost Plus 15%
10															
11	Premium Reduction For														
12	Installation Of An														
13	Employee/Family														
14	Assistance Plan?														Yes: Varies by Benefit
15															
16	Premium Level Required														
17	For Full Experience Rating														
18	Extended Health Care														$250,000 Annual
19	Dental														$250,000 Annual
20	E.H.C. + Dental Combined														$250,000 Annual
21	Weekly Indemnity														$250,000 Annual
22	Life Insurance														Not Available
23	Long Term Disabilty														Not Available
24															
25	Premium Level Required														
26	For Administrative Services														
27	Only (A.S.O.)														Not Available
28	Extended Health Care														
29	Dental														
30	Weekly Indemnity														
31	Life Insurance														
32	Long Term Disability														
33															
34	Comments														
35															
36															
37															
38															
39															
40															

The contents of this report are for comparison purposes only. The terms and conditions of the actual policy apply in the event of any discrepency. Confidential.

63. Group Insurance Financial Information, page 8: Alternate financing, ASO charges, stop-loss

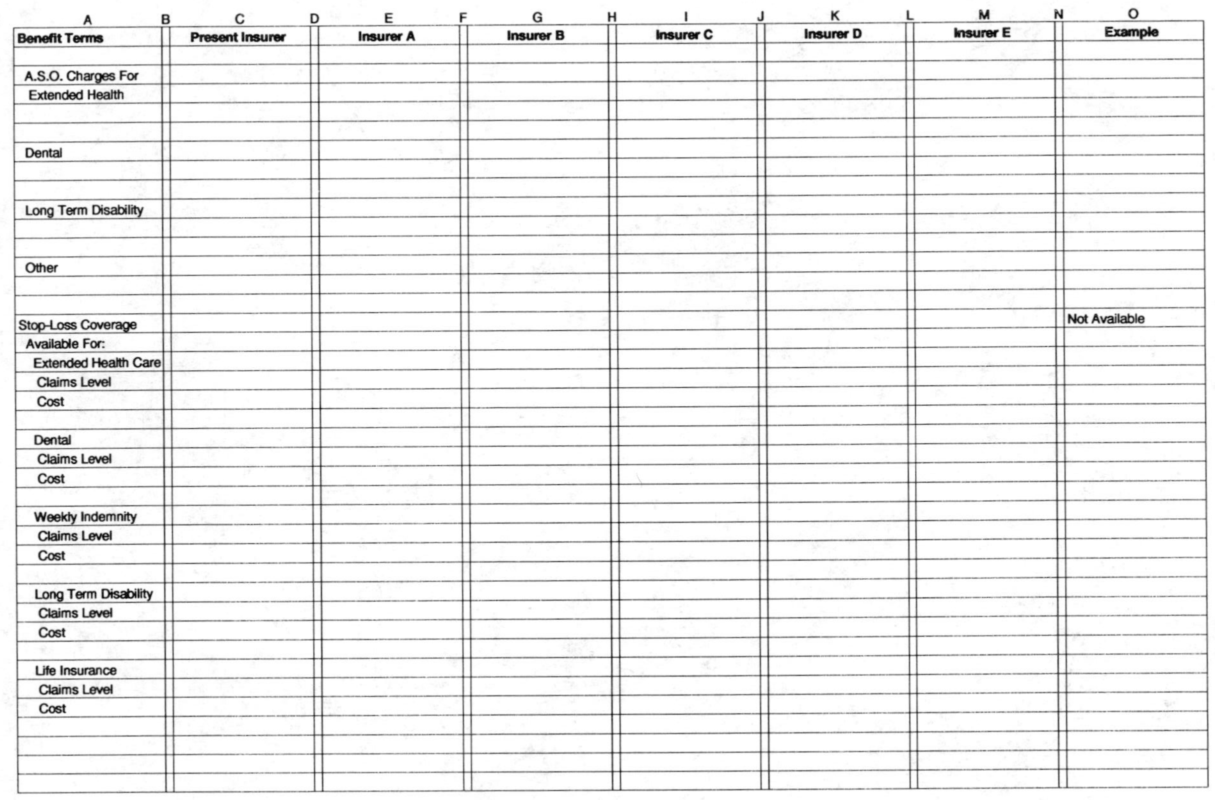

GROUP INSURANCE FINANCIAL INFORMATION: Page. 8 Alternate Financing

A	A	B	C	D	E	F	G	H	I	J	K	L	M	N	O
1	Benefit Terms		Present Insurer		Insurer A		Insurer B		Insurer C		Insurer D		Insurer E		Example
2															
3	A.S.O. Charges For														
4	Extended Health														
5															
6															
7	Dental														
8															
9															
10	Long Term Disability														
11															
12															
13	Other														
14															
15															
16	Stop-Loss Coverage														Not Available
17	Available For:														
18	Extended Health Care														
19	Claims Level														
20	Cost														
21															
22	Dental														
23	Claims Level														
24	Cost														
25															
26	Weekly Indemnity														
27	Claims Level														
28	Cost														
29															
30	Long Term Disability														
31	Claims Level														
32	Cost														
33															
34	Life Insurance														
35	Claims Level														
36	Cost														
37															
38															
39															
40															

The contents of this report are for comparison purposes only. The terms and conditions of the actual policy apply in the event of any discrepancy. Confidential.

TOPICAL INDEX

ABOUT THE AUTHOR

Richard Ackroyd was born in England in 1951, and came to Canada with his parents in 1955. After growing up in Cambridge, Ontario, he pursued studies in philosophy at the University of Waterloo. He joined a major Canadian life insurance company in the group benefits area as a group insurance and pensions representative in 1978, and spent seven years in the Maritime provinces and three years in Alberta before being promoted to Canadian Pensions Sales Manager in 1988. Richard also gained experience with the insurer's trust company division, worked as an agent specializing in employee benefits, investments and retirement savings plans, and gained experience in the consulting field with one of Canada's largest actuarial and employee benefits consulting firms. He is a Fellow, Life Management Institute, and has written several articles on employee benefit issues for Canadian employee benefits publications.

He currently runs a private employee benefits consulting practice in Edmonton, Alberta. His hobbies include scuba diving, taekwon-do, motorcycle touring and philately.

ABOUT THE AUTHOR

CONTACT THE AUTHOR

CCH Canadian Limited and the author would appreciate your comments on *Buying and Renewing Canadian Group Insurance Plans: A Practical Guide.* Please e-mail or fax:

Richard Ackroyd
Richard Ackroyd and Associates
Suite 800, 10055 106 Street
Edmonton, Alberta T5J 2Y2
Fax: (403) 420-1013
E-mail: rackroyd@freenet.edmonton.ab.ca

	Yes	No
1. Is the information on marketing group insurance plans helpful?	☐	☐
2. Is the information on renewing group insurance plans helpful?	☐	☐
3. Is the background information on the politics helpful?	☐	☐
4. Is the information on hiring agents, brokers and consultants helpful?	☐	☐
5. Did you save your organization or your clients time and/or money as a result of reading this book?	☐	☐
6. Would you recommend this book to others?	☐	☐

7. Please list areas of the book in which you would like to see more or less information or clarification.

. . . .

. . . .

Comments:

. . . .

. . . .

For further information, please fax a copy of this page to (403) 420-1013.

Your Name: . . . . Title . . . .
Organization: . . . . Voice: (. . .) . . . .
Address: . . . . Fax: (. . . .) . . . .
. . . . E-mail: . . . .
(City) . . . . Best contact time: . . . .
Prov./State . . . . Contact Date (on or after) . . . . .
Postal Code/Zip . . . .

The author is available for:
☐ speaking engagements ☐ training programs
☐ group insurance consulting ☐ pension/retirement consulting

I (we) require information on:
☐ Subject . . . .
☐ CCH Canadian Limited's other related material.
☐ Other . . . .